...ouvent marquez d'un Chifre dans cette Carte.

59. Caborcoulis	77. Angantuebuavt	99. Tuc	139. Teuriachi	184. Tomborachi
60. Baptuadaguin	78.	100. Aribac	140. Cuquiriachi	183. Temachi
61. Tucsanoday	79.	101. Guebavi	141. Cochuta	184. Tairachi
62. Hupatuduy	80.	102. S. Luis	142. Ctenupas	185. Guadalupe
63. Oidalbu	81.	103. Gabite	143. Guarabes	186. Iasucatichi
64. Tubababia	82.	104. Bu	144. Nacatobari	187. Gutu
65. Tubatcupot	83.	105. Addi	145. S. M.	188. Bacagaritiachi
66. Tudayite	84.	106. Actun	146. B. de S. Miguel	189. Porvachi
67. Nostorigiaison	85. Ojaturs	107. Babicoadam	147. Moras	190. S. Anna
68. Soalon	86. Bapatea	108. Tucubalia	148. Nure	191. Salto
69. Encarnation	87. Aribabia	109. Moicagui	149. Habas	192. Satabo
70.	88. Tacobac	110. S. Lazaro	150. Bacum	193. Cueras
71.	89. Muhuhibay	111. Son	151. Potam	194. S. Lorenzo
72.	90. Gugubupca	112. Satic	152. Belcem	195. Coxachi
73.	91. S. Marcos	113. Bangri	153. R. de S. Nicolas	196. R. Nuevo
74.	92. S. Salvador	114. Gubo	154. Iecora	197. Yepachi
75.	93. Giburi	115. Coma	155. Saguaripa	198. Tutuaca
76.	94. Oacot	116. Aubechi	156. Aubechi	199. Tomochic
	95. Pitaytutgam	117. Baipia	157. S. Matheo	200. Siloguchi
	96. Catalina	118. Concep.	158. Teopari	201. Pasiochi
	97. S. Aug.ᵗ	119. S. Ose muri	159. R. Ose muri	202. Humarilac
	98. S. Cosme	120. S. Tadeo	160. Maitoba	203. Horogachi

235. Baimena	277. Tunal	
236. Toro	278. Ponta	
237. Fuerto	279. S. Pablo	
238. Charai	280. S. Pedro	
239. S. Miguel	281. Humaza	
240. Ahome	282. Tamoriha	
241. Guasabe et Ta.	283. S. Apolonia	
mazula	284. Piastala et S. Ignac.	
242. Nio	285. Alaye	
243. Baoma	286. S. Sebastien	
244. Ocoroni	287. Mazatlan	
245. Ignacio	288. R. d. Rosario	
246. Chicorato	289. Chamella	
247. Badiraguato	290. Acaponeta	
248. Antonilo	291.	
249. Cariatapa	292. Santiago	
250. Mocorito	293. S. Catelina	
251. Cominero	294. Tepigue	
252. Badiraguatu	295. S. Po.	
253. Tamazula	296. Tetitlan	
254. R. Topia	297. Istlan	
255. Cenelac	298. Madalena	
256. R. Zanon	299. Teguila	
257. Atonilco	300.	
258. Guepuxa	301. Leon	
259. Suilupa	302. Zamora	
260. Alaye	303. Salamanca	
261. Piaya et Otatilan	304. S. Miguel	
262. Guepibugue	305. Salaya	
263. Santiago	306. Apasco	
264. Otatis	307. S. Iu. d. Rio	
265. S. Pablo	308. Guanaxuatu	
266. Tinapa	309. S. Anna	
267. S. Nicolas	310. Lagos	
268. Palpalgua	311. S. Felipe	
269. Atotilo	312. Aguas Calientes	
270. S. Catalinia	313. Tlacotes	
271. Preludio	314. R. dl. Fresnilla	
272. S. Croix		
273.		
274. Tizonazo		
275. Guatmapa		
276. Sauced		

204. Nonoaba	127. S. Crux
205. S. Felipe	128. S. Madelena
206. S. Xavier	129. Usalome
207. S. +	130. S. Ines
208. S. Ignace	131. Serocagui
209. Huextitlan	132. Guara
210. S. Matto	133. Bacca
211. S. Iuan	234. Soy
212. S. Iuan	
213. Santiago	
214. Potrero	
215. Sape	
216. Cuteco	
217. Yetsogvic	
218. Loreto	
219. Batopilas	
220. S. Anna	
221. S. Theresa	
222. Conicari	
223. Cajamo	
224. Tessia	
225. Corimpo	
226. Hethoyoa	

Map labels:

TEGUAIO
OQUI / YOQUI
NUEVO MEXICO
Lago d'Acoma
Acoma
APACHERIA
HOJOMES
JANOS
SUMAS
MERIA
R. Nacossari
Villa
TARAUM. ARE.
Parral
Rio del Norte y del Flue.
Mississippi
Rio de Mexico
SENO MEXICANO
MAYO
Cruz
Lucas
d. Everte
Farillon
Cinaloa
Cerros
Presidio del Cerro
Rio de las Nastas
Rio de Conchos
Rio de la Saucedo
Guadiana
Sombrerette
S. Luis Potosi
Culiacan
S. Barnabo
Rio d. Tavala
Rio d. Eloti
Rio d. Pias talje
Rio d. Mazatlan
Rio d. Mazatlan
Rio dl. Rosario
Rio dl. Acaponeta
Rio d. S. Pedro
Rio d. Stiago
P. d. Chacala
Co. d. Corientes
tres Marias
ZACATECAS
LA NUEVA ESPAÑA
Rio d. Saiago
S. Luis de la Paz
Rio de Tampico
Compostela
Valle de Banderas
Guadalaxara
Chapala
Queretaro
Valladolid
MEXICO
Villa Rica
Puebla / Vera Cruz

SEA GUIDE
Volume II

BAJA

Covering the waters of Baja California from San Diego to Cabo San Lucas, to San Felipe, including all the offshore and oceanic islands.

Written and compiled by

Leland R. Lewis

with charts, illustration and design by

Peter E. Ebeling

As astronaut's view of Baja California, taken aboard Gemini V, looking southward toward Cabo San Lucas with Isla Santa Cruz, Isla San Jose, Isla Espiritu Santo, La Paz and Isla Cerralvo along the left edge of the photograph.

First Edition, October, 1971.

First Impression, October 1971.
Second Impression, February 1974.

A SEA Nautical Book.
published by SEA Publications, Inc., a wholly owned subsidiary
of Columbia Broadcasting System, Inc., 1499 Monrovia Avenue,
Newport Beach, California 92663.

Library of Congress Catalogue Number 71-173041

Standard Book Number 0-88403-006-7
(Formerly 0-87930-005-1)

TABLE OF CONTENTS

PACIFIC COAST

GULF OF CALIFORNIA

CHARTS & AERIAL PHOTOGRAPHS

NOTE — Accurate navigation at sea is possible only with official Coast & Geodetic or Naval Oceanographic Office charts and publications — therefore, all sailing directions in this book should be checked against latest charts, publications and notices to mariners whenever a cruise is undertaken.

RUTTERS OF THE SEA

Rutter was the English name in the sixteenth and seventeenth centuries for a book of sailing directions equivalent to our Admiralty and Coast Pilots of the nineteenth and twentieth centuries. It was derived from the French "routier" meaning literally "route book," which came into being as the result of carefully kept ship's logs and the enduring value of the local piloting information set down therein. Having been compiled for practical use by men who were trading, fishing or fighting in sailing ships on seas that were often wild and bitter, surviving examples of early sailing directions are exceedingly rare. Most copies were worked to destruction or lost in some forgotten tragedy of the sea.

The sea is cruel, merciless to those who presume upon her kindness. One Pierre Garcie, author of early French sailing directions, knew this well, for in the Foreward to his fifteenth century *Le Gran Routier* he wrote feelingly: "From the mighty perils and great dangers which are in the waves and maelstroms of the violent sea I fled and made my escape, but only with the greatest efforts and tribulations." It was to help sailors avoid dangers of the sea that this experienced seaman set down on paper in 1483 the directions for sailing safely around the coasts of England and Wales and along those of France, Portugal and Spain.

"Common navigation" or pilotage, as opposed to "La Navigation Grande" or celestial navigation, was defined in 1581 as using no other instruments than experience, the compass and the lead. The pilot book of sailing directions was curiously overlooked as an equally important instrument of navigation though such existed from early Grecian times and several French and English editions of reliable quality had been prepared and printed before 1581. Mariners have always considered local coastal information valuable and highly desirable knowledge and often of a privileged and secretive nature. Until recent times nations considered the logs of their exploration and survey vessels exclusive state secrets and protected them with elaborate security. Navigators and their charts of routes and sailing tracks were booty of pirates and privateers as highly prized as the treasure of the captured ships themselves. And there was sound reason for such valuation, for pilotage in many ways has often been the determining factor in the life or death of a ship and its crew at sea. Vessels in ages past, though blindly feared to be doomed to inevitable disaster when they strayed for long far beyond the sight of land, have never fallen off the edge of the open sea; for a navigator at sea can make errors in calculation of the heavenly bodies and, safely floating, still be given a chance to correct his bearings; whereas in piloting along a coast with shrouded headlands and hidden dangers, any serious error may be his last.

No wonder then that such as Pierre Garcie stands in the modern world of coastal piloting as the Pharos of

Alexandria stood to safely guide the mariners of that ancient Mediterranean coast to harbor. Just as the origins of the fifteenth-century European Rutters can be traced to ancient navigational aids, so the evolution of our modern pilot books and sailing directions can be seen to be the perfection of those early Rutters of the Sea.

The art of ship's log keeping has no stop. True, all the world's continents and most of its islands have long ago been discovered but many remote coasts still stand poorly charted, and strange as it seems, some dangers not documented at all. Rocks and reefs more often than not bear the names — and the bones — of the vessels that found them by accident alone. It may be thought that a particular danger, proven such by the publicized foundering of an unfortunate vessel, would then be given a wide berth by all those who followed after; but such is too often not the case as amply illustrated by the shifting banks of Sable Island off the Nova Scotia coast, where scarcely remains a virgin spot for one more ship to newly wreck. Or treacherous and unlighted Sacramento Reef off Mexico which claimed yet another proud vessel with all hands, on a recent moonless night. Or, for that matter, along any coast where ships ply in regular trade or for pleasure and leave abundant evidence of such traffic wedged among the coastal rocks or beached above the tide.

Thus it remains the serious responsibility of the master, whether of cargo, fish or pleasure, to carefully log his ship's encounters with dangers of the sea and landmarks of the shore and to give these entries widest circulation, so that all who follow after may do so well-apprised, and thereby go with greater safety for the vessel and its crew. Then, when stowing sextant, chronometer and chart for voyaging to a strange or little-known shore be well-advised to also take the best printed Pilot of that place, a Rutter of the Sea.

*Pharos of Alexandria
280 B.C.*

THIS PILOT

Is dedicated to cruising men;
a rare breed in this modern age
content to spread their wings on the
open sea and leisurely experience
the fullness of the world.

PREFACE

The far-reaching Pacific coastline of the Baja California Peninsula sweeps southeastward from the temperate vicinity of the port of San Diego over 700 miles to Cabo San Lucas in a latitude just beyond the Tropic of Cancer. Thence around the cape, and for almost as great a length, the Gulf coast runs northwestward to San Felipe and the mouth of the Colorado River — a total distance of almost 1,400 miles. That is, of course, if one measures a straight line track between major promontories, ignoring the sweep of the land tucked behind hundreds of headlands that crown the looping shoreline and bracket the curve of the beaches. If one were to closely follow the contour of the peninsula, coasting the land and poking into every bight and bay along the way, that distance could easily be multiplied several times over before the log ticked off the last mile of the voyage.

Documenting all the detail of this great length of coastline is a monumental job, especially when it is thought important to include local information concerning the nature and depths of the anchorages, safe landing places, sources of fresh water, availability of provisions, fuel, marine services, overnight facilities, medical aid and countless other bits of knowledge that may prove helpful to the seafarer. Without doubt such a detailed documentation is a big undertaking which, if it is to be done thoroughly and accurately, is certainly beyond the compass of any one man. And so it is that the information contained in this book has been gleaned from many sources and contributed by many men who, over years of experience along this coast, have set down observations from their first-hand knowledge for the guidance and safety of all those who choose to follow.

In this tradition it has long been the practice among shipmasters to keep a careful log of conditions encountered at sea, especially the lay of the land when coasting, the set and drift of the currents, the existence and location of submerged dangers, soundings with the tallow'd lead, and when at anchor, the bearings of landmarks, protection of the headlands, shift of the wind, direction of the swell and general safety of the place. Some modern log notations are comprised of technical observations, such as areas of unusual magnetic disturbances, the quality of radio

transmission and reception in various localities, the strength of radar reflections for distinctive landmarks. There is also the sportsman's and fisherman's log, noting the abundance of clams along the beach, where lobster and abalone are to be found, the best bottom fishing holes, the location of good fishing banks and conditions encountered thereon; plankton coloration in the sea, the migration of whales, the state of the weather and the phase of the moon.

This book, then, is a compilation of all these facts and more, combed from every available source that the author has come to know through his own experience as a professional navigator along this coast. It is as accurate as observations and measurements generally taken by professional seamen, which sometimes are estimates but never guesses. It is as complete as the author has known how to make it; as complete as he has been successful in searching out primary sources of local information. It follows that some bits will be left out, some only partly included; hopefully, none in error. To rectify any lack, to include any ignored fact, to delete any facility that may pass away with disuse and time, the mariner who uses this guide is strongly urged to make navigational notes from his own observations and to record them in the margins provided for that purpose.

As a final note, it has been thought advisable to cite authority for only the more important types of information; on the other hand, no facts have been included not supported by available records or official documents unless otherwise stated. All courses should be checked and distances laid off on official government navigation charts. The set of the currents should be observed, drift calculated and compasses checked daily, the sounding lead ever employed in shoal waters and the general prudential rule of the sea should be followed at all times.

For all the comfort and security afforded by modern science, the sea is a formidable enemy. Those who spend their lives at sea, or live by its shores, or obtain a living or find pleasure from it, hold it always in unreserved respect. They know that the sea must be met on its own terms, its signs read and heeded, and the ultimate responsibility for the safe conduct of a vessel and its crew lies singularly with the ship's master.

LRL
Point Lobos
California

The Cape of the Californias

For more than 400 years Cabo San Lucas has been the focal point of expeditions to that great reach of territory that runs from Land's End to the mythical straits of Anian somewhere far to the north. At the outset of European discovery and colonization in the first decades of the sixteenth century, expeditionary traffic moved northward from the frontier that began at Cabo San Lucas. By the nineteenth and twentieth centuries the trend of exploitation had shifted polarity, and hordes of land, fortune and pleasure seekers from the newly developed northern cities turned southward, coveting the vast and undeveloped reaches of the same frontier.

Spanish and Portuguese expeditionary captains with competent navigators and pilots led the way, charting the landmarks and the dangers, the offshore islands and outlying rocks, the bays and harbors of refuge; in fact, "counting the stones along the shore," as they frequently colored the entries in their logs. On one of the first exploratory expeditions northward from Mexico in 1539, Francisco de Ulloa, formerly Hernán Cortez' pilot, sailing southward along the western shore of the Sea of Cortez, doubled a cape he called San Lucas and was credited with its discovery.

In 1542, three years after Ulloa's voyage, Juan Rodríguez Cabrillo doubled Cabo San Lucas in early July, though with some difficulty due to contrary winds, and proceeded to accomplish his renowned voyage of exploration northward up the Pacific coast of the Californias, reaching approximately the forty-second parallel of latitude in the vicinity of Cape Mendocino.

The feasibility of a northern trade route from the Philippine Islands across the Pacific to Mexico was proved with the successful transpacific voyages in 1565 of Esteban Rodríguez and his navigator Andrés de Urdaneta, and simultaneously by the voyage of Alonzo de Arellano and his navigator Lope Martín. These bold voyages initiated a regular yearly transpacific sailing of Spanish merchantmen from the Philippines to the west coast of the new world.

The Manila Galleons, or China Ships as they were commonly called, outward bound carried great cargoes of supplies sorely needed in the Spanish colonies, and gold and silver specie for the Spanish treasury on their return voyage. Leaving the Philippines in early July, these ships crossed the Pacific by sailing northeastward into the "Kuroshio" or Japan Current, reaching the California coast in the late fall near Monterey or even farther south along the Baja California peninsula. Then, in favorable northwesterly winds,

the China Ships coasted southward past Isla de Pájaros (Guadalupe Island), Cedros Island, Cabo San Lucas and Cabo Corrientes, finally to their destination port of Acapulco, arriving in late January or early February of the following year.

The Manila Galleons carried, in addition to several hundred tons of general cargo, several hundred souls comprising the passengers and crew. The lack of adequate fresh water and fresh food on these long outbound voyages inflicted great hardship on those aboard, and it was common practice for the galleons' commanders to seek shelter for brief respite and refreshment at various California coastal harbors and islands before continuing to Acapulco. The Bay of San Lucas in the shelter of the Cape was a favorite watering port until the threat of roving pirates dimmed its usefulness.

During this early maritime period when Spain commanded the sailing routes across the Pacific, the west coast of the Americas was largely free from piratical incursion and the Spanish cargo ships went unmolested; thus it remained for most of the sixteenth century. Even after the first widespread attacks along the entire sweep of the west coast by Francis Drake in 1579, Spain still considered her settlements, coastal shipping and transpacific trade routes relatively safe; such isolated plundering by foreign intruders was considered at the seats of government in Mexico City and Spain only a "transitory evil," bothersome at most. As a consequence of this myopic appraisal of the safety of their vessels, the Spanish Galleons sailed across the Pacific unescorted and virtually unarmed. In the course of capture of a number of these Spanish ships by nations officially at war with Spain, or by privateers or freebooters, the knowledge of their transpacific routes and sailing practices was extracted as a most valuable prize, for once these ocean sailing tracks were known, plans to intercept and capture other vessels could be more successfully carried out. The favored place for pirates to lay in wait for the annual passage of the Manila Galleons was along the southern segment of the Baja California coast, and the best vantage point for action combined with good shelter, a careening beach and a source of fresh water and game, was in the bight in the lee of Cabo San Lucas.

After the costly capture of one of their finest China Ships, an order was given to all captains of Manila Galleons to avoid Cabo San Lucas and to remain well offshore and out of sight of land when passing off the cape. This was an order

more easily given than obeyed, as the cape often remained the initial landfall and principal landmark depended upon by the transpacific navigators after several months of trackless crossing from the Philippines.

The Manila trade increased tenfold in the next few years but little was done to arm the transpacific galleons or to protect their trade route. The seas off the Pacific coast of New Spain were invaded by a number of foreign expeditions of various nationalities during these years. Their principal objectives were usually not the advertised ones of discovery, hydrography and survey, but rather commercial trade and barter in the lucrative Spanish colonies with the thought, secretly harbored, of capturing a rich merchantman.

To counter this threat, the Spanish decided to send a well-equipped expedition directly northward to thoroughly explore and chart the California coast in search of a port of refuge. For this job they selected Sebastían Vizcaíno, well-qualified to act as General of the expeditionary fleet. Three ships, the *San Diego,* Vizcaíno's flagship, the *Santo Tómas* and the frigate *Tres Reyes,* left Acapulco on May 5, 1602, for a voyage of exploration whose success was to establish a firm knowledge of the character of the coast from Cabo San Lucas to Cape Mendocino, and to fix the majority of the place names down to the present day.

Vizcaíno's survey was a thorough one that took the expedition far northward to within sight of Cabo Blanco before turning back. Monterey Bay was discovered and considered a suitable harbor for the Manila ships which normally raised the coast approximately in this latitude on their northern route across the Pacific. Cabrillo's previous voyage in 1542 had apparently been as thorough, but his charts did not receive the recognition accorded those of Vizcaíno. Both had passed the entrance to San Francisco Bay, so continually shrouded in fog that it lay undiscovered until 1769, and then was found only by a land party on foot.

While Vizcaíno was given rather explicit directions, including a firm policy of not changing established names of ports and landmarks, the sailing directions and charts of previous expeditions with which he was supplied were so vague that he was unable to recognize or determine the places previously named, and was therefore generally unable to comply with this place-name policy. Names given by Vizcaíno followed the established tradition of applying the name from the Roman liturgical calendar for the particular day, except in those few instances when it was thought appropriate to honor an individual or to apply a geographical name descriptive of a unique locale. Vizcaíno's charts were ably reproduced by the cartographer Enrico Martinez in 1603, and subsequently disseminated to Spanish shipmasters from whence they eventually found their way into internationally published world charts, thus establishing most of the California coastal place names as we know them today.

For over a hundred years the Manila Galleons had made their annual crossing virtually unmolested, oftentimes through sheer good fortune. Piratical attacks, however, continued to occur from time to time against Spanish shipping, notably marked by the forays of the English privateers William Dampier, in 1704, and Woodes Rogers, in 1710. It was in the course of the voyage of this latter privateer around the Horn into the Pacific and down the west coast of New Spain that Alexander Selkirk, the Robinson Crusoe of literary fame, was rescued after four years of marooned existence on Juan Fernandez Island off the coast of Chili. Selkirk came aboard as a member of the crew and accompanied Rogers in his various exploits all the way to Cabo San Lucas and eventually back to England. Roger's fleet successfully intercepted and captured one of the two Manila Galleons bound for Acapulco that year, but was driven off by the courageous resistance of the crew of the second Spanish merchantman.

Cabo San Lucas was, for the most part, during these several hundred years the northernmost point reached by the various fleets of foreign "traders" and pirates who reached the "South Sea" through the Straits of Magellan, although some of the fleets of commercial invaders came across the Pacific making landfall, as did the Spanish vessels, somewhere on the coast of Alta California. After 1750, smuggling of contraband goods became more widespread, with concomitant sea chases, sea battles and an occasional sacking of the coastal settlements, whenever and wherever possible. Throughout the rest of the eighteenth and all of the nineteenth centuries, a steady stream of adventurers, explorers, men of the church, naturalists, promoters, vagabonds and settlers came to the frontier of the new Spanish territory and found shelter in the harbors and anchorages of the Baja California coast along the way.

Today, the musty aura of exploration, commerce, religious conversion and pirating floats lingeringly over Baja California waters as modern-day adventurers ride safely at anchor in the quiet repose of remote and idyllic coves, while the strident focus of the late twentieth century moves elsewhere in the world.

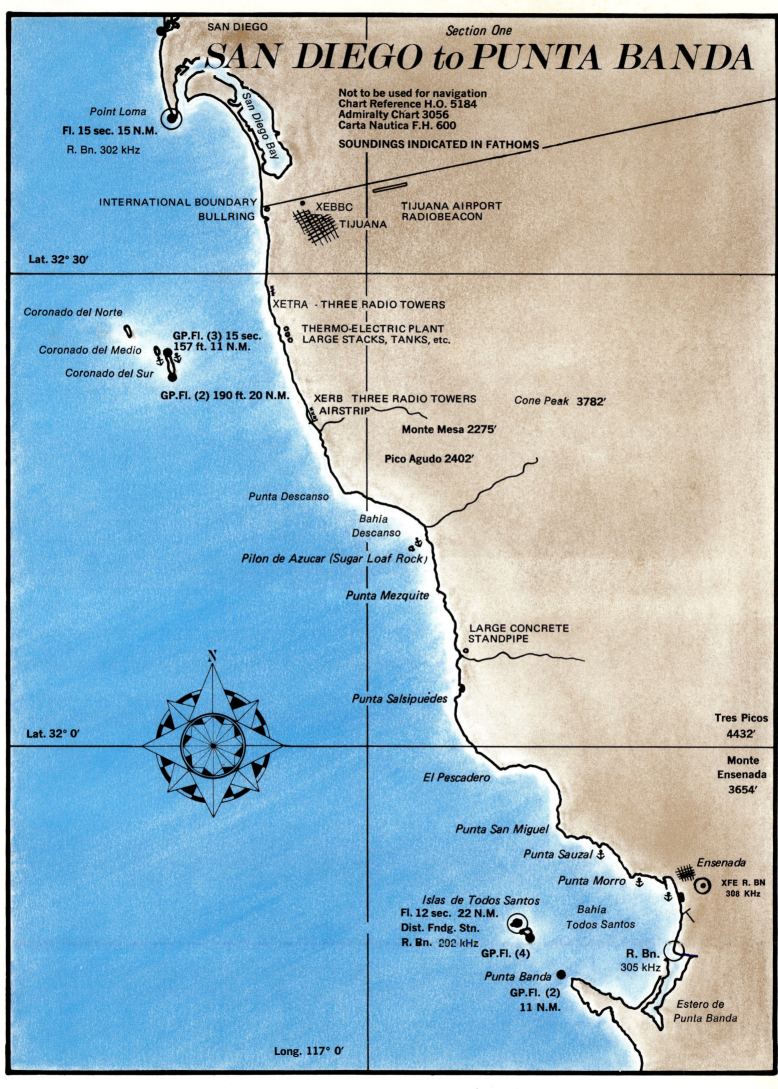

SAN DIEGO

Section One

SAN DIEGO to PUNTA BANDA

Point Loma
Fl. 15 sec. 15 N.M.
R. Bn. 302 kHz

Not to be used for navigation
Chart Reference H.O. 5184
Admiralty Chart 3056
Carta Nautica F.H. 600

SOUNDINGS INDICATED IN FATHOMS

San Diego Bay

INTERNATIONAL BOUNDARY
BULLRING

XEBBC
TIJUANA

TIJUANA AIRPORT
RADIOBEACON

Lat. 32° 30'

Coronado del Norte

Coronado del Medio

GP.Fl. (3) 15 sec.
157 ft. 11 N.M.

Coronado del Sur

GP.Fl. (2) 190 ft. 20 N.M.

XETRA - THREE RADIO TOWERS

THERMO-ELECTRIC PLANT
LARGE STACKS, TANKS, etc.

XERB THREE RADIO TOWERS
AIRSTRIP

Cone Peak 3782'

Monte Mesa 2275'

Pico Agudo 2402'

Punta Descanso

Bahía
Descanso

Pilon de Azucar (Sugar Loaf Rock)

Punta Mezquite

LARGE CONCRETE
STANDPIPE

N

Punta Salsipuédes

Tres Picos
4432'

Lat. 32° 0'

Monte
Ensenada
3654'

El Pescadero

Punta San Miguel

Punta Sauzal

Ensenada

Punta Morro

XFE R. BN
308 KHz

Islas de Todos Santos
Fl. 12 sec. 22 N.M.
Dist. Fndg. Stn.
R. Bn. 202 kHz

Bahía
Todos Santos

GP.Fl. (4)

R. Bn.
305 kHz

Punta Banda

GP.Fl. (2)
11 N.M.

Estero de
Punta Banda

Long. 117° 0'

14

SECTION 1
SAN DIEGO to PUNTA BANDA

*Anchorage at
Todos Santos*

San Diego is the southernmost United States port of departure for Mexico. Ten miles southeastward of the mouth of the harbor lies the political division between the Californias, an arbitrary geographic demarcation beyond which stretches the Baja California Peninsula some 800 miles toward the Tropic of Cancer and beyond. It is a voyage that can be safely undertaken in a small boat properly fitted out and provisioned; a voyage that can be enjoyably accomplished by those familiar with the sea and with local coastal information. It is not without its hazards, however, and those who attempt a lengthy coastal passage southward for the first time are well-advised to seek good sailing directions, to go fully prepared and with caution.

The coastline between San Diego and Ensenada, Mexico, is distinguished by many prominent landmarks. A coastal highway traverses the face of the foothills bordering the sea. Numerous settlements and some remarkable structures show prominently to seaward. The coast south of San Diego Harbor as far as Ensenada and Bahía de Todos Santos is largely clear of hidden dangers; the several offshore islands and exposed rocks are clearly marked on official navigation charts; certain other submerged rocks and reefs awash — for the most part within the 10-fathom curve — are located and identified within the pages of this book. For navigation in the ocean area described in this section use U.S. Coast & Geodetic Survey Charts 5101, San Diego to Santa Rosa Island; U.S. Naval Oceanographic Office Charts, H.O. 1006, San Francisco to Point Telmo; H.O. 5195, San Diego to Islas Todos Santos; H.O. 5184, Point Loma to Punta Colnett; and H.O. 1149, San Diego to Bahía San Quintín with Bahía Todos Santos inset; British Admiralty Charts 2324, Cape San Lucas to San Diego Bay; 2885, plans on the Coast of California; Carta de Faros e Hidrografía de México; F.H. 600, San Diego a San Quintín; F.H. 610, De Ensenada a Mazatlán Incluyendo Golfo de California.

Upon leaving San Diego Harbor and taking a departure from Lighted Whistle Buoy "1", 2.6 miles south of Point Loma, the Coronado Islands — a group of four rocky islets in Mexican waters — may be seen on the horizon on clear days, almost due south and about 13 miles distant from the point. A course taken east of south, about 165° true, will pass through the 7-mile wide coastal channel to the leeward of these islands. An alternative course may be taken west of south, about 200° true, to pass seaward of the island group. In thick weather, when electing to pass to seaward, it is advisable to lay this latter course farther to the westward, thereby passing the entire group of islands well to port. However, except when looking to better wind outside by which to sail, most mariners choose the inside coastal passage, a more direct southerly course as well as one affording a calmer sea in the lee.

About 10 miles southeastward of Point Loma Light, the International Boundary between the United States and Mexico is marked by a weathered 20-foot high white marble obelisk on a pedestal 41 feet above the sea and approximately 200 yards from the shore, near the edge of a low flat-topped bluff. It is plainly visible from seaward standing in a small grassy semicircular plot immediately northward of the Plaza Monumental, a strikingly large white circular bullring with multiple concrete columns looming on the shore. A stone mound, 365 feet above the sea and one mile eastward of the obelisk, marks another point along the boundary line. Directly northward of the border monument the coastal mesa falls to low marshy land in United States territory south of San Diego Bay. The Río Tijuana (Tijuana River) crosses the boundary about 4¾ miles inland and flows into the sea close northward of the monument. On a course to Ensenada from San Diego through the leeward passage between the mainland and the Coronado Islands, a mass of white lights may be seen at night, marking the residential and industrial development along the coast immediately south of San Diego Harbor. On a hill directly above, a **red blinking light** marks the position of the two vertical radio antennas of Radio Station XEBBC. A stretch of hills, dark at night, intervenes between these lights and two distinct clusters of white lights southward. A rotating *aerobeacon,* flashing white, may be seen near the Tijuana Airport, about 6 miles east-southeastward of the Boundary Monument, providing a good mark at night. It is situated at Latitude 32° 30′ north, Longitude 117° 01′ west.

About 7 miles offshore and 10 miles southwestward of the Boundary Monument, the four rocky islets comprising the Los Coronados Islands form the outer limit of the channel. Navigation lights are shown from the north and south ends of Coronado del Sur, the largest island in the group. An extensive kelp field extends southeastward. The navigation light on the northeastern side of South Coronado Island displays **three white flashes** every **15 seconds** and while somewhat dim, may be seen for 11 miles in clear weather; the navigation light on the south point of the island displays **two white flashes** that may be seen in clear weather for 20 miles, and provides an excellent point of departure for vessels steering south, either in the leeward channel or in the outside passage. The South Light is obscured from some northward positions by the North and Middle Islands but is plainly visible from all points southward. (For light characteristic detail see "Islas Coronados.")

The coast beyond the International Boundary Monument is generally bluff from 50 to 80 feet high and trends southward 4 miles, thence south-southeastward 13 miles to Descanso Point. A few miles inland is a range of hills about 400 feet high, backed by a range of mountains including a prominent mesa called Monte Mesa (Table Mountain), 2,275 feet high, and Pico Agudo (Sharp Peak), a triple-peaked mountain 2,402 feet high, a few miles southward of Table Mountain. About 6 miles inland is a great chain of coastal mountains which attain an elevation of 3,782 feet at Cone Peak, 3,291 feet at Double Peak and 3,572 feet at Otay Mountain, the last within the United States border, about 3 miles northward of the International Boundary Line. These landmarks, easily distinguished from seaward, provide excellent bearings for coastal navigation. Three tall steel radio towers marked by **blinking red lights** at night may be seen atop the mountain 8 miles southward of the Boundary Monument and about 2½ miles northward of a large

power generating station. These are the radio antennas of station XTRA which broadcasts on 690 kiloHertz and is geographically located at Latitude 32° 25' 30" north, Longitude 117° 05' 15" west. A second powerful rotating *aerobeacon*, flashing red, is located atop a rolling hill immediately north of the power station. Multiple concrete smokestacks, displaying fixed and **flashing red lights** at night, stand at the power station. Steel latticework electrical towers are located on either side of the smokestacks and march inland over the hills. At ground level there are numerous work-lights in and about the buildings. An oil storage tank farm is established on the north side of the station and a submarine oil pipeline marked by white mooring buoys extends offshore. A rock jetty projects seaward, its hooked extremity protecting a cooling water intake channel. A lighted bell buoy, painted red and white and exhibiting a **white flashing light** every **4 seconds,** is moored off the jetty marking the oil loading area.

El Rosarito (Rosarito Beach), a settlement comprised of a large resort hotel, adjoining motels and private residences stretching several miles along a white sand beach, is located approximately 2 miles south of the power station. Radio Broadcast Station XERB transmits on 1091 kiloHertz from an antenna tower located at Rosarito Beach. The tower is located at Latitude 31° 20.5' north, Longitude 117° 03.8' west. A *large bare rock* lies offshore within the 10-fathom curve immediately southward of the radio antenna; the tower bears 44° true, 900 yards from this rock. A paved *airstrip,* suitable for light planes, runs parallel to the beach immediately opposite the offshore rock. A small *bank* abreast Rosarito Beach, with a least known depth of 15 fathoms, is situated about 7 miles westward of Punta Descanso. Aguajito, a conspicuous turret-shaped hill near the coast on the edge of a high plateau approximately 3 miles southward of El Rosarito, provides a good mark.

International boundary, Tijuana Bull Ring and shoreline

Rosarito Beach power station and water intake jetty

Los Islas Coronados

Los Islas de Coronados (Coronado Islands) include a group of four bold, high, rocky islets lying about 4½ miles inside the territorial waters of Mexico. They are situated about 7 miles offshore at their nearest point, approximately 10 miles southwestward of the International Boundary Monument. The islands give *good radar returns* up to 20 miles and the southernmost and largest of the group displays navigation lights which are attended. The northernmost island, Coronado del Norte, is situated about 13½ miles southward of Point Loma; the southernmost island, Coronado del Sur, is located approximately 13 miles northwestward of Punta Descanso; two middle islets and a rock lie in between. The islands extend about 5 miles in a northwest and southeast orientation. The Coronados are often called the Sentinels of San Diego Bay, guarding the harbor entrance from the southward and providing an excellent landmark for vessels approaching from westward or northwestward. On September 27, 1542, a Spanish coastal survey expedition commanded by Juan Rodríguez Cabrillo, sailing up the coast from Todos Santos Bay, passed this uninhabited island group. Cabrillo noted in his log that they were 3 leagues from the mainland and afforded shelter from the west winds. After examining their bleak and barren appearance, he called them Las Islas Desiertas (Desert Islands). Sixty years later, on November 10, 1602, Sebastián Vizcaíno, on another comprehensive coastal survey of the Californias ordered by the Viceroy of New Spain, sighted the same offshore islands and called them Islas de San Martin, a name which he duly noted on his survey chart. The expedition's scribe, Father Antonio de la Ascención who kept a personal diary, gave the name Los Cuatro Coronados to the group and it is this name that has survived on modern charts. Since that time they have been referred to by various colloquial names such as Dead Men's Islands and the Sarcaphagi. The northern island has been referred to as Cortez and sometimes Corpus Christi as it was thought to resemble a body draped in a shroud.

Southeast light, Isla Sur

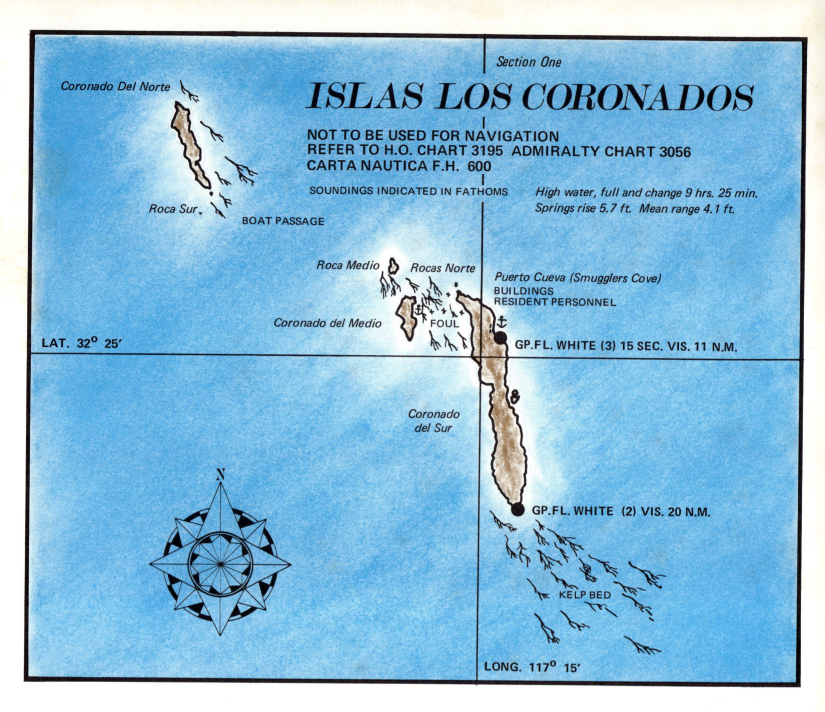

ISLAS LOS CORONADOS

Section One

NOT TO BE USED FOR NAVIGATION
REFER TO H.O. CHART 3195 ADMIRALTY CHART 3056
CARTA NAUTICA F.H. 600

SOUNDINGS INDICATED IN FATHOMS

High water, full and change 9 hrs. 25 min.
Springs rise 5.7 ft. Mean range 4.1 ft.

Coronado Del Norte

Roca Sur

BOAT PASSAGE

Roca Medio   Rocas Norte

Puerto Cueva (Smugglers Cove)
BUILDINGS
RESIDENT PERSONNEL

Coronado del Medio   FOUL

GP.FL. WHITE (3) 15 SEC. VIS. 11 N.M.

LAT. 32° 25'

Coronado
del Sur

N

GP.FL. WHITE (2) VIS. 20 N.M.

KELP BED

LONG. 117° 15'

Coastal pirates were reputed to have lain in wait in their lee for richly laden Spanish merchantmen bound from the Philippines to Acapulco via the northern sailing route. But all romance aside, Islas Los Coronados are rather bleak most of the year around; a nesting place for thousands of a variety of sea birds and some few hardy land birds. There is no fresh water save for dew or fog and as a consequence no trace of habitation of prehistoric man or modern Indians has been found. Sea lions bask on the rocks exposed at the tide line; sea elephants have been observed from time to time. The islands were once the habitat of the numerous California sea otters hunted almost to extinction in the first three decades of the 1800's for their valuable pelts. Plant life is very limited, growing with some difficulty in the dry rocky soil but, like all the California offshore islands, the group displays a surprising bloom of cactus flowers, ice plant, daisies, sea dahlias and a variety of other brightly colored flowers in the springtime, especially after a particularly rainy season.

The northernmost islet of the group, and second in size, Coronado del Norte, is about 1 mile long and rises to a

height of 467 feet. It is barren, uninhabited and unlighted, surrounded by a large bed of kelp. The passage between this islet and the middle islets to the southeastward is about 1½ miles wide but in this strait are numerous patches of kelp, thick enough to impede small craft or foul their propellers; use of this passage is not recommended without local information. There are no beaches and only one practical anchorage at North Coronado — a quiet cove on the leeward side surrounded by steep tumbled rock and usually filled with small fishing craft during the summer months. Near the landing cove is a rickety wooden structure, known locally as the lobster shack. It was erected for the use of stranded fishermen and affords a good landmark. *Landing* may be made by skiff onto the rocky ledge, thence along a rocky path to a steep trail leading to the summit. The west side of the island is a nearly perpendicular cliff about 500 feet high; a short rocky shelf forms the windward shore, home for numerous sea lions. A large number of wheeling sea birds fill the air above the cliffs, especially during the mating season. A curious ecological condition exists: North Coronado nurtures most of the sea birds of the entire group and has been found to have no rattlesnakes; South Coronado has but few nesting birds but a generous population of rattlesnakes.

The two central islets separated from North Coronado by the deep 1½-mile wide channel and lying respectively ¾ and ½ mile westward of South Coronado, are small barren rocks 101 and 251 feet high respectively, referred to as Middle Rock and Middle Island. Both islets are much alike — steep pinnacles of rock with isolated patches of weathered soil sufficient to support scattered growths of brush. Near the center of the most northerly is a basin of an old crater filled with earth. Here the brush grows more thickly and supports numerous nesting birds. There is a 100-foot cave above the tide line at the southern tip of this islet in which flocks of sea birds make their nests. On the smaller of the Middle Islets is a similar cave whose mouth is beneath the tide level providing a secure habitat for harems of seals; the cove is accessible to skin divers with local knowledge. Small vessels find shelter in a *protected anchorage* on the east side of Middle Island.

Coronado del Sur (South Coronado) the southernmost and largest islet, is about 1¾ miles long and rises near its southern end to a height of 672 feet; seen from northward or southward it appears as a wedge-shaped mass. A large rock off the north end of the South Island is called North Rock. Scrubby bushes, cactus and ice plant grow on this islet and colorful flowers appear in the early spring after the seasonal rains. Puerto Cuevo, sometimes referred to as Smuggler's Cove, is a deeply indented cove on the northeastern side of the island where the Mexican lighthouse keeper and a small army contingent are garrisoned. The Los Coronados Northeast Light stands on the bluff above the cove.

Anchorage in this sheltered cove, situated a short distance southward of the middle of the island, may be had in depths of 6 to 8 fathoms, sand bottom. The anchorage is open northward but protected from the prevailing wind; comfortable shelter may be found here in moderately heavy southwesterly weather. Boats may land safely within the cove at the old resort hotel converted to barracks but special permission to land must be obtained in advance from Mexican authorities. In this anchorage on a calm day fish and marine plants are plainly visible over the white sandy bottom.

On the south ridge of the island near the army buildings is a trail to the lighthouse and one that winds upward to Pirate Cave where José Arvaez is reputed to have once lain in wait for his victims and in which he secreted his plunder. The eastern side of the island is composed of a steep rocky cliff where sea birds nest but it is not so abrupt or so sheer as the sheer cliff on North Coronado Island. A trail is cut along these cliffs to the light on the south point of the island. A resort hotel, once known as Los Coronados Yacht Club, was laboriously constructed on pilings against the steep rocky cliff just above the water's edge at Puerto Cueva in the

early 1930's. Designed principally as a gambling casino, it failed when such operation was prohibited by enforcement of Mexican law, and now comprises the "barracks." A small rocky cove, indented beneath the cliffs on the west side of the island, is called Sea Elephant Cove and hosts a small colony of these marine animals.

Large rafts of kelp which encircle the island group provide a rich habitat for many varieties of rock fish as well as giant black sea bass, making it a favorite spot for sportfishermen. *Navigation warning: A large kelp bed, about 2½ miles long and ¾ of a mile wide, lies southeastward of South Coronado and should be avoided as a navigation hazard.*

LANDMARKS AND LIGHTS — A navigation light is shown from a white square masonry tower 157 feet above the sea at Puerto Cueva on the northeastern side of South Coronado; the light has a characteristic **white group flash of three flashes** every **15 seconds:** flash 1 second, eclipse 2 seconds; flash 1 second, eclipse 2 seconds; flash 1 second, eclipse 8 seconds. The light, while of low candlepower, can be seen for 11 miles on a clear night and is visible in the sector 169° through 341°. A second more powerful light, South Light, is shown from a white cylindrical masonry tower 190 feet above the sea on the south point of the islet; the light has a characteristic **white group flash** of **two flashes** and is visible for 20 miles seaward in clear weather in the sector 263° through 155°; North Coronado Islet obscures the light in the sector 135° through 139° and Middle Coronado Islets obscure it 148° through 151°.

A special purpose light buoy, not to be considered an aid to navigation, is moored in a position about 5½ miles westward of the boundary monument and about 7 miles north-northeastward of North Coronado. This white buoy shows a **flashing white light** and is marked **"NEL."** Various weather and special purpose buoys are anchored from time to time in the general area.

A bombing target with a danger area of a 3-mile radius lies northward of Islas Los Coronados. The target consists of a radar-rigged triangular pyramid, 20 feet high, equipped with a **fixed amber light** and **bell.**

SEA AND WEATHER CONDITIONS — The weather conditions outside San Diego Bay are generally mild with clear days most of the year; severe storms are infrequent and occur for the most part during the winter months. The prevailing winds are from the west and northwest with an average velocity of 7 knots, springing up in the morning and increasing toward the late afternoon; the velocity seldom exceeds 25 knots. Winter storms are generally from the southeast or the southwest. Reasonable shelter from severe southwesterly gales may be had in the lee of South Coronado Island. The climate is sunny and warm most of the time. Fogs are not common, consisting mainly of nightly mists that seldom persist beyond midmorning; heavy fogs occur on the average of no more than 30 days a year. There are no fog signals established on the Coronado Islands. Weather aids by radio are broadcast by the United States Coast Guard on NMQ, 2670 kiloHertz, 9 a.m. and 9 p.m., local time.

FACILITIES — There are no public facilities on the islands other than an emergency shelter for stranded fishermen at Puerto Cueva, South Island, and the Lobster Shack at North Island; resident lighthouse personnel and the small Mexican Army garrison are maintained by supply ship from Ensenada.

COMMUNICATIONS — Lighthouse personnel operate a radio network on Mexican military frequencies and will relay emergency messages. The United States Coast Guard may be reached on the emergency marine frequencies of 2182 kHz or 156.8 mHz VHF Channel 16. (See appendix for additional radiotelephone and radiotelegraph, frequencies and emergency procedures.)

TRANSPORTATION — Sportfishing vessels and sightseeing charter boats operate from San Diego daily. A Mexican Government vessel supplies the lighthouse personnel on a regular weekly run to South Coronado from Ensenada, 46 miles southeastward.

MARINE EMERGENCIES AND MEDICAL FACILITIES — The Mexican Government has authority and jurisdiction over the Coronado Islands and the waters in the vicinity as part of its sovereign territory. First aid and emergency medical treatment may be rendered by the Mexican Army garrison on South Coronado Island. Cooperative emergency arrangements exist between the United States and the Mexican Government whereby the U.S. Coast Guard will assist the Mexican Government upon official request when, by virtue of close proximity to vessels and crews in distress, they may render aid or effect rescue promptly and efficiently.

Punta Descanso (Descanso Point), situated about 1½ miles southward of Aguajito and 17 miles from the Border Monument, may be recognized by a slight hill 392 feet high on top of the bluff near the extremity of the point. Bahía Descanso (Descanso Bay) is a wide indentation in the coast southeastward of Punta Descanso; eastward of the point the coast turns sharply to the east-southeastward for a distance of 5½ miles and then continues to the southward, forming the bay.

Pilón de Azúcar (Sugarloaf Rock), 13 feet high and whitened with birdlime, is situated about 1¾ miles offshore

Pilon de Azucar (Sugarloaf Rock)

in the middle of the bay about 4 miles southeastward of Punta Descanso; it is the only offlying danger in the bay. *Anchorage* is often obtained by small coasters with local knowledge southward of this rock in 8 to 15 fathoms with good holding ground over a sand bottom. While the depths increase rapidly offshore along this coast (the 100-fathom curve lies only about 3½ miles from the shore) *anchorage* may be had by vessels with local knowledge anywhere along the shore of this bay. A kelp barge harvests the extensive kelp beds that grow along this coast and may be frequently seen cutting seaweed close inshore. The Descanso Ranch is at the mouth of the Río Descanso, about 7 miles southeastward of Descanso Point and 2½ miles northward of Mesquite Point. It comprises a small settlement which may be identified from seaward by the conspicuous sand hills to the northward. Originally the site of the Mission Descanso established in 1814 by the Dominican Fathers, it was abandoned in 1834; no ruins remain. Small vessels with local knowledge sometimes anchor here.

The coast between Punta Descanso and Punta Salsipuedes, about 15 miles south-southeastward, is low, poorly defined and generally sandy; there are occasional rocky cliffs with hills rising immediately from the beach. A new

Rosarito Beach resort, showing reef offshore with Pico Agudo in the background

Tollgate, Pueblo de San Miguel

toll road with divided lanes runs along the shore and through cuts in the coastal hills, crossing numerous arroyos on concrete trestles that show conspicuously to seaward. Campsites, cabins, motels, roadside restaurants and resorts are established along this route and show prominently to seaward. Several resorts have paved ramps for small boat launching with anchorage and access to the shore facilities afforded. Approximately 2¾ miles northward of Punta Salsipuedes, Río San Miguel flows into the Pacific through a broad arroyo opening on the shore. The coastal highway crosses the river on a long bridge inclined southward and supported on four concrete columns.

High on the brow of the bluff on the northern side of the arroyo stands the tall cylindrical concrete tower of an aqueduct ventilator. Water from wells along the bed of the Río San Miguel is pumped to the top of the hill and distributed northward through a large-diameter conduit that can be seen traversing the side of the hill below the standpipe. This is a good mark from seaward. On the banks of the Río San Miguel several miles from the mouth of the arroyo, the Mission San Miguel de la Frontera was founded by the Dominican Fathers Tomás Valdellon and Miguel López in 1782. In 1787 the site was moved closer to the coast, where adobe ruins are still in evidence. The mission was abandoned in 1834. The mission establishments were meant to be self-sustaining but at the outset required supply by sea for both food and living necessities. In most cases, after great expenditure of native labor under the direction of the missionary fathers, the missions enjoyed a degree of success and shipped their produce by the same route on which they originally depended for survival.

Two-and-a-half miles southward of the aqueduct standpipe is Punta Salsipucdes (get out if you can), a Spanish description apparently referring to a difficult lee shore for sailing vessels in earlier times. Beyond Salsipuedes Point, San Miguel Point marks the northern entrance to Todos Santos Bay. This stretch of coast consists of alternate sand bluffs and rocky cliffs about 50 feet high, backed by hills to 500 feet high. When viewed from seaward this range has the appearance of rising directly from the coast.

Punta Banda and Los Islas Todos Santos (Todos Santos Islands) are the first significant features to be discerned when approaching Todos Santos Bay. Both the point and the Todos Santos Islands lying northwestward appear to be islands on the horizon. Gradually the interval between Punta Banda and the Todos Santos Islands becomes visible. Along this coast several headlands that appear before reaching Ensenada Harbor give the navigator a false sense of position. They are in order from the west: Descanso Point, Salsipuedes Point, San Miguel Point, Saucedal Point, Morro Point, and finally Ensenada Point, marked by a rock breakwater extending seaward.

Bahía de Todos Santos (Todos Santos Bay) is formed by San Miguel Point on the north shore and by Punta Banda and the Todos Santos Islands to the south. The mouth of this bay to the northward of the islands is about 6 miles wide. A *shoal,* covered to a depth of 3 fathoms and surrounded by kelp, lies about 4 miles from San Miguel Point along a line drawn between that point and the northern island. Punta San Miguel (San Miguel Point), situated about 11 miles southward of Salsipuedes Point, is a bold headland about 150 feet high. The point of land about 6 miles northward of San Miguel Point is also referred to sometimes as Salsipuedes Point. San Miguel Village is located on a low lying flat coastal shelf at the northern perimeter of a broad arroyo that opens on the coast. A short rock jetty extends from the southern end of a sandy beach. On a low terrace above the shore, the coastal highway passes beneath the last of a series of three toll gates between Tijuana and Ensenada. There is a paved launching ramp for small boats at the San Miguel Village complex.

The coast between San Miguel and Ensenada Points, comprising the northeastern side of the bay, is characterized by bold cliffs 50 to 100 feet high closely backed by hills. Punta Morro (Morro Point), 2¾ miles southwestward of San Miguel Point, marks the opening of a valley in which there are several ranch buildings and through which winds a paved road. Neat rows of olive trees comprise several large orchards surrounding the mediterranean style mansion of the late General Abelardo Rodríguez, former governor of both Sonora and Baja California and ex-president of Mexico. A *breakwater* projecting from the point protects an anchorage for small boats between it and a long pier that extends from a shoreside complex of fish cannery buildings and warehouses. Fishing vessels warp alongside the pier for discharging their catch by bucket and pier-mounted crane; fuel and fresh water are taken here by cannery vessels. The water is somewhat shoal in the anchorage and alongside the pier, and the lead should be used when approaching the wharf. The village of El Sauzal, older than Ensenada and at one time headquarters for the Lower California Development Company, adjoins the cannery and is currently an active fishing port. A Social Security government medical

Punta and Pueblo de Sauzal

hospital is located on the northern outskirts of the town; various business establishments provide goods and services. Punta Morro (Morro Point), 2¾ miles southwestward of Saucedal Point, lies abreast a narrow valley that runs behind Ensenada. Along this shore there is an extensive kelp bed, the outer edge of which lies in depths of 10 to 13 fathoms, and the southern extremity of which lies 1½ miles southwestward of Morro Point. *Caution: Do not attempt to pass between the kelp and the shore; vessels should pass outside this kelp as breakers have been reported along the inside edge of the bed. Navigation note: In 1958 a vessel reported striking a pinnacle rock about 1¼ miles west-southwestward of, and bearing 238° from, Morro Point. A depth of 2½ fathoms has been sounded over this rock.* Eastward of Morro Point is a small bight in which fishing and pleasure boats find *anchorage* and take permanent mooring. A *reef* extends about ¼ mile southward from the point, and both eastward and westward of the point the water is shoal for a considerable distance offshore. Kelp beds fringe the point and numerous detached rocks exposed, awash and submerged, surround the shoal water off the point. Entrance into the bight for anchorage should be made from the southward and with local knowledge.

Punta Ensenada (Ensenada Point), a steep promontory 370 feet high, lies about 1¾ miles eastward of Morro Point. Halfway up the slope of Ensenada Point a prominent lookout station (a white hexagonal house with a mast) provides a good landmark. *A breakwater* protecting Ensenada Harbor extends seaward from Ensenada Point. Beyond the breakwater the land turns sharply to the northward then curves to the eastward, forming a small bay at the head of which is situated the old town and port of Ensenada.

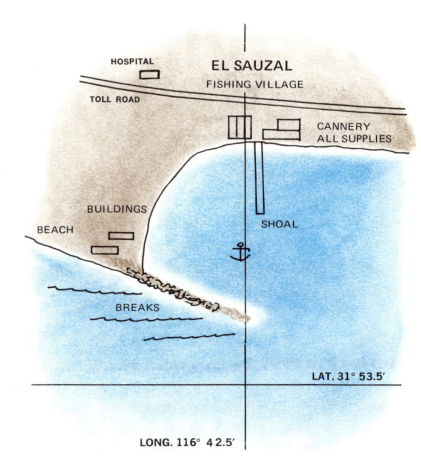

The port and town of Ensenada are located at the head of Bahía de Todos Santos, approximately 60 miles by sea southeast of San Diego. Ensenada Harbor is a modern improved ship basin protected behind a long rock breakwater that extends southeastward from Punta de Ensenada (Ensenada Point) and is sheltered from the prevailing coastal wind by the trend of the coast eastward of that same point. The southeastern end of the breakwater is located at Latitude 31° 52' north, Longitude 116° 38' west.

Ensenada Harbor is a deepwater port offering modern accommodations to cargo ships, fishing vessels and yachts. The harbor is one of the oldest ports on the Pacific coast and has a colorful history. Discovered for the Spanish in September, 1542, and called San Mateo by Juan Rodríguez Cabrillo, and 60 years later Ensenada de Todos Santos by Sebastián Vizcaíno, the bay and anchorage have been in almost continuous use over the intervening years. First utilized as a landing and watering place by the Manila Galleons crossing the Pacific from the Philippines bound for Acapulco, the landing subsequently became a supply point for the Franciscan and Dominican Fathers when establishing their missions in this part of the Baja California Peninsula. Sealers, whalers and coastal traders from around the Horn dropped anchor here, and a whaling station was established and operated in the southern reaches of the bay around the middle 1800's. Miners and prospectors during and after the California gold rush stopped for the trickle of fresh water, for mining supplies and provisions, and for whiskey and recreation in what was, at the time, an outpost of civilization. At one time controlling most of the Peninsula, the Lower California Development Company had its headquarters here. The city and harbor of Ensenada have evolved over the years into a modern and prosperous port owing to the gradual but constant development of agriculture and industry in the surrounding countryside, together with the natural attractions of the area to hunters, sportsmen and sportfishermen. While the old Spanish customs

and Latin hospitality remain, the once arid and sleepy village has become bustling and prosperous.

Ensenada Harbor is capable of accommodating behind its protective stone breakwater, moderate sized cargo and passenger vessels at modern dockside terminals, fishing vessels at a sportfishing pier, and yachts and small private craft. Once each year in May an International Yacht Race from Newport Beach to Ensenada Harbor is held, at which time the City of Ensenada plays host to four or five hundred sailing yachts and their crews. The Ensenada Race is an increasingly popular event with a three- or four-day festival celebrated by all hands.

LANDMARKS AND LIGHTS — When approaching Ensenada Harbor from the northwest quadrant, Todos Santos Islands, offshore about 8¾ miles southwest of Ensenada Harbor, provide an excellent landmark on the south side of the entrance channel into the harbor. A new lighthouse painted with white-and-orange horizontal bands has been built very near the old lighthouse on the northernmost island of the Todos Santos group. It is situated in a flat meadow on the northwestern extremity of the island. The navigation light, 230 feet above the sea and **flashing white** every 12 seconds, is visible 22 miles seaward around the horizon. A *radiobeacon* established at this light transmits the Morse code signal "TS" (— · · ·) on 292 kiloHertz. A fog siren synchronized with the radiobeacon for *distance finding* is audible in the sector 330° through 150°. (See Islas Todos Santos.) When approaching Bahía de Todos Santos in the quadrant west to north, the Ensenada entrance channel is oriented on a bearing of 124° true along the axis of another *radiobeacon* established on the shore at the north side of the mouth of Estero de Punta Banda. The radiobeacon transmits on 305 kiloHertz the Morse code signal "EN-ES" (· — · · · ·). South of the line bearing 124° toward the radiobeacon, the signal "ES" will be heard the stronger of the two; north of this bearing line, "EN" will be heard

Punta Morro and Punta Ensenada.

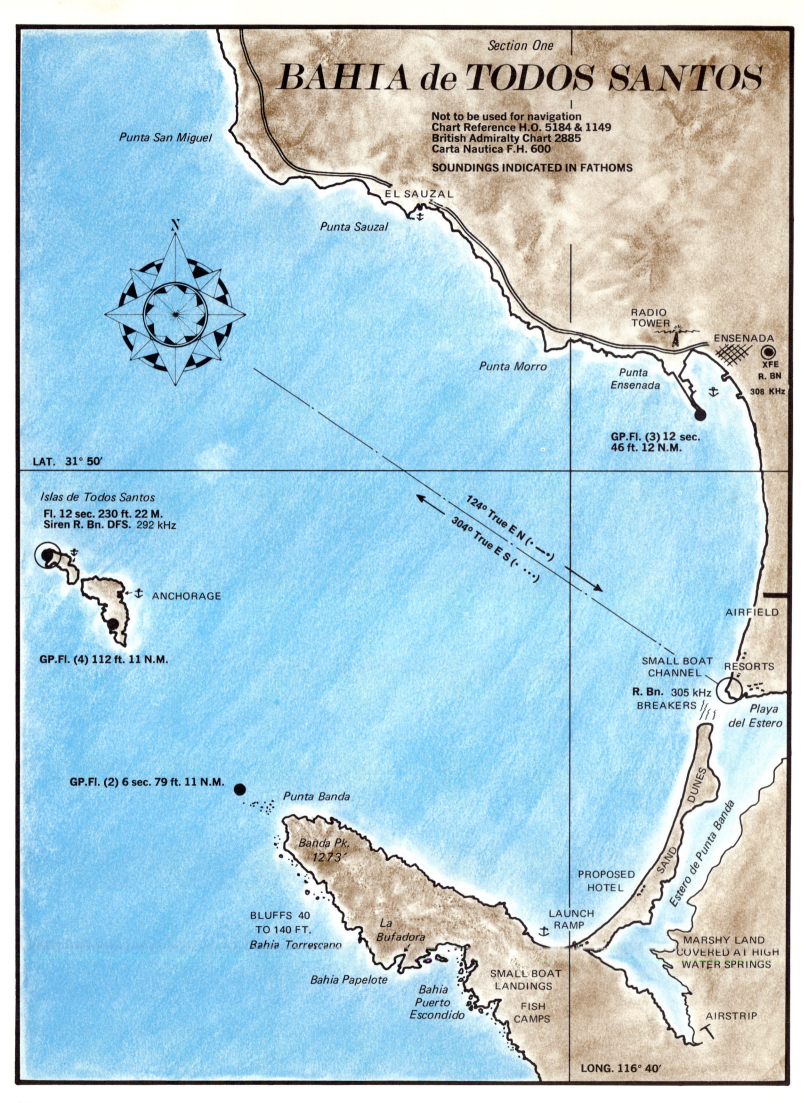

Section One

BAHIA de TODOS SANTOS

Not to be used for navigation
Chart Reference H.O. 5184 & 1149
British Admiralty Chart 2885
Carta Nautica F.H. 600
SOUNDINGS INDICATED IN FATHOMS

Punta San Miguel

EL SAUZAL

Punta Sauzal

N

RADIO
TOWER

ENSENADA

XFE
R. BN
308 KHz

Punta Morro

Punta
Ensenada

GP.Fl. (3) 12 sec.
46 ft. 12 N.M.

LAT. 31° 50'

Islas de Todos Santos
Fl. 12 sec. 230 ft. 22 M.
Siren R. Bn. DFS. 292 kHz

124° True E N (·—·)

304° True E S (·····)

ANCHORAGE

GP.Fl. (4) 112 ft. 11 N.M.

AIRFIELD

SMALL BOAT
CHANNEL

RESORTS

R. Bn. 305 kHz
BREAKERS

Playa
del Estero

GP.Fl. (2) 6 sec. 79 ft. 11 N.M.

Punta Banda

Banda Pk.
1273'

SAND DUNES

Estero de Punta Banda

PROPOSED
HOTEL

BLUFFS 40
TO 140 FT.
Bahia Torrescano

La
Bufadora

LAUNCH
RAMP

MARSHY LAND
COVERED AT HIGH
WATER SPRINGS

Bahia Papelote

Bahia
Puerto
Escondido

SMALL BOAT
LANDINGS

FISH
CAMPS

AIRSTRIP

LONG. 116° 40'

Approach to the breakwater at Ensenada   *Below, a view of the harbor and anchorage at Ensenada*

stronger. Dead on the bearing both signals will be heard at equally reduced strength. The passage through this northern entrance channel between a 3-fathom rock 2½ miles northward of the northernmost island of Islas de Todos Santos and Punta San Miguel is clear, with a least charted depth of 20 fathoms, except for a 2½-fathom *shoal* 1¼ miles westward of Punta Morro. Strong tidal currents have been encountered in this channel.

Punta Banda, the southern point of Todos Santos Bay, is a bold rocky headland. A ragged ledge extends about one mile northwest from the point. The shore of this promontory as far as the edge of the lagoon is a continuous bluff 40 to 140 feet high, back of which the land rises to between 700 and 800 feet. Banda Peak, about one mile eastward of the point, rises to an elevation of 1,264 feet and serves as an excellent mark for vessels approaching from the southward. Along the southwestern shore of the bay are numerous detached rocks and patches of kelp. When approaching Todos Santos Bay in the quadrant south to west, the navigation light located on the exposed rock offlying Punta Banda approximately ¾ mile, exhibits a **white group flash** of **two flashes** every **6 seconds:** flash 0.3 second, eclipse 1.2 seconds; flash 0.3 second, eclipse 4.2 seconds. This untended light is visible 16 miles in clear weather from 0° through 235°; it is obscured in the sector 136° through 147° by Islas de Todos Santos. When making through this southern channel into Bahía de Todos Santos, a course of approximately 60° true will bring a vessel up on a heading for the Ensenada Breakwater Light.

Among the landmarks that are useful in approaching the anchorage at the head of the bay are the lookout station on the slope above Ensenada Point, the customhouse — a triangular building with a tower at its southwestern corner — a large round mill chimney 150 feet high, and a water reservoir behind the town. Radiobeacon XFE, transmits a signal on 308 kiloHertz. If this beacon is not operating, call the Harbor Master on 2182 kiloHertz or 156.8 MegaHertz VHF Channel 16.

A stone breakwater 4,090 feet long extends southeastward from Ensenada Point, forming a protected anchorage within the curve of the beach. A navigation light is shown at the head of the breakwater and from the head of each of two moles inside at the foot of the breakwater. The Ensenada Breakwater Light is shown 46 feet above the sea from an orange iron framework tower and exhibits a **white group flash** of **three flashes** every **12 seconds:** flash 1 second, eclipse 1 second; flash 1 second, eclipse 1 second, flash 1 second, eclipse 10 seconds; it is visible all around. General depths in the bay range from 3 to 5 fathoms at the head of the bay to 10 fathoms in the center of the bay. The fairway leading into the protected portion of the

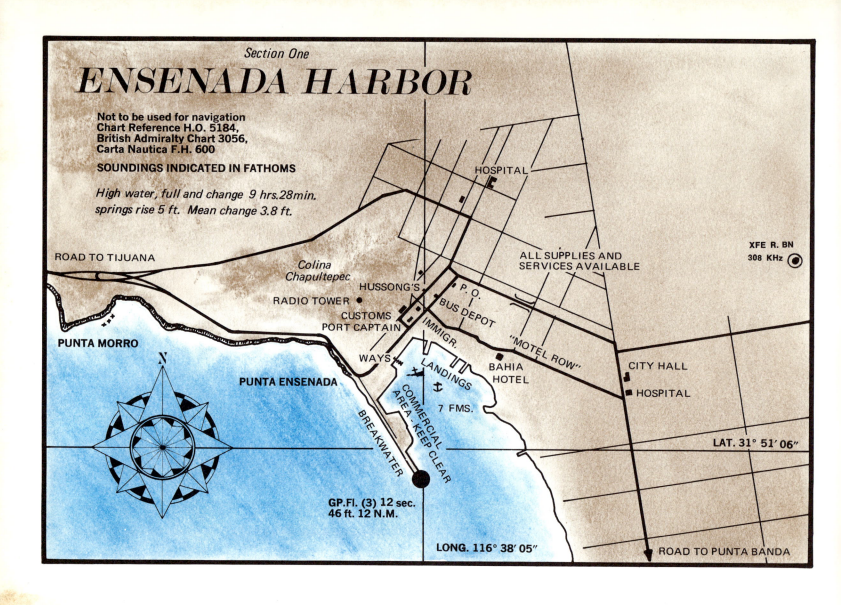

ENSENADA HARBOR

Not to be used for navigation
Chart Reference H.O. 5184,
British Admiralty Chart 3056,
Carta Nautica F.H. 600

SOUNDINGS INDICATED IN FATHOMS

High water, full and change 9 hrs. 28min.
springs rise 5 ft. Mean change 3.8 ft.

ROAD TO TIJUANA

XFE R. BN
308 KHz

Colina Chapultepec

ALL SUPPLIES AND
SERVICES AVAILABLE

HOSPITAL

HUSSONG'S

RADIO TOWER ●

P. O.
BUS DEPOT

CUSTOMS
PORT CAPTAIN

IMMIGR.

"MOTEL ROW"

PUNTA MORRO

WAYS

LANDINGS

BAHIA
HOTEL

CITY HALL

PUNTA ENSENADA

HOSPITAL

COMMERCIAL AREA · KEEP CLEAR

7 FMS.

BREAKWATER

LAT. 31° 51' 06"

GP. Fl. (3) 12 sec.
46 ft. 12 N.M.

LONG. 116° 38' 05"

ROAD TO PUNTA BANDA

harbor behind the breakwater is about 650 feet wide with a least depth of 33 feet at mean low water.

WHARFS AND BERTHS — Muelle Altura, a quay built on the inner side of the breakwater, is designed to provide berthing for cargo vessels and has depths alongside of 29 to 33 feet. General cargo is discharged. Muelle Cabotaje, a wharf on the north side of the harbor over 1,000 feet long, has depths alongside ranging from 9 feet on the northeast end to 22 feet on the southwest end. It is used by small coastal vessels and harbor utility craft. Eastward of Muelle Cabotaje are several commercial fishing piers. *Note: A recent storm destroyed the yacht dock but plans call for its rebuilding.* There is a ways and boat yard near the fishing piers. A pier, used by barges and tugs employed by the cement plant to transport raw materials from an open pit mine downcoast, extends from the eastern shore of Todos Santos Bay; the general area is frequently marked by a white cloud of dust hovering in the air over the cement plant located inland.

Ensenada is a port of entry and the Captain of the Port has jurisdiction over the west coast of Lower California north of Latitude 28°. Vessels touching at any port not a port of entry within this area must clear at Ensenada. Foreign vessels calling at Ensenada must clear Customs, Immigration, and Quarantine within 24 hours after arrival.

Estero de Punta Banda — The land on the southeastern side of Bahía de Todos Santos is low and sandy, behind which is an extensive lagoon, running about 6 miles in the north/south direction that terminates at the high land of the Punta Banda promontory. The entrance to this lagoon, situated near its northern end about 5 miles southward of the Ensenada Breakwater, threads through extensive shoals at the lagoon mouth on which the sea breaks continually. The entrance channel is narrow and follows the contour close to the eastern shore; the sea breaks along the southwestern limit on the offlying sand shoal and there are shore breakers along the northeastern limit on the beach. The depth of the channel varies with seasons and tides and is suitable at present only as a small boat channel for those with local knowledge.

The *radiobeacon* previously described is established at the mouth of the Estero de Punta Banda on the northern shore. Within the lagoon broad channels extend well up toward the southern end, divided by extensive sand shoals. The eastern shore of the lagoon is low and marshy, heavily grown with marsh reeds and covered at high water. The La Grulla Gun Club, at the southeast extremity of the Punta Banda Estero, dates back to before the turn of the century. The marshland surrounding the gun club is set aside as a hunting reservation and should not be entered without permission. The western side of the lagoon is separated from Todos Santos Bay by a long, low sandspit grown with patches of desert shrubs and ice plant. A road leads along the sandspit from the Punta Banda promontory all the way to its northern tip at the lagoon entrance. This road, however, is blocked in several places by drifting sand dunes and is negotiable only by 4-wheel drive vehicles or sand buggies. A third of the way along this sandspit, the concrete shell of a very large resort hotel of ultra modern design stands partially covered by drifting sand. Originally intended for a resort complex combined with a modern marina and yacht club, it surveys the ocean beach on one side and the protected lagoon on the other. Begun by the Mexican Government in the middle 1960's and abandoned for lack of adequate financing, it has now been purchased by private interests for completion and further development. On the opposite side of the estero near its entrance is a complex of partially dredged channels and slips for another marina development still to be completed. There are several operating motels on this eastern shore which provide small craft launching ramps. In a bight adjoining Bahía de Todos Santos, formed at the foot of the estero sandspit and the Punta Banda promontory, there is a sportfishing camp and small boat launching ramp. This was the site of the old whaling station in operation around the middle of the 1800's. Further west along the shore of the promontory is another sportfishing camp with a small boat launching ramp. Various fisherman's supplies and services are available at these camps and a paved road communicates between them and Ensenada.

SEA AND WEATHER CONDITIONS — Ensenada Harbor is open only to the west and receives the breezes and the swells that generally come from this direction. The severe storms that sometimes blow in from the southeast, south, or southwest are effectively baffled by the surrounding land and by the breakwater protecting the basin. The breakwater deflects incoming swells under most weather conditions and calm water usually prevails within the basin. There is some surge at the docks and slips but it is generally of mild degree. Anchorage in the open roadstead is subject to rolling swells.

Generally, the breezes blow from the northwest, west and southwest, springing up about midmorning, increasing toward the late afternoon, and dying out after sundown. Winds within the bay seldom exceed 25 knots, usually averaging from 8 to 12 knots. There is frequently an afternoon chop in the shallower parts of the bay that can be somewhat uncomfortable while riding at anchor in a small craft. Fogs are not common but do occur during the summer months, usually at night, clearing by midmorning. Storm warnings are displayed on the moles.

ANCHORAGE — There is adequate protected anchorage behind the breakwater in the northeastern part of the bay in 3 to 5 fathoms over a sand and mud bottom. Larger vessels may anchor ½ mile offshore south of the breakwater in deeper water. If maximum protection from a southerly gale is desired, anchorage should be shifted to the southern part of the bay in the lee of Banda Point. In the extreme southern part of the bay, 4 miles from Banda Point and just at the end of the red cliffs, is a low sand beach flanked on the south and west by hills 500 feet high, near which is the site of an old whaling station. In this Whaler's Bight there is good and comfortable *anchorage* in depths of 3 to 10 fathoms over a sand and mud bottom. The prevailing northwesterly wind in its usual force is not seriously felt here.

TIDES — The mean high water interval at full and change in Todos Santos Bay is 9 hours, 28 minutes; the mean range is 3.8 feet, the spring range is 5 feet.

FACILITIES — Ensenada is a modern city with a population of more than 50,000 and provides all general city services and supplies. (During reconstruction of the marina, fuel can be purchased at gasoline stations in town.) It is advisable to purchase bottled water, available in the town, for drinking. There is a sportfishing dock just north of the marina where as many as 36 charter and excursion boats operate throughout the year. A small ways and repair yard is established on the beach in the northern corner of the basin. Vessels up to 25 tons can be hauled for maintenance or repair. A diesel tug and a tug-fireboat are available in the port. The Captain of the Port is located at 493 Frente, telephone 8-2825. The immigration office is at Calle Ruiz, telephone 8-2116.

PORT CLEARANCE — Proper papers must be prepared before leaving Ensenada for the United States or other Mexican or foreign ports and this may be accomplished through any reputable customhouse broker. A crew list is the single most important document. (See appendix for entering and clearing procedures.) Among the agents that offer clearing services in Ensenada are: Gil Ojeda, Comisionista y Agente de Buques, Apartado Postal 22, Avenido Frente 485, telephone 8-3615 or (residence) 8-2738, office hours 9 a.m. to 2 p.m. and 4 p.m. to 8 p.m.; and Agencia Maritima del Pacifico, Ruiz 12-E, telephone 8-1125 or 8-2648.

PUBLIC ACCOMMODATIONS — Ensenada has 55 hotels and motels of varying classes located throughout the city but principally along the waterfront. First class accommodations are available. More than 30 excellent restaurants and hospitable grog houses are connected with these establishments. There are 17 trailer parks in the town with a number of excellent ones on the coast overlooking the bay. The tourist bureau located at Calle Primera may be contacted for information and direction to any class or type accommodation desired.

Entrance to the lagoon at Estero Beach

COMMUNICATIONS — Public telephones are located at the marina and in the hotels and motels and other public places within the city with service to the telephone systems throughout Mexico and the United States. Cable messages are accepted for transmission from Mexico City. The cable office is at Miramar and Sixth Avenues, telephone 8-2263. The telephone office, from which paid long distance calls may be made, is at Third Avenue and Obregón, telephone 8-2200. The post office is at Gastelum and Miramar Avenues, with a branch office at Vizcaíno No. 215. The Club de Yates de Ensenada may be addressed Apartado Postal 502, Ensenada, Baja California, Mexico, telephone 8-3876. The Port Captain may be called by telephone, 8-2825, and receives radio messages on 2182 kHz or 156.8 mHz VHF Channel 16 through radio station XFE, Ensenada.

TRANSPORTATION — The town has no railroad communication but good paved roads connect northward to Tijuana and southward for some distance to the coastal settlements. There is an *airfield* with services and facilities for commercial and private planes. Buses serve the city and provide intercity transportation. Taxis may be summoned to the dockside. Rental cars are available.

MARINE EMERGENCIES — Call the Captain of the Port at 8-2825 by landline telephone or the Port Guard at 8-2477. Call the City Police at 9-1263. Call the Mexican Coast Guard by radio on 156.8 mHz or 2182 kHz.

MEDICAL FACILITIES — There are several hospitals in Ensenada organized to provide emergency treatment. Call for an ambulance by telephone at 8-2555. The Civil Hospital, equipped with emergency receiving facilities, is located at Ruiz and 14th Avenues, telephone 8-2555 or 8-3113 or 8-3333; the Hospital Ismte is at Ruiz and 14th Avenues, telephone 8-1460; the Hospital Infantil is at Gastelum and 14th Avenues, telephone 8-3275. Social Security Hospital is on Avenue Reforma,

Fraccion Bahía, telephone 9-1701, 9-1702, 9-1703, 9-1704, 9-1705, 9-1706.

SOURCES OF ADDITIONAL INFORMATION — Direction de Turismo, Calle Primera 768, Ensenada, Baja California, Mexico; Consejo Nacional de Turismo, International y Balboa, Ensenada, Baja California, Mexico; Pemex Travel Club, Avenida Juarez No. 89, Mexico 7, D.F., Mexico; Club de Yates de Ensenada, Apartado Postal 502, Ensenada, Baja California, Mexico. (See also appendix.)

Islas Todos Santos (All Saints Islands) lie about 3½ miles northwestward of Punta Banda and extend about 1¾ miles in a northwest direction as a geographic continuation of the Punta Banda promontory. The islets are situated offshore in Bahía de Todos Santos (Todos Santos Bay) approximately 8¾ miles from the seaward end of the Ensenada Breakwater and about 6¼ miles southwestward of Punta San Miguel. Todos Santos Lighthouse on the northwestern extremity of the northernmost and smaller of the two islands is located at Latitude 31° 49′ north, Longitude 116° 49′ west.

Islas Todos Santos are comprised of two rocky islets surrounded by detached rocks and considerable kelp. The northwestern and smaller islet is relatively flat with a

Todos Santos Light

Punta Banda and offlying rocks, looking east

maximum elevation of 55 feet above the sea. Two light-houses, one old, one new, a radiobeacon antenna and several service buildings are situated at its western extremity. The southeastern and somewhat larger islet is 313 feet high with a navigation light at its highest peak, situated at the southeastern extremity. The two islets are separated by a shallow boat channel clogged with kelp and submerged rocks that bare at low water. Kelp beds surround both islets and an extensive field of kelp (the outer edge of which lies in a depth of about 20 fathoms) extends approximately 1 mile northward from the north-western islet. The islets are covered with dry brush and the rocky cliffs provide a rookery for thousands of sea birds. No fresh water has been found and the islands are uninhabited save for occasional lobster fishermen and abalone divers, who occupy small tarpaper shacks on the southeastern islet, and resident lighthouse personnel quartered on the northwestern islet.

As mentioned earlier . . . Cabrillo first discovered Bahía de Todos Santos and its offshore islands on Sunday, September 17, 1542, and named the area San Mateo. Vizcaíno, on his expedition to rechart the coast of the Californias 60 years later, named the bay and its offshore islands Todos Santos. There is no evidence of any early native habitation, no doubt due to the lack of fresh water. The islands were in every probability used by ancient Indian itinerant fisher-men as they are now, for a casual but rather good fishing spot reached easily by canoe. It is widely rumored in the town of Ensenada that Robert Louis Stevenson lived for a time just outside the city and used the offshore island group as a model for his classic adventure *Treasure Island*. However, such is not the case; Robert Louis Stevenson never lived near Ensenada, and while the Todos Santos Islands are in the character of those described in *Treasure Island,* the rugged rockbound coast of Monterey was the actual locale of Stevenson's imaginative fiction.

A mine was worked on the larger south island before the turn of the century and its old machinery and building foundations may still be seen on the flat above the cove on the eastern side. On the smaller north island in a cove on the northeastern side, a dock has been built to land fresh water and supplies for the lighthouse facility. A road leads from the landing to the northwestern end of the island and an old dilapidated truck provides transportation for supplies. A Mexican vessel of the Port Guard calls weekly and may be seen occasionally at anchor in the open road-stead off the landing.

LANDMARKS AND LIGHTS — A navigation light is shown from a new cylindrical orange-and-white banded concrete tower located several hundred yards from the old white cylindrical lighthouse at the northwestern extremity of the northernmost islet. This new light, established 230 feet above the sea, **flashes white** every 12 seconds and is visible 22 miles in clear weather all around the horizon. A *radiobeacon* situated at the light transmits a Morse code signal "TS" on 292 kiloHertz (— •••). A fog siren, synchronized with the radiobeacon for *distance finding* in thick weather, is audible in the sector 330° through 150°. The tall steel latticework antenna of the radiobeacon stands close westward of the new lighthouse. A *reef,* partially exposed at low water, extends westward from the northwestern extremity of the islet below the lighthouse and an *exposed rock,* on which the sea breaks, lies off the end of the reef. The kelp field grows for a considerable distance out beyond the end of the reef and is a good indicator of the proximity of danger when approaching the island during thick weather. A second navigation light, 112 feet above the sea on the southeastern end of the South Island, exhibits a characteristic **white group flash** of **four flashes** from a small white concrete tower, and is visible for 11 miles in clear weather in the sector 194° through 115°.

Across the deep 2½-mile wide channel between the South Island and the mainland, a navigation light is exhibited on a large exposed rock offlying Punta Banda. This untended light, shown from a white tower 88 feet above the sea, displays a characteristic **white group flash** of **two flashes** every **6 seconds:** flash 0.3 second, eclipse 1.2 seconds; flash 0.3 second, eclipse 4.2 seconds. It is visible 11 miles in clear weather from 0° through 235°; the light is obscured in the sector 136° through 147° by Islas de Todos Santos. A *submerged rock* with a least depth of 3 fathoms over it, surrounded by kelp, is charted approximately 2½ miles northward of the northwestern islet; the position of this rock is approximate, however, as it has not been possible to verify its location or existence in recent years.

The channel separating the Todos Santos Islands from Punta Banda is 2½ miles wide, very deep and free of dangers. It leads over a submarine ridge connecting the islands to the point; the least mid-channel depth is 128 fathoms. *Note: The Punta Banda Light has been moved in recent years from the promontory to the outermost reef, a little over ¾ mile off the point. Do not attempt to pass inside the light except in a small vessel and with local knowledge; generally such passage is not recommended as the area is foul with exposed and submerged dangers.* Pico Banda (Banda Peak), which attains an elevation of 1,273 feet about ¾ mile southeastward of the point, rises gently from the southward but falls abruptly northward and forms an excellent landmark from southward. The peak is frequently shrouded in early morning coastal fog and rises through the mists with the appearance of a detached island.

SEA AND WEATHER CONDITIONS — Islas de Todos Santos provide a lee along their northeastern side and afford good shelter except in winds and weather from the easterly quadrant. Weather in the area is generally that previously described for Ensenada; however, the prevailing northwesterlies blow with somewhat more force in the vicinity of Punta Banda, as may be expected around any promontory.

ANCHORAGE — Good anchorage may be had in depths of 4 fathoms, sand bottom, off the eastern side of the smaller northernmost island in the open roadstead abreast the lighthouse dock. The lighthouse supply vessel anchors here and lands fresh water and provisions once each week. Two excellent and well protected coves for small craft are located on the lee side of the larger southernmost islet about midway along its northeastern shore. The northwesternmost of the two coves is a popular shelter for fishings vessels and yachts and, while the entrance appears small when first sighted, it opens into a commodious well-protected basin capable of holding 12 to 15 small vessels. The cove is surrounded by high rock walls on all sides and is mostly free of submerged dangers. Kelp floats in the cove but all the submerged rocks are close inshore. *Anchorage* is in 5 to 8 fathoms over a rock-strewn sand bottom. A small concrete post, the remnant foundation of one leg of an old crane, is anchored on a rock ledge close to the water's edge at the head of the cove. A chain or wire strap may usually be found wrapped around this post for making fast a stern line. It is advisable not to employ a rope bridle as the sawing action of the post will usually part the stoutest line overnight, and a high tide, which sometimes covers the post, is likely to float off a rope yarn bight. The customary anchoring position is bow out, stern line ashore. *Caution: a submerged rock, covered a little more than a fathom, lies about 75 feet off the ledge near the concrete mooring block at the head of the northernmost cove; deepdraft*

Islas Todos Santos with Punta Banda in the background

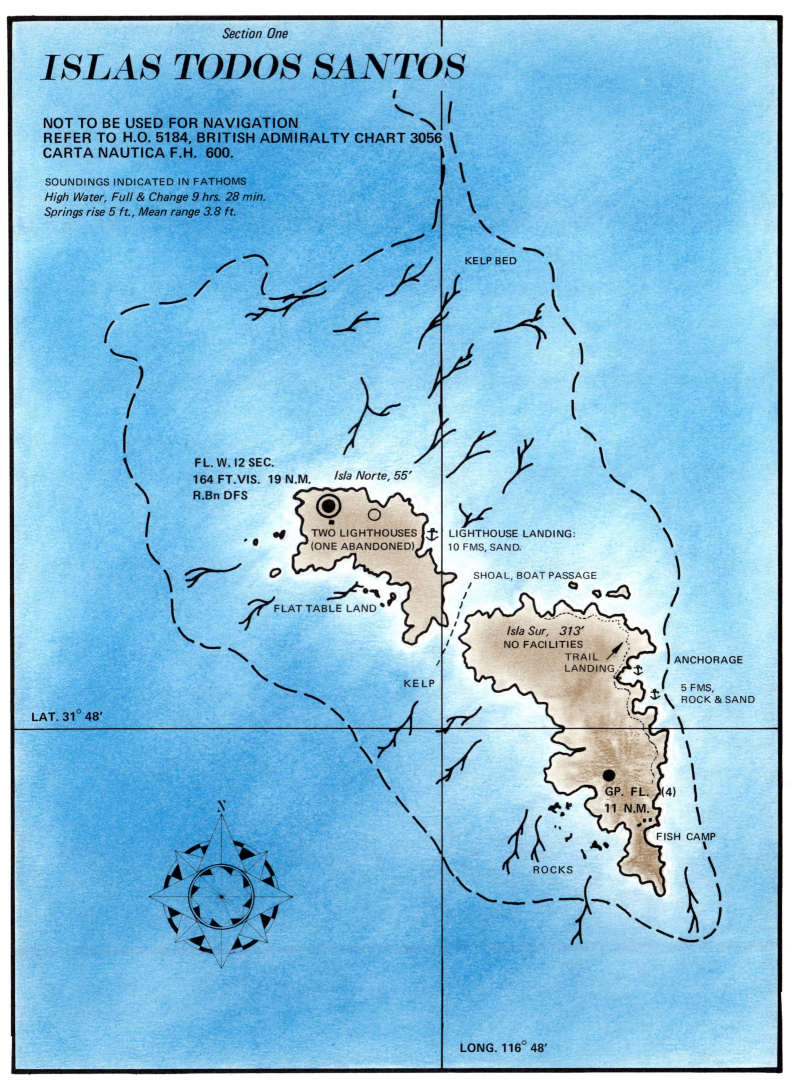

ISLAS TODOS SANTOS

NOT TO BE USED FOR NAVIGATION
REFER TO H.O. 5184, BRITISH ADMIRALTY CHART 3056
CARTA NAUTICA F.H. 600.

SOUNDINGS INDICATED IN FATHOMS
High Water, Full & Change 9 hrs. 28 min.
Springs rise 5 ft., Mean range 3.8 ft.

KELP BED

FL. W. 12 SEC.
164 FT. VIS. 19 N.M.
R.Bn DFS

Isla Norte, 55'

TWO LIGHTHOUSES
(ONE ABANDONED)

LIGHTHOUSE LANDING:
10 FMS, SAND.

SHOAL, BOAT PASSAGE

FLAT TABLE LAND

Isla Sur, 313'
NO FACILITIES

TRAIL
LANDING

ANCHORAGE

5 FMS,
ROCK & SAND

KELP

LAT. 31° 48'

N

GP. FL. (4)
11 N.M.

FISH CAMP

ROCKS

LONG. 116° 48'

31

Detail of the cove on South Island

vessels should be moored clear of this danger. If one comes upon this anchorage filled with yachts and fishing vessels, he may elect to try the next cove immediately southeastward, separated from the first cove by a high narrow ridge. Similar conditions prevail here though there are some *submerged dangers* on the southeastern side that must be given adequate berth. One need not be alarmed when moored snugly in either cove to have one vessel after another slip in the entrance and find mooring room where none seems to exist. While it is pleasant to have either cove to one's self, it is also a memorable experience to step from boat deck to boat deck across the cove. This anchorage is well protected except from the easterly quadrant and even then provides some small shelter from heavy blows; however, sailing vessels will do well to quit these coves before heavy winds make it difficult to sail free of the headlands.

Landing in the northwesternmost cove may be made on the ledge near the concrete post; the cliff, while somewhat steep, may be scaled easily to the flat ground of the island above. The old foundations of buildings and mining machinery used before the turn of the century are located closeby. All parts of the southeastern island may be reached from this point.

There is a narrow *boat passage* through a deep cleft in the high rock wall at the northern head of the larger cove; the passage is often heavily grown with kelp and a moderate to heavy surge fills through both ends. The passage opens into a second, well-protected cove with a scattering of exposed and submerged rocks. A deep cave opens in the sheer wall of rock to one side of this cove. The water is generally still and clear and the submarine gardens are rich with plant growth. There is a shingle beach at the head of this cove where a dry landing may be made with access to the top of the island.

TIDES — The mean high water interval at Bahía de Todos Santos is 9 hours 28 minutes; the mean range is 3.8 feet, and the spring range is 5 feet.

FACILITIES AND PUBLIC ACCOMMODATIONS — The lighthouse and service buildings, together with the small dock for landing supplies on the eastern side of the North Island, are the only facilities in service. There are no public facilities or accommodations of any kind.

COMMUNICATIONS — Lighthouse personnel operate a radio on a network of assigned Mexican frequencies communicating with Ensenada on a schedule several times daily. They will accept emergency messages for transmission.

MARINE EMERGENCIES AND MEDICAL FACILITIES — First aid may be rendered by lighthouse personnel; the nearest complete medical facilities are located in Ensenada. (See Ensenada for detailed medical advice.)

TODOS SANTOS COVE

FOUL

LAT. 31° 48' 18"

LONG. 116° 47' 30"

BEST LANDING: SAND 5F. WATCH FOR ROCK COVERED 7'

Section Two

PUNTA BANDA to CABO COLNETT

NOT TO BE USED FOR NAVIGATION
REFER TO H.O. 5184 BRITISH ADMIRALTY CHART 3056
CARTA NAUTICA F.H. 600

SOUNDINGS INDICATED IN FATHOMS

High water full and change 9 hrs. 00 min.
Mean range 4.0 ft.

GP.FL. White (2)
VIS. 11 N.M.
Punta Banda

Bahia Todos Santos

Playa de Estero

Estero de
Punta Banda

LANDING

Bahia Papelote

Cerro Soledad

Pico Soledad

Bahia Soledad

Rocas Soledad

LANDING

Puerto Santo Tomas

Punta China

LAT. 31° 30'

Punta San Jose

Mesa de San Jose

Los Muertos
FISH CAMP

Punta Piedras

Bahia Almejas

LANDING PLACE

San Vicente
AIRSTRIP

Punta Cabras

Pico San
Antonio
1845'

Punta San Isidro
LANDING PLACE

Erendira

VILLAGE

N

Playa San Antonio del Mar
(Scavenger's Beach)

VILLAGE

Cerro Colorado
1106'

COLNETT

FLYING SAMARITAN
HOSPITAL & AIRSTRIP

LOW & FLAT

FISH CAMP

FL. WHITE 5 SEC.

LANDING

Cabo Colnett

Bahia Colnett
Punta San Telmo

LONG. 116° 30'

33

South side of Punta Banda

SECTION 2
PUNTA BANDA to CABO COLNETT

Punta Banda marks the southern threshold of a bold coastline, much less frequented by yachts and pleasure craft than that portion of the coast which stretches northward. This is not owing to any lack of worthwhile coves, anchorages, beaches or good cruising ground, but to general lack of local information as to the nature of the coast, its facilities and available shelter. So long has Punta Banda been the southern terminal cruising point for many yachts from the north that nearly all marine insurance issued for pleasure boats in Southern California ports specifies Punta Banda as the southern navigational limit covered under their policies. It is well to bear in mind that, if one wishes to maintain valid marine insurance throughout his voyage, a separate cover policy usually must be obtained when cruising beyond Punta Banda. As small boat traffic steadily increases southward along the Baja Peninsula, which it surely must with the spread of accurate and reliable coastal information, the present navigational limits pertaining to marine insurance will no doubt be extended and voyages undertaken without hesitation or special concern.

Between Punta Banda and Punta Santo Tomás, 12 miles southward, the coast is generally high and precipitous with deep water close to shore. Kelp is abundant, surrounding numerous detached rocks, with one dominant *white rock* standing several hundred yards offshore outside the 10-fathom curve and a precipitous *rocky islet,* a little more than a mile offshore. Sportfishing is excellent throughout the area.

There are a number of small coves, beaches, bights, and landings that may be reached by both land and sea, as well as several good landmarks.

The mountains along this coast rise abruptly to a group of 3000-foot peaks, the most prominent of which, close to the coast, is Pico Soledad (Soledad Peak) rising to an elevation of 3,484 feet about 3 miles east-northeastward of the head of Bahía de la Soledad. Three miles eastward is an unnamed peak, highest of the range, with a charted altitude of 3,566 feet.

From seaward the Punta Banda Peninsula shows some 13 coastal terraces or ancient beaches in wave-cut benches that are clearly visible above the present sea level. The point derives its name from the 1862 Geological and Geophysical coastal survey expedition aboard the research vessel *Maria* under the direction of Dr. Longinos Banda, an eminent Mexican scientist. Prior to this time the point was referred to on early charts as Punta Gravero.

Immediately around the point is an indented cove, Bahía Torrescaño, the vicinity of which may be readily identified from both land and sea when any swell is running by a most spectacular and high-reaching spout of spray from a blowhole called La Buffadora (The Roarer). The natural swell of the sea submerges a tide-line rocky crevice trapping and compressing air within the cavity. As the swell recedes, air and water burst forth with a terrific roar, shooting as much as a 100 feet outward and upward from the rocky face.

When the light is right, the settling spray will often strike a miniature rainbow over the blowhole.

A fish camp with a store, refreshment stands and boats for hire is located closeby. A paved road leads from the vicinity of the blowhole 13 miles to the Ensenada highway.

Bahía Papelote, the next and deeper indentation southeastward along the shore, is a small cove with a floating mass of kelp surrounding detached rocks. Bahía Puerto Escondido, the next and largest bight to the southward, is marked by a number of large *detached rocks* close along the steep shore with some toward the center of the cove. A lobster fishery called Kennedy's Camp and also known as Nuevo Arbolitos, is located on the northwest side of the cove. Small rental boats for bottom fishing employ this landing. Above the center of the cove, just below a low spur of the peninsula, is an old eucalyptus grove, and camp ground, El Arbolitos, which may be seen from seaward. A *rocky islet* on which a colony of sea lions can usually be seen and heard, lies just offshore in this vicinity.

Piedro Blanca, a conspicuous whitened rock standing several hundred yards offshore outside the 20-fathom curve, lies just southeastward of Kennedy's Camp. Rocks, detached and awash within beds of seaweed, hug the precipitous coast until it turns southward in a sweep of sandy beach flanking the mouth of Arroyo Maximinos. A group of farm buildings may be seen just back of the beach on the north

side of the arroyo. A primitive dirt road from this beach connects with the Punta Banda Highway. The best *landing* is at the north end of the beach in the lee of Punta Banda. Southward of this arroyo lies Punta Maximinos surrounded by kelp beds and some *detached rocks*.

Bahía Soledad (Soledad Bay), just northward of the Santo Tomás promontory and about 11 miles from Punta Banda, is a roughly rectangular indentation about a mile wide, bracketed by Punta Las Maximinos on its northern extremity and by Punta Rif to the southward.

Kelp beds surround *detached rocks* at both the northeastern and southwestern entrances to this bay, extending about ½ mile offshore generally following the 10-fathom curve. Otherwise the bay is clear of dangers and affords convenient depths of 6- to 10-fathoms *anchorage* over a sand bottom. At the head of the bay a clean, wide, sandy beach flanks either side of Arroyo Soledad, dry most of the year, with runoff only after fresh rains. A primitive road leads from Bahía Soledad to the Santo Tomás Valley, but the bay is seldom visited and is usually deserted. Shelter is provided from the south and southeast, but the anchorage is fully exposed to the prevailing westerly and northwesterly winds, with accompanying swells and heavy surf except in the calmest weather. Fishing boats are sometimes seen at anchor off the beach.

Punta Santo Tomás is the southwestern extremity of a square-shaped headland that projects about 1½ miles westward from the general coastline; Punta Rif comprises its northwestern extremity. The headland is low and rocky, but the land rises quickly to a height of 395 feet within ¾ mile and 1,450 feet at Pico Acantilado (Bluff Peak) 1¾ miles northeastward of the point. The entire headland is surrounded by kelp which extends outward nearly ½ mile from its northern and western sides. A *sunken rock,* on which the sea breaks, lies 700 yards north-northwestward of Punta Santo Tomás. When rounding this headland a course allowing at least ½-mile sea room should be followed.

Rocas Soledad (El Islote, or Soledad Rocks), rising from deep water 1¼ miles westward of Punta Santo Tomás, is comprised of a group of rocks, steep-to, 20 feet high, whitened by birdlime and surrounded by kelp. The channel between Rocas Soledad and the point is deep and free of dangers; lay a course clear of the kelp, either port or starboard, for safety. There is excellent fishing most of the year in the close vicinity of these rocks.

Puerto Santo Tomás lies in the lee within a bight eastward of the headland of the same name and affords *good anchorage,* sheltered against the prevailing coastal winds. A swell, reflected around Santo Tomás Point, generally sweeps the shore cliffs.

DIRECTIONS — When making for the anchorage from the northward or westward, give Punta Santo Tomás and the land to the southward and eastward a ½-mile berth to avoid the dense kelp beds. Stand to the eastward until a small sand beach, the landing place, with a few outlying rocks at its southern end, is open to the northward of the inner point; then haul to the northward. As soon as Soledad Rocks are in range with the southern extremity of the headland southeastward of Punta Santo Tomás, about ¼ mile off the landing place, select a suitable anchoring position. Large vessels should anchor farther out with Rocas Soledad open of the point. Small yachts and fishing vessels may approach close in the lee of the bight. There are no outlying dangers in the approach from the southward; vessels coming to anchor from that direction should steer for the deepest bight under the lee of the point until the small sand beach is made out. *Anchorage* may be taken in depths of 5 to 10 fathoms over a sand bottom. There are no navigation lights in Puerto Santo Tomás but a fish camp, cantina, and motel called Vista Al Mar, are located above the landing and may show some lights at night. Due to the aforementioned swell in the anchorage, it is wise to use both bow and stern anchors to prevent rolling in the troughs.

CAUTION — Commercial lobster fishermen anchor large holding receivers in the bay. These heavy wooden-slatted boxes ride at mooring just awash and are entirely invisible at night unless spotlighted. Give the mooring cans a wide berth.

TIDES AND CURRENTS — The high water interval at full and change is 9 hours 00 minutes, the mean difference is 4 feet. The normal California current runs southward along this coast and as it sweeps past the protruding headland of Santo Tomás, a great circular whirl is created within the bay. This action causes a marine upwelling of cold water,

Bahia Soledad showing anchorage

which is as much as 10° to 12° cooler than that found northward of the headland. Abundant nutrients supporting a dense population of marine life accompany this upwelling and make Santo Tomás Bay an excellent fish habitat.

On Thursday, September 14, 1542, Juan Rodríguez Cabrillo cast anchor behind a small cape and bestowed the name Cabo de Cruz on that place we know today as Santo Tomás. His latitude description of 33° was considerably in error unless an injustice has been done in translating his log in the 429 intervening years. However, the hand-held astrolabe was the navigating instrument of the day and its reading was often in error and sometimes significantly so.

Puerto Santo Tomás became the principal port along this coast during the time of the Spanish Colonial development of the area. Unlike many of the open roadsteads at which supply and trading vessels called, this landing provided good shelter from the prevailing winds and seas. In this place cliffs drop to the water's edge and the sailing vessels that called were able to load and land their cargoes from very near the shore by high line. In contrast, the harbor at Ensenada was quite shoal for a good distance offshore and ships were forced to anchor far out, making the handling of cargo both difficult and time consuming.

The adobe ruins of the original Mission Santo Tomás de Aquino, founded in 1791, lie just a short distance inland from the landing. Coastal fogs and lack of good water were not conducive to the temperaments or the vineyards of the founding fathers and in 1794 the mission was moved farther inland to its present site in the Santo Tomás Valley, where the existence of three large flowing springs, brighter sun and warmer weather better mellowed the padres' feeling of well-being and better nurtured the grapes, olives and other crops.

Mission Santo Tomás was the last of the great California chain of early Spanish colonial settlements to be dissolved under the church secularization order of the Government of

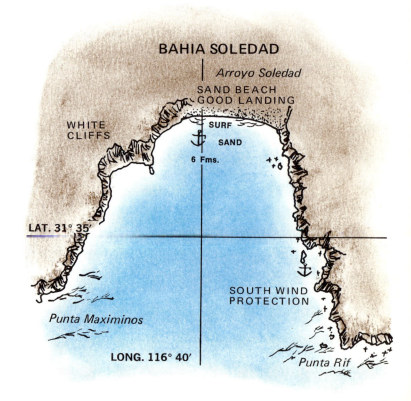

Rocas Soledad with Punta Santo Tomás in the background

Mexico. In 1849 Father Augustin Mansilla de Gamboa closed the church doors, and the mission period of Baja California ended with the departure of this last of the Dominican Order. In July of the same year the village of Santo Tomás became the first capitol of the area, called La Frontera (The Frontier), and remained the capitol for 25 years until the gold strike of the 1870's changed the seat of power to Ensenada. Under the padres, and long after their departure, the region was well known for its excellent wines and Santo Tomás was the principal vineyard along the coast. The winery and warehouse of Vinos de Santo Tomás supplied many a cask to trading vessels calling at the port. The winery and bodega have moved to Ensenada, but the Santo Tomás vineyards still produce their excellent grapes from the limestone soil. Today the village, located 11 miles inland and connected to the port by a good road, is a pleasant pastoral settlement catering to tourists. Its historical interest spans some two hundred years.

Beyond the Santo Tomás landing, a road shows to seaward running along the top of the bluff from Vista Al Mar,

following the curve of the bay southeastward. A well frame stands on the brink of the cliff near the landing and provides potable fresh water to the settlement. At the southern end of the bay, about one mile from the landing, Boca de Santo Tomás opens on the shore and the trickle of the Santo Tomás River disappears into a broad sand and pebbly beach that separates the river mouth from the sea. Sweet water is obtained from wells in the cottonwood thickets along the stream. A tree-bordered meadow is used by campers and surf fishermen; soft drinks and refreshments are sometimes available from a small tienda (store). The camp is called La Bocana (The Mouth). From La Bocana the coastal road turns inland and runs up the Santo Tomás Valley to the old Mission Village. South across the mouth of Río Santo Tomás a cluster of sand dunes below Punta Clara can be readily made out. *Detached rocks* on the south side of the river mouth lie just off this point. Kelp beds grow profusely offshore and continue for a mile southward to Punta China, sometimes called the Point of Pebbles. A limestone quarry is located back of China Point. Quarried materials are loaded here onto coastal barges moored close along the cliff

Anchorage at Santo Tomás

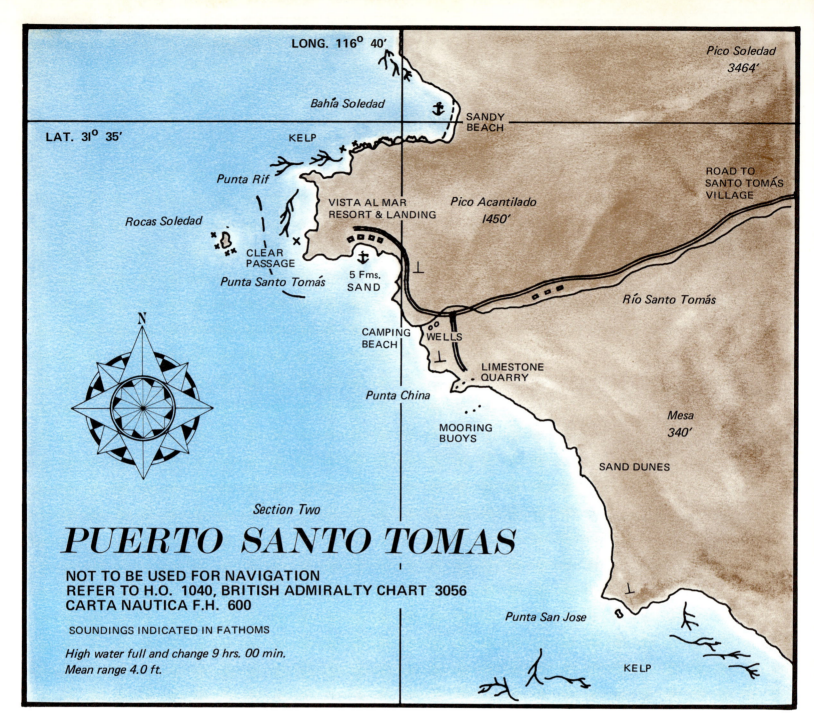

LONG. 116° 40'

Pico Soledad
3464'

Bahía Soledad

SANDY
BEACH

LAT. 31° 35'

KELP

ROAD TO
SANTO TOMÁS
VILLAGE

Punta Rif

VISTA AL MAR
RESORT & LANDING

Pico Acantilado
1450'

Rocas Soledad

CLEAR
PASSAGE

Punta Santo Tomás

5 Fms.
SAND

Río Santo Tomás

N

CAMPING
BEACH

WELLS

LIMESTONE
QUARRY

Punta China

Mesa
340'

MOORING
BUOYS

SAND DUNES

Section Two

PUERTO SANTO TOMAS

**NOT TO BE USED FOR NAVIGATION
REFER TO H.O. 1040, BRITISH ADMIRALTY CHART 3056
CARTA NAUTICA F.H. 600**

SOUNDINGS INDICATED IN FATHOMS

*High water full and change 9 hrs. 00 min.
Mean range 4.0 ft.*

Punta San Jose

KELP

and are then towed northward to the docks of the cement plant in Ensenada. Quarry buildings and rising dust of loading activities show distinctly to seaward. A company *airstrip* is situated on the coastal ledge immediately north of China Point near the quarry. A well-graded road connects the quarry to the Santo Tomás Valley road and thence to the Ensenada Highway.

Punta San José lies about 7 miles southeastward of Punta Santo Tomás with the intervening curve of the coast interrupted by the mouth of the Santo Tomás River just northward of Punta Clara, and to the southward by Arroyo Campodin midway between Punta China and Punta San José. The coast comprises a succession of bluffs backed by hills and small mesas. A great field of kelp extends about 3½ miles off San José Point; in the kelp about a mile southwestward of the point there is a *shoal patch* 5¾ fathoms, just outside the 10-fathom curve. San José Point affords good protection from the prevailing winds, but the anchorage is generally blocked by kelp. A *detached rock* lies just off the point in the kelp. On Punta San José is an abandoned

fish camp, and southward there are a number of ranchos established along the coast, generally located near arroyos and close to a constant source of ground water. There is a copper mine back of this coast among the cluster of sharp pointed peaks called Cerro Las Tetas de Cabra (Teats of a Goat), about 4 miles northeast of Punta San José. The coast trends eastward forming a shelter from the prevailing winds, then curves southeastward to Punta Piedras.

The plateau of San José lies midway between these two points backed by peaks of 2,000-foot altitude. A coastal bluff lies high above the shore, but arroyos break through to the beach. Rancho El Embarcadero is established back of the shore at the mouth of an arroyo, about 1½ miles eastward of Punta San José. A *landing* can be made on this beach. A road runs up the arroyo, connecting the landing and the ranch with the Santo Tomás road. About ½ mile southeastward, Arroyo del Encino opens onto the beach. Two *detached rocks* lie offshore just to the southeastward of the mouth of this arroyo.

Punta Cabras

Los Muertos, a fish camp, is situated on the shore below a small point approximately 2½ miles southeastward of San José Point. Fishing skiffs may be seen pulled up on the beach or out among the kelp beds for a day's work. One-half mile further south, a small arroyo breaks through to the shore; Rancho Boca del San José lies a short distance up from the sea. One-half mile southeastward, another small arroyo breaks through to the shore, and a short distance beyond, the coastal road may be seen to run in a straight line southward for several miles. A minor point of land about 2½ miles southeastward of the Los Muertos Fish Camp and five miles southeastward of Punta San José, is also called Punta San José, probably because it is located beneath the aforementioned plateau of the same name.

CHARTING NOTE — As one progresses along the coast of Baja California, he will encounter place names repeated several times over at locations geographically removed sometimes but a few miles from one another. Many such places have several names and, when known, a distinguishing local name will be applied for more positive identification. Because of the inevitable confusion to cartographers caused by these repetitious place names, some official Oceanographic Office navigation charts bear misnamed geographical locations; in some few instances these charts contradict themselves from one large scale chart to another. Corrected notation, as far as is known to the author, will be pointed out; further correction is invited from mariners, who in the course of their voyages, have made positive identification of these places. Reliable documentation of charted errors are solicited wherever they may be found.

Off Punta San José, midway along the plateau of the same name, is a *detached rock;* ½ mile southeastward, Arroyo San Juan breaks through to the shore in a small bight facing northwestward. A *detached rock* lies off the mouth of the arroyo and another *detached rock* lies offshore midway between the first arroyo and the mouth of another small arroyo ½ mile southeastward. Two miles further south is a large crescent beach of smooth sand bracketed by rocky headlands on which the surf breaks heavily. The shoreline in this vicinity is punctuated by bird rocks and sea-eroded stacks. Clams are plentiful on many of the small beaches along this shore. The large crescent beach affords a very pleasant *landing place.*

Punta Piedras (Rocky Point) variously called Punta Roquena and Punta La Cuesta del Gato, juts out on the southern extremity of the crescent beach about 3 miles northwestward of Punta Cabra. A *detached rock* lies off the point and another eastward of the point. Bahía Almeja (Clam Beach) lies immediately eastward under Punta Piedras.

The wreck of the *Tampico Maru,* a small coastal tanker with smokestack and crews quarters aft, lies bow up on the rocks parallel to the shore. It drove ashore fully loaded with diesel oil on March 29, 1957 and caused substantial damage to the marine environment in the vicinity. The flora and fauna have since almost wholly recovered and the onslaught of the waves has almost completely broken up the remains of the stranded vessel.

Southeastward of Punta Piedras 1½ miles are two fish camps where fishing skiffs may be seen drawn up on the beach or fishing close offshore. Immediately southward of the fish camps, in a bight northward of Punta Cabra, there is a large smooth beach with sand dunes showing seaward. A *landing place* is charted on the southern end of this beach. Rancho Punta Cabra is established at the mouth of Canyon de Santa Cruz which opens onto the beach.

Punta Cabra (Goat Point), a squarish formation of land, protrudes seaward at the southern extremity of the beach about 3 miles southeastward of Punta Piedras. A large kelp bed extends some distance offshore and surrounds a *detached rock* close off the point. Tucked into a bight about ½ mile southeastward of Punta Cabra is a commercial fish camp. A cluster of *detached rocks* lies close offshore about 1 mile southeastward of the fish camp; the mouth of a small arroyo opens on the shore about 1 mile farther south.

Punta Isidro is about 3¾ miles southeastward of Punta Cabra and about 2 miles northwestward of the mouth of Río San Isidro.

Puerto Isidro is located immediately eastward of the point at the mouth of Cañon del Burro. Two *detached rocks,* almost completely whitened by birdlime, are clearly visible to seaward for a distance of 5 or 6 miles and serve as landmarks for a charted *boat landing* behind the larger rock. There is a small tienda (store) at this place and a settlement of a dozen or so houses. A road leads inland from the landing 7 miles to the old Mission of San Vicente. A cluster of *detached rocks* and *rocks awash* lies southeastward close offshore, surrounded by extensive kelp beds that extend along the coast to a position beyond the mouth of the Río San Vicente.

Erendira is a small village at the mouth of the Río San Isidro, referred to locally by some as Río San Vicente and located about 2½ miles southeastward of Punta San Isidro. From this place a road leads inland up the river valley about 7 miles to the ruins of the old Mission of San Vicente and connects with the main highway from Ensenada. There is an airstrip at the village of San Vicente. Pico San Antonio rises to a height of 1,848 feet above a plateau a little over 4 miles eastward of the mouth of Río San Isidro. *Navigation caution: Kelp fringes the shore generally to the 6-fathom curve but surrounds a rocky 2-fathom patch about ½ mile offshore just northwestward of the mouth of the San Isidro River. Roca El Resuello (Spouting Rock) lies detached nearly ½ mile offshore about 5 miles southeastward of the mouth of Río San Isidro.*

Punta La Mina del Fraile, a minor but sharp point of land, juts out from the coastal cliffs immediately southward of the mouth of the Río San Isidro and marks the southern limit of the Punta Isidro kelp beds. Southward for about 3 miles to a rounded and unnamed point the coast is clear of detached rocks. Three small arroyos break through to the shore in this stretch of coast. There are numerous blowholes along the rocky ledge of the shoreline.

Southward beyond the unnamed point for approximately 8 miles as far as the mouth of Río San Antonio, *numerous detached rocks* lie close offshore, except the one previously noted as located about ½ mile offshore 5 miles southeastward of the mouth of the San Isidro River, and 1½ miles south of the unnamed point. An arroyo breaks through the coastal bluff immediately northward of this offshore rock. Another arroyo breaks through about 1½ miles southward, this one backed by an 840-foot peak above the plateau. A third arroyo in this coastal stretch breaks through to the shore about 3½ miles north of Río San Antonio. Primitive roads lead from the mouths of each of these arroyos connecting to the coastal road on the plateau.

Punta San Isidro

Punta China showing quarry and barge loading terminal

Playa San Antonio del Mar is a broad beach backed by flat and marshy land just north of the mouth of Río San Antonio. There is more than a mile of sandy beach in this vicinity with rolling dunes rising from the berm on the northern end. It is a lee shore and much of the flotsam and jetsam carried southward by the California current is cast up on the sand and left to bleach in the sun. Great glass net floats, drifted down on the California coastal current from fishing fleets buffeted by Alaskan and Aleutian winter storms, may be occasionally found. Planks and logs and ship's dunnage, and an occasional wrecked hull of an unfortunate coastal vessel, together with the usual trash of the sea, make interesting beachcombing if one is able to land through the considerable surf. Pismo clams are found in abundance along this beach. There are several resort settlements along the shore with cabins for rent and meals available. At the southern extremity of the beach a road leads inland up the Río San Antonio arroyo several miles to the Johnson Ranch, a famous fishing and hunting resort established in this region for many years. An *airstrip* is located at the ranch and extensive development, now in the planning stage, would include a modern resort, with dredging of the marsh and estero at Playa San Antonio del Mar to create a small craft refuge and marina. At the present time, there is a small village established here, and some supplies are available.

Weather dictates the suitability of any of the anchorages between Todos Santos Bay and Colnett Bay. Under the usual northwesterly wind conditions the anchorages in the lee of Punta San José and Punta Cabras are preferable. There is a fish camp at Punta San José. A coastal road leads from this landing north to Santo Tomás and Ensenada. At Punta Cabras there is a sandy strip of beach where landing is generally safe and dry through a usually calm surf. *Landing* through the considerable surf at Playa San Antonio del Mar is not recommended except when the sea is unusually calm. From Playa San Antonio del Mar to abeam the light atop the remarkable bluff of Cabo Colnett is about 7½ miles; there are no suitable anchorages in this distance until Bahía Colnett.

In the lee of the more prominent points along this stretch of coast an upwelling of cold water produced by the prevailing coastal current supports an abundant fish habitat; the growth of larger specimens of lobster and abalone are encouraged by this cold water and nutrient-rich environment. Mexican fish and game laws are strictly enforced; a government vessel closely patrols this coast for this purpose and to provide adequate security for the increasing number of small pleasure craft.

SOURCES OF ADDITIONAL INFORMATION — Captain of the Port, Operación Porturia, San Carlos, B.C., P.O. Box 170, Villa Constitución, B. Cfa., Mexico. (See also Appendix.)

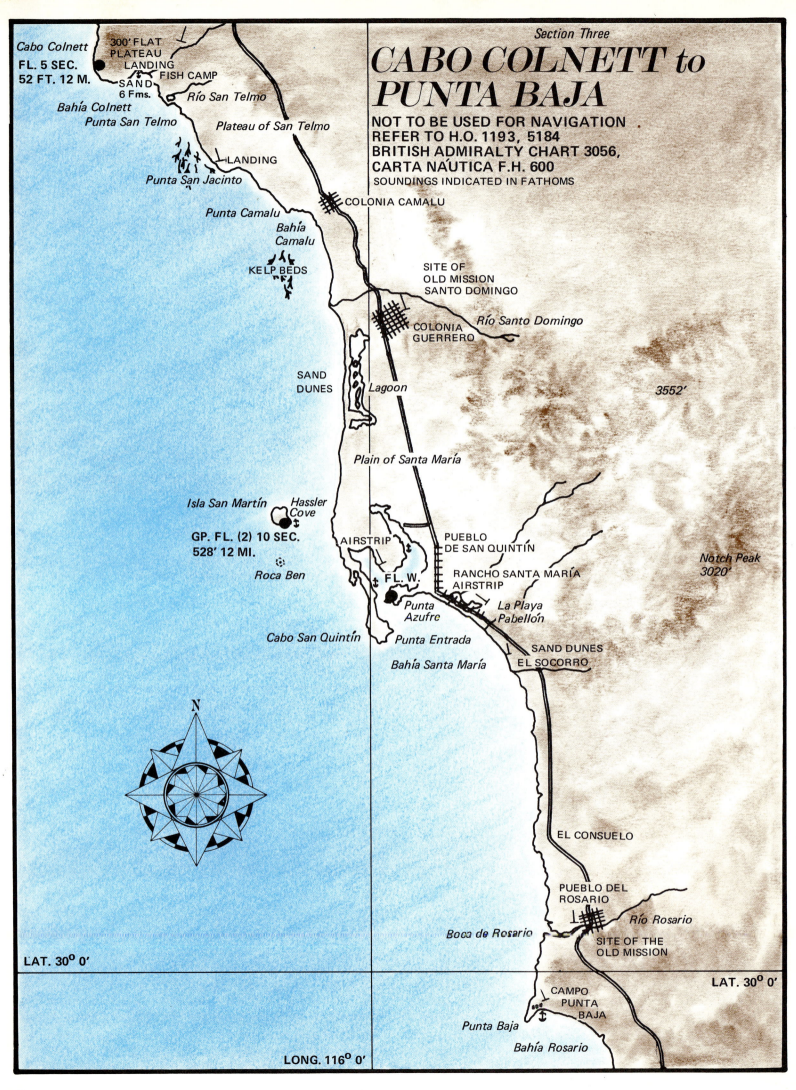

Section Three

CABO COLNETT to PUNTA BAJA

NOT TO BE USED FOR NAVIGATION .
REFER TO H.O. 1193, 5184
BRITISH ADMIRALTY CHART 3056,
CARTA NÁUTICA F.H. 600
SOUNDINGS INDICATED IN FATHOMS

Cabo Colnett
FL. 5 SEC.
52 FT. 12 M.

300' FLAT
PLATEAU
LANDING
FISH CAMP
SAND
6 Fms.

Bahía Colnett
Punta San Telmo

Río San Telmo
Plateau of San Telmo

LANDING

Punta San Jacinto

Punta Camalu

Bahía
Camalu

KELP BEDS

COLONIA CAMALU

SITE OF
OLD MISSION
SANTO DOMINGO

COLONIA
GUERRERO

Río Santo Domingo

SAND
DUNES

Lagoon

3552'

Plain of Santa María

Isla San Martín

Hassler
Cove

GP. FL. (2) 10 SEC.
528' 12 MI.

Roca Ben

AIRSTRIP

PUEBLO
DE SAN QUINTÍN

RANCHO SANTA MARÍA
AIRSTRIP

Notch Peak
3020'

FL. W.

Punta
Azufre

La Playa
Pabellón

Cabo San Quintín

Punta Entrada

Bahía Santa María

SAND DUNES
EL SOCORRO

N

EL CONSUELO

PUEBLO DEL
ROSARIO

Boca de Rosario

Río Rosario

SITE OF THE
OLD MISSION

LAT. 30° 0'

LAT. 30° 0'

CAMPO
PUNTA
BAJA

Punta Baja

Bahía Rosario

LONG. 116° 0'

Cabo Colnett looking toward the south

SECTION 3
CABO COLNETT to PUNTA BAJA

For navigation use United States Oceanographic Charts H.O. 1006, San Francisco to Point Telmo; H.O. 1193, Bahía de San Quintín to Isla Cedros; H.O. 1043, Bahía de San Quintín; H.O. 1044, Plans on the West Coast of Baja California; British Admiralty Charts #2324, Cape San Lucas to San Diego Bay; #3056, Bahía Rosario to San Diego Bay; Mexican Cartas Náuticas de Faros e Hidrógraphia F.H. 610, de Ensenada a Mazatlán; F.H. 601, Cabo San Quintín a Punta Eugenio.

Cabo Colnett (Cape Colnett) is located approximately 40 miles southeastward of Punta Santo Tomás and approximately 32 miles northwestward of Isla San Martín. It is a remarkable headland and an excellent landmark. It is a great bulk of land that rises abruptly from the sea in perpendicular cliffs to a plateau 300 to 400 feet high, the cliffs are remarkably stratified. On a base of light-colored sandstone more than 50 feet above the sea lies a stratum of broken rock, nearly black and markedly resembling coal, above which is sand. The height and sharp outline of the cape is visible at a great distance when approaching from either northward or southward. Punta Colnett has been reported to give *good radar returns* up to 29 miles. A *navigation light* established on the point at Latitude 30° 59.0′ north and Longitude 116° 20.0′ west **flashes white** every **five seconds:** flash 0.5 second, eclipse 4.5 seconds. The light

is exhibited 52 feet above the sea from a red tower and can be seen for 12 miles on clear nights. Cabo Colnett was named after Captain James Colnett of the British Royal Navy whose 374-ton survey sloop *Rattler* visited these waters in 1793 on a coastal charting expedition to reconnoiter new whaling grounds and suitable ports of refuge.

Bahía Colnett (Colnett Bay) is a large bight eastward of Punta Colnett, situated between the cape and Punta San Telmo, 4 miles east-southeastward and sheltered from the prevailing coastal winds by the bulk of the cape. The plateau of San Rafael, 200 feet high, is situated on the eastern side of the bay; it is also known as Mesa Altar.

To make the anchorage from the northward or westward, round the cape at the 10-fathom curve and stand to the east about 1½ miles until abreast of the mouth of a short deep gorge that slashes the cliffs on the southern face. Best *anchorage* is in 6 fathoms off the mouth of the gorge, good holding ground in sand and shell. Best *landing* is several hundred yards to the east behind a gravel shoal where the cliffs taper off to the shingle beach at the mouth of the Río San Rafael; there is a sand spit in front over which the sea breaks occasionally at low water. A ranch settlement is located back of the landing. The anchorage is subject to sudden blasts of wind driving down the face of the shore cliff from the mesa above. Ocean swells diffracted around the curve of the cape frequently sweep the anchorage. Breakers and surf pound the southeast shore of the bight toward the mouth of the Rio San Telmo.

Shoal water fringed by kelp extends ¾ mile offshore to the west of Punta San Telmo and the mouth of the river. There are several *detached rocks* just offshore southeast of Punta Telmo and a great patch of kelp that extends to the 10-fathom curve as far as Punta San Jacinto. A primitive road connects Cabo Colnett with the Peninsular Highway and runs along the shore to the southeast. A fish camp is established near the landing by commercial lobster fishermen. There are clams to be found in the beach.

Near the town of Colnett, located on the Peninsular Highway several miles inland from the landing, are two graded dirt *airstrips:* Colnett West, utilized for the town, and Colnett East, utilized by the Flying Samaritans.

MEDICAL FACILITIES — At the village of Colnett about 7 miles northeast of the landing along a dirt road leading inland from the shore, there is a medical clinic maintained by a local North American resident in conjunction with an organization known as Samartinos Voladores (The Flying Samaritans) a group of medical doctors, dentists, and specialists who make a regular monthly visit to the clinic by private small aircraft to attend to medical needs of the local residents. Colnett is one of four Flying Samaritan clinics established in Baja California and one of seven locations visited on a regular monthly basis; eleven other locations are visited as the need arises.

The facilities at Colnett include waiting rooms, examination rooms, operating rooms, X-ray laboratory, pharmacy, laboratory, dental office, and a small ward. The clinic has a fairly complete variety of serviceable, if not modern, medical equipment — such things as an X-ray machine, operating tables and lamps, dental chair and tools, surgical equipment, and so forth — all contributed by the medical members of the Flying Samaritan group. There is a gasoline engine-driven electrical generator which supplies power for lights, operating lamps and medical equipment. In cases of emergency members of this medical team fly to their nearest Baja based clinic or other accessible location to render medical aid and treatment; severe cases requiring facilities other than that available in the field are flown to San Diego for treatment and care.

Communication in Baja California is somewhat limited but there are a certain number of locations equipped with landline telephone to either Ensenada or La Paz or radio-telegraph or radiotelephone circuits that will relay messages. (See Appendix for detailed information.)

TIDES AND CURRENTS — A significant cold water upwelling condition in the bay, due to an eddy of the south-flowing California current past the cape and similar to that described at Puerto Santo Tomás, creates a very favorable fish habitat. The same California coastal current sweeps in to brush the land and creates a lee shore at the mouth of the San Telmo River, depositing a variety of flotsam and jetsam along the beach. The mean high water interval at Colnett Bay is 9 hours, 27 minutes; the spring range is 5.8 feet, the mean range is 4.4 feet.

Punta San Jacinto is situated about 6 miles southeastward of Punta San Telmo; the coast between is characterized by a great growth of kelp that floats as far as the 10-fathom curve, reaching 3 to 4 miles in places. There is a *landing* charted under the lee of this point. Two 4¾-fathom spots are located, respectively, 1¼ miles southward and 2½ miles northwestward of San Jacinto Point. Rancho San Francisquito is established in this vicinity and the coastal plain is tilled in a grain-field pattern. An old mission outpost was once situated nearby. Punta Camalu, 4½ miles southeastward of Punta San Jacinto, shelters a small bight, Bahía Camalu. The Plateau of San Jacinto rises behind. The character of the shore along this stretch of coast is somewhat different than that to the northward of Cabo Colnett, comprising sand hills and bluffs backed by low mesas as far as the Río San Ramón alternatively called Santo Domingo River. Beyond is a low sandy shore behind which there is a lagoon, and stretching southward, the plain of Santa María extending to the shores of Bahía Camalu, the combined coastline stretching about 7 miles southward to Boca de Santo Domingo.

Camalu-By-The-Sea is a fishing resort overlooking Bahía

Isla San Martín showing Hassler Cove on the left

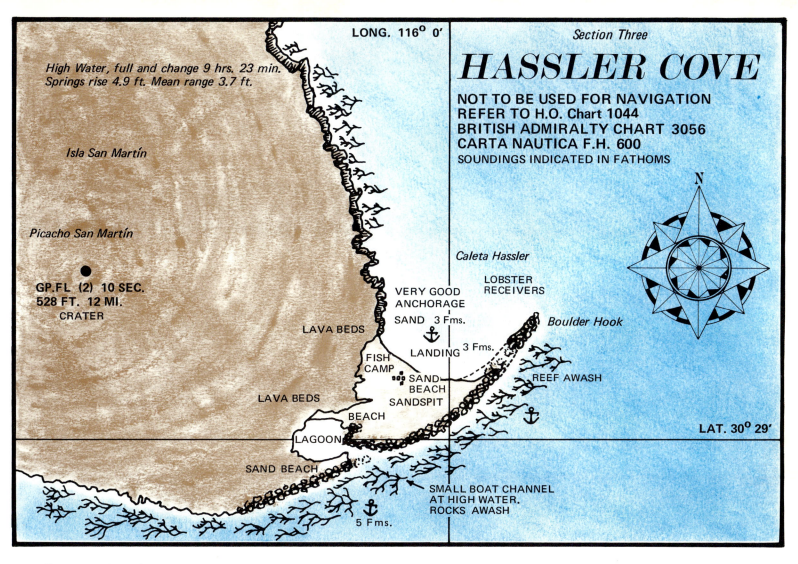

HASSLER COVE

NOT TO BE USED FOR NAVIGATION
REFER TO H.O. Chart 1044
BRITISH ADMIRALTY CHART 3056
CARTA NAUTICA F.H. 600
SOUNDINGS INDICATED IN FATHOMS

High Water, full and change 9 hrs. 23 min.
Springs rise 4.9 ft. Mean range 3.7 ft.

LONG. 116° 0'

Isla San Martín

Picacho San Martín

GP.FL (2) 10 SEC.
528 FT. 12 MI.
CRATER

Caleta Hassler

LOBSTER
RECEIVERS

VERY GOOD
ANCHORAGE
SAND 3 Fms.

Boulder Hook

LAVA BEDS

3 Fms.

LANDING

FISH
CAMP

SAND
BEACH

REEF AWASH

LAVA BEDS

SANDSPIT

BEACH

LAT. 30° 29'

LAGOON

SAND BEACH

SMALL BOAT CHANNEL
AT HIGH WATER.
ROCKS AWASH

5 Fms.

N

Camalu and Bahía San Ramón to the southward. Two miles inland from this resort is a small village on the Peninsular Highway, Valle Camalu, with cafes, cantinas, tiendas (stores), a post office and a Pemex gasoline station. There are several other small villages in the near vicinity, San Telmo, Abajo, Rubén Jaramillo, Santo Domingo, Colonia Guerrero, all located on or near the highway. Río San Ramón or Río Santo Domingo, opens on the shore about 7 miles south of Punta Camalu. A rancho is situated just south of the river mouth. The ruins of the old Mission Santo Domingo are located in the town of the same name about 5 miles inland from the coast on the highway. A wide sandy beach stretches 12 or more miles from Boca Santo Domingo southward to the cliffs opposite San Martín Island. Mount Calamahue (La Encantada or Providence Peak) about 37 miles from the coast eastward of San Ramón Bay near the middle of the peninsula in the San Pedro Mártir Range, is the highest point of land in Baja California. Its charted altitude is 10,126 feet; it is an excellent landmark and can be seen clearly from a great distance at sea — as far as 100 miles in clear weather. Mount Calamahue has a whitish appearance and a jagged peak which is snow-covered during the winter and spring. Mexico's new national observatory is situated on this peak.

Isla San Martín (San Martín Island), offlying the coast about 3 miles, is about 30 miles south-southeastward of Cabo Colnett and about 10 miles northwestward of Cabo San Quintín. It is circular in form having a diameter of about 1 mile. The island slopes gently to a central volcanic peak rounded by wind and weather to an appearance of a smooth convex shape with a central knob. This is actually a double peak, the southernmost of which is the remnant of an extinct volcano 497 feet above the sea with a crater at its summit 350 feet in diameter and 40 feet deep. A *navigation light* is established on the rim of the crater, mounted on a white metal tower 528 feet above the sea, and can be seen around the horizon. It displays a **white group flash** of **two flashes** every **10 seconds** and can be seen for a distance of 12 miles in clear weather. Its geographic position is Latitude 30° 29' north, Longitude 116° 07' west. The island is surrounded by thick beds of kelp in which are a number of *detached rocks*.

Anchorage may be taken at several places around the island. Caleta Hassler (Hassler Cove), a small bight on the eastern side of the island, is recommended for small vessels as the best shelter from southeasterly winds and with the least swell from the open sea in most weather. Boulder Hook forms the rocky eastern protection for the cove, projecting northwestward in a natural and effective breakwater of smooth volcanic stones. The romantic at heart have attributed this natural configuration to the industry of freebooters who are reputed to have used San Martín Island for a lair of refuge. While freebooters possibly sometimes did lie in wait in the lee of Isla San Martín for the annual passage of the Manila Galleon, no evidence from any logs or records or scholarly work available to the author bears out this claim other than oft-repeated folklore. The galleons kept well off the coast making landfall at Cedros Island or Cape San Lucas, with orders eventually to avoid even those places for security on their coastwise passage to Acapulco.

Within the cove there is good holding ground in from 3 to 9 fathoms, sand bottom over rock. During a southerly gale with the anchor paying into the bight toward the head of the cove, a second anchor should be dropped underfoot as a safety precaution to guard against a change of wind to the northwestward. Easy *landing* may be effected on the long sand beach at the head of the cove. Lobster fishermen use this cove to moor their holding receivers. These heavy wooden-slatted boxes, usually awash, are difficult to discern, but are generally anchored with buoys close inshore. On the flat above the beach are more than a dozen wood and tarpaper shacks of a seasonal fish camp surrounded by a jumbled junkyard of broken lobster traps scattered amidst a litter of fish boxes, floats and pieces of driftwood.

On the southeastern side of the island back of the sandspit that forms the bight of Hassler Cove is a small circular lagoon which is open to the sea at half tide. *Anchorage* may be taken abreast this lagoon in 5 to 10 fathoms outside the kelp and *landing* effected through the mouth of the lagoon on the broad sandy beach within. No dangers are known to exist in this anchorage area but the mouth of the lagoon is foul and passage by small boat alone is possible. *Anchorage* may also be taken anywhere on the northeast side in 4 to 5 fathoms outside the kelp, the best protection being within Hassler Cove. The island itself is rather barren, supporting cactus, ice plant, and a few stunted bushes among the loose masses of lava. Great numbers of seabirds that use the island for a nesting habitat wheel overhead. Care should be exercised not to disturb their rookeries during nesting season. Elephant seals abound and are especially numerous on the shores of the cove and lagoon.

Cabrillo visited the island and anchored off its shore on August 27 and again from August 30 to September 4, 1542.

The Coast Survey expedition that reconnoitered these waters in 1880 under Lt. Commander H. E. Nichols, USN, conducting magnetic survey along the coasts of Mexico and Central America, found the cove at San Martín Island a fine shelter but apparently unnamed. They bestowed the name Hassler after the name of their vessel and the Coast and Geodetic bureau's first director, appointed in 1807, Ferdinand Hassler.

Cemetery - San Quintín

The passage between San Martín Island and the mainland is about 2½ miles wide with depths of 10 to 13 fathoms and no known dangers. To the southward, however, there are three known shoals. Ben's Rock a *dangerous submerged rock* with a covering depth of 1½ fathoms, is located at Latitude 30° 26′ north, Longitude 116° 07′ west, 3 miles distant from the central peak of the island on a true bearing of 177°. There are depths of 11 fathoms close aboard the rock and 25-fathoms 200 yards from it; no kelp grows in the vicinity and in moderate weather the sea breaks on it only occasionally. Ben's Rock lies about 4 miles from the mainland. A 6½-fathom *patch* about 100 yards in extent was reported by a vessel's captain in 1929 to lie 4½ miles south-southwestward of San Martín Island which would put it about 2¼ miles 238° true bearing from Ben's Rock. The position of this patch is approximate. In 1964 a *submerged rock* was reported in this area, located approximately Latitude 30° 19½′ north, Longitude 116° 06′ west. About 5 miles, 278° from Cabo San Quintín and outside the 50-fathom curve is a small *rocky bank* with a least depth of 15 fathoms; between the bank and the coast 4 miles distant,

Cabo San Quintín

View of Bahía San Quintín looking northward

the water is deep and the sounding regular. The great bay formed by the curve of the coast between Cabo Colnett and the mainland point opposite Isla San Martín was called Bahía de Las Virgenes on early charts and the point opposite the island Punta Zuniga.

SEA AND WEATHER CONDITIONS — The prevailing winds along this coast are northwesterly and generally blow steadily from that direction for about 8 months out of the year. From November through February, winds from the southeast to southwest are frequent, with occasional moderate southeasterly gales that are accompanied by considerable rain. Before the subsidence of these gales the wind hauls to the southwestward, sometimes blowing very hard for a few hours, and then comes out from the northwestward with fine weather. In December and January strong northers are likely to occur, blowing from the direction between north and northeastward and lasting 1 to 3 days. The tail ends of local but fierce hurricanes called "Chubascos" generated in the region around the Revillagegido Islands between June and November occasionally lash this coast. Winds approaching 100 miles per hour may be experienced but are usually of short duration.

The coast northeastward of San Martín Island rises from the lowland southward of Río San Ramón, to a sheer cliff of dark-colored rock which extends 2½ miles farther southward; thence the cliff breaks to a low sand beach for ½ mile. Beyond this beach and as far as Colina del Sudoeste (Southwest Hill) 380 feet high, which rises directly from the edge of the sea, the coast is comprised of bold rocky bluffs. Southward of the hill the coast is again low and sandy for 3½ miles. Beyond this sandy shelf as far as Cabo San Quintín, the shore is low and rocky with numerous projecting points and low detached rocks on which the sea breaks heavily.

Cabo San Quintín is the southeastern extremity of the long narrow peninsula that forms the western barrier against the sea and creates the calm waters of Bahía San Quintín and its interior estuary. Just southward of Southwest Hill the peninsula is low and only a few yards wide, but near its terminal end it widens to about 1½ miles and rises to an elevation at Mount Mazo of 160 feet. On the western side of the peninsula abreast Mount Mazo are two rocky points, Punta Arrecife (Reef Point) and an unnamed point to the northward; *rocky reefs* extend nearly ½ mile off each of these points. Punta Afuera is the southern extremity of the peninsula and is about ¼ mile westward of Cabo San Quintín. Between the two points is a narrow strip of sand beach; *detached rocks* extend nearly ¼ mile outward from both the point and the cape.

On the eastern side of the peninsula a low rocky beach extends for some distance northward of the cape, breaking to a low sandy beach running in a northeasterly direction to Punta Entrada and forming a bight between it and the cape. Two large *detached rocks* lie about 300 yards southwestward of Entrada Point well within the bight; numerous *sunken rocks,* over which the swell breaks, lie across the mouth. Punta Entrada (Entrada Point), about ½ mile northeastward of Cabo San Quintín, is a low rocky point surrounded by *shoal water;* it should be given a berth of at least ¼ mile. About 600 yards northwestward of Entrada Point is an unnamed point of rocky configuration, and 500 yards beyond in the same direction there is a low and sandy point, Punta Sextante. Situated ¾ mile farther northwestward is Punta Roca (Rocky Point), a conspicuous point of land that appears in contrast to the intervening low sand beach. In the bight beyond Entrada Point the water is very shoal with a bed of kelp surrounding a *detached rock* to the northwestward. Inasmuch as it is well protected against the swell, the bight affords *fair landing* for small boats. Off Punta Sextante a sandspit projecting about 500 yards eastward into the entrance channel dries at low water. The hulk of the old San Diego ferryboat *Moreno* lies stranded in the shallow water northwest of the sandspit offlying Punta Sextante. It was brought to San Quintín for use as a cannery tender, but was abandoned with the cannery project. *Good anchorage* may be had in the bight close by the old ferryboat. Beyond Rocky Point there is a succession of sand dunes as far as Laguna Point, a distance of about 1½ miles northward. Laguna Point together with Punta Azufre (Sulfur Point), the opposite sandy point ¾ mile southeastward across the entrance channel, forms the entrance to Puerto San Quintín. A *navigation light* which exhibits a *white flash* that is visible for 15 miles is shown from Punta Azufre on the southeastern side of the mouth of the inner lagoon. The extensive bay eastward of Cabo San Quintín and outside the lagoon is called Bahía Santa María and affords moderately protected *anchorage* for large vessels unable to cross the rather shallow bar to the inner harbor. The area immediately within the entrance to the lagoon is called Bahía San Simón; the northwestern arm of the interior estuary is called Bahía Falsa; the southeastern arm of the estuary leads through a shoal and tortuous channel into San Quintín Bay proper and to the old cannery dock.

Puerto de San Quintín and the various estuaries that comprise the rather extensive landlocked lagoon may be compared to Newport Bay of 50 years ago. The kind of dredging and channel improvement accomplished over the years in that northern harbor applied to this bay could create the same commodious and well-protected type of small craft harbor so much needed on this coast as a harbor of refuge. The inner bay affords to very small vessels of shallow draft a perfectly secure and well-protected shelter from all directions. The entrance channel, however, is a maze of shoals that shift from time to time, subject to the currents of the sea. This narrow and tortuous channel, with seldom more than 1½ fathoms over the bar, is consequently subject to change of depth and direction with every southerly gale. The channel is marked in part by spar and barrel buoys, and by stakes and pilings, but it should not be attempted without a pilot familiar with local conditions. At high water, a draft

of 10 feet can generally clear the bar if the channel through it is well known. A small boat can be lowered and the channel conned and buoyed for a larger vessel to follow, but this is a nerve-racking and time-consuming procedure, and it is better-advised to make prior arrangements for a harbor pilot. There is a good one in residence at San Quintín Village and his services are available through the operator of the fishing resort at the head of the bay. Pilot services are reasonable and a safe passage better-assured with less concern. The bay is very well worth a visit and if present plans of various developers continue apace, Puerto San Quintín will undoubtedly become one of the most important way stops for coastal vessels bound south or north.

Bahía Santa María, generally referred to as San Quintín Bay, situated eastward of Cabo San Quintín affords spacious *anchorage* for larger vessels seeking shelter from prevailing winds outside the inner harbor. Although shoal water extends for a considerable distance from the head of the bay, good holding ground in from 4 to 8 fathoms over a mud bottom is to be had under the lee of the cape. A long swell diffracted around the headland usually sweeps the anchorage. There are no known dangers in this anchorage. The best *anchorage* for vessels of moderate draft outside the bar may be had with Mount Ceniza, easternmost of the cluster of five hills, bearing 355°, and Mount Mazo, on the cape, bearing 274°. This large bay embraced in the sweep of the coast southeastward of San Quintín was known on early charts as Bahía de San Francisco.

Old Railroad Bridge – San Quintín

TIDES AND CURRENTS — The mean high water interval at San Quintín Bay is 9 hours, 23 minutes; the spring range is 4.9 feet; the mean range is 3.7 feet. Ebb and flood tide across the bar and through the restricted channel abreast the old railroad bridge causeway near the abandoned mill can be of considerable velocity, and should be reckoned with on entering or leaving the inner harbor or traversing its narrow channels.

The large water area in the port comprises mostly sand and mud flats which dry in a surprising number of places at low water. A *narrow channel* with depths of 1½ to 2 fathoms winds for several miles to the head of the bay. The surrounding land is low and sandy and, with the exception of cactus and a few stunted bushes, is entirely without vegetation. Five volcanic hills, ranging in height from 280 to 876 feet, to the northward of the port appear from seaward as islands. Successful farming has been recently undertaken on the land behind the port and the character of the countryside should gradually grow greener with the spread of these farms. Fresh water has been recently developed through the drilling of deep wells providing adequate supplies for both domestic use and irrigation in a previously arid region.

San Quintín Village at the head of the bay is the old settlement of the once flourishing California Development Company of London whose enterprise began a railroad, built a flour mill and facilities to serve an anticipated influx of settlers on 30-acre tracts of land subdivided by the company. The wheat crop failed for lack of adequate rainfall or irrigation during an extended drought and the flour mill deteriorated, unused. The railroad bridge across the estuary eventually washed out and the franchise let by the Mexican Government in 1890 was ultimately cancelled in 1918. Ruins of the old mill, the relic of a large steam engine with its great flywheel, and the remains of the railroad causeway, now without its bridge, are mute evidence of prior exploitation that failed. A fish cannery and wharf were built in recent years, but this investment failed.

Today an enterprising group of Mexican nationals and foreign investors under liberalized laws are bringing a renais-

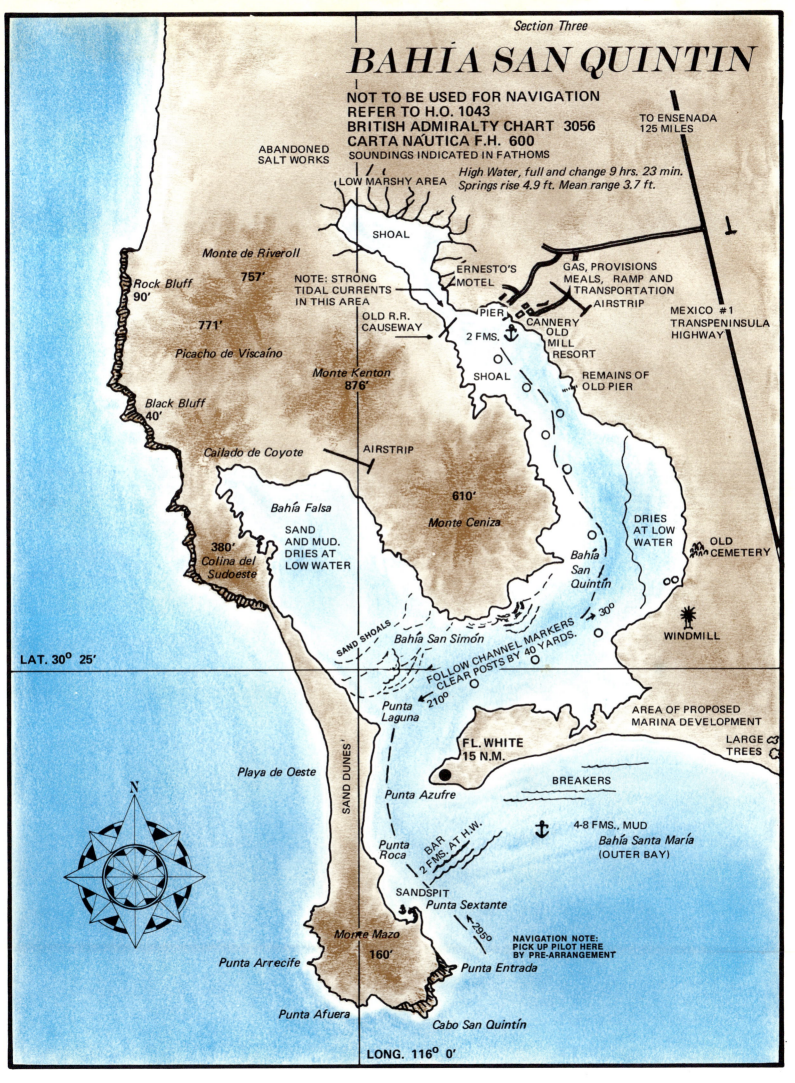

BAHÍA SAN QUINTIN

NOT TO BE USED FOR NAVIGATION
REFER TO H.O. 1043
BRITISH ADMIRALTY CHART 3056
CARTA NÁUTICA F.H. 600
SOUNDINGS INDICATED IN FATHOMS

High Water, full and change 9 hrs. 23 min.
Springs rise 4.9 ft. Mean range 3.7 ft.

ABANDONED SALT WORKS

LOW MARSHY AREA

SHOAL

TO ENSENADA 125 MILES

Monte de Riveroll
757'

Rock Bluff 90'

771'

Picacho de Viscaíno

NOTE: STRONG TIDAL CURRENTS IN THIS AREA

OLD R.R. CAUSEWAY

ERNESTO'S MOTEL

PIER

2 FMS.

GAS, PROVISIONS MEALS, RAMP AND TRANSPORTATION
AIRSTRIP

CANNERY OLD MILL RESORT

MEXICO #1 TRANSPENINSULA HIGHWAY

Monte Kenton 876'

SHOAL

REMAINS OF OLD PIER

Black Bluff 40'

Cailado de Coyote

AIRSTRIP

Bahía Falsa

SAND AND MUD. DRIES AT LOW WATER

610'

Monte Ceniza

DRIES AT LOW WATER

OLD CEMETERY

380'
Colina del Sudoeste

Bahía San Quintín

30°

WINDMILL

SAND SHOALS

Bahía San Simón

FOLLOW CHANNEL MARKERS
CLEAR POSTS BY 40 YARDS.

210°

Punta Laguna

AREA OF PROPOSED MARINA DEVELOPMENT

LARGE TREES

Playa de Oeste

SAND DUNES'

FL. WHITE 15 N.M.

Punta Azufre

BREAKERS

Punta Roca

BAR 2 FMS. AT H.W.

4-8 FMS., MUD
Bahía Santa María (OUTER BAY)

SANDSPIT
Punta Sextante

295°

NAVIGATION NOTE:
PICK UP PILOT HERE
BY PRE-ARRANGEMENT

Monte Mazo 160'

Punta Arrecife

Punta Entrada

Punta Afuera

Cabo San Quintín

N

sance to an area long neglected, but with great potential for agriculture, industry, commercial fishing, sportfishing, and tourism. Well-graded and hard-surfaced roads are steadily being developed southward to facilitate transportation and travel. Several resort motels that offer deep-sea sportfishing and comfortable accommodations are presently operating, with others building and more in the planning stage. Several *airstrips* have been built to accommodate light planes for crop dusting, transportation and tourism. San Quintín Bay, visited by Cabrillo on August 22, 1542, was the first land in Baja California to be claimed by him in the name of the Spanish Crown and was given the name Posesión.

FACILITIES — Toward the head of the southeastern arm of the inner bay opposite the old causeway there is a small settlement comprising a number of houses, a large warehouse, and a wharf in usable condition. Gasoline and diesel fuel in limited quantities are available here. Mechanical repairs can be had and some provisions are available. Two *airstrips* for light planes are in operation nearby, but aviation gasoline must be arranged for in advance. El Molino Viejo Motel (Old Mill), operated by Al Vela near the wharf, provides comfortable accommodation, excellent food and sportfishing boats. Ernesto's is equally hospitable. Boats may be rented or launched. The Peninsular Highway, paved to within a few miles of San Quintín Bay, passes within 3½ miles of this landing.

The open roadstead eastward of San Quintín Bay is officially named Bahía Santa María although it is called out on the U.S. Hydrographic Charts #1149 and #1193 as Bahía de San Quintín. The shore of this bay from Punta Azufre to the mouth of the Río Santa María — a small stream about 4 miles eastward of the point — is comprised of a low sandy beach with hills about 300 feet high rising a short distance inland and, beyond these, a mountain range with peaks rising from 1,500 to 3,000 feet. The highest of these is Cerro Ciprés ("Notch Peak") 3,020 feet high, rising almost due east of El Socorro (see below) and about 12 miles from the coast.

A ranch is established at the mouth of the Río Santa María just back of the beach. A few miles inland from this place is the Santa María Skyranch, a resort complex providing comfortable tourist accommodations, meals and an *airstrip* regularly used by light planes. Another resort, Playa del Oro, with tourist accommodations and an *airstrip,* is located just westward of Skyranch. The Robertson Ranch and Campo Gronado are also in the near vicinity. A road leads from the beach inland to these places.

There is a marshy area in the low flat land midway between the mouth of the Río Santa María and the mouth of the Río Pabellón, 3 miles to the southeastward. The stretch of beach along this section of the coast is called El Pabellón, (Pavilion Beach). The sand is hard packed and suitable for motor vehicles; it is not unusual to see dune buggies and motorcycles traveling along the shore above the tide at high speeds. Pismo clams are plentiful.

Between the mouth of the Río Pabellón and the mouth of Arroyo Socorro, a distance of about 3½ miles, the character of the coast begins to change to sand bluffs and dark-colored cliffs 50 to 100 feet high, alternating for several miles and gradually decreasing in height toward Punta Baja. Lateral sand dunes run back of the shoreline southward of El Pabellón. A patch of *white sand* shows to seaward just northward

Pueblo de San Quintín showing the main channel

of Arroyo Socorro. Rancho El Socorro is located at the mouth of the Arroyo and provides tourist accommodations for sportfishermen. An *airstrip* at the ranch can accommodate light planes. Nearby Rancho Socorrito also provides accommodations for tourists.

From El Socorro, about 6 miles southward, there are six small arroyos opening on the shore. The sixth arroyo is called Cañón Hondo (Hondo Canyon) also known locally as Arroyo Amargo. From Punta Azufre to within a mile of Hondo Canyon there are no known dangers off the coast. Seaweed beds grow offshore at the mouth of Hondo Canyon; *sunken and detached rocks* extend along the shoreline from about a mile north of this point to about 3 miles north of Río del Rosario. About 2 miles south of Hondo Canyon an Arroyo breaks through to the shore and about 2 miles farther south Cañón del Rosario opens to the sea.

Black Sea Bass

At Rosario Canyon the small settlement of El Consuelo may be found astride the coast road that runs very near and parallel to the shore at this point. From El Consuelo a road turns inland up Rosario Canyon and leads to the village of El Rosario, located about 4 miles inland and established on both banks of Río El Rosario. Between Cañon Rosario and La Bocana (mouth of the Rosario River) about 7 miles southward, an extensive plateau rises to a height of 600 feet about 1 mile from the shoreline. The old El Rosario *airstrip,* built atop the plateau during World War II, is now abandoned although light planes may still land if pilots have local knowledge. A newer *airstrip,* several miles eastward, still atop the plateau, is the airport developed by the Flying Samaritans to serve their clinic at the hospital in the town. It is the airstrip generally used to communicate with the area by light plane. A third *airstrip,* located at the mouth of El Rosario River just back of the shoreline, is also used by the Flying Samaritans but it is badly maintained and recommended only to those with local knowledge. (See Appendix.)

La Bocana, about 6 miles north of Punta Baja, a small indentation in the coast marked by a dark-colored hill 349 feet high on its southern side, is the sandy mouth of the Rosario River which runs most of the year, fed by numerous small tributary streams draining into the Rosario Valley. The river mouth is fairly wide, generally with a sizable fresh water estero (lagoon) separated from the sea by a sandbar but which is washed out from time to time by heavy rains. *Anchorage* is in an open roadstead outside the surf line and on calm days a *landing* may be attempted on the sand beach through the breakers. The flat bottomland back of La Bocana is cultivated to some extent today as it has been since the time of the Spanish Mission which was first established there in 1774. The ruins of mission buildings at several sites may readily be seen. Paleontologists conducting a scientific dig on a hillside about 8 miles south of El Rosario recently found the nearly complete skeleton of the largest duck-billed sea-going dinosaur ever found: an animal 100 feet long and about 75 million years old. More recently the same team found tiny fossilized teeth from a mole-like animal that lived in this area when it was a land of smoking volcanoes and steamy jungle swamps some 80 million years ago. The fossils are said to be the oldest mammal remains ever found along the west coast of this hemisphere.

The village of El Rosario is located about 4 miles from the coast on the northern bank of El Rosario River although there is also a settlement at the site of old mission ruins about 1½ miles closer to the landing on the southern bank. A primitive road runs from the coast at the sandy mouth of the river up the northern bank to the settlements, called, respectively, Rosario de Arriba (Upper Rosario) and Rosario de Abajo (Lower Rosario). The nature of the town is fundamentally agricultural with a small population of between 300 and 400 persons. Cultivated fields of chili peppers, olive groves and palm trees surround a scattering of small adobe houses. Upper Rosario is the principal business center of the community with two gas stations, a cafe and tiendas (stores), tourist cabins and a *hospital* looked after in part by the Flying Samaritans. There is weekly bus service to Ensenada as well as a government post office, mail and telephone service, all of which communicate through Ensenada, El Rosario being the end of the line.

El Rosario Abajo (Lower El Rosario), located on the south side of the river, is the interesting site of the ruins of the second mission, as well as the location of a number of sizable homes and commercial buildings still in use, that date from the early 1800's. Before the advent of the Spanish Colonial settlement, the valley supported an Indian rancheria called Vinadaco. The Dominican Monks founded their first mission on this site in 1774. The largest part of the Indian population was wiped out by a series of epidemics between 1777 and 1782. Subsequently, one of the great recurring floods coursed down the arroyo and destroyed much of the improvement to fields and buildings wrought by the Spanish colonizers, and in 1802 the mission was rebuilt downstream on the opposite bank at Rosario Abajo. El Rosario continued as an important mission center until it was secularized and subsequently abandoned about 1832.

LIGHT, Isla San Martín

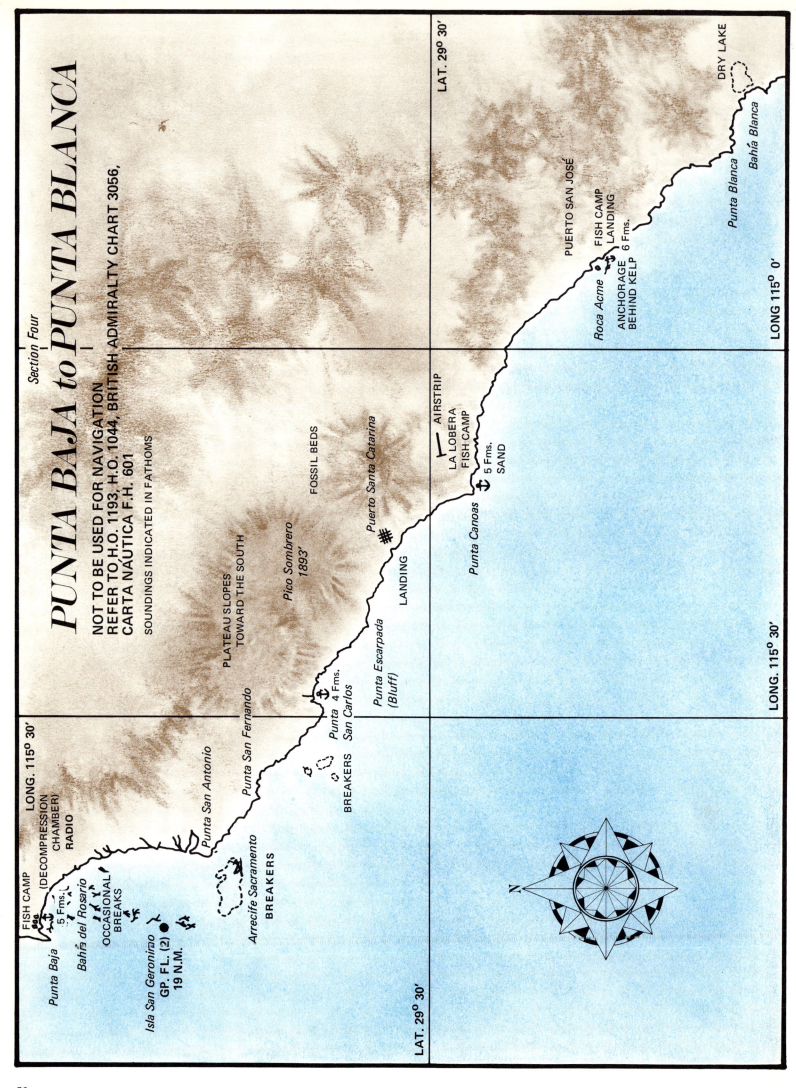

PUNTA BAJA to PUNTA BLANCA

Section Four

NOT TO BE USED FOR NAVIGATION
REFER TO H.O. 1193, H.O. 1044, BRITISH ADMIRALTY CHART 3056,
CARTA NÁUTICA F.H. 601
SOUNDINGS INDICATED IN FATHOMS

LAT. 29° 30'

DRY LAKE

PUERTO SAN JOSÉ

FISH CAMP
LANDING
6 Fms.

Roca Acme

ANCHORAGE
BEHIND KELP

Punta Blanca

Bahía Blanca

LONG. 115° 0'

AIRSTRIP

LA LOBERA
FISH CAMP

5 Fms.
SAND

FOSSIL BEDS

Puerto Santa Catarina

Pico Sombrero
1893'

PLATEAU SLOPES
TOWARD THE SOUTH

Punta Canoas

LANDING

Punta Escarpada
(Bluff)

Punta
San Carlos
4 Fms.

Punta San Fernando

Punta San Antonio

LONG. 115° 30'

LONG. 115° 30'

FISH CAMP
(DECOMPRESSION
CHAMBER)
RADIO

Punta Baja

Bahía del Rosario
5 Fms.

OCCASIONAL
BREAKS

Isla San Geronimo
GP. FL. (2)
19 N.M.

Arrecife Sacramento
BREAKERS

BREAKERS

LAT. 29° 30'

N

LAT. 29° 30'

Punta Baja, looking to the north

SECTION 4
PUNTA BAJA to PUNTA BLANCA

For general navigation along this coast use United States Oceanographic Charts H.O. 1006, San Francisco to Point Telmo; 623, Cabo San Quintín to Punta Eugenia; H.O. 1193, Bahía de San Quintín to Isla Cedros; H.O. 1044, Plans on the West Coast of Baja California; British Admiralty Charts #2324, Cape San Lucas to San Diego Bay; #3056, Bahía Rosario to San Diego Bay, #3055, Bahía San Hipólito to Bahía Rosario; Mexican Cartas Náuticas de Faros e Hidrografía F.H. 610, De Ensenada a Mazatlán; F.H. 601, Cabo San Quintín a Punta Eugenio.

Punta Baja lies about 26 miles in a straight line course south-southeastward of Cabo San Quintín. It is a long finger of land with a low sand cliff about 30 feet high at its terminal end off which there are numerous *detached rocks*. A *reef* surrounded by kelp projects southward a short distance from the point. Vessels rounding the point into Rosario Bay should lay a course well clear of the headland.

On Sunday, August 20, 1542, the vessels of Cabrillo's expedition approached this point of land from their previous night's anchorage at Isla San Geronimo, and the headland was given the name Engaño (Tricky). It was duly described in the log and passed abeam for better anchorage further northward. The land on Punta Baja is flat with a low rise of darker hills at the foot of the point. Just below these hills on the southern exposure is a commercial fish camp consisting of about a dozen shacks and a processing plant located above an indifferent *landing·*

Medical Note: There is an emergency decompression chamber to relieve divers' bends available at this place.

Bahía del Rosario (Rosario Bay) is formed by the sweep of the coast eastward of Punta Baja. Shoal water extends about ½ mile offshore and kelp grows heavily throughout the bay but *good anchorage,* sheltered from the prevailing coastal winds, may be found in depths of 5 to 6 fathoms over a sand bottom. A prominent *white patch* in the hills about 1¾ miles northward of the bay provides a good bearing when making into the anchorage.

Punta Baja and Bahía Rosario, looking eastward

TIDES — In Rosario Bay the high water interval at full and change is 9 hours 19 minutes; the spring range is 6.4 feet and the mean range, 4.8 feet. *Landing* may be effected at low water in the small cove below the fish camp or at the mouth of a small arroyo ¼ mile to the eastward. As in many of the bays of this configuration along the Peninsula's Pacific coast, ocean swells are diffracted around the point and sweep the anchorage. An eddy of the southward-running California current produces an upwelling of cold ocean water within the bay bringing with it basic nutrients that support a rich marine life cycle. Lobsters are plentiful and, at one time, there were extensive beds of abalone close inshore on rocks that dried at low water. Bottom fishing is excellent throughout the bay. The anchorage at Rosario Bay is about a 67-mile run from Cabo Colnett, approximately 37 miles from Hassler Cove at Isla San Martín and some 27 miles from Entrada Point, Bahía San Quintín. Coastal cruising vessels frequently anchor here.

From Punta Baja the coast bends to the eastward for about 5 miles and then to the southward about 10 miles to Punta San Antonio. The character of the shore consists of sand bluffs 50 to 100 feet high, backed at a distance of 1½ to 2 miles by hills 300 to 500 feet high. Several canyons break through to the shore of which the most conspicuous are, Cañón Penga Quemada, about 4½ miles eastward of Punta Baja, Cañón de San Vicente, about 6½ miles farther southward, and Cañón de San Antonio, approximately 2¼ miles still farther southward. Several smaller canyons show to seaward along the shore. Picacho San Vicente (San Vicente Peak), 1,511 feet high, rises 10½ miles east-southeastward of Punta Baja and about 3 miles inland.

Between Punta Baja and Punta San Antonio, a straight line distance of approximately 13 miles, there is a welter of kelp surrounding several 3- and 4-fathom shoal spots that break occasionally. About 9¼ miles southward of Punta Baja and about 5 miles offshore lies Isla San Geron-imo, surrounded by fields of kelp, except on its southeastern side, where the shore offers shelter from prevailing coastal winds and a *landing place*. Beyond the island, about 4 miles off Punta San Antonio to the westward, is Arrecife Sacramento (Sacramento Reef) with *rocks exposed* and *awash* breaking heavily when the seas are running, and surrounded by thick beds of kelp. *Caution: The area is navigable but dangerous; courses must be laid carefully, a sharp watch kept, patches of kelp avoided and a wide berth given the charted dangers.* A course may be laid either inside Rosario Bay close inshore, and passage made through the 1½-mile wide channel between Sacramento Reef and Punta San Antonio, or outside well clear of the shoals, the kelp, the island and the reef.

Isla San Geronimo (San Geronimo Island), about 9¼ miles southward of Punta Baja and 5 miles offshore, is a totally barren piece of land, whitish in color and covered with sand and birdlime. It is ¾ mile long and about ¼ mile wide at its greatest width, with rocky shores and cliffs 10 to 20 feet high. A rocky spine runs the length of the island rising to a maximum height of 130 feet, from which place a *navigation light* is shown 154 feet above the sea from a cylindrical masonry tower. The characteristic of the light is a **white group flash** of **two flashes every 10 seconds** that can be seen unobstructed around the horizon for 19 miles in clear weather. The Sacramento Reef is covered by a *red sector* of Isla de San Geronimo Light. The light is attended and a reliable aid to navigation although from time to time it has been reported extinguished. Its geographic location is Latitude 30° 29′ north, Longitude 116° 07′ west.

The island is surrounded by extensive kelp beds and *detached rocks* with a reef of *submerged rocks* extending from the southern end some 750 yards southwestward, over which the swell breaks; at the outer end of this *reef* is a 15-foot high rock against which the sea breaks heavily. *Navigation note: Give this rock a wide berth when rounding the southern end of the island as breakers have*

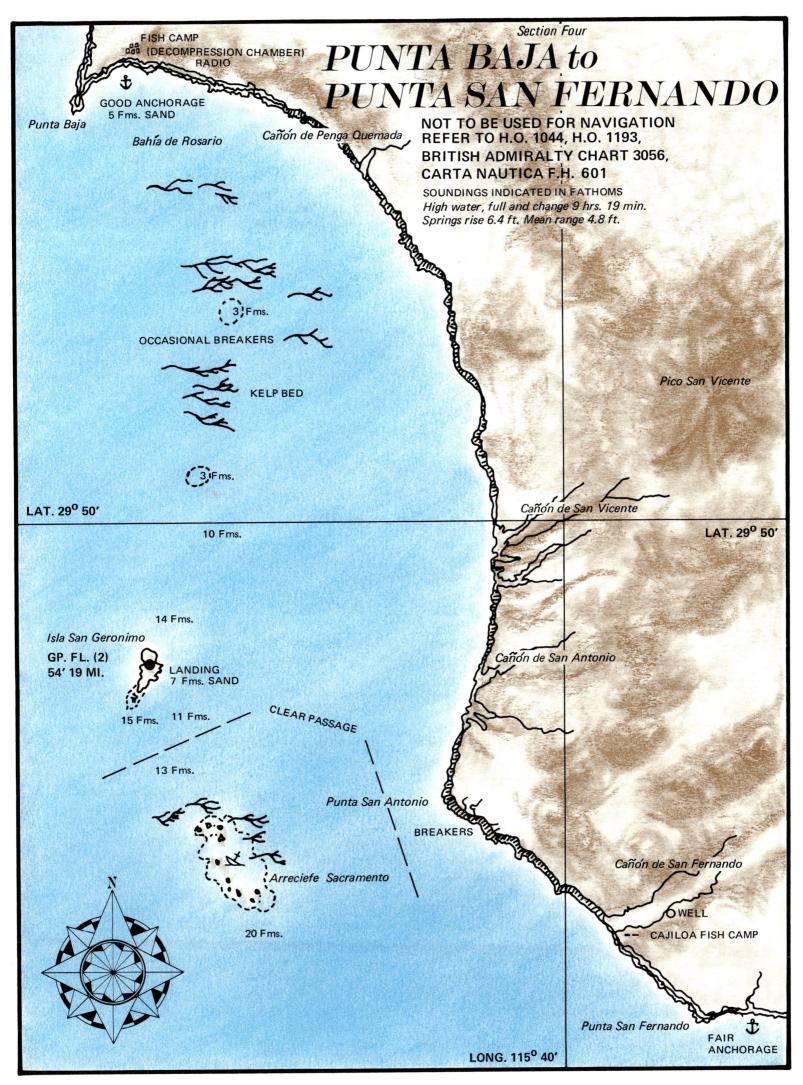

FISH CAMP
(DECOMPRESSION CHAMBER)
RADIO

GOOD ANCHORAGE
5 Fms. SAND

Punta Baja

Bahía de Rosario

Cañón de Penga Quemada

Section Four

PUNTA BAJA to
PUNTA SAN FERNANDO

NOT TO BE USED FOR NAVIGATION
REFER TO H.O. 1044, H.O. 1193,
BRITISH ADMIRALTY CHART 3056,
CARTA NAUTICA F.H. 601
SOUNDINGS INDICATED IN FATHOMS
High water, full and change 9 hrs. 19 min.
Springs rise 6.4 ft. Mean range 4.8 ft.

3 Fms.

OCCASIONAL BREAKERS

KELP BED

Pico San Vicente

3 Fms.

LAT. 29° 50'

Cañón de San Vicente

LAT. 29° 50'

10 Fms.

14 Fms.

Isla San Geronimo
GP. FL. (2)
54' 19 MI.

LANDING
7 Fms. SAND

Cañón de San Antonio

15 Fms.   11 Fms.

CLEAR PASSAGE

13 Fms.

Punta San Antonio

N

BREAKERS

Arreciefe Sacramento

Cañón de San Fernando

20 Fms.

WELL

CAJILOA FISH CAMP

Punta San Fernando

FAIR
ANCHORAGE

LONG. 115° 40'

*been observed from time to time, 200 yards southwest-
ward.* A great field of kelp in which there are numerous
rocky shoal patches extends southward from Bahía Rosario to Isla San Geronimo. One of these *shoals,* a
3-fathom patch on which the swell breaks occasionally,
lies about 4 miles south-southeastward of Punta Baja;
another, covered by 3¼ fathoms, lies about 2¾ miles
north-northeastward of the northern end of the island.
The bottom is rocky and irregular in the kelp-covered area
and other equally shoal patches may exist. The outer edge
of the kelp follows, in general, the 10-fathom curve which
is as much as 5 miles offshore along this stretch of coast.
An open-water channel about 1 mile wide, with mid-
channel depths of 13 to 15 fathoms between the southern
end of this kelp field and that extending off the north side
of Isla Geronimo, may be used with safety.

north, keeping well clear of the kelp. On August 19, 1542,
Cabrillo anchored his two caravels, *Salvador* and *Victoria,*
in the lee of this island and bestowed the name San Ber-
nardo upon it. However, Vizcaíno's place names con-
ferred 60 years later are generally the ones that have come
down to us and appear on present-day charts.

Arrecife Sacramento (Sacramento Reef), which has
claimed the lives of a number of vessels, lies about 1½
miles southeastward of Isla San Geronimo, its most seaward edge a little more than 5 miles offshore abreast
Punta San Antonio, and directly in the track of north-
bound vessels keeping close along the coast. The reef is
steep-to and covers an area that is about 2¼ miles long,
northwest and southeast, and 1¼ miles wide. It lies between the 10- and 20-fathom curves with numerous *rocks*

Isla San Geronimo

A *fishing bank* with a least depth of 37 fathoms lies 13
miles due west of the island and another *bank* with a least
depth of 39 fathoms lies about 14 miles in the south-southwestward direction from the island. Schools of yellowfin
tuna and skipjack are frequently fished for in this general
area by commercial Tuna Clippers. Local fishermen in
small skiffs frequent the island and the reef to the southward for lobster and bottom fish and commercial divers
take abalone which is abundant in the area. Sport fishermen angle for giant black sea bass which are plentiful.

Shelter may be had from the prevailing coastal winds
in a *fair anchorage* eastward of the island in about 7
fathoms, sand bottom. Ocean swells diffracted around the
ends of the island sometimes create a considerable trough
in which a vessel may roll uncomfortably. There is a *good
landing place* on a small shingle beach in a slight indentation on the southeastern side of the island below the
light. Vessels making for the anchorage may pass from
the open sea around to the south, keeping well outside
the reef, or they may use the open-water channel to the

submerged, awash and *protruding* from the sea, which
boil at low water and break in several patches of white
surf when a heavy swell is running. The entire reef area
is surrounded by extensive fields of kelp which include
shoal patches of 3 to 5 fathoms several hundred yards
eastward of the main body of the reef. The 20-fathom
curve follows the seaward edge of the reef on its outermost side. *Navigation note: A red sector of the light on
Isla San Geronimo covers Sacramento Reef.*

A *wreck* marked on the navigation charts lies on the
southern side of the reef. Several Tuna Clippers and a
number of other vessels from time to time have struck
this reef and ground out their lives on the jagged rocks
hidden in the kelp. The particular wreck charted, and from
which the reef gained its name, was the 271-foot side-
wheeler S.S. *Sacramento* bound up the coast from Panama
in 1872. Existence of the reef was known, but uncharted,
at that time, and general knowledge of its extent and
exact location fell into the realm of "local information",
special knowledge contained in the navigation notes of

ship's masters who frequented these waters. The *Sacramento* was following a course laid safely along the 20-fathom curve offshore, except for the dangerous shoal directly in her track, shortly to be known as Sacramento Reef. Within less than 30 minutes after striking the reef, water filled through the badly breached hull and the vessel settled to its freight deck. The 80 passengers and crew aboard made their way safely to Isla San Geronimo and within five days were picked up by a rescue vessel, the S.S. *Montana*. The *Sacramento's* 268 tons of general cargo and $1,500,000 in gold coin bound for San Francisco from Mazatlán were salvaged but the sunken remains of the ship's hull is still fair game for adventurous divers willing to brave the treacherous currents around the reef. Countless other wrecks are strewn on the reef from the latter part of the 1500's onward.

The most recent victim to have gone to a watery grave on this reef carried her entire crew with her, leaving an aura of mystery to settle over her steel bones. Late in the night of May 25, or early in the morning of May 26, 1969, the well-known 150-foot steel schooner *Goodwill,* on a passage from Cape San Lucas to San Diego, wrecked on Sacramento Reef with a loss of all hands. It is known that at approximately 1700 hours on May 25, 1969, radio contact was had between the *Goodwill* and the Tuna Clipper *Karen Mary* out of San Diego. At that time the *Goodwill*

indicated that she was approximately 50 miles northwest of Cedros Island and was proceeding under power toward Ensenada at approximately five knots. Neither the ship nor any of its crew were ever heard from again; its sunken hull with jagged tophamper protruding above the reef was discovered in an overflight by airmen searching for the overdue yacht. Aerial photographs revealed its lifeboats still lashed on deck. Two members of the crew were found drowned in their life preservers, floating near the reef; others were found washed ashore several weeks later, having drifted down in the coastal current to Sebastián Vizcaíno Bay. A conclusion must be drawn that the vessel's course set shoreward by current drift or through the master's miscalculation carried her hard upon the reef and to a watery grave.

Passage between the northern edge of the kelp surrounding the reef and the southern edge of the kelp fringing San Geronimo Island is about 1½ miles wide with mid-channel depths of 11 to 15 fathoms; a clear channel passage between the eastern side of the reef and Punta San Antonio is about 1½ miles wide with mid-channel depths of 7 to 11 fathoms. Large dense masses of kelp grow profusely in the general area with a proclivity for shoal water and the prudent navigator will give the kelp beds a wide berth. Punta San Antonio comprises a low cliff from which shoal ground marked by kelp extends nearly ¾ mile westward. There is a 3-fathom *patch* about 2½ miles westward of San Antonio Point and ½ mile eastward of the reef, and with the exception of the additional shoal area ¾ mile off Punta San Antonio, there are no other known dangers through this passage.

Southward from Isla San Geronimo to Puerto San José at Acme Rock is a run of about 60 miles along a coast where shelter from prevailing winds may be sought in any one of three or four safe anchorages. From San Antonio Point to Canoas Point, a distance of 33 miles, the coast has a general southeasterly trend with a succession of curves to the eastward at Punta San Fernando, Punta San Carlos and Punta Escarparda (Bluff Point), on some charts Punta Acantilado. Although the water is somewhat shoal, *anchorage* with good holding ground and some protection from the prevailing winds may be taken in the lee of these points. Immediately southward of Arroyo San Fernando is the Cajiloa Fish Camp, seasonally occupied by coastal fishermen. There are no permanent shacks or buildings here but a *spring,* tapped by a small well that produces a somewhat brackish water, is located about 1 mile inland on the primitive dirt road that runs up from the fish camp. Of the above mentioned *anchorages* the one eastward of Punta San Carlos is the best and most frequented by small vessels seeking shelter, although in choosing an anchorage one should consider the state of the sea and the weather and not overlook any of these places. In calm weather, except for the swells that nearly always sweep the open roadstead along this coast and diffract around the headlands, any of these anchorages can provide a pleasant stopover with *safe landings* possible nearby. *Anchorage note: Be wary of a shift of wind; buoy a tripline to the anchor flukes for quick departure and examine the area of the anchorage carefully for pinnacles around which your scope will allow you to swing.*

The mouth of Arroyo San Fernando opens on the shore just south of Punta San Antonio. Approximately 30 miles inland up the San Fernando Canyon is the site of the only Franciscan mission to have been established by that order in Baja California. The site, originally an Indian settlement, was called variously "'Guircata," "Velicata" or "Villacutta," depending upon the particular translation. It was first discovered in Spanish colonial times by the Jesuit padre, Wenceslao Link, in 1766. The Jesuits were expelled from the country before that order could establish a mission here. However, in 1769, Father Junípero Serra on his way to Alta California did establish the

Mission San Fernando and under the Franciscans and their successors, the Dominicans, it developed into a large and important settlement. The Indian population, which reached a peak of about 1,500 persons, was decimated by the great epidemics of 1777-1780 and the mission was virtually abandoned by 1818. Remnants of adobe walls and an old irrigation ditch mark the site.

This stretch of coast is generally characterized by sand bluffs, 50 to 100 feet high, breaking to low shelving beaches at the intersecting arroyos. The coast is backed by moderately high hills and tablelands 1,000 to 2,000 feet high with numerous peaks. Sombrero Peak, 1,893 feet high and shaped remarkably like a hat, is situated 2½ miles northeastward of Punta Escarparda (Bluff Point) and provides an excellent landmark from seaward.

Puerto de San Carlos, in the lee of the point of the same name, is a sloping shelf of coastal land beneath the 2,000-foot Mesa de San Carlos (San Carlos Plateau). The plateau may be recognized by its slightly sloping profile toward the south and the 2,424-foot peak, called Hat Peak, eastward of Punta de San Carlos and northwestward of Sombrero Peak. There is a seasonally occupied fish camp on the shelf back of the beach. During the lobster fishing season there is considerable activity here and the bay may be filled with moored lobster receivers holding the fishermen's catch for shipment. *Anchorage*

Punta San Carlos Anchorage

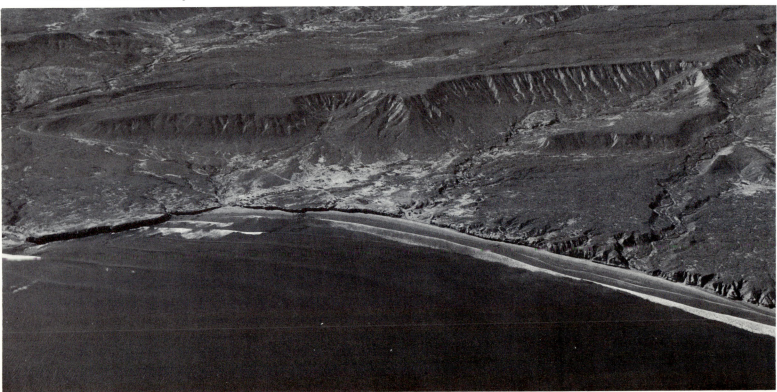

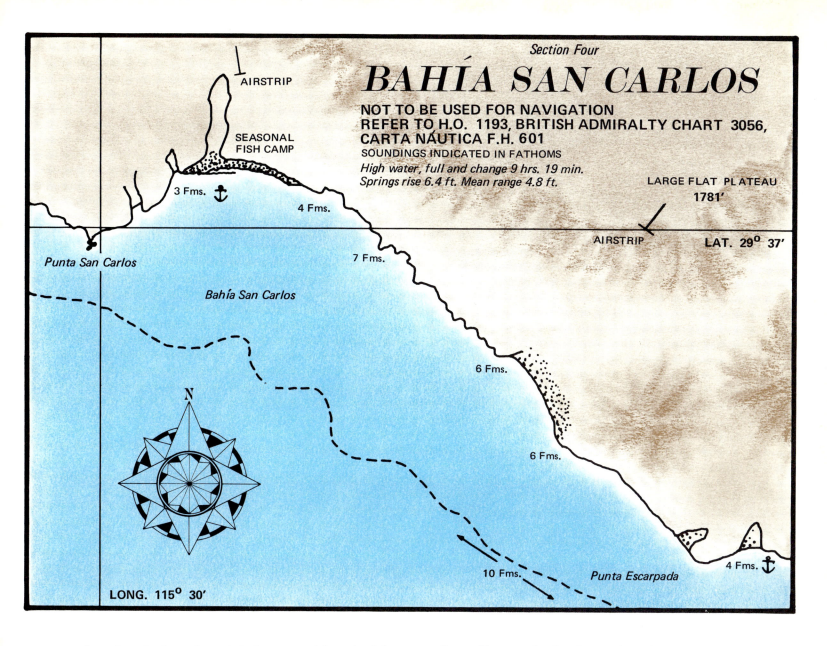

BAHÍA SAN CARLOS

**NOT TO BE USED FOR NAVIGATION
REFER TO H.O. 1193, BRITISH ADMIRALTY CHART 3056,
CARTA NÁUTICA F.H. 601**
SOUNDINGS INDICATED IN FATHOMS
*High water, full and change 9 hrs. 19 min.
Springs rise 6.4 ft. Mean range 4.8 ft.*

AIRSTRIP

SEASONAL FISH CAMP

3 Fms.

4 Fms.

LARGE FLAT PLATEAU
1781'

AIRSTRIP

LAT. 29° 37'

Punta San Carlos

7 Fms.

Bahía San Carlos

N

6 Fms.

6 Fms.

10 Fms.

Punta Escarpada

4 Fms.

LONG. 115° 30'

may be taken in from 3 to 4 fathoms, avoiding the lobster receivers that are awash and sometimes hard to see, but usually buoyed. The anchorage is not protected from the southwest or from the southeast and occasionally north winds with velocities of 50 knots or above may sweep down the 2,000-foot mountain wall from the mesa above, making the anchorage untenable. There are no supplies available and there is no fresh water to be had.

The open roadstead of Puerto San Carlos was used about 100 years ago to land cargo from coastal trading vessels to supply the many mines and mining settlements in the interior. Tentative consideration has been given to the planning of a coastal way port of refuge at San Carlos for yachts and pleasure fishing vessels. A large field of *kelp,* about 2½ miles in length and extending about 5 miles offshore, lies west-southwestward of Punta San Carlos. Depths of 6 to 10 fathoms hard sand and rock have been sounded in this field. No dangers are known to exist but as with all kelp-covered, relatively shoal areas along this coast, *caution* should be observed in and around the kelp beds, since submerged pinnacles may exist. A *fishing bank* with a least sounded depth of 9 fathoms is located about 3¼ miles westward of Punta San Carlos and another *bank* with a least sounded depth of 9 fathoms, marked by a field of kelp, lies about 4¼ miles west-northwestward of Punta San Carlos.

Punta Escarparda (or Punta Acantilado), 20½ miles southeastward of Punta San Antonio, is a bold sand bluff about 100 feet high that is closely backed by hills rising to the San Carlos Mesa. Pico Sombrero, 1,893 feet high atop the mesa, is directly behind the point about 2½ miles distant.

Puerto Santa Catarina (Santa Catarina Landing), located at the mouth of the arroyo of the same name, about 8 miles northwestward of Punta Canoas, is a seasonally occupied fish camp comprised of tarpaper shacks. It is an *open roadstead* with a small stone jetty once used, around 1900, for exporting copper and lightering onyx marble blocks produced at the quarry of El Mármol to vessels offshore. Some scattering of these black marble blocks may still be seen discarded along the beach, and close southward large pieces of a wrecked ship lie stranded on the shore. The butt ends of a few wooden pilings that may be seen at low tide are all that remain of a wooden pier that once extended from the shore; a disused road runs down to the foot of the old pier site. There is a small brackish lagoon in the mouth of the arroyo that opens on the coast at the landing. A dozen or so graves marked by weathered wooden crosses may be seen on a knoll beside the lagoon. In 1957 a pier capable of accommodating vessels drawing 20 feet was built. Vessels may *anchor* in good holding ground of mud, sand and boulders about 300

Roca Acme

yards north of the pier; however the beach is not a good landing place for small boats because of the surf. There is a small *spring* of poor water near this site. An *airstrip* suitable for light planes is located near the landing.

Rich and world famous fossil beds are located on the road to the old quarry at El Máramol but quite close to the coast. The remarkable fossils to be found here were discovered a great many years ago and specimens collected have gained world-wide recognition. Back in the hills in a small arroyo, eroded by the fierce runoff of infrequent flash floods, the surface is strewn with the exposed fossils of what appear to be giant snail shells curled in a single plane. These "snails" are commonly 2 feet in diameter, with some greater in size to be found. The snail-like creatures are ancient cephalopods, long extinct relatives of the squid and octopus. These abundant fossilized marine animals, which apparently congregated in the shallows of an evaporating primordial sea, have left an articulate record of their existence here for those who care to study the Sanskrit of evolution.

Punta Canoas, about 7 miles southeastward of Santa Catarina Landing, is a sharp perpendicular sand bluff, 224 feet high, that is surrounded by hills 700 to 1,200 feet high, behind which is a mountain range more than 2,000 feet high. A hill shown on the chart as Bracket Peak, attains an elevation of 306 feet about 5 miles northward of Punta Canoas. San Pedro and San Pablo peaks in this range, respectively 2,620 and 2,615 feet high, are situated fairly close together about 17 miles northeastward of Canoas Point. San Miguel, the highest peak of the range, located about 13 miles northward of San Pedro and San Pablo Peaks, is 3,598 feet high. *Caution: In 1930 a vessel struck a submerged pinnacle rock with a least depth of 5 to 7 feet at low water about 600 to 700 yards south-southwestward off Punta Canoas. Anchorage* may be taken in the lee of this point in depths of 5 to 7 fathoms, sand bottom, about ½ mile offshore. The bottom shelves gently so that one may approach closer than ½ mile if a shallower anchorage is desired. In good weather this shelter provides partial protection from the prevailing coastal winds. Ocean swells generally sweep across the anchorage and vessels lying-to will experience the discomfiture of rolling in the trough. Bow and stern anchors properly placed will prevent a good bit of this problem.

La Lobera, a seasonal fish camp, may be found on the mesa above Punta Canoas, and another seasonally occupied fish camp is established in the lee of the point. An *airstrip,* in a broad flat valley a little over ½ mile back of the point and reached by a primitive dirt road, was once utilized by air freighters for transportation of the catch to market. On August 15, 1542, Cabrillo anchored his vessels overnight in the lee of this point and, perhaps because of the unfavorable weather in the anchorage, he applied the name Mal Abrigo (Poor Shelter) to the point.

The coast between Punta Canoas and Punta Blanca, 32 miles to the southeastward, is composed of sand bluffs and rocky points alternating with sand beaches. Three distinct mountain ranges are discernible from seaward along this stretch of coast; the first is 500 to 1,000 feet high; the second is 2,000 feet high; the third exceeds 3,000 feet. Pico San Miguel and Pico San José, 6 miles westward, attain elevations of 3,598 and 2,972 feet, respectively, about 25 miles north-northeastward of Punta Canoas. The coastal road, a primitive track for the most part, runs close along the shore here and connects to the interior settlements at Punta Canoas and Puerto de San José.

Los Morros, a seasonally occupied fish camp, is located about 12 miles southward of Punta Canoas. A little more than half way between these two points, approximately 19 miles southeastward of Punta Canoas, lies a small rocky islet, whitened by birdlime, about 20 feet high and ½ mile offshore, known locally as Acme Rock. The islet is surrounded by a heavy growth of kelp and this, together with *reefs awash* that project out from the headland to the northward, provide a shelter for Puerto San José, once one of the principal cargo landing points for the region's interior ranches, mines and settlements, now the site of a commercial fish camp.

Immediately southward of the islet is an extensive field of kelp in the lee of which a very smooth *anchorage* may be had in depths of 6 fathoms. Commercial fishing boats frequent this anchorage for overnight shelter. Rolling is minimal and the early morning calms frequently show a sea smooth as glass.

WIND AND WEATHER — The sea breeze normally springs up around 11 o'clock in the morning and blows with gently increasing velocity until just before sunset when it begins to die, giving way to light offshore night breezes. *Landing* can be most always effected safely upon the beach in all but stormy weather and very rough seas. A dirt road runs up the Arroyo de San José from the landing and connects to the Transpeninsular Highway. An *airstrip* near the landing is sometimes used by light planes.

SECTION 5
PUNTA BLANCA to
MORRO SANTO DOMINGO

For navigation along this stretch of coast use United States Oceanographic Charts H.O. 623, Cabo San Quintín to Punta Eugenio; H.O. 1193, Bahía de San Quintín to Punta Eugenio; H.O. 1193, Bahía de San Quintín to Isla Cedros; H.O. 1044, Plans on the West Coast of Baja California; British Admiralty Charts #2324, Cape San Lucas to San Diego Bay; #3055, Bahía San Hipólito a Bahía Rosario; Mexican Cartas Náuticas F.H. 610, De Ensenada a Mazatlán; F.H. 601, Cabo San Quintín a Punta Eugenio; F.H. 603, Golfo de California — Parte Norte.

Punta Blanca presents the whitish face of a steep sandstone cliff about 100 feet high, immediately behind which is a plateau about 200 feet above sea level; several peaks between 500 and 600 feet are located just back of the plateau, and the coast range of mountains rises immediately behind to a little over 2,000 feet. About ¾ mile northwestward is a similar point which projects seaward about ¼ mile surrounded by detached rocks.

Bahía Blanca, eastward of Punta Blanca and sheltered somewhat from the prevailing winds by the point, is an open roadstead that affords *good anchorage* in depths of 6 to 8 fathoms. *Safe landing* can be made immediately eastward of the point in the lee on a small sandy beach between the hills. A ridge reaches outward toward the point and flattens to a sloping plateau about 200 feet high just back of the point. On the northeastern shore of the bay is the dry basin of a small lagoon whitened by deposited salt; about 1½ miles southeastward of the first is another larger dry basin in a plain that extends back several miles between the hills. The coast between Punta Blanca and Punta Cono, 10 miles southeastward, is a succession of bluffs and sand beaches. El Salinito, a seasonal fish camp about 7 miles southward of Punta Blanca, may be recognized by a muddy salt flat behind a pebbly beach. The coastal road touches the shore at this point.

Punta Cono (Cone Point) is a steep and rocky double-pointed headland. Cono Roja (Red Cone), a conspicuous reddish-colored hill 169 feet high, lies close northward of Cone Point. This point first appears to southward bound vessels as an island. Bahía Falsa (False Bay) lies indented

Punta Blanca, looking toward the southeast

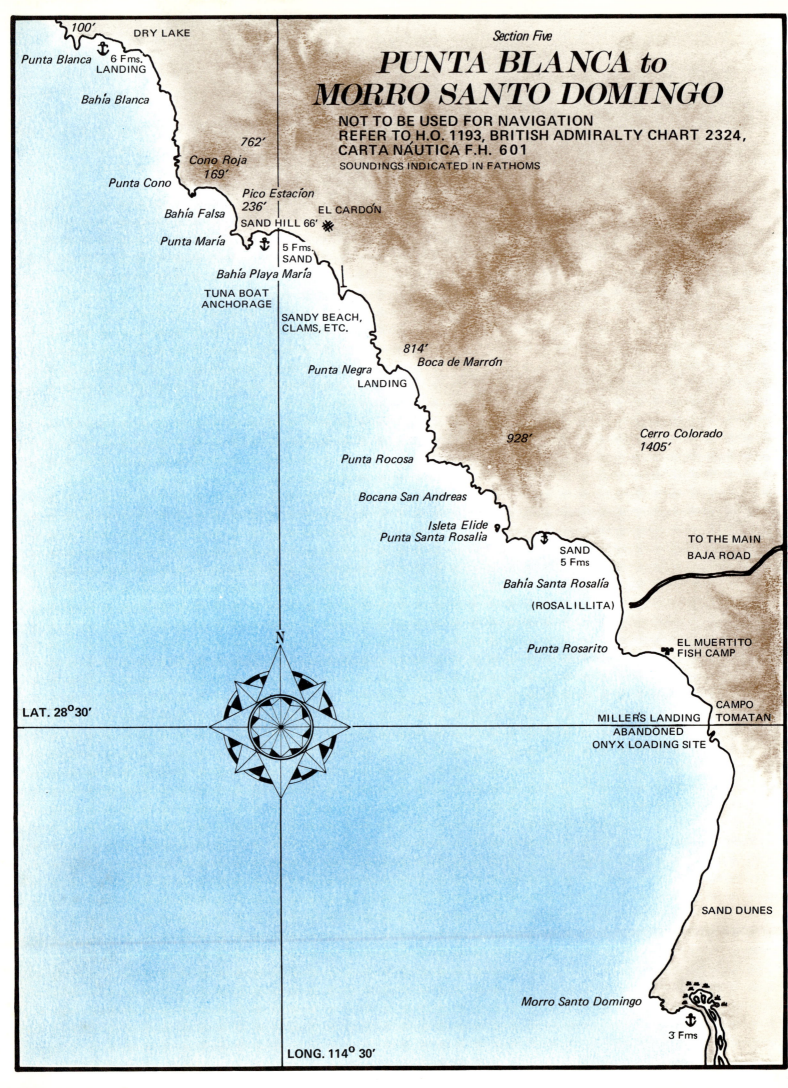

PUNTA BLANCA to
MORRO SANTO DOMINGO
NOT TO BE USED FOR NAVIGATION
REFER TO H.O. 1193, BRITISH ADMIRALTY CHART 2324,
CARTA NÁUTICA F.H. 601
SOUNDINGS INDICATED IN FATHOMS

100'

DRY LAKE

Punta Blanca   6 Fms.
LANDING

Bahía Blanca

762'

Cono Roja
169'

Punta Cono

Pico Estación
236'   EL CARDÓN

Bahía Falsa

SAND HILL 66'

Punta María   5 Fms.
                     SAND

Bahía Playa María

TUNA BOAT
ANCHORAGE

SANDY BEACH,
CLAMS, ETC.

814'
Boca de Marrón

Punta Negra
LANDING

928'   Cerro Colorado
                          1405'

Punta Rocosa

Bocana San Andreas

Isleta Elide
Punta Santa Rosalia

                    SAND   TO THE MAIN
                    5 Fms   BAJA ROAD

Bahía Santa Rosalía

(ROSALILLITA)

Punta Rosarito   EL MUERTITO
                        FISH CAMP

N

LAT. 28° 30'   CAMPO
                                          TOMATAN
              MILLER'S LANDING
              ABANDONED
              ONYX LOADING SITE

SAND DUNES

Morro Santo Domingo

3 Fms

LONG. 114° 30'

eastward of Punta Cono with a low shoreline comprised of sand and shingle beaches that curve around to Punta Falsa, a round rocky point 1¼ miles northwestward of Punta María; thence as far as Punta María the coast is steep and rocky. A wide conspicuous arroyo with sand hills on either side opens on the bay 1¾ miles eastward of Punta Cono. Bahía Falsa affords *anchorage* in depths of 4 to 6 fathoms with fair protection from the prevailing winds. A *landing strip* back of the bay is sometimes used by light aircraft. Because of the *better anchorages* to be found in Bahía Blanca northward and Bahía Playa María southward, Bahía Falsa is seldom sought for shelter. Punta María, a low rocky point about 4 miles southeastward of Punta Cono and about 1¼ miles southeastward of Punta Falsa, may be identified by a *sand mound* 66 feet high, approximately ½ mile to the northward.

Bahía Playa María, tucked in behind this point and well-sheltered from the prevailing coastal winds, provides a *good anchorage* for small vessels in spite of the fact that most of the bay is comprised of open roadstead. *Anchorage* may be taken in the northern part of the bay in from 3 to 7 fathoms over a sand bottom, the best protection being well in the lee of Punta María. *Directions: When making for the anchorage an excellent landmark is a conspicuous cone-shaped hill rising abruptly from the northern shore of the bay, 236 feet high, referred to on navigation charts as Pico Estación (Station Peak). An uncomfortable swell sweeps around the point and reaches across most of the bay, the calmest anchorage being close under the lee.* The lengthy stretch of sandy beach affords a landing in most weather for small boats and the place is well-known for an abundance of clams that may be easily obtained at low water.

TIDES — The mean high water interval at full and change at Playa María Bay is 9 hours 15 minutes; the spring range is 7.6 feet, the mean range 5.7 feet.

Bahía Playa María is frequented by fishing vessels seeking live bait through use of beach nets cast close to the surf. At one time Tuna Clippers from San Diego and San Pedro were to be found frequently at anchor in the open roadstead. Smaller vessels are more apt to be found at anchor here at the present time.

A Tuna Clipper is a unique community in itself with a sharp-freezing plant aboard, a large-volume seawater circulating system for maintaining bait alive 10 days or more far offshore, and on many modern clippers, a giant turntable aft, piled high with great nylon nets. These vessels

Punta Cono and Bahía Falsa

are all powerfully diesel-driven and capable of speeds from 12 to 15 knots with a non-stop range of 5,000 to 6,000 miles and comfortable living facilities for from 12 to 20 men. Their radiotelephone range is 1,000 miles or greater, and for those few vessels left which carry C. W. radiotelegraph operators, the range is worldwide from any point at any time.

The crews are made up of first, second and third generation Portuguese, Italians, Scandinavians, Japanese, and an increasing number of Mexican nationals. On most of the vessels a beautifully appointed chapel is located in one of the deck cabins for the crews' communion with the Creator of All Things to give thanks for a good catch and to pray for fine weather. Almost without exception, the boats are spotless, scrubbed thoroughly by every member of the crew after each day's foray on the fishing banks. The flow of warmth from their hospitable galleys is a most welcome experience when one has been invited aboard. Tuna boats homeward bound will gladly carry mail, fetch spare parts on their next trip out and most importantly relay radio messages home.

Agua Cardón, the remains of an abandoned fish camp with a dry well nearby, is situated in Playa María Bay, approximately halfway between Punta María and Punta Ositos, 5½ miles southward. Punta Negra (Black Point), called Punta Prieta on some charts, 10 miles southeastward of Punta María is a dark-colored rocky point distinguished by a hill 609 feet high that rises to it. Another hill, 517 feet high, stands close to the shore about ¾ mile northward of Punta Negra. A steep, rocky, rounded point, with a *conspicuous sand hill* 688 feet high rising from it, is situated about 2 miles southeastward of Black Point. About 1¼ miles farther on is another bluff point and close to it a detached hill 386 feet high. *Detached rocks*

Punta Ositos

lie close off both of these last described points. Two more smaller points interrupt the stretch of sand beaches that chiefly characterize the coast from Punta Negra to Punta Rocosa (Rocky Point) a distance of 5 miles south-southeastward.

Boca de Marrón, a beautiful crescent beach at the mouth of a small arroyo, lies just southward of Punta Negra. *Safe landing* for small boats may be made upon the beach in fine weather. A coastal road runs along the shore and communicates with the village of Punta Prieta about 12 miles inland.

Punta Rocosa is a steep cliff 75 feet high, the abrupt termination of a ridge of hills that extends eastward from the coast and includes a *conspicuous conical hill* 928 feet high, situated nearly 2 miles eastward of the point. The high peaks of Cedros Island, some 60 miles distant, are clearly visible from this vicinity.

Bocana San Andreas, a fish camp at the mouth of the Arroyo San Andreas, is located about 5 miles southeast of Punta Rocosa. The coastal road runs to the camp and communicates with Rancho San Andreas, a little over 13 miles inland by road. An *airstrip* suitable for light planes is situated along this road near the camp. *Safe landing* is afforded on the sand beach in good weather. For nearly 3½ miles southeastward of Rocky Point the coast is bold and rocky with cliffs 50 feet high; thence to abreast Elide Islet it is comprised chiefly of a low sand beach.

Isleta Elide (Elide Islet) lying ¾ mile northwestward of Punta Santa Rosalillita (Punta Santa Rosalía) and about ¼ mile offshore, is a barren rocky islet about ¼ mile long and 40 feet high, whitened with birdlime. At various times the southward-flowing California current and its eddy builds a connecting sandspit between the islet and the nearest shore over which the sea breaks. Prominent buildings, once used as a meteorological station, are located on the eastern side of the islet. Vessels sometimes *anchor* in the lee off the southeast side but a heavy swell is usually experienced there and the anchorage is not recommended.

Anchovy

Bahía Playa Maria

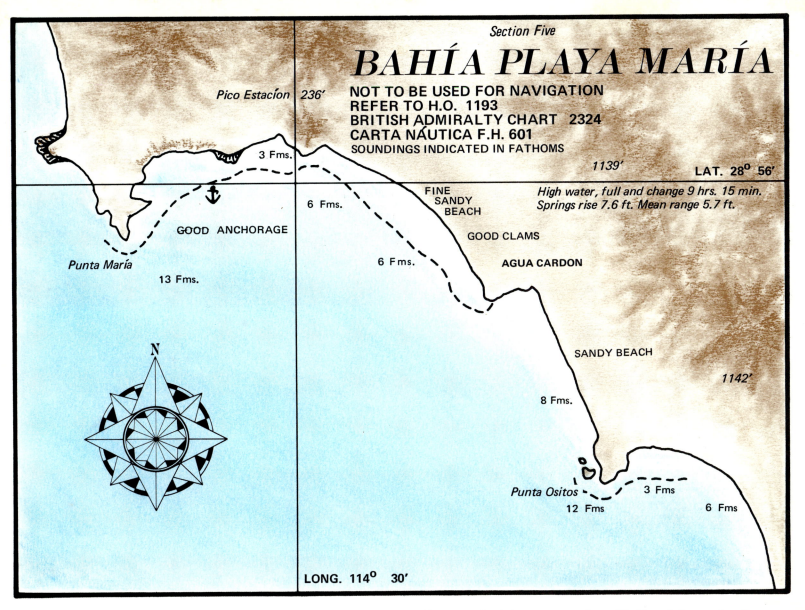

BAHÍA PLAYA MARÍA

NOT TO BE USED FOR NAVIGATION
REFER TO H.O. 1193
BRITISH ADMIRALTY CHART 2324
CARTA NÁUTICA F.H. 601
SOUNDINGS INDICATED IN FATHOMS

Pico Estación 236'

1139'

LAT. 28° 56'

High water, full and change 9 hrs. 15 min.
Springs rise 7.6 ft. Mean range 5.7 ft.

3 Fms.

6 Fms.

FINE
SANDY
BEACH

GOOD CLAMS

AGUA CARDON

GOOD ANCHORAGE

6 Fms.

6 Fms.

Punta María

13 Fms.

SANDY BEACH

1142'

8 Fms.

N

Punta Ositos

3 Fms

12 Fms

6 Fms

LONG. 114° 30'

Punta Santa Rosalillita (Rosalía), 6 miles southeastward of Punta Rocosa, is a bluff 87 feet high, the abrupt termination of a plateau that extends back several miles from the coast. Another point, sharp and angular in contour and with steep sides, lies one mile to the eastward of Punta Santa Rosalillita projecting southward about ¾ mile. A sandy wash breaks through the rocky shore midway between the two points. No known dangers exist off either point but *shoal water* extends about ½ mile eastward of the eastern point.

Bahía Santa Rosalillita (Santa Rosalía Bay), eastward of Rosalillita (Rosalía) Point, affords a good and spacious *anchorage* in depths of 5 to 8 fathoms, sand bottom, well-sheltered from the coastal winds. *Landing* may be made almost anywhere in the bay in good weather; the best place is on the pebbly beach at the mouth of the Arroyo Santa Dominquito that breaks through the plateau in the northern part of the bay. Westward of the arroyo is a smaller break in the plateau opening onto a shingle beach and occupied by a seasonal fish camp. The coast road runs down to this landing and communicates with the Rancho San Andreas about 12 miles inland, presently unworked. The fading marks of an abandoned *airstrip* may be seen atop the plateau just back of the fish camp, where air freighters at one time loaded the lobster catch for market. The name Santa Rosalillita is used locally in the diminutive form and distinguishes this Pacific coast bay from the like-named mining port on the gulf side of the peninsula.

The eastern shore of Bahía Santa Rosalillita is comprised of a low sand beach backed by the bold rocky cliffs of a broad plateau 90 to 150 feet high. Clams are plentiful on this beach and may be easily gathered at low water. No fresh water has been found in the vicinity.

Punta Rosarito, about 8 miles southeastward of Santa Rosalillita Point at the southern end of the bay, is a low projecting point with numerous outlying rocks. A *dangerous reef and shoal* marked by a field of kelp extends about ½ mile southward and westward from the southwestern side of the point. Southward of Rosarito Point the coast recedes eastward, forming between this point and Morro Santo Domingo (Lagoon Head) 19 miles distant, a large open bay with a bluff shore 50 to 100 feet high rising to about 200 feet near Lagoon Head. A low flat country bor-

Boca de San Andreas

Roca Elide and Punta Santa Rosalía

ders on the shore but high hills rise a few miles inland and the Sierra Calmalli range of mountains are visible in the interior, the most conspicuous being a high leaning peak, the jagged top of which seems to overhang, situated about 2.2 miles east-northeastward of Punta Rosarito. Several fish camps are located along this shore, occupied seasonally by groups of fishing cooperatives taking lobster, abalone, clams and bottom fish for shipment by truck or airfreighter to market. An *airstrip* suitable for cargo planes is located near El Muertito Fish Camp.

El Muertito (The Dead Boy) Fish Camp, in the lee of Punta Rosarito, is so named for a solitary grave along the side of the road that passes near the camp. It is carefully fenced with pickets and rails of driftwood, a rough wooden cross at its head. The white hulls of abalone shells cover the mound. Abalone fishermen discovered the body washed ashore from some ship at sea and gave it proper burial; it was never identified. Altamira, another fish camp established somewhat back from the coast, is about 13 miles southward of El Muertito. El Tomatal Fish Camp is situated back of a small cove in the lee of a minor point just beyond El Muertito; a road runs down to the camp.

Miller's Landing, situated on the beach roughly midway between Punta Rosarito and Morro Santo Domingo, is a long-abandoned loading point for onyx marble from the quarry at El Marmolito in the interior. Large slabs of the stone were at one time to be seen strewn along the beach. Sand dunes characterize the shoreline between Miller's Landing and Morro Santo Domingo.

Morro Santo Domingo (Lagoon Head) is a bold dark-colored headland of volcanic origin 502 feet high that is clearly visible from a distance of 30 to 40 miles, in contrast to the low shoreline both to the north and east; when first seen from seaward it appears as an island. The coastal road threads along the top of the bluff.

Bahía Santa Rosalía

Morro Santo Domingo (Lagoon Head)

SECTION 6

MORRO SANTO DOMINGO to PUNTA SAN EUGENIO (Including Scammon's Lagoon)

Captain Scammon

Bahía Sebastián Vizcaíno, a vast expanse of bay encircled by a great hook of the coast running from Morro de Santo Domingo on the north around to Punta Eugenio and Isla Cedros on the west, is a fascinating area in which to cruise. For navigation in this area see United States Oceanographic Office Charts H.O. 623, Cabo San Quintín to Punta Eugenio; H.O. 1193, Bahía de San Quintín to Isla Cedros; H.O. 1310, Cedros Island to Abreojos Point; H.O. 1044, Plans on the West Coast of Baja California; British Admiralty Charts #3055, Bahía San Hipólito to Bahía Rosario; Mexican Cartas Náuticas F.H. 601, Cabo San Quintín a Punta Eugenio; F.H. 603, Golfo de California — Parte Norte; F.H. 602, Punta Eugenio a Cabo San Lázaro.

Fondeadero Morro Santo Domingo (Lagoon Head Anchorage) is in the small bay eastward of the headland of the same name. The northern and eastern parts of the *anchorage* are quite shoal but vessels may anchor well up into the bight in depths of 3 to 8 fathoms, sand bottom, with fair protection from the prevailing wind. There is a good *landing place* for small boats on a sand beach at the foot of the bluff about 1 mile within the southernmost

point of the headland. *Directions: The anchorage should be approached with care, and on the lead, since the low shoreline and shelving beach make judgment of adequate offing deceptive, as would encourage vessels to go aground.*

Laguna Manuela (Manuela Lagoon), eastward of Morro Santo Domingo and the northernmost of the three large lagoons that open into Bahía Sebastián Vizcaíno, is a long narrow body of water with its entrance situated about 4 miles southeastward of Lagoon Head. A long narrow spit of white sand beach curving southward from Lagoon Head Anchorage, partially covered with a stunted bushy growth, separates the lagoon from the bay. The passage into the lagoon crosses a *bar* which extends off the entrance about 1 mile and has about 5 feet of water over it at low tide; the sea usually breaks on the *bar* even in fine weather. A tidal current ebbs and flows through the entrance at considerable velocity and entrance or exit should be planned for slack water. These swift tidal currents, together with storm-shifted sand and silt, constantly change the character of all the lagoon entrances and channels along this coast, therefore prudence should be exercised when making a decision to enter. The passage should not be attempted without a local

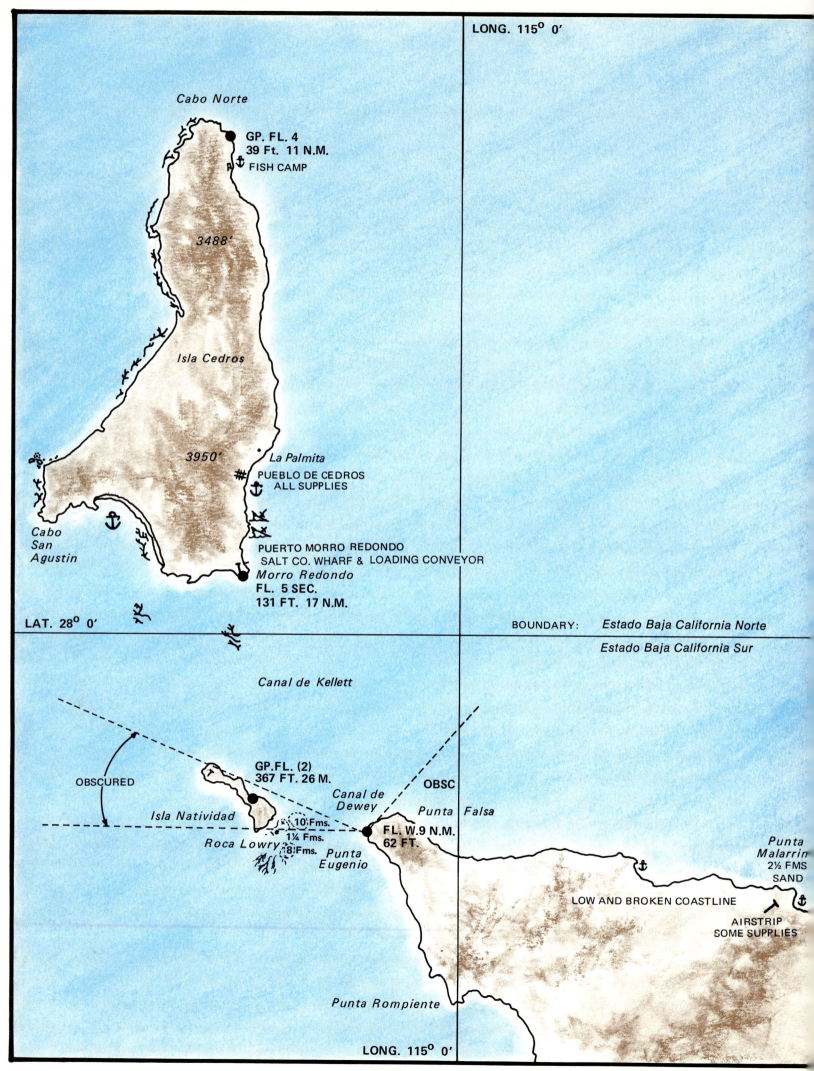

LONG. 115° 0'

Cabo Norte

GP. FL. 4
39 Ft. 11 N.M.
⚓ FISH CAMP

3488'

Isla Cedros

3950' • *La Palmita*

⚓ PUEBLO DE CEDROS
ALL SUPPLIES

*Cabo
San
Agustin*

⚓

PUERTO MORRO REDONDO
SALT CO. WHARF & LOADING CONVEYOR
Morro Redondo
FL. 5 SEC.
131 FT. 17 N.M.

LAT. 28° 0'

BOUNDARY: *Estado Baja California Norte*

Estado Baja California Sur

Canal de Kellett

OBSCURED

GP. FL. (2)
367 FT. 26 M.

*Canal de
Dewey*   OBSC

Isla Natividad   *Punta Falsa*

10 Fms.
1¼ Fms.   FL. W. 9 N.M.   *Punta
Malarrin*
Roca Lowry   8 Fms.   62 FT.   2½ FMS
⚓
*Punta
Eugenio*   SAND

LOW AND BROKEN COASTLINE

⚓
AIRSTRIP
SOME SUPPLIES

Punta Rompiente

LONG. 115° 0'

Section Six

MORRO SANTO DOMINGO
to
PUNTA SAN EUGENIO

REFER TO H.O. 1193, H.O. 1310, H.O. 1044, BRITISH ADMIRALTY 3055, CARTA NAUTICA F.H. 601

High water, full and change 9 hrs. 5 min.
Springs rise 7.5 ft. Mean range 5.9 ft.

SOUNDINGS INDICATED IN FATHOMS

N

Morro Santo Domingo

Puerto de
Santo Domingo

3 FMS.

Laguna Manuela

BUOY —
R.W. Vert. Stripes
Bell, Ra. Ref.
10 Fms.

Puerto
Venustiano
Carranza

SCAVENGER'S
BEACH

Laguna Guerrero Negro

ENTRANCE BUOY
BLACK CAN, LIGHTED
Ra. Ref.

Guerrero Negro
ALL SUPPLIES

Campo Chaparrito

DRY LAKE - SALT PONDS

Bahía de Sebastian Viscaíno

Fl. W.
Ev. 10 Sec.

SCAVENGER'S
BEACH

Laguna Ojo de Liebre
(Scammon's Lagoon)

SAND DUNES

NDING

DRY
LAKE

DRY LAKE

LONG. 114° 30'

Boca de Laguna Manuela

pilot or prior experience. There are no services, supplies, fresh water, or aids to navigation in this lagoon. The average range of the tide is about 6½ feet.

Laguna del Guerrero Negro (Black Warrior Lagoon) is the next and considerably larger lagoon southward. It is about 8 miles long, north and south, and approximately 3 miles wide. The entrance lies about 9 miles southward of Morro Santo Domingo, and on some charts it is designated as Estero de San José and is also known as Salina Vizcaíno. Natural salt deposits have been exploited in this region since about 1860. The modern wharf facilities at Puerto Venustiano Carranza are no longer in use and the access channel no longer regularly dredged. Small vessels may still safely enter through the natural channel with local knowledge but the passage should not be attempted without a pilot or prior experience.

DIRECTIONS, LANDMARKS AND LIGHTS — Vessels approaching the lagoon entrance from the north should take cognizance of the California current, running 140° from 1 to 2½ knots depending on the season and tidal reinforcement, which may be encountered southward of Isla San Geronimo.

Approaching the entrance of the lagoon from the west, the north end of Cedros Island is a good point of departure but a southerly set should be expected. When approaching from the south lights are exhibited on both sides of Kellett Channel. On near approach, Morro Santo Domingo (Lagoon Head Point) offers a prominent mark visible against a low shoreline by day and a good *radar target* both by night and day. From a fix on this point the *entrance Buoy* can be located, Latitude 28° 8½′ north, Longitude 114° 11′ west, about 7 miles, 208° true from Lagoon Head and about 3 miles west-northwestward of the *entrance range* marking the seaward end of the channel. This *buoy* is a *red and white* vertical striped *can* with *bell* and *radar reflector*. The sea buoy was lighted but it is presently extinguished. Depths in the vicinity of the approach buoy are approximately 10 fathoms and with adquate scope *good anchorage* may be had over a hard sand bottom in spite of the exposed appearance of the place. From the sea buoy to the dock within the lagoon there was a well-defined channel 8 miles long marked by buoys and ranges; however dredging has been suspended and the channel partially silted. The channel buoys remaining on the port hand entering are painted black with odd

numbers and red with even numbers on the starboard hand. The buoys were illuminated by white and red flashing lights respectively but are at present extinguished. A tidal current ebbs and flows at considerable velocity through the entrance channel reaching a rate of around 4½ or 5 knots during spring tides, and it is therefore prudent to plan passage at slack water.

The Laguna Guerrero Negro entrance channel is marked by a *range,* the front tower of which is located on the south side of the channel and marked by a *red triangular daymark,* point down; the *rear range tower* is located 540 yards, 124° true from the front tower and is marked by a *red triangular daymark,* point up. From the sea buoy the *entrance range,* when in *range* 124° leads over the bar to the junction of the *second range reach.* (See CAUTION). The south side of the entrance channel is marked by a *range of black and white* horizontally banded towers; the north side of the channel is marked by a *range* of beacons with *black triangular daymarks.* The ranges and beacons formerly lighted are at present extinguished.

The *second range reach,* located about 1½ miles south-southwestward of the entrance range on the western shore of the lagoon, is comprised of a *front range* wooden post with a dark-colored *diamond daymark;* the *rear range* wooden post with a dark-colored *rectangular daymark* is 333 yards, 187° true from the front post. The *second range reach,* when in *range* 187° leads to the junction of the *third range reach.*

The *third range,* located about 4 miles southward of the entrance on the southern shore of the lagoon, is comprised of a *front range black beacon* with a *rectangular daymark;* and a *rear range black beacon* with a *diamond daymark* located 430 yards, 164° true from the front beacon. The *third range reach* when in *range* 164°, leads to the junction of the fourth range reach.

The *fourth range,* located about 2½ miles south-south-eastward of the entrance on the southeastern shore of the lagoon, when in *range* astern 044° true, leads to the junction of the fifth range reach.

The *fifth range,* about 2 miles westward of the third range, when in *range* 239½° true, leads to the large steel "T" pier of Puerto Venustiano Carranza.

Two anchorages are designated: One facing the "T" pier with a depth of about 23 feet at low water; the other located in the third section of the channel in the vicinity between buoys 9, 11, 13, 14 and 16 with a minimum depth of about 32 feet. The anchorages have good holding ground over sand and mud.

CAUTION — Dredging of this channel has been discontinued; enter only with an experienced pilot.

TIDES — The average range of the tide is 6½ feet.

WIND AND WEATHER — The prevailing winds in the vicinity of the port are northwesterly, calm in the early morning, coming up around 11 a.m. and frequently reaching force 4 or more in the afternoon. Vessels may encounter fog in the winter months near the entrance to the lagoon, usually clearing about midday; the air is generally clear for most of the year with a very hot sun.

FACILITIES — The town of Guerrero Negro, about 6 miles by road from Puerto Venustiano Carranza, consists of a small industrial factory settlement of about 1,000 plant workers, supervisory management and shop keepers. The road from the wharf is hard surfaced with a mixture of salt and gypsum. Taxis are available in the town and may be used to transport supplies to the wharf. There is a hotel, a public restaurant and a variety of retail clothing and general merchandise stores with a surprising stock of goods and supplies; meat, fresh fruits, vegetables, ice, and other general provisions are available. There is a government radiotelegraph station and postal service, a 5-room school house and church services on Sunday. La Espinita, a few minutes out of the village by taxi, is the site of the local bar and poolroom providing refreshment and recreation to the factory workers and townspeople, and to the crews of visiting vessels when in port. A small company *hospital* with a doctor and nurse in residence is maintained for emergency medical treatment.

There are two *airports,* one accommodating small private planes and the other serving regular scheduled DC-3's from Tijuana and La Paz, as well as a company-owned Lodestar. Passenger flights arrive and depart twice weekly. A motel is located at the commercial airport. A hard-surfaced road connects across the salt pond dikes to the barge wharf at Chaparrito in Scammon's Lagoon to which the salt loading operations have been shifted.

Communication Note — Radio transmission and reception on low frequencies in this area is poor, the signals attenuated severely by the vast expanse of surrounding salt marsh.

The low sandy shore-island that separates the Laguna Guerrero Negro entrance from Scammon's Lagoon entrance immediately southward is quite a remarkable lee shore. The objects found on the beach have drifted for months or even years before they are washed ashore to be bleached by the sun, to be buffetted by wind and sand, and ultimately to be covered by drifting dunes. A common, highly prized item is the Japanese green glass fishing float.

At Estero de San José, the hulk of a British sailing vessel, the *Black Warrior,* lies wrecked ashore at some forgotten spot. It is from this shipwreck that the middle lagoon got its popular name: Laguna Guerrero Negro. The *Black Warrior* was reputed to have aboard several million dollars in gold bullion, now long buried beneath the shifting sands. This vessel, originally out of New London, was on a whaling voyage when wrecked and probably did not have aboard any cargo other than barrels of whale oil.

Laguna Ojo de Liebre (Eye of the Jack Rabbit), better known as Scammon's Lagoon, the southernmost and by far the largest and most important of the three lagoons that open into Bahía Sebastián Vizcaíno, is studded with low islets and numerous sandbars, many of which uncover at low tide. While the lagoon is well-known and has been frequented by ships since before the time of the great whale slaughter in the latter half of the nineteenth century, its precise limits and dimensions have been surveyed only recently.

The narrow entrance expands into a body of water covering more than 156 square miles of channels and tidal flats surrounded by the lower reaches of the dune-studded Sebastián

Entrance to Laguna Guerrero Negro

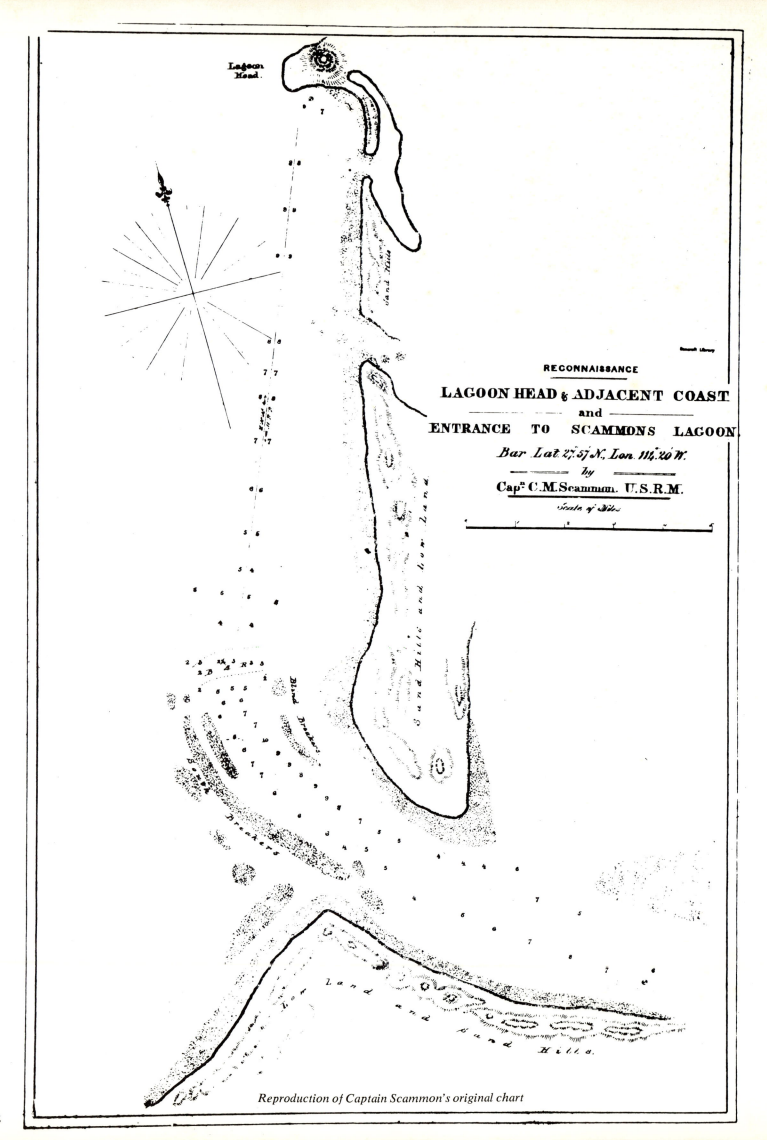

RECONNAISSANCE

LAGOON HEAD & ADJACENT COAST

and

ENTRANCE TO SCAMMONS LAGOON.

Bar Lat. 27°57′ N., Lon. 114°20′ W.

by

Capⁿ C. M. Scammon. U.S.R.M.

Scale of Miles

Reproduction of Captain Scammon's original chart

Vizcaíno Desert. The eastern edge of the lagoon, including the tidal shallows now diked off into solar evaporation pans by the salt works, is about 35 miles from the entrance bar and has a width of up to 12 miles. A navigable branch, known as Fort Lagoon, extends about 8 miles southward of the main lagoon. During the era of whale fishery, other branches of the lagoon were known as the Fishpond, Cooper's Lagoon, and the nursery. Present-day scientists studying the mating habits of the whale population refer to a certain shallow neck as Fornication Hole.

WILDLIFE REFUGE — On January 14, 1972, President Luis Echeverria Alvarez of Mexico declared Scammon's Lagoon and the southern portion of Bahía Sebastián Vizcaíno a wildlife refuge for the special protection of the California gray whale. As such, entrance is prohibited except by special permit, issued primarily to expeditions engaged in scientific study. Vessels may enter otherwise only on official business or in emergency or distress.

DIRECTIONS, LANDMARKS AND LIGHTS — The entrance to Scammon's Lagoon, about 15 miles southwestward of Laguna Guerrero Negro, is distinguished on either side by white sand dunes 30 to 40 feet high. Extensive shoals, with depths of less than 2 fathoms over them, project northward about 7½ miles and about 4 miles offshore fronting the entrance.

CAUTION: OFFLYING SHOAL — A 2-fathom shoal, about ¾ mile long lying along a northwest/southeast line and about ¼ mile wide, is situated about 6½ miles north-northwestward of the entrance to Scammon's Lagoon; depths of 10 fathoms have been sounded only 200 yards eastward.

Refer to Laguna Guerrero Negro for approach to the general vicinity of the lagoon mouths. The *entrance buoy* to Scammon's Lagoon is a *black can* anchored in 6 fathoms, fitted with a *radar reflector* and exhibiting a *flashing white light* at night. The buoy is located at latitude 28° 00′ 29″ north, longitude 114° 16′ 03″ west, about 11½ miles, 215° true from the Laguna Guerrero Negro sea buoy. As the Scammon's Lagoon entrance buoy is approached, the surf line comes into view and steel *range towers* can be seen at regular intervals along the beach. From the entrance buoy passed on the starboard hand, a course along *range 154°* true, marked by two lighted steel towers set in line on the beach will carry a vessel past a 3-legged wooden dolphin well off on the starboard hand, fitted with a *radar reflector* and exhibiting a *fixed red light* at night, to the juncture of a *second range reach* about 1 mile offshore. The *second range* is comprised of two steel towers set in line on the beach well off on the port hand in *range 74°* true astern; the front tower exhibits a *red light* at night, the rear tower exhibits a *white light*. When the second range draws in line astern, approximately a 90° starboard turn to a course of 254° true will carry a vessel along a dog-leg reach approximately parallel to the shore and across the entrance bar in 3½ fathoms at high water. A rolling surf breaks on the shore beach on the port hand and combers break on the bar on the starboard hand with the entrance course threaded between. Running swells will hump across the bar to a degree depending upon the weather and the state of the sea. The 3-legged dolphin previously mentioned will be passed on the starboard hand along this course to a taller 3-legged dolphin fitted with a *radar reflector* and exhibiting a *fixed white light* passed on the port hand. This second dolphin marks a turn in the channel southward along a course marked by a series

of 3 additional dolphins fitted with radar reflectors and exhibiting *fixed white lights* at night. The last dolphin along this course on the port hand marks a turn southeastward to a point abeam a tall white steel tower exhibiting a navigation light that *flashes white every 10 seconds* 60 feet above the sea, visible for 5 miles in clear weather; the tower is fitted with a *radar reflector* and marks the passage through the mouth and into the main body of the lagoon.

CAUTION — Tidal currents ebb and flow through the lagoon entrance at a considerable velocity up to 4 or 5 knots; safest passage for maneuverability should be planned at slack water. The state of the sea should be carefully determined before entering or leaving the lagoon to avoid dangerous humping swells across the bar. Since tidal currents and the effect of severe storms alter the extent and the configuration of the bar from time to time, as well as affecting the surrounding shoals and channels both outside and inside the lagoon, prudence should be exercised and the lead or sounding machine constantly employed. Salt barges are towed in and out of the lagoon around the northern entrance point and should be carefully watched for, both here and at the sea buoy.

Beginning abeam the navigation light on the northern entrance point of the lagoon, a barge canal dredged along the northern shore to depths of from 20 to 38 feet leads to a commercial loading wharf marked by a remarkable mound of bulk salt glistening white several miles distant. The barge canal is marked by dolphins and wooden posts exhibiting *fixed white lights* at night along its course and by amber and green and red *ranges* in the last third of its length. The salt company, Exportadora de Sal, presently owned by a large Japanese Company, operates a mechanized bulk loader on the modern wharf. Fresh water is piped to the wharf; a limited stock of diesel oil and gasoline is kept for company use, although fuel may be purchased from private stocks in town and trucked to the wharf. There are some supplies and fresh provisions in the nearby village of Chaparrito, and a variety of ship's stores and provisions in the village of Guerrero Negro, as well as a small company *hospital* with attending nurse and doctor for emergency treatment. There is also

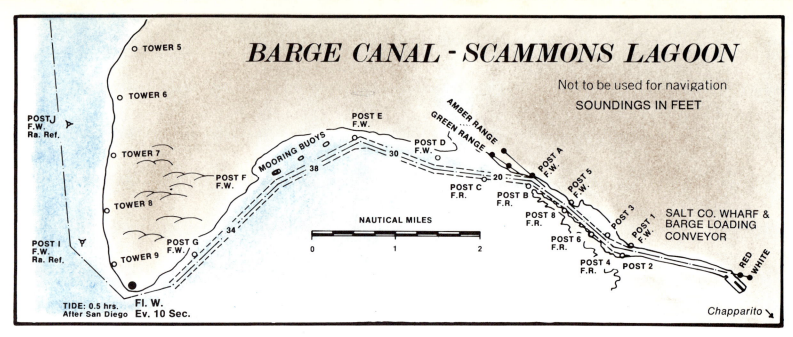

Not to be used for navigation
SOUNDINGS IN FEET

TOWER 5

TOWER 6

POST J
F.W.
Ra. Ref.

TOWER 7

MOORING BUOYS

POST E
F.W.

AMBER RANGE

GREEN RANGE

POST D
F.W.

POST A
F.W.

POST F
F.W.

38

30

POST 5
F.W.

SALT CO. WHARF &
BARGE LOADING
CONVEYOR

TOWER 8

POST C
F.R.

POST B
F.R.

POST 3

POST 8
F.R.

POST 1
F.W.

NAUTICAL MILES

POST I
F.W.
Ra. Ref.

POST G
F.W.

34

TOWER 9

0   1   2

POST 6
F.R.

RED
WHITE

POST 4
F.R.

POST 2

TIDE: 0.5 hrs.
After San Diego

Fl. W.
Ev. 10 Sec.

Chapparito

a government telegraph and postal service as previously mentioned. Regularly scheduled *air transportation* is maintained to Guererro Negro from Ensenada and La Paz. A hard-surfaced road connects the two villages and the loading wharf.

Except for the navigable barge canal, the northern portion of the lagoon is filled with low sandy islets and numerous sandbars. Laguna Guerrero Negro and Scammon's Lagoon are connected by a meandering tidal channel that can be negotiated in a skiff at high water. There is a good natural channel along the south shore of Scammon's Lagoon ranging in depth from 10 to 60 fathoms with various branches winding about in a complex pattern among numerous shoals that dry at low water. Vessels commonly run up to Isla Piedra (Stony Island) and a good channel of 4 to 5 fathoms runs all the way in to Estero Norte (The Nursery). The lagoon has been roughly charted over the years by a number of scientific research organizations through the means of actual soundings and by use of aerial photographs which clearly show the delineation of the channel network. The sketch chart that accompanies this text embodies a composite of these surveys.

ANCHORAGE — The lagoon affords good anchorage in depths of 4 to 6 fathoms, good holding ground over a sand and mud bottom in several popular places. The anchorages are completely sheltered against the sea but not the wind, which may and frequently does blow force 4 or greater in the afternoons. The strong tidal currents that ebb and flow through the channels within the lagoon require a Northhill or Danforth type sand and mud hook with enough scope rove out to cope with the tidal conditions; care should be exercised to avoid riding up on a tidal flat covered at high water and bare at low. Anchorage may be taken safely on the southwestern side of the lagoon about ¼ mile off the beach near the mouth of a tidal slough that penetrates this shore in 5 fahoms sand and mud; care should be taken to avoid the *sand shoal* that makes out from the mouth of the slough. The remains of an abandoned fish camp are to be found just back of the beach opposite this anchorage, the place marked by the shank of a large rusty grapnel hook sticking up out of the water at high tide, and uncovered at low water.

Anchorage may also be taken in 5 fathoms, sand and mud, in the protection of the northern entrance point being careful to avoid the fairway in the dredged barge canal as tows regularly enter and leave the lagoon by this route. Good

anchorage may also be had in 4 fathoms, sand and mud, off the abandoned turtle camp on the southwestern side of Isla Brozas (Brushy Island), about ¾ mile off the beach; the tidal flat uncovers and dries in front of the camp. Anchorage may be had off the southwestern side of Isla Piedra (Stony Island) in 4 fathoms sand and mud, within a channel leading through the surrounding shoal and approached by means of a range comprised of a white, rock-filled 55-gallon drum on the beach set in line with a rock mound painted red to be seen behind and on the crest of the low island in approximate *range* 87° true.

Modern salt production in the lagoon, as important as it is to the economy of Baja California in general and the lagoon area in particular, is dull indeed in comparison to the great whale hunts of the old whaling days 100 years ago. Captain Charles M. Scammon is credited with the discovery of the entrance to the lagoon that accommodates a large proportion of the annual migration of the California gray whales between December and March; more whales come to this particular lagoon each year than any other in Baja California. Laguna Ojo de Liebre was known to earlier whalers, but some were not as fortunate as Captain Scammon. The record shows several wrecks as a result of early attempts by whaling vessels to negotiate passage into the lagoon without success. Nonetheless, it is to Captain Scammon whom we owe a colorful and authentic picture of the place, for he was a thorough man of keen intellect and his logs, charts and sketches describe an exciting and historically important era in a most remote place.

Captain Scammon aboard the brig *Boston,* accompanied by the small tender *Marin,* arrived at Sebastián Vizcaíno Bay in December 1856 and anchored in the lee of Morro Santo Domingo to the northward of the still unknown lagoon. Reconnoitering the mouth of the lagoon, the shallow draft *Marin* and three whaleboats went ahead to sound the entrance channel and reported sufficient depth for the brig to pass over the bar. The passage proved difficult and dangerous as the wind died when but halfway through; both vessels had to anchor uncomfortably close to wild breakers for the night.

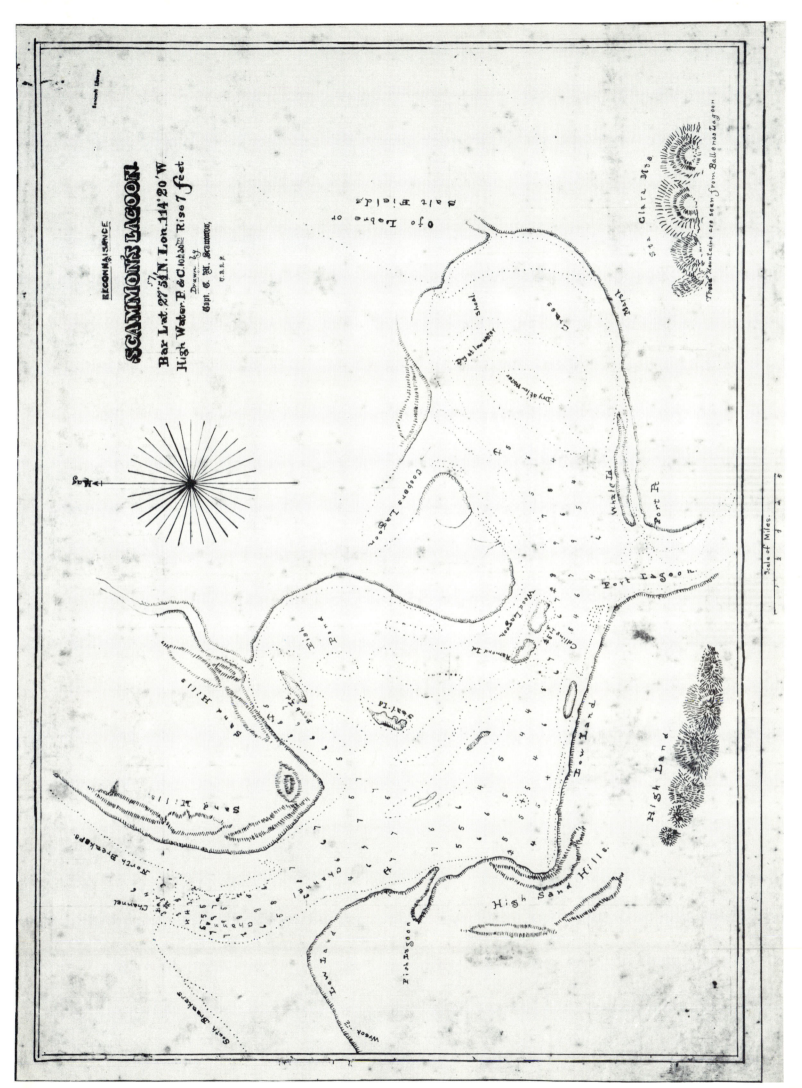

Reproduction of Captain Scammon's original chart   75

LAGUNA OJO DE LIEBRE (SCAMMON'S)
LAGUNA GUERRERO NEGRO
LAGUNA MANUELA

NOT TO BE USED FOR NAVIGATION
REFER TO H.O. 1193, H.O. 1044, H.O. 1310, H.O. 623
BRITISH ADMIRALTY CHART 3055   CARTA NÁUTICA F.H. 601

SOUNDINGS INDICATED IN FATHOMS
High water full and change, 9 hrs. 5 min.
Springs rise 7.5 ft. Mean range 5.9 ft.

LONG. 114° 0'

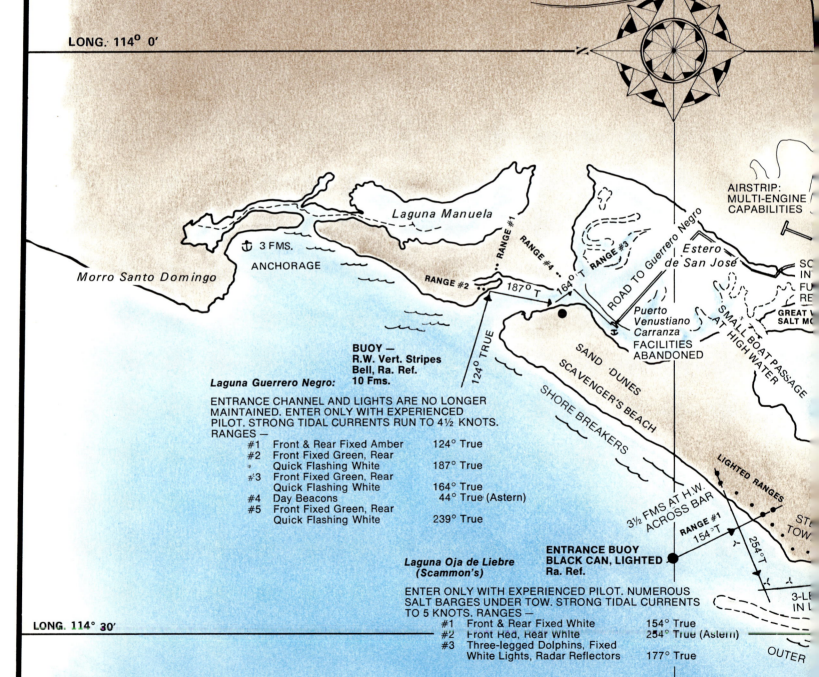

Las Bombas

Espiña

AIRSTRIP:
MULTI-ENGINE
CAPABILITIES

Laguna Manuela

RANGE #1
RANGE #4
RANGE #3
164° T

Estero
de San José

ROAD TO Guerrero Negro

GREAT V
SALT M

⚓ 3 FMS.
ANCHORAGE

RANGE #2
187° T

Morro Santo Domingo

SMALL BOAT PASSAGE
AT HIGH WATER

124° TRUE

Puerto
Venustiano
Carranza
FACILITIES
ABANDONED

SAND   DUNES

SCAVENGER'S BEACH

SHORE BREAKERS

BUOY —
R.W. Vert. Stripes
Bell, Ra. Ref.
10 Fms.

Laguna Guerrero Negro:
ENTRANCE CHANNEL AND LIGHTS ARE NO LONGER
MAINTAINED. ENTER ONLY WITH EXPERIENCED
PILOT. STRONG TIDAL CURRENTS RUN TO 4½ KNOTS.
RANGES —

#1	Front & Rear Fixed Amber	124° True
#2	Front Fixed Green, Rear Quick Flashing White	187° True
#3	Front Fixed Green, Rear Quick Flashing White	164° True
#4	Day Beacons	44° True (Astern)
#5	Front Fixed Green, Rear Quick Flashing White	239° True

LIGHTED RANGES

3½ FMS AT H.W.
ACROSS BAR

RANGE #1
154° T

254° T

ST
TOW

Laguna Oja de Liebre
(Scammon's)

ENTRANCE BUOY
BLACK CAN, LIGHTED
Ra. Ref.

ENTER ONLY WITH EXPERIENCED PILOT. NUMEROUS
SALT BARGES UNDER TOW. STRONG TIDAL CURRENTS
TO 5 KNOTS. RANGES —

#1	Front & Rear Fixed White	154° True
#2	Front Red, Rear White	254° True (Astern)
#3	Three-legged Dolphins, Fixed White Lights, Radar Reflectors	177° True

3-L
IN L

OUTER

LONG. 114° 30'

Bahia de Sebastian Viscaino

LAT. 28° 0'

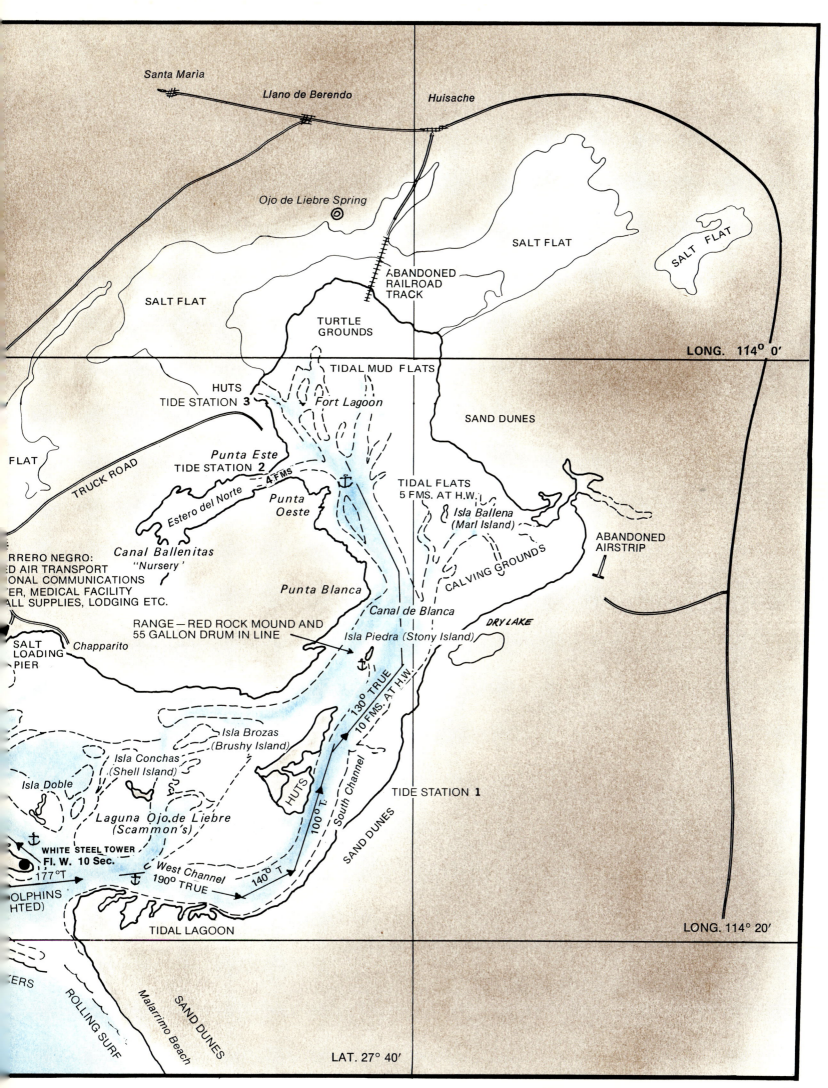

Santa Maria

Llano de Berendo

Huisache

Ojo de Liebre Spring

SALT FLAT

SALT FLAT

SALT FLAT

ABANDONED
RAILROAD
TRACK

TURTLE
GROUNDS

TIDAL MUD FLATS

SAND DUNES

HUTS
TIDE STATION 3

Fort Lagoon

FLAT

TRUCK ROAD

Punta Este
TIDE STATION 2

4 FMS.

TIDAL FLATS
5 FMS. AT H.W.

Estero del Norte

Punta
Oeste

Isla Ballena
(Marl Island)

ABANDONED
AIRSTRIP

Canal Ballenitas
"Nursery"

Punta Blanca

CALVING GROUNDS

RRERO NEGRO:
ED AIR TRANSPORT
ONAL COMMUNICATIONS
ER, MEDICAL FACILITY
LL SUPPLIES, LODGING ETC.

Canal de Blanca

DRY LAKE

SALT
LOADING
PIER

Chapparito

RANGE—RED ROCK MOUND AND
55 GALLON DRUM IN LINE

Isla Piedra (Stony Island)

130° TRUE
10 FMS. AT H.W.

Isla Brozas
(Brushy Island)

Isla Conchas
(Shell Island)

HUTS

100° T.

South Channel

TIDE STATION 1

Isla Doble

Laguna Ojo de Liebre
(Scammon's)

SAND DUNES

WHITE STEEL TOWER
Fl. W. 10 Sec.

177°T

West Channel
190° TRUE

140° T

OLPHINS
HTED)

TIDAL LAGOON

KERS

ROLLING SURF

SAND DUNES

Malarrimo Beach

LAT. 27° 40'

LONG. 114° 0'

LONG. 114° 20'

Entrance to Laguna Ojo de Liebre (Scammon's Lagoon)

Exploration of the inner channels began by taking soundings from a boat and it was soon discovered that here was a whaling ground beyond anything Scammon had ever seen. The inner reaches of the lagoon were alive with countless whales, particularly cows with calves. It was a major breeding ground for the gray whale, and an era of fabulously profitable slaughter opened that was to be both short-lived and almost irreversibly destructive to the California gray whale population. To this day Laguna Ojo de Liebre (Eye of the Jackrabbit Lagoon) is popularly known as Scammon's where the California "grays" still come to breed and give birth to their young. One of Captain Scammon's own logbooks is inscribed on the front cover "Whales Taken in Scammon's Lagoon, Voyage Number Three 1860-61." For those interested in a picture of whaling as it was in Captain Scammon's time, the description from his book *Marine Mammals of the Northwestern Coast,* published in 1874, cannot be bettered. It reads:

As the season approaches for the whales to bring forth their young, which is from December to March, they formally collected at the most remote extremities of the lagoons, and huddled together so thickly that it was difficult for a boat to cross the waters without coming in contact with them.

The first streak of dawn is the signal for lowering the boats, all pulling for the headwaters, where the whales are expected to be found. As soon as one is seen, the officer who first discovers it sets a "waif" — a small flag — in his boat, and gives chase. Boats belonging to other vessels do not interfere, but go in search of other whales. When pursuing, great care is taken to keep behind, and a short distance from the animal, until it is driven to the extremity of the lagoon, or into shoal water; then the men in the nearest boats spring to their oars in the exciting race, and the animal, swimming so near the bottom, has its progress impeded, thereby giving its pursuers a decided advantage: although occasionally it will suddenly change its course, or "dodge," which frequently prolongs the chase for hours, the boats cutting through the water at their utmost speed. At other times, when the cub is young and weak, the movements of the mother are sympathetically suited to the necessities of her dependent offspring. It is rare that the dam will forsake her young one, when molested.

California Gray Whale

By the 1890's whaling along the Pacific coast had all but ceased because of the unprofitable "harvest" from a thoroughly decimated and rapidly disappearing species. Some shore whaling stations and one or two floating whale processing ships, however, continued sporadically to ply the trade until the 1930's when American and Russian ships again launched a concentrated effort to take whales off the California coast and once again almost wiped out the species. Only the international agreement of 1938 to which Japan, Russia, and the United States were among the signatories, saved the California "grays." They have had a surprising ability to survive and once again number as many as 4,000 to 5,000. In December, January, February, and March one can see from many headlands of the California coast the passing of the migratory whales, "blowing" as they make their 6,000 or 7,000-mile passage to the whale nursery; and again in June, July and August, their return passage to the Arctic feeding grounds. None has the vantage point of a small boat sailor, however, who may pass right through the middle of a school of whales, feel the wet spume blow down upon him when in the lee of a spouter; or hear the mysterious and somewhat frightening "blow" exhaled quite close by in the black of night.

Toward the easterly edge of Scammon's Lagoon is an old causeway, a long abandoned narrow gauge railway used in an early salt works, and the Ojo de Liebre *spring,* a tiny water hole used by man and beast for countless years in an otherwise arid desert. The spring gets its name from many long-eared rabbits that refresh themselves from it and in turn the lagoon gets its colorful colloquial, and official name from the spring.

Outside the lagoon the great curve of the coast runs southwestward, then westward hooking toward the off-shore islands lying northwestward which complete the embrace of Bahía Sebastián Vizcaíno. From the entrance to Scammon's Lagoon the coast is comprised of a low and sandy lee shore backed by low sand hills for about 7 miles, at which point it rises to bluffs. It is along this beach, about 5 miles from the entrance channel, that a stranded ship lies hard aground.

About 6 miles along the bluffs there is a hill 632 feet high that marks Punta Malarrimo. *Shoal water* along this entire stretch of shoreline extends up to a mile offshore as far as Punta Malarrimo; thence to Punta Falsa, 28 miles westward, the coast is clean with no offlying dangers except a *rocky reef* close offshore at the boat landing and a *rock* ½ mile offshore in a small bight 12 miles eastward of Punta Falsa. Under Punta Malarrimo is a lobster camp with a few temporary shacks ashore. *Anchorage* here is afforded some distance from the shore in shoal water with sand bottom. The anchoring ground is open to the swell however and can be most uncomfortable.

An *airstrip* suitable for light planes is situated close to the camp. (See Appendix.) Punta Malarrimo may be identified by a 632-foot hill that rises from the point. Better anchorage with good shelter from the sea may be taken off an old shore whaling station, now a cooperative lobster camp, in the lee of a point about 10 miles westward of Punta Malarrimo marked "Boat Landing" on the navigation chart. There is a cluster of shacks back of the beach and an 827-foot hill 3 miles west-southwestward of the point for identification. A *reef,* the inshore end of which dries, extends about ½ mile offshore for a distance of about 1 mile along the coast westward of this point. A smooth *anchorage* for small vessels is afforded in 2 to 2½ fathoms, sand bottom, behind the rocky reef that projects from the point. The reef is not marked on navigation charts but the water is usually quite clear and by carefully conning into the lee, safe passage to anchorage may easily be made. A dirt *landing strip* is located back of the fish camp here.

Punta Falsa (Falsa Point), the northernmost part of the Punta Eugenio Promontory, about 1½ miles northeastward of Punta Eugenio, is steep and rocky. About ½ mile northward of the point lies a dangerous oval-shaped *reef,* ¾ mile long and ½ mile wide surrounded by a field of kelp; near the middle of the reef is a *rock awash* over which the sea breaks heavily. Depths of 7 to 8 fathoms were sounded over a rocky bottom between the reef and the point, and also between the reef and the western Chester Islet.

Barge Canal, Scammon's Lagoon

The Chester Islets are comprised of two rocks, 18 feet high, whitened by birdlime. The western islet, lying ½ mile northeastward of Punta Falsa, has a small outlying *rock* close off its north side; the eastern islet lies 1,300 yards east-southeastward of the western islet, 1 mile from the point and 1,000 yards offshore. The passage between the two islets and the shore is filled with a thick bed of kelp and, although no hidden dangers have been found, this passage is not recommended without local knowledge.

Punta San Eugenio, the northwestern extremity of the tongue of land that forms the southern shore of Bahía Sebastián Vizcaíno, is a dark rocky promontory surrounded by a *reef of rocks* that extends about ¼ mile offshore. There was formerly a whaling station in a small cove about ½ mile southeastward of the point; some remnant of the station may still be seen. A *navigation light* is shown from a white pyramidal masonry tower 23 feet high on Punta San Eugenio. The light, 62 feet above the sea, **flashes white every 1½ seconds** and is visible in clear weather for 9 miles in an arc 329° to 221°; it is obscured by Isla Natividad from 90° to 113°. As around any major promontory, the wind blows forcibly a great percentage of the time, early morning, if any, being the calmest period for easy passage.

Upon leaving Sebastián Vizcaíno Bay southward bound vessels have several options: they may sail through Dewey Channel around Punta Eugenio bound for the *protected anchorage,* facilities, provisions and fuel at Turtle Bay; or they may call at Cedros Island where *anchorage* is available only in an open roadstead, but provisions, facilities, fuel and fresh water may be had.

SECTION 7
ISLAS NATIVIDAD, CEDROS and SAN BENITO

Punta Norte, Cedros I.

The western limit of Sebastián Vizcaíno Bay is marked by a string of offshore islands that form a very effective shelter against the prevailing wind and sea. These include Isla Natividad, a low flat island about 3¾ miles westward of Punta Eugenio across Dewey Channel; Isla Cedros, a large high island about 12 miles northwestward of Punta Eugenio, and Islas San Benito, a group of three small islands outside the bay about 14 miles westward of Isla Cedros. The southern entrance to Bahía Sebastián Vizcaíno lies between Punta San Eugenio and the southeastern end of Isla Cedros, forming a channel about 14 miles wide. Isla Natividad is situated between the point and Cedros Island, dividing this entrance into two channels: Canal de Dewey to the eastward and Canal de Kellett to the north.

Isla Natividad (Natividad Island) about 3¾ miles long lying northwest and southeast, and ½ to 1½ miles wide, is barren and hilly rising near the middle to an elevation of 491 feet. A group of buildings and a tall steel mast, which are only visible when approaching from southward, stand on the southeastern end, the widest part of the island. The shores of the island are mostly steep and rocky, fringed by detached rocks and kelp; several *reefs* extend off the northwest side of the island.

A more accessible shoreline is presented at the southeastern end of the island where there is a sand beach about ½ mile long. A fishing village consisting of several dozen huts is established on a low bluff above a cove abreast Roca Plana (Flat Rock). The small boats of the village may be frequently seen tending lobster traps or abalone diving gear close offshore. An unpaved *airstrip* parallels the sand beach on the flat above the sea just southeastward of the village. Roca Plana, 24 feet high, lies about ½ mile eastward of the southern point of the island at the extremity of a *reef* connecting the rock with the island and on which the sea swell may be seen to break almost continually. *Anchorage* may be taken off the fishing village.

Roca Vela (Sail Rock) 56 feet high, with a pointed configuration like a marconi sail, lies about 400 yards westward of the same point, with a *reef* extending southeastward from it and on which the sea breaks only occasionally when the weather is fair. Great patches of kelp as much as ½ mile in extent grow about 2 miles west and south of Sail Rock but may be broken up and dispersed from time to time by coastal storms. A *detached rock submerged*, with a depth over it of about 4 fathoms, was reported in 1927 about 1 mile southwestward of Sail Rock.

Roca María (Maria Rock), 15 feet high, stands on a *reef* which projects about ½ mile westward from the northwestern tip of Isla Natividad. A *dangerous wreck* lies sunk 1¾ miles northwestward of the southern extremity of the island. A *navigation light* is shown from a gray pyramidal masonry tower 367 feet above the sea, situated on the southeastern side of the island about 1 mile northward of its southern end. The light exhibits a **white group flash** of **2 flashes every 12 seconds:** flash 1 second, eclipse 1 second, flash 1 second, eclipse 9 seconds, and in clear weather may be seen for 26 miles all around the compass except for sector 122° through 137° where it is obscured by an intervening peak. Natividad Island has been reported to give *good radar returns* up to 20 miles distance.

Isla Natividad

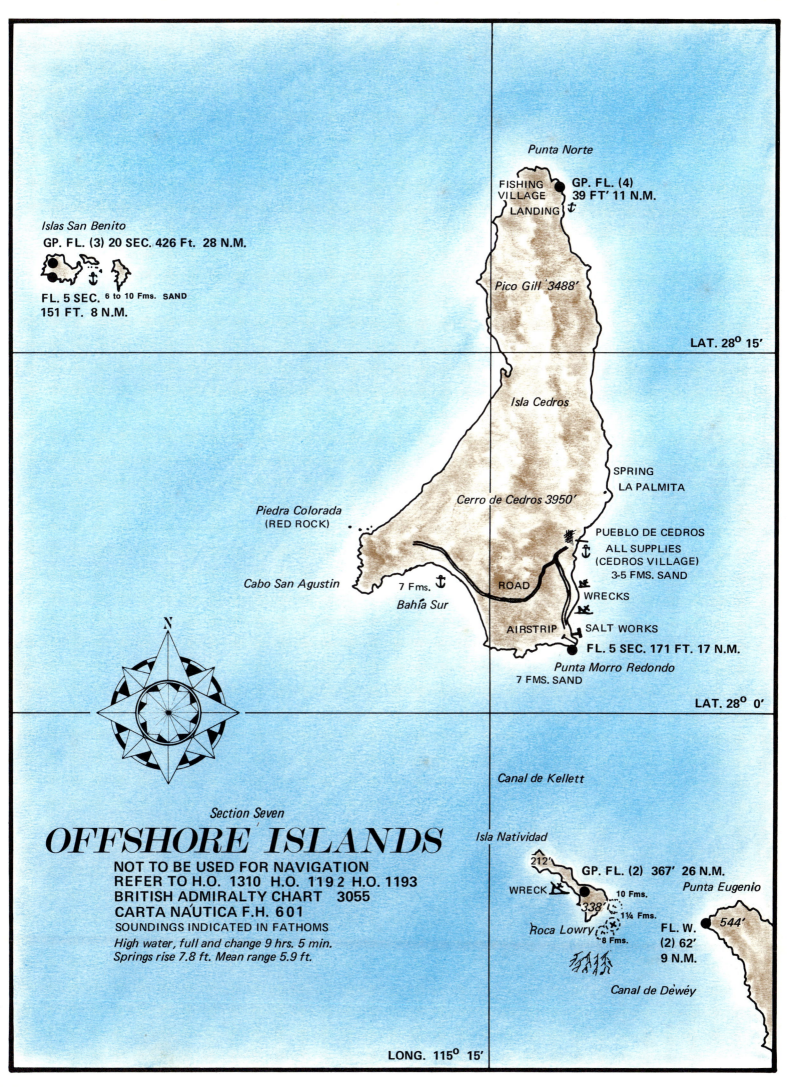

Islas San Benito
GP. FL. (3) 20 SEC. 426 Ft. 28 N.M.

FL. 5 SEC. 6 to 10 Fms. SAND
151 FT. 8 N.M.

Punta Norte

FISHING
VILLAGE
LANDING

GP. FL. (4)
39 FT' 11 N.M.

Pico Gill '3488'

LAT. 28° 15'

Isla Cedros

SPRING
LA PALMITA

Piedra Colorada
(RED ROCK)

Cerro de Cedros 3950'

PUEBLO DE CEDROS
ALL SUPPLIES
(CEDROS VILLAGE)
3-5 FMS. SAND

Cabo San Agustin

7 Fms.
Bahía Sur

ROAD

WRECKS

AIRSTRIP

SALT WORKS

FL. 5 SEC. 171 FT. 17 N.M.

Punta Morro Redondo
7 FMS. SAND

LAT. 28° 0'

N

Canal de Kellett

Section Seven

OFFSHORE ISLANDS

Isla Natividad

NOT TO BE USED FOR NAVIGATION
REFER TO H.O. 1310 H.O. 1192 H.O. 1193
BRITISH ADMIRALTY CHART 3055
CARTA NÁUTICA F.H. 601
SOUNDINGS INDICATED IN FATHOMS
*High water, full and change 9 hrs. 5 min.
Springs rise 7.8 ft. Mean range 5.9 ft.*

212'

WRECK

GP. FL. (2) 367' 26 N.M.

Punta Eugenio

10 Fms.

338'

1¼ Fms.

FL. W.

544'

Roca Lowry

8 Fms.

(2) 62'

9 N.M.

Canal de Dewey

LONG. 115° 15'

Isla Natividad showing Roca Plana to the right. Isla Cedros in the background

Navigation caution: Sebastián Vizcaíno Bay, Punta Eugenio and the offlying islands are often shrouded in mists and sometimes by heavy fogs, particularly in the early morning through forenoon, usually burning off by 11 or 12 o'clock, but sometimes persisting throughout the day and evening. Visibility of the navigation lights during periods of fog or mist is greatly reduced and often obscured altogether. Extreme caution must be employed when running these channels under adverse weather conditions.

Canal de Dewey (Dewey Channel) is about 4 miles wide between Punta San Eugenio and Isla Natividad and with prudence may be traversed with safety. On the western side of the channel *foul ground* extends about 1¾ miles southeastward off the Isla Natividad shore and the soundings are very irregular. On the eastern side of the channel off Punta Eugenio, there is clear passage about a mile wide through which a least depth of 17 fathoms has been sounded about 1 mile from shore, except for a 10-fathom patch sounded in 1952, about 1¾ miles west-northwestward of Punta San Eugenio Lighthouse. A heavy growth of kelp on either side plainly marks the channel most of the time. *Tidal currents* set through this channel with considerable strength and should be given particular attention at spring-tide intervals. Vessels bound northward may avoid the strong northwest winds that usually blow and the strong leeward currents that usually set in this general area by passing through Dewey Channel and along the east side of Cedros Island. The water here is generally calm and smooth in the lee, in sharp contrast to the swells and chop of the open sea. It is a pleasant relief to steer this course and an opportunity to wash down, mend sail or make repairs while smoothly underway. Vessels which make this coastal run regularly, usually choose this course on their northward passage to enjoy the comfort of the lee and a brief respite from the open sea.

Roca Lowry (Lowry Rock) is a circular *rocky shoal* about ½ mile in diameter, with a depth over it of less than 6 feet and with 6 to 10 fathoms around it, and on which the sea breaks only occasionally. It lies on the western side of the center line drawn through the Dewey Channel, about 1 mile eastward of Roca Plana (Flat Rock) and presents a hazard to the careless navigator. This *shoal* is recognizable by the light green color of the water over it. There is a sounding of 8 fathoms about ¾ mile eastward and a sounding of 5½ fathoms about 1½ miles southward of Lowry Rock.

Canal de Kellett (Kellett Channel), about 8 miles wide between Isla Natividad and Isla Cedros to the north, has a least depth of 21 fathoms along a course slightly south of the mid-channel that leads into Sebastián Vizcaíno Bay. There are no known dangers in this deep, wide channel, but a bank with depths of less than 10 fathoms over it, and on which fields of kelp grow, extends about 3½ miles southward from Cedros Island, with a 5-fathom patch near its southern edge.

Isla de Cedros (Cedros Island), sometimes called Cerros, is a rather large island of volcanic origin, mountainous and with numerous high peaks; uptilted sedimentary strata on the island are of great age, mute evidence of tremendous geological disturbance occurring in the dim past. Cedros Island is about 20½ miles long oriented north and south, with a width varying from 2 miles near its northern end to 9 miles near its southern end. The southeastern extremity lies about 12 miles northwestward of Punta San Eugenio to which it was attached as part of the mainland at one time. Monte Cedros (Cedros Mountain), the highest peak on the island and known locally as Cerro Cenizo

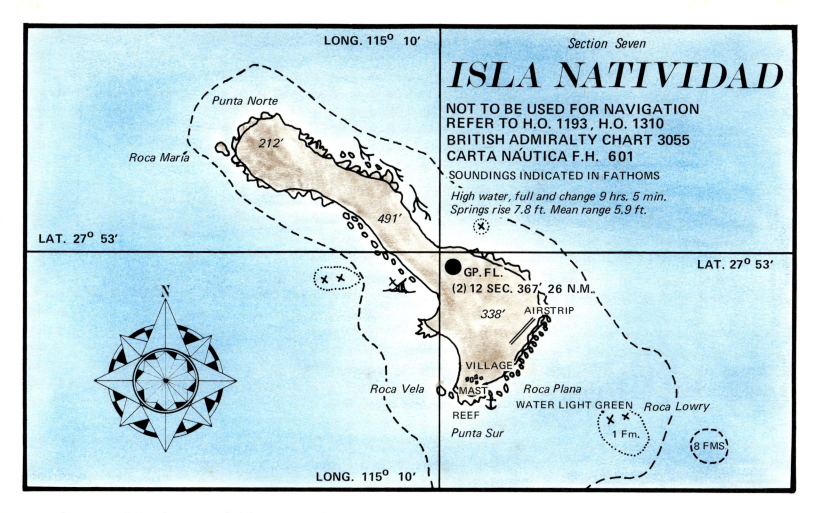

(Volcano Hill), rises to a height of 3,950 feet.

Pico Gill (Gill Peak) rises to an elevation of 3,488 feet in the northern part. The peaks are separated by deeply eroded arroyos. The island can be seen in clear weather for a distance of about 60 miles and appears as a very irregular broken outline. *Good radar returns* may be observed at a distance of 18 miles.

When approaching from the north a *navigation light,* shown 39 feet above the sea from a white pyramidal concrete tower on the northeastern end of the island, displays a **white group flash** of **4 flashes every 12 seconds:** flash 0.3 second, eclipse 1.7 seconds; flash 0.3 second, eclipse 1.7 seconds; flash 0.3 second, eclipse 1.7 seconds; flash 0.3 second, eclipse 5.7 seconds. This light is visible in clear weather for 11 miles in the sector 329° through 221° except as it is obscured by Isla Natividad in the sector 90° through 113°.

When approaching from the south a *navigation light,* shown 131 feet above the sea from Punta del Morro Redondo on the southeastern tip of Cedros Island, displays a **white flashing light every 5 seconds:** flash 0.5 second, eclipse 4.5 seconds, visible for 17 miles in clear weather but obscured from the north and west. Both of these aids to navigation are generally dependable.

Isla Cedros appears, upon first sighting, to be a somewhat barren island which it is for the most part in the southern portion; the northern part, in contrast, is relatively fertile and well wooded. The island gets its name from numerous scrub junipers found growing in some high parts of the island, and these have been traditionally called

"cedars" after the early Spanish identification. The higher ridges and western slopes of the mountains at the north end, and in the central portion have some extensive groves of Bishop pine that attain a height of 60 to 70 feet and constitute one of the most interesting growths of island vegetation. There are also a species of dwarf oak, and many varieties of shrubs and flowers to be found in the arroyos. Around the sources of fresh water may be found groves of palms. There are several *springs* which flow abundantly with good sweet water that have been known and used by coastal vessels for the replenishment of their water stores since the Manila Galleons of early Spanish Colonial times. Prior to that time the flowing springs comfortably supported a large indigenous Indian population. Whalers and crews of coastal trading vessels with local knowledge anchored in the lee of the island to water, gather firewood and forage for game.

Deer, goats, pigs, and many smaller animals run wild, their ancestors having been brought to the island by the whaling fleet in order that they might flourish and multiply to provide fresh meat on subsequent voyages. Of course most of the domestic type animals to be seen are presently kept by residents of the island as private herds and are not to be molested.

Gold and copper mines were once worked on the island and the remnant structures of buildings and machinery are still in evidence on the northern end, located well up an arroyo that opens on the shore at a fishing village near the lighthouse. The remains of a masonry wharf used by the mining company around 1910 is situated in front of the village. A brick-lined cistern, now in disuse, is located back of the wharf. A wagon road leads toward the mine

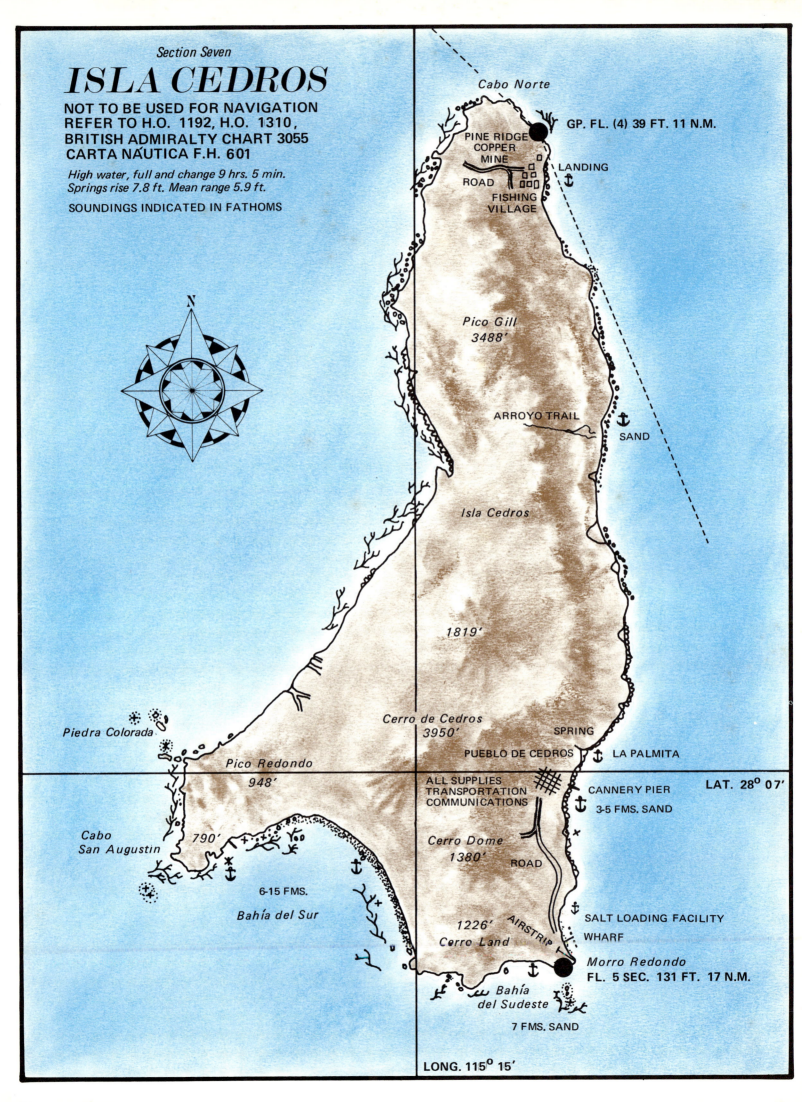

but is mostly washed out in the arroyo. Mountainous heaps of salt are presently stockpiled on the southern end of the island, brought in by barge from the coastal salt works at Laguna Guerrero Negro and Scammon's Lagoon for loading onto ocean-going freighters.

A large fish cannery, which operates almost continuously and supports a sizable village of about 200 to 300 residents, is located just northward of the salt loading wharf. Provisions, fuel and water in limited quantity are available here. There is a government radiotelegraph station in the village

There is an *airstrip* for commercial and private planes and *regularly scheduled passenger flights* operate several times weekly to and from Guerrero Negro, Tijuana, Ensenada and La Paz. A motor vessel communicates with Ensenada on a regular schedule, carrying mail, passengers and supplies; commercial fishing vessels serve the cannery. Tuna Clippers out of San Diego and San Pedro call frequently and private yachts in their passages up and down the Baja California Peninsula anchor occasionally around the island in any of several coves.

In short, Cedros Island is a much frequented way station with a good bit of activity ashore and in its roadsteads; a good place to call, to rendezvous or to lay over in fair weather. There are a number of *anchorages,* mostly open roadsteads in the lee of the island, but the wind and weather are changeable and, very often, that anchorage which was sheltered becomes uncomfortably exposed, necessitating an unscheduled move around to another place.

Main Plaza, Cedros Island

WIND AND WEATHER — The climate is generally temperate and similar to Ensenada's but somewhat warmer; there are periods, however, when, for weeks on end it is quite hot and dry. There is very little rainfall and not infrequently an entire year will pass without any at all. In the vicinity of the island there are often low mists sometimes forming into light fog banks that occur in the evening or in the morning, especially during the summer months; furnace-like currents of air move outward from the Sebastián Vizcaíno desert back of the lagoons and meet the cool moisture-laden ocean air in the bay precipitating clouds of vapor. During these dense fogs, most of the features of the land bordering Sebastián Vizcaíno Bay are obscured, but the high peaks of Cedros Island can nearly always be seen showing clearly above the mists. These fogs usually clear off by noon restoring visibility all around the compass.

On near approach to Cedros Island its volcanic and rocky character weathered by time can be made out. The shores of the island are formed by high cliffs, occasionally broken by rocky beaches at the mouths of the arroyos. The west side, exposed to the open sea, is washed by heavy surf; the southern and eastern shores are sheltered from the prevailing coastal winds that blow generally out of the north-

west. Most of the *sheltered anchorages* are to be found on the southern and eastern sides in the lee. Along the western shore are great beds of kelp where, in the early days of California, vast herds of sea otters were taken for their highly prized pelts. As was typical of nineteenth century exploitation, wanton greed marked the taking of these otters to the almost complete extinction of the species. Since the animals have been protected by international treaty from further slaughter, the herds are making a slow comeback and may be seen in small groups frolicking in the kelp along the central California coast between Monterey and Cayucas.

The northern point of the island, Cabo Norte, is formed by broken bluffs off which there are numerous detached rocks. A sharp peak, 1,714 feet high, with a grove of juniper trees (cedars) showing along its crest, rises immediately behind the point. The *navigation light* previously described is on this point. On the northeast side near Cabo Norte, the coast is comprised of a succession of rocky bluffs and arroyos with short stretches of gravel beach; the land rises abruptly in sharp ridges and precipitous cliffs to mountain peaks upwards of 3,000 feet high. The coast on this side is generally steep-to and free from kelp. About 3 miles from the northern end there is a low sandy point. *Good anchorage* sheltered against the prevailing winds can be taken southward of this point. A small stream of fresh water flows along the bottom of the arroyo near this anchorage but the water is heavily mineralized with salts leached out of the great heaps of copper slag high up the arroyo at the site of the abandoned mine.

Approximately 7½ miles south of the North Light is a sand beach at the mouth of a long arroyo that penetrates the island for some distance, and forms at its upper end a divide just northward of Cedros Mountain. A trail leads up this arroyo and through a pass across the divide to the western side of the island where there are some remnants of houses and a small *spring,* all that is left to be seen of an abandoned rancho called San Luis. *Anchorage* may be taken off this beach over a sand bottom.

About 14½ miles south of the North Light, along the eastern shore of the island, is a beach with a palm grove known as La Palmita. In the grove is the fresh water *spring* previously mentioned, well-known for centuries by navigators and used from the time of the Manila Galleons by passing vessels for the replacement of their water stores. Francisco Ulloa lost six anchors in 1539 on this bottom and according to his log recovered only one. Between 1850 and 1880, whalers pursuing their prey along this coast and usually in from Scammon's Lagoon or Guerrero Negro, refilled their ship's casks at this spring. At the present time Tuna Clippers out of San Pedro and San Diego, fishing the offshore banks, may be found here, frequently anchored overnight in search of the live bait that schools around this fresh water source. A system of bright lights hung at night in a cluster at the end of a long pole close over the surface of the sea attracts a large "ball" of live bait that can then be readily encircled by a net. Sometimes a great wad of waste, wired tightly to a steel rod, soaked in diesel fuel and lighted off in a smoky orange ball of flame, is rowed slowly about in the black of night, protruding over the transom of a small skiff. Attracted by the flickering light, as by

Isla Cedros showing the eastern shoreline and profile

the Pied Piper, the bait follows in an accumulating "ball" until the water is slashed to a fiery iridescence by the countless mass of their shimmering bodies, and the fishermen close the walls of their net in final capture.

Not only do tuna and skipjack abound in the area, but also albacore, yellow tail, bonito, dolphin, mackeral, black sea bass and sardines exist in great abundance. Lobsters and abalone are commercially caught off the shores of the island and airfreighted to San Diego where they command a good price. The local fishermen work in "cooperatives" for the canneries and the packing houses at Cedros Village. Their numerous fishing skiffs and diving boats may be seen in small fleets close offshore around the island.

On the eastern shore of Cedros Island about 2 miles south of La Palmita and 4½ miles northward of Punta Morro Redondo, Cedros Village, a sizable settlement with a long wharf, a large warehouse and a goodly number of wooden houses crowding down to the water's edge, lies nestled at the foot of Cedros Mountain.

The population of Cedros Village varies seasonally from 400 to 600 persons, most of whom are employed either by the fish cannery established at the foot of the wharf or by the salt works deepdraft loading terminal at Morro Redondo 5 miles away and connected to the village by the only road on the island. An unpaved but quite serviceable *airstrip* for private and commercial multiengine planes is located at Morro Redondo close to the salt loading terminal. Air service to Ensenada is available about 4 times a week as well as service to Guerrero Negro, Santa Rosalia, La Paz and mainland Mexico. A customs officer, a health officer and a Mexican Army officer, in charge of the military radio, comprise the port officials.

Anchorage may be taken in the open roadstead about ¼ mile off the wharf over a sand bottom which provides good holding ground. The pier, which extends some 500 feet offshore and has a depth of about 16 feet at its outer end, can accommodate small vessels which may tie up to take on gasoline, diesel fuel, and water in limited quantities, providing the weather is calm. Cargo for larger vessels is normally handled by lighters to and from the roadstead. Water is piped to the pier from a *spring* above the village; quite a large stock of gasoline and diesel fuel is stored in drums at the foot of the wharf. General engine repairs can be made in the village; the cannery has a well-equipped machine shop. Competent divers with hard-hat rig are employed by the cannery in the abalone fishery and can be hired when needed. Small quantities of fresh and staple supplies are available in the village but at rather high prices; meat is scarce. Various fresh and canned fish products are available in season at the cannery. The *military radio,* established in the village, accepts private messages for transmission to mainland circuits; mail is carried by a regularly scheduled motor vessel that calls at the village weekly. It carries passengers and supplies to and from Ensenada.

The south shore of Cedros Island from the eastern limit of South Bay to Morro Redondo Point, a distance of about 4 miles, is bold and rocky, off which there are many detached and outlying rocks. The offshore soundings are very irregular; depths of 10 to 15 fathoms are found within a mile of the coast and patches of 4¾ to 10 fathoms, rocky bottom, lie as far as 3 miles off-shore to the southward. These *rocky shoals* are marked by patches of kelp.

Punta Morro Redondo (Morro Redondo Point), the southeastern extremity of Cedros Island, is a rocky cliff

Village and anchorage on Isla Cedros

about 30 feet high capped by a round hill just back of the cliff. *Detached rocks* lie southward about 1,250 yards from the point and westward of it. The point is situated about 12½ miles north-northwestward of Punta San Eugenio. A *navigation light,* previously mentioned, is established on this headland. *Anchorage* may be taken off a shingle beach northward of a low point about ½ mile northward of Punta Morro Redondo in depths of 7 to 10 fathoms, sand bottom, about ½ mile off the beach; beyond that distance a vessel will be carried off soundings as the water deepens suddenly. *Caution: there are detached rocks immediately off the low point near the anchorage.*

Wrecks lie stranded along the rocky shore about 1½ miles and 3 miles northward of Morro Redondo Point, between it and the village, and can be readily observed.

The northwestern part of this bay, designated Puerto Morro Redondo, is used by the salt works to stockpile bulk salt ashore and to load ocean-going freighters by use of mechanized loading equipment situated on a long "T" pier that extends about 600 feet into the bay. The great mounds of snow white salt are the first things that catch the eye on approach and they provide a distinctive landmark. Several barges employed to transport the salt across Sebastián Vizcaíno Bay from the evaporation ponds and processing plant, located in Laguna Guerrero Negro and Scammon's Lagoon on the mainland, may be frequently seen anchored in the roadstead or alongside the "T" pier. At regular intervals ocean-going freighters may be seen warped against the deepwater face of this pier, working several hatches. The depth alongside is approximately 60 feet.

Warping buoys are moored off the face of the pier for handling the freighters. A barge wharf is located within the head of the pier to facilitate unloading the salt transported from the salt works on the coast. Two seagoing tugs used for barge hauling are stationed at the port; and an additional 1,000-horsepower tug is available for towing and berthing vessels and can be called in emergency to aid in freeing stranded small vessels anywhere in the area. The steel tower of the mechanized loader on the pierhead provides a good landmark against the mounds of salt. Several groups of buildings are established at the loading site: an *airstrip* runs across back of the site and a road winds down to the shore and across to the village.

A *medical clinic* with a *doctor* in attendance is located at the salt works. Minor repairs can be made at the terminal's machine shop. Very limited provisions are available here; diesel oil is available on an emergency basis only. Freighters awaiting a pilot or their turn at the loading pier generally anchor in a depth of 20 fathoms, mud bottom, about ¾ mile north-northeastward of the terminal pierhead. Deepdraft vessels enter and clear the port from the north, avoiding Kellett Channel, and the possibility of un-

Salt loading Terminal at Morro Redondo

Morro Redondo, Cedros Island

charted dangers. The approaches to the terminal are clear with the exception of the rocks southward of Morro Redondo Point.

Bahía del Sudeste (Southeast Bay), the indentation in the coast between Punta Morro Redondo and the southernmost point of the island, affords *anchorage* with shelter from the prevailing wind in depths of from 7 to 8 fathoms. The two hills shown on the chart as Land Peak, 1,226 feet high, and Dome Peak, 1,380 feet high, are situated, respectively, about 1¼ and 2¾ miles northward of the southern point of the island.

Bahía del Sur (South Bay) is the wide open bay between a point 1½ miles west-northwestward of the southernmost point of the island and Cabo San Agustin, the southwestern point.

The shore of Bahía del Sur is formed by a succession of rocky bluffs and arroyos backed by hills and fronted on the eastern and northern sides by sand beaches. There is much kelp near the southeastern shore and a group of *rocks* lies about ½ mile offshore and about the same distance northwestward of the eastern point. The bay offers *good anchorage* in depths of from 6 to 15 fathoms and affords some protection from the prevailing winds, but is open to the southerly gales that sometimes occur in early winter. The shelter is considered uncomfortable for small vessels, the eastern side of the island being preferred. The best *landing place* other than at the commercial pier is in a cove

about 250 yards northward of a conspicuous black rock, 158 feet high, situated onshore close northward of the southeastern extremity of Cabo San Agustin.

Cabo San Agustin, the southwestern extremity of Cedros Island, is a bold rocky headland terminating a range of hills separated by a gap from the island's main mountain range to the northeastward. Pico San Agustin (San Agustin Peak), 790 feet high and situated on the cape, rises abruptly from the shore; Pico Redondo (Redondo Peak) rises to an elevation of 948 feet about 2¼ miles farther northeastward.

A *reef,* on which the sea breaks in heavy weather, lies about 1 mile southwestward of the cape surrounded by a field of kelp that extends about 2 miles from the cape in the same direction. In 1951 a depth of 15 fathoms was reported outside the 100-fathom curve about 16 miles southwestward of Cabo San Agustin.

The western coast of Cedros Island for about 8 or 9 miles from Cabo Norte has the same general character as the eastern side: a succession of broken bluffs backed by sharp ridges and precipitous slopes that rise to mountain peaks. However, the off-lying rocks are more numerous and extend farther offshore. There is generally a heavy surf on this side of the island and dense fields of kelp grow along the shore within the 10-fathom curve; especially is the kelp growth heavy at the southern end. Beyond a distance of 8 or 9 miles, the shore of the island curves around to the southwestward in an almost continuous line of steep cliffs fronted by a stony beach as far as the point that lies 2¼ miles northward of Cabo San Agustin, except for a 2½-mile

Lighthouse Landing, West San Benito Island

stretch about halfway between, where a rocky ledge with many detached rocks extends into the sea.

A *reef* extends about 2 miles northwestward from a point 2½ miles northward of Cabo San Agustin. Piedra Colorada (Red Rock), a conspicuous reddish-colored rock 44 feet high, stands on this reef about ½ mile from its extremity. An off-lying *bank,* with depths from 9 to 14 fathoms, has been sounded on a line between a point 17 miles westward of Cabo San Agustin and a point 15 miles southwestward of Cabo San Eugenio.

Navigation caution: Soundings in this general area are irregular and caution should be employed when coasting the island; patches of kelp should be avoided unless prior local knowledge enables the navigator to know with certainty that they are free of hidden dangers.

Coasting Cedros Island on a clear day, one can see on nearly every habitable flat, on the points and headlands and in the hills above the sea, the remnant shell debris of the ancient Indian inhabitants who occupied the island for centuries before its discovery by the early Spanish explorers. A rather numerous tribe of Cochimi Indians, who called the island Amalgua (or Isle of Fogs), hunted and fished the year around and traveled to and from the mainland in well-made, seaworthy canoes called "balsas" by the Spanish.

Cedros was discovered for the Spanish by Francisco de Ulloa who sailed on orders from Hernán Cortez in three ships from Acapulco in 1539, charged to explore the coast of California and to chart sheltered bays and the general lay of the land. After surveying the Gulf of California as far as the Colorado River delta, he doubled Cabo San Lucas and proceeded northward along the Pacific coast, reaching Isla de Cedros in April of 1540. After spending some months exploring the island, locating its major springs and having some difficult brushes with the Indian inhabitants,

Ulloa sent one of his ships back to Acapulco with news of his voyage thus far. In the other ships he sailed northward to continue his coastal exploration, but was never heard from again.

Due to its combination of good water and sheltered lee, Cedros Island became a regular way port for coastal explorers who followed Ulloa; Juan Rodríguez Cabrillo anchored off Cedros between August 5 and 10, 1542, on his voyage of coastal exploration. With the discovery of the northern transpacific sailing route from the Orient, the Manila Galleons, after raising the California coast on their eastward voyage (usually near Monterey), would frequently call at Cedros Island for fresh stores of water and firewood, depleted on their long Pacific passage. It also provided a welcome relief for the usually scurvy-ridden crew before continuing southward to their destination port of Acapulco. Pirates and privateers used the coves and anchorages of this island and of the off-lying San Benito Islands to lay in wait for the annual arrival of these richly laden galleons.

Various interesting animals are indigenous to the island; others have been brought by crews of ships over the years and have thrived. Deer, rabbits, and several kinds of wild rats and mice are to be found; also rattlesnakes, gopher snakes, several kinds of lizards, and a tree frog. Goats, cats and dogs have been liberated on the island, and they have turned to the wild state where not domesticated by the inhabitants of the village. The cats have had a somewhat difficult time, because the birds are scarce and are extremely wild and wary.

Great activity of waterborne traffic has always been focused in this general area, from the time of the indigenous Indian inhabitation, through the Spanish occupation, the sealing and whaling period, the continuing fishing efforts, and now most recently, the development of the bulk salt loading facility at Puerto Morro Redondo. As a result of the

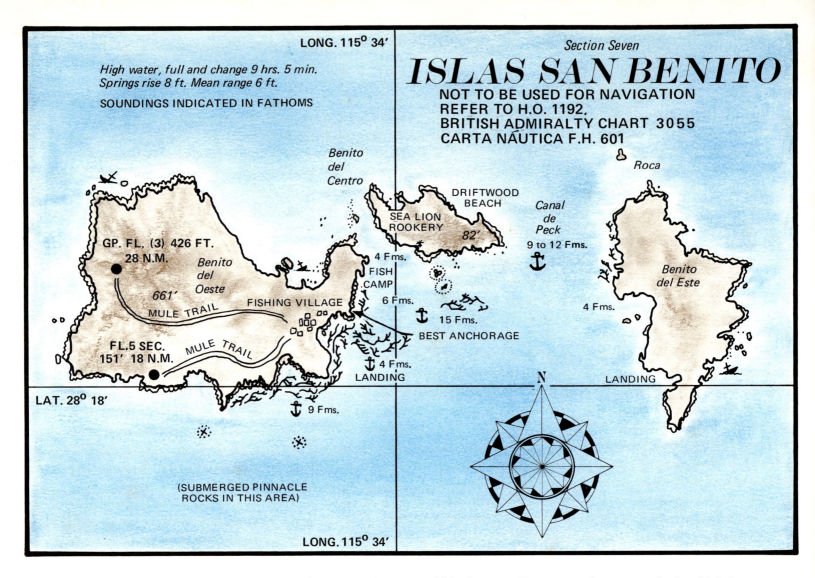

Section Seven

ISLAS SAN BENITO

NOT TO BE USED FOR NAVIGATION
REFER TO H.O. 1192,
BRITISH ADMIRALTY CHART 3055
CARTA NÁUTICA F.H. 601

LONG. 115° 34'

High water, full and change 9 hrs. 5 min.
Springs rise 8 ft. Mean range 6 ft.
SOUNDINGS INDICATED IN FATHOMS

Benito del Centro

DRIFTWOOD BEACH

SEA LION ROOKERY

82'

Roca

Canal de Peck
9 to 12 Fms.

GP. FL. (3) 426 FT.
28 N.M.

Benito del Oeste

661'

MULE TRAIL

FISHING VILLAGE

4 Fms.

FISH CAMP

6 Fms.

Benito del Este

4 Fms.

FL.5 SEC.
151' 18 N.M.

MULE TRAIL

15 Fms.

BEST ANCHORAGE

4 Fms.
LANDING

LANDING

LAT. 28° 18'

9 Fms.

N

(SUBMERGED PINNACLE ROCKS IN THIS AREA)

LONG. 115° 34'

current marine activity, large freighters may be seen coming or going at frequent intervals and, coupled with the activity of the tuna fishing fleet and small coastal freighters that ply regularly north and south, there is a daily passage of several vessels of one kind or another through the Bahía Sebastián Vizcaíno area the year around.

Islas de San Benito (San Benito Islands), a group of three barren, rocky islands surrounded by detached rocks and kelp, lie offshore westward of Cedros Island. The group is comprised of West Benito, Middle Benito and East Benito, all situated in close proximity to one another, surrounding a protected and partially enclosed bay. The easternmost island of the group lies about 14½ miles westward of the northern end of Isla Cedros. The group is *lighted* and gives *good radar returns* up to 21 miles.

Benito del Oeste (West Benito), the largest island of the group, is in the form of a high plateau with a mound near its center, 661 feet high. Its shores are bold and rocky with some submerged rocks offshore. A *submerged rock,* with a depth of 10 feet over it, lies about 400 yards, 205° from the southern end of the island. Rocas Pináculo (Pinnacle Rocks), comprised of 2 *rocks submerged* with depths over them of about 6 feet, lie close together about 1 mile westward of the southwestern extremity of West Benito Island. These rocks are about 80 feet apart along a northeast-southwest line, steep-to and nearly always marked by a breaking sea. Bottom has been sounded at 12 fathoms about 100 feet eastward of the rocks but at no other place

within the same distance was bottom touched at 20 fathoms.

There is an *anchorage* on the south side of the island in 10 fathoms, sand bottom, a little westward of the southeastern point of the island; a better *anchorage* is to be found off the east side in the bay between West and Middle Benito, in about 10 fathoms, sand bottom, where there is excellent shelter from the prevailing wind and swell. The best *landing place* is behind some rocks in an indentation along the east coast of West Benito, about ¼ mile northward of the southeast point, the site of a permanent fishing village and the *lighthouse landing. Navigation lights* are shown on the southern and northwestern sides of West Benito. A **group flash** of **3 white flashes every 20 seconds** is shown 426 feet above the sea from a cylindrical concrete tower on the northwest side of the island. The light is visible 28 miles in the sector from 3° around to 276°; it is obscured by the peaks of the islands through the remaining sector of the compass. This light is one of the principal coastal aids to navigation; it is attended and reliable. A second *navigation light* shown 150 feet above the sea from a gray cylindrical masonry tower on the south side of the island **flashes white every 5 seconds** with an 0.8 second flash followed by a 4.2 second eclipse. This flashing light is visible for 18 miles in the sector 277° through 107°; it is obscured through the remaining sector of the compass.

The *wreck* of the wooden Tuna Clipper *Southern Pacific* lies strewn along the north shore of West Island opposite the fishing village, having struck a pinnacle rock.

Breakers have been reported 9 miles west-northwestward of the San Benito Islands and a quantity of kelp has been observed growing in this vicinity. *Breakers* have also been reported 2 miles south of San Benito Islands. Depths of 9 fathoms have been sounded about 3 miles southwestward of the southwesternmost point of the island; depths of 12 fathoms lie about 3½ miles west-northwestward of this point and a depth of 17 fathoms has been sounded about 10 miles westward of this same point.

Benito del Centro (Middle Benito Island), separated from Benito del Oeste by a boat channel about 200 yards wide and 2 fathoms deep, is a low flat island with a low hill about 82 feet high. Its southern coast is bordered by foul ground; a prominent isolated *rock* above water is situated about 250 yards southward of the southern point of the island; about ¼ mile westward of this rock, directly opposite the passage, there is a smaller *rock;* both rocks serve as useful marks when anchoring in this area. There are no known dangers southward of the line joining these two rocks. The north coast of this central island is a lee shore strewn with flotsam and jetsam and the accumulated wreckage of a number of foundered vessels. The island is also a breeding ground for Californila sea lions and in the spring hundreds of pups are born and suckled.

Benito del Este (East Benito), close eastward of Benito del Centro and separated from it by Canal de Peck, is distinguished by four well-defined hills of which the highest attains an elevation of 421 feet. *Foul ground* extends out from the northwestern side for a distance of 250 yards; a prominent *rock* is situated about ½ mile west-northwestward of the southern end of East Benito Island and there is another rock about ¼ of a mile northward of the northern end. Canal de Peck (Peck's Channel) has least depths in the fairway of from 9 to 12 fathoms and no known dangers except a 4-fathom patch, which lies on the eastern side about 400 yards west-southwestward of the prominent westernmost point of Benito del Este. This passage may be safely used by holding a course through mid-channel. The eastern side of this island is rocky but with a number of coves in which *safe landing* may be made. The wreckage of a fishing vessel lies in one of these coves.

Ranger Bank, with a least known depth of 38 fathoms, rock bottom, lies about 6¼ miles northward of East Benito Island and has a length, north and south within the 100-fathom curve, of 11¼ miles and a width of 1¼ to 3½ miles. Between the bank and the San Benito Islands a maximum depth of 304 fathoms has been sounded. Ranger Bank is a well-known fish habitat and large schools of migrating tuna and skipjack feed here in season. Tuna Clippers may be seen frequently fishing the immediate area.

Fur seals, elephant seals, and sea otters were once found on the islands in abundance but have since disappeared, save a small number of sea elephants, since their indiscriminate exploitation by nineteenth century sealers. California sea lions, however, are abundant, covering many of the outlying rocks with their colonies and setting up a furious chorus of barking when disturbed. In the late 1930's and early 1940's the sea lions as well were hunted and slaughtered by American vessels, exploiting the seal colonies for meat packed as a well-known brand of dog food. Early globes charting these islands designated them as Islas de Lobos, a Spanish description for sea lions.

There are no indigenous land animals on the San Benitos nor are there any snakes; a small variety of lizard thrives; insects and land snails are abundant. The flora and fauna were first made known to the world through a visit here by the officers of the British survey ships *Pandora* and *Herald* between 1845 and 1851. An unusual land shell was named Helix Pandorae. In the 1920's Japanese fishermen industriously gathered abalone, which was quite abundant, from the rocks between the tides and dried the meat in the sun on great drying racks. The dried meat brought a fancy price in San Francisco and in the Orient where most of it was shipped. The Japanese fishermen brought all their fresh water with them from San Diego and made do with these stores for the several months they stayed.

The characteristic plants of the San Benitos are cacti, of which there are several species. One of the most annoying to shore expeditions is the cholla — pronounced choya — the barbed thorns of which are as sharp as steel needles and are very difficult to extract once they have penetrated the skin.

SOURCES OF ADDITIONAL INFORMATION — Pesquera Isla de Cedros, S. de R. L., Ruiz 62 Sur, Fte. Paseo Hidalgo, Ensenada, B. Cfa. Mexico, telephone 3-2681. San Diego Museum of Natural History, Director in Charge of Public Voyages to Scammon's Lagoon, Balboa Park, San Diego, California. (See also Appendix.)

WEST BENITO COVE
HOUSES
CONCRETE CISTERN
ROCKY CLIFFS
ROCKY BEACH
LONG. 115° 34' 30"
2 Fms.
CLEAR CHANNEL
LAT. 28° 18' 15"
7 Fms.
SKIFFS ANCHORED OUT

West San Benito Island

SECTION 8

PUNTA SAN EUGENIO to PUNTA ABREOJOS

Puerto San Bartolomé (known locally as Tortugas or Turtle Bay) is 343 miles southeastward of San Diego, about 28 miles southeastward of the southern tip of Cedros Island, and about 15½ miles south-southeastward of Punta San Eugenio. It is the best all-weather harbor between San Diego and Magdalena Bay, completely landlocked and one of the three best shelters on the Peninsula's Pacific Coast in severe southeasterly weather. Magdalena Bay, 272 miles to the southeastward, and for smaller vessels, Hassler Cove, San Martin Island, about 188 miles to the northwestward, also provide protected refuge in southeast gales, as do Todos Santos and Sebastián Vizcaíno Bays, to some extent.

The entrance to Puerto San Bartolomé lies approximately at Latitude 27° 40′ north, Longitude 114° 53½′ west. For navigation see U.S. Oceanographic Office charts; H.O. 623, Cabo San Quintín to Punta Eugenio; H.O. 624, Punta Eugenio to Cabo San Lázaro; H.O. 1310, Cedros Island to Abreojos Point; H.O. 1204, Port San Bartolomé; British Admiralty Charts #3055, Bahía San Hipólito to Bahía Rosario; #2885, Plans on the Coast of California; Mexican Cartas Náuticas F.H. 601, Cabo San Quintín a Punta Eugenio; F.H. 602, Punta Eugenio a Cabo San Lázaro.

Juan Rodríguez Cabrillo was the first European to sail into Turtle Bay, where he cast anchor on Tuesday, August 1, 1542, calling the bay Bahía de San Pedro Vinculla, a name which he duly entered in his log. Sixty years later on August 23, 1602, Sebastián Vizcaíno entered Turtle Bay and called the place Bahía de San Bartolomé, the name by which it has been officially called since that time. Fray Antonio de la Ascención, who accompanied Vizcaíno's expedition, reported that large amounts of ambergris were found on the beach, attesting to the seasonal presence of the migrating California gray whale. Around the middle of the 1800's, it was one of the important whaling bays regularly visited by whalers of all nations. During the whaling season surprisingly large numbers of vessels could be found at anchor within the bay at one time, their whaleboats overside pursuing the calving whales.

Great sea turtles called Caguamas or Tortugas — for which the bay was named by local fishermen — were taken in large numbers by the crews of the whaling vessels and others for food, the meat being of good taste, likened in its various parts to chicken, mutton and veal. Today, turtles are extremely scarce in Turtle Bay.

LANDMARKS AND LIGHTS — The coast southeastward of Punta San Eugenio for 8¾ miles, as far as Punta Rompiente (Breaker Point), is marked by a succession of rocky bluffs with projecting points and *off-lying rocks* surrounded by kelp. Sharp bare hills stand close to the coast, the highest of which, Monte Eugenio, rises to an elevation of 690 feet, about 1½ miles northwestward of Punta Rompiente. A conspicuous mountain, 933 feet high, situated

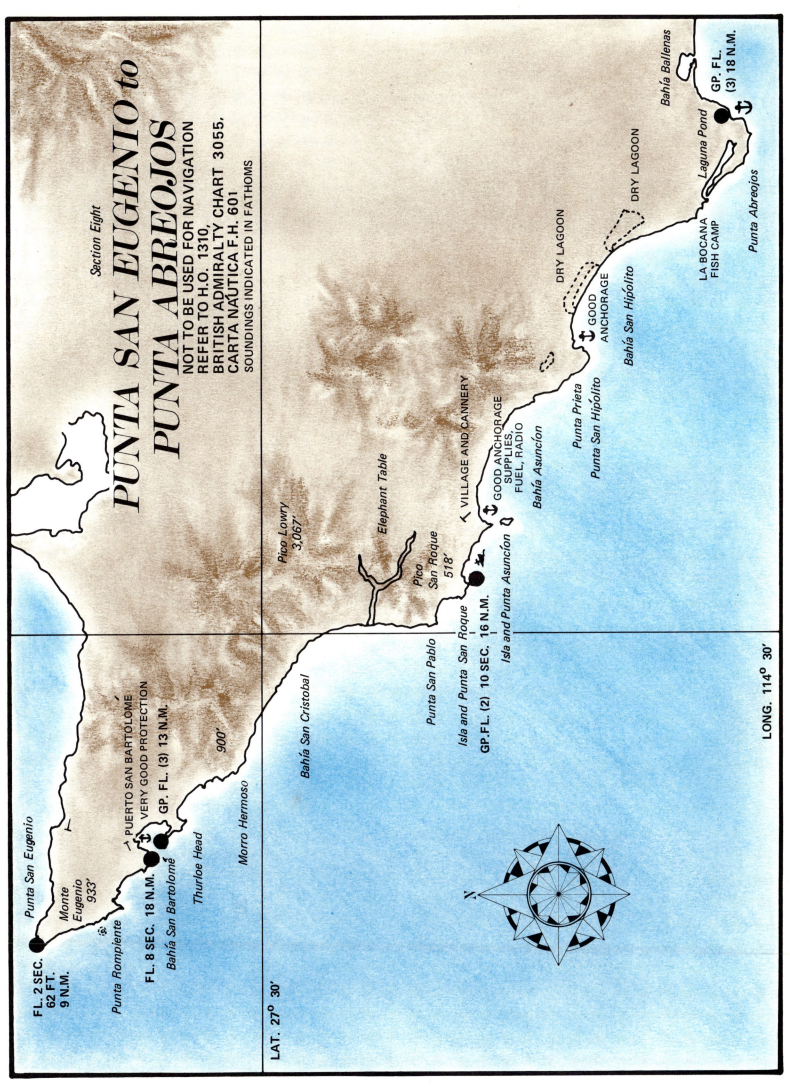

PUNTA SAN EUGENIO to PUNTA ABREOJOS

Section Eight

NOT TO BE USED FOR NAVIGATION
REFER TO H.O. 1310,
BRITISH ADMIRALTY CHART 3055,
CARTA NÁUTICA F.H. 601
SOUNDINGS INDICATED IN FATHOMS

Punta San Eugenio

Monte Eugenio 933'

Punta Rompiente

PUERTO SAN BARTOLOMÉ
VERY GOOD PROTECTION

GP. FL. (3) 13 N.M.

FL. 8 SEC. 18 N.M.

Bahía San Bartolomé

Thurloe Head

Morro Hermoso

FL. 2 SEC. 62 FT. 9 N.M.

900'

Pico Lowry 3,067'

Elephant Table

Pico San Roque 518'

Bahía San Cristobal

Punta San Pablo

VILLAGE AND CANNERY

GOOD ANCHORAGE SUPPLIES, FUEL, RADIO

Isla and Punta San Roque
GP. FL. (2) 10 SEC. 16 N.M.

Isla and Punta Asuncíon

Bahía Asuncíon

Punta Prieta

Punta San Hipólito

Bahía San Hipólito

GOOD ANCHORAGE

DRY LAGOON

DRY LAGOON

La Bocana FISH CAMP

Laguna Pond

Punta Abreojos

Bahía Ballenas

GP. FL. (3) 18 N.M.

LAT. 27° 30'

LONG. 114° 30'

93

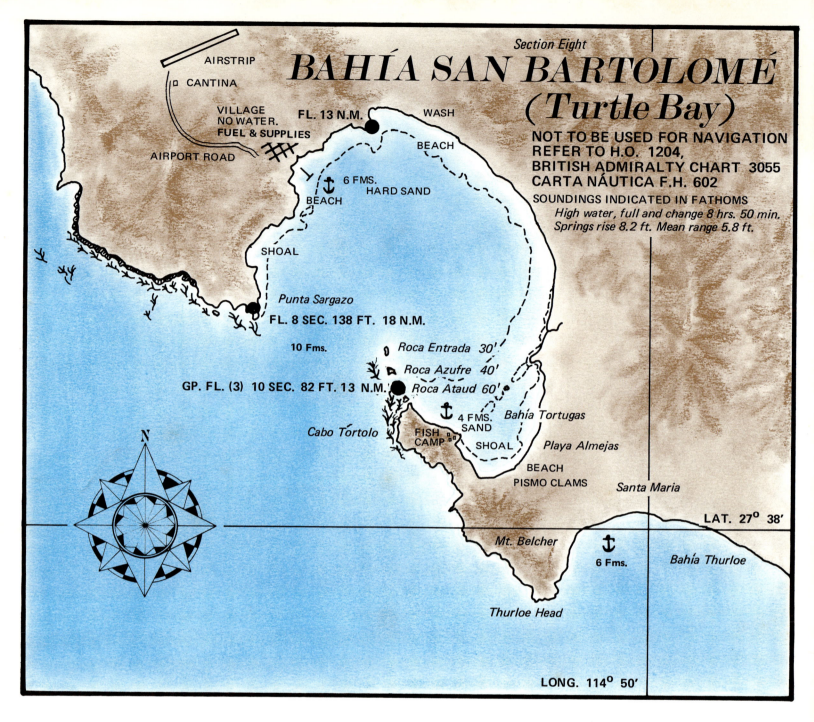

AIRSTRIP
CANTINA
VILLAGE
NO WATER.
FUEL & SUPPLIES
AIRPORT ROAD
FL. 13 N.M.
WASH
BEACH
6 FMS.
HARD SAND
BEACH
SHOAL
Punta Sargazo
FL. 8 SEC. 138 FT. 18 N.M.
10 Fms.
Roca Entrada 30'
Roca Azufre 40'
GP. FL. (3) 10 SEC. 82 FT. 13 N.M.
Roca Ataud 60'
4 FMS.
SAND
Bahía Tortugas
Cabo Tórtolo
FISH
CAMP
SHOAL
Playa Almejas
BEACH
PISMO CLAMS
Santa Maria
LAT. 27° 38'
Mt. Belcher
6 Fms.
Bahía Thurloe
Thurloe Head
N
LONG. 114° 50'

about 3¾ miles northeastward of Punta Rompiente, shows three distinct peaks when approached from the westward or northward, and two distinct peaks when approached from the southward. An abandoned whaling station, last operated in the latter part of the 1800's, is located on a flat above the sea about 1 mile southeastward of Punta Eugenia.

Punta Rompiente is a steep rocky headland southward of which there are numerous detached rocks over which the sea breaks heavily and suggests its name, Breaker Point. The land eastward of Punta Rompiente is lower than that northwestward of it and likewise is rugged and barren, receding about 1½ miles to form a bay which affords *anchorage* to vessels with local knowledge and shelter from the prevailing wind. Some kelp grows in this bay and the floating patches should be avoided when seeking an anchorage, as submerged and uncharted dangers may exist. *Navigation warning: A ship struck a submerged obstruction in 1965, 1½ miles west-northwestward of Punta Rompiente.*

Punta Sargazo (Kelp Point), the northwestern entrance

point of Puerto San Bartolomé, lies 6¾ miles southeastward of Punta Rompiente. It is a flat point about 30 feet high on a bed of sandstone that rises steeply toward Mount Bartolomé, 871 feet high. Close off the point there are many detached rocks surrounded by dense beds of kelp; *foul ground* with numerous shoal and rocky patches extends nearly ½ mile offshore in places for a distance of about 2 miles northwestward of Punta Sargazo; the entire area is heavily grown with dense kelp beds. The entrance to Puerto San Bartolomé (Turtle Bay) lies between Punta Sargazo and Cabo Tórtolo, about 1¾ miles southeastward.

A *navigation light,* Kelp Point Light shown 138 feet above the sea from a red tower situated on Punta Sargazo on the northern side of the entrance, **flashes white every 8 seconds:** flash 0.8 second, eclipse 7.2 seconds, and can be seen in clear weather for a distance of 18 miles.

Another *navigation light,* Roca Ataud Light, shown 92 feet above the sea from a white tower standing on Roca Ataud, sometimes listed as Roca Féretro (Coffin Rock) is situated about 700 yards off Cabo Tórtolo on the southern side of the entrance. It displays a **white group flash of 3 flashes every 10 seconds:** flash 0.3 second, eclipse 1 second; flash 0.3 second, eclipse 1 second; flash 0.3 second, eclipse 7.1 seconds. This light can be seen in clear weather for a distance of 15 miles.

The navigable entrance channel is about ¾ mile wide between the dangers extending from the entrance heads and leads into an almost circular harbor of about 2½-miles in diameter. There are shoals within the harbor that are to be avoided, especially by vessels of deepdraft. A *detached shoal* with a depth over it of 25 feet lies about ½ mile northeastward of Punta Sargazo, and a *shoal sandspit* extends about 400 yards offshore south-southeastward from a point about 1 mile northeastward of Punta Sargazo.

are numerous smaller rocks in this vicinity, some awash and some above water, that form an almost continuous, natural breakwater. *Detached shoals* have been sounded in the entrance bearing from Entrada Rock as follows: 4½ fathoms, 260 yards, 1°; 5 fathoms, 300 yards, 335°; 4½ fathoms, 1,460 yards, 297°; and 3¼ fathoms, 800 yards, 278°. The location of these shoals is marked on the navigation charts.

The general depths in the harbor decrease gradually from about 10 fathoms at the entrance toward the northwestern shore, from which the 5-fathom curve is sounded about 1 mile distant,and the 3-fathom curve about ¼ mile distant. The northern and eastern sides of the bay consist of low shingle and gravel beaches behind which the land is generally low and sandy, gradually rising to a higher broken country with but few traces of vegetation. The

Punta Rompiente, looking southward

Cabo Tórtolo, the southern entrance of the port, is a rocky point about 20 feet high that marks the abrupt termination of a narrow promontory 417 feet high. The cape gives *good radar returns* up to 19 miles. A *reef* on which there are a number of rocks, some above water, extends nearly 1 mile north-northwestward from the point and forms a natural breakwater on which the seas break heavily when running. This *reef,* which extends well into the harbor entrance from the southern side, has a depth of 5 fathoms over its northern end. Roca Entrada (Entrance Rock), exposed 2 feet above water and situated about 100 yards within this shoal, marks the terminal point of the visible reef.

Standing on the reef between Entrance Rock and Cape Tórtolo are three large prominent rocks: Roca Azufre (Sulfur Rock), the outermost, is 30 feet high and has two dark projecting horns forming a noticeable contrast when viewed against the light color of the rest of the rock. The middle rock, Roca Ataud or Roca Féretro (both names translate as Coffin Rock) is 40 feet high; upon it is erected the white steel tower of the Roca Ataud navigation light, characteristics of which have been previously noted. An unnamed rock nearest the cape is 60 feet high. There

western shore is comprised of high bluffs. There is a dry wash, running during the rainy season, situated in the northern extremity of the bay immediately eastward of a ridge of eroded hills that terminate in a point extending into the waters of the bay. A *navigation light* which exhibits a **white flash** and is visible for 13 miles is shown from this point. The beach eastward of this point is low and flat and affords *good landing.* The broad sandy bed of this wash reaches a number of miles inland toward a range of mountains that backs the bay.

ANCHORAGE — Anchorage may be taken within the entrance but the northern part of the bay is somewhat exposed to the long regular swell from seaward. *Safe anchorage* may be had over sand bottom inside the reef that extends northwestward from Cabo Tórtolo but the area is often windy with an uncomfortable swell. *Landing* may be made on either of two sandy beaches along the near shore. Pangas (fishing skiffs) may be frequently found riding on moorings off this shore, sometimes drawn up on the sand in front of several fishermen's shacks.

In southwesterly weather the *best anchorage* is in the

Entrance to Puerto San Bartolomé (Turtle Bay)

lee of Cabo Tórtolo, eastward of the reef in Bahía de Tortugas (Turtle Bay), in 3½ to 6 fathoms over a sand bottom that shoals gently to a *good landing* on a long stretch of sand beach. This beach is called Playa Almejas (Clam Beach) and large pismo clams are plentiful here. The bottom is quite shoal a good distance from the shore in this part of the bay; however *anchorage* in 6 fathoms may be made with Cabo Tórtolo bearing 203° and Roca Entrada bearing 282°. This anchorage is subject to gusty northwest winds that sometimes blow across the low sandy neck that separates Turtle Bay from Thurloe Bay and one must look to the ground tackle well. *Anchorage* may also be taken in the lee of Punta Sargazo (Kelp Point) on the northwestern side of the bay, but here too the area is subject to northwest winds that sometimes blow quite strongly down from the hills. Fishing and commercial vessels *anchor* off the cannery wharf in 3 to 6 fathoms over a hard black sand bottom.

Navigation note: Puerto San Bartolomé has shoaled in places to a greater extent than the mean depths shown on current navigation charts. Caution should be exercised when piloting deepdraft vessels within the harbor and careful soundings should be made before selecting an anchorage.

FACILITIES — Commercial vessels warp against a pier that extends about 400 feet from the shore in front of the cannery town situated on the northwestern side of the bay. Two smokestacks protrude from the roof of the metal cannery building at the foot of the wharf; short electrical poles stand out to the end of the pier providing a good mark for locating the anchorage off the cannery. The pier deck is substantial and accommodates a motorized tractor that pulls a train of small cargo trailers to facilitate cargo handling.

The *Hidalgo,* a small coastal motorship serving the cannery, calls at the port fortnightly, bringing supplies, fuel and fresh water, which is unavailable naturally anywhere in the area. Small fish boats anchor in the bay off the head of the pier and a fleet of fishing skiffs powered by outboard motors are moored to one side.

Marine and aviation gasoline is stored in steel drums behind a fenced enclosure at mid-wharf and is available in limited quantities. Diesel fuel is sold independently from a floating barge, anchored off the pier, not equipped with transfer pumps or hoses. Arrangements for a special fuel drop may be made through the company office in Ensenada (see sources of additional information at end of section) and required quantities of fuel and other supplies may be brought to the cannery wharf aboard the company freighter on its regular biweekly call. Some common engine and marine parts, lubricating oil and engine room supplies are available for purchase from the cannery warehouse. Aviation fuel (100 or 80 octane) and aviation lubricating oil are likewise available in limited quantities. Butane gas may also be purchased when available. Engine repairs and machine work can be had and professional divers are available for hire.

In the village there is a bakery. A limited selection of other provisions is available but fresh water is unavailable except in emergencies, and then only in very limited quantities, as all fresh water in the port must be brought in or distilled from sea water when the cannery is in operation. Ice may be obtained at the cannery but it is advisable to use it only for refrigeration and not to put it directly into drinking liquids.

The cannery, comprised of 4 or 5 large metal buildings and a number of smaller wooden ones grouped together at the foot of the wharf, handles live, fresh-frozen and canned fish products, shipped to market by cargo plane or in the refrigerated hold of the company motorship. The population of the village is supported almost wholly by the fishing enterprise of which the cannery is the focal point. A sizable number of people are employed year around including fishing cooperatives, cannery workers and a managerial staff.

Abalone is the principal product procured along the coastal shelf and around the offshore islands beneath the beds of kelp by divers organized into "cooperativas" or independent cooperative unions. Each cooperative is assigned a specified coastal zone in which to conduct its fishing operations. The divers, working at depths of from 60 to 90 feet in full dress from motorized skiffs, pry the abalone from the rocky bottom and pass them to the surface in baskets handled by their tenders. After each morning's diving expeditions, the catch is brought to the cannery where it is shucked from its shells, cleaned and trimmed before being packed and frozen for marketing under the label "Southern Seas." Lobsters are taken in season and flown to market live by cargo planes from an unpaved *airstrip* back of the town.

The first commercial fishing operations in Turtle Bay, the name by which the entire port is referred to locally, was first established by the Japanese in the early 1920's on concession from the Mexican Government. While they took a variety of fish species, their principal catch was abalone which, when dried, was highly prized in the Orient. Abalone fishing and drying operations were carried on at first in much the same manner as the Japanese effort on Islas San Benito: boiling the meat first, then air drying in the sun on chicken-wire racks. The Japanese brought all their fresh water with them as no source was discovered anywhere in the area. Ultimately a cannery was built by the Japanese and several deep wells were drilled in an attempt to locate fresh water but none succeeded in tapping an aquafer.

In the 1930's the concession to the Japanese was cancelled and the cannery was taken over by the Mexican Government. In the 1940's the cannery was reorganized under private Mexican management and has flourished with increasing productivity since. A new search for fresh water is underway with improved drilling technology, and plans are

under study for a totally adequate water distillation plant incorporating power, refrigeration and seawater distillation in one integrated system.

PUBLIC ACCOMMODATIONS — There is a small restaurant in the village where meals are served, and a cantina outside the village proper is located on the road to the airstrip. Overnight sleeping rooms, generally reserved for cannery visitors on business, may be rented at very low rates. From May to September a sportfishing enterprise flies guests from Ensenada to Turtle Bay and provides accommodations, meals and fishing launches at a resort motel.

TRANSPORTATION — A number of automobiles may be seen in the village and a taxi is available, although the entire village is easily accessible on foot. There is regular *air service* out of Puerto San Bartolomé to Ensenada, Cedros Island and Guerrero Negro. Small private planes frequently land at the *airstrip* back of the town and cargo planes make regular runs during the lobster season.

An unpaved road connects to the fish camp at Punta Malarrimo on Sebastián Vizcaíno Bay, to the salt works at Scammon's Lagoon and Laguna Guerrero Negro to the northward, and to the cannery at Asunción Bay. There is regular cargo truck traffic on these roads and passengers will be taken on an unscheduled basis.

SEA AND WEATHER CONDITIONS — The prevailing winds along this stretch of coast are northwesterly and blow predominantly from that direction for about 8 months of the year. During November, December, January, and February winds from southeast to southwest are frequent with occasional moderate southeasterly gales that are accompanied by some rain. Before the breaking up of these gales the wind hauls to the southwestward, sometimes blowing very hard for a few hours, then comes out from the northwestward with fine weather.

In December and January heavy northers are likely to occur, blowing from a direction between north and north-

Cabo Tórtolo showing from the left, Entrance Rock, Sulphur Rock, Coffin Rock, and one unnamed

Anchorage in the lee of Cabo Tórtolo

east and lasting 1 to 3 days. The prevailing northwesterly winds tend to be modified by local land and sea breezes, except when they blow above their normal strength, at which time the land breeze is often absent and the sea breeze only apparent by virtue of a slightly increased onshore component. The sea breeze along this coast blows from the sea to the land during daylight hours, and is generally strongest in the afternoon; it occasionally reaches force 5 and sometimes extends 20 miles or more seaward. The land breeze does not usually begin until a few hours after sunset but may continue for an hour or two after sunrise. It seldom exceeds force 4 and does not usually extend more than 5 miles seaward.

Strong winds blowing around the promontory of Punta San Eugenio may be expected from September to March; gusty winds within the harbor of San Bartolomé may be expected, blowing down off the hills in the northeastern portion of the bay and sweeping the southeastern portion in the afternoons. Light fogs may be expected in the night

Approach to the village of Turtle Bay

and the early mornings during the summer months, usually clearing off by midday.

TIDES — During December, January and February the California current sets 25 to 50% of the time southeastward at a rate of approximately 12 nautical miles per day; during March, April and May it runs southeastward along this coast 51 to 74% of the time at approximately 11 miles per day; during June, July and August it runs 51 to 74% of the time southeastward at about 10 miles per day; during September, October and November it runs 25 to 50% of the time about 9 miles per day. The current may be found to accelerate somewhat from these rates off the headland of Punta San Eugenio, in the passages between the off-lying islands and between the islands and the mainland. The strength and direction of the daily currents are affected strongly by the prevailing winds. A weak indraft into Turtle Bay on the rising tide may be experienced. The average time of high water at full and change is 8 hours 50 minutes; the average time of low water after either transit of the moon is 14 hours 38 minutes; mean rise and fall of the tide at Turtle Bay is 5.8 feet. The spring range is 8.2 feet.

Navigation note: A common juncture of north-south commercial freight ship routes lies close off the coast in the near vicinity of Turtle Bay and a careful watch should be kept by small vessels passing through the area at night. (See Appendix and "Ocean Passages of the World" Chart 5307, British Admiralty.)

Anchorage at Turtle Bay Village

MARINE EMERGENCIES — Mexican Naval vessels visit the port at irregular intervals, but none is permanently stationed at Turtle Bay. The nearest Mexican Naval facilities are in Ensenada, about 285 miles to the northward, and in Magdalena Bay, about 272 miles to the southward. Coastal traffic along the Pacific side of the Baja California Peninsula is nearly always quite heavy, including numerous Tuna Clippers from San Diego and San Pedro as well as coastal freighters of many nationalities. Contact can usually be made with low power on the intermediate frequency radiotelephone bands 2182 and 2638 kHz or on VHF channel 16, 156.8 mHz. Vessels with more powerful transmitters may relay messages.

MEDICAL FACILITIES — A small company clinic is maintained for medical emergencies at the cannery.

COMMUNICATIONS — The cannery operates a point-to-point and ship-to-shore high frequency radio station and will handle public messages. The Mexican government has activated several coastal patrol vessels which maintain safety and security surveillance between Ensenada and Cabo San Lucas. Contact these vessels on 2182 kHz and 156.8 mHz, VHF Channel 16. Other yachts or fishing vessels can relay emergency messages on 2638 and 2738 kHz or VHF.

SOURCES OF ADDITIONAL INFORMATION — Empacadora de Baja California, S. de R.L. de C.V. Espinoza 843, Ensenada, B. Cfa., Mexico, telephone 9-1401, 9-1402, 9-1403. (See also Appendix.)

The coastal bays, off-lying shoals and reefs, and offshore banks south of Turtle Bay comprise a region of rich fishing grounds. Live bait is abundant along the shorelines and beaches of the many bays and within the mouths of the lagoons; several varieties of edible clams may be dug from the sand and mud of this littoral. Lobster and abalone thrive beneath the kelp beds immediately offshore; schools of tuna, skipjack, bonita, albacore, yellowtail, and other game fish feed on the offshore banks; a small red lobster-like crustacean called "langostina" that proliferates in these waters, provides a substantial portion of the food necessary to this abundant life cycle. Sea turtles may be seen in large numbers swimming offshore; bottom fish are abundant. Tuna Clippers from the north and from the cape may be seen fishing in these waters. Several fish canneries situated along the coast operate at full capacity during the season.

Morro Thurloe (Thurloe Head), situated a little more than 2½ miles southeastward of Cabo Tórtolo, is a bold rocky point about 150 feet high from which foul ground extends seaward for a distance of about 400 yards in all directions. The intervening coast consists of a long irregular cliff 25 to 100 feet high that is rocky and steep and closely backed by high hills. Monte Belcher, with an elevation of 401 feet, is situated about 1 mile northwestward.

Eastward of Thurloe Head, the coast sweeps around through the northeast, east and southeast and forms Thurloe Bay. The land along the northwestern and northern shores of the bay is low and sandy with a shingle beach that is backed by a number of small sand hills. *Anchorage* may be had eastward of Thurloe Head in depths of from 6 to 7 fathoms, with shelter from the prevailing wind.

Morro Hermoso is a headland rising abruptly to an elevation of 900 feet from a bare rocky cliff at the turn of the coast about 8 miles southeastward of Thurloe Head. From the southern end of Thurloe Bay to Morro Hermoso the coast is comprised of steep bluffs, 50 to 100 feet high, behind which is a range of hills that rises to elevations of

1,400 to 2,000 feet. Pico Hermoso rises to an elevation of 2,018 feet near the coast about 2 miles east-northeastward of Morro Hermoso.

OFF-LYING BANKS — A detached bank with a depth over it of 38 fathoms is charted within the 100-fathom curve about 5¾ miles west-southwestward of Morro Hermoso, bearing 240°. A depth of 9 fathoms was sounded in 1953 southwestward of Morro Hermoso in approximate position Latitude 27° 19′ north, Longitude 114° 54′ west; within 6½ miles north-northwestward of this shoal, depths of 63 and 65 fathoms were sounded in 1943 and 1960; a depth of 42 fathoms was sounded about 3 miles eastward of this 63-fathom bank. In 1957 a depth of 15 fathoms was sounded about 5½ miles westward of Punta Sargazo; in 1966, a depth of 18 fathoms was sounded 19 miles west-northwestward of Punta San Pablo.

Between Morro Hermoso and Morro San Pablo, 23 miles southeastward, the coast recedes 5¾ miles forming Bahía de San Cristobal. The shores of this bay are comprised chiefly of sand cliffs and bluffs 50 to 100 feet high. Immediately behind, the coast range rises to a height of several hundred feet. A sandy beach about 4 miles in length

Morro San Pablo and Punta San Roque

breaks the procession of sand cliffs along the northern part of the eastern shore of Bahía de San Cristobal.

Rocas de la Gaviota (Gull Rocks) are situated close offshore about 1 mile east-southeastward of Morro Hermoso; Roca de Pájaros (Bird Rock) lies close inshore about 4½ miles east-southeastward of Gull Rocks. A conspicuous canyon breaks through the cliffs about midway between Gull Rocks and Bird Rock. An arroyo leads down to the sea about 6¼ miles northward of San Pablo Head. *Note: A depth of less than 10 fathoms has been sounded near the 50-fathom curve at a spot situated about 12 miles west-northwestward of San Pablo Head.*

Morro San Pablo (San Pablo Head) is a dark slate-colored bluff from which a prominent hill rises to an elevation of 760 feet directly above it. Extensive tablelands rise to elevations of from 1,000 to 2,000 feet a few miles inland from San Pablo Head, and behind these is a remarkable

range of peaks of variegated colors from 2,000 to 3,000 feet in height, including Pico Lowry (Lowry Peak) 3,067 feet high. Morro San Pablo gives *good radar returns* up to 16 miles. A *reef* projects ½ mile southward from the point; outside this reef the depths increase rapidly: 50 fathoms is sounded at 1 mile and 100 fathoms at 1½ miles offshore.

Bahía de San Pablo (San Pablo Bay) lies between Morro San Pablo and Punta San Roque, 3¼ miles to the southeast. At the head of the bay is a sand beach bracketed by steep bluffs. Except for a *reef* extending southward from San Pablo Head, San Pablo Bay is free of all dangers and affords *good anchorage* about ¾ mile offshore in depths of from 10 to 15 fathoms.

Punta San Roque is a light-colored bluff about 50 feet high backed by Pico San Roque, which rises to an elevation of 518 feet. Punta San Roque gives *good radar returns* up to 21 miles. The point is steep-to; a depth of 20 fathoms is sounded a little more than ¼ mile seaward, but for 1¼ miles southeastward *foul ground* extends for a distance of about ¼ mile offshore. Kelp beds grow off the point and mark shoal water. Bahía de San Roque, eastward of the point, affords a *fair anchorage* sheltered in the lee in depths

Punta San Roque

of 10 to 12 fathoms. The shore of the bay is comprised of shingle and rocky beaches backed by sand bluffs. The adjacent country is hilly and there are tablelands in the interior. A sizable fishing village is located at the head of the bight at the north end of the beach. A number of pangas may usually be seen anchored out. San Roque Bay was employed as a landing place for the Santa Clara placer mines in the 1800's until Asunción Bay was made a port.

Isla de San Roque (San Roque Island) situated 3¾ miles southeastward of San Roque Head and about 1¾ miles offshore, is a rugged rocky islet ¾ of a mile long, east and west, ¼ mile wide and 50 feet high. A *reef*, over which the sea breaks, projects ¼ mile from the eastern end of the island; at a point ½ mile farther eastward there is a *patch of rocks* separated from the reef by depths of 8½ to 9 fathoms. Nearly ¼ mile northward of the rocky patch there is a *shoal* with a depth of less than 2 fathoms. A vessel drawing 13½ feet reported striking on this shoal in 1946.

Anchorage at Punta San Roque

About ¼ mile farther northward, a *shoal* with an estimated depth of 5 feet was reported in 1946. A depth of 1¾ fathoms was reported about 1¼ miles north-northwestward of the western extremity of San Roque Island. Although the passage between the island and the shore to the northeast appears to have mid-channel depths of from 6 to 8 fathoms, it should not be attempted without knowledge as parts of it are foul. *Breakers* extending off from the mainland northward of the island mark *shoal water* that borders the shore. Kelp beds surround the island and patches of kelp mark the adjacent shoals; all kelp should be avoided for hidden and uncharted dangers.

Isla San Roque. Bearing 056°

Anchorage may be had, protected from the prevailing wind, between Isla de San Roque and the mainland northwestward in depths of from 10 to 12 fathoms. *Caution: A patch of kelp in a depth of 10 feet was observed in 1961 near the center of this anchorage in a position about 1¼ miles northwestward of the island; other similar areas of kelp exist between the above position and the island.* A depth of 24 fathoms has been sounded about 4 miles southward of Isla San Roque just inside the 50-fathom curve. A *navigation light,* shown 118 feet above the sea from a red tower situated on the western extremity of San Roque Island, displays a **group flash of 2 white flashes every 10 seconds:** flash 0.3 second, eclipse 1 second; flash 0.3 second, eclipse 8.4 seconds. The light can be seen for a distance of 16 miles in clear weather.

A *stranded wreck* lies in a position approximately 250 yards southward of the southeastern extremity of San Roque Island. A *sunken wreck,* with a portion of the mast showing, lies in about 7 fathoms about 700 yards northeastward of the same point.

Navigation note: A strong current occurring at irregular intervals has been observed to set eastward at a rate of from 4 to 5 knots off San Roque Island. The observing vessel noted the current at full strength for a period of over 6 hours, thence a gradual slackening to still water. The current is thought not to be of tidal origin.

Three conspicuous huts are located about ¼ mile eastward of the western extremity of the island, seasonally occupied by lobster fishermen. The island is essentially a seabird island; gulls, cormorants and pelicans nest by the thousands and much of the land is white with guano. A considerable amount of this valuable fertilizer has been stripped from San Roque Island and its near neighbor, Asunción Island, and shipped to Gulf of California ports in years gone by.

Punta Asunción (Asunción Point), about 8 miles southeastward of Punta San Roque, is a low, sharp sandy point with a conical mound about 75 feet high on its outer end; moderately high hills are situated a short distance inland. *Reefs and detached rocks* on which the sea breaks lie off the point, and shoal water extends ½ mile on either side.

Isla Asunción (Asunción Island), nearly ¾ mile southward of Punta Asunción and connected to it by a shallow bank, is approximately ¾ mile long north and south, ¼ mile wide and rises to a height of 165 feet at its southern end. A group of *rocks awash* is situated on this connecting bank about midway between the point and the island, and a *rock* which dries from 3 to 4 feet lies about a half mile

Isla San Roque with Punta Asunción in the background

westward of the northern end of the island. The island is composed of sandstone formation and is entirely barren. Asunción Island is surrounded by detached rocks and kelp which extend about ¼ mile southward from its southern end. From its northern end a *reef of rocks,* some awash and many above water, projects 600 yards to the northward and ½ mile to the westward. The sea breaks continually over the reef. A *submerged rock,* over which there is a depth of 6 fathoms, lies about 3¼ miles 127° from the island, about 4½ miles southeastward of Punta Asunción. *Anchorage* up into the bight on the eastern side of Asunción Island on its inshore end may be had in about 4 fathoms over a hard sand bottom, protected from the prevailing northwesterly weather. *Directions: Vessels making for this anchorage should steer southward of the island and not attempt the passage betwen Asunción Island and the point, which is foul with rocks.* At the eastern end of Asunción Island is a precipitous, flat-topped rock, Roca Ángulo, frequented by numerous seals and countless seabirds.

Navigation note: Both Isla San Roque and Isla Asunción are so situated along this coast as to blend with the features of the shore and are thereby most difficult to distinguish as separate landmarks from seaward; only on close approach and with a fair degree of piloting accuracy is the observer able to raise these islands.

Bahía de la Asunción (Asunción Bay) lies close east-

ward of Punta Asunción, extending 1¼ miles northward of the point and more than 3 miles northward of the southern end of Isla Asunción. In moderate weather Bahía de la Asunción affords *good anchorage* well up in the lee of the point in depths of from 5 to 10 fathoms, sand bottom, about ½ mile from shore. *Anchorage* sheltered from the prevailing weather in all but southerly winds may also be taken off the cannery, situated at the head of the bight. Lobster holding receivers moored in the bay during lobster season, and awash, must be avoided. A swell usually sweeps across the anchorage area, and the beach, being somewhat steep-to, causes the surf to break in a sharp, strong surge. *Landing* by dinghy can be wet and sometimes moderately dangerous; a rubber life raft is the ideal shoreboat at Asunción Bay. The sandy beach back of the surfline to the eastward of the village is a perfect place for a camp, a campfire, and a lobster-boiling feast.

Punta Asunción (to the left) and Isla Asunción

Cabrillo notes in his log between July 25 and 27, 1542; "The party continued voyaging along the same route up the coast to Latitude 28° (sic) and there they anchored under the shelter of a point, where there were groups of trees such as they had not seen since the point of California. ... the mountains are high and rough with some groves of trees. The point was called Santa Ana, and a small island lay about one league from the land."

Here again, Cabrillo's calculation for latitude misses the mark by about a degree, due, according to knowledgeable scholars, to the very rough celestial observations taken by means of the thumbhole astrolabe employed at that time for determining latitude. Sixty years later, on August 13, 1602, Vizcaíno exploring the same coast, named the bay and island, Asunción.

Isla de la Asunción Bearing 053°.

Asunción Village (San Rafael), sheltered by the point and island to the westward, is a fishing village of about the same size and importance as Turtle Bay. There is a church in the town boasting two steeples, and an automobile junkyard on the beach. The town of about 1,500 people is supported entirely by the abalone cannery and the lobster fishery. The cannery and the entire town receive all supplies by small freighter from Ensenada. Canned and fresh-frozen abalone are transported to Ensenada on the freighter's return trip. Lobsters are flown alive to Ensenada by cargo planes utilizing an unpaved *airstrip* about 3 miles from the village. At one time there was a wharf at Asunción Bay but it has long since disintegrated; a few jagged pilings rising at the water's edge are all that remain. All loading and unloading of supplies and delivery of the abalone and lobster catch to the cannery is accomplished by a fleet of amphibious motorized "ducks," a lighter-type, self-powered barge fitted with pneumatic rubber tires in addition to a marine propeller. These land-and-water-borne vehicles rumble over the beach and into the bay, powering out to freighter or fishing vessel to receive or deliver cargo; thence back to the shore and over the beach to the cannery or warehouse.

The abalone cannery has its headquarters in Ensenada and operates at full capacity during the abalone season. It is considering the processing of other fish products including the abundant pismo clam that occurs in great quantities south of Asunción Bay.

FACILITIES — While the facilities that exist at Asunción Village are established primarily for the operation of the cannery and use of the villagers, certain services and some supplies are available to visiting yachtsmen or fishermen. Gasoline and diesel fuel may be had in limited quantities. Lubricating oil, engine room supplies and some engine parts are kept in stock. Butane gas can sometimes be obtained. Provisions are available in limited variety and quantity. Fresh and canned abalone may be purchased from the cannery and fresh lobster in season is available from the fishermen. Clams may be dug from the beach. There is no fresh water for filling ships' tanks as most of the water used by the village and cannery is distilled during cannery operations, or brought in by freighter from Cedros Island. Divers are available for hire. Some machine work may be had at the cannery shops, and engine mechanics may be hired.

PUBLIC ACCOMMODATIONS — Overnight accommodations ashore may be had, when not in use by visiting company officials for whom they are principally intended.

TRANSPORTATION — Air cargo planes land regularly at the *airstrip* about 3 miles southeast of the village. Charter planes can be hired from Tijuana or Ensenada. The unpaved coastal road connects Asunción Village with Turtle Bay to the north and Abreojos Village to the south thence to inland towns and villages. There are some cars and trucks in the village and cargo trucks make regular runs from Asunción Bay northward. The coastal freighter *Hidalgo* calls fortnightly and runs to ports both north and south of Asunción Bay.

COMMUNICATIONS — The cannery maintains a point-to-point and ship-to-shore radio that operates on high frequency with scheduled communication to the company's home base in Ensenada; schedules are also maintained with Turtle Bay. The radio is open to public use.

MEDICAL EMERGENCIES — A *doctor* is sometimes available in the village, or can be summoned by radio and flown from Ensenada or Santa Rosalía by small plane.

SEA AND WEATHER CONDITIONS — Similar to Turtle Bay; see that section.

SOURCES OF ADDITIONAL INFORMATION — Empacadora Baja, California, S. de R.L. de C.V. Espinoza 843, Ensenada, B.Cfa., Mexico. (See also Appendix.)

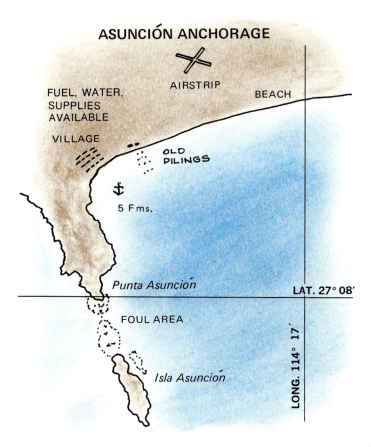

ASUNCIÓN ANCHORAGE

AIRSTRIP

FUEL, WATER, SUPPLIES AVAILABLE

VILLAGE

BEACH

OLD PILINGS

5 Fms.

Punta Asunción

LAT. 27° 08′

FOUL AREA

LONG. 114° 17′

Isla Asunción

Anchorage at Bahía Asunción showing the village

Punta San Hipólito (San Hipólito Point), 18½ miles southeastward, is a low black rocky point backed by barren sand hills from 50 to 100 feet high. The intervening coast between Punta Asunción and Punta San Hipólito is low and sandy with an occasional bluff. Hills and tablelands of moderate elevation rise a short distance inland. *Monte Mesa* (Table Mountain), 1,327 feet high, stands 6 miles northward of the point on flat terrain and provides an excellent navigation mark by which to steer when approaching the coast from off-soundings. Punta Prieta, a seasonally occupied fish camp, is situated in the southeastern end of the bay about 4 miles northwestward of Punta San Hipólito.

Bahía de San Hipólito (San Hipólito Bay) is formed by the bight close eastward of the point. On August 13, 1602, 60 years after Cabrillo explored the same coast, Vizcaíno sheltered his vessels in this bay and gave the anchorage its present name.

Good anchorage may be obtained by vessels with local

knowledge about ½ mile offshore eastward of Punta San Hipólito, in depths of from 5 to 6 fathoms, sand bottom. A *shoal* with a least depth over it of 6 fathoms was reported in 1937 to lie in the approach to the bay, about 4½ miles southeastward of Punta San Hipólito. A *shelving reef,* over which the sea breaks, projects about ½ mile southward from the point. Depths of 25 fathoms lie about 11½ miles southward and 9½ miles south-southwestward of Punta San Hipólito. Kelp beds, which grow abundantly along the coast to the northward of Punta San Hipólito, suddenly disappear to the southward of this bay.

The coast between Punta de San Hipólito and Punta Abreojos, 28 miles southeastward, is low and sandy and recedes to form a great open bight at the head of which there are several lagoons with openings to the sea, all of which are dry except Pond Lagoon. The land behind rises gradually to hills and tablelands 600 to 1,000 feet high, with high and broken mountains in the distance. Soundings are regular and deep water carries to within about 10 miles

Punta Hipólito with Bahía Hipólito in the background

Bahía Hipólito showing Table Mountain

of Punta Abreojos; nearer the point the bottom becomes irregular and shoals considerably.

At the turn of the coast, 10 miles northwestward of Punta Abreojos, a *reef* projects ¼ mile southward. At about 9 miles northwestward of the point a larger *reef,* over which the sea breaks heavily, projects from the coast more than a mile southward; this *reef* forms the west side of an extensive bank (with depths of less than five fathoms on it) that skirts the shore for a distance of about 8 miles northwestward of Punta Abreojos; off the entrance to Pond Lagoon this *shoal bank* extends offshore about 1½ to 3 miles in a southerly and southwesterly direction.

Laguna Pond (Pond Lagoon) is situated just back of the beach, its northern end open to the sea about 7¾ miles northwestward of Punta Abreojos; from its entrance the lagoon runs parallel to the coast for almost 6 miles in a southeasterly direction; the head of Pond Lagoon is situated close behind Punta Abreojos. There is a *stone monument* established on a hill near the mouth of the lagoon and on the western shore is a sizable fish camp called La Bocana comprised of 30 or 40 small houses and several fish processing buildings. An *airstrip* for cargo freighters close by serves the camp during lobster season.

The coastal road runs along the shore, thence along the northern edge of the lagoon to Punta Abreojos. Small fishing vessels anchor within the lagoon, crossing the bar and entering through the shifting channel. *Caution: Vessels should be taken into the lagoon only with local knowledge and experience.* In 1963 a *shoal* with a least depth of 2 feet and marked by *breakers* was sounded in a position 12½ miles west-northwestward of the entrance to Pond Lagoon. The lagoon is a year-round habitat for large schools of a number of varieties of small fish and they may be seen frequently churning the surface of the water close by the mouth. Many offshore banks attract schools of larger fish and the entire coastal area has been frequented for many years by Tuna Clippers in a rich and continuing harvest of one of the peninsula's most productive fishing grounds. A trolling line in these waters is almost a guaranteed source of seafood for the galley.

Mahi Mahi

Entrance to Pond Lagoon

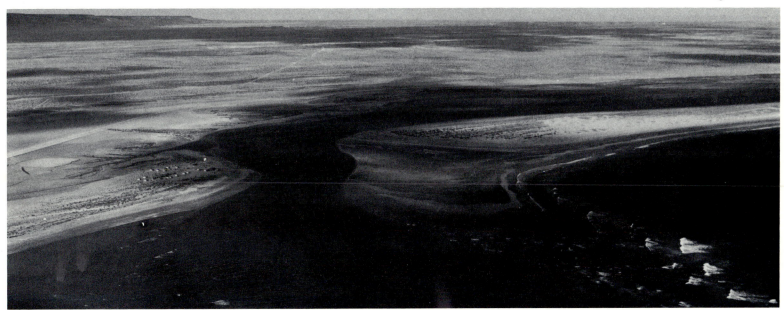

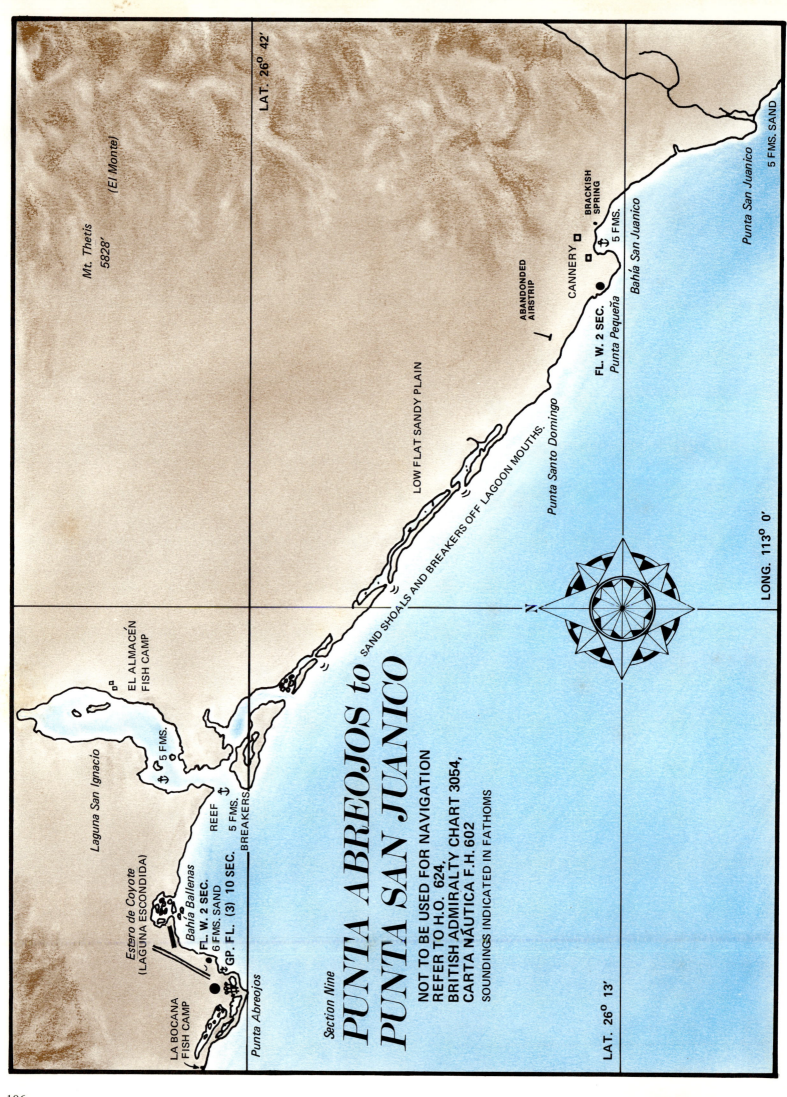

Section Nine

PUNTA ABREOJOS to PUNTA SAN JUANICO

NOT TO BE USED FOR NAVIGATION
REFER TO H.O. 624,
BRITISH ADMIRALTY CHART 3054,
CARTA NÁUTICA F.H. 602
SOUNDINGS INDICATED IN FATHOMS

LAT. 26° 42'

Mt. Thetis
5828'

(El Monte)

LOW FLAT SANDY PLAIN

BRACKISH
SPRING

ABANDONDED
AIRSTRIP

CANNERY

5 FMS.

FL. W. 2 SEC.
Punta Pequeña

Punta Santo Domingo

SAND SHOALS AND BREAKERS OFF LAGOON MOUTHS.

Bahía San Juanico

Punta San Juanico

5 FMS. SAND

LONG. 113° 0'

N

Laguna San Ignacio

EL ALMACÉN
FISH CAMP

5 FMS.

REEF
5 FMS.
BREAKERS

Estero de Coyote
(LAGUNA ESCONDIDA)

Bahía Ballenas

FL. W. 2 SEC.
6 FMS. SAND

GP. FL. (3) 10 SEC.

LA BOCANA
FISH CAMP

Punta Abreojos

LAT. 26° 13'

Punta Abreojos showing shoal, and Whale Rocks

SECTION 9
PUNTA ABREOJOS to PUNTA SAN JUANICO

Punta Abreojos circa 1939

Punta Abreojos (Abreojos Point) was appropriately named by Juan Rodríguez Cabrillo on July 25, 1542. After reconnoitering the lay of the land off this point his log entry reads: "There lie some very dangerous reefs and rocks which can only be seen when the sea breaks on them." Originally, Abre Ojos (Open the Eye), his name for the point, has come down to us relatively unchanged; Cabrillo's admonition is clear!

Punta Abreojos is a low and sandy bluff on which some stunted bushes grow. The surrounding country is low, flat and sand-covered. A barren detached hill 312 feet high rises about 3 miles northward of the point and is backed by a prominent tableland 600 feet high; these coastal features provide a good navigational landmark when approaching from seaward. A *reef* projects from the point about ½ mile southward and numerous *detached rocks* lie close inshore along the eastern side of the point.

A *navigation light,* Punta Abreojos Light, is shown 170 feet above sea from a pyramidal gray stone tower above a building complex, situated on a flat sandy plain about 2½ miles northward of the point and set a distance back from the shore. The light displays a **white group flash of 3 flashes every 10 seconds:** flash 0.3 second, eclipse 1.7 seconds, flash 0.3 second, eclipse 1.7 seconds, flash 0.3 second, eclipse 5.7 seconds. It is visible in the sector 235° through 106° and may be seen 18 miles in clear weather.

Roca Ballena (Whale Rock), 10 feet high, stands on a *detached reef* about ¾ mile long and ½ mile wide, situated about 2 miles offshore in a position about 4 miles westward of Punta Abreojos and on which the sea breaks heavily. A *rock* 3 feet high lies about ¼ mile southeastward of Roca Ballena in the same shoal patch. A *dangerous reef* of similar extent with *rocks awash,* over which the sea breaks at times, lies about 1 mile west-southwestward of Roca Ballena. This *reef* is separated from Whale Rock by a passage ¾ mile wide and depths of 6 to 8 fathoms.

Bajo Knepper (Knepper Shoal), with a least depth over it of 2¼ fathoms, lies about 1 mile offshore in a position about 2½ miles east-northeastward of Punta Abreojos.

Bajos Wright (Wright Shoals) include several detached shoals consisting of a number of *dangerous submerged rocks* with depths of from 2 to 3 fathoms over them lying in a position of from 1 to 1½ miles southward and southeastward of Punta Abreojos, bearing between 180° and 146°. The *passage* between the shoals and the point has a width of about 1,250 yards and depths of from 6 to 7 fathoms.

Fondeadero Abreojos (Abreojos Anchorage), eastward of Punta Abreojos, affords *good anchorage* protected from the prevailing winds in about 6 fathoms, sandy bottom, about ½ mile from the beach. In moderate weather boats may *readily land* on this beach. *Directions: Vessels making*

(Above) *Punta Abreojos with Pond Lagoon in the background*

(Below) *Punta Abreojos anchorage*

for the anchorage from the northwest steer a course of 45° for the point of land that is situated 1¾ miles northeastward of Punta Abreojos, passing about midway between Wright Shoals and the reef off Abreojos Point. Safe anchorage in 6 fathoms may be taken when the light bears 354°. When making an approach from the south or southeast pass well southeastward of Wright Shoals with a course laid about midway between Knepper Shoal and Wright Shoals directly to anchorage in the bay about midway between Punta Abreojos and the point of land 1¾ miles northeastward. For masters of vessels lacking local experience, this latter course is the safer to anchorage. Mind the ground tackle well as this place is sometimes swept by gusts of wind.

A *quieter anchorage* may be had for smaller vessels in the next cove eastward. *Note: When approaching from the northwest, passage into the anchorage may be made between the point of land immediately eastward of Punta Abreojos and Knepper Shoal, avoiding the sandbar extending seaward off the point; when approaching from the south, a course may be laid directly into the anchorage passing southward of Knepper Shoal. With the lighthouse bearing 290° cast anchor in 5 fathoms, sand, in the lee of the shoal. The sea breaks heavily on the point southward and on the shoal; ocean swells diffract around the point and sweep through the passage between the shoal and the point. A current sets through this passage and prevailing wind blows offshore with considerable force. Two anchors are recommended spaced well apart. Anchorage at Abreojos is uncomfortable at best but can be had when necessary.*

SEA AND WEATHER CONDITIONS — The land and sea breezes are regular and strong. The northwest pre-vailing sea breezes sweep across the flat land almost constantly and often with great force. Strong northeast winds blow out of the San Ignacio Lagoon, a few miles eastward, fairly often from September to March. Fogs are somewhat common at night and in the early morning during the winter months, usually clearing by midday.

CURRENTS AND TIDES — The mean high water interval at Abreojos Anchorage at full and change is 9 hours 00 minutes; the spring range is 6.7 feet, the mean range 4.7 feet. The California current flows offshore in this vicinity at an average of about 1½ knots in a predominantly southerly direction; the shoals and reefs of Punta Abreojos alter and intensify these currents, however, and render their effect in an irregular pattern causing them to flow in diverse directions but with enough velocity to be reckoned with. Careful bearings on passing landmarks are strongly advised when coasting the vicinity of this point. (See Coastal Currents, below.)

FACILITIES — A small fishing village is situated on the beach front immediately eastward of Punta Abreojos. The villagers, principally fishermen who ply the lobster trade from small outboard-powered skiffs, are supplied by cargo truck from the village of San Ignacio about 65 miles to the northeast. Limited supplies and gasoline are available in emergency. Aircraft gasoline is stored in limited quantity in 55-gallon drums and can sometimes be purchased. The water for the town must be brought in by tanker truck; there is none to spare for ship's stores. The Mexican fishermen are good mechanics, mainly concerned with keeping their outboard motors and the engines of their automobiles running under difficult conditions; they are quite willing to lend a hand or spare part when asked. As decoration before the doors of their homes there is displayed a curious collection of smooth watermelon-shaped stones as large and larger than the melons they are brightly painted to represent. The stones are obtained from the back country and are odd enough to induce the local fishermen to carry them, heavy as they are, to Punta Abreojos over many miles of dirt road.

COMMUNICATIONS AND TRANSPORTATION — In addition to the road connecting inland to San Ignacio and traveled by truck and car, a good and rather long, smooth *airstrip,* capable of handling cargo planes, serves the village. Abreojos Village does not now have radio communication but a system for all of Baja California is in the planning stage. The Abreojos Lighthouse has facilities for resident personnel.

MARINE EMERGENCIES — There are no medical facilities in Abreojos Village but a *doctor* and *medical facilities* are found at San Ignacio, about 65 miles inland and at Santa Rosalía about 85 miles distant on the Gulf coast. In emergency a doctor may be reached through the use of one of the cars or trucks in the village, and if necessary, a doctor flown to Abreojos by small plane. The nearest *medical assistance* by sea is Turtle Bay, approximately 100 miles northwestward and, sometimes, when the doctor is visiting the cannery, at Asunción Bay, about 47 miles northwestward. The Flying Samaritans based in San Diego will respond in emergency situations and can be reached by radiotelephone. (See Appendix.)

COASTAL CURRENTS — Close along the coast near the shore between Abreojos Point and the entrance to Magdalena Bay ocean currents set predominantly to the south; farther offshore they are frequently found setting to the north. The line of demarcation between southward setting currents and northward setting currents is rather sharply defined, the change being sometimes marked by a sudden change in ocean depth. A vessel running along this coast with a spring flood setting into the mouths of the many lagoons that open to seaward would be carried toward the beach. This is often apparent when running down to make Cape San Lázaro, when a ship's master will frequently find his vessel fetching into the coast north of the cape. Masters of vessels bound southward to Magdalena Bay or beyond should lay a course that includes a generous compass course factor to compensate for inshore set and which will carry them well clear of Cape San Lázaro. Numerous vessels, large and small, lie stranded on this coast, the wrecks concentrated for the most part in the hook just northward of Cape San Lázaro.

Bahía de Ballenas (Whale Bay) is an open bay situated between Punta Abreojos and Punta Holcombe at the western end of the low sand island at the entrance to San Ignacio Lagoon. This bay, open to the south, is about 16½ miles wide between the two points and recedes about 5½ miles northward. At the head of the bay, about 8½ miles northeastward of Punta Abreojos, is the entrance to a small lagoon, Estero del Coyote, sometimes referred to as Laguna de Escondida, which extends several miles in a northerly direction. Small vessels may enter this lagoon through a shifting access channel across a shoal bar on which the sea breaks. The eastern side of the entrance to this lagoon is marked as Punta Nieves on old whaler's charts. An extensive *sand bank* extends about 1 mile offshore for about 4 miles westward of the lagoon entrance. A seasonally occupied fishing village is located on the western shore of the lagoon and is called locally, El Coyote.

The entrance to Laguna de San Ignacio, a considerably larger and more important lagoon, lies in the eastern part of Ballenas Bay. About 2 miles inland from the coast and 5½ miles northwestward of Punta Bronaugh at the entrance to the San Ignacio Lagoon there is a conspicuous conical sand hill of yellowish color rising to a height of 179 feet. It provides a good approach mark.

The shores of Ballenas Bay are low and sandy, marked by sand dunes about 10 feet high covered with sagebrush; except on the western side where two rocky points are connected by a low bluff from which the land slopes up gradually to the higher land northward of Punta Abreojos. In clear weather the high volcanic peaks of Las Tres Virgenes, 6,547 feet high, situated about 60 miles northeastward near the gulf coast of the peninsula, are plainly visible from the bay. The land northward and eastward of Bahía Ballenas and lagoons is nearly level and extremely barren, although a few stunted mesquite trees, patches of rush grass and a large species of cactus occasionally are to be seen. The soundings in the bay are regular with moderate depths close to the shore except off the entrance to the lagoons where there are *extensive shoals* on which the sea breaks. With strong winds, a heavy swell rolls into the bay and a high surf breaks heavily on the beach, making landing hazardous.

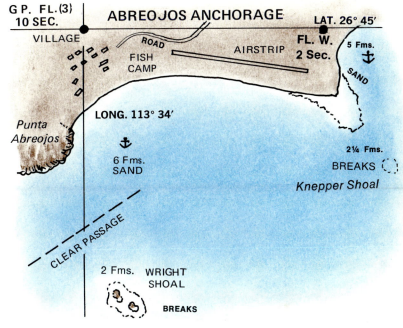

Laguna San Ignacio, looking southward

Cabrillo anchored his survey vessels, *San Salvador* and *Victoria,* in this bay on July 25, 1542, and named it the Port of Santiago. Vizcaíno's two ships *San Diego* and *Tres Reyes,* stood off this same bay on July 30, 1602, and on August 2, the *Tres Reyes* was ordered to enter the lagoon and explore. The frigate returned the following day, having sighted a large number of whales, therefore naming the bay Ballenas; however, since no fresh water was found the expedition continued northward.

Ballenas Bay was the site of extensive whaling operations in the latter half of the 1800's. Scores of vessels anchored in the bay during the whaling season. Captain Scammon was one of the vanguard of early whalemen that pursued their quarry in Ballenas Bay. His charts of the area were some of the first to be drawn with accuracy and contained a wealth of local information.

The German World War I raider *Leipzig* lay in Ballenas Bay, August 27, 1914, awaiting a rendezvous with the SS *Mazatlán* and her badly needed supply of bunkering coal. Hunted by the Australian cruiser *Newcastle* and the Japanese cruiser *Idzumo,* the raider was playing a deadly game of cat-and-mouse along the Pacific coast and into the Gulf of California, sinking Allied merchant ships at the outset of the war.

Laguna de San Ignacio (San Ignacio Lagoon) (H.O. Chart 1493) is a large lagoon from 2 to 4 miles wide, running northward from Punta Bronaugh at its western entrance and penetrating the low, flat coastal plain to an extent of about 16 miles. The lagoon is fronted by a long, low island about 8 miles in extent, lying in the curve of the shore and called on early whaler's charts Sand Island; a salt pond is situated in the middle of the island.

Punta Holcombe is the western extremity of Sand Island which is separated from the mainland by a shallow channel ½ fathom deep and from 1 to 1½ miles wide. Punta Parmenter, sometimes referred to as Rocky Point, on the eastern shore, and Punta Bronaugh on the western shore of the lagoon entrance (situated respectively about 4 miles north-northeastward and 3 miles northward of the western extremity of Sand Island) form the entrance points at the mouth of the San Ignacio Lagoon, the approach to which lies westward of Punta Holcombe. The yellowish sand hill, previously described, 179 feet high and situated about 5½ miles northwestward of Punta Bronaugh, is a good mark to steer by when approaching the lagoon. *Extensive shoals* which partly dry at low water project southward about 4 miles from Punta Bronaugh and about 1¾ miles from Punta Holcombe, forming a bar about 800 yards wide with depths over it of about 3¼ fathoms. The channel through this bar is clearly marked by lines of breakers on either side which serve as the best guides for entering. No directions can be fairly given for crossing the bar which is subject to frequent and sudden changes of contour due to ocean currents, and no vessel other than those whose masters have local knowledge should attempt to enter without first sending a small boat to reconnoiter

The channel through the shoals, across the bar and into the lagoon has generally been found to be a straight one with a least depth of 3¼ fathoms over a width of 750 yards, and a depth of 3½ fathoms over a lesser width. Within the bar the depths increase to 4 and 5 fathoms and the channel opens out to a width of about ¾ of a mile, but again narrows to about 750 yards abreast Punta Holcombe. A *reef* which dries and is steep-to on its southeastern side lies on the western edge of the channel nearly opposite Punta Holcombe.

Entrance to Laguna San Ignacio

Entrance to Laguna Escondida

Beyond Punta Holcombe the channel again deepens, becoming broader until it enters the lagoon. A course of 35° leads from the bar on a mid-channel course nearly abreast Punta Bronaugh, where the course must be altered northward to avoid the *shoal* on the eastern side of the channel. After passing Holcombe Point and the reef opposite, an entering vessel should use as landmarks the north point of Sand Island, Punta Bronaugh, and the point on the east side of the channel inside Punta Parmenter, 2½ miles northeastward of Punta Bronaugh. *Navigation note: A small boat channel in which there are depths of 1¼ to 2½ fathoms leads in a northeasterly direction through the shore bank close along Punta Bronaugh, thence to the main channel north-northeastward of the point. Within the lagoon about 2 miles above Punta Bronaugh there is an open area about 1 mile square with a depth of 5 to 8 fathoms throughout. Here the fairway divides into three channels, the easternmost being the best and leading toward the head of the lagoon with a least depth of 3¼ fathoms along a narrow and somewhat tortuous course for a distance of 7 miles; thence to the head of the lagoon the depths in the channel vary between 2½ and 1¼ fathoms.*

On the eastern side of the main branch of the lagoon two small turtle fishing camps are located hard by the shore, La Laguna and El Almacén. About 30 miles northeast from the head of the lagoon, at the foot of a series of gradually rising mesas, is the small village and former Mission of San Ignacio. The mission called San Ignacio de Kadakman or Cadacaaman, after the name of the Indian ranchería originally found there, was established in 1728 by Father Juan B. Luyando. The shade of the old date palm groves planted then still provide, in this well-watered oasis, a welcome surcease from the heat and brittle dryness of the desert country. San Ignacio has a population of about 1,500 persons.

To the San Ignacio Lagoon in the mating season, after migrating almost 7,000 miles from the Arctic Ocean, come the now ever-increasing pods of California gray whales which run in through the lagoon mouth and up the deeper channels to lie in the shallows and give birth to their young. The lagoon supports a sizable turtle population and is a veritable aquarium for small schoolfish. Clams abound in the sand and mud of the tidal flats; bottom fish are plentiful.

Islas Ballena (Whale Islands), situated in the upper part of the lagoon, are two low islands with a maximum width of about ½ mile that are almost connected and lie parallel to the shores of the lagoon for a distance of about 3 miles. At the head of the boat channel on the northwest shore is Sham Island Point projecting into the lagoon. Punta Bell is situated on the western shore about 7 miles from Punta Bronaugh. Caleta Curlew, a small, very shallow cove formed by the bight southward of Punta Bell is situated on the western shore of the lagoon about 5 miles above Punta Bronaugh. The shores of the lagoon on the western side are bordered by a low barren sandy plain and on its eastern side by a plain elevated about 15 feet above the surface of the lagoon, and covered with sagebrush.

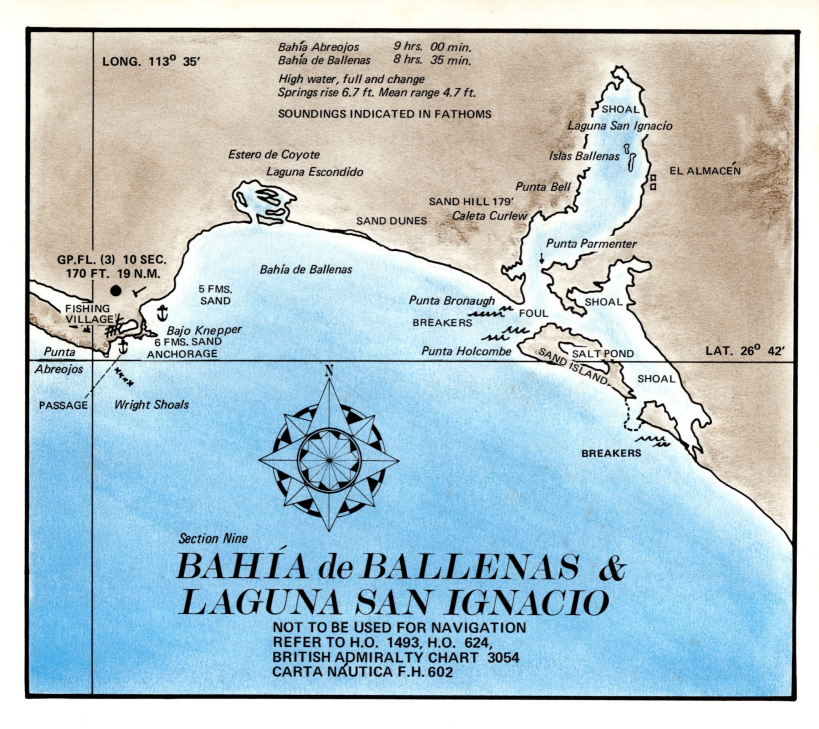

LONG. 113° 35'

Bahía Abreojos   9 hrs. 00 min.
Bahía de Ballenas   8 hrs. 35 min.

High water, full and change
Springs rise 6.7 ft. Mean range 4.7 ft.

SOUNDINGS INDICATED IN FATHOMS

SHOAL
Laguna San Ignacio

Estero de Coyote
Laguna Escondido

Islas Ballenas

EL ALMACÉN

Punta Bell

SAND HILL 179'
Caleta Curlew

SAND DUNES

Punta Parmenter

GP.FL. (3) 10 SEC.
170 FT. 19 N.M.

Bahía de Ballenas

FISHING
VILLAGE

5 FMS.
SAND

Punta Bronaugh

SHOAL

BREAKERS

FOUL

Bajo Knepper
6 FMS. SAND
ANCHORAGE

Punta Holcombe

SAND ISLAND

SALT POND

Punta
Abreojos

LAT. 26° 42'

PASSAGE

Wright Shoals

SHOAL

N

BREAKERS

Section Nine

BAHÍA de BALLENAS & LAGUNA SAN IGNACIO

NOT TO BE USED FOR NAVIGATION
REFER TO H.O. 1493, H.O. 624,
BRITISH ADMIRALTY CHART 3054
CARTA NÁUTICA F.H. 602

Navigation note: Ballenas Bay and the San Ignacio Lagoon were originally surveyed by the U.S.S. Thetis in 1892 and a hydrographic survey chart H.O. 1494 was issued as a part of the portfolio of charts covering this area. H.O. 1494 has been discontinued for some years as whaling is no longer pursued in the shoal waters of the lagoon and general navigation is limited by its depth.

ANCHORAGE — During good weather anchorage may be had outside the lagoon entrance with Punta Bronaugh bearing 57° distant about 3½ miles in depths of from 5 to 6 fathoms. Within the lagoon about 2 miles above Punta Bronaugh in the area about 1 mile square, there is good anchorage in calm water in depths of from 5 to 8 fathoms.

TIDES AND CURRENTS — Tidal streams run over and along the bar and off the lagoon mouth with considerable velocity, particularly during spring tides; a heavy swell sometimes sweeps the bar and allowance should be made for set when carrying a light vessel or a deep draft through the entrance channel. High water at full and change occurs at 8 hours, 35 minutes; maximum rise of the tide is 6' 5".

SEA AND WEATHER CONDITIONS — The land and sea breezes are fairly strong and regular, enabling sailing vessels to enter and leave the lagoon in a fair wind. Strong winds blowing out of the lagoon may be expected frequently from September to March. Fogs are somewhat common at night and in the early morning during the winter months, usually clearing by noon.

Punta Santo Domingo

FACILITIES — There are no facilities at San Ignacio. Some little gasoline is stored in 55-gallon drums by the fishermen at La Laguna and El Almacén Fish Camps for use in their outboard motors. Fresh turtle meat is available at the camps when a catch is brought in; otherwise it is hung in the sun to dry and shipped to San Ignacio by truck and thence to the Gulf port of Santa Rosalía. A dirt road communicates with San Ignacio 30 miles to the northeast where there is a telegraph to Santa Rosalía; the road connects also with a coastal road passing through Punta Abreojos to the northwest and San Juanico to the southeast. Truckers use this coastal road during the dry season and truck traffic is considerable for such an out-of-the-way place. There is no fresh water in the immediate vicinity but *good drinking water* is obtainable at a ranch along the road to San Ignacio.

The coast between the entrance to San Ignacio Lagoon and Punta Santo Domingo, situated about 40 miles to the southeast, is low and sandy, penetrated at several places by long narrow lagoons that lie parallel to the coast. The lagoons are separated from the sea by ½- mile wide strips of sand beach through which there are passages at irregular intervals. These "bocas," or "mouths" of the lagoons, are shallow and fronted by sand shoals on which the seas break, often a considerable distance offshore. Small boats may enter in fine weather but coasting vessels should beware of standing in too close against the offshore bars. The coast, being low and sandy, is not easily distinguished but the depths, though irregular, increase gradually offshore and sounding is the best piloting guide, especially at night.

Within the 100-fathom curve, which lies 33 to 37 miles off this part of the coast, there are two banks, Hutchins Bank with a least depth of 18 fathoms, and Moore Bank with a least depth of 54 fathoms located, respectively, 21 and 38 miles south-southwestward of Holcombe Point.

Navigation caution: A current setting onshore is generally prevalent along this shore especially at the mouths of the lagoons and precaution should be exercised by the master as to his vessel's relative position to the coastline along the compass course. Often the master of a small vessel coasting too close inshore is surprised and dismayed to observe breakers rolling in on the offshore bars outside the projected track of his course, necessitating a quick maneuver to double back and gain more sea room adequately clear of these coastal dangers.

A series of irregular tablelands from 800 to 1,000 feet high rise abruptly from the lowland at a distance of about 10 miles from the coast in the vicinity of San Ignacio Lagoon and gradually converging, meet the coast at Santo Domingo Point. Mount Thetis, a remarkable peak 5,828 feet high known locally as El Monte, rises about 35 miles north-northeastward of Punta Santo Domingo and has been seen from vessels 70 miles offshore. The southern slope of this mountain is very abrupt revealing a gap in the mountain range

Punta Santo Domingo (Santo Domingo Point) is a conspicuous, perpendicular rocky cliff of dark color, 175 feet high, backed by a tableland 400 feet high. Cliffs extend for several miles on either side of the point; the northern cliff

Bahía San Juanico and Punta Pequeña

is formed by a very remarkable white sand bluff. A *reef* projects a short distance southwestward from the point and the sea breaks heavily on the rocks at the foot of the cliff, making landing dangerous except in moderate weather. The best *landing place* is on the open beach at the foot of the white sand bluff avoiding rocky patches along the shore. *Anchorage,* with some protection from the prevailing wind, may be taken eastward of the point in depths of from 5 to 6 fathoms about ½ mile offshore, but little comfort is found when anchoring where there are depths of less than 12 fathoms, due to the heavy ground swell which prevails. This anchorage has an easy access however, and a marvelous beach for swimming.

From Punta Santo Domingo to Punta San Juanico, about 26 miles southeastward, the coast is comprised principally of sand hills 100 to 200 feet high, with tablelands and mountains farther inland. The peaks of the Sierra de la Giganta which form the backbone of the Baja California Peninsula, overtopping the intervening range of mountains, are distinctly visible from seaward. Punta Pequeña, 11½ miles southeastward of Punta Santo Domingo, is a rocky point with bluffs from 15 to 60 feet high. A stone beacon exhibiting a navigation light, that flashes every 2 seconds, with a 12 mile range is situated on the southwestern side of Punta Pequeña. A rocky ledge, over which the sea breaks, extends for a short distance from the point, the shoal water deepening quickly, 20 fathoms being found ¾ mile from the point. *Note: Punta Pequeña and Punta San Juanico, 16 miles southeastward, have an almost identical appearance and may be easily confused with each other when approaching from southward.*

Bahía San Juanico showing cannery

Punta San Juanico with Boca de San Gregorio to the right

SECTION 10

PUNTA SAN JUANICO to CABO SAN LÁZARO

Cabo San Lázaro light.

Bahía de San Juanico, formed by a deep indentation in the coast eastward of Punta Pequeña, affords an *excellent anchorage* northeastward of the point about 1 mile offshore in depths of 5 to 6 fathoms sheltered from the prevailing wind. A fishing village and a cannery are situated at the head of San Juanico Bay but the cannery has operated only sporadically in the last several years and the village is rather sparsely occupied at the present time. There is a *spring of good water* among some date palms near the beach where vessels can replenish their fresh water stores, but transport is somewhat difficult. Some few provisions are available and limited amounts of gasoline at times may be purchased. Lobsters are plentiful and can usually be traded from the fishermen; clams abound along the beach. Shrimp occur near here seasonally, San Juanico being the farthest point to which shrimp vessels from Guaymas and Mazatlán voyage in search of a catch. The *anchorage* in San Juanico Bay under the lee of Punta Pequeña is a pretty place and a pleasant layover when voyaging in either direction along this coast. The main coastal road reaches the cannery site and connects to a transpeninsular road a few miles south that in turn communicates with the town of Mulegé on the Gulf coast. An *airstrip* about one mile northwest of the cannery is utilized by cargo planes for transport of the catch of live lobster to market. There is a radiotelegraph at the cannery through which public messages may be sent.

On July 19, 1542, Cabrillo anchored his caravels in this bay and explored the countryside. He called this particular bay Bahía Magdalena. Its present name — Bahía San Juanico — derives from the subsequent voyage of Vizcaíno.

Arroyo Mesquital opens to the sea at Boca de Mesquital, about 6 miles southeastward of Punta Pequeña. There is a source of *fresh water* in a *spring* located about 10 miles up the arroyo at the foot of a sandstone bluff; 1 or 2 miles farther up the arroyo there are several ponds containing good, clear water, frequented by horses and cattle pastured in the surrounding countryside.

Punta San Juanico (San Juanico Point), about 15 miles southeastward of Punta Pequeña, is a steep sand bluff about 50 feet high sparsely covered with sagebrush. The surf rolls in on a *shallow bank* and breaks at the foot of the bluff. The *bank* extends about ¾ mile offshore and for a distance of about 2 miles northward of the point. A *dangerous shoal,* over which the sea breaks at low water, lies inside the 3-fathom curve about ½ mile southeastward of Punta San Juanico; there is at times a heavy rolling swell that breaks occasionally on this shoal. The bight eastward of Punta San Juanico is shoal with *numerous sandbars* formed off the mouth of the San Gregorio Lagoon; however vessels may find *anchorage* protected against the prevailing winds,

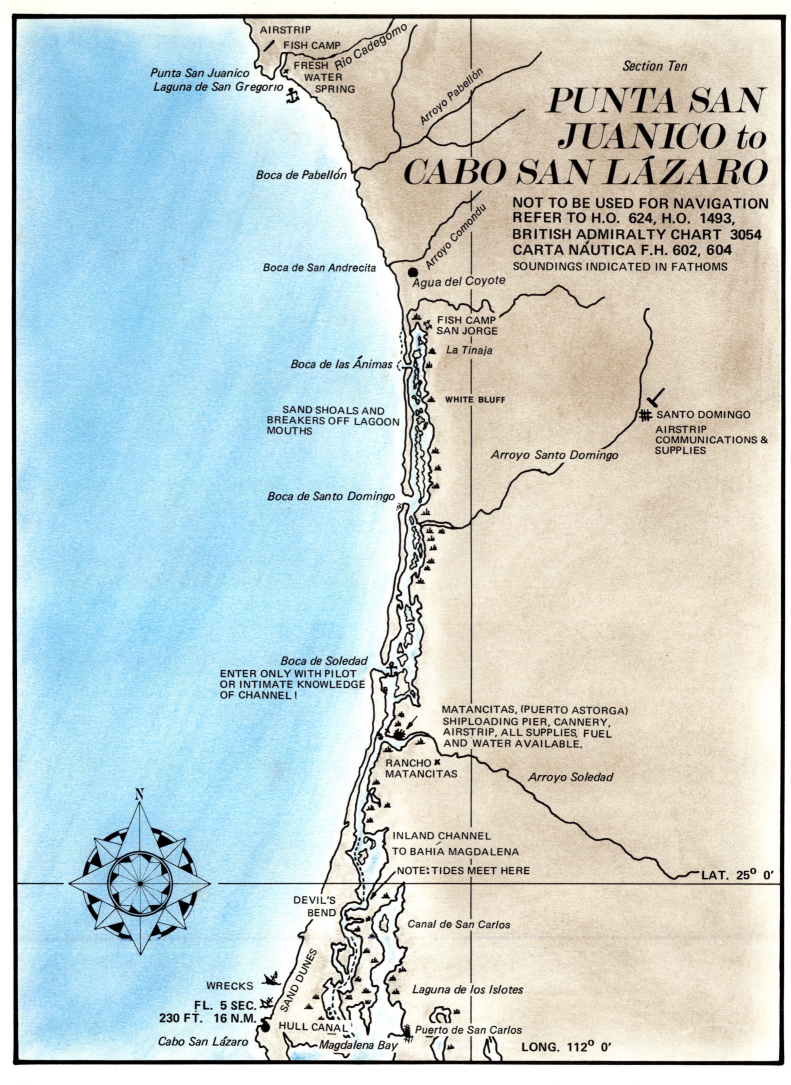

southeastward of Punta San Juanico beyond the lagoon mouth, in depths of 5 to 6 fathoms, sand bottom. The anchorage is not recommended to vessels without local knowledge due to constantly shifting shoal bars that extend a considerable distance offshore here. *Note: If anchorage in this bight is sought, approach with caution and continual sounding, preferably in fair weather.*

Laguna San Gregorio (San Gregorio Lagoon) entered close eastward of Punta San Juanico, is the estuary of Río Cadegomo and Arroyo San Gregorio. The entrance is quite narrow with depths of about 3 feet over the bar. There are depths of from 1 to 3 fathoms within the lagoon which runs northward for about 3¼ miles, gradually narrowing; the southern portion is encumbered with shoals and sandbars. Small local coasters of 6- to 7-foot draft cross the bar into the lagoon at highest springs.

La Bocana, a fish camp at the mouth of the San Gregorio Lagoon, is situated above a sand beach on the western shore of the estero. A dirt *airstrip* is located just above the head of the lagoon on the north side of the river. A dirt road runs from La Bocana and connects to the coastal road leading southward to Magdalena Bay as well as across the peninsula to Bahía Concepción on the Gulf coast. About 20 miles along this latter road, following the Cadegomo River, the village of La Purísima is located near the site of La Purísima Mission. Government telephone facilities are available here, supplies are sold and refreshment may be had.

Arroyo de San Gregorio penetrates between the Cavellezera and Purísima Vieja Mesas and opens onto the head of Laguna San Gregorio. There are several ranches along the bottomland of the arroyo and, near the foot of Monte Subida Alta, situated about 11 miles northeastward of Boca San Gregorio are several fresh water ponds. Eastward of Arroyo de San Gregorio the Cadegomo River, whose source waters rise near the Gulf coast, runs with a considerable flow through narrow gorges and valleys and empties into the San Gregorio Lagoon about 2¾ miles from the coast. The Cadegomo River is an almost constant stream, and although near its mouth it has only the dimensions of a small brook, at 12 to 15 miles above its mouth it is a river of considerable size. For many miles above this distance the river is a beautiful stream that varies in width from 25 to 100 feet and in depth from 1 to 10 feet. On its banks and in its valleys thousands of head of horses and cattle, mules and goats find good pasturage; oranges, lemons, figs, dates, sugar cane and other crops grow luxuriantly. The Cadegomo is called a "river" as distinguished from "arroyo," the latter being a watercourse through which a stream flows only during the period of heavy rainfall, after which it again becomes a dry watercourse with scattered ponds remaining. These ponds, called pozos by the local inhabitants, are natural reservoirs which freqently preserve visible water for periods of as long as 2 to 3 years after the flow of water down the arroyo has stopped.

Mission La Purísima Concepción was first established in this locale in 1719 by Father Nicolás Tamaral at a place now called Purísima Vieja (Old Purísima). In the 1730's the mission was moved to a more favorable location on the banks of the Río de Cadegomo and an unrecognizable mound of adobe, all that is left of the buildings, is known as Mission La Purísima Concepción de Cadegomo. In 1822 the last missionary in residence died and the place was deserted for several years before being repopulated by settlers from the mainland. The small village of La Purísima established just below the mission site now supports a population of approximately 1,000 persons.

From Punta San Juanico to Cabo San Lázaro, about 75 miles southward, the coast sweeps around in a gradual curve eastward, then westward, receding about 11 miles. The character of this coast is at first somewhat rugged and uneven with hills and low rocky tablelands close by the sea; thence southward, the mesas recede from the coast giving way to predominantly level land with rolling plains rising gradually to segmented tablelands of a whitish hue that merge with the higher mesas and mountain peaks of the interior. Numerous arroyos cut through, dividing the mesas, then open out on the shore, forming a series of coastal lagoons beginning about 20 miles southward of Punta San Juanico. The mouths of these lagoons are marked by rolling breakers curling over shoal bars, blocking passage into most except by small boat in calm weather.

The *seaward shoals* fronting the lagoons are subject to constant change due first to the contouring action of ocean currents and shifting sand; the secondary action of outrushing rain-swollen water runoff intermittently tends to cut relatively deep channels through the shoals and to wash away the deposited sand. The daily rhythmic tidal flow in and out of the lagoons completes the cycle, creating a tidal bore, which though relatively weak, shapes the contour of the sandbars with a constant scouring action. Vessels of surprising draft cross the bars and enter many of these lagoons to find calm and protected anchorage within. However, without specific local knowledge or careful reconnaissance first by ship's boat to ascertain the depth and configuration of the channels, entry is ill-advised even for the best seaman. Various yachtsmen through accident or mistake combined with sheer luck have successfully entered some of these lagoons, striking and bumping across the bars, but this is a foolhardy adventure, risking vessel, equipment and crew, even when successful. With adequate knowledge, proper precaution, and positive soundings of the depth and configuration of the entrance channels, safe passage can be achieved into many of the lagoons at flood on a spring tide.

Beyond the lagoons of Cabo San Lázaro the coast is low and sandy with high land to be seen far in the interior, creating a perspective from seaward difficult to judge as to distance of a ship's track offshore, especially at night. The swell is deep and broad and breaks in a many-tiered line of heavy surf on the sandy beach. The 100-fathom curve lies 13 to

49 miles offshore; soundings of 40 to 76 fathoms lying about ½ to 22 miles outside the 100-fathom curve mark the existence of a *bank* of considerable extent. The northern limit of the bank is 39 to 53 miles southwestward of Punta Santo Domingo and the southern limit, where depths of 40 to 75 fathoms have been sounded, lies about 23½ miles northwestward of Cabo San Lázaro.

OFFSHORE BANKS — Between Punta Abreojos and Cabo San Lázaro there is a series of *detached banks,* some quite extensive in area and others with shoal patches or pinnacles with 10 fathoms of water or less over them. Rosa Bank, with a depth of 275 fathoms, lies about 85 miles west-southwestward of Punta Abreojos in surrounding ocean depths of over 1,500 fathoms. Hutchins Bank, with a least depth over it of 18 fathoms, lies 21 miles offshore southeastward of Punta Abreojos. Moore Bank, with a least depth over it of 54 fathoms, lies about 61 miles westward of Punta San Juanico. Uncle Sam Bank with a least known depth over it of 36 fathoms, lies about 65 miles west-southwestward of Punta San Juanico, and within 15 miles northeastward of it, depths of 8 and 9 fathoms have been sounded in the vicinity of Latitude 25° 38′ to 41′ north, Longitude 113° 17′ to 21′ west. Depths of 13 and 11 fathoms have been sounded in the vicinity of Latitude 25° 44′ north, Longitude 113° 09′ west. Rosa Bank, Uncle Sam Bank and the 8-, 9-, 11-, and 13-fathom spots all lie outside the 100-fathom curve; Hutchins Bank and Moore Bank lie within the 100-fathom curve.

Thetis Bank, discovered in 1895 by U.S.S. *Thetis,* lies about 18 miles west-northwestward of Cabo San Lázaro. Thetis Bank is about 1½ miles long north and south and

cape and from the northern ports of San Pedro and San Diego frequent these banks, taking thousands of tons of fish annually. A small red crustacean, which may be observed on the surface of the sea in large colonies, flourishes in the vicinity of these banks; a proliferation of game fishes feed on these tiny crustaceans, one link in the life cycle of the myriad of sea forms that thrive in these waters.

Boca de Pabellón, the mouth of the arroyo of the same name, opens to the sea about 10 miles southeastward of Boca de San Gregorio. Ocean currents frequently close this mouth with a sandbar during the dry season which is washed away again during the rainy season. About 1½ miles toward the head of the lagoon formed at the mouth of this arroyo is a cattle ranch, El Pabellón, at which there is a pond with slightly brackish but *potable water.*

Boca de San Andrecita, the mouth of Arroyo Comondú, opens to the sea about 17½ miles southeastward of Punta San Juanico. A spring-fed mountain stream rises at the head of this arroyo but the water is mostly drawn off by the inhabitants of San José Comondú and San Miguel Comondú, small farming villages situated across the river from one another well up into the mountains about 21 miles from the mouth of the arroyo. About 5½ miles from the sea, a road cuts in along the northern side of the arroyo and leads to the villages. Mission San José was first established in 1708 at Comondú Viejo by Father Julián de Mayorga, thence moved in 1737 to its new location by the river; Mission San Miguel grew from a visiting station and cattle ranch first established there by Padre Juan Ugarte in 1714. Some of these mission buildings are still in use. These communities are surrounded by barren lava mesas; the valley

Adobe huts

¾ mile wide within its 50-fathom curve. The bottom is very irregular with many jagged rocks, but sand, shells and coral have been brought up with the sounding lead. The least known depth on this bank is 6½ fathoms but it is possible that shallower water may exist; a small patch of seaweed was observed to be apparently growing on the bank in 1931. A depth of 6 fathoms was sounded in 1955 about 15 miles westward of Cape San Lázaro in the vicinity of Latitude 24° 48′ north, Longitude 112° 35′ west. A depth of 10 fathoms was sounded immediately northwestward of Thetis Bank in the vicinity of Latitude 25° 04′ north, Longitude 112° 45′ west.

Petrel Bank, with depths over it of from 10 to 40 fathoms, fine gray sand, was discovered in 1904 by the U.S.S. *Petrel* about 27 miles west-southwestward of Cabo San Lázaro. The *bank* has a length of about 10 miles northwest to southeast and a width of about 6 miles and is situated about 14 miles outside the 100-fathom curve. The general area around these *banks* and *shoal patches* is rich fishing ground, attracting tuna, skipjack, bonita, albacore, and a large and abundant variety of bottom fish. Tuna Clippers from the

floor is a narrow but lush ribbon of green, fed by several never-failing *springs* which rise nearby. Large crops of dates, figs and grapes and sugar cane are grown; raisins and wine are made from the grapes. The isolation of this place and its picturesque whitewashed adobe houses and quiet groves of date palms give it a Shangri-la character well worth a visit from the coast. A stream of water reaches the sea at Boca de San Andrecita but only when heavy rains produce an abundant flow in Arroyo Comondú, at which time the sandbar at the mouth is washed away opening the lagoon to the sea. A *deep well* dug to 190 feet is situated on the second road back from the coast, about 5 miles northeastward from Boca de San Andrecita.

Boca de las Ánimas, about 8 miles southward of Boca de San Andrecita and about 25 miles southward of Punta San Juanico, is the northernmost of the three entrances to a series of extensive and interconnected lagoons that run parallel to the shore southward, ultimately opening into Madgalena Bay with which they are connected by an inland waterway navigable to small boats of shoal draft. These lagoons are separated from the sea by narrow strips of sand

Boca de las Ánimas

Coastline near Boca de las Ánimas looking southward

beach, the entrances fronted by *shoals* and *bars* which are constantly shifting and which consitute a danger to small vessels running close along the coast.

Boca de las Ánimas is about ¾ mile wide fronted by *shoals* upon which rolling swells break in several tiers; a further line of breakers may be encountered between the two sand points that form the entrance. Narrow channels thread through the breakers close aboard both the north and south shoreline of the lagoon mouth; the northern channel is the most open of breaking surf. *Shoals* exist within the mouth, some marked by surf; the principal navigable channel after passing southward of the outer sand shoal, cloverleafs to the north, east and south. The deeper channels follow close along the sandspit, while shallower portions of the estuary penetrate the Magdalena Plain with an intricate pattern of marshlands and tidal channels for some distance inland from the mouth.

Although the use of these lagoons as an inland waterway is largely confined to small craft, vessels of considerable size utilize the deeper channels to serve the various small ports established as fishing or shipping points within the lagoon. While local vessels are known to occasionally enter the lagoon under certain conditions through Boca de las Ánimas and Boca de Santo Domingo, the principal and safer entrance channel is at Boca de Soledad, the last entrance southward before Cabo San Lázaro. The lagoons may also be approached from Magdalena Bay into which there is a clear deepwater channel.

Arroyo de San Bernacio opens into the northernmost estero of the lagoon 3¾ miles north of Boca de las Ánimas.

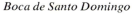

Boca de Santo Domingo

San Jorge, a fish camp and loading port for shipment of produce and supplies to and from La Purísima and Comondú, is situated on the eastern shore of the lagoon 3 miles north-northeastward of Boca de las Ánimas; small shoal draft vessels carry cargo from this port to Bahía Magdalena, 60 miles southward.

Boca de Santo Domingo, about 10½ miles southward of Boca de las Ánimas, along an intervening coast comprised of a low sand beach with occasional low hills sparsely covered with bushes, is the middle entrance to the coastal waterway connecting to Magdalena Bay. Entry into the lagoon through Boca de Santo Domingo is not recommended without thorough reconnaissance and sounding of the depths in the channel. *Caution: When a sea is running, the rolling breakers on the bar can be dangerous.* While local vessels negotiate this entrance frequently, those masters without thorough knowledge of the channel are better-advised to use Boca de Soledad or the deepwater entrance to Magdalena Bay. The entrance channel through Boca de Santo Domingo is both deeper and broader than that through Boca de las Ánimas and it is less obscured by the turbulence of breakers over the bar. A small sand island that dries marks the center of an extensive crescent-shaped sand shoal that has formed in the middle of the mouth midway between the two sandy entrance points. The broader, deeper channel is on the south side of the mouth and will carry a vessel in on a straighter course than the northern channel. Breakers mark the limits of both channels and shoal water

reflects a distinctly lighter hue than the deeper channels. Within the lagoon the channel widens both to the north and south but there are shoals and sandbars to be avoided. An estuary reaches several miles inland at the mouth of Arroyo de Santo Domingo, which opens into the coastal lagoon about 2 miles south of Boca de Santo Domingo. A *ranch* is situated above the head of this estuary, about 7 miles inland, and *fresh water* in pools is found nearby. The dusty, wind-swept farming village of Santo Domingo is situated on the old coastal highway, about 10 miles from the coast up Arroyo de Santo Domingo. There is an *airstrip* for light planes, as well as government radio communication facilities open to the public, airmail service to La Paz and accommodations, gasoline, and supplies are available. The new coastal highway passes close by the village.

In June, 1965, the master of a shoal draft, Block Islander *Mary V,* mistaking Boca de Santo Domingo for Boca de Soledad, attempted the entrance channel with almost dire results:

"To the right, 200 feet away, surf broke heavily on the beach; less than this distance, huge crests broke to our left. In this narrow passage, formed by the breakers, we were running parallel to the beach to make the entrance [to the lagoon]. As the 90° starboard turn [we had calculated would take us through the pass] approached, our vessel was lifted by a great comber and dropped hard on one of the many guardian sandbars [situated off the entrance]. At

Boca de Soledad looking eastward

Puerto Astorga on the inland waterway, looking south

first shock, our 38-foot double-ended Block Island cutter turned 90° and headed for the beach. The relatively quiet passage vanished; on all sides was white water. In rapid succession we were lifted up and dropped heavily on the bar, each time coming closer to the beach. With the boat first on one beam then the other and the waves breaking over the deck [we all strapped on our life preservers]. Papers and money were hurriedly brought on deck and the dinghy made ready for the last short trip to safety. During the first dozen shocks the rudder had raised in its pintles, jamming the propeller. We were without power so the anchor was dropped to keep us from going any farther onshore. Just as all hope had vanished, the backsurge from a huge onshore wave pushed us out a good 20 yards. At this point the rudder dropped down in its usual position and for the moment we were free. The anchor was [quickly] cut loose; with full power from our 115-h.p. [engine] and one final bounce and we were over the bar and into the serenity of quiet waters [within the lagoon. While we were now safely sheltered in calm water with our spare anchor down, the ultimate realization was with us that] there was just one way out, the way we had come in. Early the next morning

[with the dinghy] we made an effort to retrieve the jettisoned anchor and 100 feet of chain . . . but the tide had come in and gone out and the anchor and chain were buried beneath the sand. At 10 a.m., when we judged the tide was as high as it was going to get, the skipper climbed the mast for a final look [before attempting the entrance]. The best bet seemed straight out, a different route from our [near disastrous] entry. Even so, the new route led over two solid rows of breakers at a distance of 150 yards from shore. We weighed anchor and out we went with the skipper in the spreaders [to con the vessel] and a [helmsman] at the tiller as the boat began to rise and fall with the swells. [A course was chosen] where the waves broke least heavily. Two great lurches and we were over and out, but all hands could see sand being churned up in the breakers on each side of us. The whole operation had taken about 12 minutes. [We were thankful] for an inordinate amount of luck [and] for a well built, sturdy boat."

Boca de Soledad, the southernmost and principal entrance to this chain of coastal lagoons, is situated 13½ miles southward of Boca de Santo Domingo, about 50 miles southward

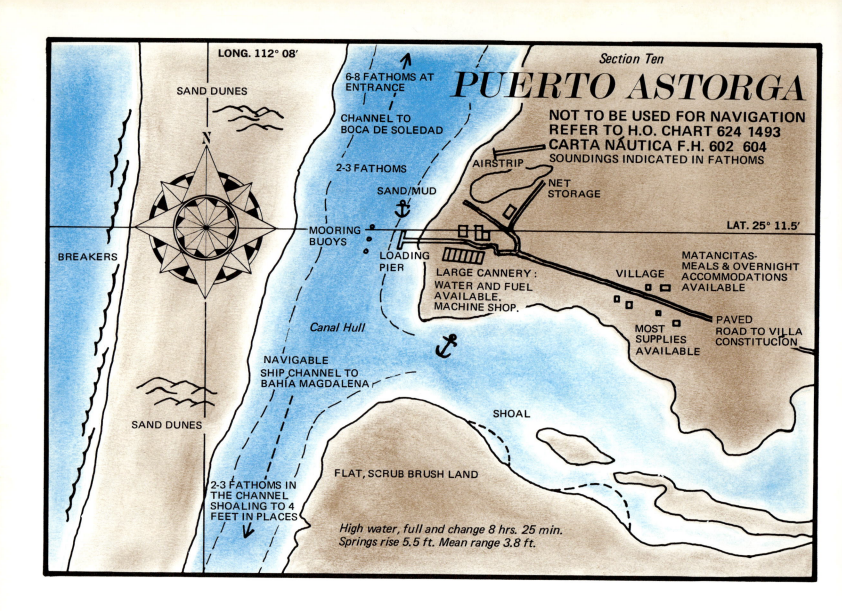

Section Ten

PUERTO ASTORGA

LONG. 112° 08'

SAND DUNES

6-8 FATHOMS AT ENTRANCE

CHANNEL TO BOCA DE SOLEDAD

2-3 FATHOMS

SAND/MUD

AIRSTRIP

NET STORAGE

LAT. 25° 11.5'

N

BREAKERS

MOORING BUOYS

LOADING PIER

LARGE CANNERY: WATER AND FUEL AVAILABLE. MACHINE SHOP.

VILLAGE

MATANCITAS-MEALS & OVERNIGHT ACCOMMODATIONS AVAILABLE

Canal Hull

MOST SUPPLIES AVAILABLE

PAVED ROAD TO VILLA CONSTITUCION

NAVIGABLE SHIP CHANNEL TO BAHÍA MAGDALENA

SAND DUNES

SHOAL

2-3 FATHOMS IN THE CHANNEL SHOALING TO 4 FEET IN PLACES

FLAT, SCRUB BRUSH LAND

High water, full and change 8 hrs. 25 min.
Springs rise 5.5 ft. Mean range 3.8 ft.

of Punta San Juanico and about 30 miles northward of Cape San Lázaro. The entrance is marked on either side by a ridge of sand hills 50 to 100 feet high. A *shallow bank,* over which the sea breaks, extends about 3 miles westward and southward from the northern side of Boca de Soledad. At high water and in moderate weather the entrance channels will generally be plainly marked by smooth water between the lines of breakers; at low water and in heavy weather the entrance is almost totally obscured by breakers extending for a considerable distance offshore. The broadest and deepest channel into the lagoon is situated on the southern side of the entrance although passage may be had close aboard the northern shore. A *shoal bank,* marked by breakers, lies between the two entrance channels just outside the mouth. When making for the entrance from northward, breakers appear from offshore to completely cover the entire mouth. The *entrance channel,* close along the northern shore, is narrow and doesn't open up to view until a vessel is well inside the outer breaking shoals. For this reason it is well-advised to sail southerly of the entrance, then enter through the southerly channel from the southwest; the *channel* here is wider and deeper with breakers on both sides less hazardous marking the entrance more clearly. *Shoal water* borders the seaward side of the southern entrance point and extends westward for a considerable distance offshore; a 2½-fathom spot about 1 mile southward of the southern entrance point breaks at half tide as does most of the rest of the shoal water at the mouth of the en-

trance channel. Passage through this channel is made with breakers close aboard both port and starboard and way must be kept on a vessel to avoid being carried aground by the turbulent currents. There is a bight just inside the southern

TYCHEE

Hull Canal with Puerto Astorga and Matancitas in the background

entrance point large enough for several small craft to swing at anchor.

When attempting the entrance to the lagoon, anchors and cable should be rigged and ready for instant emergency use to prevent broaching in case of grounding in the surf line. Entrance or exit should be scheduled at high water and slack tide as the ebb and flow of tidal currents through the mouth run at times as much as 5 knots. As heretofore cautioned, the entrance channel should be first carefully conned from a small boat and buoyed, if necessary. One should not attempt to enter under sail alone if his vessel is equipped with adequate and reliable mechanical power. Familiarity with the conditions at Boca de Soledad after an initial passage will ease the effort of crossing the bar and negotiating the entrance channel. A small coastal freighter as well as several commercial fishing vessels use this entrance regularly and tie up at the cannery wharf about 5 miles down the channel.

Within the lagoon the navigable channel broadens to the southward as far as the estuary at the mouth of Arroyo de Soledad about 5 miles from the lagoon entrance; thence the channel narrows, and twisting and turning with some few buoy markers, communicates with Magdalena Bay about 30 miles southward. There are several ports and shipping points along the way with improved facilities. Puerto Astorga, referred to as Matancitas by the local inhabitants after the name of a small settlement nearby and as Puerto Adolfo Lopéz Matéos on some charts, is an important fishing port with a modern cannery, refrigeration plant and wharf established on the mainland side of the lagoon at the mouth of the estuary at Arroyo Soledad. Some dredging of the channel to broaden and deepen it has been done in the vicinity of the wharf. The fish plant, when in full operation,

employs about 250 people and mostly supports the adjacent village of 1,200 people. A very good *airstrip* is located adjacent to the cannery alongside a large flat net drying area. A deep well provides an adequate quantity of *water* but the quality is poor. A road connects Puerto Astorga cannery and village with Villa Constitución, a large farming center about 28 miles inland, as well as connecting to the trans-peninsular highway.

Inland from Matancitas, about 12 miles up Arroyo de Soledad at the meeting of four dirt roads, is a collection of shacks clustered around a garden and orchard, once the headquarters of the Lower California Company, an enterprising group of American speculators who in 1866 controlled about five-sixths of the entire Lower California Peninsula through a concession from the Mexican Government. Around 1870 three shiploads of American colonists arrived to settle and develop the land, but their high expectations born of the promoters' oversell and their lack of preparation to deal with an essentially arid environment rendered the colonizing effort a complete failure, and left the colonizers to straggle back home as best they could.

Mantancitas is served by a fleet of three small purse seiners of 35- to 50-ton capacity and a small coastal freighter that brings supplies and loads processed fish products for shipment to market in Ensenada, La Paz and mainland Mexico.

ANCHORAGE — Secure anchorage may be taken north of the cannery wharf with the stern kedged ashore over a bottom of sand and mud. Be careful to sound the depth and allow for tidal variation; keep sufficiently clear of the fairway approaching the wharf so as not to obstruct the oc-

Approach to "Devil's Bend", looking south

Boca de Soledad, Matancitas

casional ship traffic utilizing the wharf. When taking water, fuel, or provisions, vessels may tie up along the face of the wharf with permission from the manager of the cannery. A *better anchorage* closer to the town is available for shoal draft vessels within the Arroyo de Soledad estuary that extends inland off the main lagoon ¼ mile south of the wharf.

CURRENTS AND TIDES — Tidal currents ebb and flow in this estuary and in the lagoon and precaution must be taken to prevent swinging and fouling the anchor. Anchorage fore and aft is recommended. The mean high water interval in the lagoon is 8 hours, 25 minutes; the spring range is 5.5 feet, the mean range is 3.8 feet.

INLAND WATERWAY — Boca de Soledad to Magdalena Bay. While shoal draft boats regularly use the northern part of La Laguna (the local name for the interconnecting lagoons beginning just north of Boca de las Ánimas) for water transport of small cargo, the principal and deeper channel begins at Boca de Soledad and runs for 40 miles southward connecting to Bahía Magdalena. This navigable channel, completely protected from the sea for its entire length, varies from about 50 feet in depth at the mouths of the lagoons to a little more than 4 feet in some shoal places, and has a width of as much as several hundred yards to as little as 30 feet. A local vessel has carried a draft of 4 feet regularly from Boca de Soledad through to Magdalena Bay in cargo. A spring tide would allow a vessel of somewhat deeper draft to make the same passage if properly piloted through the twisting channels. Local fishermen at Matancitas who know the navigable channels may be hired for such pilotage though care should be taken to ascertain the validity of their knowledge.

The waterway runs broad and very nearly straight for about 13 miles southward of Boca de Soledad with some sand islets and shoals located principally on the mainland side of the channel. The lagoon then broadens into a larger

open expanse of water for the next 5 miles with a number of shallow coves and inlets. Tidal flow entering from the north at Boca de Soledad and from the south at Magdalena Bay meet in relatively slack water at the southern end of this section of La Laguna. The ebb and flow of the tidal currents increase in velocity as one approaches either the entrance at Boca de Soledad or Magdalena Bay. The continuation of the navigable channel twists and turns as it threads its course through a 4-mile maze called Devil's Bend where 90° turns through an extremely short radius are required to keep to the channel, which is bouyed in places. Beyond Devil's Bend to the southward the channel connects to Hull Canal which bends to the westward threading its way through 8 miles of mangrove islets and shoal bars to the northern end of Magdalena Bay. About 17 miles southward of Punta Edie, the northern entrance to Hull Canal, one may gain access to the sea through the deepwater entrance of Magdalena Bay.

SEA AND WEATHER CONDITIONS — South of Boca de las Ánimas and as far as Magdalena Bay, a significant change in weather may be encountered. During the fall

"Devil's Bend", looking toward Magdalena Bay

and early winter months fogs are frequent, forming over the lagoons and Bahía Magdalena, then driven seaward by easterly winds which rise in the night and blow during the early morning hours, covering the coastal areas with light to moderately heavy mists. When the sea breeze begins to blow, it drives the fog back over the land; this coastal strip usually clears around noon. Warm weather with light southwesterly and northwesterly winds accompanied usually by a very smooth sea prevails during these months. Northers do not generally blow this far south. After the rains of the late summers the otherwise barren, sage-covered desert of the Magdalena Plain may bloom with abundant green vegetation and wild flowers.

FACILITIES — Fuel, both diesel and gasoline, water (poor quality), fresh and dry provisions, canned fish products (sardines, herring, shrimp, bonita, skipjack, tuna) when the cannery is operating, lubricating oil, butane and ice, are all generally available at the cannery or in the town; there are no boatyard facilities as such but welding and machine work are available at the cannery in emergency.

COMMUNICATIONS — Radio communications are maintained at the cannery with all points.

TRANSPORTATION — A company plane is based at the cannery when it is in operation. Supply trucks make regular runs between Matancitas, Villa Constitución, Puerto San Carlos on Magdalena Bay and La Paz.

PUBLIC ACCOMMODATIONS — Meals and refreshments are available in the town; overnight accommodations, when not in use by visiting cannery personnel for which they are principally provided, may be had at very reasonable rates.

MARINE EMERGENCIES — A Mexican Naval Station is maintained and manned at Puerto Cortez in Magdalena Bay about 60 miles distant by inland waterway or by open sea. A Mexican Naval vessel is permanently stationed there ready to render aid if needed. The station may be contacted by radio on 2182 kHz or 156.8 mHz, VHF Channel 16 ship-to-shore radiotelephone.

MEDICAL FACILITIES — First aid is available in the village at Matancitas; a *doctor* is in residence and there is a small *hospital,* at Villa Constitución; a *hospital* is located at La Paz and may be reached by plane.

SOURCES OF ADDITIONAL INFORMATION — Pesquera Matancitas, S. A., Puerto Astorga, B. Cfa., Mexico. (See also Appendix.)

The coast, between Boca de Soledad and Cabo San Lázaro is low and sandy with sand dunes from 10 to 25 feet high, and tends in a southerly direction, a distance of about 30 miles. This coastal strip is actually a part of 50-mile-long Magdalena Island, isolated from the mainland through the channel at Boca de Soledad. The waterways of the interconnecting lagoons that extend southward just back of the intervening strip of beach ultimately join Magdalena Bay. The surf rolls in heavily on a broad and shallow shelf with many tiers of breakers cresting a good distance offshore. The current sets inshore along this coast at times as much as 1½ knots, and numerous vessels over the years have been lost by stranding on the lee shore. A large freighter, upright and stern-to, stands wedged ashore 3½ miles northward of Cabo San Lázaro. Other wrecks, some since covered by sand, litter the hook of the strand northward of Cape San Lázaro. *A good example of the danger posed by this lee shore may be read from the log of Gamin, racing southward in 1961 with a sizable fleet of yachts from Los Angeles to Mazatlán:*

In an effort to keep up speed, on Thursday we stayed on an onshore tack a little too long perhaps but [finally] came about as we dropped down to six knots. We were holding a course of 135° and for a short time making a slower but comfortable 5½ knots. There is something beautiful about the night sea with its white-crested waves, the wind making small whistlings in the rigging, the creak of the hull as a boat settles into a long swell or sticks her nose up out of a bow wave. All of us felt the beauty of it; it was difficult to leave the helm.

The . . . spinnaker was drawing well and the big main was quiet and full of wind. It was a satisfying time to be at sea. Despite [minor problems] we had come over 600 miles safely.

Then all hell broke loose! [We] heard a roaring behind [us] and looked back to see a tremendous wave bearing down on us at what seemed a terrific speed and high over our hull. [A crew member] shouted, "My God, we're on a reef! With a yell he jumped for the companionway and shouted to the below-deck watch, "Emergency! Emergency! Get on deck! Quick! We're on a reef!" Then we hit! Two quick jolts and *Gamin* was free. [We] thought thank God, she's bounced over into deep water! Then she hit again with a tremendous crash. One huge comber had picked her up, held her for a moment high in the air, then thrown her violently into the hard bottom of the sea. Another breaker did the same. Then another. The noise was terrific.

The *Gamin* began to come apart. The mast came down with a crunch and flailed away in the tumbling sea like a demoniacal thing trying to escape the wire shrouds holding it. Huge pieces of the mast swung through the darkness as though wielded by devils. The main billowed out in the water, was flung back into the boat with a mad fury. Breakers came incessantly high overhead and plunged down on us to fill our throats with water, twist us from side to side in the narrow cockpit and wrench at our arms. The noise was . . . deafening with the surf roaring down on us, the hull pounding in the surf, the men cursing the balky life raft fastenings, the skipper shouting, "Cast off the damn raft before someone gets killed!" [Then] we were in the sea."

We were all rocked pretty hard and consumed with remorse, thinking that something could have been done to avoid the grounding. [We soon began to] realize that during [that] last half hour on the wheel nothing could have been done; the die had long been cast, everyone said. As we were to learn later, it had been cast for us since sunset when the tropical darkness would keep us from seeing the land as we were set into it by uncharted (sic) currents. With the spinnaker guy, foreguy and top-ping lift, and mainsail set with preventer, a boom vang and the mainsheet, there wasn't a chance in the minute or so between the time we saw the first huge wave and the time we hit the beach, to get *Gamin* around. If we had gotten her pointed nearer the wind, could we have gotten out through those huge seas? None of us thought so. [At dawn] the rugged height rising from the beach to the south was quickly identified as Mount San Lázaro; from it Cabo San Lázaro jutted out [to sea]. The *Gamin* had gone aground about 9 miles north of the Cape.

Richard Fenton's well-told experience in 1961 stands as a tragic but eloquent warning to guard against inshore sets along this open coast.

Navigation note: When running southward with big following seas, a conventional taffrail log has a tendency to underread actual distance run, the percentage of error dependent on the size of the vessel.

Cabo San Lázaro is the northwestern extremity of a remarkable headland of volcanic origin; the cliffs about this headland are bold and rocky, the land within rising abruptly to rugged mountainous hills of which Monte San Lázaro, the highest, attains an altitude of 1,275 feet. When first sighted upon approaching from seaward, Cabo San Lázaro appears as an island in contrast with the surrounding low-lying land from which it rises. The cape has been reported to give *good radar returns* up to 43 miles. A *navigation light* is shown 230 feet above the sea from a square white concrete tower and exhibits a **flashing white light every 5 seconds,** visible in an arc from 330° through 242° for a distance of 16 miles in clear weather. A small light-keeper's dwelling is built as part of the light tower; the light is attended and generally reliable.

Along the shore of this headland there are numerous outlying rocks, and strong tide rips have been encountered about 1½ miles southwestward of San Lázaro Light. The current near the cape sets southeastward at about 1 to 1½ knots.

Cabo San Lázaro

The Cape San Lázaro area is frequently windswept, as is common around all promontories, and is known as one of the most dangerous capes of the Pacific coast. On February 22, 1870 the American steamer *Golden City,* carrying as part of her cargo ½ million dollars worth of gold and silver bullion and specie, foundered and sank in 9 fathoms off the cape; none of this cargo has ever been reported as salvaged nor is the exact location known.

From Cape San Lázaro the coast runs southeastward about 3½ miles to Punta Hughes (Hughes Point) the low, rocky southeastern extremity of the Monte San Lázaro volcanic formation. Beyond Hughes Point the land abruptly recedes to the northward, sweeping around to the east and to the south in a great semicircular basin with a low sandy beach forming Bahía Santa María (Santa María Bay) 7 miles wide between the headlands, and indented more than 4 miles from a line projected between them. The shore of this bay is comprised of a low, narrow sand beach with low sand hills grown with patches of bushes, behind which is the channel leading from the northwestern end of Bahía Magdalena to the lagoons farther northward. Santa María Lagoon, a small marshy saltwater inlet, opens in the northwestern corner of the bay and penetrates the shore along the northwestern side of the Monte San Lázaro formation. *Good Anchorage* may be had in the northwestern bight of the bay in the lee of the abrupt cliffs northward of Punta Hughes, about midway between the point and the lagoon estuary in 4 to 8 fathoms, sand bottom, ½ to ¾ miles from the beach. The soundings in the bay are very irregular, increasing from 3 fathoms near the shore to 20 fathoms across the entrance. This bay is protected from all but southerly weather, but a rather heavy surf with large breakers rolls in along the 12-mile arc of the sandy beach. *Landing is* best made near the mouth of the lagoon. The bay has a strange fascination: stark in its seclusion, primordial in its isolation, clean, unused and rarely visited. Gulls wheel overhead fishing the bay; whales may be frequently seen during the spring and summer months close ashore on their way into Bahía Magdalena immediately southward.

Cabo Corso, at the southern end of Bahía de Santa María, is a bold rocky point formed by dark-colored hills that rise abruptly 600 feet and, in marked contrast, is fronted by white sand bluffs 70 to 80 feet high.

Morro Howland (Howland's Bluff) is situated about 1 mile north-northeastward of Cabo Corso. The coast between Cabo Corso and Punta Entrada, about 9 miles southeastward, is a succession of rocky points and intervening sand beaches fringed in places with numerous detached rocks close offshore. The land rises abruptly to heights of more than 1,000 feet; Monte Isabel, the highest peak, rises to an elevation of 1,250 feet. Punta Roja (Red Point) is situated about 2½ miles southeastward of Cabo Corso; and Punta Magdalena about 2½ miles west-north-westward of Punta Entrada; between the two points the coast recedes slightly, forming a shallow bay about 4½ miles wide.

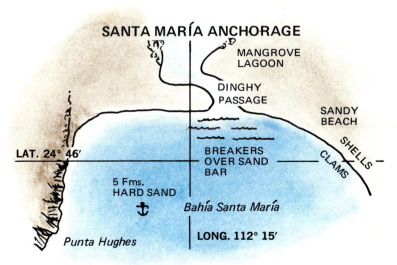

SANTA MARÍA ANCHORAGE

MANGROVE LAGOON

DINGHY PASSAGE

SANDY BEACH

SHELLS

CLAMS

LAT. 24° 46'

5 Fms. HARD SAND

BREAKERS OVER SAND BAR

Bahía Santa María

Punta Hughes

LONG. 112° 15'

SECTION 11
CABO SAN LÁZARO to
CABO TOSCO
(Including Bahía de Magdalena)

Cabo San Lázaro with Punta Hughes and Cabo Corso in the background

Bahía Magdalena (Magdalena Bay) is the largest deepwater, all-weather harbor on the Pacific coast of Baja California. It is located 615 miles southeastward of the Port of San Diego; 272 miles from Turtle Bay; 165 miles northwestward of Cabo San Lucas. The deepwater entrance to the bay is situated 22 miles southeastward of Cabo San Lázaro at Latitude 24° 32′ north, Longitude 112° 03′ west. For navigation see United States Oceanographic Office Charts H.O. 1006, H.O. 624, H.O. 1493, and H.O. 1636; British Admiralty Charts #2323, #2324, #3053, and #3054; Mexican Cartas Náuticas F.H. 602, F.H. 604, and F.H. 610.

The northern portion of Magdalena Bay is sheltered behind Isla Magdalena, the coastal strip of land beginning at Boca de Soledad and terminating southward at Punta Entrada which comprises the northern entrance point of the deepwater passage into the bay. The southern portion of the bay is protected behind Isla Santa Margarita, the western end of which, Punta Redondo, forms the opposite entrance point into the bay. Bahía Magdalena is thereby completely protected on all sides, easily accessible from the open sea through a clear deepdraft channel 2½ miles wide and 10 to 19 fathoms in depth, and large enough to accommodate, at safe anchorage, several hundred of the largest vessels presently afloat.

The bay is about 17 miles long northwest and southeast and 12 miles wide with an area of about 80 square miles measured beyond the 5-fathom curve. A narrow but navigable channel runs from the southeastern end of the bay opening beyond Mangrove Island into a large connecting body of water, Bahía Almejas (Almejas Bay) which in turn is protected behind Isla Santa Margarita.

At the northwestern end of Magdalena Bay a series of coastal lagoons extend northward more than 60 miles and provide sheltered inside passage for shoal draft vessels for much of this distance. Access to the northern end of this passage may be had through Boca de Soledad, some 35 miles to the northward of Magdalena Bay and fully described in the previous section.

Punta Hughes with Bahía Santa María to the right

In the 1850's and 60's whalers regularly ascended the canals along these coastal lagoons for a distance of 40 miles in pursuit of their quarry. Several other lagoons open on the northern part of the bay and *shoal water* extends 1 to 2 miles from the northern and eastern shores.

"Narwhal" circa 1883

The land on the northern and eastern sides of the bay is flat, low and sandy, and is covered with cactus and brush, part of the desert vegetation that covers most of the Magdalena Plain. The surrounding countryside is quite barren with a scarcity of fresh water that has discouraged agriculture and settlement. Magdalena Bay, however, provides an important and useful harbor with natural deepwater access for coastal freighters, and a good deepdraft port, Puerto San Carlos, has been developed within the bay for cargo handling.

Bahía Magdalena is entered between Punta Entrada and Punta Redondo. Punta Entrada is a dome-shaped hill about 200 feet high, the southeastern extremity of a high and narrow peninsula that extends southeastward 10 miles from Santa María Bay and forms the western entrance point to Magdalena Bay. The point is connected to the peninsula by a narrow strip of sand and rock only a few feet above high water. Near the point are several outlying rocks 10 to 20 feet high. Roca Vela (Sail Rock) is a small pinnacle rock close southeastward of the point, well defined, which provides a useful mark when approaching from westward. A *reef* over which the sea breaks extends southeastward from the rock for a distance of about 600 yards. A *prominent wreck* lies wedged among the rocks on the shore approximately ½ mile westward of the point. This vessel was attempting to enter Magdalena Bay for shelter during extremely heavy weather, missed the entrance channel and was blown ashore.

Punta Redondo, the eastern entrance point of the bay and the western extremity of Santa Margarita Island, is a round rocky headland about 100 feet high 3¼ miles southeastward of Punta Entrada; the land rises from it to a height of 841 feet at a distance of 1 mile and to 1,691 feet at 5½ miles. A *reef,* at the outer end of which is a *rock awash* and on which the sea breaks heavily, extends about 700 yards westward from Punta Redondo. At the beginning of the spring flood a heavy overfall has been observed at least 400 yards from the extremity of the reef, where there are depths of 7 to 9 fathoms. *Caution: The turbulence of this tidal current can pose a severe danger to small boats and the area should be given a wide berth. There is a clear passage 10 to 19 fathoms deep and about 2¾ miles wide between the dangers on either side of the entrance. Sailing vessels should keep well up toward Entrada Point when making for the entrance, as both wind and current tend to set them down toward Redondo Point.*

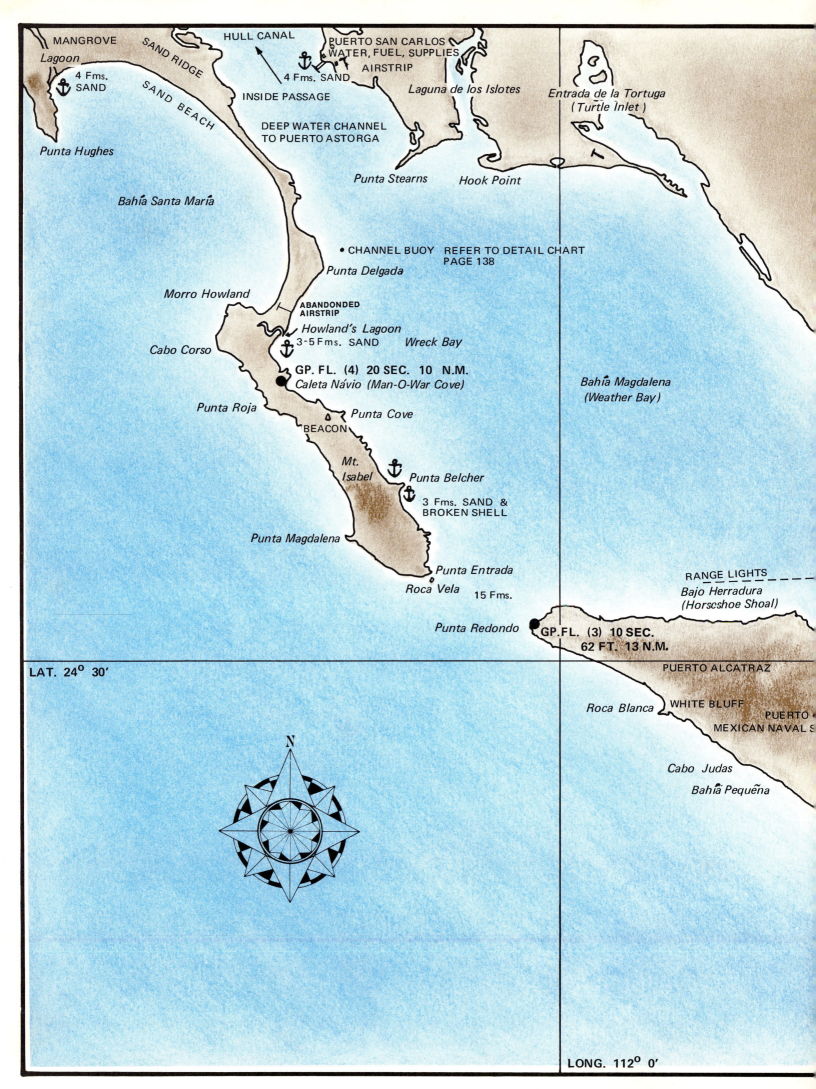

MANGROVE
Lagoon
4 Fms.
SAND
Punta Hughes

SAND RIDGE
SAND BEACH

HULL CANAL
INSIDE PASSAGE

PUERTO SAN CARLOS
WATER, FUEL, SUPPLIES
AIRSTRIP
4 Fms. SAND

DEEP WATER CHANNEL
TO PUERTO ASTORGA

Laguna de los Islotes

Entrada de la Tortuga
(Turtle Inlet)

Bahía Santa María

Punta Stearns   Hook Point

• CHANNEL BUOY   REFER TO DETAIL CHART
PAGE 138

Punta Delgada

Morro Howland

ABANDONDED
AIRSTRIP

Howland's Lagoon
3-5 Fms. SAND   *Wreck Bay*

Cabo Corso

GP. FL. (4) 20 SEC. 10 N.M.
Caleta Návio (Man-O-War Cove)

Bahía Magdalena
(Weather Bay)

Punta Roja

Punta Cove
BEACON

Mt.
Isabel   *Punta Belcher*
3 Fms. SAND &
BROKEN SHELL

Punta Magdalena

Punta Entrada
Roca Vela   15 Fms.

RANGE LIGHTS
Bajo Herradura
(Horseshoe Shoal)

Punta Redondo   GP.FL. (3) 10 SEC.
62 FT. 13 N.M.

LAT. 24° 30'

PUERTO ALCATRAZ

Roca Blanca   WHITE BLUFF   PUERTO
MEXICAN NAVAL S

Cabo Judas
Bahía Pequeña

N

LONG. 112° 0'

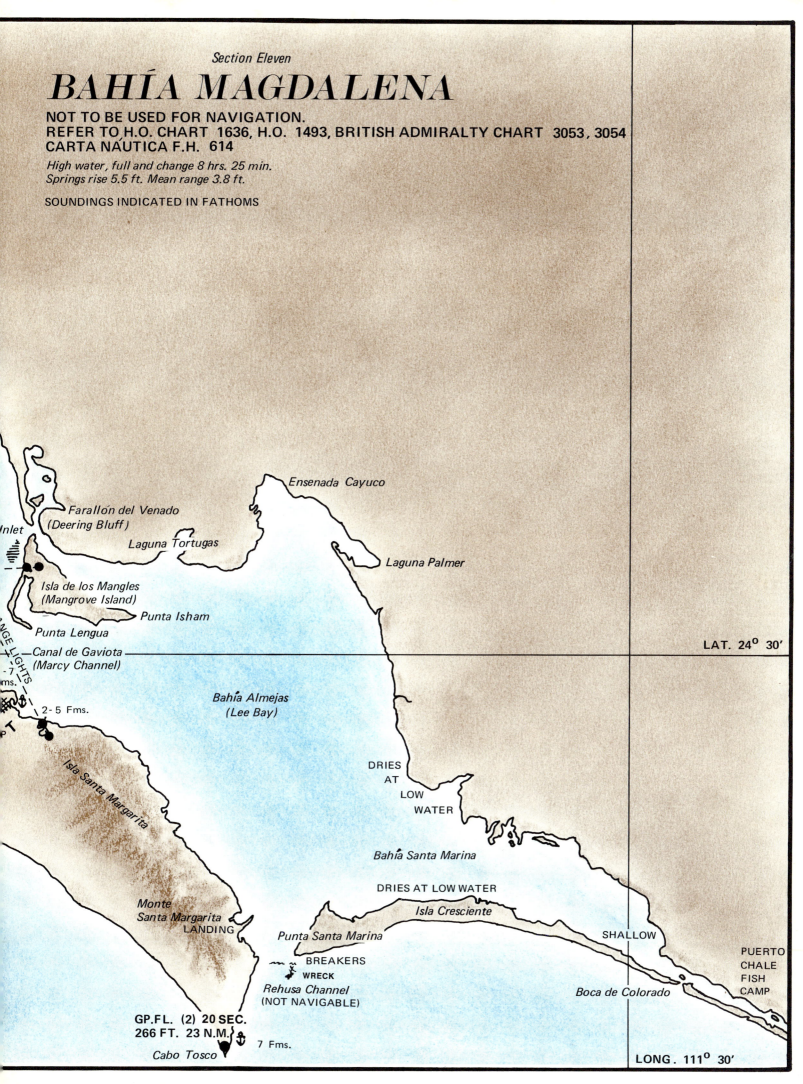

BAHÍA MAGDALENA

NOT TO BE USED FOR NAVIGATION.
REFER TO H.O. CHART 1636, H.O. 1493, BRITISH ADMIRALTY CHART 3053, 3054
CARTA NÁUTICA F.H. 614

High water, full and change 8 hrs. 25 min.
Springs rise 5.5 ft. Mean range 3.8 ft.

SOUNDINGS INDICATED IN FATHOMS

Ensenada Cayuco

Farallón del Venado
(Deering Bluff)

Laguna Tortugas

Laguna Palmer

Inlet

Isla de los Mangles
(Mangrove Island)

Punta Isham

Punta Lengua

Canal de Gaviota
(Marcy Channel)

NGE LIGHTS

7
ms.

LAT. 24° 30'

Bahía Almejas
(Lee Bay)

2- 5 Fms.

DRIES
AT
LOW
WATER

Isla Santa Margarita

Bahía Santa Marina

DRIES AT LOW WATER

Isla Cresciente

Monte
Santa Margarita
LANDING

Punta Santa Marina

SHALLOW

PUERTO
CHALE
FISH
CAMP

BREAKERS
WRECK

Rehusa Channel
(NOT NAVIGABLE)

Boca de Colorado

GP.FL. (2) 20 SEC.
266 FT. 23 N.M.

7 Fms.

Cabo Tosco

LONG. 111° 30'

Entrance to Bahía Magdalena showing Punta Entrada to the left and Punta Redondo to the right

A *navigation light* shown 62 feet above the sea, from a white square masonry tower with a red top on Punta Redondo, displays a **white group flash** of **three flashes every 10 seconds:** flash 0.3 second, eclipse 1.5 seconds; flash 0.3 second, eclipse 1.5 seconds; flash 0.3 second, eclipse 6.1 seconds. It is visible for 13 miles in the sector 330° through 242° in clear weather. The light structure does not stand out clearly against the background of the point and it is difficult to make out when approaching from the northward; it may easily be seen, however, when approaching from the southward. *Navigation note: In the past this light has been reported to be unreliable in that it is often extinguished due to technical difficulties.*

Vessels entering Magdalena Bay for the first time or for temporary shelter enroute along the Pacific coast of the Baja California Peninsula usually make for an easy anchorage under Punta Belcher, about 3 miles northwestward of the entrance after passing Sail Rock abeam, or for Caleta Návio (Man O'War Cove) about 5 miles further northwestward. The bay is deep and clear of dangers to within 250 yards of the shore here, except in the bight close southward of Punta Belcher where *shoal water* extends ½ mile from the shore and ¼ mile outside the point. *Directions: A vessel should keep Punta Entrada aboard when entering Bahía Magdalena as both the prevailing wind and the current tend to set towards Punta Redondo. If bound for Man O'War Cove care must be taken to avoid the shoal close southward of Punta Belcher. A course paralleling the shore*

at a distance off of about 1 mile should be steered between Sail Rock and Man O'War Cove. A course line drawn from Sail Rock tangent to the shore northward clears the outer edge of the sandspit off Belcher Point and may be used as a danger bearing.

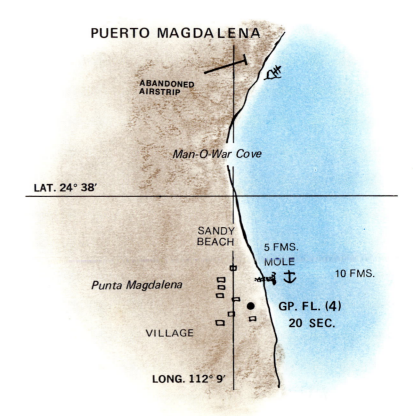

Punta Redondo

Belcher Point is a flat, sandy triangular-shaped shelf of land projecting from the shore about ½ mile eastward of Mount Isabel which looms above it. The land is sparsely covered with low bushes and a group of fishermen's shacks occupies the seaward tip back of a very gradually sloping sand beach with scarcely a ripple of surf along its shores. On the northwestern shore of the point a group of large black iron tanks stand, together with rusting winches, mincing tables, boilers and trying pots, the remnant works of large-scale whaling operations conducted in Magdalena Bay principally during the 1850's and 60's, and to a diminishing degree as late as the first part of the 1930's.

Belcher Point

Morro Howland and Cabo Corso

Punta Belcher and Mount Isabel

Dozens of whaling vessels plied the waters of the bay during the whaling seasons, and the activity here exceeded in number of ships and men, even that carried on in Scammon's Lagoon 300 miles to the northward. While Scammon's Lagoon attracted a greater concentration of the migrating whales, it was far more difficult for a ship's captain to safely negotiate the tricky lagoon entrance than to enter through the deep, wide mouth of Magdalena Bay, open to the sea and free of dangers. A great pile of large whalebones, bleached by the wind and sun, is still to be seen along the beach at Belcher Point.

Good anchorage may be taken in the center of the bight southward of Belcher's Point in 2½ to 3 fathoms over a sand and broken shell bottom. The regular ebb and flow of the tidal current sweeps around the point and into the bight, setting over the sandspit off Punta Belcher at a rate of from 1 to 2 knots. The prevailing breeze blows from north to south. *Landing* is safe and easily effected anywhere along the shore. There is no fresh water and there are no developed facilities; the area is quite barren but the old whaling station works is worth a look. Sebastián Vizcaíno anchored the vessels of his expedition under the lee of this

Punta Entrada and Punta Belcher, looking north

Man O'War Cove

point in July, 1602. Belcher's Point was named after Captain Edward Belcher, commanding the British survey vessels HMS *Sulfur* and *Starling* in 1837 and 1839. On an old English chart surveyed for the British Admiralty by Captain Belcher, a source of fresh water is shown at Belcher Point and at Cove Point.

Caleta del Navio (Man O'War Cove) is situated about 5 miles northwestward of Belcher Point. It lies between Punta Cove and Punta Delgada, the former situated 2½ miles northwestward of Punta Belcher, the latter 3½ miles northward of Man O'War Cove. A *shoal spit* extends about 2½ miles south-southeastward from Punta Delgada.

Puerto Magdalena is a small village situated on the west shore of Man O'War Cove, 7½ miles northwestward of Entrada Point. A scattering of shacks accommodates a handful of fishermen and their wives and families. A short stone mole in disrepair extends a few feet into the bay. Once a Port Captain was permanently stationed here and had the authority to clear foreign vessels as their first or last port of call in Mexico. Now clearance is obtained at Puerto San Carlos or at the Naval Base at Puerto Cortez.

The ruins of a sizable warehouse, with little left save the concrete foundation, is located on the rise near the Port Captain's residence. Puerto Magdalena was formerly the headquarters for Flores, Hale & Company which, after a failure in 1870-71 in a colonization attempt at Matancitas, engaged in an enterprise collecting the Orchilla plant, a common looking gray moss that grows abundantly throughout the area surrounding Magdalena Bay. Orchilla is a parasitic lichen that hangs in festoons from the native trees and bushes and from which a valuable organic dye was extracted. The warehouse was constructed for storage of the baled dye plant and a long wooden pier, long since carried away by storm, was built out into the bay from the head of the mole.

A *navigation light,* shown 30 feet above the sea from a red metal column on the mole in Man O'War Cove, exhibits a **white group flash** of **four flashes every 20 seconds:** flash 0.5 second, eclipse 1 second; flash 0.5 second, eclipse 1 second; flash 0.5 second, eclipse 1 second; flash 0.5 second, eclipse 15 seconds. While the light is of very low candlepower, it is visible in clear weather for 10 miles through the sector 262° - 296°. *A wooden beacon* with a *triangular topmark* stands on a stone base surmounting a bluff about 1¾ miles southeastward of the Man O'War Cove light structure.

Anchorage may be taken in 3 to 5 fathoms, good holding sand bottom several hundred yards offshore; *anchorage* in depths of 9 to 10 fathoms may be had ½ mile from shore with the light bearing 274°; *anchorage* in a depth of 13 fathoms may be had ¾ to 1 mile offshore, with Belcher Point and the right tangent of Redondo Point in range bearing 140° and Man O'War Cove Light bearing 254°. Tidal streams in Man O'War Cove generally run nearly northward and southward and at a rate considerably less than in other parts of the bay. This is considered the best anchorage in the bay for all seasons but if the wind should be southerly, which is not often the case, sheltered *anchorage* may be obtained in the southern part of the bay under the lee of Isla Santa Margarita described in a further paragraph.

TIDES — The mean high water interval at full and change in Magdalena Bay is 8 hours, 25 minutes; the spring range is 5.5 feet, the mean range, 3.8 feet.

The northwestern portion of Magdalena Bay is much encumbered with *shoals* and *sandbanks* separated by navigable channels in which there are depths of 3 to 12 fathoms. These channels lead to the inland waterway of the coastal lagoons to the northward, previously described. The entrances to these channels lie between Punta Delgada, situated about 9½ miles north-northwestward of Punta Entrada, and Punta Stearns, which lies about 3½ miles further northeastward. *Shoal water* extends about 5 miles southward from Punta Stearns. Punta Edie is situated about 7 miles northward of Punta Delgada and about 5½ miles north-northwestward of Punta Stearns; Canal Hull and Canal San Carlos lead, respectively, westward and eastward of Punta Edie.

Thouars Spit, with a fathom of water over it at the southern end of Tessan Bank, and Dupetit Spit, covered 1½ fathoms at the southern end of Venus Bank, are situated about 5 miles southeastward of Punta Delgada and 5 miles south-southeastward of Punta Stearns, respectively. They should be given an adequately wide berth by deep-draft vessels. In the middle 1800's an English whaling vessel ran aground on Punta Delgada which is so low that in foul weather the sea breaks over the land. The first buildings erected at the village of "Wreck Bay" were constructed from the wrecked ship's timbers.

Deering Inlet, opening at the southern end of the eastern shore, is a shallow inlet much encumbered with shoals.

Tortuga (Turtle) Inlet, opening at the northwestern end of the eastern shore, is a larger inlet but also shallow and encumbered with shoals, particularly at its mouth where tide rips run sometimes with considerable turbulence during ebb and flow. Small boats can negotiate these inlets to their heads, and among the dense growth of mangrove a great variety of birdlife can be seen. Shellfish abound in the mudbanks and flats along the shores and around the shoals that dry at low water. Laguna de Los Islotes, opening just eastward of Punta Stearns on the northern side of the bay, has an entrance bar with 7 feet of water over it and is navigable for a considerable distance inland at high water, with 2½ to 4½ fathoms in the navigable channel.

Punta Stearns (Stearns Point) is situated about 11½ miles northward of Punta Entrada. A small islet overgrown with a mangrove thicket lies southward of the point, separated by a shoal and narrow channel. *Very shoal water* extends a little over a mile eastward and southeastward from the islet forming Venus Bank. An irregular channel with a least depth of 1 fathom leads into Laguna de Islotes between Punta Stearns and Punta Hook. A dirt road communicates with the point from the town of El Refugio about 10 miles inland.

Opposite Stearns Point 2 miles eastward across the mouth of Laguna de Islotes lies Hook Point, a low flat sandy spit encompassing the basin of a small inlet at the mouth of the lagoon. Eastward of Hook Point about 2¼ miles is another small round inlet backed by drainage canals that cut through a mangrove swamp. Eastward of this inlet about 2 miles, and 5½ miles from Punta Stearns, is Punta Médano Amarillo, a yellow bluff 40 to 50 feet high, useful as a piloting mark. A poor *dirt airstrip* is established on the plain back of the point. A *shoal,* portions of which dry, extends over 2 miles eastward of Punta Médano Amarillo nearly to the opposite shore, all but closing off the entrance to Turtle Inlet.

Navigation note: Each occurrence of a severe storm in the area creates a torrential runoff with wind-whipped tides that sometimes tend to cut new channels and silt in the old ones, wash away tidal islets and form new ones. Charts showing detailed channel, shoal and shore configuration are subject to minor annual change. Therefore, when piloting within the shoal portions of Magdalena Bay, careful observation must be exercised at all times and soundings with the lead continually taken.

The Puerto San Carlos facilities are situated on the eastern side of the entrance to Canal de San Carlos, 1½ miles east-southeastward of Punta Edie. It is approached from Bahía Magdalena through a buoyed channel, narrow in places, with a least dredged depth of 25 feet. Landfall Light Buoy, painted white and exhibiting a **white group flashing light** showing Morse code "A," **(short flash, long flash)** is moored with a second light buoy (both equipped with radar reflectors) about 2 miles south-southeastward of Punta Delgada; they mark the entrance to a narrow channel leading northward to Puerto San Carlos. From Landfall Light Buoy the channel leads north-northeastward for about 7 miles, passing Tessan Bank on the starboard hand to a position 2¼ miles southward of Punta Edie; here the channel turns sharply east-southeastward for about 1¾ miles, whence it again leads north-northwestward for 2 miles to the pierhead. The channel is marked inbound on the starboard hand by red-painted light buoys marked with even numbers showing **white or red flashing lights** together with red buoys with triangular topmarks bearing lettered identification. On the port hand the channel is buoyed with black-painted light buoys marked with odd numbers showing **white or green flashing lights** together with black buoys with can-shaped topmarks bearing lettered identification. No. 15 Black Light Buoy exhibiting a **white flashing light** is moored 350 yards west-southwestward of the pierhead and marks the western limit of the turning basin abreast it. *Note: Numbered buoys are lighted; lettered buoys are unlighted.*

When approaching Puerto San Carlos a sharply defined metal warehouse grows steadily larger, looming above the low profile of the flat surrounding land. A squat steel water tank stands high on metal legs close northwestward; a second tank stands farther along the shore. The steel framework of a mechanized bulk loader rises in the foreground on the pierhead and a gantry crane stands alongside the warehouse. Beacons are fixed atop steel poles at either end of the wharf's face. *Anchorage* may be taken off the wharf outside the black can buoy in 4 fathoms, sand, but the area can be windy; adequate scope is well advised.

PORT CLEARANCE — It is customary for foreign vessels to clear their ship's papers with the Captain of the Port permanently stationed here. He is authorized to clear yachts, fishing vessels and commercial cargo ships in and out of Mexico as their first or last port of call. However, there is no immigration or health officer at the port. If such an officer is required, he must be summoned from La Paz with travel time and expenses added to the regular charge.

About 4 miles northeastward of Punta Stearns, at the entrance to Canal de San Carlos, is a modern, recently constructed deepwater port, Puerto San Carlos. It is the shipping port for the agricultural community surrounding Villa Constitución, also known as El Crucero, some 30 miles inland in the Santo Domingo Valley, to which it is connected by a straight, hard-surfaced 2-lane road heavily travelled by cargo trucks.

Canal de San Carlos, noted on early charts as Ballenas Lagoon because of the rich whale fishery conducted along its 12 miles of twisting mangrove-lined canals, extends inland in a northerly direction. For those who have local knowledge of its configuration and its shoals and bars, there is a navigable channel, with a depth of 3 fathoms or more, that runs for a distance of about 9 miles to Punta Providencia and the village of San Carlos. A road connects San Carlos to Matancitas and to the old coastal road which, in turn, enters the new straight, paved highway connecting to Santa Rita, southward, and Santo Domingo, northward. Punta Banderita is situated about 5 miles up the lagoon from Puerto San Carlos, and a small village is located on the shore near Laguna Claco.

At Puerto San Carlos there is a broad dirt mole, Muelle Fiscal, built about 700 yards out on the shore bank to the edge of a deep channel. An "L" shaped jetty and pierhead about 330 feet long extends from the head of the mole; there is a depth of about 42 feet a short distance off the pierhead. A least depth of 17 feet has been reported alongside the pier, causing large vessels to lie aground at low water. Dolphins are placed along the edge of the channel to increase the berthing length to about 500 feet, and mooring buoys are established off both ends of the pierhead for warping cargo vessels alongside and to facilitate shifting.

A steel belt-fed bulk loading tower stands at the end of the jetty and provides a good mark to steer by when making for the dock. A long metal cargo storage shed, painted white, is built at the outer end of the mole. A hard dirt *airstrip* is established at the foot of the mole. A dockmaster and maintenance personnel are in residence and occupy a group of buildings located at the foot of the mole.

Puerto San Carlos

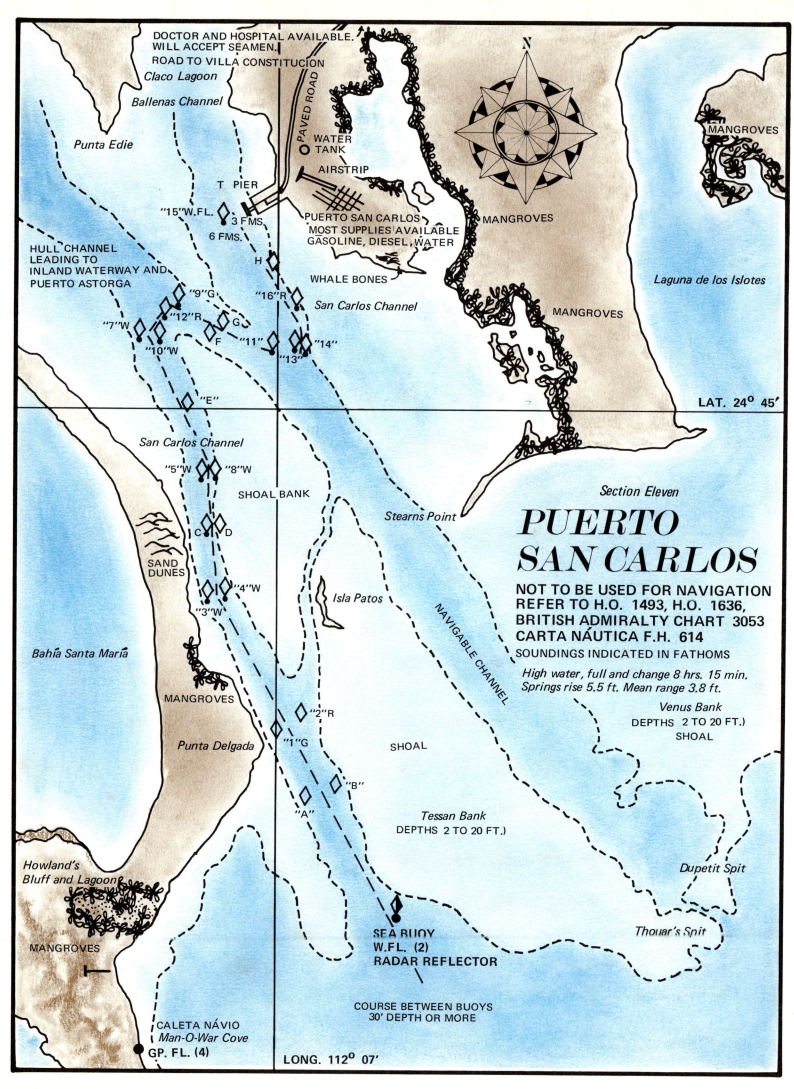

DOCTOR AND HOSPITAL AVAILABLE.
WILL ACCEPT SEAMEN.
ROAD TO VILLA CONSTITUCION

Claco Lagoon

Ballenas Channel

Punta Edie

PAVED ROAD

WATER TANK

AIRSTRIP

T PIER

"15"W.FL.

3 FMS.

6 FMS.

PUERTO SAN CARLOS
MOST SUPPLIES AVAILABLE
GASOLINE, DIESEL, WATER

MANGROVES

MANGROVES

Laguna de los Islotes

HULL CHANNEL
LEADING TO
INLAND WATERWAY AND
PUERTO ASTORGA

H

WHALE BONES

"9"G

"16"R

San Carlos Channel

"7"W

"12"R

"10"W

G

F

"11"

"14"

"13"

MANGROVES

"E"

LAT. 24° 45'

San Carlos Channel

"5"W

"8"W

SHOAL BANK

Stearns Point

Section Eleven

PUERTO SAN CARLOS

NOT TO BE USED FOR NAVIGATION
REFER TO H.O. 1493, H.O. 1636,
BRITISH ADMIRALTY CHART 3053
CARTA NÁUTICA F.H. 614
SOUNDINGS INDICATED IN FATHOMS

*High water, full and change 8 hrs. 15 min.
Springs rise 5.5 ft. Mean range 3.8 ft.*

C

D

SAND DUNES

"4"W

"3"W

Isla Patos

NAVIGABLE CHANNEL

Venus Bank
DEPTHS 2 TO 20 FT.)
SHOAL

Bahía Santa María

MANGROVES

Punta Delgada

"2"R

"1"G

"B"

SHOAL

Tessan Bank
DEPTHS 2 TO 20 FT.)

Dupetit Spit

"A"

Howland's
Bluff and Lagoon

MANGROVES

SEA BUOY
W.FL. (2)
RADAR REFLECTOR

Thouar's Spit

COURSE BETWEEN BUOYS
30' DEPTH OR MORE

CALETA NÁVIO
Man-O-War Cove
GP. FL. (4)

LONG. 112° 07'

Puerto San Carlos

Detail of pier and anchorage at Puerto San Carlos

FACILITIES AND SERVICES — The modern concrete wharf, lined on its face with rubber truck tires, warps ocean-going freighters alongside, utilizing offlying mooring buoys. Sacks of grain and bales of cotton grown on nearby farmland are frequently piled at dockside. Good potable water is piped to the dock under a considerable head; there is no charge for the small amounts taken aboard yachts but the fire hose supply with no reducer presents a problem of loading. Diesel fuel is piped to the wharf; gasoline may be purchased in 55-gallon drums, regular or premium. A machine shop and competent mechanics are available. A 375-horsepower tug is available at all times for service within the bay. Divers are available and an electronic technician can be obtained. Various stores, supplies and fresh provisions may be purchased but the selection is small and the quantities limited.

COMMUNICATIONS — The Port Administration Office maintains a radio watch on 2182 kiloHertz and 500 kiloHertz at 15 to 18 minutes and 45 to 48 minutes after each hour from 0900 to 1300 and 1500 to 1800 local time (7 hours slow of Greenwich) and will respond in Spanish or English when called. A good paved road links Puerto San Carlos with Villa Constitución, distant 34 miles, and with La Paz, 162 miles. Regularly scheduled passenger and cargo flights link Tijuana, Ensenada, Guerrero Negro, Santa Rosalia, Loreto, Villa Constitución, Puerto San Carlos, and La Paz; air flights also leave Villa Constitución

Laguna de los Islotes

for Los Mochis and Guaymas on the mainland. Aero taxis are available from La Paz.

MEDICAL FACILITIES — There is a Navy physician at the port; a 6-bed hospital and two 5-bed clinics at Villa Constitución will accept seamen. There are several additional Navy physicians and a military hospital at Puerto Cortez, across the bay on Magdalena Island.

SOURCES OF ADDITIONAL INFORMATION — Captainia del Puerto, Operación Portuaria, San Carlos B.C., P.O. Box 170, Villa Constitución, B. Cfa., Mexico. (See also Appendix.)

The old-time whalers who frequented the bay around the middle 1800's called the natural division between Magdalena Bay proper and Almejas Bay southward "Weather" and "Lee" Bays, respectively.

Within the bay a *shoal,* with a least depth over it of 4¼ fathoms, lies about ¾ of a mile offshore about 4½ miles eastward of Punta Redondo. Canal de Gaviota (Marcy Channel) described below, is situated in the southeastern corner of the bay and leads into Bahía de Almejas. *Two shoals* on either side, with less than 1 fathom in places, confine this channel to narrow limits. Mangrove Island is situated on the eastern side of Marcy Channel. *Navigation caution: While the largest portion of Magdalena Bay is deep and navigable, shoals extend from 1 to 2 miles offshore on its eastern and northern sides, and caution should be exercised when approaching this shore.*

Canal de Gaviota (Marcy Channel), off the southeastern end of Magdalena Bay, is a deep but narrow channel connecting Bahía Magdalena and Bahía Almejas. The channel is about 1 mile wide between the shoals that restrict its navigable width and it has charted mid-channel depths of 12 to 16 fathoms. From deep water in Magdalena Bay to the western entrance of the channel, a distance of about 4½ miles, there is a least charted depth of 5¼ fathoms.

The western approach to Canal de Gaviota lies between Bajo de la Herradura (Horseshoe Shoal), extending out from the southwestern side of the channel, and Bajo California (California Shoal) on the northeastern side. Horseshoe Shoal, with depths over it of less than 3 fathoms, extends about 1 mile northeastward from the northern shore of Isla Santa Margarita, about 8 miles eastward of Punta Redondo; there is a very *shoal spot,* with a depth over it of 3 to 4 feet on its outer edge, that extends further into Gaviota Channel than is shown on H.O. Chart 1636. California Shoal, with a least depth of 1 fathom over its southern edge, lies about 1 mile northward of Horseshoe Shoal. With an ebbing tidal stream there are breakers on both California Shoal and Horseshoe Shoal, even when the sea is smooth

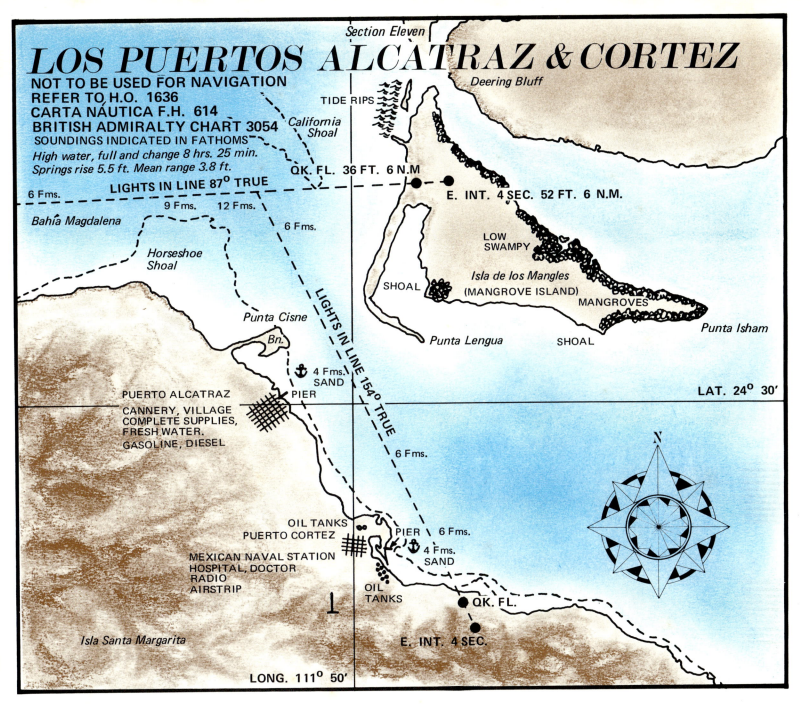

LOS PUERTOS ALCATRAZ & CORTEZ

Section Eleven

NOT TO BE USED FOR NAVIGATION
REFER TO H.O. 1636
CARTA NÁUTICA F.H. 614
BRITISH ADMIRALTY CHART 3054
SOUNDINGS INDICATED IN FATHOMS
High water, full and change 8 hrs. 25 min.
Springs rise 5.5 ft. Mean range 3.8 ft.

Deering Bluff

TIDE RIPS

California Shoal

QK. FL. 36 FT. 6 N.M.

E. INT. 4 SEC. 52 FT. 6 N.M.

LIGHTS IN LINE 87° TRUE

6 Fms.

Bahía Magdalena

9 Fms.   12 Fms.

6 Fms.

Horseshoe Shoal

LOW SWAMPY

Isla de los Mangles
(MANGROVE ISLAND)

SHOAL

MANGROVES

LIGHTS IN LINE 154° TRUE

Punta Cisne

Bn.

Punta Lengua   SHOAL   Punta Isham

4 Fms. SAND

PUERTO ALCATRAZ
CANNERY, VILLAGE
COMPLETE SUPPLIES,
FRESH WATER.
GASOLINE, DIESEL

PIER

LAT. 24° 30'

6 Fms.

N

OIL TANKS
PUERTO CORTEZ

PIER   6 Fms.

4 Fms. SAND

MEXICAN NAVAL STATION
HOSPITAL, DOCTOR
RADIO
AIRSTRIP

OIL TANKS

QK. FL.

Isla Santa Margarita

E. INT. 4 SEC.

LONG. 111° 50'

and the swell hardly perceptible.

The northeastern side of the channel is bordered by shoal ground extending southward from Mangrove Island. A *bank,* with depths over it of less than 5 fathoms, extends to a position about 3½ miles westward of the western end of California Shoal.

Range lights are established in *two ranges* to guide the mariner safely through the channel. Mangrove Island Range, about 1 mile southward of the northern extremity of Mangrove Island, comprises a **range front light,** exhibiting a **quick white flash** from a red iron tower 36 feet above the sea and visible for 6 miles in clear weather (a *red and white checkered square daymark* is affixed to the light structure); and a **rear range light** 650 yards eastward of the first in range 87°, exhibiting an **equal interval white light flashing every four seconds,** 52 feet above the sea from a red iron tower and visible for 6 miles in clear weather.

Directions: Upon entering Gaviota Channel from Magdalena Bay, a course along the Mangrove Range Line should be carried to within about 1½ miles of the western shore of

Mangrove Island whence the Gaviota (Marcy) Channel Range Lights should bear true 154° and the course altered to starboard along this second range line.

The Gaviota (Marcy) Channel Range, established about 3¼ miles southward of Punta Lengua on the northeastern shore of Santa Margarita Island, comprises a **range front light** exhibiting a **quick flashing white light** shown from the top of a black steel pipe set in a white triangular concrete base; and a **range rear light,** located ½ mile southeastward in range 154°, exhibiting an **equal interval flashing white light** shown from the top of another black steel pipe set in a concrete base. These light structures have been reported to be difficult to distinguish in daylight and are rather dimly lit by night. A course aligned along this range carries abeam Punta Cisne, Puerta Alcatraz and Puerto Cortez; the range lights are situated about 1¼ miles southsoutheastward of Puerto Cortez. There is a least known depth of 6 fathoms in the channel along the range line. The narrowest part of Canal de la Gaviota (Marcy Channel) lies between Punta Lengua on the southwestern end of Mangrove Island bnd Punta Cisne on the shore of Isla de

Puerto Alcatraz

Santa Margarita, opposite, about ¾ mile wide between the shoals. A *black pole beacon* stands on Cisne Point. *Note: The ebb and flow of the tidal stream in this channel is sometimes severe and caution should be observed to maintain sufficient way to prevent being set onto shoal ground.*

Bahía Almejas, about 12 miles long and 8 miles wide, is well protected by the high, dormant, volcanic Isla de Santa Margarita (Santa Margarita Island). On the northern and eastern sides of this bay are *extensive shoals* and the southeastern portion of the bay is filled with *shoals* and *sand bars* which block Rehusa Channel and prevent free passage at any tide between the southern end of the bay and the open sea beyond except by small boat.

Almejas Bay embraces a large area of deep navigable water with the exception of the aforementioned shoal portion at its southernmost end. There are two large lagoons at the northern end of the bay, Laguna Palmer and Laguna Tortugas, and between them is Caleta Cayuco; all three dry at low water except for shallow channels. Punta Ricketson is the western entrance point of Caleta Cayuco. Mangrove Island lies on the shoal extending from the northern shore southward of Deering Bluff which is situated about 11½ miles east-northeastward of Punta Redondo. The narrowest part of Canal de la Gaviota (Marcy Channel) lies between Punta Lengua on the southwestern end of Mangrove Island and Punta Cisne on the shore of Isla de Santa Margarita, opposite. Punta Isham is the eastern extremity of Mangrove Island.

Puerto Alcatraz is a cannery village sheltered in the bight southward of Punta Cisne on the eastern shore of Santa Margarita Island. The cannery buildings are closely grouped at the water's edge at the south end of the village; an iron legged pier with a wooden deck extends into the bay about 350 feet from the cannery and narrow gauge rails run to the pierhead. Depths alongside range from 10 feet to 31 feet at its outer end. The cannery, La Maritime, S.A., is served by three small fishing vessels and the catch, augmented by casual fishermen, enables the cannery to operate year around. It is primarily a fish-meal and fish-oil plant utilizing a species of herring found in great abundance in the bay; the cannery also packs sardines. About 50 people are employed at the height of the season and the adjacent village is supported by the cannery activity.

Anchorage may be taken in the bight northeastward of the pier in 3 to 7 fathoms over a mud and sand bottom. For the most part the weather is mild and equable with a light prevailing wind during the day out of the north or northwest. The anchorage is usually calm but can boil up in a blow to be very uncomfortable with gusts sweeping the bay and

Lobster Receiver

Puerto Cortez

setting a vessel up over its ground tackle. The ebb and flow of the tidal stream runs heavily in the channel off the anchorage and resultant eddy currents have a tendency to stream a vessel on its anchor first one way, then another. Anchors fore and aft are therefore advisable with the bow of the vessel looking in toward the mouth of the shallow lagoon enclosed behind Punta Cisne; this lagoon is suitable for small boats only, as the passage through its mouth is quite shoal.

FACILITIES — Diesel fuel and gasoline are available at the cannery most of the time and may be purchased from the cannery manager. Fuel may be taken alongside the pierhead through hose and nozzle. Fresh water is scarce and must be thoroughly boiled before drinking. A limited stock of engine parts and engine room supplies may be had. Divers and mechanics can be hired. Minor machine work is available. Some provisions are available in the village but in limited supply. Fresh meat, vegetables and fruit may be purchased when available. *Note: Mexican pesos are the only form of money usually acceptable here.*

PUBLIC ACCOMMODATIONS — Overnight accommodations may be had in the village when not in use by visiting cannery officials; meals are served.

COMMUNICATIONS — The cannery operates a radio telephone and will accept public messages. A road connects to Puerto Cortez 2 miles south. A hard-packed sand *airstrip*

serves the village at Puerto Cortez.

MARINE EMERGENCIES — The Naval Base at Puerto Cortez located 2 miles south of the cannery will render emergency aid to vessels or crews in distress.

MEDICAL FACILITIES — First Aid may be rendered at the cannery; more serious sickness or injury should be treated at the Naval Base at Puerto Cortez.

HEALTH CAUTION — The cannery dumps fish refuse directly into the bay and drawing of salt water for any use on board while anchored in the close vicinity is ill-advised.

Puerto Cortez, an important Mexican Naval Base, is situated in a bight 2 miles southeast of Puerto Alcatraz. There are several dozen permanent buildings and metal sheds and warehouses built on a flat rounded point that extends into the bay. Four large oil tanks, three white and one black, rise on the northern side of the point and provide a useful mark when piloting through Canal de Gaviota. A wooden pier carrying six-inch fuel pipelines extends several hundred feet into the bay opposite the oil tanks. Part of the length of the original pier has been destroyed by storm in recent years and the depths alongside and at the pierhead are 22 feet or less. There are several Mexican Naval vessels moored in the bight at all times, their number frequently reinforced by other naval vessels when in from coastal patrol. On the southern side of the point there is a small stone mole extending a few feet out from the shore, formerly for the use of small boats and landing craft. The pier has been destroyed by storm and this facility is now not in use. Southward of this mole on the shore of a small bight is an airplane hangar and boat shed and, at one time, there was a small marine railway. A flagpole stands before the Naval Headquarters building and two steel radio masts rise behind the building. Back of the Naval Base is a good *hard-packed airstrip.*

Anchorage may be taken southward of the point in the shelter of the large bight in 2 to 5 fathoms, good holding ground on a bottom of sand and shell. The anchorage is usually quite calm but wind can whip up a considerable chop and, coupled with the ebb and flow of tidal currents through the narrows, require ground tackle fore and aft. Tidal ranges are the same as for Magdalena Bay. Puerto Cortez bight provides good shelter from heavy southeast weather, and vessels usually run in when anchorage in other parts of the bay is untenable.

Puerto Cortez was named by Sebastián Vizcaíno who sailed into the bay July 16, 1602, naming it Bahía de Almejas for the great number of shellfish to be found in the sand of the beaches along the shore. He called the port Puerto del Marqués for Fernando Cortez, Marqués de Valle de Oaxaca; today it is known as Puerto Cortez.

Puerto Cortez is outstandingly clean and hospitable; landing may be made with the permission of the Naval Commandante. A two-story colonial style concrete building houses an elementary school on the lower floor and the offices of the naval officials of the headquarters of the Third Naval Zone on the upper floor. The Naval Base accommodates the families of the personnel and makes for quite a lively community. There is a post office and a radiotelegraph office and a military PX-type store where a variety of goods may be obtained at very reasonable prices. When the supply ship is in from Ensenada or La Paz, fresh provisions of many kinds are available for purchase. Repair parts can be ordered here from La Paz and received via truck and boat in a very few days. Diesel fuel may be obtained by application to the Naval Commandante, as well as minor engine repair by diesel mechanics stationed at the base. *Fresh water* is available here but it is of a poor brackish quality and should be boiled before use.

Puerto Cortez was formerly a whaling station and the beach is still littered with the whitened whalebones that may be found among the plentiful supply of driftwood. During World War I an American company operated a magnesite mine on Santa Margarita Island and the ore was brought to Puerto Cortez by truck for loading.

Magdalena Bay was first discovered for the Spanish in 1539 by Francisco de Ulloa, commanding an expedition for Hernan Cortez and charged with the search for the rich pearl island of Ciguatan where Amazons were fabled to live in a sovereign state. Ulloa named the bay San Abad and

sailed on to Cedros Island. Juan Rodríguez Cabrillo reconnoitered Magdalena Bay on July 18, 1542, naming it Bahía San Pedro. Cabrillo's log read: "This is a good port and it is sheltered from west winds, but it has not water or wood." The bay received its present name, Magdalena, from Sebastián Vizcaíno who sailed in on July 21, 1602, and spent about a week exploring and charting it.

The Jesuit missionary Padre Guillen conducted an overland expedition to Magdalena Bay in 1719, with the intention of developing a port of refuge in the bay for the annual passage of the Manila Galleons which, as mentioned earlier, coasted the peninsula on their way to their destination port of Acapulco. A missionary visiting station was founded about 1734 near the eastern shore of the bay, and the great China ships occasionally entered for shelter and refreshment and traded with the missionaries. This settlement was short-lived, however and further development abandoned principally for the lack of a good and reliable source of fresh water.

In the opening years of the 1800's a great prosperity was stimulated at Bahía Magdalena in consequence of an active smuggling trade between the Baja residents settled around the mission and the Yankee and European ship masters and traders flaunting the commercial embargo enacted by Spain. Mules and donkeys, laden with hides, furs, pearls, fruits and honey and driven to the shore of the bay, met the traders in their longboats which freighted manufactured goods of all kinds, including cloth, hardware and staples, from the trading ships anchored in the bay. For a third of a century this contraband trade flourished, dying out only after Mexican independence had been won from Spain and the Secularization Act brought on the decline of the chain of Baja Mission settlements.

Admiral DuPetit-Thouars on the *Venus,* Captain Edward Belcher on the H.M.S. *Starling* and Captain Kellett for the Hydrographic Office of the British Admiralty visited Magdalena Bay during the 1830's and 40's and surveyed its waters.

Shortly after 1850 the bay again experienced a great prosperity when fleets of whalers, sealers and guano gatherers made it the center of their operations. Magdalena Bay was their favorite anchorage for "trying out the oil." The masts of the many ships appeared as forests of poles and rigging; oily black smoke from beneath the trying pots filled the sky.

Magdalena Bay provided such a naturally good and sheltered harbor that it was not to be deserted for long. The notorious William Walker, who attempted to capture Baja California with his independent company of adventurers shortly after the Mexican-American War, anchored his bark *Caroline* in Magdalena Bay to draw up plans for attack. In 1874 George Dewey, then Commander in the United States Navy, visited Magdalena Bay on the U.S.S. *Narragansett* engaged in the Hydrographic Survey of the West Coast of Mexico; this survey forms the basis of the H.O. Charts still published by the U.S. Naval Oceanographic Office. In the early 1900's The Great White Fleet of United States Men-of-War on a world cruise was accorded the privilege, through the courtesy of Mexico, to enter Magdalena Bay and lay over for target practice, their great cannon rending the calm of these silent waters. At the very outset of World

War I on August 5, 1914 the German light cruiser *Leipzig*, took the British freighter *Cetriana* into Magdalena Bay, removed all her bunker coal and her radio and stood out to sea the day after Britain declared war on Germany.

Bahía de Santa Marina (Santa Marina Bay), sheltered behind Cresciente Island, is the eastern extension of Bahía de Almejas. The bay is shoal and filled with sand bars among which run a network of channels enabling shoal draft navigation as far as the vicinity of Puerto Chale and El Dátil.

Puerto Chale is a small coastal fish camp, seasonally occupied. A fresh water tank and some brick salting bins stand on the site. There is a rough dirt *airstrip* back of the camp, little used, and a road connecting to the village of Santa Rita, thence to the main coast road which leads to Cabo San Lucas, San José del Cabo and La Paz. El Dátil, another seasonally occupied fish camp on the northern shore of Santa Marina Bay, is situated about 2 miles southward of Puerto Chale. Santa Marina Bay is connected with the sea by a narrow and shallow passage at Boca de Colorado, situated about 7½ miles southeast of Puerto Chale.

The fish life within Magdalena, Almejas and Santa Marina Bays is indeed prolific. Great schools of sardines and herring break the surface of the waters of the bay by day, and at night, a milky bright luminescence punctuates the dark waters with great patches of pulsating light. Sierra, a very tasty species of bonita, are abundant and easy to catch. A variety of game fish and bottom fish may be taken throughout the bay.

All the connecting lagoons and inlets are well worth exploring by small boat, as the wildlife is abundant among the mangrove thickets and in the salt marshes; clams and oysters are plentiful. Porpoise play singly and in schools, and seals are frequent visitors. During the late winter and early spring months the spouting of the migrating gray whales is a common sight, with often a spectacular display of broaching and lobtailing. Manta Ray, from the very young to full grown adults weighing tons or more, leap clear of the water, whacking their wide-spread wings on a surface school of small fish so as to stun them and thereby render them more amenable to being eaten. Great sea turtles frequent the bay and may be seen lazily swimming on the surface. Shark are also numerous. Both inside the bay and outside the mouth, on the relatively shallow banks offshore, a small red crayfish-like crustacean proliferates and provides the food for many of the larger creatures of the sea, including whales.

When conditions are just right, a biological phenomenon called a burst-of-life occurs within these drifting colonies and a report of the following kind is registered by a ship's master on a passage through the area: "On June 1, 1961, while off the coast of Lower California, the Chief Engineer reported his main condenser clogged, possibly from small fish; we switched to the auxiliary. At 7 a.m. on June 2 when 10 miles northwest of Cape San Lázaro the auxiliary also went out of action. The ship was stopped and the condensers were cleaned of 12 buckets of small crustaceans, similar to crayfish. The sea around us had millions more, in fact, in the sunlight it was colored red for miles around. On getting underway I ran straight for deep water but before reaching it, say some 10 miles, I had to have the condensers cleared twice again."

SOURCES OF ADDITIONAL INFORMATION — Captain of the Port, Operación Porturia, San Carlos, B.C., P.O. Box 170, Villa Constitución, B. Cfa., Mexico. (See also Appendix.)

Punta Laguna and Punta Cisne

Isla Cresciente and Boca de Colorado

SECTION 12
CABO TOSCO to CABO SAN LUCAS

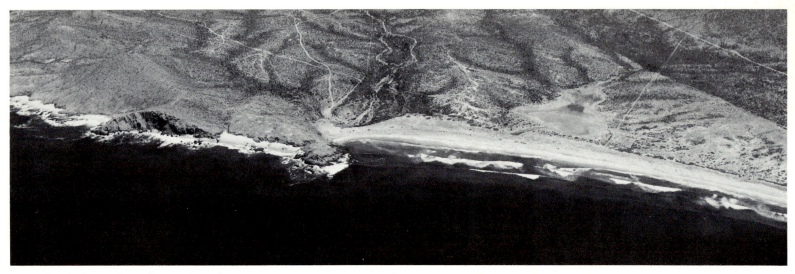

Typical coastline, Punta Pescadero

Southward from a seaward position off the entrance to Bahía Magdalena, Isla de Santa Margarita (Santa Margarita Island), high and barren and of volcanic origin, stretches 21 miles from its northwestern end at Punta Redondo to its southeastern end at Cabo Tosco. The seaward side of Santa Margarita Island presents a barren coastline, bare of trees and bushes and the usual ground cover to be seen on most of the islands off the Pacific coast of Baja California. The high hills are cut with numerous arroyos joining to form broader valleys as they open onto the sea. Several levels of wave-cut terraces and elevated sea-carved grottos give ample evidence of past geological emergence of the coastline of this island. The seaward face at both ends of the island is high, bold and rocky with high hills rising directly from the shores; the middle of the island for a distance of about 6 miles, however, is comprised of a low sandy plain and has a deceptive appearance from a distance, as if receding within the hills and forming a bay. This low plain, gradually narrowing, extends across the island at a minimum width of 3¼ miles, causing the profile of the land to appear from seaward as two islets bracketing an apparent opening which can easily be mistaken for the entrance to Magdalena Bay.

A *navigation light,* previously described, is shown from Punta Redondo. At 4¾ miles southeastward of Redondo Point there is a remarkable cliff about 200 feet high, Acantilado Blanco (White Bluff) which can be made out a good distance offshore. *Caution: Two submerged rocks lie offshore ½ mile westward of White Bluff.* Immediately back of this cliff is Pico Acantilado Blanco (White Bluff Peak), 1,074 feet high. Cabo Judas (Cape Judas) is a promontory situated about 2¼ miles southeastward of the White Bluff; thence 2½ miles further southeastward is Bahía Pequeña (Pequeña Bay), a small indentation in the weather coast at the low portion of Santa Margarita Island. Las

Hermanas (The Sisters) are two remarkable peaks 1,631 and 1,413 feet high, respectively, situated near the coast a short distance southeastward of the low plain and about 7 miles westward of Cabo Tosco. Monte Santa Margarita (Santa Margarita Mountain), near the southeastern end of the island, is the highest point and has an elevation of 1,858 feet.

Cabo Tosco (Cape Tosco), the southeastern extremity of Santa Margarita Island, is a sharp, bold rocky point from which a *reef,* on which the sea breaks heavily, extends about ½ mile southward. A *navigation light* exhibiting a **white group flash of two flashes every 20 seconds** is shown 266 feet above the sea from a white quadrangular masonry tower and dwelling, about 600 yards northward of the extremity of Cabo Tosco, and is visible through the sector 191° to 118°. The cape gives *good radar returns* up to 21 miles. *Anchorage* may be had about ½ mile eastward of Cabo Tosco in 7 to 9 fathoms but *caution is advised on account of the strength of the tidal currents that ebb and flow through the narrows of the Rehusa Channel.* Extensive silting northward of the point has reduced the anchorage area considerably from that historically reported. *Breakers* have been reported about 2 miles northeastward of Cabo Tosco, 1½ miles off the eastern shore of the island.

Obstruction: In 1941 it was reported that a submerged pinnacle rock, covered to a depth of 2 to 3 fathoms, was observed in a position approximately 1½ miles southward of Punta Tosco Light. Offlying rock — A pinnacle rock with a depth of 22 fathoms lies about 8 miles south-southwestward of Cabo Tosco. There is a *spring* of brackish water on the northeast side of the island near the beach, and there is another *spring* of excellent water at the southern end of the island, near the site of a small ranch situated on the shores of a shallow cove just inside Rehusa Channel.

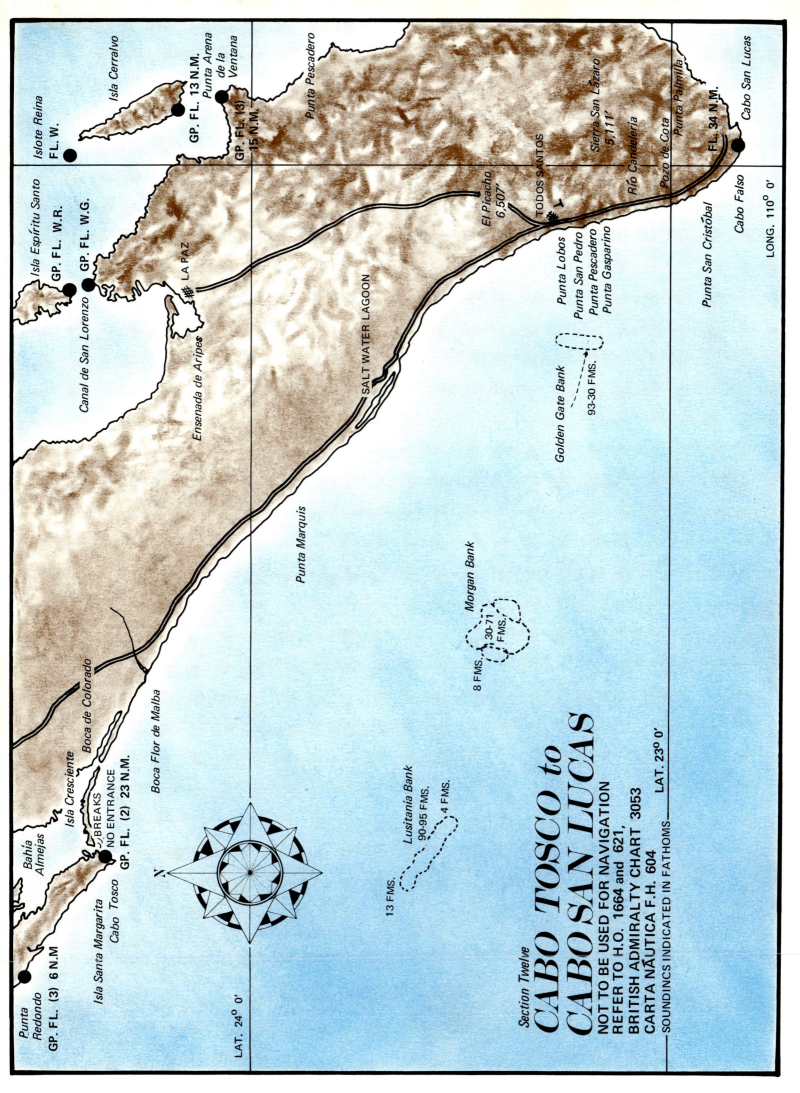

Section Twelve
CABO TOSCO to CABO SAN LUCAS

NOT TO BE USED FOR NAVIGATION
REFER TO H.O. 1664 and 621,
BRITISH ADMIRALTY CHART 3053
CARTA NÁUTICA F.H. 604
SOUNDINGS INDICATED IN FATHOMS

LAT. 24° 0'
LAT. 23° 0'
LONG. 110° 0'

Punta Redondo
GP. FL. (3) 6 N.M.
Bahía Almejas
Isla Santa Margarita
Cabo Tosco
GP. FL. (2) 23 N.M.
Isla Cresciente
NO ENTRANCE
BREAKS
Boca Flor de Malba
Boca de Colorado

Isla Espíritu Santo
Islote Reina
FL. W.
Isla Cerralvo
GP. FL. 13 N.M.
Punta Arena de la Ventana
GP. FL. (3) 15 N.M.
GP. FL. W.R.
GP. FL. W.G.
Canal de San Lorenzo
LA PAZ
Ensenada de Aripes

Punta Pescadero
Punta Marquis
SALT WATER LAGOON

El Picacho 6,507'
TODOS SANTOS
Sierra San Lázaro 5,111'
Río Candelaria
Pozo de Cota
Punta Palmilla
FL. 34 N.M.
Cabo San Lucas

Punta Lobos
Punta San Pedro
Punta Pescadero
Punta Gasparino
Golden Gate Bank
93-30 FMS.

Morgan Bank
30-71 FMS.
8 FMS.

Lusitania Bank
90-95 FMS.
4 FMS.
13 FMS.

Cabo Falso
Punta San Cristóbal

N

147

Landing at Punta Lobos

San Pedro Ranch and Cove

The flow of these springs is sometimes severely limited after a long drought, which occurs at intervals in the area. Cabrillo anchored his expeditionary vessels here on Wednesday, July 12, 1542, and entered in his log: "This was a good port, protected from the west-northwest winds. The port is at the head of the island on the southeast side, and is clean and good for anchoring, but it has no water."

On September 13, 1931, the American steamer *Colombia* carrying $320,000 worth of gold and silver bullion and specie, in addition to her regular cargo of general freight, wrecked and sank in 8 fathoms off Cabo Tosco. The original salvagers recovered approximately $200,000 for the owners; subsequently an additional $5,460 was recovered from the master's strongbox. The wreck is still there, noted on most coastal charts.

Canal de Rehusa (Rehusa Channel), known locally as Bocana de Estequeros, is the southern entrance to Bahía de Almejas; it lies between the southeastern extremity of Isla de Santa Margarita and Punta Santa Marina, the western extremity of Isla Cresciente. Santa Marina Point lies 3½ miles northeastward of Cabo Tosco and about 1 mile eastward of the easternmost point of Santa Margarita Island. *Breakers* have been observed in a position about 2 miles southward of Punta Marina and there are other *shoal patches,* over which the sea breaks, in the approach to Rehusa Channel. The channel itself is encumbered with shoals, and the tidal streams in it are of considerable strength, causing tide rips and overfalls and preventing passage through it except in small boats for navigators with local knowledge, but then at some peril. (See Magdalena Bay.) A *wreck* lies stranded on the shore about ¾ mile eastward of Santa Marina Point.

The coast between Punta Santa Marina, the eastern entrance point to Rehusa Channel, and Boca del Colorado, 11½ miles eastward, is formed by Isla Cresciente (Crescent Island). It is a low sand island, the northern side of which comprises the southeastern side of Almejas Bay and the southern shore of Bahía de Santa Marina. Crescent Island is about 12 miles long east and west with a growth of mangroves on its northern side; the 10-fathom curve lies ½ to ¾ mile seaward and in thick weather, sounding is the best practice to keep a safe offing.

Boca del Colorado at the eastern end of Crescent Island is the southern entrance to Bahía de Santa Marina, but only for small boats and navigators with local knowledge as the passage is shoal and the bay itself, lying between Crescent Island and the mainland is blocked by shoals and sandbars. Punta el Conejo (Conejo Point), opposite the eastern extremity of Crescent Island and forming the eastern point to Boca de Colorado, is the western end of a long, narrow peninsula that lies parallel to the mainland and is separated from it by Laguna Rancho Bueno (Rancho Bueno Lagoon). The lagoon is about 7 miles long, very narrow and navigable by boats for about half its length, whence it becomes a tidal marsh grown with thickets of mangrove. El Conejo is a dome-shaped mound about 50 feet high that is located on the north side of the lagoon about 5 miles northward of El Conejo Point. El Conejo Point gives *good radar returns* up to 20 miles. Southeastward of Cabo Tosco for about 90 miles as far as Punta Lobos, there is a broad, relatively shoal shelf. It extends a good distance offshore, beyond which there are numerous banks and rather shallow patches as well as submarine pinnacles, some of which are charted and others reported in the standard published Pilots covering the area. For about 60 miles southeastward of Punta Conejo the 100-fathom curve closely parallels the coast at a distance of 10 to 12 miles. Beyond that distance it sweeps outward and lies more than 23 miles from the coast at a position west-southwestward of Punta Lobos, forming a broad bank southeastward of which, in less than a mile, the depths increase from 73 to 323 fathoms. From this latter position the 100-fathom curve jogs sharply in toward the coast again and parallels it at a distance of 1 to 4 miles as far as Cape San Lucas.

Caution: When navigating along this coast, the depths are a good guide as to the proximity of the land, and a regular series of soundings should be made, especially while running at night or during thick weather as the coast, being comparatively low, is not easily seen.

ANCHORAGE — In fine weather vessels may anchor anywhere along this part of the coast between Punta Conejo and Punta Lobos at about 1 mile offshore in depths of 8 to 10 fathoms; the depths are regular and there are no hidden dangers but *breakers* extend some distance offshore and landing is somewhat difficult.

CURRENTS — The California current off this coast is irregular and often weak; a southerly set is more frequent in the spring and least frequent in the autumn. Rates up to about 1½ knots may occur. Onshore sets are often experienced, particularly off the mouths of the lagoons. Tidal currents may reinforce the normal coastal current at certain times of the month and such increase of velocity may be further emphasized by the submarine configuration of the offshore banks over which they flow, to produce isolated currents of surprising strength.

OFFSHORE BANKS — An extensive bank, the limits of which are not well defined, lies about 14 miles southward of Cabo Tosco. Depths on this bank range from 20 to 70 fathoms, with a least depth of 3¼ fathoms sounded in 1952 at approximately Latitude 24° 02' north, Longitude 111° 30' west; a depth of 9 fathoms was reported in 1961 at approximately Latitude 23° 39' north, Longitude 111° 21' west. Soundings of 6 to 15 fathoms were reported in 1960 on this bank in an area about 30 miles south-southeastward of Cabo Tosco. Numerous ship's reports of soundings over a period of years indicate that the 100-fathom curve appears to lie farther offshore than charted along this part of the coast. Outside this bank about 25 miles, and about 60 miles southward of Cabo Tosco, lies Lusitania Bank where depths of 90 to 95 fathoms extend about 4 miles in an east and west direction. About 3 miles northeastward of these soundings on Lusitania Bank, depths of 13 to 44 fathoms extend about 10 miles in a northwest-southeast direction; the southeast limit of these soundings has not been charted. The least charted depth of 13 fathoms lies at the northwestern extremity of this bank; however, a depth of only 4 fathoms was reported in 1968 about 3 miles eastward at approximately Latitude 23° 43' north, Longitude 111° 43' 15" west. On a still day with clear water one could easily see the bottom over this pinnacle, and by fishing around with the ground tackle, anchorage could be effected if desired, but the bottom is quite rocky.

Another bank with depths sounded at 18 to 37 fathoms was reported in 1963 to lie with its center at approximately Latitude 23° 22' north, Longitude 111° 37.7' west. This bank is about 10 miles long and extends in a northwest-southeast direction. Morgan Bank with depths of 30 to 71 fathoms is situated about 51 miles westward of Punta Lobos. A depth of 8 fathoms was sounded in 1964 on the western edge of Morgan Bank at Latitude 23° 24' north, Longitude 111° 09' 12" west. A depth of 13 fathoms was reported in 1968 on the southeastern part of this same bank at Latitude 23° 24' 30" north, Longitude 111° 08' 30" west.

There is an extensive area of undefined banks, with depths ranging from 4½ to 90 fathoms, about 34 miles westward of Punta Lobos. Depths of 4½ fathoms were sounded in 1963 about Latitude 23° 22' north, Longitude 110° 50' west. Depths of 5 fathoms have been reported at about Latitude 23° 20' north, Longitude 110° 45' west, and Latitude 23° 21' north, Longitude 110° 46' west. Depths of 8 fathoms have been sounded at about Latitude 23° 22' north, Longitude 110° 59' west, and Latitude 23° 24' north, Longitude 110° 59' west. Depths of 14 fathoms were reported in 1967 at about Latitude 23° 10' north, Longitude 110° 47' west. *Note: As these shoal patches have been reported by the masters of various vessels passing through the area at different periods, employing an approximation of their Latitude and Longitude description for each position of observation, some of the reported soundings may coincide with a small difference of depth or position noted. Charting the above information, however, will develop a pattern indicating the general delineation of the banks and depths sounded.*

Caution: Vessels passing through the area between 22 to 37 miles west-southwestward, and 30 to 55 miles westward of Punta Lobos are advised to navigate with caution as less than charted or reported depths may exist.

The entire offshore area of banks and submarine pinnacles are natural feeding grounds for tuna, skipjack, bonita, marlin, and other game fish. The commercial Tuna Clippers out of San Pedro, San Diego, Cape San Lucas, Guaymas and Mazatlán frequent these banks in search of a catch. Dozens of commercial fishing vessels may be seen plying these waters back and forth in their fishing runs, their electronic sounding devices continuously recording the bottom configuration. Large patches of small red crayfish-like crustaceans may be seen floating in the water on these banks, supported in their life cycle by nutrients brought to the surface by upwelling currents; the crustaceans in turn provide a rich harvest of food for the larger school fish.

The coast between Punta El Conejo and Punta Lobos, about 90 miles to the southeastward, is low, sandy and barren backed by a low, rolling country 50 to 100 feet high that is cut by gullies and arroyos. Within about 15 miles of

Punta Lobos the land, which is covered with cactus, rises gradually from the coast to an elevation of 500 to 1,100 feet. The land in the interior rises gradually toward the Gulf coast and is characterized by scattered, conspicuous mesas. There is a coastal road, El Camino Real, that runs along the shore connecting many small settlements and ranches; branch roads lead inland, some communicating across the relatively narrow intervening plain with La Paz on the Gulf coast.

Boca Flor de Malba, the entrance to Estero Salada, situated at the seaward end of Arroyo Flor de Malba, lies about 12 miles east-southeastward of Boca de Colorado. There is no navigable passage from the sea through this entrance. Pools of fresh water stand a short distance up the arroyo and a ranch is located on the northwest side of the dry bed of the river.

Punta Marqués (Marquis Point), situated about 28 miles southeastward of Boca Flor de Malba, is a low, rocky point bracketed by sandy bluffs just back of the beach on either side; a *reef of rocks* extends about ½ mile southward from the point. *Good radar returns* may be had from the point up to about 18 miles. There are some isolated tablelands that break through to the ocean during the rainy season, are situated 18 miles, 13 miles and 7 miles, respectively, northwestward of Punta Lobos. Ranches are established at each of these places. Punta Lobos is the northwestern extremity of Los Lobos, a high rocky promontory, 682 feet high, that stretches about 1¼ miles along the seafront, bracketed on both sides by white sand beaches. The point projects at a sharp angle from the sand beach on the northern side of the promontory, forming a small cove in the hook of the point. *Landing* can be made here in favorable weather but when a sea is running, the surf on the beach is somewhat discouraging and, in addition, the sand shifts at certain seasons, leaving bare rocks uncovered. There is an *airstrip* immediately back of the beach.

About 1956, the Territorial Government built an elaborate fish smoking plant about a quarter of a mile from the Punta Lobos beach landing. The well-constructed concrete building has several smoke ovens and a large filleting and salting room as well as a residence for the manager. An adequate water supply is available and a large variety of game and bottom fish as well as great sea turtles abound close offshore along the entire coastal area. This plant never produced any quantity of smoked fish, however, and

Todos Santos Village and Punta de la Poza

from 500 to 600 feet high, situated from 7 to 11 miles eastward of Punta Marqués.

Bahía de La Paz (La Paz Bay) on the gulf coast of the Baja California Peninsula lies about 23 miles northeastward of Punta Marqués across low, flat land covered with small clumps of desert bushes, cactus and stunted trees. La Aguja Ranch is located immediately northward of Punta Marqués and has a source of *fresh water*. Cunaño, Tiputati and Inocentes Ranches, situated 5, 12 and 16 miles, respectively, southeastward of Punta Marqués, are also sources of *fresh water*. From Inocentes Ranch a road leads to La Paz.

Boca de Canisal, Boca de Palmarito, and Boca de Playita, openings at the seaward ends of small fresh water esteros

has long been abandoned for organized commercial production; it is used now by the local fishermen on a sort of squatter basis. Tortoise and shark fishing from small pangas by independent fishermen is carried on and the meat is salted, dried and trucked to La Paz.

Punta Gasparino, looking southward

a steady flow, makes its way to the springs below through fissures in the lava strata and cracks in the bedrock, producing low but voluminous "fountains" at the points of emergence. The largest of these springs flows out of Bartolo Canyon on the gulf side in Las Palmas Bay and another, almost as great in volume, comes to the surface within 3 miles of the Pacific shore at the springs of Todos Santos. An attempt to raise the level of the Todos Santos spring a few feet, in order to irrigate more land by gravity alone, very nearly proved disastrous; for the effort somehow shifted the pressure in the subterranean passages and the spring vanished from its age-old location. When it reappeared, it issued through an opening a mile away at a level lower by 12 feet than at its previous outlet, thus isolating from irrigation a number of acres of land that had been tilled previously.

Palm trees, fruit trees, mangoes, for which the area is noted, and waving fields of cane characterize the countryside. The town, with a population of about 2,500, is comprised principally of one-story adobe houses laid out in an orderly pattern and dominated by a large white-washed church originally built about 1840. It was completely remodeled after 1941 at which time it was severely damaged in a particularly violent chubasco that swept the cape region. The site of Todos Santos was first developed in 1724 as a farm and visiting station by Padre Jaime Bravo, a missionary from La Paz. In 1734 it became an independent mission called Santa Rosa but was completely destroyed by an Indian rebellion shortly thereafter. A series of virulent epidemics wiped out several subsequent Indian populations at the mission, which was rebuilt as Mission Todos Santos. The village was finally resettled by an influx of settlers from mainland Mexico shortly after secularization of all church lands in 1834. The original site of the mission church is about a mile above the town at Mission Viejo; a faint trace of a stone foundation is all that remains.

In the town today there are a number of stores where a variety of supplies may be purchased; there is a gasoline and diesel distributor, a bar, a restaurant, a hotel and a movie theatre. On the south edge of town there is a new *Government Hospital*. There is a *telephone office* in the town and a road communicates with La Paz. There are several *airstrips* in the close vicinity in good repair and in frequent use.

Río de Todos Santos is an all-year stream that flows through a fertile valley and reaches the sea about ½ mile northward of Punta Lobos. The southern side of its mouth, known as Punta de La Paz, is a perpendicular bluff about 50 feet high at the northern end of a tableland that extends from the vicinity of Punta Lobos. Off La Poza Point there are numerous *outlying rocks*. Todos Santos Village is situated on the bank of the river 2 miles from its mouth; a road leads to the village from a sand beach.

Anchorage may be had in moderate weather by vessels with local knowledge about 600 yards offshore in a position about ½ mile northward of Punta Lobos, with the point bearing about 150° in depths of from 6 to 10 fathoms, sand bottom.

Todos Santos Village, located almost exactly on the Tropic of Cancer, is a very pleasant farming village on the southeastern side of the Todos Santos Arroyo, overlooking a patchwork of growing fields of sugar cane. Three *springs* at San Juan in the upper part of the valley provide adequate irrigation for part of the year, and a small dam below retains enough more water to carry on undiminished farming in the lower valley throughout the year. Irrigation canals are constructed to enable cultivation of a large area of the fertile valleys around the village. The emergence of these springs, which have a considerable year round flow, have a great effect on the verdure of the cape region of the peninsula. The springs derive from the porous volcanic nature of the high range of mountains, where there is considerable rainfall. The watershed, held back sufficiently to provide

From offshore, when abreast Punta Lobos, the high mountains back of La Paz and the sharp peaks of the Sierra de la Laguna are plainly visible; La Aguja and Picacho, the most northerly and conspicuous peaks of this range are, respectively, 6,432 and 6,507 feet high and from the southwest they appear as two steep-faced cliffs.

Navigation note: In 1966 a magnetic disturbance was reported southwestward of Punta Lobos in Latitude 23° 10′ north, Longitude 110° 24′ west, with abnormal deviations up to 15° noted at this time. Careful attention to compass headings and relative bearings should be kept when in this vicinity.

Cabo Falso with Cabo San Lucas in the background

The coast for about 20 miles southward of Punta Lobos is comprised of a series of sand beaches broken by rocky bluffs that project slightly from the coastline. There are *sunken rocks* off these points and they should be given a berth of not less than ½ mile; elsewhere no hidden dangers have been found outside ¼ mile from shore. The water in most places is deep close-to but *shoal water* extends offshore at the mouths of some of the arroyos. The sand beaches are mostly steep and landing is difficult, with considerable surf even in moderate weather. Immediately back of the coast the land is hilly with high and broken mountains in the interior.

Punta San Pedro, a steep rocky bluff, backed at a distance of about ½ mile by a hill 618 feet high, lies about 2 miles southward of Punta Lobos. Between Punta San Pedro and the southern end of Los Lobos there is a white sand beach about ¾ mile long, back of which is located the San Pedro Ranch with a small cultivated area. An *airstrip* is located alongside the ranch. The rocky coast continues 1¼ miles southward of San Pedro Point, whence a sand beach extends nearly to Pescadero Point.

La Bocana, the mouth of a large stream that is closed in the dry season, is situated midway along this beach, about 2 miles southward of San Pedro Point. About 2 miles inland from La Bocana is the village of Pescadero.

Punta Pescadero is rocky with off-lying ledges; it rises steeply to a hill 347 feet high. It should not be approached closer than a distance of ½ mile.

Punta Gasparino is a rocky bluff 75 feet high, surrounded by sunken rocks that project all along the general line of the coast from about 4 miles southeastward of Pescadero Point; a sand beach lies between the two points. Like Pescadero Point, Gasparino Point should be given a berth of at least ½ mile to avoid *submerged rocks*. Close northward of the point and 1½ miles inland is the village of Palmar, a small settlement surrounded by a large grove of palms.

Punta La Tinaja, about 9 miles southward of Gasparino Point, is a rocky bluff about 75 feet high, backed by a steep hill 541 feet high. Between Gasparino Point and La Tinaja Point are three arroyos that break through to the sea during the rainy season. On the banks of the northernmost is a small settlement marked by palm trees. There are a number of ranches along the coast in the mouths of the arroyos between Punta Gasparino and Boca de la Tinaja. Boca de las Matancitas (distinguished from the cannery town of similar name north of Magdalena Bay) at the southernmost of these arroyos, is situated about 5 miles southeastward of Punta Gasparino and may be identified by yellowish-colored bluffs with cactus-covered slopes that rise on either side toward the hills. A small village set among a grove of palms is located about 2½ miles northward of Boca de las Matancitas.

Boca de la Tinaja lies just southward of the point of the same name; the name is derived from the numerous rock basins or tinajas in the vicinity. La Tinaja Ranch is located about 1 mile inland from the mouth of the arroyo. Monte el Guatamote rises to an elevation of 2,367 feet about 4 miles eastward of the point and provides a conspicuous landmark for the area. Arroyo de la Candelaria runs down to the sea about 4 miles southeastward of Punta Tinaja. *Fresh water* is available quite near the surface of the dry stream bed; and on each side of the arroyo near the beach, there are ranches; at a distance of about 5 miles from the coast is Candelaria Village. The coastal road connecting all the villages and ranches along this part of the coast crosses the arroyo just back of the berm.

Monte Calabasa, which rises to an elevation of 1,770 feet about 2½ miles from the coast northward of Arroyo Candelaria, will give *good radar returns* up to 36 miles, and provides a good navigation mark from offshore. The 100-fathom curve lies only about 1¼ miles off this part of the coast. About 1 mile southeastward of Arroyo de Candelaria is a rocky bluff 75 feet high from which Cerro de la Playa, a conical hill, rises to an elevation of 504 feet. There is a ranch and a source of *fresh water* about ½ mile southward of Cerro de la Playa and ¾ mile inland. About 2½ miles southward of this point is a rocky red-colored bluff about 50 feet high, with numerous rocks at its foot; between this bluff and Punta San Cristobal, next southward, two streams discharge at the mouths of arroyos San Cristobal and Suspiro. Punta San Cristobal, about 5 miles southward of Cerro de la Playa, is a bold rocky bluff 200 to 300 feet high. About 1½ miles eastward of this point is El Suspiro, a projecting spur of hills 795 feet high.

The coast bending gradually to the eastward between Punta San Cristobal and Punta Falso, a distance of about 7 miles, is comprised of steep sand beaches backed by high whitish-colored sand bluffs, 150 to 330 feet high, covered with patches of low shrubs which show dark against the white background; the land behind rises gradually to the coastal range the height of which decreases somewhat toward Cabo Falso.

OFFSHORE BANKS — Two banks off this part of the coast, San Jaime Bank, about 14 miles offshore and about 15 to 25 miles westward of Cabo Falso, at approximately Latitude 22° 50′ north, Longitude 110° 15′ west, and Golden Gate Bank, about 8 miles offshore and about 20 miles westward of Cabo Falso, at approximately Latitude 23° 02′ north, Longitude 110° 15′ west, have been sounded extensively, principally by commercial fishing vessels.

San Jaime Bank is comprised of three principal submarine pinnacles and several minor ones, all within 4 miles or less of each other. The outermost pinnacle has been sounded at 70 fathoms with a least depth of 20 fathoms reported in 1937; the southernmost pinnacle has been sounded at 63 fathoms with a least depth of 5 fathoms reported in 1948; the northernmost pinnacle has been sounded at 60 fathoms with a least depth of 28 fathoms reported in 1946. A depth of 11 fathoms was sounded near this pinnacle in 1967. Isolated pinnacles of 70, 86 and 70 fathoms have been sounded within the area of San Jaime Bank.

Golden Gate Bank was reported in 1939 and named after the fishing vessel from which it was first sounded; depths over the bank are 93 to 30 fathoms, the last and least depth reported in 1962. A bank with a depth of 35 fathoms was reported in 1948 to lie about 112 miles westward of Cabo Falso Light at Latitude 22° 40′ 30″ north, Longitude 111° 58′ 00″ west. When running through the area in which these banks are located, soundings are useful in determining a vessel's position. At the same time a trolling line trailed astern seldom fails to catch some kind of edible fish.

Cabo Falso, situated at Latitude 22° 52′ north, Longitude 109° 58′ west, is the southernmost point of the Baja California Peninsula. It is a rocky bluff about 50 feet high, covered for the most part by drifted sand blown up from the long sand beach that stretches to the eastward; there is a conspicuous sand slide close eastward of the *old lighthouse,* now no longer in use. The *new lighthouse,* a red and white banded concrete tower, stands on a conical hill, 656 feet above the sea, immediately behind the point and ½ mile above the old lighthouse; it exhibits a powerful **flashing white light every 0.6 second** that is visible for 36 miles in clear weather through the sector 191° to 118°. The light tender's dwelling is built alongside the new light. This part of the coast is bold, with many detached outlying rocks, but may be approached to within ¼ mile, where there are depths of 5 to 6 fathoms. Cabo Falso gives *good radar returns* up to 20 miles. A new hotel, La Finisterra, perched on a rocky ridge overlooking the sandy beach close westward of Cabo San Lucas, surveys the infinity of the Pacific Ocean; its lights may be observed to seaward at night.

The aspect from seaward when approaching the southernmost tip of Baja California from the northward or westward is indeed an exciting and spectacular moment in the long voyage down the peninsula. The bold sand-strewn cliffs of Cabo Falso mark the turning point when doubling the cape; 4 miles eastward along a broad stretch of white sand beach at the foot of a short range of hills is the triangular peak, La Vigia and the twin sharp rocks called the Friars, which stand at the very extremity of the peninsula, Cabo San Lucas; the final reach of rock: lands end!

Cabo Falso

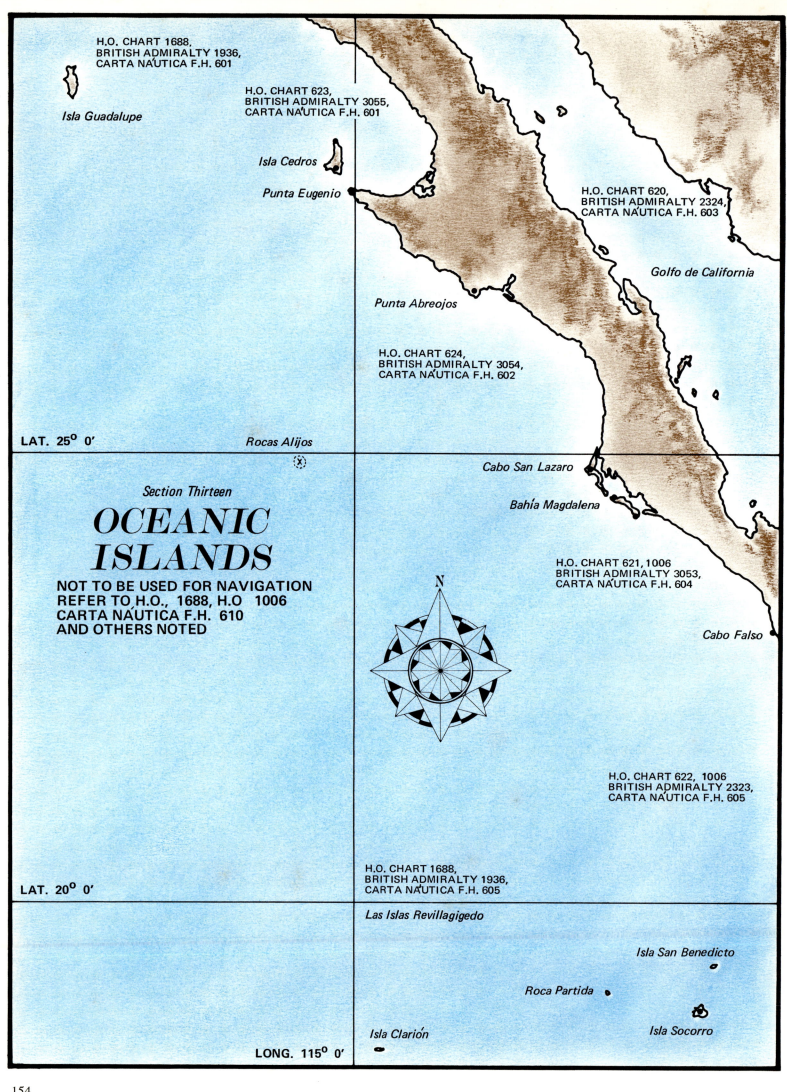

H.O. CHART 1688,
BRITISH ADMIRALTY 1936,
CARTA NAÚTICA F.H. 601

Isla Guadalupe

H.O. CHART 623,
BRITISH ADMIRALTY 3055,
CARTA NAÚTICA F.H. 601

Isla Cedros

Punta Eugenio

H.O. CHART 620,
BRITISH ADMIRALTY 2324,
CARTA NAÚTICA F.H. 603

Golfo de California

Punta Abreojos

H.O. CHART 624,
BRITISH ADMIRALTY 3054,
CARTA NAÚTICA F.H. 602

LAT. 25° 0'   *Rocas Alijos*

Cabo San Lazaro

Section Thirteen

OCEANIC
ISLANDS

**NOT TO BE USED FOR NAVIGATION
REFER TO H.O., 1688, H.O 1006
CARTA NAÚTICA F.H. 610
AND OTHERS NOTED**

Bahía Magdalena

H.O. CHART 621, 1006
BRITISH ADMIRALTY 3053,
CARTA NAÚTICA F.H. 604

Cabo Falso

N

H.O. CHART 622, 1006
BRITISH ADMIRALTY 2323,
CARTA NAÚTICA F.H. 605

H.O. CHART 1688,
BRITISH ADMIRALTY 1936,
CARTA NAÚTICA F.H. 605

LAT. 20° 0'

Las Islas Revillagigedo

Isla San Benedicto

Roca Partida

Isla Socorro

Isla Clarión

LONG. 115° 0'

154

SECTION 13
OCEANIC ISLANDS

The Revillagigedo Islands lie in an isolated archipelago off the tip of Baja California between 220 and 368 miles south and southwest of Cabo San Lucas. The group is comprised of three islands: San Benedicto, Socorro, Clarión, and a large double-headed rock, Roca Partida, all of volcanic origin and uninhabited, save for a small Mexican Naval contingent and village on the southern tip of Socorro, the largest of the group. These are desert islands and oceanic in the classic sense, high-peaked and barren although somewhat green during certain seasons of the year, except for double-headed, guano-covered Roca Partida and recently volcanic, ash-covered San Benedicto which displays a large new cinder cone and a great lava flow. The islands are remote patches of truly virgin soil as untouched today by the inroads of civilization as they were when Hernando de Grijalva first discovered them in 1533 and took possession for the Spanish crown.

The Revillagigedo Islands have been the object of many scientific expeditions over the last several hundred years because their isolation lends a unique interest to the flora and fauna to be found there. Undisturbed over countless centuries save for wind, weather and occasional volcanic activity, the life cycles of the terrestrial and marine plants and animals proceed from year to year in elemental evolutionary patterns. Life on these remote specks of ocean-bound land is fascinating to behold. Large flights of birds fill the air around the islands and make their aerial nests along the cliffs, among the rocks or in the low stunted bushes growing on the slopes of the peaks. Great marine turtles emerge from the sea, lumber up the beaches to the berm, and deposit a nest of eggs to hatch in the sun-warmed sand. Some of the pods of California gray whales on the annual migration from the Arctic to the warm waters of Baja California come to the archipelago and give birth of their young. Seals sun on the wave-washed rocks, a myriad of game fish school in the surrounding sea. A multitude of colorful bottom fish lace the shallows close inshore; shark are numerous, blackfish and killer whales cruise the islands and porpoise weave the sea in vast schools.

The descriptions of many of the islands' features derive from the names of the vessels, the scientific expeditions, or their leaders who have called over the years. Today, the area is visited principally by Tuna Clippers and occasionally by an Oceanographic Research Vessel, a sport-fishing boat or a cruising yacht. Tuna Clippers are almost always to be found in the vicinity, or between the coastal banks and the island fishing grounds.

There is, however, the wreckage of more than one small vessel bleaching in the sand above the tide, as tropical cyclones affecting the general area of the Pacific Coast of Baja California are sometimes severe and broad of track when occurring in the exposed vicinity of the Revillagigedo Islands.

WIND AND WEATHER — Nine-tenths of the tropical cyclones of this region are encountered in an area which is roughly the shape of a triangle whose base is the coastline extending from Point Eugenio near the middle of Baja California to the middle of the Costa Rican coast, and whose apex lies near Latitude 10° north and Longitude 125° west. It is during the rainy season in this region that tropical cyclones are most prevalent. Occasionally a cyclonic storm occurs in May, and about every 2 or 3 years one may be expected in each of the months of June and July. The average number for August is about one annually. The height of the cyclone season is in September when two or three normally occur. In October the average number is about one annually, and only rarely does one occur in November. These storms, after forming in the more southern portion of the cyclone region, tend to move toward the northwest at various distances off the Mexican coast. The September storms tend to continue farther, on a northwesterly course than do those of other months, and on reaching Baja California they pass to one side or the other of the cape. The areas of the Pacific cyclones are often small, sometimes less than 50 miles across, and winds of gale force are confined to a very narrow zone. In the vicinity of the Revillagigedo Islands, however, there are observed occasionally violent storms which have a wide belt of extreme storminess, with a total affected width of 200 or more miles; the coastal storms are rarely that extensive.

Cyclonic storms affecting the Mexican coast in general and the Baja California Pacific coast in particular are described in this section at length to give the small craft mariner adequate understanding of the severity of the wind and weather he may have to deal with when undertaking this totally exposed offshore passage between his departure from coastal shelter and anchorage in the lee of one of the islands of the Revillagigedo group. Adequate preparation for such a passage, common sense in observing the signs of the sea, and timely knowledge of accurate weather conditions through radio forecast will generally enable safe and comfortable, and thereby enjoyable cruising off soundings.

It is well to observe the state of the sea for indications of approaching weather. The existence of a nearby storm may be discovered from the appearance of the sea swells, the barometer change, and the character of the clouds. The sea swell affords one of the first indications of an approaching storm. At sea it is manifested as a long unbroken wave, usually with the time interval between crests much longer than normally observed. In the tropics the barometric pressure, except for diurnal fluctuation, tends to remain the same from day to day. On the approach of a tropical storm the barometer falls slowly at first and then more rapidly as the center of the weather disturbance approaches. The rate of fall depends on the size of the storm, the ultimate depth of the barometric depression, and the progressive rate of the storm. The character of the clouds may also be read as clear indication of weather disturbance. The appearance of the high, feathery, cirrus-type clouds indicates the outer edge of the storm. These clouds usually appear in advance of the lower clouds. The cirrus clouds are often brilliantly colored at sunset and sunrise so that a red sky is one of the signs of the approach of a cyclone.

Tropical cyclones off the Mexican coast are referred to locally as *chubascos.* They are generally much smaller in size and duration than full-fledged cyclones of other tropical regions but they have the same characteristics and can pose a most violent threat to vessels at sea and wreak considerable damage ashore. *Chubascos* are characterized by very strong cyclonic winds which rotate about a calm center of low atmospheric pressure with an overall storm configuration that is generally circular. Cyclonic storms in the northern hemisphere spiral inward in a counterclockwise direction. At the outer limits of the weather disturbance the winds are gentle to moderate and blow intermittently; they increase in strength toward the center, with their greatest violence usually just outside the small, relatively calm center or "eye" of the storm. The velocity of these winds is gale force or more, often even attaining 100 knots or greater. The eye of the storm is frequently ominously calm in comparison to the violence of the elements just beyond. The sea is almost always confused and mountainous. The diameter of this central calm varies, a full-fledged tropical cyclonic storm having an average diameter of about 14 miles; for a local Mexican Chubasco, it is generally somewhat smaller.

One weather phenomenon that may be observed as characteristic of the eye of the storm, and by which it may be recognized, is the slackening of the wind from a given direction to a relative calm, which in turn gives way to a rising wind but from the opposite direction as the inner periphery of the cyclonic wheel passes a given position. This central zone is sometimes cloudless so that the sun is visible by day and the stars by night. The air is usually warmer and drier by comparison and the barometer generally at its lowest dip. Barometer readings below 29 inches almost always exist; readings below 28 inches are not uncommon. In some full-fledged storms readings below 27 inches have been observed. Along this section of the coast the normal barometric pressure in January is about

30.05 inches; in July it averages about 29.90 inches. This type of storm is usually accompanied by heavy to excessive rains. Showers occur near the outer limits of the disturbance but as the storm approaches the characteristic squalls begin and the showers increase in frequency and intensity. As the center continues to approach, the rain becomes continuous and falls in heavy torrents.

Understanding the characteristics of a local tropical hurricane or *chubasco,* and realizing its potential for damage to a boat and its equipment are important prerequisites for avoiding contact with one, if possible, or handling a vessel wisely if caught in a severe blow at sea. Weather forecasts may be obtained for this region from the following sources: United States National Weather Service, Los Angeles Radio Facility; United States Coast Guard, San Pedro Radio, Notice to Mariners, Hydrographic Information, Weather and Storm Warnings; Coastal Radio Stations KMI, Oakland, and KOU, San Pedro, Pacific Coastal Weather Bulletins and Summaries; informal local aviation and marine weather conditions through radio contact with Baja California aircraft and vessels at sea. (See Appendix for schedule of weather broadcasts and frequencies of transmissions.)

View of the north end of Gudalupe Island, distant 5 miles

Isla Guadalupe (Guadalupe Island), comprising Mexico's westernmost possession, is situated at Latitude 29° 10′ north, Longitude 118° 17′ west, approximately 144 miles west-southwestward of Punta Baja, the nearest point on the mainland coast. It is about 222 miles southwestward of San Diego, 180 miles southwestward of Punta Banda, and 164 miles northwestward of Cedros Island. At various times Guadalupe Island has been reported by ships' masters to lie northeastward of its charted position. According to the latest determination of its geographic location, the island is situated 1.7 miles 58° from its present position as charted on H.O. 5760, First Edition, March 1942, corrected to September 1968. For navigation see U.S. Oceanographic Office Charts H.O. 1688, 5760, 623 and 1006; British Admiralty Chart #1936; Mexican Carta Náutica F.H. 601.

Navigation note: Submarine transit lane Sierra Pluto passes in a north-south track off the west coast of the island; a close watch should be kept for submersible vessels in the sea lane.

Guadalupe Island first appeared upon maritime charts in 1837 after a visit to the West American coast by French Admiral Dupetit-Thouars in his frigate *La Venus* bound on a 'round the world expedition. It was sighted in 1602 on Sebastián Vizcaíno's second voyage of discovery to California. His flotilla of three vessels, *San Diego, Santo Tomás,* and *Tres Reyes,* had become separated in a severe northeast blow. The *Santo Tomás,* under the command of Toribio Gómez de Corbán, was blown offshore "about 40

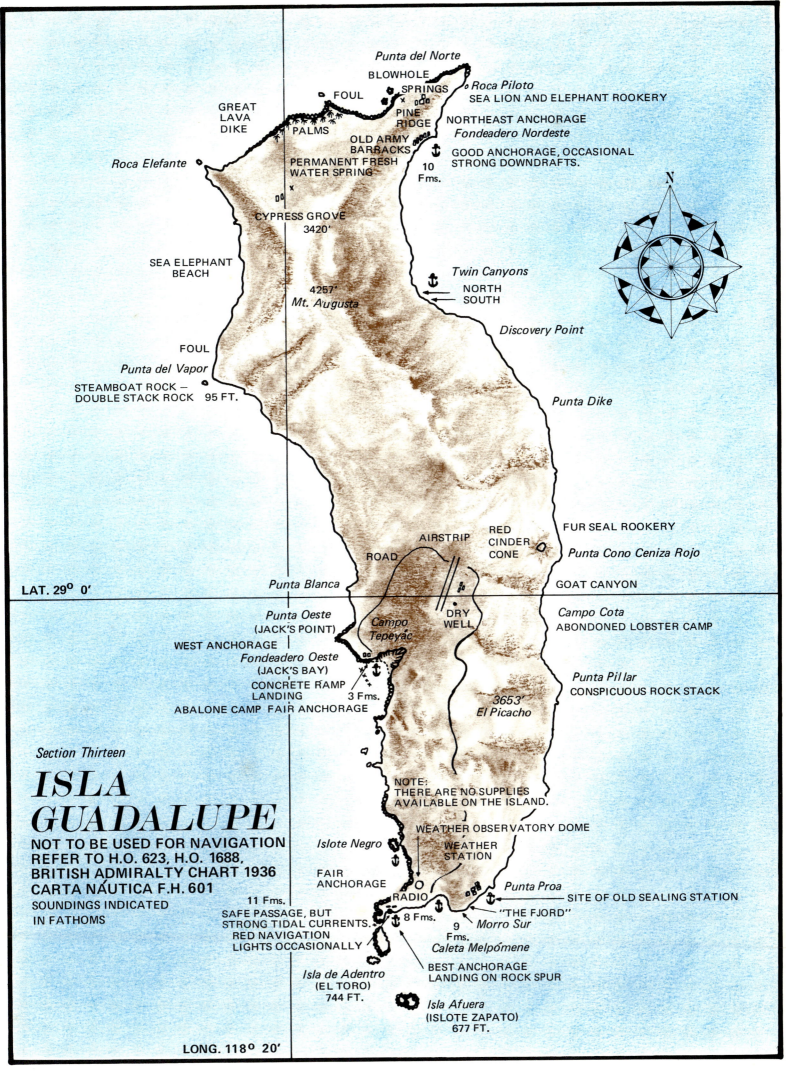

Punta Norte, Isla Guadalupe

leagues" where a large island was sighted, but due to a dangerous leak in his ship's hull, Gómez returned to Cedros Island without thoroughly reconnoitering the island. Later in the voyage, upon conferring with Vizcaíno and his navigators and analyzing the course of his vessel's track during the preceding weeks, it was determined that the "Isla Grande" that Gómez had raised was actually "Isla de los Pájaros" (the Isle of Birds) "approximately 40 leagues offshore," as had been noted in the logs of some of the Manila Galleons crossing from the Philippines in the latter half of the sixteenth century. Isla de los Pájaros, the name by which Guadalupe Island was originally known, was first sighted in 1565 by Andres de Urdaneta, pilot aboard one of the first Spanish merchantmen to make the crossing.

Guadalupe Island has a length of 20 miles north and south and a maximum width at its northern end of a little over 6 miles; it has a minimum width at its southern end of a little less than 2 miles. The southern half of the island is dotted with many volcanic mounds and cinder cones of a variety of sizes, scientific observations of which indicate that the island's central volcano may only be dormant and not extinct. The coasts consist generally of bold rocky bluffs and sheer volcanic cliffs revealing a random pattern of great lava flows. The sea has eaten its way into the volcanic cliffs and exposed a myriad of caverns, lava bubbles, and vents which spout great sprays of mist in response to the surge of the sea. Many of the canyons are so full of caves festooned with weird lava shapes that they seem to present a landscape from another world. Some detached rocks lie close off the island's coast but there are few known dangers outside a distance offshore of more than ¼ mile; however, there is a 5-fathom patch about ¾ mile offshore on the western side, approximately 3½ miles northward of the southernmost point. Discolored water has been observed to extend for a considerable distance off North Point but very deep water surrounds the island with the 50-fathom curve never much more than ½ mile off and in some places much closer-to.

Between the island and the mainland the general depths sounded are more than 2,000 fathoms, but in 1919 the United States Coast & Geodetic Survey vessel *Lydonia* sounded 176 fathoms on what is known as the Ferrel Sea-mount, about 60 miles east-northeastward of Punta del Norte or about 80 mile west-southwestward of Isla de San Geronimo; the position of the Ferrel Seamount is approximately Latitude 29° 28′ north, Longitude 117° 15′ west. In 1929 a least depth of 47 fathoms was sounded in this same vicinity.

Because of the unusual climate created by this land mass projecting abruptly from the deep surrounding ocean, the upper parts of the island are usually enveloped in clouds the greater part of the year, and its peaks are obscured for the most part.

Guadalupe Island represents approximately the top one-third of a great volcanic mountain that rises some 12,000 feet from the surrounding ocean floor. Geologically, Guadalupe is considered to be approximately 7,000,000 years old. Geographically, it has never been connected with other shores and in its relatively remote position may be considered as one of the world's true oceanic islands in every respect. The great abysmal depths of the surrounding ocean have been highly effective barriers to the natural distribution of plant and animal life. As a consequence, the flora and fauna of Guadalupe are severely limited in variety as compared to the coastal area of Baja California; but as a result of this biological isolation there are many endemic species of plant and animal life unique to Guadalupe, and their singular characteristics provide a rich and fascinating study for naturalists.

The climate is essentially of a desert character, such conditions having prevailed since the time of cooling of the volcanic stuff of which the island is made; surface erosion has been so slight over the ages that original features of the landscape have been preserved in almost undisturbed detail. The southern part of the island is quite barren but that part of the northern portion which projects high above the sea, and is almost constantly swathed by the lower strata of clouds, is bountifully supplied with moisture, chiefly in the form of a watery mist. This phenomenon in an otherwise desert environment supports some fine groves of pine, cypress, oak and fruit-bearing palms, all species found only on Guadalupe. The particular species of oak, unique to this oceanic island, is said to bear the largest acorns of

(Above) Looking southward toward Punta Proa

(Below) Anchorage off the meteorological station

any oak in existence, being fully 2 inches in diameter.

View of the south end of Guadalupe Island, distant 26 miles

Below the northern peaks are some wonderfully fertile valleys watered by scant but sufficient seepages from the moistured heights. An early naturalist visiting the island in 1875 camped in one of the cypress groves and observed a paradise of beautiful shrubs and flowering plants, with wild birds so abundant and so tame that he called it an isle of dreams. But the wildlife conditions have vastly changed since that time due to the proliferation of a few goats, introduced by whalers in the mid-1800's as a source of fresh meat for their crews; the goats now comprise a vast roaming herd that has converted the entire island into their private and exclusive pasture. Incessant herbivores, they have eaten almost every living plant and have reduced the vegetation to a closely nibbled grassland, with but few exceptions; branches of the pine, cypress, oak and other mature trees above their reach have escaped annihilation as have plants and shrubs growing on cliffs or offshore islets, inaccessible to grazing. But seedlings of the full-grown trees flowering on Guadalupe are quickly nipped off at the ground so that presently, only some fine old pine and oak growing along the ridges of the highlands on the northern portion of the islands, and the low wide-spreading Guadalupe cypress on the north central plateau, all of which reached their maturity before the goats were introduced, persist to represent their species. When these trees have lived out their lives and are gone, there will be no others to grow in their stead unless the goat population is severely cut back and thereafter carefully controlled.

A few lonely burros, left by the Mexican Army contingent once stationed on the island, were at one time still to be seen near the water hole located in a high valley at the north end of the island. How much of the water contained in the reedy, rock-rimmed basin is remnant rainwater caught during the seasonal downpour, and how much due to seepage from the spring, is a moot question; however, it very nearly dries up in parched years. Closeby the water hole are the weathered remains of two adobe buildings, one with a ragged and deteriorating roof, the other with its roof entirely blown away. House cats brought as pets by the whalers and later by the Mexican Army quickly turned into wild cats, small in size and in number but deadly to the island's once populous birdlife. The cats proceeded to subsist almost wholly upon the island's generous variety of birds and have been the direct cause of the disappearance of most of them. House mice, introduced in cargo brought from the mainland, also overran the island and probably provided a more than adequate food supply for the cats, once the majority of the birds had fallen prey. As yet there is no archaeological evidence to indicate that the coastal Indians ever occupied or visited Guadalupe Island and while any such evidence would be an exciting and fascinating find, it wouldn't be too surprising, considering the demonstrated boat-building ability and remarkable seamanship of California's coastal Indian population.

Isla Afuera

Punta del Norte (North Point) is a high rocky promontory, the seaward extremity of the mist-covered northern ridge of the island. Close southward and off-lying Punta del Norte stands Roca Piloto (Pilot Rock), a jagged, leaning rocky pinnacle that affords a good mark when approaching this side of the island. On the west side of North Point a spouting blowhole sends cascades of water vapor into the air as the heavy Pacific swell rises against the cliffs. Along this northern rockbound shore of the island, about 3¾ miles westward of Punta del Norte, a detached rock stands about ½ mile offshore; close westward another *detached rock* is situated close to a dominant rocky point.

Roca Elefante (Elephant Rock), situated a little over 2 miles southwestward, stands off the northwestern extremity of the island. The intervening coast is comprised of precipitous lava cliffs against which the sea breaks heavily; a great lava dike intersects the cliffs about midway along this northwest wall. On the slopes above the cliffs, groves of palm may be seen growing among Guadalupe pine and island oak. Clouds carried by the northwest winds sweep over this end of the island, bathing the high ridge in dense water vapor; two small springs of sweet water result from the watershed high on this northwest slope.

Along this northwestern stretch of the island's coast, about 2½ miles southwest of Punta del Norte, at a slight indentation in the massive walls of lava that rise two thousand feet above the sea, there is a narrow beach encompassed by a rockbound shore accessible only from the sea. Here a sizable colony of huge, clumsy marine animals

called sea elephants, protected by the precipitous cliffs that back their rookery, have had an opportunity to regenerate their once numerous population. These animals were at one time widely distributed and abundant on many of the remote islands in the Antarctic region as well as the coastal islands of California, but whalers learned early in the 1800's that a fair quantity and quality of oil could be obtained from the blubber of each carcass. So the slaughter began and the species was soon commercially exterminated. More than once it was thought that the last living representative of their species had been killed, but each time a small group escaped to extend their survival.

Sea Elephant

Wildlife Reservation — It is important to note that in 1922 President Obregón of Mexico declared Guadalupe Island a Wildlife Reservation. Unauthorized landing has been prohibited since that time, and among other wildlife

(Above) Isla Afuera and Isla Adentro

(Below) Morro del Sur

species, no elephant seal or fur seal is permitted to be taken, killed or molested within 3 miles of its shore. Heavy fines have been fixed for violations of these conservation measures and in some few cases have been levied against violaters to enforce future adherence.

Punta del Vapor (Steamboat Point) is situated along the western shore of the island, about 4½ miles southward of Roca Elefante. Roca del Vapor (Steamboat Rock), a double rock stack 95 feet high, lies close off this point; from seaward this rock has the appearance of a two-funnel steamer. Between Roca Elefante and Punta del Vapor, a narrow rockbound beach called Elephant Seal Beach, accessible only from the sea and backed by precipitous cliffs, supports a huge sea elephant colony. From Punta del Vapor the coast trends southward for 5½ miles to Punta Blanca, a whitish point close northward of which there are numerous *detached rocks*.

Punta del Oeste (West Point), referred to on early whalers' charts as Jack's Point, a low, rugged lava delta, is situated about 1¼ miles southward of Punta Blanca and about 6 miles northward of the southwestern extremity of the island. Fondeadero del Oeste (West Anchorage) referred to on early charts as Jack's Bay, lies in a bight immediately southward of the point. Campo Tepeyác, a permanent lobster and abalone fishing camp, is situated at the head of the bight protected by a lava reef that fronts the *landing*. *Anchorage* may be taken in this bight about 300 yards off a rockslide close southeastward of the landing, in depths of 3 fathoms, lava rock bottom. A Navy-type anchor is recommended, rigged with a buoyed trip line and a rode of chain or wire. Some protection from the northwest is afforded in this anchorage by the *lava reef awash* which projects southeastward from the shore just

above the landing. The open roadstead, however, is exposed to the heavy swell from northwestward, rendering it somewhat uncomfortable.

There is a boat channel around the southern end of the *lava reef* that leads in a dog-leg course to a concrete *landing ramp* on the beach fronting the fish camp. There are *rocks awash* and *rocks submerged* that can be seen in clear water and which must be avoided. One trip through the channel, piloted by a fisherman from the camp, is sufficient to familiarize a boatman with the dangers. Lobster pots are set out with bouys close by the reef and *lobster receivers floating awash* are anchored in the fairway.

Campo Tepeyac consists of about a dozen fishermen's wood and tar-paper shacks situated along the rocky slope of the beach; a small warehouse stands on the rise above the shacks, and a diesel-powered refrigeration plant cools a large walk-in box which holds the daily catch for air cargo shipment to Ensenada. An abalone shucking shed and lobster preparation and packing tables stand beside the walk-in refrigerator. About a dozen well-made skiffs, with good outboard motors and gasoline-driven air pumps for the hookah equipment of the abalone divers, operate from this camp.

About 30 fishermen, some with their wives and children, occupy the camp on a permanent basis. A white wooden cross may be seen erected high on a red cinder hill above the camp. There is a shortwave radio at the camp and a scheduled communication is maintained between Fishing Cooperative Headquarters in Ensenada and branch Cooperative Fish Camps at Bahía Rosario, Punta Baja and Bahía Tortugas. The manager of the camp will relay emergency messages. There is a four-wheel drive truck at the camp,

Punta de Oeste, Jack's Point

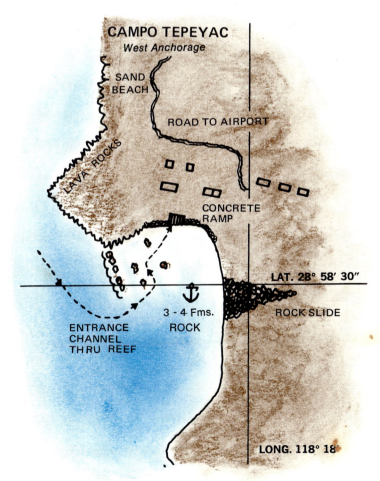

utilized to transport fish products to the airstrip. A rough, rocky road has been built through jagged fields of lava rocks and boulders to a large flat-dished crater situated at the top of a mountain in the center of the island, the site of an *airstrip*. All supplies and personnel are transported by air on a weekly schedule from Ensenada. The *airstrip* is capable of handling multi-engine cargo planes of moderate size and was recently built for the goat meat enterprise previously referred to. A C-47 Aerocarga freight plane lies with its landing gear wrecked beneath it off the northeast end of the runway, a casualty of the goat meat operation. There is a well dug alongside the airstrip but it is a dry hole. All fresh water at the fish camp must be brought in from visiting ships or trucked from the *spring* below the cypress grove, about 10 miles northwest of the airport. Water is the one commodity in short supply on the island and frequently in critical supply at the camp.

A *shoal,* covered to a depth of 5 fathoms, lies about ¾ mile offshore in a position approximately 2 miles southward of West Anchorage, opposite a sharp point of rocks distinguished by a whitish cliff above; immediately northward of this point are two sunken rocks on a *submerged reef* that breaks heavily with white water. The area should be given a wide berth when making for West Anchorage.

About 2 miles southward of the reef and the whitish point off which it is situated, and 1½ miles northward of the southwestern extremity of the island stands *Islote Negro,* (Black Islet), with a large *detached rock* close-to and separated from the main island by only a narrow boat passage. White metal buildings and a steel framework antenna of a meteorological station show to seaward on the ridge above *observation point* at the southwestern extremity of Guadalupe Island; the white round dome of the Meteorological Observatory may be seen high on the ridge.

Off Observation Point stand two sizable islets and five lesser rocks above water. Islote de Adentro (Inner Islet), referred to locally as El Toro, is 744 feet high and appears in profile like a bull's head. The islet is situated close southward of Observation Point and is separated from it by a passage about ¼ mile wide in which there are depths of 11 fathoms; however, there are *rocks submerged* on the northern side of the passage and three above water that must be avoided. There are two *detached rocks* each 40 feet high, that lie close off the southern side of Isla de Adentro.

Islote de Afuera (Outer Islet), called El Zapato on charts drawn in the early 1800's, is 677 feet high and its sheer volcanic sides rise vertically from deep water to a crater that may be seen from below, the profile of the whole looking very much like a giant shoe. Islote Afuera is situated northeastward of Islote Adentro, being separated from it by a deep channel about a mile wide.

Navigation note: Safe passage may be had between Isla Adentro and Observation Point. Directions: Head southward until the passage is well open, then steer for it, keeping Inner Islet close aboard; strong tidal currents run in this passage, generally setting in a westerly direction. Three rocks above water on the northern side of the channel are marked on the chart, the highest of which is about 35 feet;

the westernmost has a *submerged rock* close eastward of it. *Anchorage* may be had off the rock breakwater protecting the weather station village, in depths of 8 fathoms over a rocky bottom. When making for *anchorage* in Caleta Melpómene, proceed westward toward the great cliff at the southeastern extremity of the island.

Caleta Melpómene (Melpómene Cove) is situated between Isla Adentro and Morro del Sur (South Bluff), an imposing mountain of steep rock that comprises the southeastern extremity of the island and presents a great towering cliff that faces off the eastern side of the cove and drops precipitously to the sea below. The cove affords *anchorage* with shelter from all winds except those from between east and southwest, in depths of 9 fathoms. H.M.S. *Melpómene,* a British survey vessel, anchored here in 1892 in depths of 14 fathoms with the southeastern point of the island bearing 98° and the southern extremity of Isla de Adentro bearing 234°. With strong westerly or northwesterly winds the anchorage is swept by a heavy ground swell and the ground tackle must be carefully attended; violent gusts of wind frequently sweep the anchorage blowing down from the heights of the island and may be experienced by day or night. Volcanic cliffs 100 to 150 feet high, against which the swell breaks with great foaming turbulence, ring the cove.

The best *landing place* is near the western end of the cove around a rocky promontory in a small protected bight in the lee of the three offshore rocks; passengers can be disembarked on the natural breakwater. At the landing, above a black stone beach, is a small settlement of about a dozen buildings, some made of brick, occupied by a contingent of marines of the Mexican Navy. A flagpole stands before the settlement and a radio mast is erected alongside the easternmost building. Meteorological equipment is mounted on a second steel mast and shows two *red navigation lights* while

Red Cinder Cone Point

Isla Adentro, Guadalupe Weather Station, Melepómene Cove

the generator is running at night. A religious shrine is built on the slope above the buildings and a sportsfield has been cleared on the terrace just above the shrine, at the site of a former sealing station.

The meteorological station functions in the capacity of a crucial weather outpost, the westernmost of a series of Mexican observation posts that participate in an international program of exchange of meteorological information. Guadalupe Island lies approximately in the path of the sometimes severe ocean storms that form between the months of July and November in the general vicinity of the Revillagigedo Islands, some 750 miles southeastward. Guadalupe Weather Station provides a valuable early warning service to ship and aircraft movement along the Baja California coast, as well as to ports and harbors in the north. Forty-six daily entries, including data on wind, barometric pressure, precipitation, temperature and state of the weather, comprise each report. The information is radioed to Ensenada on a frequent schedule. The information thus forwarded is included in the nationwide sequence of network weather reports teletyped to all stations.

Approximately 50 people occupy the Guadalupe Island Naval Base and Weather Station, including a medical corpsman. All supplies are brought from Ensenada once every three weeks, although the island's goat herds provide an unending supply of fresh meat. There is no fresh water on the southern tip of the island where the weather station is located and the colony is completely dependent on the Mexican Navy which brings fresh water along with necessary provisions. *Health caution: All water obtained for drinking or cooking at the weather station should be boiled before drinking.*

Permission to land on the island must be obtained from the Commandant at the Naval Base, and clearance to the island beforehand obtained from any official port of entry in Mexico. It is important to remember that the wildlife and shellfish are assiduously protected by the Mexican Government and a substantial fine levied against taking them illegally. The genuine graciousness of Mexican hospitality is nowhere more warmly displayed than at such a remote outpost as this, for the men and families of the Naval contingent, serving their country month on end in lonely isolation, are exceedingly happy to receive and entertain good guests from the mainland.

Along the southeastern shore of the island about a mile northward of Morro del Sur, between that major landmark and Punta Proa, at the lowest point of the cliffs, there is a very good *boat landing* from which it is possible to gain access to the interior of the island. Near the landing is the site of what was once one of the four major fur seal rookeries on the island, referred to by scientific expeditions as South Rookery or Sealers' Camp. Great colonies of these animals thrived at one time on Guadalupe Island and other of the offshore islands, as well as along the coast of the Californias. Long months were spent pursuing the fur seal, processing the pelts and loading a full cargo for home port. Records show that as many as 30,000 pelts and more were taken by a single ship in one year; frequently battles and armed boarding that amounted to piracy and open warfare flared amongst the sealers. Harpoon guns were loaded and at the ready, not for whale but to repel interlopers from sealing grounds considered exclusive and inviolate territory of first comers, hotly challenged by crews of ships with empty holds hungry for a lucrative catch. The great colonies of fur seals that inspired this deadly rush to the sealing grounds were quickly decimated and after a few years of uncontrolled slaughter, ceased to be particularly profitable.

Twin Canyons

At South Rookery the stone foundations of 16 sealers' huts are still to be found, with rusty square boat nails and some redwood roofing shingles scattered about, evidence of the relatively large operation that was conducted at the height of the sealing operations. On the walls of these same stone huts the sealers and whalemen left the petroglyphic evidence of their presence down to the month and year of their visits. Carefully carved into the building rock are the names of men and their ships with home ports for years from 1811, to 1881. One inscription reads: "Ship Essex '35 Oct. Henry Waldbon, Bristol, R.I." Significantly the chronology ends in the first part of the 1880's.

Long thought totally extinct by scientists, a small colony of fur seal was discovered on Guadalupe in 1927, and more than a quarter of a century later a breeding colony was observed by Dr. Carl Hubbs of Scripps Institution of Oceanography, on a scientific expedition to the island in 1954. *Important note: To reiterate an important and assiduously enforced regulation: fur seals, elephant seals, and all wildlife on Guadalupe Island are protected by strict Mexican law; the taking, trapping, or molesting of any wildlife within three miles of the shore is prohibited.*

Close southward of the landing at South Rookery there is a narrow and deep indentation in the shore with a sand beach at its head called The Fjord. A boat may enter and land on the beach almost completely sheltered from the sea.

Northward of South Rookery along the eastern shore of the island, the predominant volcanic character of the land may be seen in a succession of steep rocky cliffs in which there are many sea-scoured caves and lava tubes at tidal level that form spouting blowholes plainly to be seen and heard. Punta Proa, northward of the old sealing station, appears in profile as the prow of a ship; this point is sometimes referred to as Yellow Point or Double Point.

About 5 miles northward of South Rookery is a conspicuous rock stack called Pillar Point or Boxing Glove Point, immediately above which is a red cinder cone on the slope. About 2 miles northward of Pillar Point there is a deserted lobster camp called Campo Cota, situated at the mouth of an arroyo that opens on the shore between two reddish cinder cones. An old wooden shack with a few timbers remaining may be seen at the camp. An old fur seal rookery,

with telltale beach rocks worn to a glistening smoothness by the seal colony's incessant activity over many hundreds of years, lies along the shore between the lobster camp and Goat Creek, about ½ mile northward.

Punta Cono Ceniza Rojo (Red Cinder Cone Point), immediately northward of Goat Creek, affords an excellent navigational mark. El Picacho, about 3,200 feet high, the highest peak in the southern portion of Guadalupe Island, rises to a turret-shaped crest above this part of the coastline. Occlusion Point is situated about 2 miles northward of Red Cinder Cone Point, thence 1½ miles farther northward is Dike Point, site of a remarkable volcanic dike in the coastal formation. In the vicinity just north of Dike Point, the water-washed deck timbers of a sizable wooden vessel lie cast up on the rocky beach.

From Dike Point the coast trends in a northwesterly direction to Discovery Point, a distance of about 2 miles. Discovery Point was so named for the finding of the small colony of Guadalupe fur seals in 1954 by Dr. Carl Hubbs of Scripps Institution of Oceanography. Twin Canyons, comprised of North and South Canyon, open onto the shore about 1¼ miles northwestward of Discovery Point. While the sea breaks on detached rocks and outlying reefs all along this coast, there is deep water with no hidden dangers outside ¼ mile offshore, except for a *sunken rock* about ¼ mile offshore approximately 5 miles southward of Punta del Norte and on which the sea breaks heavily.

Northeast Anchorage, an indentation about 3 miles northwestward of Twin Canyons and 1½ miles southward of Punta del Norte, affords the most comfortable *anchorage* to be found at Guadalupe Island. There are no sunken rocks in the cove and depths of 4 fathoms are found within 200 feet of the beach, although the coastal shelf is quite steep and at 100 yards the depths fall steeply to 25 fathoms. This cove offers good protection from the prevailing west and northwest winds and is not exposed to the violent gusts which descend from the heights of the island in most all the other anchorages. The bottom is comprised of gravel without any weed and provides good holding ground, where vessels anchored close inshore may secure fore and aft by carrying a stern line ashore to be made fast to the boulders on the beach. In the bight itself the surf breaks so heavily that landing through it is dangerous but a *safe landing* can be easily effected alongside the point of rocks at the southern end of the cove, taking care to avoid the *reef awash* that extends several hundred yards seaward off the point. There is a white wooden cross erected on the point with the legend in white letters painted on the rock, "Senador."

The narrow beach is backed by a precipitous 1,500-foot rock wall; deeply hued strata of browns and yellows and reds run through the rock and suggest a rich mineral content crudely smelted by the intense heat of ancient volcanic activity. Beyond the landing place south of the reef, there is a small sand beach where *good anchorage* in a depth of 10 to 15 fathoms, sand bottom, may be obtained ¼ mile offshore, and vessels are well-sheltered against wind.

In a shallow canyon that opens onto this beach, on rocky terraces above the landing, stand the decaying military buildings and barracks of a Mexican garrison once stationed on Guadalupe Island. Above the barracks and overlooking the site is a dilapidated white stucco building known locally as The Fort, with a round turret pierced by gun slits. A series of rock stairs leads to a higher rocky terrace farther up the bluff, where — surveying the entire landing and roadstead — is a two-story building of later vintage, but also falling into ruins, that once served as the Army officers' quarters. This military camp, occupied by a Mexican military establishment for a number of years, was finally abandoned around 1947. Northeast Landing was also the locale for a short-lived enterprise organized to process canned goat meat utilizing the vast herds of wild goats that populate the island. The enterprise struggled to succeed for several years in the early 1900's and then was abandoned. All that remains of the cannery is an old rusty steam boiler alongside a scattering of crumbling foundations. A rock-walled well of brackish water stands on the rocky shore between the iron boiler and the barracks. A small *spring* of sweet water is located above the landing in the arroyo but runs only in wet years; it decreases to a bare seepage in years of drouth.

A hundred years before this time the beach was a thriving rookery for the black fur seal and had been so for countless hundreds of years. The smooth and polished surface of the lava rock bears mute testimony to the countless generations of tens of thousands of these animals that once densely populated the rookery. With great labor the sealers that exploited this colony constructed a massive rock-walled roadway that works its way from the beach up the mountainside to a drying flat high above; there on the smooth ground the seal skins were stretched out for processing, held securely in place by wooden pegs driven into the earth. The roadway is still usable and in good repair.

A Mexican cooperative abalone diving vessel, *Senador,* at one time visited Guadalupe Island at regular intervals with a nest of small skiffs. Hookah divers, tended from the skiffs, gathered the abundant shellfish from the rocky depths and fetched them to the "mother" ship for processing and freezing.

Northwestward of this anchorage and landing, the northeastern extremity of the island, Punta del Norte (North Point) juts seaward from a curving coastline that sweeps around to form the point; off-lying and close southward of Punta del Norte stands the aforementioned Roca Piloto (Pilot Rock), a jagged leaning rocky pinnacle around which the sea abounds with fish. Yellowtail, a favorite fighting gamefish of many coastal bays, may be caught here in great numbers and good size, anywhere from 10 to 40 pounds. Sportfishing boats from San Diego may be seen frequently in this vicinity. Pilot Rock Beach, close south and inshore of Pilot Rock, is a black sand beach on which a landing can be made in fine weather.

Approach to Northeast Anchorage

Roca Piloto

Cabo Norte

SEA AND WEATHER CONDITIONS — Throughout the year winds from west and north predominate, greatly outnumbering those from any other quarter. The winds are mainly moderate in strength, reaching force 7 or greater, less than one day per month in the winter, on the average, and even less frequently in other seasons. Local tropical hurricanes or *Chubascos,* small in extent and short in duration but with fierce winds, have their genesis in the ocean area southwest of Guadalupe Island; for the most part these storms move roughly parallel to the coast before turning either seaward or toward the mainland, and have a greatest incidence in the month of September, with somewhat lesser occurrence in the three preceding months and the one succeeding month. Guadalupe Island is situated in such an oceanic position as to be shielded, for the most part, from these violent storms, their tracks generally passing well southward, the winds slacking with any northward movement and nearly all having lost their hurricane force upon approaching the latitude of the island. Rain is infrequent but low stratus clouds gather around the peaks of the island a large percentage of the summer months, due to a chilling of moisture-laden sea air by a relatively cold ocean layer around the island. While snow at sea in the north Pacific Ocean is practically unknown south of 40° north latitude, near the top of Guadalupe Island, frosts in the winter months are common and a light snow may be seen at rare intervals, showing a delicate white mantle on the peaks at the northern end of the island.

COMMUNICATIONS — Radio contact with Ensenada is maintained daily from the Mexican Naval Weather Station located at the south end of the island. Upon application to the Commandant of the station, messages may be accepted for transmission and replies delivered. The fishing cooperative at Northwest Anchorage maintains a reliable radio schedule with Ensenada three times daily. They will relay emergency messages.

MARINE EMERGENCIES — Closest Mexican Naval base is located at Ensenada, approximately 180 miles northeastward of the island. Coastal fishing vessels will render aid in the best tradition of the sea and can generally be reached by radiotelephone on 2182, 2638 and 2738 kilo-Hertz. The United States Coast Guard will render seaborne or airborne aid, under emergency conditions, by treaty with Mexico. Messages should be sent or relayed on emergency frequencies in accordance with international rules.

MEDICAL EMERGENCIES — There is a medical corpsman stationed at the Meteorological Base at the south end of the island where emergency medical aid may be rendered. The *Flying Samaritans* maintain a medical clinic at San Quintín, about 140 miles northeastward on the mainland. A DC-3 Aerocarga plane based at Ensenada calls weekly at Guadalupe Island and may be reached by road from either the weather station or Campo Tepeyác.

SOURCES OF ADDITIONAL INFORMATION — Sociedad Cooperative de Produción Pesquera, Avenue Lopéz Mateos 466, Ensenada, B. Cfa., Mexico; Aerocarga Aviación, S.A. Km. 116 Cipres, B. Cfa., Mexico, telephone Ensenada 9-1825; Servicios Navales, Gobierno Federal, Álvaro Obregón No. 860, B. Cfa., Mexico, telephone 8-2245.

Scrub Oak

Roca Partida, looking Northeast

Roca Partida, looking South

Isla Roca Partida, the smallest of the four islands of the Revillagigedo Archipelago belonging to Mexico, is situated about 60 miles west-northwestward of Cabo Henslow, Socorro Island, and about 153 miles eastward of Isla Clarión; it is about 860 nautical miles southeast of San Diego and about 260 miles southward of Cabo San Lucas. Roca Partida is the remnant of a very old volcano, the summit of which has been eroded by wave action to what now appears as a barren divided rock rising 110 feet above the sea, its two rocky pinnacles are connected by a solid bridge about 20 feet high, and are covered with a thin layer of birdlime that whitens it to the appearance, from a distance, of a disabled ship under jury rig. The rock is steep-to and it is possible for vessels to lie as close as desired because of the near-vertical 40-fathom dropoff to the shelf beneath. The average width of this supporting shelf is about 5,000 feet, with the break to deep water occurring at about 80 fathoms all around. The whole of this rocky islet is about a hundred yards in length by not more than 50 yards wide.

Roca Partida was discovered by the Spanish explorer Ruy López de Villalobos in 1542; Captain Colnett, Royal Navy, drew the first reconnaissance chart in 1793, which was slightly modified by the U.S.S. *Naragansett* survey under Commander George Dewey in 1874 for use on all U.S. Navy Hydrographic Office charts. A scientific study, undertaken in 1953, '55 and '57 by the University of California, Scripps Institution of Oceanography expedition, resulted in the most accurate charting of Roca Partida and soundings of the surrounding shelf made to this date.

The first known landing on Roca Partida was made by this expedition in 1953 for the purpose of collecting rock samples for analysis and classification. Such a "first" land-

ing so long after its initial discovery can readily be understood, for other than a precarious nesting place for birds, it poses only a danger to navigation, or possibly a terrestrial fix by which to prove up one's navigation. In any case, its position relative to a ship's track should be prudently noted on the pilot chart and its rocky dangers avoided. *Note: A strong westerly set in the vicinity of the islet has been experienced, reinforced at periods by the lunar tide.* Commercial fishermen from the coast visit the area. The sea roundabout is frequently alive with small red crabs in clustered patches. Schools of tuna and skipjack thrash the water to a frothy turbulence as they feed on these tiny crustaceans.

Roca Partida is situated geologically in the Clarión Fracture Zone which extends over 2,000 miles westward of Isla Clarión. It is believed to be related to the trans-Mexico volcanic belt, which includes the newly erupted volcanoes at Isla San Benedicto, Paracutín and Orizaba on the Mexican mainland, and extends at least to the smoking cone of Popocatépetyl in the Valley of Mexico. All evidence above the sea indicates volcanic activity dormant at Roca Partida for the past several thousand years but there are two submarine volcanic pinnacles in the near vicinity (one 12 miles to the northeast) which are unavailable to easy examination.

Rocas Alijos, looking toward the west

Rocas Alijos, looking toward the north

Rocas Alijos (Alijos Rocks), "The Lighters," situated at Latitude 24° 57′ north, Longitude 115° 45′ west, are a dangerous group of barren rocks protruding from the surface of the sea in complete isolation from any other landmark. They lie off the coast of Baja California, 152 miles south-southwestward of Punta San Roque, the nearest point on the coast, about 186 miles westward of Cape San Lázaro, and 343 miles west-northwestward of Cabo Falso. The group is comprised of three principal rocks and numerous smaller ones clustered in a single group, both exposed and submerged. They extend about ⅓ of a mile in a north-south orientation with a width of less than 200 yards. Sunken rocks lie both southward and northward of the visible rocks. The northernmost of the larger rocks stands 72 feet high; South Rock, the largest and southernmost of the group stands 112 feet high. The sheer character of their configuration makes landing on these rocky pinnacles impossible even in the calmest weather. Soundings of 50 fathoms are found at a distance of about ½ mile both eastward and westward of the rocks, and 36 fathoms at a little greater distance northward. Depths of more than 1,300 fathoms are found within 6 miles of the group.

Alijos Rocks appear to be the weathered remnant of a once substantial island, long since eroded by wind and wave, leaving only these bare, rocky pinnacles standing in the sea. Seen from a distance, they appear to be a ship under sail, or as observed by their discoverer in 1791, Captain Marquina, enroute from the Philippines in a Spanish Merchantman: "A string of Lighters." These rocks are neither buoyed, lighted nor marked in any way and give no warning of their existence, save for the wash of the surf against them and the shrill cry of the night birds that wheel about them; such sounds to be heard only in close proximity by an alert watch and then only in the stillness that accompanies calm weather aboard a sailing craft. The rocks should be given a wide berth, their position relative to the track of a vessel carefully marked, and a sharp lookout kept while running in their vicinity. *Navigation warning: the geographic position of Alijos Rocks on H.O. Charts 1006 and 1688 as well as British Admiralty Chart #1936 is displaced from their charted position about 2 miles, 290°.*

The French Frigate *La Venus* under French Admiral Dupetit-Thouars surveyed this ocean area in 1837 and sketched a chart of Alijos Rocks which formed the basis of international charts still published. More precise observations were taken by a scientific expedition in 1957 and noted on the latest charts. The Alijos Rocks are visited frequently by Tuna Clippers from San Diego, San Pedro and Mexico, in search of the large schools of tuna and skipjack that often feed around them. Game fish frequent the area; whales, seals, porpoise and blackfish pass this way and a variety of sea birds make their aerial nests on the precarious shelves of rocks. Other than this activity Alijos Rocks stand their lonely vigil in the vastness of the surrounding ocean from century to century slowly being swallowed by the eroding sea.

Isla San Benedicto, September 20, 1952

Isla San Benedicto, the third largest and most north-easterly of the four islands of the Revillagigedo group, lies 220 miles southward of Cabo San Lucas in Latitude 19° 18′ north, Longitude 110° 49′ west. It is a volcanic island that has recently had a series of eruptions that began on the morning of August 1, 1952, and remained active intermittently for a number of months, changing considerably some previously existing physical characteristics of the land.

The violent and spectacular birth of the volcano on San Benedicto Island was observed from its onset by the crew of the Tuna Clipper *Challenger* who were fishing in close proximity to the island. Their original reports and photographs were followed by a full-scale scientific study by members of teams from Scripps Institution of Oceanography as well as by leading scientists of Mexico, all of whom have kept the island under close watch since and have collected a continuing record of valuable information, much of which has been published in scientific journals.

The first marine chart known to have been made of Isla San Benedicto was drawn by Captain James Colnett of the British Royal Navy during a hydrographic expedition in 1793. A survey sketch made by the officers and men under Commander George Dewey of the U.S.S. *Narragansett* in 1874, produced a chart of the island in more comprehensive detail. This original American sketch is still in use today by the British Admirality in their chart #1936, Islands of the North Pacific, and was in use by the U.S. Hydrographic Office on H.O. 1688 as recently as the edition of 1951. The latest detailed charts have been made by scientists from the U.S. and Mexico, primarily studying the island's volcanic activity, and these data have been made available for the most recent charts published.

The new dimensions of San Benedicto Island, calculated

after the eruption of 1952, are 2.8 miles long, roughly oriented north by east and south by west; 1.6 miles wide across the widest point of the new Bárcena volcanic cone, which is situated toward the southern end of the island and named in honor of the Mexican geologist Manano Bárcena. The maximum height of the Bárcena Volcano, the highest point of land, is about 1,100 feet above sea level built up from an initial 975-foot altitude shown on pre-eruption hydrographic charts. The new volcanic cone dominates the profile of the island and cinder ash has largely bridged the area northward toward the Herrera Crater.

Prior to the volcanic eruption and formation of the Bárcena Volcano the only names of geographic features in general use were Montículo Cinerítico (Ash Mound) above Punta Sur on the southern end of the island; Herrera Crater, situated in the center of the island; White Bluffs, on the southern end of the island, and Black Bluff, on the eastern side of the island toward the southern end. The latter two designations, "White Bluffs" and "Black Bluff," are no longer descriptive of the island's features as they were obliterated during or shortly after the eruption.

It is possible to land on the southeast side of the island, in a small skiff, immediately adjacent to the Delta Lavico (Lava Delta) west of the lava flow which protects the black sand beach from the prevailing northerly seas; or on a small pocket beach north of the prominent volcanic dikes at Punta Órtolan. The former landing is sometimes beset with a short crashing surf and the beach has been named Caletilla Volteadura (Turnover Beach) after a swamping of their skiff in the surf by two Scripps' scientists, some of the first men to set foot on this newly formed beach after the eruption of 1952. It is difficult to reach other parts of the island from these landing places, the sides of the new volcanic cone being crumbly and subject to slide.

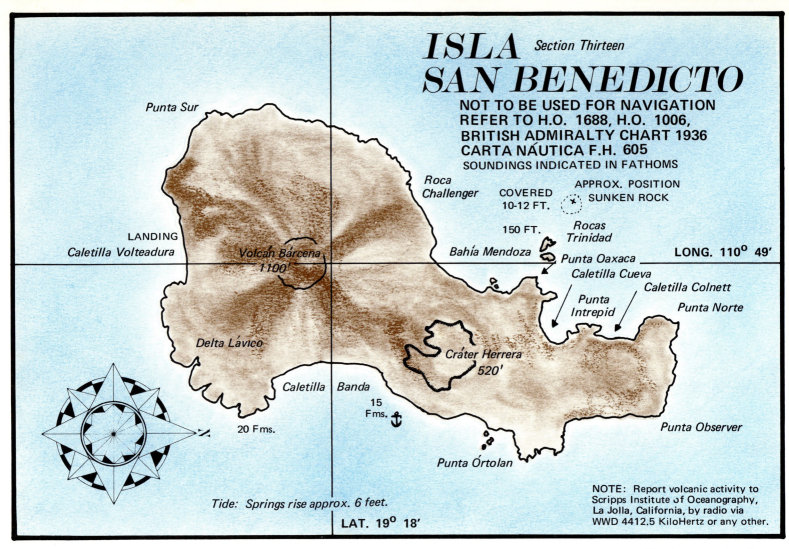

NOT TO BE USED FOR NAVIGATION
REFER TO H.O. 1688, H.O. 1006,
BRITISH ADMIRALTY CHART 1936
CARTA NÁUTICA F.H. 605
SOUNDINGS INDICATED IN FATHOMS

Punta Sur

Roca Challenger

COVERED 10-12 FT.

APPROX. POSITION
SUNKEN ROCK

LANDING
Caletilla Volteadura

150 FT.

Rocas Trinidad

Bahía Mendoza

Punta Oaxaca

LONG. 110° 49'

Volcán Bárcena
1100'

Caletilla Cueva

Caletilla Colnett

Punta Intrepid

Punta Norte

Delta Lávico

Cráter Herrera
520'

Caletilla Banda

15 Fms.

20 Fms.

Punta Observer

Punta Órtolan

Tide: Springs rise approx. 6 feet.

NOTE: Report volcanic activity to Scripps Institute of Oceanography, La Jolla, California, by radio via WWD 4412.5 KiloHertz or any other.

LAT. 19° 18'

Except for the new Lava Delta below the southeast side of the Bárcena volcanic cone and several pocket beaches on the east and west sides, the island presents an almost unbroken array of precipitous rocky cliffs rising directly out of the sea. The northern extremity of the island is composed of precipitous and broken rocky cliffs that extend eastward and westward of Punta Norte (North Point) which slopes downward from Cerro López de Villalobos (Villalobos Hill) to a rough bench above a sheer bluff.

Southward of Punta Norte on the western side of the island is an indentation forming Colnett Cove. Punta Intrepid divides this cove from a second and deeper cove to the southward, Cueva Cove, which is backed by the sheer walls of a cliff that rises vertically to a volcanic plateau above. An *exposed rock* lies detached close northward of Punta Intrepid. Cueva Cove is foul with rocks close off the cliffs upon which the seas wash in white foam. On the southern side of Cueva Cove stands a tall conspicuous column of rock, attached to a knob at the end of a projecting ridge which comprises Punta Oaxaca. Lying off this point about ¼ mile are Rocas Trinidad (Trinity Rocks), two rather large sheer-faced stacks and one smaller rock, 200, 150, and 60 feet high, respectively.

Southward of Punta Oaxaca is a broad indentation, Bahía Mendoza, that runs beneath the Herrera Crater and is bracketed on its southern extremity by Roca Challenger (Challenger Rock). At the northern end of this bay, standing close seaward of a white cliff, is a needle-like pinnacle rock. On the southern extremity of Bahía Mendoza is the

spectacular bluff outcropping of Roca Challenger, several hundred feet above the sea. Since the eruption of the Bárcena Volcano and the formation of its dominant cone, Roca Challenger is almost wholly incorporated in the slope of the cone, projecting now as sort of a rocky balcony from its northwestern side.

From Challenger Rock southward, southeastward, and eastward, the deeply eroded cone of the Bárcena Volcano curves around toward Punta Sur (South Point), the southernmost extremity of the island. The seaward edge of the cone falls precipitously into the sea, with *submerged and detached rocks* close offshore. Punta Sur, a conspicuous bluff rising steeply from the sea and showing patches of white material near its foot, is situated immediately below Montículo Cinerítico (Ash Mound) which rises to a little over 1,000 feet above sea level. *Detached rocks* lie close along the shore at the foot of this bluff. Northward of Punta Sur, on the eastern side of the island, is Caletilla Volteadura (Overturn Beach), a relatively flat black sand-and-pumice strand upon which a landing can be made through the surf in good weather. It is bounded by Punta Sur at its southern extremity and by the Delta Lavico (Lava Delta) on the north. Delta Lavico is a broad fan-shaped flow of black lava rock, extruded in 1952 from a vent at the base of the Bárcena Volcano which rises directly above the Lava

Volcanic eruption on San Benedicto August 1, 1952

Delta; the surface of the cone is deeply furrowed by recent erosion. The delta is about 1,400 yards wide at its widest point and extends seaward about 700 yards. Soundings to determine the submarine extent of the Lava Delta have been made; the 100-fathom curve is located no more than 1,000 feet off the central most seaward portion of the flow. *Anchorage* was taken in 20 fathoms abeam the Lava Delta by the yacht *Observer* in December, 1952, but this anchorage was made for the convenience of the scientists aboard studying the eruption then still in progress. *Better anchorage areas* are yet to be surveyed and reported. On the northeastern side of Delta Lavico is another black sand and pumice beach, Caletilla Banda, on which landing is not recommended due to prevailing northerly weather.

Along the eastern side of the island, Crater Herrera rises steeply from the sea, joined on its southern side to the new Bárcena cone. The seaward side of the Herrera Crater is a whitish bluff several hundred feet high and about ½ mile long. At the northern end of the crater, the cliff turns slightly outward to form an inconspicuous point off which a *reef of rocks,* submerged and awash, extends several hundred yards seaward. A cluster of *three exposed rocks* is located off the end of this reef. Immediately northward of this inconspicuous point and reef is a prominent point, Punta Órtolan, a sharp rocky bluff with detached rocks at its foot. Arroyo Fragata, on the northern side of Punta Órtolan, drains the upper slope of the volcanic plateau between Herrera Crater and Cerro López de Villalobos on the northern end of the island.

Northward along the cliffs toward Punta Observer, several *detached rocks* stand close offshore, including a tall needle-like pinnacle. Punta Observer is a relatively flat-topped knob above a sheer rocky cliff at the north-

eastern tip of the island; it forms a sort of opera-box platform of land protruding from the cliffs slightly below Cerro Villalobos. Viewed from the southward, the cliff below this knob is distinctly of a dark color as sharply contrasted to the whitish-colored cliffs adjoining. Westward of Punta Observer, the precipitous cliffs comprising the northern end of the island fall steeply to the sea from Cerra Villalobos.

Caution: A dangerous sunken rock, with 10 to 12 feet of water over it, lies about ¾ mile southwestward of the extreme northwestern point of the island; a depth of 15 fathoms was sounded about 15 miles northward of the northern point of the island.

In the early morning hours of August 1, 1952, Isla San Benedicto was indeed a sight to behold. The Tuna Clipper *Challenger* had arrived at 0530 to try its luck with the schools of yellowfin tuna that were feeding about 2 miles west of Punta Norte. About 0745, volcanic activity suddenly erupted in the form of a thin white pencil-like column of gas rising skyward behind Roca Challenger; low rumblings were heard by some of the crew but for the most part this unique phenomenon seemed soundless. A few minutes later, the steam column had been displaced by a dark cement-colored column of ash and steam that shot first skyward and then immediately began to spread over the profile of the island, enveloping the peaks and headlands, and thereafter the entire island, in dense volcanic smoke. Meantime an unfolding cauliflower plume had risen to almost 5,000 feet altitude over the island. Several inches of powdery dust and volcanic cinders the size of tennis balls rained on the decks of the *Challenger* as it held a course at full speed away from the violently erupting volcano. The ocean, previously clear and blue,

Roca Challenger

Punta Norte, Roca Challenger

now continually receiving a heavy rain of volcanic ash, became turbid and murky. Splashes that could clearly be observed in the sea southwest of Montículo Cinerítico indicated that sizable volcanic bombs were being ejected quite forcibly from the maw of the new volcano, as the *Challenger* left San Benedicto for Isla Socorro, 27 miles southward. A column of dark ash from San Benedicto seemed to be rising very high into the sky and volcanic dust continued to fall on the decks of the *Challenger*.

In the afternoon, the Tuna Clipper left Isla Socorro for Roca Partida, 60 miles to the west; on the way large pieces of pumice were seen floating in the water, carried by the westerly set of the prevailing current. A transpacific drift of floating pumice ejected by the erupting volcano was found ashore on the Hawaiian, Johnston, Wake and Marshall Islands, and is believed to have reached the Palau Islands, which are located in the Western Pacific Ocean. The eruption plume was estimated to rise higher than 10,000 feet and volcanic dust still fell on the deck of the ship, now more than 70 miles away from San Benedicto. At night, on August 4, flashes of fire from the new volcano were seen from Socorro to which the ship had re-

turned. The skipper of the *Challenger* had notified the U.S. Hydrographic Office by radio of the eruption shortly after it began and ultimately the news reached the scientific world, which launched a systematic airborne and seaborne observation.

Rarely do volcanoes put on such a fiery show and seldom are spectators on hand in such remote areas to observe and record the phenomenon. The crew of the *Challenger* was doubly fortunate in witnessing the volcanic violence from a front row seat and escaping it with whole skins. Many vessels have followed after to view the eruption but it has seemingly subsided to a sphinx-like repose, leaving a formidable new cone that now dominates the island. *Scientific note: Mariners observing a renewal of volcanic activity on San Benedicto Island, or anywhere in the Revillagigedo group, are requested to notify the Mexican Government or Scripps Institution of Oceanography, La Jolla, California, by radio via station WWD on the frequency 4412.5 kiloHertz, or by any other radio channel or relay available, as it is desired to scientifically observe any eruption by aircraft as soon after the onset as possible.*

Isla San Benedicto, looking south

Isla San Benedicto looking to the northwest, October, 1954

Cabo Middleton and Academy Bay

Isla Socorro is the largest of the four islands of the Revillagigedo Archipelago and lies 27 miles south-south-west of San Benedicto, 246 miles southward of Cabo San Lucas, in Latitude 18° 47′ north, Longitude 110° 58′ west. It is a volcanic island showing abundant evidence of past volcanic activity and some signs of mild recent eruption. The central peak of the island, Cerro Evermann, rises to an elevation of 3,707 feet, the greatest height of any of the peaks in the archipelago, and may be sighted in clear weather from a distance of 70 miles. The high central peak of Socorro is frequently cloud-capped, bearing witness to the impression given the early explorer, López de Villalobos who named the island Anublada (Cloudy) in 1542.

Upon close approach during certain seasons of the year, and especially after considerable rainfall, the island has a rather pleasant appearance of green slopes, contrasting to the black lava and reddish ash that comprise the greater part of the terrain. As viewed from seaward during the dry season and generally for the most part of the year, Socorro has a barren and uninviting appearance. The ground along most of the shore is covered with a thick and almost impenetrable growth of cactus and sage-like brush.

The volcanic nature of the island is everywhere apparent; quantities of lava are strewn along the slope in isolated patches and the red soil is plentifully mixed with ashes. The hill on the east side of Braithwaite Bay is composed entirely of ashes. The surface of the island is broken by hummocks and crater-like mounds, and in some places is furrowed by deep ravines that are walled with lava. There is some grass, but the vegetation in general is of a low order. On the northern slope of the island, however, the prospect is somewhat more pleasing. A kind of bean, which grows abundantly along the ground on this part of the island, appears to be wholesome if cooked and eaten in moderation. Prickly pears or "cactus apples" also grow in abundance and may be gathered and eaten, their ripeness revealed by a bright red coloration; they are generally somewhat tart but can be quite sweet.

The western side of the island is comprised of a series of precipitous cliffs in which the sea has worked numerous caves and formed many blowholes which spout rhythmically to the surge of the sea. About ½ mile northward of Punta Tosca (Rugged Point) is a natural stone bridge, eroded by the sea, plainly visible from shipboard. To the southward of Cape Middleton is a conspicuous sandy beach, a *good landing place* in easterly and southeasterly weather. There is an abundance of small animal and bird life on the island and some few sheep, remnant of a herd kept by an American company in the late twenties. For about a

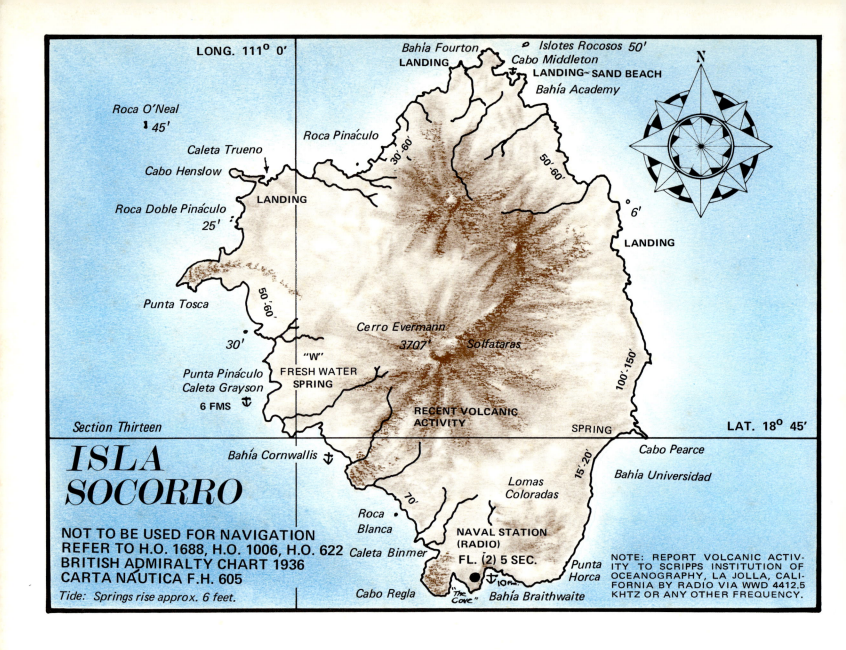

Section Thirteen

ISLA SOCORRO

NOT TO BE USED FOR NAVIGATION
REFER TO H.O. 1688, H.O. 1006, H.O. 622
BRITISH ADMIRALTY CHART 1936
CARTA NÁUTICA F.H. 605

Tide: Springs rise approx. 6 feet.

NOTE: REPORT VOLCANIC ACTIV-
ITY TO SCRIPPS INSTITUTION OF
OCEANOGRAPHY, LA JOLLA, CALI-
FORNIA BY RADIO VIA WWD 4412.5
KHTZ OR ANY OTHER FREQUENCY.

year, in 1927 or 1928, a sheepherder and his wife resided on the island, the only known residents until the establishment of the Mexican naval garrison in 1957 at Cabo Regla and a supporting settlement at Bahía Braithwaite.

Cabo Middleton, northernmost point of Socorro Island, is a peninsular piece of land about 50 feet high and ½ mile wide, situated at the end of a spur running down from Mount Evermann; it is connected to the island by a narrow neck of sand and a dry salt flat partly overgrown by low scrub brush. This isthmus separates two deep bights on either side of the cape. *Detached rocks* lie off the seaward face of the cape and an *exposed reef,* several hundred yards long and against which the swell breaks, extends northeastward from the southeastern end of the cape.

Islotes Rocosos (Rocky Islets) are two detached rocks separated from each other by approximately ½ mile, lying about 1 mile east-northeastward of Cabo Middleton; the outer islet is about 50 feet high. The swell breaks heavily on these rocks and breakers have been reported to extend ¾ mile westward of the islets toward the reef.

In the bights, well sheltered from the prevailing weather by the cape and the reef, are coves with gently sloping white sand beaches where *safe anchorage* may be taken and an easy *landing* effected through calm surf. Bahía Fourton, the western bight, affords no anchorage owing to the detached rocks but small boats may enter by keeping westward of Arch Rock, situated about 200 yards offshore, until the bight opens. A course may then be taken directly to the sandy beach at the head of the cove where a *landing* can be made. Tucked behind a shorebound curving reef is a flat pocket of white coral sand very pleasant to use as a swimming beach; the water is crystal clear, and warm.

Bahía Academy, comprised of two coves in the eastern bight, spans about ½ mile between its entrance points; the *reef,* which extends seaward from the southeastern end of the cape, forms a partial breakwater sheltering the bight. A vessel entering the bight must keep clear of *two sunken rocks* lying about 50 yards from the southern shore between the red cliffs on the starboard hand and the outer sandy cove on the port hand; a rounded conical hill just up behind the cove is a good landmark by which to steer. *Anchorage* may be taken in the deeper cove on the western side of Academy Bay in 2 to 5 fathoms, over a rock-strewn bottom, bow out with the stern kedged ashore on the sandy beach. The 75-foot schooner *Idalia,* drawing twelve feet, anchored in this cove stern kedged ashore, for several weeks during the

Grayson Cove. Source of fresh water

(Below) *Detail of Grayson Cove*

month of May, well-protected from wind and weather by the cliffs on both sides of the cove. Ready access to Fourton Bay may be had across the intervening isthmus; the white sand beaches on both sides of the cape afford good swimming, camping and beachcombing.

Southwestward of Cabo Middleton, along the western side of the island, the shoreline is comprised of a bluff 30 to 60 feet high, with offlying *detached rocks* upon which the swell breaks moderately. The configuration of this bluff is uneven with numerous indentations and protruding points. About 3 miles southwestward of Cabo Middleton, protruding from the cliffs, are two prominent points; the southwesternmost is attached at its base to the precipitous cliff by a narrow neck. A quarter mile southwestward of this point are *two detached rocks,* several hundred yards apart and close offshore in the curve of a bight; the larger rock to the southwestward is of a tall roundish tapering shape and is designated Roca Pináculo. A third *detached flat-top rock* stands close off the bluff face of an old lava delta comprising the southwestern limit of the bight. There are *submerged rocks* along this shore. Immediately around the lava-delta point, and tucked in a bight on its western side, is a small shallow lagoon, protected from the sea by a lateral lava flow forming a perfect breakwater. The lagoon is flooded at high tide through a narrow and shallow entrance. A draw runs up behind the lagoon in which there is a growth of scrub brush. From the lagoon the bluff runs northwestward to a whitish rocky point against which the swell breaks heavily. Westward of this point, *detached rocks* close offshore are awash.

Cabo Henslow (Cape Henslow), about 1 mile westward of this rocky point, is a dog-legged peninsula composed of volcanic rocks in perpendicular cliffs 100 feet high, surmounted by a mesa at its outer end. On the northeastern side of this peninsula, at its inner end is the entrance to a shallow rectangular lagoon called Caleta Trueno. A coral reef blocks the mouth of this lagoon and *detached rocks,* exposed and submerged, lie off the broken shoreline to the northeast, but a safe and sheltered *landing* can be made in all but heavy weather. At the head of Caleta Trueno is a white coral-sand, fan-shaped beach and opposite the entrance is a sandy isthmus that connects Cabo Henslow to the island. On the southwestern side of the cape there is an open bight;

on the northeastern side of the bight, at its inner end, boulders are strewn along the seaward edge of the sandy isthmus. A *landing* can be made here in fine weather but the lagoon entrance on the opposite side of the cape affords a more sheltered landing opportunity, and is generally preferred. *Detached rocks,* submerged and awash, lie close offshore in the southwestern part of the bight, under the hook of a rocky, black-lava point against which the swell breaks in a froth of white water.

Looking northward, Cape Henslow appears from a distance as a saddle with a very flat seat, the dip of the saddle toward shore. The western end of the cape terminates in a sheer cliff-sided flat knob. Roca O'Neal (O'Neal Rock), 45 feet high and about ½ mile long with deep water close-to, lies about 1 mile north-northwestward of Cape Henslow; breakers have been observed to extend for a distance of 500 yards northwestward and 700 yards southeastward of the rock, with a northwest swell running. O'Neal Rock shows a jagged profile and is entirely barren.

Roca Doble Pináculo (Double Pinnacle Rock), situated about ¾ mile southward of Cape Henslow and close offshore between Punta Tosca and the cape, is a conspicuous, sharp, double-pinnacle rock about 25 feet high, an excellent landmark from seaward. *Two rocks awash* lie northeastward of Double Pinnacle Rock. Southward of Roca Doble Piná-culo is a bight, partly closed on its southwestern side by a hook formed by a lava flow off the northern side of Punta Tosca. A natural stone bridge has been worked through the lava rock by the sea at the inner end of this hook and presents a second landmark opposite Double Pinnacle Rock. This bight affords excellent shelter from northeast through south, although the soundings in the bight are unknown to this writer and the quality of the anchorage must be determined; the shore cliff is steep.

Punta Tosca (Rugged Point), the western extremity of the island, is comprised of a rather remarkable old lava flow that extends seaward in a westerly direction and curves to the southwestward at its outer end. The point is broad and flat with bluff sides and a procession of lava terraces that march up the flow for some distance inland, where it dog-legs to a rounded hill. The pattern of these lava terraces appears as the giant tracks of an outsize tractor. The seaward end of the point is broken, with a *rocky reef* projecting several hundred yards from its southern face.

Profile of Cabo Henslow

Immediately southeastward of Punta Tosca a narrow bight is deeply indented in the lava bluffs; the shoreline is precipitous, broken and rocky, with the swell breaking heavily at its foot. A dormant volcanic cone, with inter-leaved lava flows clustered about its central peak, is situated just above the bluffs at the head of this bight. Close south-ward of this cove is a rounded knob with a precipitous face; a *large detached rock*, several smaller ones, and *rocks submerged* lie off this point. An open bay with a small cove tucked into the steep surrounding cliffs lies close southward of the aforementioned point. A double forked arroyo with a heavy growth of scrub brush runs upward from the head of this cove, but landing is difficult and *submerged rocks* lie within the entrance and in the approach to the cove.

At the southern limit of this bay, a precipitous ridge of rock projects seaward from a bluff that runs southward to the entrance of Caleta Grayson (Grayson Cove). At the northern entrance to Caleta Grayson stand several *pinnacle rocks* off Pinnacle Point; one prominent tall, sharp rock casts a sundial shadow on the cliff before which it stands, when backed by a late afternoon sun. When approaching Caleta Grayson from the northward, the pinnacles make an excellent landmark; holding a course to the southward, one may make out a growth of bushy trees at the head of the cove as it opens to view.

Inside the cove there is *safe anchorage* in a depth of 6 fathoms, over a rocky bottom, for vessels of 100 feet in length or less; this anchorage is exposed only to westerly winds. There are *sunken rocks* on the northern and southern sides of the cove which must be avoided; there are numerous *coral heads* at the inner end of the cove but no well-developed reef. *Caution: A dangerous shoal of submerged rocks, on which the swell breaks, projects off the southern headland of the cove and should be given a wide berth.* This headland is comprised of a roughly fan-shaped old lava flow, with a thin-ridged finger of black lava protruding from its face, and it separates Caleta Grayson from Bahía Corn-wallis to the south. A *landing* can be made on the steep boulder beach at the head of the cove, but with some dif-ficulty if the swell is running. Fresh water trickles from a *spring* at the foot of a sloping cliff at the northern end of the rocky beach at the head of the cove. High up on the cliff the legend "AGUA" with an arrow pointing downward appears in white paint; below, the figure "W" with an arrow beneath pointing downward is carved in the face of the rock. Casks can best be filled at low water, as the spring issues forth from among the rocks on the beach just above the tide. An old and efficient trick in watering at such a spring is to fill the dinghy to the thwarts, first having scrub-bed the bilges spotlessly clean. A great cleft in the bluffs is a good locating landmark; the *spring* is closeby to the left when rowing in from the mouth of the cove. A clump of cac-tus grows on the brow of the cliff above the sea, immediately to the left of the spring. Numerous names and dates of visitors to the cove are carved and painted on the rocks all around. The spring is called Venero Damian Garcia, the fountainhead of Damian Garcia.

Upon approaching an intended anchorage at Grayson Cove in May 1951, Bill and Phyllis Crowe, aboard the schooner *Lang Syne*, observed volcanic activity from a small cinder cone just back of the beach. According to their report, brick-red smoke began to roar from the cinder cone, turning quickly jet black and roaring still higher. It stopped sud-denly, then white issued forth, then red again. Expecting a violent upheaval at any moment, they headed for Clarión Island, about 209 miles distant. As Socorro fell astern, the smoke mushroomed high into the upper atmosphere where the setting sun tinted it gold and pink. This volcanic activity, observed by chance, proved to be the forerunner of the more violent eruption at San Benedicto in 1952. Thereafter for a number of months, as late as 1957, hot gasses and vapors issued from volcanic vents near the summit of Cerro Ever-mann and steam issued from the walls of two lava tunnels on the south side of the island. Since the islands are remote and the coincidence of volcanic activity and a human ob-server to note and report it is somewhat rare, no doubt many eruptions over the last 400 years have gone unnoticed and unrecorded. However, many dome-in-cone volcanic struc-

Binmer's Cove, Isla Socorro

tures occur on Socorro similar to those found on San Benedicto, especially near the summit of Cerro Evermann, and it is likely that many of the eruptions on Socorro were similar to the Bárcena Volcano on San Benedicto; it cannot be assumed that, although presently dormant, Socorro is inactive. *Scientific note: As stated in the previous chapter, mariners observing a renewal of volcanic activity on Socorro, or anywhere in the Revillagigedo Archipelago, are requested to notify the Mexican Government and Scripps Institution of Oceanography, La Jolla, California by radio.*

Immediately southwestward of the old lava-flow headland on the southern side of Caleta Grayson is a rocky indentation in which the swell breaks ashore in a frothy surf. *Detached rocks and rocks awash* lie close offshore on both sides of this indentation; thin-ridged fingers of black lava protrude from the inner shore and a long, low ridge of rock, about 30 feet high at its northern end, lies detached close offshore on the southeastern side of this point. While this detached rock is of no particular distinction, a number of standard navigation charts in current publication give it the name "Roca Doble Pináculo," identical to the name more properly applied to the rock of that actual physical description located between Cabo Henslow and Punta Tosca.

In fairness to the early cartographers, who may have applied this dual name to what might have been at one time a similar physical feature off this coast, it can be assumed that the double pinnacles on this second rock, if ever they did exist prominently, were eroded away by the sea, leaving it without any distinctive pinnacles at all. Thus this name, as applied to this particular rock on whatever chart so designated, should now be properly deleted to prevent confusion of landmarks.

A *submerged rock,* covered by a depth of less than 6 feet,

lies about ¼ mile offshore, approximately ½ mile southeastward of this rock.

Bahía Cornwallis (Cornwallis Bay) stretches about 1½ miles southeastward of this detached, long, low ridge of rock and the point off which it is situated, to a broad flat point comprised of an old lava flow projecting seaward from the shore; it includes within the bracket of these headlands *several good anchorages.* Between Cornwallis Bay and the bay immediately southeastward, which holds Binmer's Cove under the lee of Punta Regla, sheltered as they are on the southwestern side of the island, these *anchorages* are considered safest during the months of June through December, as the wind then seldom blows from a direction more than two points southward of east. *Anchorage* may be taken off the first two white coral-sand beaches in the lee of the lava flow northwestward of Cabo Regla, but quite close to the beach, as the depths increase rapidly offshore. There are several shallow indentations and a somewhat sizable *detached rock* along the shoreline of bay between Bahía Cornwallis and Punta Regla. The rock designated Roca Blanca is just northwestward of a cliff-sided ridge of lava rock that protrudes at right angles from the shore, close northwestward of Caleta Binmer. Between this protruding lava ridge and Binmer's Cove, just above the shoreline, is a volcanic hill designated Monte Radioactivo; immediately above the head of the cove is a larger volcanic hill designated Monte Medina. Both these hills and the protruding lava ridge afford good landmarks when approaching the anchorage in Binmer's Cove from either a northwesterly or southerly direction. *Good anchorage* may be taken for larger vessels in this cove in depths of 8 or 9 fathoms, with better holding ground and more protection than the anchorage opposite the two white coral-sand beaches in Cornwallis Bay. At the head of Binmer's Cove is a coarse coral-sand beach and, near shore, some *coral heads.* The surf here is moderately heavy and landing through it is sometimes difficult. A *good landing place,* sheltered from the surf in most weather, may be found at the head of the cove on the southeastern side of Punta Regla. The shoreline along this entire section of the island is largely comprised of steep cliffs with few coves for landing, with access to the interior.

There is a Mexican Naval Station established on the lava flow above the southern shore of Binmer's Cove with radio-telegraph and radiotelephone facilities to military and commercial circuits on the mainland; the steel antenna can be seen closeby the station. The Commandant and his small garrison are quite helpful and hospitable, as one would expect from men minding such a remote outpost, and in particular from Mexican Nationals who are universally known for their warmth and hospitality. Binmer's Cove was named in 1793 by Captain Colnett who made the first detailed chart of the archipelago.

Indented on the southeastern side of Cabo Regla, and sheltered between it and the high rocky bluff of a lava ridge that also projects seaward from the shore immediately to the eastward of the cape, is a deep "V"-shaped cove called Bahía Vargas Lozano, which is considered one of Socorro's most sheltered anchorages for small vessels; on some charts this anchorage is referred to as The Cove. The beach is mixed coral sand and boulders, the surf is moderate and a *landing place* prepared by the naval garrison affords easy access for small boats. Both shores of the cove are rocky, the westerly side more so, and *detached rocks,* both exposed and submerged, must be given sufficient berth upon entering. A clear and unobstructed broad central channel runs from the entrance all the way to the head of the cove, and vessels making for an anchorage will do well to lay their approach course along a line bisecting the central angle of the cove. At the head of the cove is a pair of *range markers* placed about 350 yards apart; the *front range* which stands on the shore has a *square daymark painted red and white checks;* the *rear beacon* has a *red and white triangular daymark. When in range the markers bear 355°. Caution: A rocky shoal lies about 200 yards offshore close westward of the range line.*

Navigation note: Scientific expeditions recently surveying the geographic locations of the principal headlands of Isla Socorro report Cabo Regla as lying about ¼ mile southward of its position as charted on H.O. Chart 1688 and British Admiralty Plan #1936.

Bahía Braithwaite (Braithwaite Bay), the second indentation eastward of Cabo Regla and immediately adjacent to Bahía Vargas Lozano, affords *good anchorage* during the dry season from December to June, sheltered against all but southerly and easterly weather, which latter makes the anchorage all but untenable. It may be easily identified by the beach at the head of the bay, a mixture of stones and rocky ledges; it is the only beach on the southern side of the island except that in the cove westward. Boats can land here without much trouble in fair weather as the surf is quite moderate. *Fair anchorage* on a bottom of sand and shell with patches of rock may be had about ¼ mile from the beach, in depths of from 10 to 11 fathoms, the highest peak of the island bearing 335°. A *navigation*

light displaying a **white group flash of two flashes every 5 seconds,** visible 20 miles, is shown 180 feet above the sea on the southern headland of the island, close eastward of Braithwaite Bay. A *landing light* is also shown on the western shore of Braithwaite Bay.

A volcanic cone, Monte Arnaud, whose sheer western face falls directly to the water on the eastern side of this bay, is a good landmark, but the mariner must beware of *detached rocks* and a *reef awash* upon which the sea breaks heavily at the foot of this cone. A steel antenna tower stands 450 yards westward of the head of the bay. Cerro Colorado, a reddish volcanic hill, is situated above and to the northeastward of Bahía Braithwaite. On the western shore a raw volcanic cliff broken by a lesser ridge of rock shows to seaward upon entering the bay. Eastward of Bahía Braithwaite, Punta Horca surmounted by a volcanic hill, comprises the southernmost point of Socorro Island.

Northward from Punta Horca to Bahía Universidad, a large open bay under the hook of Cabo Pearce about 3 miles distant, the coast is comprised mostly of sheer rocky cliffs 15 to 25 feet high. Cabo Pearce, the easternmost point of Socorro Island, is a long, narrow, sheer ridge of lava rock curving seaward to form the northern extremity of Bahía Universidad. The top of this ridge is overlayed by a white layer of volcanic deposit, especially toward its landward end as well as on the shelf above the sea immediately to the southwest. A fresh water *spring* flows from near the top of the cliff, approximately ½ mile southwest of Cabo Pearce, but is not as readily accessible as the spring in Grayson's Cove on the opposite side of the island.

When approaching Socorro Island from eastward, a prominent white patch on the cliffs directly below the summit of the highest point on the island, Mount Evermann, may be readily discerned in clear weather. From certain angles of observation, the white patch appears in the shape of the head and horns of a steer; it makes a good landmark when approaching Cabo Pearce which is situated in a line directly below the patch.

There are several indentations close northward around Cabo Pearce, with some detached and exposed rocks. Behind and above Cabo Pearce is a range of table mountains about 1,000 feet high. The coast northward of Cabo Pearce is composed principally of sheer rocky cliffs 100 to 150 feet high, overhanging in places and scooped out in numerous small indentations. *Detached rocks,* submerged and awash, lie close off the cliffs. About 4 miles northward of Cabo Pearce, in a small cove formed at the edge of a great lava flow that can be readily identified by huge furrows running down the mountainside, is a sandy beach on which a *landing* can be made readily.

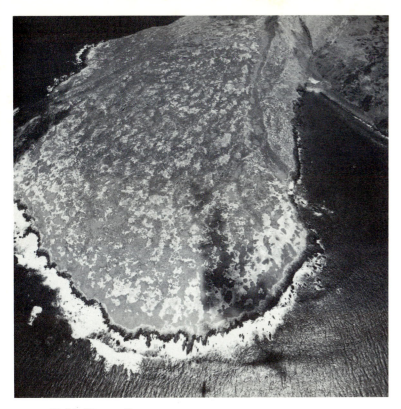

Bahía Vargas Lozano

The Cove

Northwestward, beyond the lava flow, the coast continues to Cape Middleton in cliffs of varying heights, from 20 to 80 feet, with some detached rocks on which the sea breaks heavily when it is running. A *large rock* close offshore, about 6 feet high, is situated about 4 miles northwestward of Cabo Pearce.

CURRENTS — A southerly setting current which flows at a rate of from ½ to 1 knot may be observed in the vicinity of Socorro Island. Tidal currents during the lunar month may reinforce the velocity of the southerly setting current or reverse it when in opposition.

TIDES — The tidal range is about 1 foot for neaps and about 6 feet for springs.

Note: Seamounts extend over 300 miles south of Socorro Island in the general direction of Clipperton Island. Various banks have been discovered only to have been "lost" and never found again. Such a one is Passion Rock at approximately Longitude 109° west and Latitude 16° 30' north, as shown on James Imray's chart of the Coasts of California, published in 1849. New pinnacles with as little as 11 fathoms of water covering them have been sounded in recent years. For detailed information reference is made to H.O. Publication 26, Sailing Directions For the West Coasts of Mexico and Central America, and to the British Admiralty Pilot for the West Coasts of Central America.

Socorro Island is by far the most interesting of the Revillagigedo Archipelago, with protected coves, a number of good anchorages, several excellent white sand beaches, several easily accessible landing places, a small settlement, radio communication through an established Mexican Naval Station, good camping places ashore close-by the anchorages, fresh water in all seasons, and one of

the most spectacular bottom and game fishing areas north of the Galápagos Islands. There is considerable traffic between the Mexican coast and the general vicinity of this island group, principally by Tuna Clippers from San Pedro, San Diego, and Cape San Lucas. The friendliness and general will to helpfulness within their means of the skippers and crews of these clippers is comforting indeed in this otherwise remote offshore area. For sailing vessels, the prevailing westerly winds provide a long reach from the vicinity of Cape San Lucas to the Revillagigedo Islands and return; a quartering run from the vicinity of Cedros Island. Returning to San Diego, the northeast trades may be encountered only a few miles westward of these islands, allowing a comfortable reach on the starboard tack northwestward to the latitude of San Diego, then a broad reach on the port tack through the northwesterly coastal breezes into port. See the current pilot charts for the North Pacific Ocean, Oceanographic Office Publication 1401 for prevailing winds, directions, and intensities. See also British Admiralty Publication *Ocean Passages of the World*. This can be ocean sailing at its best but requires good seamanship, accurate navigation and a staunch vessel rigged for offshore cruising.

Roca Monumento, Isla Clarión, looking toward the northwest

Isla Clarión (Clarión Island) also known as Isla de Santa Rosa, is the westernmost of the Revillagigedo Archipelago. Remote and uninhabited, it is of volcanic origin similar to Socorro Island. It is situated about 209 miles westward of Cabo Regla, Socorro Island from which it bears 263°; 153 miles from Isla Roca Partida from which it bears 255°; 226 miles from Isla San Benedicto from which it bears 224°. The island is a little over 5 miles long oriented east and west, with a greatest width of 2 miles at its western end. There are three prominent peaks of which the highest and westernmost, Cerro Gallegos, is about 1,100 feet; the other two peaks, Monte de la Marina in the center of the island and Pico Tienda de la Campana (Tent Peak) at the eastern end, are 933 and 959 feet high, respectively. The eastern tip of Clarión Island is geographically located at Latitude 18° 23′ north, Longitude 114° 41′ west.

Isla Clarión is precipitous, rocky, and virtually inaccessible all around except in the vicinity of Sulphur Bay on the southern side, midway between the southwest and southeast points. The northern side of the island is comprised of perpendicular rocky cliffs rising straight up from the sea as high as 600 feet. The eastern and western sides of the island are also precipitous and inaccessible from the sea. Off the northwest point of the island, Roca Monumento (Monument Rock), 200 feet high, stands as a remarkable and prominent landmark plainly visible for a considerable distance; it is comprised of a broken pyramidal shaft of alternate layers of red and white rock rising 200 feet above a great square base. Pinnacle rocks of various heights stand close off the corners of the base. Between Monument Rock and the northwest point of the island are a number of smaller pinnacle rocks. One great cluster of variegated pinnacles surmounts a lofty stone bridge through which the sky can be seen when bearing properly; this group is known as Rocas Pináculos. Above Rocas Pináculos the island rises in a white striated cliff several hundred feet high. *Caution: A rocky shoal covered to a depth of 3 fathoms lies about ¾ mile northeastward of Monument Rock.* Off the north side of the island, about 1¼ miles east-northeastward of the northwest point and standing about 375 yards from the cliffs, is a *detached rock* 25 feet high.

Detached rocks, submerged, awash and exposed, lie scattered off the cliffs that comprise the island's northern shore. A *rock* over which there is a depth of less than 6 feet, is situated about 400 yards off the northeastern end of Clarión Island. On the eastern side of Clarión Island, near its northeastern point, is a prominent rounded hump forming a volcanic cliff with multiple layered strata folded downward at a sharp angle. This landmark is called Escarpa de Escoria and is easily recognized when approaching from the eastward.

Roca del Cuervo (Crow Rock), designated Shag Rock on many marine charts, is situated close off the eastern side of the island about midway between the northeastern and southwestern points. The rock is 40 feet high with numerous smaller rocks close around it.

Roca Pirámide (Pyramid Rock) stands close off the southeastern point of the island. The coast between Pyramid Rock and Sulphur Bay, situated about 2¼ miles westward, is a sweeping indentation backed by a white coral-sand beach and fronted by *foul ground* which extends as much as 600 yards offshore in places, and upon which breakers curl heavily shoreward. Farallón de la Bandera, about 2½ miles westward of Roca Pirámide, is a black lava headland 173 feet high, connected to the island by a broad neck of white coral-sand beach. This headland stands at the eastern entrance to Bahía Sulphur, a protected bay backed by a wide, sandy beach, indented between Farallón de la Bandera and Roca Cresta de Gallo, the latter a high rocky point, about ½ mile westward, that looks very much like a coxcomb. Bahía Sulphur affords the only tolerable *anchorage* at Clarión Island and there are several *landing places* in its vicinity. Immediately westward of Roca Cresta de Gallo is a deep, very narrow indentation where a *landing* on a protected rocky ledge may be made when the sea is calm.

Punta Rocosa (Rocky Point), 1¾ miles westward of this landing place, comprises the southwestern point of the island. Rocky cliffs 75 to 200 feet high run about 1¼ miles in a northwesterly direction along the western shore of the island, then round up to an almost 1½-mile stretch of cliffs oriented north and south; thence break to a northeast and southwest alignment, where the most remarkable landmark of Clarión Island, the 200-foot high massive Roca Monumento, stands off the northwest extremity of the island.

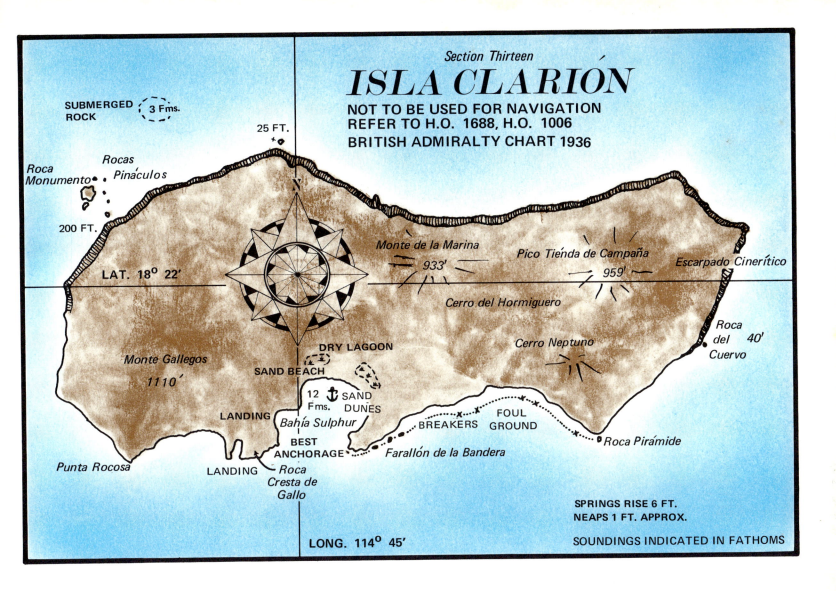

SUBMERGED ROCK   3 Fms.

25 FT.

Roca Monumento   Rocas Pináculos

200 FT.

LAT. 18° 22'

Monte de la Marina   933'

Pico Tienda de Campaña   959'

Escarpado Cinerítico

Cerro del Hormiguero

Monte Gallegos   1110'

DRY LAGOON

SAND BEACH

Cerro Neptuno

Roca del Cuervo   40'

12 Fms.   SAND DUNES

LANDING

Bahía Sulphur

BEST ANCHORAGE

BREAKERS   FOUL GROUND

Farallón de la Bandera

Roca Pirámide

Punta Rocosa

LANDING   Roca Cresta de Gallo

SPRINGS RISE 6 FT.
NEAPS 1 FT. APPROX.

LONG. 114° 45'

SOUNDINGS INDICATED IN FATHOMS

Standing well off the southern side in clear weather, a silhouette view of Clarión Island shows Cerro Gallegos, the predominant peak near the western end, Roca Cresta de Gallo, a rocky headland at the western entrance to Sulphur Bay; Farallón de la Bandera, a black lava hill at the eastern entrance to Sulphur Bay; Monte de la Marina, the highest rounded peak of three in the center of the island; Pico Tienda de Campaña, the largest dominant peak on the eastern end of the island; Cerro del Hormiguero, a flat-topped peak just westward of Pico Tienda de Compaña; Cerro Neptuno, a lower hill southward and beneath Pico Tienda de Compaña; and Escarpa de Escoria, the volcanic headland comprising the most significant feature of the eastern end of the island.

A well developed *coral reef* fringes the south side of Clarión Island. It is especially well developed in Bahía Sulphur and along the shore eastward from Farallón de la Bandera. The *reef* in Bahía Sulphur extends westward from the landward side of Farallón de la Bandera to the opposite side of the bay, so that the inner half of the bay is well protected from the surf, especially at low tide. The *reef* lies within a few inches of the ocean surface at low tide and forms a bold underwater scarp some 20 or 30 feet high, from the base of which the ocean floor descends rapidly seaward. It forms a similar platform eastward of Farallón de la Bandera extending several hundred yards from shore. Soundings obtained off the southern side of Clarión Island show 20 fathoms at ½ mile from shore, increasing to 50

fathoms at 1 mile. Between Clarión and Socorro the general depth is nearly 2,000 fathoms.

Sulphur Bay was named by Captain Edward Belcher of the British Royal Navy who anchored at Clarión Island in 1837 in the course of a zoological and botanical expedition aboard the H.M.S. *Sulphur*. This *anchorage* affords fair holding ground during northerly winds in depths of 12 or 13 fathoms at a distance of about 600 yards from the sand beach. The inner ⅔ of Sulphur Bay is blocked by the *coral reef* upon which the surf breaks heavily.

TIDES AND CURRENTS — There is a strong westerly set in this anchorage, reinforced at periods of lunar tides. Tide staff measurements on Isla Clarión indicate that the tidal range is about 1 foot for neap tides and about 6 feet for springs.

Whales frequent this bay in the spring and surprisingly large numbers may be seen in the proper season. Rowing ashore becomes a hazard at these times as the humps of the California gray whales break the surface of the bay while rising to blow. It is not unusual to see a great bull whale leap clear of the sea bringing his powerful tail down hard upon the water with the sound of a cannon. Great sea turtles, 200 to 500 pounds, also swim these waters, mate in the shallows, the female then trundling herself up the sandy beach to lay her fertilized eggs in the warm sand near the berm of the beach. In the months of March, April and May

Isla Clarión, north side

Isla Clarión, east side

Sulphur Bay, Isla Clarión

when the turtle eggs are hatching, one can dig his fingers beneath the soft sand and uncover the hatched turtles by the handfuls.

A *landing* may be made in moderate weather on a steep beach of coarse coral and volcanic cobbles on the west side of the bay, preferably at high tide; no attempt should be made to land straight on through the breakers toward the central part of the beach, as a small boat is most surely to be swamped in the surf. Once landed upon the beach, it stretches eastward in a graceful curve to Farallón de la Bandera. At the head of the bay the beach is composed of fine white coral sand; the beach eastward of Sulphur Bay beyond Farallón de la Bandera is composed of coarse frag-

ments and white coral sand intermixed with cobbles and pebbles of volcanic rock. Near the center of this beach where the surf is the heaviest, the coral is banked up in three well-defined terraces; the breakers extend out ½ mile from this beach. Near this point is the dry bed of a brook leading toward the foothills in the central part of the island. The bed of a small dry mud-caked lagoon is situated just back of the berm that rises from the beach. The lagoon appears to be briefly a fresh water pond during rainy periods; no flowing or ponded water source seems to exist on Clarión Island during the dry season, which is most of the year. The only flowing fresh water source in the entire archipelago is that described at Grayson Cove, Socorro Island, 209 miles to the eastward.

Isla Clarión from a point directly south of Sulphur Bay: 1. Cerro Gallegos;
2. Farallón de la Bandera; 3. Monte de la Marina; 4. Roca Cresta de Gallo;
5. Cerro del Hormiquero; 6. Pico Tienda de Compaña; 7. Cerro Neptuno;
8. Escarpa de Escoria

The land back of the two sand beaches is relatively flat and covered with a growth of head-high bushes which in places are so thick as to be virtually impenetrable. A kind of booby, a large white island bird, makes a great basket-like nest on the top of this brush, interweaving the branches into a tangled mat, and crowning the achievement with several white duck-size eggs that look inside like chicken's eggs, but taste strongly of fish.

In 1905 the Schooner *Academy,* on a scientific voyage through this area, dropped anchor in Sulphur Bay, Clarión Island. Just back of the landing place, the shore party saw a grave with a marker bearing the date 1897 and a tablet erected by the U.S.S. *Boston* noting her arrival there while in search of the lost brigantine *Tahiti.* The grave marker and the tablet have long since disappeared but a relatively new bronze tablet was erected by the officers and men of a Mexican expedition in 1948. The tablet commemorates Escuela Superior de Guerra and reads: ISLA CLARIÓN — ISLAS REVILLAGIGEDO — ESTADE DE COLIMA, REPÚBLICA MEXICANA EXPEDICIÓN ESCUELA SUPERIOR DE GUERRA, MAYO DE 1948.

The island westward of Sulphur Bay is thickly covered with cactus and is difficult to penetrate. The relatively level terrain directly behind Sulphur Bay rises gently in a broad plateau to the foot of the hills, then through a canyon, Cañon de los Madrones, situated between Domo de Andesita on the west and Monte de la Marina on the east, toward a ridge running east and west between Cerro Gallegos and Monte de Marina. Beyond the ridge to the northern side of the island the land falls steeply to the precipitous cliffs of the northern shore, which are 200 to 600 feet high.

The vegetation of Clarión Island includes, besides an abundance of cactus and long grass, a dense growth of weed which has a thick fleshy leaf, a type of trailing vine having red and yellow flowers, a species of bean, low thorny bushes and morning glories. Despite the apparent absence of water, animal life is abundant and the island is a breeding place for thousands of seabirds. Besides gulls and gannets there are doves, owls, crows, numerous song birds and a number of additional species of seabirds. Good, edible bottom fish abound along the shores of the island and great schools of skipjack and tuna feed in the waters close offshore. Clarión is visited frequently by Tuna Clippers from the coast in pursuit of a catch.

While volcanic eruptions and fumarole activity have been recently observed on San Benedicto and Socorro Islands to the eastward, Clarión has apparently been dormant for a great length of time. It does give its name to a major volcanic fracture zone and, since it was apparently formed above the sea in violent eruption ages past, could again manifest activity at any time.

Allaire Bank with depths of 71 and 114 fathoms, rocky bottom, was sounded by Captain Allaire of the French ship *Germaine* in 1916 and reported to exist about 300 miles west-northwestward of Clarión Island in approximate Latitude 20° north, Longitude 120° west. No one has since found this bank in that general area and its existence today is doubtful. Volcanic activity may have destroyed this underwater peak or it may exist as a sharp pinnacle, difficult to find in the vastness of the open sea. Many vessels have ranged the area with excellent depth sounders to no avail; if found it would constitute an excellent fishing ground, and be of scientific interest.

"E.D." (Existence Doubtful) appears on official navigation charts, signifying a bank or shoal or submarine pinnacle in a locality observed or sounded by a qualified shipmaster in some prior time but never found again for verification. Earthquakes, volcanic activity or the immensity of the ocean's surface, combined with a less than precise navigational fix, may account for such charting discrepancies. In the meantime, the ocean bottom contour charting continues with new seamounts, submarine pinnacles and an occasional rocky shoal discovered from time to time and reported to the U.S. Navy Oceanographic Office for inclusion in Notice to Mariners and ultimately, upon proper verification, for integration into official charts.

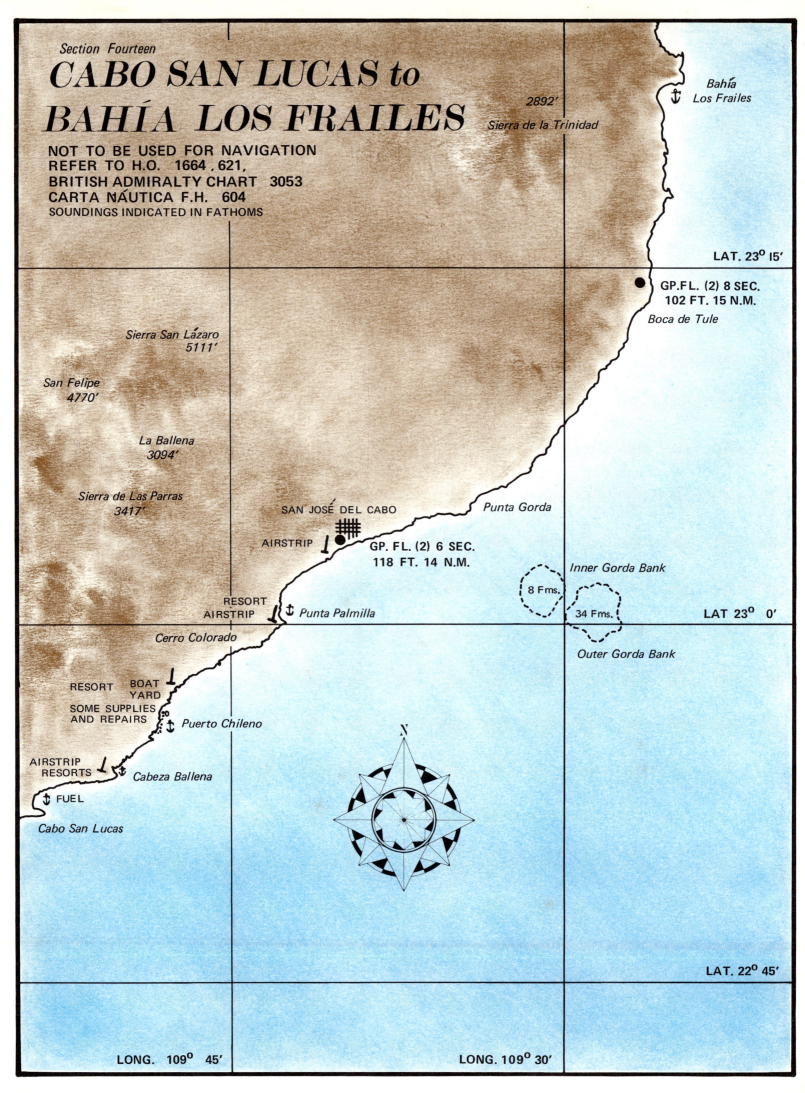

Section Fourteen

CABO SAN LUCAS to BAHÍA LOS FRAILES

NOT TO BE USED FOR NAVIGATION
REFER TO H.O. 1664 , 621,
BRITISH ADMIRALTY CHART 3053
CARTA NÁUTICA F.H. 604
SOUNDINGS INDICATED IN FATHOMS

Bahía
Los Frailes

2892'
Sierra de la Trinidad

LAT. 23° 15'

GP.FL. (2) 8 SEC.
102 FT. 15 N.M.

Boca de Tule

Sierra San Lázaro
5111'

San Felipe
4770'

La Ballena
3094'

Sierra de Las Parras
3417'

SAN JOSÉ DEL CABO

AIRSTRIP

Punta Gorda

GP. FL. (2) 6 SEC.
118 FT. 14 N.M.

Inner Gorda Bank

8 Fms.

RESORT
AIRSTRIP

Punta Palmilla

34 Fms.

LAT 23° 0'

Cerro Colorado

Outer Gorda Bank

RESORT   BOAT
         YARD
SOME SUPPLIES
AND REPAIRS

Puerto Chileno

AIRSTRIP
RESORTS

Cabeza Ballena

FUEL

Cabo San Lucas

N

LAT. 22° 45'

LONG. 109° 45'

LONG. 109° 30'

184

Bahía San Lucas, with Cabo San Lucas in the foreground

SECTION 14
CABO SAN LUCAS to BAHÍA LOS FRAILES

Until recently, despite short-lived mining bonanzas and sporadic colonization attempts, the Gulf coast of the cape region from Cabo San Lucas northward to La Paz has been isolated from the slow current of progress in other portions of the Baja California Peninsula. Perhaps because of its very isolation and certainly due to the riches to be found there—a wealth of matchless pearls, a most salubrious climate just within the Tropic of Cancer, a generous sweep of white sand beaches and a sparkling sea boasting some of the best game fishing waters in the world — it has steadily exerted a powerful attraction on all adventurous souls since Hernando Cortez first sailed the Vermillion Sea over 400 years ago.

Barren and sharp rocky hills line the coast between Cabo Falso and Cabo San Lucas; the sea breaks heavily against the bold rocky bluffs and on the sand beaches at their bases. A sandy beach which runs through a gap in the hills to Bahía San Lucas is situated about ¾ mile westward of the land's end. Between this beach and the cape there is a wedge-shaped mass of steep rocky hills the highest of which,

La Vigía, rises to a height of 500 feet. Two high, bold rocks, Los Frailes (the Friars), with a number of small outlying rocks near them, stand in the sea at the eastern extremity of the cape. The westernmost of these two rocks, connected with La Vigía and the main ridge of the cape by a narrow strip of sand, is 291 feet high and through its eastern side there is worked, by the constant onslaught of ocean waves, a well-weathered archway through which the sea breaks at high water. The eastern rock, a nearly vertical pillar of stone 222 feet high, forms the bitter end of the 800-mile long Baja California Peninsula; about 100 feet easterly lies a rock 8 feet high surrounded by deep water, separated from the cape by a 10-fathom channel. A *dangerous sunken wreck* lies about 100 yards southward of the 222-foot rock. These distinctive rocks comprising Cabo San Lucas, somewhat whitened by birdlime, show clearly in profile when approaching from westward or southward, with Punta Cabezo Ballena extending farther eastward in the background. Cabo San Lucas gives *good radar returns* up to 28 miles; it is not lighted; however, lights of the hotels and village in and around the bay may be seen when the cove is open to

San Lucas Cove

view, and *red dock lights* are displayed at the end of the cannery wharf when packing operations are in progress. For navigation in this area see H.O. 621, H.O. 622, H.O. 1666; British Admiralty Chart #3053; Cartas Náuticas F.H. 604, F.H. 605.

Bahía San Lucas (San Lucas Bay) is a large sheltered bight tucked into the northward behind the hook of the cape; a long, white curving sand beach sweeping around to the eastward creates a partially sheltered bay about 2 miles across. It affords *anchorage* with good shelter from north-westerly winds, but it is exposed to the south around to the east and quite vulnerable to the fierce southerly weather that is apt to blow up during the summer months anytime between July and October. *Directions: When making for an anchorage in Bahía San Lucas from the westward or south-ward, round the cape at a distance of about 400 yards and steer into the anchorage on a course of 335°.* A narrow trough, the northern end of the deep San Lucas submarine canyon, runs up the middle of the bay to within 600 yards of the shore, rendering the depths irregular, quite deep in the middle and close along the south and west shores, and moderate along the north shore, with a short sandy shelf close to the beach. Inasmuch as the slope of this trough is quite steep, the lead should be on the bottom when the anchor is let go.

Anchorage may be taken in depths of 6 to 12 fathoms about ¼ mile off the north shore of the bay, sand bottom. The western part of the bay is much better protected from the sea, but as the 50-fathom curve here lies within ¼ mile of the beach, this anchorage is good only for small vessels. A stern anchor toward shore is advisable to keep a vessel's head into the incoming swell, as swinging on the ground tackle can be uncomfortable with the west wind in the afternoon frequently blowing across a southerly swell. Southeasterly weather creates a dangerous lee shore and safer anchorage is to be had in the eastern part of the bay. This position is farther away from the landing at the pier,

with access to the village, but more comfortable in the sea-way. When taking water, fuel or provisions *anchorage* may be taken about 200 yards north of the cannery wharf in 4 fathoms, warping the vessel's stern to the pierhead. The wharf has a depth of about 20 feet off its head and 14 feet alongside. *Anchoring caution: Since the bottom is soft sand, a patent anchor such as a Danforth is advised.*

TIDES — The mean high water interval at full and change is 8 hours 8 minutes; the mean rise and fall is 2.8 feet; the greatest spring range is 6.8 feet.

The wharf, about 60 feet long, is built at the head of the bight on the southern shore of the bay below the fish can-nery. A *flashing red light* is shown from the head of the wharf when the cannery is in operation and expecting one of its fishing vessels. Fresh water is piped to the head of the wharf and may be taken aboard small vessels alongside; larger vessels must transport it to anchor in steel drums; fuel oil and gasoline are also supplied in drums. The can-nery, situated above the foot of the wharf, has been in con-tinuous daily operation under various management since about 1929.

FACILITIES — San Lucas Village, with a population of about 400, is located behind the sand hills on the north-western side of the bay. There are a main plaza, a new stone building housing a cantina and dance hall, several grocery stores, a bakery, a gasoline distributor, a machine shop and the customs house, as well as various service bus-inesses, an elementary school and the residences of the villagers. San Lucas Village, once located in a hollow near the shore of the bay — a pleasant place with much foliage and trees — was virtually wiped out by a fierce chubasco of September 13, 1939. The old cantina, located in a stone building, was almost the only structure to survive. The village has been entirely rebuilt; in fact, moved well back from sea to the hillside beyond the airstrip behind the Hotel Camino Real. On the eastern edge of the village a Japanese family operates a very productive garden farm. Fresh fruits

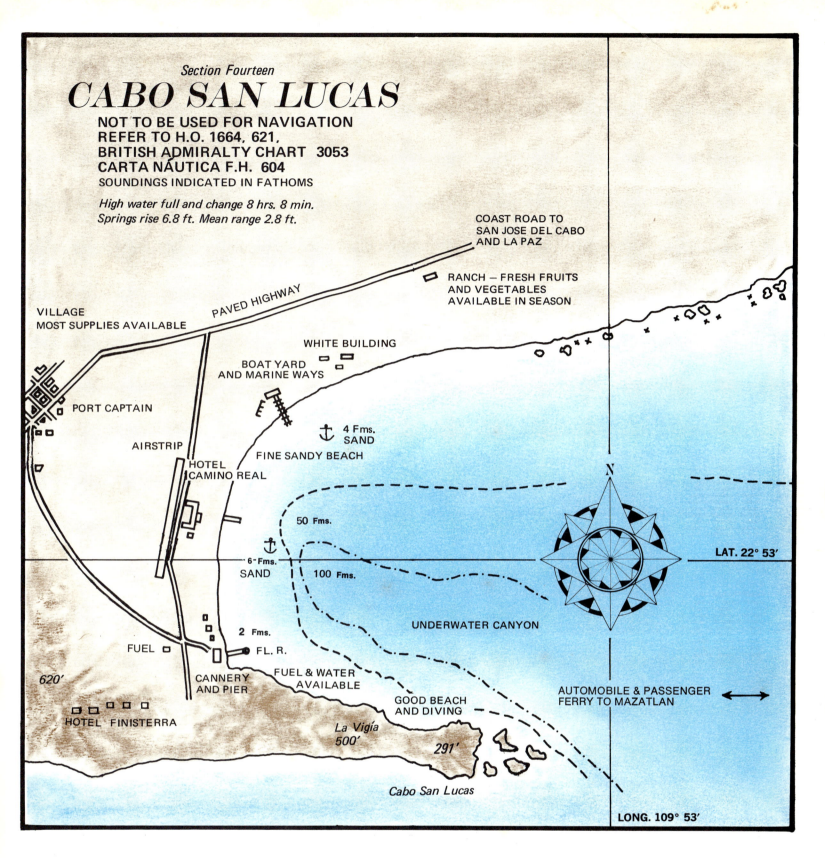

Section Fourteen

CABO SAN LUCAS

*High water full and change 8 hrs. 8 min.
Springs rise 6.8 ft. Mean range 2.8 ft.*

COAST ROAD TO
SAN JOSE DEL CABO
AND LA PAZ

RANCH — FRESH FRUITS
AND VEGETABLES
AVAILABLE IN SEASON

PAVED HIGHWAY

VILLAGE
MOST SUPPLIES AVAILABLE

WHITE BUILDING

BOAT YARD
AND MARINE WAYS

PORT CAPTAIN

4 Fms.
SAND

AIRSTRIP

FINE SANDY BEACH

HOTEL
CAMINO REAL

50 Fms.

6 Fms.
SAND

100 Fms.

N

LAT. 22° 53'

UNDERWATER CANYON

FUEL

2 Fms.

FL. R.

CANNERY
AND PIER

FUEL & WATER
AVAILABLE

AUTOMOBILE & PASSENGER
FERRY TO MAZATLAN

620'

GOOD BEACH
AND DIVING

HOTEL FINISTERRA

La Vigía
500'

291'

Cabo San Lucas

LONG. 109° 53'

and vegetables are to be had in great abundance; fresh eggs are also available. There is a cattle ranch nearby and fresh meat in quantity may be purchased on order. The Japanese garden farm is a two-mile walk by dirt road from town; closer access may be had by landing on the beach about 1¾ miles northeastward of the cannery wharf and walking about ¾ mile inland to the farm, situated back of the sand hills. The surf on the beach may be heavy however, at which times landing is difficult.

PORT OF ENTRY — Bahía San Lucas is an official port of entry for Mexico, and the Port Captain, Immigration and Customs officials will clear vessels during working hours as first or last port of call; yachts should present their cruising permits for validation.

PUBLIC ACCOMMODATIONS — A very modern and luxurious hotel, Hacienda Cabo San Lucas (now called Hacienda Camino Real Cabo San Lucas) is situated just above the shore in the bight northward of the pier, on a broad white sandy beach. Accommodations are luxurious, service excellent, prices reasonable on American plan. Hacienda Camino Real Cabo San Lucas is the first of several elegant cape resorts newly built in the region to rival those of the European Cote D' Azur. Accommodations may be had by reservation; dinner for the crew by prearrangement. A well-kept *airstrip* for small planes is maintained immediately back of the hotel; a *second airstrip* capable of accommodating multiengine aircraft is located nearby. A second luxury hotel, La Finisterra, is located at the break in the ridge to the westward of the wharf; it is reached by the road to the village that begins back of the cannery. It is also a first-class resort.

FACILITIES — Fresh water may be taken at the cannery dock; it is potable, plentiful and safe, although all water taken aboard for drinking and cooking purposes should be tested for purity, chemically treated or boiled. The pipeline at the cannery wharf is valved at the pierhead and requires a 1½-inch nipple and appropriate reducer to ship-supplied filling hose. Water is also available from a *courtesy buoy* moored off the beach, to which a fresh water hose is run. Fuel oil may be purchased at the cannery and taken alongside the wharf from drums. The fuel oil delivery system at Cabo San Lucas incorporates a water drainage sump in its storage tanks and supply lines and is one of the only fuel stops in Baja California that provides relatively water-free fuel. Arrangements to take on fuel must first be made with the Captain of the Port. Engine repair parts and engine room supplies are also available from several sources in the village and in emergency can be flown in from La Paz, Ensenada or San Diego. A small boat yard with repair facilities and a track and wheeled ways is located on the beach beyond the Hotel Camino Real. There is quite a good machine shop in the village; engine mechanics and divers may be hired.

COMMUNICATIONS — There is a government post office in the village; telegraph and telephone circuits connect the cape with San José del Cabo and La Paz; there is radiotelephone communication with Ensenada, La Paz and San Diego; the cannery operates ship-to-shore radiotelephone on 2638 kiloHertz; the hotel operates UNICOM 122.8 megaHertz to aircraft and ship-to-shore on 2620 kiloHertz. A road connects to all cape settlements: San José del Cabo, Todos Santos and La Paz. Automobiles may be rented; taxi service is available.

MARINE EMERGENCIES — Mexican Naval and Coast Guard vessels operate out of Magdalena Bay, 165 miles to the northeastward; and from La Paz, 135 miles around the cape and to the northwestward. Radio contact can usually be made with commercial fishing vessels in the general area with request for aid or relay of messages. Tugs are available out of Magdalena Bay or La Paz.

MEDICAL FACILITIES — There is a complete pharmacy in Todos Santos Village. First aid may be obtained in the village and the services of a doctor are available; hospitals and specialized care are available at Todos Santos Village, 37 miles northwestward by road or by sea, and at La Paz, 135 miles around the cape.

SOURCES OF ADDITIONAL INFORMATION — Hotel Camino Real Cabo San Lucas, 10250 Santa Monica Blvd. Suite 199, Century City, Los Angeles, California 90067, telephone (213) 879-0830; Compañia Productos Marinos, S. de R.L., Territorio del Sur, B. CFA., Mexico. Hotel La Finisterra, Apartado Postal #1, Cape San Lucas, B. CFA. Sur, Mexico.

Puerto Chileno

Upon leaving the anchorage at Bahía San Lucas, a wide, white, sandy beach stretches eastward giving way to a rocky shoreline that sweeps outward beyond two minor points to Cabeza Ballena (Whale Head) a precipitous rocky point closely fringed by outlying rocks. The point of a dark-grayish color, rising in a steep bluff 188 feet above the sea, is situated about 3 miles northeastward of Cabo San Lucas and, together with the two preceding minor points, forms the eastern limit of San Lucas Bay. Bearing southwestward it looks remarkably like the head of a giant gray whale. Close westward of the highest point of Cabeza Ballena, a remarkable cone-shaped rock rises from the shore behind which the coastal hills attain an elevation of about 1,200 feet. A partially protected cove close northeastward of Cabeza Ballena affords *fair anchorage* for small boats in depths of about 7 fathoms, sand and rock bottom. Three sandy beaches within the cove provide a *safe landing* in calm weather but a moderate swell generally runs into the cove and breaks onshore; when such condition exists landing through the surf must be carefully timed to avoid an upset. A *reef of exposed rocks* extends about 100 yards northeastward from Cabeza Ballena and should be given adequate sea room. On a rocky point at the northeastern end of the largest beach within this cove, a steel vessel is wrecked ashore, and stranded in the outlying rocks; in September, 1966, the Japanese fishing vessel *Inari Maru No. 10* drove ashore in the dark of night in a southeasterly blow. A resort development has been projected for construction in this vicinity. A heavy surf runs on the beach just westward of the wreck. Northward of Wreck Point several large trees grow in a wash just back of the beach and the coastal road runs close along the shore.

For about 2½ miles northeastward of Cabeza Ballena the shore is scalloped by small indentations with white sand beaches at their heads; *outlying rocks* and *submerged reefs,* on which the sea breaks, fringe this coast. Cerro de Santa María (Santa María Hill) rises from the shore about 2½ miles northeastward of Cabeza Ballena to a height of 465 feet. Close southward of Santa María Hill a small rock-bound cove, Caleta Santa María, affords *fair anchorage* for small vessels in good weather; the entrance is encumbered with *rocks submerged and awash* and care must be used in threading a course through a clear channel to the anchorage close inshore. Hotel Bajo Colorado, a cabana-style resort is located in this cove on Santa María Beach. The hotel utilizes the Hotel Cabo San Lucas airstrip about 2 miles northeast and monitors both 122.8 kiloHertz UNICOM and 2620 kiloHertz marine band. Puerto Chileno, a small cove immediately northward, opens into an *anchorage* for small craft. Hotel Cabo San Lucas, a luxury hotel situated on the ridge of a point of land that juts seaward on the northern side of the cove about 1 mile northeastward of Santa María Hill, can readily be made out from seaward by day behind a screen of palms and is conspicuously lighted at night. Puerto Chileno is situated about 7 miles northeastward of Cabo San Lucas.

ANCHORAGE — The hotel's fleet of sportfishing launches lies at moorings in the cove on the north side of an *exposed rocky reef* that extends several hundred yards seaward from the shore. The reef provides an effective natural breakwater attenuating the sea swell somewhat as it runs into the cove. Visiting yachts may anchor in this partially protected basin but the bottom is rocky and suitable ground tackle should be employed with a buoyed trip line to retrieve the tackle. Because there is usually a considerable surge in the anchorage, it is prudent to maintain an onboard anchor watch at all times. The swell breaks upon the reef and against rocks that fringe the point beneath the hotel. *Safe landing* can be made on the crescent of sandy beach in the cove during calm weather. Several blasts on a horn will usually bring shore boat service, provided by the hotel for their guests. There has been some talk of constructing a small service pier to facilitate landing.

FACILITIES — Yachtsmen are welcome in the hotel's dining room but prior arrangements should be made for both the number of guests and an appropriate hour. The hotel provides first-class accommodations on American plan. A fresh water swimming pool is provided for enjoyment of guests. A *landing strip* serves the hotel and air transportation is available to the International Airport at La Paz. Closeby Hotel Cabo San Lucas is the old ranch site of El Tule situated just back of the mouth of the wash on the north side of the hotel site. The coastal road runs along the shore here and communicates with the town of San José del Cabo, 15 miles northward and La Paz, 125 miles farther northward.

Connected with the hotel is an ambitious and successful boat-building yard where modern and seaworthy sportfishing launches are constructed. Engine, hull and running gear repairs as well as some marine supplies and parts are available here. Small shallow draft vessels can be hauled out by boat trailer over the beach for emergency hull repairs.

COMMUNICATION — There is telephone communication from Puerto Chileno through San José del Cabo to La Paz. Telegraph messages are accepted for relay through La Paz to the mainland and to all international points. Best practical method for voice communication with least delay is by use of shipboard high frequency equipment through ship-to-shore public communications circuits. See Appendix. There is frequently some high frequency radio equipped vessel in the area willing to allow use of its facility in emergency. Radio watch is maintained on UNICOM frequency 122.8 megaHertz and ship-to-shore frequency 2620 kiloHertz.

SEA AND WEATHER CONDITIONS — The anchorage, open to the southward and eastward, is vulnerable to the late summer storms that blow in from this quarter; it is also generally beset by ocean swells that sweep the vicinity. The cove is uncomfortable, and a rough and hazardous lee shore when high winds blow from the southerly or easterly quarter; vessels will do well to stand offshore or seek anchorage elsewhere, under such conditions, until unfavorable weather abates.

Cerro Colorado (Red Hill) rises to an elevation of 437 feet about ½ mile from the beach at a position 5½ miles northeastward of Santa María Hill and affords an excellent mark from seaward. About 2½ miles northeastward of the wash at El Tule, a second larger wash opens onto the beach at Rancho El Bledido. At the northeastern end of a white sand beach the gable of a whitewashed ranch house shows up well from seaward. The coast beyond El Bledido is comprised of a white sand beach interrupted by a number of rocky points fringed with off-lying rocks. The beach sweeps toward the northeast as far as Cerro Colorado, thence it is broken and rocky.

Punta Palmilla (Palmilla Point), 1½ miles northeastward of Cerro Colorado, is a low rocky bluff fringed with detached and sunken rocks on which the sea breaks; it is backed by a mound 353 feet high that is covered with scrub desert growth. Hotel Las Cruces Palmilla, a modern luxury resort hotel whose white moorish architecture with red-tiled roofs shows conspicuously to seaward, stands on Palmilla Point; its lights are readily distinguished at night. A small white colonial-style church surmounted by a cross stands on a knoll back of the hotel. The first of the cape resorts to be constructed, Las Cruces Palmilla has an elegant but comfortable old-world charm with continental luxury and hospitable Mexican warmth much welcomed by yachtsmen.

ANCHORAGE — There is a bight indented close northward of Punta Palmilla where vessels may anchor in depths of 8 to 9 fathoms and boats may *land* on a curving sandy beach at its head; however care must be exercised to avoid a *reef of submerged rocks* which extends several hundred yards eastward from the southern end of the beach, terminating in a *rocky patch awash*. Small vessels may anchor closer to shore in 3 to 4 fathoms, sand. The hotel's fleet of sportfishing cruisers is moored southward of the reef and abreast

Punta Palmilla

its seaward end. There is a small marine ways just south of the foot of the reef on the beach. A small lightweight steel pier with a wooden top about 4 feet wide was constructed to facilitate a dry landing, but the structure was destroyed recently in a late summer storm. All that remains are a dozen or so steel supports, rising from the beach at the foot of a concrete jetty that extends from the shore alongside the marine railway. *Landing* may be effected on the beach. The hotel management operates a shore boat for their guests, which may be summoned by horn signal. Fuel supplies are maintained for visiting aircraft and for the hotel's sportfishing launches but in emergency may be obtained in quantities dictated by current supply.

Back of the cove on its northerly side, protected by the hook of Palmilla Point, is a small shipyard and marine railway operated to service the hotel's sportfishing fleet and other small vessels in need of haul-out or repair. Some engine parts and marine supplies are available here; special parts and supplies may be ordered from La Paz. An excellent *airstrip* is carved into the hills back of the cove and accommodates both private planes, air-taxi, and commercial multiengine equipment from La Paz and Tijuana. The coastal road communicates with the village of San José del Cabo, about 3 miles to the northward, and the city of La Paz, 125 miles further northward.

The town of San José del Cabo is situated about a mile inland on the slope of a small rise above the Río San José (the San Jose River) which empties into the sea about 3 miles northeastward of Punta Palmilla. For most of the year the mouth of the river is isolated from the sea by a wide sand berm thrown up by the action of the breakers; a large fresh water estero is formed behind this barrier. The river breaks through the berm during the rainy season, which usually occurs in or around the month of September, at which time it flows freely into the sea for a period of several months. The river rises abruptly as a full-blown stream from beneath a ledge of rocks about 19 miles inland, fed by one of the three most important fresh water springs on the cape. The river drains through the extensive San José Valley which is one of the best watered and most fertile agricultural areas in Baja California.

In the latter part of the 1600's and throughout the mission period of the 1700's, San José del Cabo served as a way port of the Manila Galleons making their long perilous Pacific passage from the Philippines to Acapulco. Water and fresh provisions were taken aboard, the sick were attended and the passengers and crew refreshed. An old mission cathedral with a colorful but tumultuous history is located here, founded in 1730 by the Jesuit Nicolás Tamaral. The mission was first established at the west end of the estero near the beach and adjacent to the present location of the cemetery. The site was moved several times due to its open exposure to seasonal storms from the sea and finally, in 1753, it was moved to where the church stands today on the hill in the town next to the plaza. On May 19, 1769, there arrived at the Mission San José del Cabo the noted French Astronomer Chappe d' Auteroche, to observe the passage of Venus across the disc of the sun, a phenomenon that occurred on June 3, 1769. In the weeks of preparation prior to the day of the observation, d' Auteroche contracted a disease that had become epidemic among the native Indians, sweeping away more than one third of them in quick fatalities and ultimately costing the astronomer his life as well. On February 7, 1822, shortly after Mexico won her independence from Spain, San José del Cabo was attacked by an English sea lord, Thomas Cochrane who, as far as the natives were concerned, was a dangerous and destructive freebooter to be dealt with as any pirate and as their means enabled them to. On March 29, 1847, during the war between Mexico and the United States, the quiet port of San José del Cabo was startled when the frigate *Portsmouth,* under United States Naval Commander Montgomery, anchored in the roadstead and landed a contingent of marines. Although the initial occupation and raising of the American flag was without incident, the small garrison of United States Marines was soon confronted by a determined band of Mexican patriots and soldiers bent on wresting control of their town from this foreign occupation force. The marines were besieged for two months and almost annihilated before reinforcements arrived. The Mexican soldiers occupied the mission church, while the marines converted the missionary's house, Casa Cural (present site of the electric plant), into a fortress. Both buildings were demolished during the siege. The death of a Mexican naval

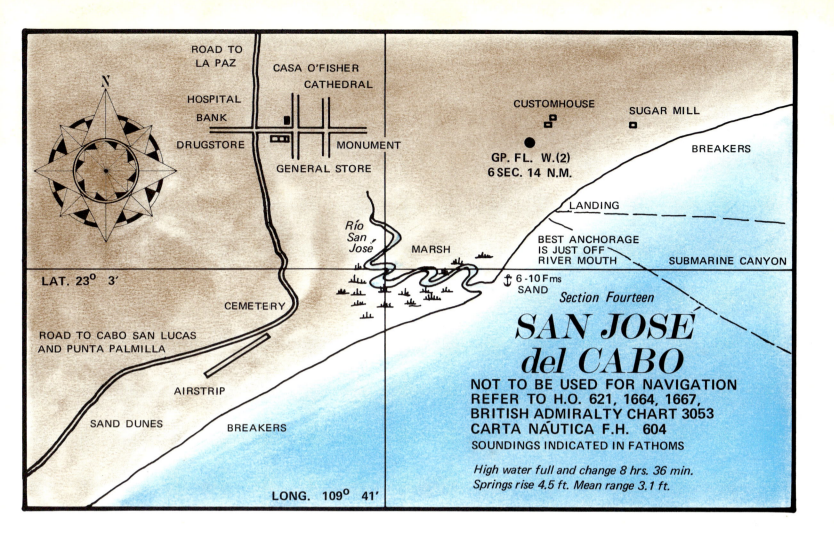

lieutenant, José Antonio Mijares, killed in an attempt to rush the American positions, is commemorated in the name of the town's main street and by a monument in the plaza. The present church was built in the 1940's. A mosaic above the entrance represents the martyrdom of the Jesuit Father Tamaral who was murdered along with his converts at nearby Santa Rosa Mission in 1734 by the Indians of the region, in revolt against the church's authority.

Today the population is close to 3,000 persons principally engaged in agriculture and cattle raising, products of which are loaded for export aboard small coastal freighters in the open roadstead or taken by truck to La Paz. The town has a regular telephone and telegraph service, a general store, a branch of the Banco National de Mexico, a well-equipped *municipal hospital,* an overnight hotel and guest house, a motion picture theater, an *airstrip* capable of accommodating medium-sized multiengine planes and a well-traveled, paved road that communicates with La Paz, Cabo San Lucas, Todos Santos and other coastal and inland points.

LANDMARKS AND LIGHTS — Palmilla Point forms the southwestern limit of Bahía San José del Cabo (San José del Cabo Bay), a large open bay formed by an indentation in the coast between Punta Palmilla and Punta Gorda, about 9 miles northeastward. *Rocky patches* are situated at either end of the bay and the sea breaks off both Punta Palmilla and Punta Gorda; the surf also breaks heavily on the long, steep intervening sand beach; landing through it in an ordinary ship's boat is a hazardous undertaking and not prudent to attempt except at specified places. A short distance back of the bay, hills rise to a moderate height and

further northwestward, Sierra de San Lázaro (the San Lázaro Mountain Range) attains an elevation of 5,111 feet at a remarkable pinnacle peak. Los Picachitos, a cluster of three conspicuous gray conical hills that resemble small craters, are situated about 2 miles westward of Punta Gorda and about ½ mile inland; the westernmost is 722 feet high and can be made out for a considerable distance from seaward. A *navigation light* exhibits a **white group flash of two flashes every 6 seconds:** flash 0.3 second, eclipse 1.2 seconds; flash 0.3 second, eclipse 4.2 seconds. It is shown 118 feet above the sea from a concrete tower painted with orange and white bands. The light is situated about 1½ miles eastward of the cathedral, close northward of the river mouth and about ½ mile back of the beach. New service buildings have been constructed closeby the old lighthouse tower. The light is visible in the sector 262° through 37° and can be seen in clear weather for a distance of 14 miles. At one time a sugar mill with a prominent detached chimney was situated about 550 yards westward of the navigation light structure and was operated to process the crops of sugar cane grown inland in the valley. An old customhouse, a small wooden building with a striped roof, stood near the shore closeby the navigation light. These old landmarks have mostly disappeared. An *airstrip* is located on the southwest side of town about ½ mile from the beach (see Appendix). Between the *airstrip* and the bay shore, about ¼ mile back of the beach on a slight rise, is a new government-sponsored fish processing plant designed to receive the catch of a fishermen's cooperative. Fishing skiffs may be seen drawn up on the beach in this location or working offshore during the fishing season. The plant was designed with modern equipment, primarily to process shark and ex-

San José del Cabo

tract liver oil. A small quantity of shark are caught during the summer season, but there is a far greater catch of cabrilla which is dried and salted to be sold as "bacalao." The plant however, is operated only sporadically and then only at a fraction of its capacity. The processing of fish meal for fertilizer is planned.

Cabrilla

SEA AND WEATHER CONDITIONS — The bay is entirely open to the southward and eastward with a heavy swell that sets into the bay at all times, particularly in the season of the southeasterly gales from May to October. Northwesterly winds prevail in the fine season from November to May. *Chubascos,* severe local hurricanes, occur only sporadically and may skip several years.

ANCHORAGE — The heavy swell that sets into the roadstead renders the anchorage uncomfortable; during the season of the southeasterly gales, usually in late summer, anchorage is somewhat hazardous, with poor holding ground on a lee shore and a heavy surf that breaks on a steep beach. During the calmer part of the year (early winter through late spring) *anchorage* may be safely taken anywhere in the bay at a distance of 600 to 1,000 yards offshore in depths of 6 to 10 fathoms, sand bottom, except just southward of the old customhouse site, where the head of the San José submarine canyon approaches the shore and the 50-fathom curve bends to within a ½ mile of the beach. The San José submarine canyon, even larger in extent than the one at Bahía San Lucas, extends outward for about 22

miles to a depth of 6,400 feet, cut at some early geological time by the flow of the San José River.

Directions: On a leading course to the commercial anchorage area bring the large whitewashed rock on the slope of Mount La Ballena, 3,084 feet high, situated 6½ miles northwestward of San José village, in range with the pinnacle summit of Sierra San Lázaro; thence with the light structure near the old mill chimney site bearing 331°, the cemetery bearing 263° and the palms near the old landing shed site on the beach bearing 295°, cast anchor in 9 fathoms. Landing barges for lightering cargo were at one time to be seen on the beach. The *best anchorage* for small vessels, however, is about ¾ mile northward of Punta Palmilla in the bight north of the resort hotel. A *dry landing* may be made safely at the head of the bight and a taxi taken to the village of San José del Cabo.

LANDING — The best landing near the commercial anchorage area is between the two thatched sheds on the beach southwestward of the customhouse, a small wooden building with a striped roof. The surf either eastward or westward of this place is generally bad and a landing can be made here when it would be unsafe 200 yards away on either side. The landing place, however, may shift during the rainy season when the river is discharging into the sea. A safer landing can be made in the small cove 750 yards northwestward of Punta Palmilla near the resort hotel.

TIDES — The mean high water interval at San José del Cabo is 8 hours 36 minutes; the spring range is 4.5 feet; the mean range, 3.1 feet.

PORT FACILITIES — Puerto de San José del Cabo is a port of entry for foreign vessels entering or leaving

Mexico as first or last port of call. Clearance is required of all foreign vessels calling at the town as a way port, including yachts en-transit under cruising permits. Quarantine and Customs officials come out and board vessels which have dropped anchor in the bay. Pilots are available and advisable for commercial vessels. Yachts must clear their cruising permits with the Captain of the Port before leaving. Cargo is worked at the anchorage in the open roadstead from small landing barges which are beached for unloading. Cattle are swum through the surf to the ship's side and hoisted aboard by the horns.

SERVICES AND SUPPLIES — Fuel oil, diesel and gasoline are available in the town, and arrangements may be made to transport these supplies in 55-gallon steel drums by landing barge to the anchorage in the bay. Lubricating oil, engine room supplies and parts are available in stock to some degree or may be ordered from La Paz. Fresh provisions including meats, vegetables, fruits and bread may be purchased in the town. Several well-stocked department stores carry a variety of goods from hardware to drygoods. Fresh water is available for ship's stores, brought out to the anchorage in steel drums. San José del Cabo has been a ship's watering place for 4 centuries and in earlier times vessels called at a ranch just westward of Punta Gorda to refill their casks.

COMMUNICATIONS — Commercial vessels call for and deliver cargo at irregular intervals communicating with other coastal ports both in the gulf and on the Pacific side of the peninsula. An *airstrip* on the west side of town accommodates both private planes and medium-size multi-engine commercial aircraft that maintain service routes to La Paz and other peninsula towns and resorts. A well-traveled paved road used both by passenger vehicles and cargo trucks connects southward to the cape resorts and villages, and northward to La Paz, thence by sea-going ferry to Mazatlán on the mainland. There is telephone service to La Paz and telegraphic messages are accepted for relay through international circuits in La Paz. The airport communicates by radiotelephone with aircraft, on UNICOM frequency of 122.8 megaHertz.

PUBLIC ACCOMMODATIONS — The Casa Fisher provides overnight accommodations on the American plan. Meals may also be taken at several restaurants in the town. The Las Cruces Palmilla Hotel at Palmilla Point, five miles southward of the town, provides first-class accommodations and meals at resort prices.

MEDICAL FACILITIES — There is a well-equipped *municipal hospital* at San José del Cabo and a *doctor in residence*. There are several larger *hospitals* in La Paz, ½ hour distant by plane.

MARINE EMERGENCIES — The Mexican Navy has several coastal vessels based at La Paz, 125 miles distant by sea. Emergency requests for aid may be made on 2182 kiloHertz, or relayed through local vessels in the vicinity. (See Appendix.)

SOURCES OF ADDITIONAL INFORMATION — Hotel Cabo San Lucas, P.O. Box 48747, Briggs Station, Los Angeles, California 90048, telephone (213) 655-4760; Las Cruces Palmilla, P.O. Box 1775, La Jolla, California 92037, telephone (714) 454-0600; Casa Fisher, San José del Cabo, Baja California Sur, Mexico; Hotel Bajo Colorado, Apartado Postal #50, San José Del Cabo, B. CFA. Sur, Mexico or 2701 Alcott, Denver, Colorado 80211, Telephone (303) 433-7308.

The northeastern limit of Bahía San José del Cabo is Punta Gorda, a round rocky bluff about 50 feet high from which a flat-topped hill rises to a height of 311 feet, nearly a half mile westward. Many *detached rocks* lie close off the point and a *shoal* with a least depth over it of 3 fathoms is situated about 700 yards southeastward. Within a distance of 400 yards outside this shoal the soundings increase to 19 fathoms. It is advisable to give Punta Gorda a berth of at least ½ mile.

Punta Palmilla, Punta Gorda

Punta Los Frailes

OFF-LYING BANKS — Inner Gorda Bank, a large rounded bank, with a least depth reported over it in 1949 of 8 fathoms, lies about 5 miles eastward of Punta Gorda. Outside Inner Gorda Bank and about 2¾ miles further southwestward is Outer Gorda Bank, over which the least depth sounded is 34 fathoms. On the two banks the bottom is rocky and irregular; around and between them there are depths of over 100 fathoms. The Gorda Banks are feeding grounds for large schools of tuna and skipjack and are popular fishing grounds for commercial Tuna Clippers;

Sealife note: Basking Sharks frequent the area of the sea around and near these banks. The Japanese call these great somnolent creatures "Babaa" meaning Old Woman because they appear to have no teeth. They are to be seen most often lazily finning on the surface of the sea; their heads are exceedingly blunt and quite broad with a huge mouth fully six feet across. The tail fin is enormous and sweeps regularly back and forth slowly as if propelled by a giant, slow-speed engine. The skin of this marine animal appears to be entirely smooth, speckled with whitish spots. Thousands of small teeth, about ⅛ inch long, are set in great sheets, file-wise around its jaws. Its mouth, acting like a trawling net, strains small sea life and school fish into its maw by the ton. This giant species of whale shark is encountered in surprisingly large numbers in March and April and through the ensuing months through September, but rarely in October or through to the spring of the next year. They run 40 feet or more in length; sometimes as large as 60 or 70 feet. They should be avoided and certainly left unmolested.

The coast between Punta Gorda and Los Frailes situated about 21 miles north-northeastward, is moderately low and rocky with occasional sand beaches on which the surf often breaks heavily; the land within slopes gradually to the Sierra de la Victoria mountain range in the interior. Along this coast there are no prominent points easily recognizable from seaward. *Navigation caution: Many sunken rocks lie close inshore but there are no known dangers except one beyond a distance of ½ mile offshore. A rock, with a depth over it of 2 fathoms and the position of which is approximate, was reported struck in 1941 by a schooner drawing 12 feet at a position about 1 mile offshore and 5 miles southwest of Los Frailes. The rock is marked on navigation chart H.O. 1664 but one must look closely to discern it.* The surf along this stretch of coast is often quite heavy but boatmen with local knowledge, and familiar with the passes between the sunken rocks close along the shore, land boats at La Laguna (El Zacaton Ranch) 1¼ miles northward of Punta Gorda. A coastal road runs from San José del Cabo to La Laguna.

Punta Cardoncito, a low rocky point that projects only slightly from the general line of the coast but upon which a heavy surf breaks most of the time, is situated about 4 miles northeastward of Punta Gorda. The *wreck* of the coastal freighter *Morelia* lies stranded bow on near the point. El Cardoncito Ranch is situated back of the beach near a sandy wash in close proximity to the wreck. Northeastward, along an 8-mile stretch of coast comprised of sand beaches with *off-lying rocks*, several dry sandy arroyos cut through the low, sagebrush covered land and open onto the beach. These are Arroyo de la Fortuna in which is

Wreck of "Morelia" at Cardoncita

located the La Fortuna Ranch; Arroyo de Manto; Arroyo de San Luis in which is located the San Luis Ranch and to which a spur of the coast road runs; and Arroyo de la Vinorama, with a wide sandy mouth and a stream of *good water* at about 1,500 yards inland, where the Vinorama Ranch is located. At the seaward end of a lateral spur of the coastal range of hills there is a low sandy beach between Arroyo del Manto and Arroyo San Luis. The water is discolored to a distance of more than a mile offshore at this point and is shoaler than sounded to either the southwestward or northeastward. Depths of 12 fathoms are found at a mile, and 17 fathoms at 1½ miles, offshore. From the vicinity of Punta Gorda the 100-fathom curve trends gradually outward until it reaches a distance of 7 miles offshore, and then curves shoreward approaching to within 1 mile off Boca del Tule. About 1 mile northeastward of Arroyo de Vinorama, there is a bold rocky bluff about 60 feet high which may be identified by its lighter gray color than other points in the vicinity. *Numerous detached rocks* lie close off this bluff, immediately northward of which is Boca de Tule where a *coastal navigation light* is established. The Boca de Tule light exhibits a **white group flash of two flashes every 8 seconds:** flash 0.5 second, eclipse 1 second; flash 0.5 second, eclipse 6 seconds. The light is shown 102 feet above the sea from a red metal framework tower and can be seen to seaward for 15 miles in clear weather.

LANDING — There is a boat landing at Boca de Tule where a safe, dry landing may be made on the beach in good weather. A small fish camp is located here and a spur of the coastal road runs out to the beach at this place.

Arroyo de las Ardillas and Arroyo del Salada open on the coast, respectively, 1½ and 2¾ miles northward of Boca del Tule. There is a ranch at the mouth of each of these arroyos. *Navigation warning: The submerged rock with a depth of 2 fathoms over it, previously noted to have*

been struck by a schooner, lies at an approximate position 4 miles northward of Boca de Tule, 5 miles southward of Los Frailes, and about 1 mile offshore; this area should be avoided.

Punta Los Frailes (Los Frailes Point), a bold, light-gray rocky bluff 410 feet high, with a hill rising 755 feet from it, forms a bold headland isolated by lowland between it and the coastal range of hills farther inland. It is the easternmost point of land of the peninsula and forms an oceanographic gateway between the Pacific Ocean and the waters of the Gulf of California, which slowly assume a set of unique characteristics as one cruises northward. Los Frailes headland provides a good landmark.

Bahía Los Frailes (Los Frailes Bay) lies indented within the point just southward of the headland and provides *good shelter* from the prevailing northerlies; in southerly weather the bay on the north side of Los Frailes affords *good shelter*.

ANCHORAGE AND LANDING — Fair anchorage protected from the northerly winds and sea may be had over a rocky bottom, in depths of 4 to 10 fathoms, about 200 yards offshore in a position just off the eastern end of the sand beach, where it joins the hill of the headland. Small vessels may *anchor* closer to the beach in depths of 3 to 9 fathoms. Further eastward the depths increase very rapidly, the waters off Los Frailes and in the bay being very deep, due to a submarine canyon whose head lies close to shore in the cove. However, shallow water that breaks when the seas are running, extends ¼ mile offshore in the southern part of the bay. Safe and *dry landing* may be made upon the beach at the head of the bay.

Above the landing the mouth of a small stream, dry except during the rainy season, opens on the shore. A small cattle ranch is located just eastward of the mouth of the stream at the intersection of the coastal roads; a seasonal fish camp is established along the shore. A *well of good water* is in use but there are no other supplies available at Los Frailes except the fish and lobster that may be bartered from the local fishermen or seafood that one catches for himself. Los Frailes is a popular shelter for cruising vessels bound north or south, and yachts may be frequently found at anchor here. A fishing resort is planned for the area sometime in the future and two *airstrips* are in use. One parallels the beach in the southern part of the bay; the other is cut into the foot of the headland hill, just eastward of the ranch. The Tropic of Cancer, Latitude 23° 23″ north, bisects the region in the near vicinity of Los Frailes Bay.

SECTION 15
BAHÍA LOS FRAILES to BAHÍA de los MUERTOS

Anemone

Cabo Pulmo showing the coral reef

Immediately northward around the point, the land sweeps inward to form a small bay which is open to the north around to the east, providing protection from southeasterly weather. *Caution: A small white rock 12 feet high and steep-to with 12 fathoms all around, protrudes from the sea about ⅓ mile northward of the sharp point of land that juts seaward about a mile northward of Los Frailes head.* There are some rock outcroppings in the bay but it affords *sheltered anchorage* with ample room for a number of small boats. The coast between this bay and Cabo Pulmo, lying 3 miles farther northward, is comprised chiefly of sand bluffs about 20 feet high with some *rocky patches* and a few *detached rocks* close inshore. The shore is at first rocky, giving way to a white sand beach as it approaches Cabo Pulmo. A small ranch with an *airstrip* is located just back of the beach close southward of the cape. Cabo Pulmo is a sharp rocky headland with a southward knob rising to a height of 75 feet and connected by a low sand covered ridge with a hill behind that rises to an elevation of 830 feet; this hill forms the terminal end of a range of mountains that rises inland to an elevation of more than 2,000 feet. *Shoal water* extends off the cape in every direction with numerous detached rocks close-to.

Navigation warning: Rocks on which a small vessel struck were reported in 1939 to extend about a mile off the cape. The wreck of the Mexican coastal freighter Colima, driven ashore in the fierce chubasco of 1939, lies sunk in 7 fathoms about 1½ miles northward of Cabo Pulmo, near the north

end of the reef; the hull can be seen from the surface. A second wreck is reported sunk in the same vicinity.

An *extensive coral reef* projects in a northeasterly direction from the shore at a position just southward of the vicinity of the previously mentioned ranch and ending in depths of 10 feet about ½ mile eastward of the cape.

ANCHORAGE — Between this reef, known as Arrecife del Pulmo (Pulmo Reef) and the cape is an *anchorage* suitable for small boats with depths of 2½ to 3 fathoms, entered through a channel between the outer end of the reef and the cape.

Bajo El Pulmo (Pulmo Shoal), with a least depth over it of 5½ fathoms, lies about 1¼ miles northeastward of Cabo Pulmo.

Navigation warning: A dangerous shoal about 1 mile in length, on which the sea breaks and over which the least charted depth is but 6 feet, lies about ½ mile offshore, about 2 miles northward of Cabo Pulmo. The seaward extremity of Los Frailes, bearing not less than 186°, clears this shoal. The coast in this vicinity should not be approached within a distance of less than 1½ miles unless with local knowledge.

The waters close about these reefs and shoals and over them usually reflect a marked lighter blue coloration than

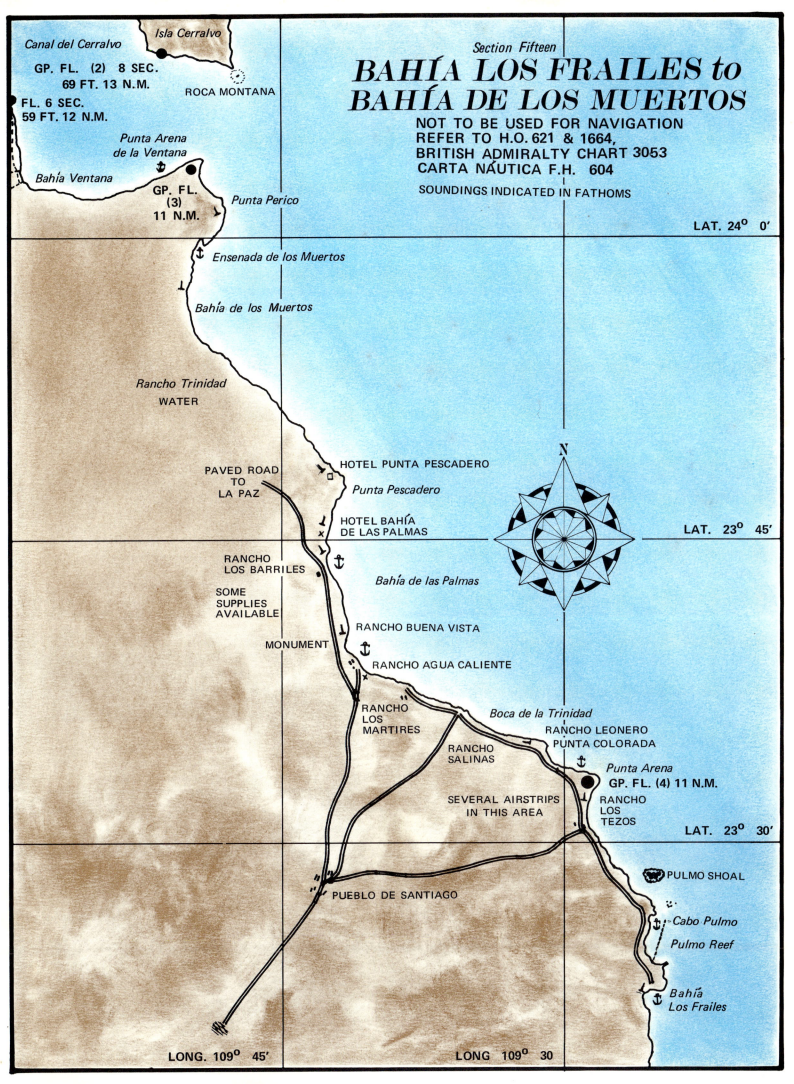

BAHÍA LOS FRAILES to BAHÍA DE LOS MUERTOS

NOT TO BE USED FOR NAVIGATION
REFER TO H.O. 621 & 1664,
BRITISH ADMIRALTY CHART 3053
CARTA NÁUTICA F.H. 604

SOUNDINGS INDICATED IN FATHOMS

LAT. 24° 0'

Canal del Cerralvo

Isla Cerralvo

GP. FL. (2) 8 SEC.
69 FT. 13 N.M.

FL. 6 SEC.
59 FT. 12 N.M.

ROCA MONTANA

Punta Arena
de la Ventana

Bahía Ventana

GP. FL.
(3)
11 N.M.

Punta Perico

Ensenada de los Muertos

Bahía de los Muertos

Rancho Trinidad
WATER

PAVED ROAD
TO
LA PAZ

HOTEL PUNTA PESCADERO

Punta Pescadero

HOTEL BAHÍA
DE LAS PALMAS

N

LAT. 23° 45'

RANCHO
LOS BARRILES

SOME
SUPPLIES
AVAILABLE

MONUMENT

Bahía de las Palmas

RANCHO BUENA VISTA

RANCHO AGUA CALIENTE

RANCHO
LOS
MARTIRES

Boca de la Trinidad

RANCHO LEONERO
PUNTA COLORADA

RANCHO
SALINAS

Punta Arena
GP. FL. (4) 11 N.M.

SEVERAL AIRSTRIPS
IN THIS AREA

RANCHO
LOS
TEZOS

LAT. 23° 30'

PULMO SHOAL

PUEBLO DE SANTIAGO

Cabo Pulmo

Pulmo Reef

Bahía
Los Frailes

LONG. 109° 45'

LONG 109° 30

197

that of the surrounding seas and visual cognizance during daylight hours, combined with a reliable depth sounder or the use of the lead, will enable a vessel in fine weather to safely approach for close reconnaissance. Pulmo Reef is an excellent spot for underwater diving exploration, its outward face a precipice on which living coral provides the ecological base for an interesting and exotic underwater world of flora and fauna. A remarkable species of sea plants, Gorgonians, which the natives call arbolitos del mar (little trees of the sea), grow profusely and undulate in the slow motion of the marine currents, among which an endless variety of marine creatures make their way.

TIDES — The tidal range is about 4½ feet.

The coast between Cabo Pulmo and Punta Arena, situated about 7 miles northward, recedes about 1½ miles within a line joining these points to form an open bay encompassed by a long sweeping strip of sand beach which flattens to a very low-lying profile in the vicinity of Punta Arena. Rancho Las Barracas is situated close by the shore at the foot of Cerro Las Barracas, a hill 1,500 feet high in a position about 2½ miles northwestward of Cabo Pulmo. Small local vessels *anchor* off the beach and land here. The coastal road is joined by a road leading inland to the village of Santiago, located about 15 miles westward.

Punta Arena (Point of Sand) is a low, sandy, looping point backed by an extensive plain covered with a generous growth of cactus, low desert trees and bushes. A heavy surf breaks all around the point but there are no off-lying dangers. Eastward of the point the soundings are very deep close offshore, the 100-fathom curve being only about ½ mile off, but the depths shoal rapidly northward of the point, and it should not be rounded at a distance off of less than ½ mile. A *navigation light* is shown from a concrete tower 39 feet high, painted with black and white bands, alongside a masonry light keeper's house, just back of the wide sand beach at the tip of the point. The light displays a **white group flash of four flashes every 12 seconds,** visible in the sector 150° through 324° for 11 miles seaward in clear weather.

ANCHORAGE — With fair protection from northerly winds, anchorage may be taken near Las Lagunas, a ranch situated about 1¼ miles southwestward of Punta Arena in a position about ¼ mile offshore with the extremity of the point bearing 009°, distant about 1 mile, in depths of 8 to 10 fathoms, sand bottom. Small vessels may *anchor* farther westward and closer inshore using appropriate ground tackle to insure against dragging in poor holding ground. The area is frequently beset by uncomfortable winds. When the weather is fine, vessels may anchor off Rancho Los Tezoz or Rancho de las Abundancias about 3 miles southward of Punta Arena. An *airstrip* is in use at Rancho de las Abundancias.

Punta Arena

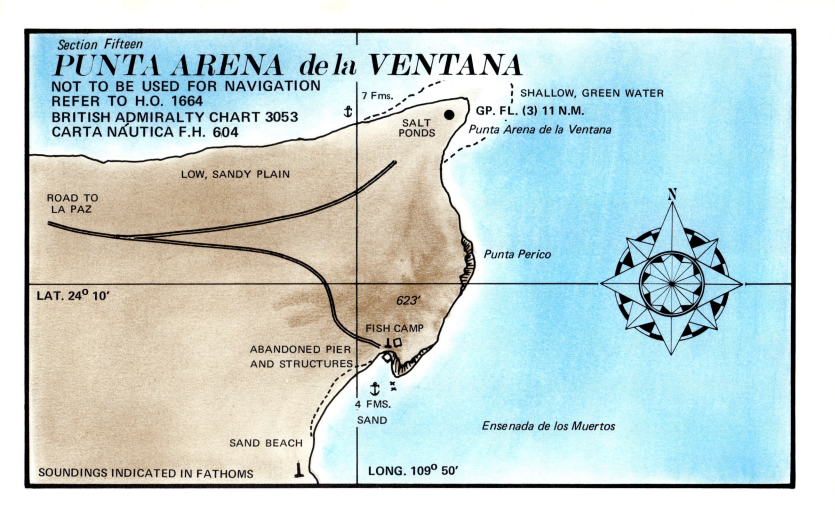

PUNTA ARENA de la VENTANA

NOT TO BE USED FOR NAVIGATION
REFER TO H.O. 1664
BRITISH ADMIRALTY CHART 3053
CARTA NÁUTICA F.H. 604

7 Fms.

SHALLOW, GREEN WATER
GP. FL. (3) 11 N.M.
Punta Arena de la Ventana

SALT PONDS

LOW, SANDY PLAIN

ROAD TO LA PAZ

Punta Perico

N

LAT. 24° 10'

623'

FISH CAMP

ABANDONED PIER AND STRUCTURES

4 FMS. SAND

Ensenada de los Muertos

SAND BEACH

SOUNDINGS INDICATED IN FATHOMS

LONG. 109° 50'

Punta Arena is the peninsula's final land buttress against which the Pacific swells break with the force of the familiar coastal surf; northward of this point and on into the Gulf, ocean swells rapidly attenuate and the shore breaking surf subsides. The waters of the gulf assume more the character of an inland lake and, in the absence of a driving wind, the surface of the sea may be quite smooth and remain so for long periods, with but a gentle ripple lapping the shore. Given enough breeze for driving a sailing vessel along its course — which there frequently is — the advantages afforded by such smooth sailing are welcome but there exists under these conditions a navigation danger that must be warned against. *Navigation note: In the absence of the usual ground swell and under conditions with no sea running, submerged rocks, reefs and shoals are unmarked by the familiar and warning break common to the Pacific. Since no surface-floating weed grows in these latitudes, the only indication of the existence of submerged dangers is a lighter hue of the sea color in their vicinity.*

Punta Colorada (alternatively called Punta Dorada) is a steep and rocky point situated about 3½ miles northwestward of Punta Arena. *Detached rocks lie close off the point* and *shoal water* extends about 1 mile offshore in the bight

Punta Colorada

between the two points. About 1¼ miles northwestward of Punta Arena there is a 2¼ fathom spot with deeper water between it and the shoal extending along the shore. Between Punta Arena and Punta Colorada a course should be followed not less than 1¼ miles offshore to avoid these shoals. Boatmen with local information thread a course through these *coastal shoals and rocky patches* to a wide sandy beach, just southward of Punta Colorada, where a fishing resort, Hotel Punta Colorada, is established. Comfortable accommodations are offered on an American plan. A spur of the coastal road communicates with the resort and a well-maintained *airstrip* is in use. (See Appendix.) Thatched umbrellas may be seen along the beach and a rock-paved walkway runs diagonally from the beach up the scrub-covered hillside to the hotel buildings above.

Bahía de las Palmas (Las Palmas Bay) is a large open bay situated between Punta Colorada and Punta Pescadero, about 16 miles northwestward, receding approximately 5 miles from a line joining these points. In the southern part of the bay soundings are relatively shallow, the 50-fathom curve extending between 3 and 4 miles off the coast in the vicinity of Boca de la Trinidad. Here the land rises gradually from the low sandy beach to the coastal mountain range. In the northern part of the bay the water is deeper with soundings of 50 fathoms within ½ mile or less of the shore, deepening rapidly thereafter. A series of stony beaches front the rocky cliffs of spurs that reach inland toward the coastal range of mountains. The largest of the *fountain springs* emerging along the Gulf coast, whose source is the high mountain range watershed, flows clear and cool at the

rate of 8 cubic feet per second out of San Bartolo Canyon, back of Las Palmas Bay. This strong flow of pure mountain water irrigates the land 'round about and makes quite habitable a terrain that would otherwise lie unproductive and parched. Several large arroyos intersect the land and their broad mouths open onto the shore of the bay. In the roadstead there is some protection afforded from the northerly winds in the northwestern part of the bay but no protection from southeasterly gales; it is entirely open from the north around to the east. When severe northerly weather threatens, vessels anchored along this coast make for the shelter of Ensenada de los Muertos, about 22 miles northwestward around Punta Pescadero; when southeasterly gales are in the offing the more protected lee of Cerralvo Island about 30 miles northwestward is sought.

Las Palmas Bay is noted for an abundance of sizable game fish. A deep submarine canyon with several narrow arms reaches close inshore from the middle of the bay toward Punta Pescadero. Large schools of fish feed close inshore in the protection of these depths. Flocks of birds "work" the schools of feeding fish and indicate their presence to sport and commercial fishermen. An upwelling from the canyon's depths provides nutrients for smaller fish and crustacians which support the cycle of sea life. This is truly one of the most remarkable angling areas in the gulf.

Boca de la Trinidad is the mouth of a small stream which opens into the southern part of the bay near a remarkable clump of trees about 3 miles westward of Punta Colorada; the arroyo is well watered and cultivated, a ranch being

Las Palmas Bay

Rancho Buena Vista

situated just back of the beach. Punta Soledad, situated about 2 miles further westward, is a low sandy point which projects but little beyond the general line of the coast. Here the Arroyo de Santiago opens onto the shore and a stream breaks through the sand berm during the rainy season. The land is well cultivated and the small village of La Rivera is established at the intersection of the coastal road and the road leading inland to the town of Santiago 11 miles southward. The village lies just eastward of Punta Soledad at the mouth of the Arroyo de Santiago. Some fresh provisions are available here. A *landing* may be made on the beach but a *shore bank* extends several hundred yards offshore, over which the depths are shoal. During the rainy season a fresh water estero forms at the mouth of the arroyo behind the berm of the beach. Close westward of Soledad Point immediately beyond the mouth of a wash that opens onto the shore, is a small angular bight with a sandy beach at the foot of a group of sharp coastal hills that rise above a brush-covered bluff. Two ranches are located along this shore, the westernmost, above the head of the cove, called Rancho Leonero, has an *aircraft landing strip* which is cut into the flat that reaches down to the beach. (See Appendix.)

Rancho Buena Vista — About 5 miles northwestward of Punta Soledad, is the famous sportfishing resort of Rancho Buena Vista. It is roughly the halfway point between the cape and La Paz, situated about 70 miles north and west of Cabo San Lucas, and about 75 miles south and east of La Paz. A prominent monument, a steel and stone pylon of modernistic design, stands in a small level clearing on the seaward end of a spur of the hills that rises back of the resort. The monument is more than 100 feet high and several hundred feet above the sea and may be clearly seen from seaward. A steel flagstaff stands to one side. Erected in 1968 it stands in a spacious stone-walled court and bears the following inscription: *LA BANDERA ES SÍMBOLO DE LA PATRIA SÍNTESIS DE NUESTRA HISTORIA — GUSTAVO DÍAZ ORDAZ, PRESIDENTE DE LA REPÚBLICA 24 FEBRERO 1968* ("The Flag is the symbol of our Country and the synthesis of our History"). Just

eastward of Rancho Bueno Vista, sportfishing launches are anchored in a small bight and there is a boatshed on the beach.

ANCHORAGE — Convenient anchorage may be taken close to the beach, *with care to avoid submerged rocks,* but the area is exposed to the north and east and in severe weather is untenable. Fortunately, the benign climate that prevails most of the months of the year makes Buena Vista a pleasant place to lay over. During stormy weather which may occur anytime between June and November, but which is most apt to occur in the latter part of September or October, the small fishing cruisers attached to the resort are pulled out of the water and up on the beach for safety; larger vessels at anchor in the roadstead make for deep water or the shelter of the cove at Ensenada de los Muertos, about 22 miles northwestward. In severe southeasterly *chubascos* the safest shelter is in the protected lee behind Cerralvo Island, about 30 miles northwestward.

LANDING — Safe landing may be made on the sandy beach, usually through a minor swell. Swimming, skindiving and sportfishing are unusually productive with many

From the left: Agua Caliente, Rancho Buena Vista, and Hotel Bahía de las Palmas

deep-sea record catches brought in from the immediate vicinity. The swimming beach is broad and clean, the water a perfect refreshing temperature, and there is a shell collector's beach nearby. However, sharks are prevalent, especially during the summer months, and care should be exercised when swimming or skin diving.

Native sportfishing bait, consisting of mullet and flying fish, is available at Buena Vista. In a scientific program to discover the habits of spawning and migration of sportfish species, a fish tagging program is in operation at Rancho Buena Vista under the official auspices of the Woods Hole Institute of Oceanography, Massachusetts, and the Tiburon Marine Laboratory of the United States Fish and Wildlife Service. It is also an effort to encourage sportfishermen to engage voluntarily in a catch-and-release program for fish caught obviously under record size and not desired for food or for trophy mounting. Comfortable accommodations are available at this resort, meals are served in family style in a community dining room. The principal residence of the ranch is situated on a hill above the community buildings. An *aircraft landing strip* is in use immediately westward of the ranch and close by the monument. Fuel is available dependent on the ranch's supply, which is trucked in from

La Paz. The new coastal road runs close along the shore and communicates with the cape settlements to the south and La Paz to the west, as well as the inland towns of Santiago and Miraflores, approximately 9 and 11 miles inland.

There are government offices in Santiago, telegraph and telephone service to La Paz, San José del Cabo and Cape San Lucas, and an *airstrip* capable of handling medium-size multiengine aircraft. General supplies and provisions are sold and *medical facilities* are available. Santiago is the point of departure for a trek to the modern-day valley of Shangri La in the Sierra de la Laguna called Canyon de la Zorra.

About a mile southward of Rancho Buena Vista there is a large private villa called Agua Caliente with a *landing pier* extending from the beach before it. A dry arroyo opens onto the shore between Agua Caliente and Buena Vista and discharges a stream of water during the rainy season. The village of Los Barriles Sur is situated close westward of Rancho Buena Vista. The village has a store where general supplies may be obtained, a post office, a telegraph office and a gasoline pump. Not far from Los Barriles there are several inland valleys where mangos, oranges, avo-

Landing at Agua Caliente

Punta Pescadero

cados, lemons, dates, and other fruits and vegetables are grown. These provisions are available in quantities dependent upon local supply, or larger quantities may be ordered in advance for later delivery.

ANCHORAGE — Convenient anchorage may be taken off the village in the roadstead open to the north and east. The anchorage is safe enough in fine weather but the approach must be made with care, sounding continuously, as the depths decrease suddenly from 15 fathoms to 3 and 4 fathoms along a narrow sandy shelf.

Hotel Bahía de las Palmas is situated close northwestward of Los Barriles and Rancho Buena Vista. A freshwater *spring* at Las Palmas irrigates a small grove of palms and has produced a green oasis sprouting from an otherwise desert landscape of low brush-covered hills. The coastal road from the south reaches Hotel Bahía de las Palmas thence turns inland at this point. It is a sportfishing and skindiving resort hotel with comfortable accommodations and modern conveniences. Meals are served; sportfishing launches are chartered; fresh native bait is available. The hotel boasts an outdoor bar and a fresh water swimming pool available to its guests as well as its own *airstrip*. (See Appendix.) The legend "Bahía de Palma" is constructed in large white letters alongside the aircraft runway back of the hotel. The sportfishing launches of the hotel may be seen anchored close off the beach during the fine season but are pulled up on the shore for storage and repair during the hot summer months. *Fuel* is available in quantities dictated by current supply on hand; minor mechanical repair may be had.

ANCHORAGE — Convenient anchorage may be taken off the beach but the water deepens rapidly close offshore. As elsewhere along this particular stretch of coast there is no protection against northerly or easterly weather. Northward of Hotel las Palmas, deep water lies close offshore and no anchorage is available until near Punta Pescadero. There is an *anchorage* for small vessels with some protection from northerly winds close inshore, about ½ mile southward of Punta Pescadero.

Punta Pescadero, the northern limit of Bahía de las Palmas, is a bold and rocky point of a reddish color and is backed by hills, the highest of which rises to a height of 858 feet. Off the point the bottom is rocky and irregular; a 5-fathom shoal lies about ¾ mile northeastward of it with deep water all around. The point should not be approached within less than a mile except with local knowledge. Close southward of the point Hotel Punta Pescadero is situated on a projecting bluff, its several buildings showing prominently to seaward. *Detached rocks* break off the bluff in front of the hotel and should be given a wide berth. The *anchorage* is situated southward of the hotel. *Safe landing* can be made on the beach in fine weather. An *aircraft landing strip* is located northwestward of Punta Pescadero. (See Appendix.) Accommodations, meals, sportfishing facilities, a well-appointed bar and warm Mexican hospitality are part and parcel of this resort establishment.

Las Palmas Bay is a most popular resort area with great activity throughout the year and especially during the fine season between late October and the end of May. Marine traffic along the coast between Cabo San Lucas and La Paz is considerable and the exchange of weather information, cruising conditions, the relay of radio messages between small craft, all contribute to a great overall safety factor.

Bahía de los Muertos lies between Punta Pescadero and Punta Perico, situated about 15 miles northward, and is formed by the wide indentation in the coast that recedes approximately 3¾ miles from a line joining the two points. The land behind the bay rises gradually to a mountain range of which the most prominent peak is El Palmar, which attains an elevation of 3,600 feet about 9 miles west-north-westward of Punta Pescadero and a little over 4 miles from the shore at the center of the bay. In the southern portion of the bay, a sandy beach extends along the shore; in the northern part of the bay, the beach is broken.

ANCHORAGE can be taken in the southern part of the bay, about ½ mile from shore, in depths of 6 to 10 fathoms, sand bottom; in the northern part of the bay, the 50-fathom curve approaches to within ⅓ mile of the shore and the shore bank is steep-to except in Ensenada de los Muertos under the hook of Punta Perico. In emergency, *fresh water*

may be obtained at La Trinidad Ranch, about 5 miles westward of Punta Pescadero. An *airstrip* is in use near this ranch. (See Appendix.)

Ensenada de los Muertos, situated about 2½ miles southward to Punta Perico, is a small cove tucked into the northern corner of Los Muertos Bay. The shore of the cove is low and sandy, rising gently to a brush-covered plain. Several small arroyos break through to the shore, the largest opening onto the beach near the head of the bay, just southwestward of the hill that rises from Punta Perico. At the northern end of the cove, a warehouse shed stands on a flat bench cut into the side hill. A mole fronts the shed and extends over the water. A road that traverses the arroyo passes a fish camp then runs out to the dock. The mole and shed facilities were built around 1925 to land cargo and supplies for the construction and operation of a silver mine, but fell into disuse shortly thereafter. Salt, gathered in the vicinity, was subsequently stored and shipped from the warehouse and dock at one time, but the port is no longer used for commercial trade, facilities at La Paz having supplanted their use. Ensenada de los Muertos is within the jurisdiction of the port authority of La Paz, and commercial vessels intending to use the port are required to notify La Paz port officials sufficiently before arrival to enable proper supervision during the time cargo is being worked. Los Muertos Bay is one of the sites tentatively selected for the establishment of one of a series of way ports and harbors of refuge for small craft, planned under the auspices of the Mexican Government. Private interests will build and operate the marine facilities to serve the needs of cruising yachts and their crews.

Bahía de los Muertos, anchorages in the foreground; Punta Perico on the right and entrance to Cerralvo channel in the background

Ensenada de los Muertos

ANCHORAGE — Good anchorage completely sheltered from northerly winds and seas may be obtained in depths of 8 to 10 fathoms, or for smaller vessels, closer inshore in about 4 to 6 fathoms, sand, where the anchorage is protected from all directions but the south.

LANDING — A dry landing can be safely made on the short stretch of sand beach at the south end of the cove. Severe southeasterly gales or *chubascos,* are more safely ridden out in the lee of Cerralvo Island about 5 miles northwestward around Punta Perico. Ensenada de los Muertos is a popular anchorage and way stop for coastal cruising vessels; small fishing vessels and yachts may be frequently found anchored in the cove. There is good *scuba* diving in the cove and an old massive anchor lies submerged in 4 fathoms just off the mole.

TIDES — The interval of high water at full and change is 8 hours, 8 minutes; the mean tidal difference is 2.8 feet; the spring range is 3.8 feet.

Punta Arena de la Ventana, Canal de Cerralvo

SECTION 16
BAHÍA de los MUERTOS to CANAL de SAN LORENZO

The run from Ensenada de los Muertos to La Paz is a distance of approximately 50 miles, with several good *anchorages* and protected passages along the way. H.O. Chart 1664, Magdalena Bay to La Paz; British Admiralty #3053, Bahía La Paz to Bahía Magdalena; Carta Náutica F.H. 604, Parte Sur del Golfo de California will serve well for accurate navigation along this coast.

Punta Perico, the northern limit of Bahía de los Muertos, is a steep-to rocky bluff of whitish color 40 to 60 feet high, rising abruptly to a hill 623 feet high. Immediately northward of the head of Los Muertos Cove there are *detached rocks,* but the water deepens close off Perico Point, with depths of 10 to 14 fathoms sounded at 200 and 300 yards, and 135 fathoms at ½ mile off the point.

The coast northward of the rocky bluffs of **Punta Perico** gives way to a receding low sandy shore as far as **Punta Arena de la Ventana,** 2 miles northwestward. This low, sandy point is the eastern limit of Bahía de la Ventana (Ventana Bay) and forms the southern entrance at the mouth of Canal de Cerralvo (the Cerralvo Channel) that runs west, thence northwest between the mainland and Isla de Cerralvo (Cerralvo Island). A *navigation light* that displays a **white group flash of three flashes** is shown from a concrete tower 33 feet high, painted with black and white bands, standing on Punta Arena de la Ventana. The light is visible for 11 miles in clear weather in the sector 210° through 319° and is an important navigational aid.

Punta Arena de la Ventana projects a considerable distance from the general run of the coastline and is quite low and flat, lacking any distinguishing features visible from seaward except the navigation light and its structure. Shoal water surrounds the point extending several hundred yards off the tip and well back off both sides. The shoal water reveals itself by distinctive color gradation of dark to light green, as one approaches the point. Several shallow lagoons and salt pans are situated abreast the light structure and back from the point. The coastal road branches and runs out to the salt pans and to a fish camp situated along the shore to the southward of the light. *Anchorage* may be taken on the northern side of the point in the open roadstead off the beach sheltered to some degree from southerly weather.

SEA AND WEATHER CONDITIONS — The prevailing winds along this section of the coast are northerly be-

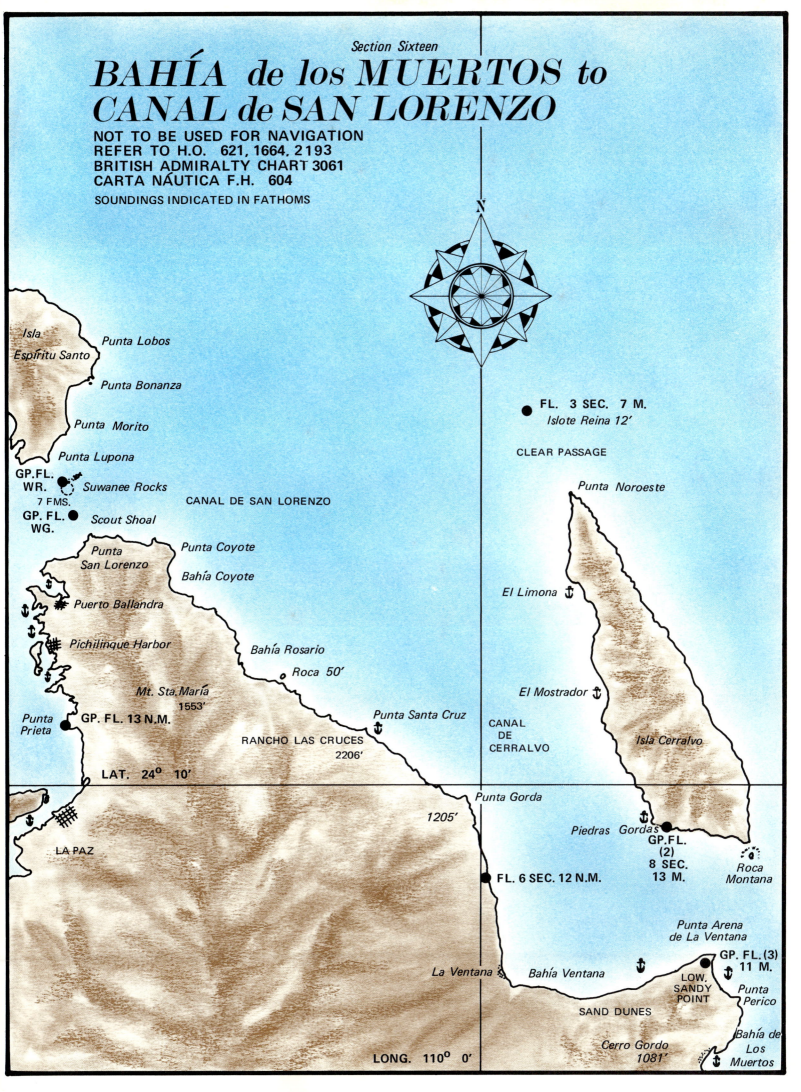

BAHÍA de los MUERTOS to CANAL de SAN LORENZO

NOT TO BE USED FOR NAVIGATION
REFER TO H.O. 621, 1664, 2193
BRITISH ADMIRALTY CHART 3061
CARTA NÁUTICA F.H. 604
SOUNDINGS INDICATED IN FATHOMS

N

Isla
Espíritu Santo

Punta Lobos

Punta Bonanza

Punta Morito

Punta Lupona

GP.FL.
WR.   Suwanee Rocks
7 FMS.

GP. FL.   Scout Shoal
WG.

CANAL DE SAN LORENZO

Punta
San Lorenzo   Punta Coyote

Bahía Coyote

Puerto Ballandra

Pichilinque Harbor

Bahía Rosario

Roca 50'

Mt. Sta. María
1553'

Punta
Prieta   GP. FL. 13 N.M.

RANCHO LAS CRUCES
2206'

Punta Santa Cruz

LAT. 24° 10'

FL. 3 SEC. 7 M.
Islote Reina 12'

CLEAR PASSAGE

Punta Noroeste

El Limona

El Mostrador

CANAL
DE
CERRALVO

Isla Cerralvo

LA PAZ

Punta Gorda

1205'

Piedras Gordas
GP.FL.
(2)
8 SEC.
13 M.

Roca
Montana

FL. 6 SEC. 12 N.M.

Punta Arena
de La Ventana

GP. FL. (3)
11 M.

La Ventana   Bahía Ventana

LOW.
SANDY
POINT

Punta
Perico

SAND DUNES

Cerro Gordo
1081'

Bahía de
Los
Muertos

LONG. 110° 0'

tween November and May; during the remainder of the year the northerly winds are often supplanted by southeasterly or southwesterly winds which sometimes generate full-blown gales which most often sweep the gulf in the latter part of September or during the month of October. The severest local gulf storm of this nature is known as *El Cordonazo* (The Whip) which blows with great violence for a relatively short duration, accompanied by much lightning and thunder. Normally there is an interval of several years between such severe storms. The *cordonazo* is distinguished from the *chubasco* in locale, the latter occurring off the Pacific coast and in the mouth of the gulf with its origin generally out at sea, and the former generating within the gulf proper. The rainy season in this area occurs during this storm-prone period with most of the rainfall around the month of September. During the dry season, which lasts most of the year, the weather is most always fine; the northerly winds blow regularly during the day, generally following the direction of the coast, supplanted by a light night breeze off the land or by calms.

TIDES — The tides ebb and flow regularly along this coast but the velocity and direction of the tidal currents depend greatly upon the prevailing wind. At the mouth of Cerralvo Channel the tidal streams sometimes attain a rate of 2½ knots; the set of the tidal current is usually irregular, often northerly in May and June; southerly from January to March.

FACILITIES — Marine facilities are principally comprised of those small beach ways and repair yards connected with the various coastal resorts for maintenance of their own fleets of sportfishing launches. Minor repairs, marine and engine parts may be obtained in emergency depending on current supply and activity of these facilities. Regular boat yards, marine supply houses and engine repair shops are established at La Paz.

PUBLIC ACCOMMODATIONS — Several classes of accommodations are available at coastal resorts and in the adjacent villages, generally offered under the American plan. Rancho Buena Vista, Hotel Las Palmas, Hotel Punta Pescadero, Hotel Punta Colorada and Rancho Buenas Aires generally offer cabaña accommodations with central or community dining rooms and refreshment bars. During the season it is advisable to make reservations well ahead of an expected visit, although each of the resorts welcomes the crews of visiting sportfishing vessels and yachts to the bars and for dinner on a space available basis. Prior arrangements should be made as to time and number of guests.

COMMUNICATIONS — Telephone, telegraph and postal facilities are established in the villages of La Rivera and Los Barriles. A paved road from Bahía San Lucas connects the coastal villages and resorts with La Paz. *Airstrips* capable of handling a range of small private aircraft to medium-size, multiengine commercial equipment are established at the various coastal villages and resorts. Each resort has radio facilities to communicate with aircraft on UNICOM frequency 122.8 megaHertz. The sportfishing fleet communicates on 2638 and 2738 kiloHertz; the hotels intercommunicate on 2620 kiloHertz. Some of the resorts have high frequency marine radiotelephone equipment capable of communicating with KMI, Oakland, California, for a telephone patch to international circuits. The citizen's band frequencies are also utilized. (See Appendix.)

TRANSPORTATION — Air transportation is the principal means of travel in Baja California. Major airlines maintain regular schedules from both United States and Mexican cities to La Paz; shuttle planes and charter service fly to all Baja Peninsula points. Charter service is also available in Tijuana. Several of the cape resorts fly their own guest planes to Tijuana. Taxis are available at all resort establishments and buses and trucks serve all the villages and ports along the coast on a fairly regular basis, and carry passengers at a nominal fee.

MARINE EMERGENCIES — Nearest Mexican Naval Base is located at La Paz, approximately 140 miles distant from Cabo San Lucas. The general area of the coast is frequented by commercial Tuna Clippers out of Cabo San Lucas, La Paz, and San Diego. These vessels, when nearby, traditionally render emergency aid when requested. The sportfishing launches connected with the various resorts along this coast will also readily render aid when requested. The common radio frequency for emergency communication with any of these sources is the ship emergency marine band 2182 kiloHertz. Radio messages to ship or shore may be relayed through any radio-equipped coastal vessel.

MEDICAL FACILITIES — A federal hospital and medical staff are located at San José del Cabo. Several private and public hospitals as well as a number of physicians, surgeons, dentists and medical specialists in the various fields of medicine are available in La Paz. Emergency first aid and some medical attention may be obtained at Bahía San Lucas, La Rivera, and Los Barriles.

SOURCES OF ADDITIONAL INFORMATION — *Rancho Buena Vista,* P.O. Box 1486, Newport Beach, California 92663, telephone (714) 673-4638; *Hotel Las Cruces Palmilla,* Box 1775, La Jolla, California 92037, telephone (714) 454-0600; Hotel Bahía de Las Palmas, Los Barriles via La Paz, B. Cfa., Mexico; *Hotel Punta Pescadero.,* P.O. Box 362, La Paz, B. Cfa., Mexico or 3630 Sunswept Drive, Studio City, California 91604, telephone (213) 763-9041; *Hotel Bajo Colorado,* 2701 Alcott, Denver, Colorado 80211, telephone (303) 433-7308; *Camino Real Cabo San Lucas,* 10250 Santa Monica Blvd., Suite 199, Century City, Los Angeles, California 90067, telephone (213) 879-0930; *Hotel Punta Colorada* (Punta Dorada) Los Barriles via La Paz, B. Cfa., Mexico; *Rancho Buenas Aires,* P.O. Box 1486, Newport Beach, California 92662; *Hotel La Finisterra,* Apartado Postal No. 1, Cabo San Lucas, B. Cfa., Mexico or 809 Shreve Bldg., 210 Post Street, San Francisco, California 94108, telephone (415) 397-1718.

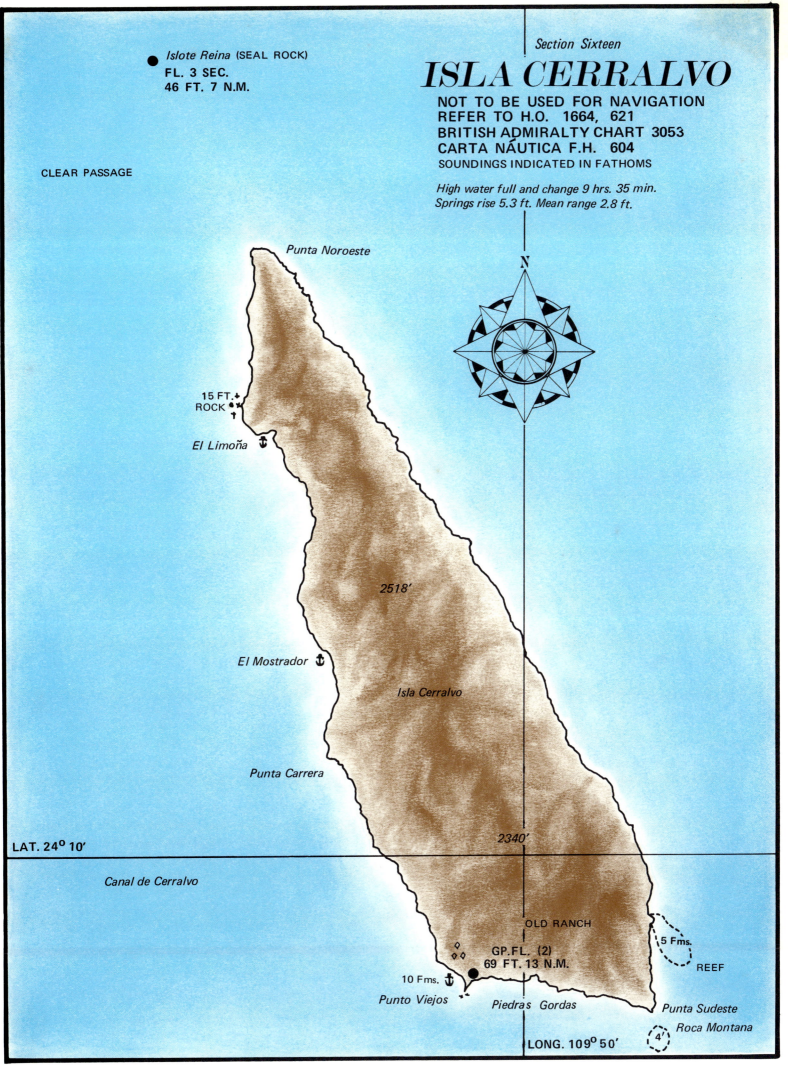

Islote Reina (SEAL ROCK)
FL. 3 SEC.
46 FT. 7 N.M.

ISLA CERRALVO
NOT TO BE USED FOR NAVIGATION
REFER TO H.O. 1664, 621
BRITISH ADMIRALTY CHART 3053
CARTA NÁUTICA F.H. 604
SOUNDINGS INDICATED IN FATHOMS

High water full and change 9 hrs. 35 min.
Springs rise 5.3 ft. Mean range 2.8 ft.

CLEAR PASSAGE

Punta Noroeste

N

15 FT.
ROCK

El Limoña

2518'

El Mostrador

Isla Cerralvo

Punta Carrera

2340'

LAT. 24° 10'

Canal de Cerralvo

OLD RANCH

5 Fms.

GP.FL. (2)
69 FT. 13 N.M.

REEF

10 Fms.

Punto Viejos   Piedras Gordas   Punta Sudeste

Roca Montana

LONG. 109° 50'   4'

Punta Viejos, Isla Cerralvo

The coastal passage that leads through the protected channel between the Peninsula shore and Isla Cerralvo is a run of about 30 miles. Cerralvo Channel is provided with lighted aids to navigation and there are safe and protected shelters along the way.

Bahía Ventana is a deep indentation that lies between Punta Arena de la Ventana and Punta Gorda, situated about 12 miles northwestward. The bay is sheltered from the east by Cerralvo Island which lies offshore about 9 miles from the center of the bay. At the eastern end of the bay Cerralvo Island is separated by but 5 miles of intervening channel from Punta Arena de la Ventana. The bay recedes about 6 miles within a line joining Punta Arena de la Ventana and Punta Gorda; its southern shores are low and sandy, bordered by an extensive desert plain that is covered with a growth of cactus and low bushes. On its western side the land is more abrupt with hills rising from the shore and blending into mountainous country extending to Bahía de La Paz. Two prominent peaks visible from a great distance, North and South El Mulato in the Cacahiles Range, rise to 3,829 and 4,144 feet elevation, respectively, about 7½ miles southwestward of Punta Gorda.

A *navigation light* **flashes white every 6 seconds:** flash 0.5 second, eclipse 5.5 seconds. It is exhibited 59 feet above the sea at Punta La Luz from a white metal tower on the shore of Bahía Ventana about 3½ miles southward of Punta Gorda. The light, visible for 12 miles in clear weather, is one of three lights established as an aid to navigation in the Cerralvo Channel.

Punta Gorda (Gorda Point), the western limit of Ventana Bay, is a bold rocky bluff 50 to 75 feet high, with high land immediately behind it. The point is steep-to with depths of 5 fathoms or more close offshore, and vessels may run in quite close.

ANCHORAGE — In moderate weather, vessels may anchor westward of Punta Arena de la Ventana, in depths of 6 to 8 fathoms, sand, taking care to avoid a sandbank which extends about 400 yards from the northwestern side of the point. Elsewhere *anchorage* may be obtained within ½ mile of the shore anywhere in the bay in depths of 5 to 8 fathoms; farther offshore the depths increase rapidly, except near the village of La Ventana, in ruins near the head of the bay. Here it is necessary to anchor a little farther out on account of a 3-fathom bank which extends about ½ mile offshore. Some *fresh water* may be obtained at the site of the village.

Isla de Cerralvo (Cerralvo Island) is the southernmost island in the Gulf of California off-lying the Baja California Peninsula. The island was first discovered for the Spanish by Fortun Jiménez on a voyage of exploration into the gulf in 1533 and was named Isla de Santiago. The island was inhabited at that time by the Pericu Indians who lived primarily on the seafood gathered along the shore and from the fruit of the cactus pitahaya that grows abundantly on the island. Extensive pearl beds along the west coast of the island were particularly rich and pearling was heavily engaged in by the Spanish almost from th time of its discovery. In 1632, a Spanish pearler, Francisco de Ortega, called here to work the beds and gave Isla Cerralvo its present name in honor of the Viceroy of New Spain. No one at present lives on the island permanently.

Cerralvo Island is a large, mostly barren island of volcanic character situated with its southerly end about 5 miles eastward of Punta Coyote, forming between its northwesterly side and the mainland shore Canal de Cerralvo (Cerralvo Channel), a deep navigable channel with a minimum width of about 5 miles. Cerralvo Island is about 16 miles long and a little over 4 miles wide at its widest point in the southerly portion, tapering toward its northern extremity. The island rises to several high peaks, of which the highest and most northerly has an elevation of 2,518 feet, situated about 7 miles from the northern extremity. Both sides of the island consist of a succession of bold, rocky bluffs with small stretches of sand and gravel beach at the mouths of steep arroyos that open between lateral spurs running down from the central mountain ridge. There is deep water close to the shore. The southeastern point of the island is a steep rocky bluff. About ¾ mile southward of this point lies Roca Montana (Montana Rock), a *dangerous sunken rock* with a depth over it of but 4 feet and on which the S.S. *Montana* struck in 1874. There is a depth of 10 fathoms close-to and between the rock and the island there is a clear passage with depths of 5 to 6 fathoms; outside Montana Rock the depths increase rapidly.

A *reef* with depths of not more than 5 fathoms over it, and the inner end of which dries at low water, extends about 1 mile east-southeastward from a position on the eastern side of the island about 1½ miles northward of the south-eastern end. Piedras Gordas, off which a *rocky reef* projects about ¼ mile, is a bold rocky point on the western side of the island, situated about 3½ miles northwestward of the southeastern end. *Anchorage* may be taken in a small bight closeby.

About ¾ mile northwestward of Piedras Gordas is a low sandy point, the southwestern extremity of the island. Deep water lies close to the point but *anchorage* may be taken about 400 yards off the northern side in depths of 10 fathoms. A *well* with brackish water is located in this vicinity and several weathered wooden crosses mark the graves of itinerant shark fishermen who frequented the island.

Punta Viejos is a bold rocky point, situated about 3½ miles northwestward of Piedras Gordas. A *navigation light* is shown 69 feet above the sea from a red tower situated on Punta Viejos. It exhibits a **white group flash of two flashes every 8 seconds:** flash 0.3 second, eclipse 1 second; flash 0.3 second, eclipse 6.4 seconds. The *light* is visible for 13 miles in clear weather. *Anchorage* may be taken in an open bight on the northwest side of the point, giving adequate berth to the numerous rocks offlying the point. Several huts are situated near the light structure. Approximately 2¼ miles northward of this point is a steep, high, whitish-colored bluff, Farallónes Blancos, a landmark at the southern limit of El Mostrador, itself a small indentation in the island's western coast, about 6½ miles northwestward of Piedras Gordas. At the head of this latter cove there is a small sandy beach. El Limona is another slight indentation in the coast in which there is a small sand and gravel beach located about 2½ miles northward of El Mostrador and about 4¼ miles from the northern extremity of the island. *Anchorage* may be taken in this bight and a dry *landing* effected upon the beach at its head. *Detached rocks* lie close offshore on both sides of the bight. The northernmost point of the island is a high bluff from which a *rocky reef* projects nearly ½ mile. Small vessels with local knowledge frequently anchor eastward of, and close under this point obtaining some protection from northwesterly winds.

Navigation Caution: Islote de la Reina (Seal Rock), located in a position about 4 miles north-northwestward of the northern point of Cerralvo Island, is a rock about 100 feet long, 50 feet wide and 12 feet high. A smaller rock awash at low water lies about 100 yards off the northwestern side of Islote de la Reina; a second rock with a depth of 2 fathoms over it lies about 200 yards eastward. There are also a few smaller rocks in the immediate vicinity and the group should be given an adequate berth.

A *navigation light* exhibited 46 feet above the sea from a metal tower on Islote de la Reina **flashes white every 3 seconds:** flash 0.5 second, eclipse 2.5 seconds. It can be seen for a distance of 7 miles in clear weather. Between this group of rocks and the northern tip of Cerralvo Island there is a deep and navigable channel which is believed to

Rancho Las Cruces

be free of dangers. Depths of 25 fathoms have been sounded ¼ mile southward of Seal Rock, increasing rapidly beyond that distance.

Canal de Cerralvo (Cerralvo Channel) is the deepwater navigable channel between Cerralvo Island and the mainland shore. Its eastern mouth, about 5 miles wide, lies between the southern end of Cerralvo Island and Punta Arena de la Ventana; its northwestern mouth, about 6½ miles wide, lies between the western side of the island and Punta Gorda. The water in the channel is too deep for anchorage which, if necessary or desired, must be found along either shore. Cargo freighters and other large vessels use this channel safely by laying a course in mid-channel. Montana Rock, the only offshore danger, may be given a safe berth by keeping to the southern side of the entrance. El Mulato peaks about 9 miles inland from Punta Gorda, bearing 270° lead into Cerralvo Channel well southward

Coast Northwest of Punta Santa Cruz

Canal de San Lorenzo with Isla Espíritu Santo in the background

of Montana Rock. The navigation lights previously described on Punta Arena de la Ventana and Piedras Gordas, at the eastern mouth and at the northwestern sweep of Ventana Bay, are an aid to navigation through the channel at night; however, unless well acquainted with the coast, it is not advisable to attempt to pass through the channel at night or in thick weather. Sailing vessels with a fair wind can negotiate the channel with ease and safety but should not attempt a passage with a head wind as the tidal currents, which run with a strength of up to 2½ knots, make a beat through the channel both difficult and dangerous. Calms are also frequent in the channel, especially at night, and sailing vessels must expect to rely on auxiliary power under adverse conditions. Without adequate auxiliary propulsion it is advisable to lay a course outside Cerralvo Island.

The coast between Punta Gorda and Punta Coyote, situated about 16 miles northwestward, is bold and rocky with occasional sand beaches; the country inland is broken and mountainous. Punta de Santa Cruz projects slightly from the general line of the coast about 5 miles northwestward of Punta Gorda; there are no outlying dangers. The point is sometimes called El Sena de la Cruz. Three large commemorative stone crosses are erected on the bluff that rises from the point and serve as an excellent landmark for locating the small bay situated immediatly to the west. While the crosses are of modern design and recent origin, they supplant a previous cross of wood which since the first memory of the local inhabitants has marked this spot as the original landing place of the first Spanish expedition across the gulf to the Peninsula of Baja California. Extending from the southern shore of the point in a small sandy bight are a short irregular rock breakwater and mole which provide *good landing* for small boats. There is a settlement back of the beach at the foot of the mole and several small ranch houses scattered around the bight; immediately southward a large flat wash, Arroyo de Santa Cruz, opens onto the shore, An *airstrip* is located in the center of the arroyo, one end extending to the shore of the bay. (See Appendix.)

Rancho de las Cruces is a large, old and well-established plantation, shaded with palms and dating back to well before the turn of the century; it is located on the southern edge of the arroyo just back of the shore, about a mile south of Punta Santa Cruz. The main ranch building is a "U"-shaped, Spanish-style ranch house with the "U" open to the gulf and enclosing a wide palm-shaded terrace and an oval salt water swimming pool. A well-appointed sportfishing resort was at one time operated in conjunction with the ranch but since 1962 it has become an exclusive private sportfishing club. It was originally the home of the late president of Mexico, General Rodríguez. A number of private vacation homes are built in the hills immediately behind the club. In front of the club buildings two short *rock jetties* extend from the shore, curving at their outer ends toward one another to form a narrow mouth to an enclosed boat basin. A *marine railway* is built on the shore of the bay to service the club's sportfishing launches. *Good water* is available at the ranch in emergency. Las Cruces is connected by road to La Paz which is about 22 miles distant.

A *sandspit* with a large white rock standing about 50 feet high on its outer edge projects about ½ mile from the shore, about 4½ miles northwestward of Punta de Santa Cruz. A *shoal rocky patch* lies exposed close northwestward of the 50-foot high rock. A small white crescent beach lies between two rocky headlands immediately southeastward of the sandspit and offlying rock. *Good landing* may be made.

Between Punta Santa Cruz and the sandspit there are several indentations in the coast at the heads of which small arroyos open onto the shore. Bahía del Rosario is the larger indentation, just westward of the sandspit with a width of about 2½ miles. There are depths of 4 fathoms close to the western shore and 15 fathoms in the center of the bay. At the head of the bay, just back of the shore, is the old village of San Rosario, at one time, in the latter part of the nineteenth century, a principal silver mining settlement along this coast. La Sopresa is a small village in the same vicinity, with an excellent beach. A *coral shoal,* with depths of less than 3 fathoms over it, extends a short distance offshore at the head of the bay. A rocky bluff backed by a prominent hill 984 feet high forms the northern limit of the bay. From this position to Punta Coyote, a distance of about

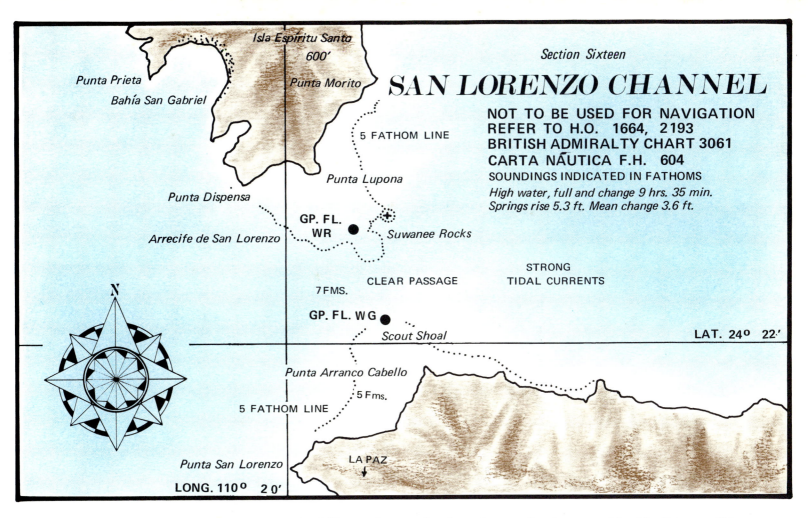

SAN LORENZO CHANNEL

Isla Espíritu Santo
600'

Punta Prieta

Punta Morito

Bahía San Gabriel

5 FATHOM LINE

Punta Lupona

Punta Dispensa

GP. FL.
WR

Arrecife de San Lorenzo

Suwanee Rocks

**NOT TO BE USED FOR NAVIGATION
REFER TO H.O. 1664, 2193
BRITISH ADMIRALTY CHART 3061
CARTA NÁUTICA F.H. 604**
SOUNDINGS INDICATED IN FATHOMS
*High water, full and change 9 hrs. 35 min.
Springs rise 5.3 ft. Mean change 3.6 ft.*

CLEAR PASSAGE

7 FMS.

GP. FL. WG

Scout Shoal

STRONG
TIDAL CURRENTS

LAT. 24° 22'

Punta Arranco Cabello

5 Fms.

5 FATHOM LINE

Punta San Lorenzo

LA PAZ

LONG. 110° 20'

N

5 miles, the coastline tends inward and the hills recede considerably. About ½ mile southeastward of Punta Coyote is a bold rocky bluff, backed by moderate high hills. This bluff is frequently mistaken for Punta Coyote which is moderately low and rocky, with a small outlying white rock close-to and a *reef of rocks* projecting a little more than 200 yards from its outer end. Punta Coyote is the southeastern entrance point of Canal de San Lorenzo, a somewhat shallow and narrow, but navigable and lighted channel leading between the headlands and off-lying Espíritu Santo Island to the Bay of La Paz. La Coyote, a small settlement comprised of ranches and small farms connected by road to La Paz, is situated in the bight just southeastward of Punta Coyote. Puerto Mejia is a small cove at the mouth of an arroyo that opens on the shore close southeastward of Punta Coyote. A dog-leg *airstrip* (see Appendix) is located between the two coves just above the shore.

Upon reaching abreast Punta Coyote, the land rounds up to the westward, forming a peninsular-shaped coast off which lies Isla Espíritu Santo (Espíritu Santo Island) to the north; a 3½-mile wide passage between the coast and the southern tip of the island leads westward, opening onto the broad expanse of Bahía de La Paz (Bay of La Paz). A narrow but navigable channel threads the passage, encumbered on either side by *rocks* and *shoals,* but the ship channel is straight, permanently marked with *two lighted towers* on either side, and carries a least depth of 42 feet through a mid-channel track.

From Punta Coyote the coast trends in a general westward direction for about 5 miles to Punta San Lorenzo and comprises the southern shore of the San Lorenzo Channel. A *shore bank* fringes the coast all along the southern side of

the channel, extending for a considerable distance offshore in several places. The shoal water over the bank reflects an emerald-greenish hue of a lighter shade than the deeper water toward the center of the channel; in fair weather a lookout aloft can readily discern the deepwater limits of this channel by its color. A bluff point that may be readily made out projects northward from the coast, about 2¼ miles westward of Punta Coyote. Las Galeras, a shelving rocky ledge, projects about ½ mile off this point, and from it the coastal bank, with depths over it of a little less than 5 fathoms, extends northward for about ½ mile. Punta Arranco Cabello (meaning "scalped") is a quite bald point, situated about 1¼ miles westward of Las Galeras; it is a steep and rocky projection, backed by a hill 164 feet high that is quite bare of vegetation. A *shore bank,* with depths of 2 fathoms over its outer edge, extends a little more than 1,200 yards northwestward of this point.

Puerto Mejia

San Lorenzo Channel, looking eastward

Scout Shoal, a rocky patch composed chiefly of loose stones, about ¼ mile long and 175 yards wide with a least depth over it of 9 feet, lies about 1 mile northwestward of Punta Arranco Cabello. It is marked by a *light* shown 10 feet above the sea from a *white tower* that exhibits a **white-green group flash of two flashes every 7 seconds;** the *green sector* of the light marks the shoal and it can be seen in clear weather at a distance of 11 miles. Between Scout Shoal and the outer edge of the 2-fathom *shore bank* that extends off Punta Arrano Cabello, there is a ⅓-mile wide passage in which a depth of 3½ fathoms may be safely carried. Vessels negotiating the San Lorenzo Channel generally keep to the center of the main channel with Scout Shoal southward of their track.

Punta San Lorenzo is a moderately high bluff, situated about 1¾ miles southwestward of Punta Arranco Cabello and forms the northwestern extremity of the eastern shore of Bahía de La Paz; over the shore bank, *shoal water* extends about 400 yards off the point. A *pinnacle rock,* covered by a little over 7 fathoms of water lies about 1 mile northwestward off San Lorenzo Point. On the opposite or northern shore of San Lorenzo Passage, Punta Lupona (Lupona Point) projects at the southern tip of Espíritu Santo Island. Off-lying this point is Arrecife de San Lorenzo (San Lorenzo Reef), the northwestern edge of which is about 1 mile southeastward. Between Punta Arranco Cabello on the southern shore and Punta Lupona on the northern shore, the San Lorenzo Passage is about 3½ miles wide at its narrowest point; the *navigable channel,* however, is limited to a width of about 1,000 yards between the 6-fathom soundings off Scout Shoal and San Lorenzo Reef; mid-channel depths are 7 to 8 fathoms, although in 1965 less water than charted was reported to exist. Adequate depths exist throughout the mid-channel track for all small coastal vessels and cruising yachts, and passage may be had as well between the two shoals and the respective adjacent shores, where depths of 3 to 4 fathoms can be safely carried; such passage is not advised, without local knowledge.

Arrecife de San Lorenzo (San Lorenzo Reef), on the northern side of the channel, is a rocky ledge about 800 yards in width, with a least depth over it of 9 feet; a 1½-fathom *submerged pinnacle* lies close southeastward of this reef but between the reef and Lupona Point, about a mile northwestward, there is a clear passage with depths of 4 fathoms. A *navigation light* shown from a *white concrete tower* painted with *orange bands,* stands on San Lorenzo Reef and exhibits a **white-red group flash every 10 seconds;** the *red sector* marks the reef. This light can be seen for 13 miles in clear weather. Rocas Suwanee (Suwanee Rocks), with a least depth over them of 4 feet, lie about ½ mile northeastward of San Lorenzo Reef, with 5 to 6 fathoms sounded close around.

TIDES AND TIDAL STREAMS — The mean high water interval at full and change in the San Lorenzo Channel is 9 hours, 35 minutes; the rise and fall of the tide has a spring range of 5.3 feet, and a mean range of 3.6 feet. The tidal streams in the channel are strong, sometimes attaining a rate of 2¼ knots and, from October to February, even as much as 3 knots. They set in a northeast-southwest direction depending on the tidal period. Masters of sailing vessels should plan their passage to coincide with a favorable tidal flow and to sail through with a fair wind; lacking these it is safer to use auxiliary power in order to avoid being dangerously set by the currents.

WIND AND WEATHER — Winds in the channel and in La Paz Bay are regular during the greater part of the year — November to May — blowing northwesterly from about 9 a.m. to 4 p.m., succeeded toward evening by southerly winds which last all night. During the rest of the year southeast and southwest winds prevail. Calms are frequent in spring and summer months; fogs infrequent.

SECTION 17
LA PAZ

The City of La Paz is located on the flat plain extending several miles southeastward of the harbor, laid out in orderly streets and avenues that extend 4 or 5 miles in a broad strip back of the waterfront. La Paz, with a population of about 35,000 (1971), is the largest and most important town of the southern part of Baja California and the seat of government for the Southern Territory; it has a most colorful history that reaches farther back in time than any other city in Baja or Alta California.

La Paz was the site of the earliest Spanish settlement on the peninsula when California was still believed to be an island called Santa Cruz, separated from the mainland by the Sea of Cortez on the west and the mythical Straits of Anian to the north. The Bay of La Paz was originally called Refugio de la Santa Cruz in the log of the *Concepción,* one of the exploration ships of an expedition sent from Tehuantepec in 1533 by Hernando Cortez under the command of Hernando Grijalva and Diego Becerra. The two vessels *San Lázaro* and *Concepción* were separated by a storm at the outset of the voyage, Grijalva's ship *San Lázaro* being driven considerably offshore to the near vicinity of the heretofore unknown and undiscovered island which he called Santo Tomás, later to be called Isla Socorro. Becerra's ship, *Concepción,* was left to continue the coastal exploration alone. Becerra was a strict, arbitrary and unreasonable captain and in the course of the first stages of the voyage was killed by his pilot Fortun Jiménez during a fight by the crew in mutiny.

It was under the leadership of Jiménez that the expedition reached and entered the bay later to be known as La Paz, thus was he the first European to discover and land on the "island of Santa Cruz," as the expedition recorded the event, later to be proven the Peninsula of Baja California. Upon going ashore Jiménez and 22 members of the crew were attacked by Indians and killed, but the remainder of the crew survived and returned to the coast of New Spain with news of their discoveries and tales of a great wealth of pearls to be found there, thus bringing "California" into history. Based on the reports of Jiménez, Cortez assembled another expedition and with three vessels built in Tehuantepec, the *San Lázaro,* the *Santo Tomás* and the *Santa Agueda,* took supplies and colonists to La Paz where he founded a settlement on the shores of the bay near what is now Pichilinque Harbor, taking formal possession of the land for the Spanish Crown on May 3, 1535. The colony lasted only a little more than a year, however, before it was abandoned due to lack of supplies precipitated by political differences between Cortez and the Viceroy of Mexico. In succeeding years, Francisco de Ulloa, Hernando Alacrón, Juan Rodrígucz Cabrillo and others explored the peninsula and its surrounding seas in a continuing series of expeditions in a search for new lands, new riches and the elusive Straits of Anian.

In 1596 Sebastián Vizcaíno, commanding an expedition to explore the peninsula, entered La Paz Bay which he so named because of his friendly reception by the Indians. While searching along the shore for a suitable site at which to establish a settlement he found, at Bahía Pichilinque, old rusted horseshoes, nails, knife blades and keys which were identified as remains of the Cortez expedition of 1535. Vizcaíno left Captain Rodrigo de Figueroa with supplies and men at La Paz with orders to establish a permanent colony. A strong stockade was erected and trenches were dug to defend the encampment, but a series of mishaps befell the colony. They culminated when a strong north wind blew up, carrying sparks from a cooking fire, igniting the thatch roof of one of the houses in the settlement. Spreading rapidly to all the huts and tents, the fire consumed over half the colony before it was extinguished. Faced with this great loss of shelter, arms, clothing and food, Vizcaíno decided to abandon the settlement at La Paz.

Various expeditions granted pearling licenses in the Gulf of California by the authorities in Mexico visited La Paz over the ensuing decades, but it wasn't until the missionary period that another attempt was made to establish a permanent colony at La Paz. In 1683 Fathers Kino, Copart and Goni, accompanied by Admiral Isidro Otondo y Antillón on orders from the Governor of the Mexican province of Sinaloa, crossed the gulf from Mazatlán to the Bay of La Paz. A small chapel was hastily built, but the natives attacked the missionaries with arrows, and in retaliation, Otondo was guilty of a cruel folly: When sixteen of the warriors later appeared at the settlement he invited them to partake of a feast and, while they were eating, ordered his marines to fire a cannonball into their midst. It exploded, killing three and wounding several others. The hostility of the Indians after this incident and the difficulty of obtaining supplies from across the gulf, upon which the colony was almost entirely dependent, put an end to this first shortlived missionary adventure at La Paz.

A more permanent mission was established at La Paz in 1720 by Jesuit Fathers Jaime Bravo and Juan de Ugarte called Nuestra Señora del Pilar de La Paz. One of a series of Indian uprisings against their Spanish masters in 1734 saw the destruction of all of the principal southern missions, including the mission at La Paz; all of the converts in residence who chose not to flee with the Father and his followers to barren Espíritu Santo Island were murdered. The La Paz Mission was shortly rebuilt but what Spanish ecclesiastical love, swords and gunpowder did not accomplish, the white man's diseases did, for the Indians of the region were all but wiped out in a series of epidemics. As a consequence of these severely decimating epidemics a curious racial dichotomy exists; for while Mexico is an Indian country, Baja California is the only part of it which has

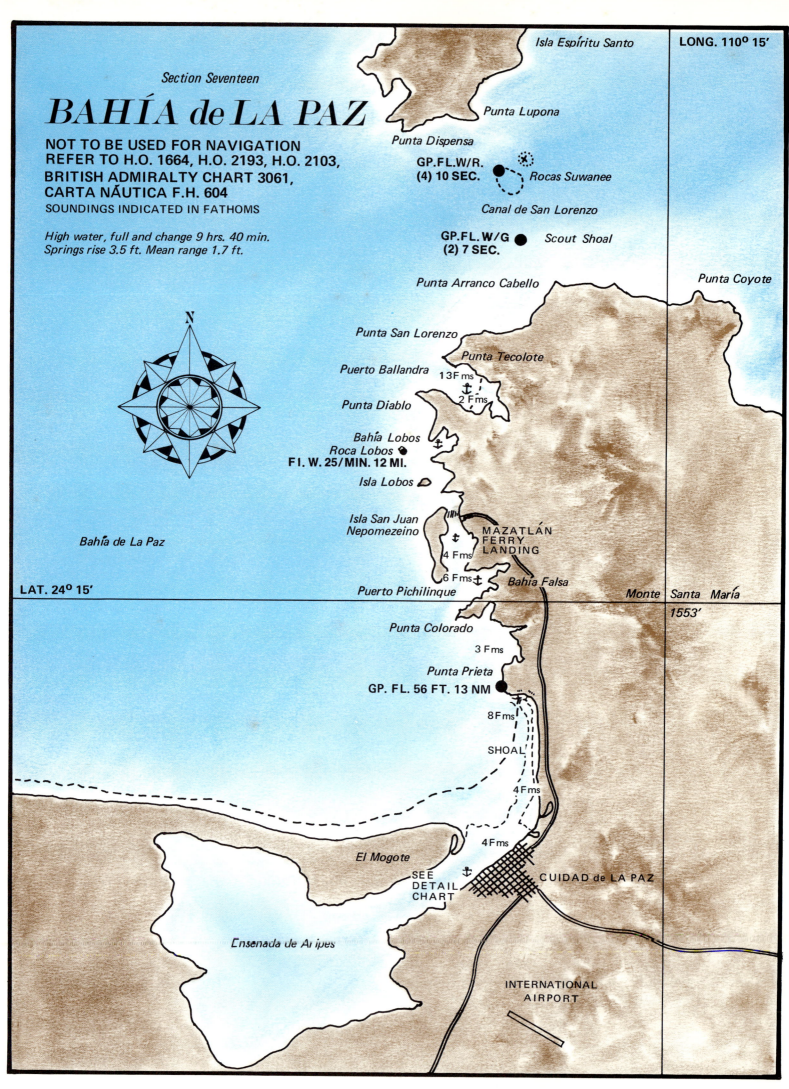

Section Seventeen

BAHÍA de LA PAZ

NOT TO BE USED FOR NAVIGATION
REFER TO H.O. 1664, H.O. 2193, H.O. 2103,
BRITISH ADMIRALTY CHART 3061,
CARTA NÁUTICA F.H. 604
SOUNDINGS INDICATED IN FATHOMS

High water, full and change 9 hrs. 40 min.
Springs rise 3.5 ft. Mean range 1.7 ft.

N

Bahía de La Paz

LONG. 110° 15'

Isla Espíritu Santo

Punta Lupona

Punta Dispensa

GP.FL.W/R.
(4) 10 SEC.   Rocas Suwanee

Canal de San Lorenzo

GP.FL. W/G   Scout Shoal
(2) 7 SEC.

Punta Coyote

Punta Arranco Cabello

Punta San Lorenzo

Punta Tecolote

Puerto Ballandra   13 Fms

Punta Diablo   2 Fms

Bahía Lobos
Roca Lobos
Fl. W. 25/MIN. 12 MI.

Isla Lobos

Isla San Juan
Nepomezeino   MAZATLÁN
FERRY
4 Fms   LANDING

6 Fms   Bahía Falsa

LAT. 24° 15'

Puerto Pichilinque   Monte Santa María

1553'

Punta Colorado

3 Fms

Punta Prieta
GP. FL. 56 FT. 13 NM

8 Fms

SHOAL

4 Fms

4 Fms

El Mogote

SEE
DETAIL
CHART   CUIDAD de LA PAZ

Ensenada de Aripes

INTERNATIONAL
AIRPORT

216

almost no descendents of the indigenous tribes represented among the present inhabitants. This critical loss of native labor depended upon by the Missionary Fathers, combined with a period of persistent drouth in which the water supply of La Paz gave out, resulted in the abandonment of the mission in 1749, only 29 years after its establishment.

The harbor continued to be used as a supply point for the missions and mines of the peninsula, but La Paz remained without permanent inhabitants until 1811 when a retired soldier, Juan José Espinoza, was granted the lands encompassing the entire site of La Paz. This was to be a reward for his services to the Spanish Government, but on the condition that he reside there and cultivate the land in order that ships putting into that port might be afforded a source of fresh provisions and sweet water. He was to be the Port Guard and in charge of the mail that arrived from time to time from Loreto, as well as caretaker of the Royal House, which was a stone structure of substantial size built during the sway of the mission. (It occupied the present site of the jail and courthouse, but was completely destroyed in 1847 when the Naval forces of the United States bombarded the city during the Mexican-American War.) Time and dereliction of duty proved Juan Espinoza unable to meet all his obligations and other colonists were invited by the Territorial Authority to settle at La Paz, each being given a tract of land with the stipulation that it be cultivated. The people slowly grew with an influx of settlers, constituted in a large proportion of English, French, German and American nationals after Mexico declared independence from Spain in 1822.

There were about 400 citizens in La Paz in 1829 when a great cloud burst almost completely destroyed the town of Loreto which was at that time Capitol of the Territory. Great fear caused most of the people of Loreto to flee and, because of instability of the social institutions brought on by this natural misfortune, it was decided in 1830 to move the Territorial Government to La Paz, passing over Puerto Escondido and San Antonio as alternative choices. Thus, from a small village dependent for its life on the mining town of San Antonio, La Paz was raised to the dignity of the Capitol of Lower California. After this its growth was much more rapid.

In 1847, during the war between Mexico and the United States, La Paz was occupied by a United States Army regiment, The New York Volunteers. Although the initial raising of the American flag was without incident, the American soldiers soon found that they were not to wrest the town so easily from the Mexican patriots and soldiers who regrouped to the south and attacked with fierce determination to dislodge the American forces. Pitched battles were fought in the streets of La Paz at the same time that the occupying American force was besieged in San José del Cabo. A street in La Paz honors José Mijares, a Mexican Naval lieutenant who lost his life attempting to storm the American position at San José. American Lieutenant E. Gould Buffum reported the occupation: "We landed at La Paz on July 21, 1847, and I was surprised to find the prettiest town I had seen in California . . . If an epicure desires to enjoy life at a low cost, I would advise him to go to Lower California. The climate is equal to that of Italy or Persia.

. . . It is eternal summer. The healthiness of the place is remarkable . . . The people of Lower California are a curious race of people; isolated from their mother country and neglected by her, they have an independence of thought and action which I never found in Upper California or elsewhere."

The intention of the occupying force in response to American statement of policy was to secure the peninsula until annexation by the United States. But by the treaty of Guadalupe Hidalgo, which formally ended hostilities between the two countries, the Peninsula of Baja California was officially returned to Mexico. It was again taken by force five years later when a disgruntled and self-styled American revolutionary, William Walker, briefly occupied the city by force of arms before being driven out.

Commander George Dewey explored the coasts of Lower California in the years 1873, 1874 and 1875 and much of the basic information contained on the U.S. Naval Oceanographic H.O. Charts currently in use is based on the surveys of his expeditions. The American Navy held a concession for and operated a coaling station in La Paz Bay at Pichilinque Harbor for a period including the first World War and for sometime after.

In spite of all the political disruption it has been subjected to, La Paz has been for many years a sleepy village of picturesque cobbled streets, unpaved lanes and horse-drawn vehicles; a city of adobe buildings of colonial architecture mixed with whitewashed residences splashed with faded Mediterranean colors. Palms and bougainvilla and arbo de fuego cast their pleasant shade over a village and its people in quiet repose. But recently the city has been emerging from this long period of somnolence. The new Interpeninsular Highway paved through the rich agricultural center of Villa Constitución, thence to the new Pacific Port of San Carlos on Magdalena Bay, has loaded the docks both of San Carlos and La Paz with bales of cotton and sacks of grain, picked up on regular schedule by domestic and foreign vessels calling at these harbors. Winter vegetables in rich and newly irrigated valley farmland are exported to mainland Mexico and to the United States. Cooperative fisheries account for a sizable annual catch of seafood delicacies, quick-frozen and shipped to domestic and foreign markets. And last, but by no means least, is the rapid development of the superb natural bays and beaches as international riviera resorts. The sportfishing in the Gulf of California is considered to be some of the most exciting in the entire world. The easily accessible gulf resorts offer first-class accommodations available at moderate prices. La Paz is the center of all this activity, with a new international airport established to receive the largest of the world's jet passenger airplanes with secondary shuttle transportation to all parts of the peninsula.

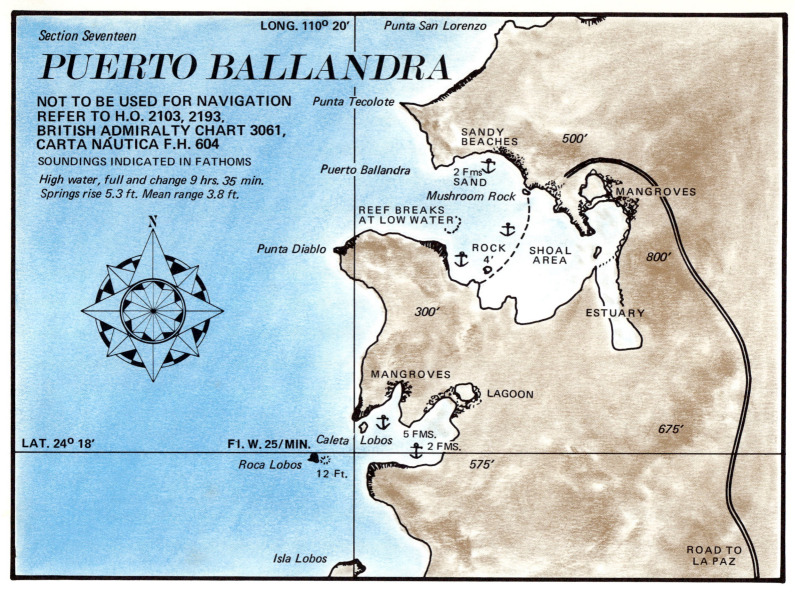

Section Seventeen

PUERTO BALLANDRA

**NOT TO BE USED FOR NAVIGATION
REFER TO H.O. 2103, 2193,
BRITISH ADMIRALTY CHART 3061,
CARTA NÁUTICA F.H. 604**
SOUNDINGS INDICATED IN FATHOMS

*High water, full and change 9 hrs. 35 min.
Springs rise 5.3 ft. Mean range 3.8 ft.*

LONG. 110° 20'
Punta San Lorenzo

Punta Tecolote

SANDY BEACHES   500'

Puerto Ballandra

2 Fms SAND

MANGROVES

Mushroom Rock

REEF BREAKS AT LOW WATER

Punta Diablo

ROCK 4'   SHOAL AREA   800'

300'   ESTUARY

MANGROVES

LAGOON

N

675'

LAT. 24° 18'   Fl. W. 25/MIN.   *Caleta Lobos*   5 FMS.   2 FMS.

Roca Lobos 12 Ft.   575'

Isla Lobos

ROAD TO LA PAZ

There are many who mourn the passing of the old La Paz, to be displaced by a modern emerging resort center characterized by feverish international activity, and for good and ready reason; nevertheless, for all the centuries of past repose, the city and its environs are coming apace with the latter half of the modern twentieth century. The durable character of La Paz, however, forged for over four centuries in a history both tumultuous and somnolent, brings something of a sense of a fine vintage, both to its inhabitants and its visitors, and there are few who come to stay for even a little while who do not leave refreshed and subtly changed in their view of the world.

Bahía de La Paz is the largest bay on the western side of the Gulf of California. It lies between Punta San Lorenzo and Cabeza de Mechudo some 34 miles northwestward, and recedes westward over 18 miles from Espíritu Santo Island which shelters the bay on its eastern side. There is deep water throughout the bay and in it there are no known dangers except those close along the shore and close off the protective group of islands. Bahía de La Paz can be entered through the San Lorenzo Channel when approaching from southeastward; or, when approaching from northward, between Mechudo Head and the northern end of Isla Partida where the channel is both wide and deep. The Port of La Paz is situated in the southeastern corner of the bay, sheltered behind a broad permanent sandspit, El Mogote. The harbor of Pichilinque, where the La Paz-Mazatlán ferry docks, is situated on the eastern shore of the bay about 6 miles northward of the town of La Paz. There are a number of *good anchorages* and coves within the Bay of La Paz where small coastal vessels may find safe and comfortable shelter. For navigation see United States Naval Oceanographic Office Charts H.O. 1664, Magdalena Bay to La Paz. H.O. 2193, San Lorenzo Channel; H.O. 2103, La Paz Harbor and Vicinity; British Admiralty Charts #3053, Bahía La Paz to Bahía Magdalena; #3061, Plans in the Golfo de California, La Paz Harbour and Approaches; Carta Náutica F.H. 604, Parte Sur del Golfo de California.

When approaching through the San Lorenzo Channel after rounding Punta San Lorenzo and Punta Tecoloté, ½ mile southwestward, a pretty little cove called Puerto Ballandra opens on the port hand bracketed between Punta Tecoloté and Punta Diablo, a sharp rocky bluff situated about ¾ mile southwestward. A white sand beach stretches between Punta San Lorenzo and Punta Tecoloté; four other inviting, fine white sandy beaches lie tucked in small indentations within the mouth of Puerto Ballandra. The cove fronts a shallow water inlet that penetrates almost a mile inland and which is encumbered with rocks and shoals that reflect a very light-green hue of water when observed from aloft, as contrasted to the darker shades of the deeper water off the mouth. The entrance to the cove is about 800 yards wide and close off the mouth a depth of 12 fathoms has been sounded, shoaling to 3 fathoms 400 yards inside.

Puerto Ballandra

Anchorage may be safely taken in 3 to 4 fathoms, sand bottom, just within the mouth of the cove taking care to avoid a *submerged reef* which is visible just below the surface at low water and which extends in a northerly direction within the cove close off Punta Diablo. *Directions: When entering the cove, keep to the middle of the mouth and steer for the high point of the white sand beach at the head of the cove.* Small vessels may find *anchorage* in 2 fathoms just off the rocks situated at the head of the cove on the south side of the high point of sand. A shallow water inlet grown with mangrove thickets opens off the north side of the cove and can be negotiated by boat for some distance back of the cove. Clams, rock oysters, and hachas (a large shellfish) are plentiful here. Gusty winds from the southern quadrant sometimes sweep over the anchorage at night but the waters of the cove are well sheltered by the configuration of the surrounding land and the holding ground is good. The shore road from La Paz runs to the north side of the cove.

TIDES — The mean high water interval at full and change at Puerto Ballandra is essentially the same as that of the San Lorenzo Channel: 9 hours, 35 minutes, but the tide is chiefly diurnal, the spring range being 3.8 feet.

Roca Lobos (Lobos Rock), a broken rock 12 feet high, lies ½ mile offshore a mile southwest of Punta Diablo. The rock is steep-to with deep water on its western side, but a shoal at 2 fathoms lies off its eastern side. On this rock, a navigation light, white flashing 25 times per minute, stands on a metal column. Between this shoal and the mainland, there is a *channel* about 800 yards wide and 5 to 10 fathoms deep. A small cove, 2 to 5 fathoms deep, east of Lobos Rock offers *anchorage* for small vessels with local knowledge. A *detached rock* lies close off the north point at the mouth of this cove. The cove's northern side is shoal. A shallow inlet at the head of the cove penetrates the shore .

Isleta Lobos (Lobos Islet or La Gaviota, The Seagull, as it is sometimes referred to locally) is about ¼ mile long and 300 yards wide, whitened by birdlime and thereby easily recognizable. It lies about ¼ mile southeastward of Lobos Rock and ¼ mile northwestward of Punta Base to which it is connected by a shallow bank; along its western side there is deep water close-to.

Punta Base (Base Point), about 2 miles southward of Punta Diablo and situated at the northern mouth of Pichilinque Harbor, rises to an elevation of 170 feet about 600 yards northeastward of its narrow peninsular extremity. Do not attempt to pass between La Gaviota Islet and Punta Base unless in a skiff as there is no clear channel and the water is quite shoal. The northern mouth of Pichilinque Harbor is likewise quite shoal and not open to passage except in a skiff. However, *good anchorage* may be taken well up into the lee on the southern side of Punta Base in 5 to 6 fathoms, with La Gaviota Islet(Isleta Lobos) providing shelter from the northwest and Isla San Juan Nepomezeino from the south. *Landing* may be made on a white sandy beach at the head of the cove.

Isla San Juan Nepomezeino (Nepomezeino Island), a long, low, narrow island of irregular shape lying parallel to the coast and embracing Pichilinque Harbor, is situated a little more than ½ mile southward of La Gaviota Islet (Isleta Los Lobos). San Juan Nepomezeino Island is 1⅜ miles long, north and south and about 600 yards wide, with a maximum elevation above the sea of about 80 feet. The northern end of the island is joined to the mainland eastward by a shallow bank over which the depths vary from 1 to 8 feet, blocking entry into Pichilinque Harbor from the north. The top of Nepomezeino Island is quite flat and an *airstrip* has been bulldozed there for small planes. (See Appendix.) The western side of the island is a steep bluff within 200 yards of which there are depths of 5 fathoms. A gravel beach extends around the southern end of the island and the 5-fathom curve at the edge of the shore bank extends out to about ¼ mile southwestward of this extremity. Near the southeastern point there is a rocky bluff with a hill 65 feet high behind, sloping down to a shallow salt pan about 500 yards long and 300 yards wide, which yields quantities of commercial salt. On the eastern side of the island within Pichilinque Harbor, the shore is comprised mostly of shelving sand and gravel beach; there are two old piers in a bight near its southern end and two buildings ashore near the foot of the piers, in need of repair, that once comprised a coaling station utilized by the United States Navy before and after World War I.

be taken most anywhere in the harbor, keeping clear of the fairway and turning basin marked by buoys used daily by the La Paz-Mazatlán-Topolobampo Ferries. *Best anchorage* for small yachts and coastal fishing vessels is either off the old coaling station wharves in the bight on the port hand immediately after entering, in 3 to 4 fathoms, or in the bight about 800 yards farther northward along the island's shore, in about 3 to 4 fathoms. There is a sand beach at this latter position where landing may be readily made.

WIND AND TIDE — The mean high water interval at full and change at Pichilinque Harbor is 9 hours 35 minutes. The tide is chiefly diurnal, the spring range being 3.8 feet. Pichilinque Harbor, while small, offers excellent protection and is considered one of the best harbors on the coast for small and deep-draft vessels alike. Shelter is afforded from winds blowing from all quarters, as well as providing good protection from the fierce southeasterly *chubascos* which sometimes blow with gale force in the later summer. The wind blows fair toward La Paz Harbor during the greater part of the day and toward Pichilinque Harbor in the late afternoon and night, making communication with La Paz by small sailing boat convenient with a fair wind both ways. La Paz bound yachts arriving too late in the day to negotiate the La Paz entrance channel during daylight hours (which is preferable without local knowledge) find Pichilinque Harbor a pleasant stopover; frequently vessels from La Paz Harbor run over and anchor here in the evening to avoid the *coromuel* winds that often blow uncomfortably throughout the night in La Paz Bay.

Pichilinque Harbor is included within the port district of La Paz and both Customs and Quarantine regulations apply. Foreign vessels calling at Pichilinque Harbor as the first port of call in Mexico must obtain clearance from the port authorities for both the vessel and its crew before anyone is landed. Prior contact by radio advising estimated time of arrival is appropriate and may expedite clearance; failing that, a hail to the dockmaster at Pichilinque, requesting official inspection and clearance will bring proper port authorities from La Paz in due time; however, the cost of clearance at Pichilinque may be greater than at La Paz owing to possible overtime and travel charges. Deepwater vessels unable to carry their draft through the La Paz access channel regularly anchor and clear at Pichilinque Harbor.

Blue shark

Bahía Pichilinque (Pichilinque Harbor) is entered between the southern end of San Juan Nepomezeino Island and Punta Falsa on the mainland about 600 yards eastward. The passage leading into the harbor is clear with 3 fathoms being sounded within 50 yards of the shore on either side, deepening to 4¾ and 5½ fathoms midway between the entrance points. When approaching the passage and entering the harbor, care must be taken to avoid the tail of the *shore bank* previously noted, which extends southwestward from the southwestern end of the island. *Anchorage* may

The La Paz-Mazatlán-Topolobampo Ferry Landing on the northeastern perimeter of Pichilinque Harbor is comprised of a concrete wharf backed by a modern steel, glass and concrete terminal building. A well-paved road runs along the shore and connects the terminal with La Paz, about 6 miles distant, southeastward. The terminal is well lighted at night and buoys mark the fairway and turning basin. There are three ferry boats which serve La Paz and the mainland. The motor vessel *La Paz,* a sleek 360 foot, 4,200 ton craft built in Japan especially for this service,

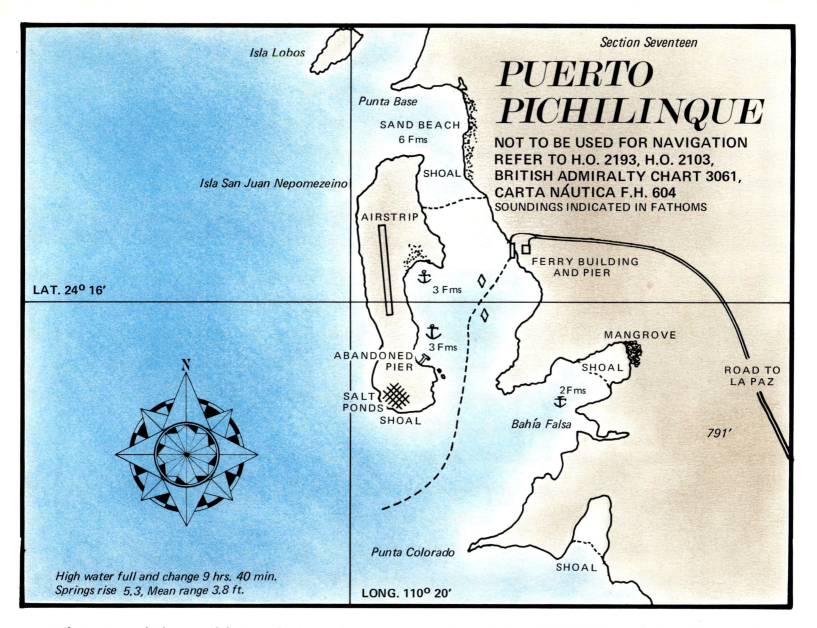

Section Seventeen

PUERTO PICHILINQUE

NOT TO BE USED FOR NAVIGATION
REFER TO H.O. 2193, H.O. 2103,
BRITISH ADMIRALTY CHART 3061,
CARTA NÁUTICA F.H. 604
SOUNDINGS INDICATED IN FATHOMS

Isla Lobos

Punta Base

SAND BEACH
6 Fms

SHOAL

Isla San Juan Nepomezeino

AIRSTRIP

FERRY BUILDING
AND PIER

LAT. 24° 16'

3 Fms

MANGROVE

SHOAL

ROAD TO
LA PAZ

3 Fms

ABANDONED
PIER

2 Fms

SALT
PONDS

SHOAL

Bahía Falsa

791'

N

Punta Colorado

SHOAL

High water full and change 9 hrs. 40 min.
Springs rise 5.3, Mean range 3.8 ft.

LONG. 110° 20'

makes two round trips a week between La Paz and Mazatlán. The *La Paz* can carry 370 passengers in 3 classes and has a capacity for 114 cars and 60 trucks. A second ferry the *President Díaz Ordaz* has recently been added to this service providing a daily sailing schedule. A third ferry, the *Salvatierra* serves La Paz and Topolobampo carrying both passengers and vehicles.

As previously mentioned, the vicinity of Pichilinque Harbor is believed to be the site of the first Spanish colonization attempt in La Paz Bay by the Hernando Cortez expedition of 1535. Originally called Refugio de la Santa Cruz and believed to be part of the great island of "California" the colony was shortly abandoned for lack of supplies from the mainland and a subsequent shortage of vital provisions. Several other attempts at colonization failed in the first 200 years after the bay's initial discovery but during this time it provided a haven for pearlers and pirates, the latter preying upon the Manila Galleons. It was from the extensive use of the harbor by various groups of pirates that Pichilinque got its name, one certainly not of Indian or Spanish origin. It is thought to have been derived from the Spanish mispronunciation of Vlissingen or Flushing, home port of a group of Dutch pirates who used the harbor for refuge and for careening their ships, or possibly from the two words "pecho lengua" meaning "throaty voice" which characterized the Dutch buccaneers. All pirates raiding the

coast came to be called "Pichilinques". A certain group of French buccaneers used the harbor for refuge sporadically over a period between 1687 and 1691, accumulating a great deal of treasure from their coastal sorties. Altogether the French spent about 7 months at Bahía Pichilinque and a legend of buried treasure in the vicinity of the bay persists to this day. Sebastián Vizcaíno called at the bay in 1569 and named it Puerto del Marqués in honor of Cortez, after discovering traces of a prior colony which he believed to be that of the Cortez expedition of 1535. In 1768 the bay was established as an official port and formally named Puerto de Cortez, but the more romantic name of Pichilinque has prevailed. The same Spanish penchant for mispronunciation of foreign names has contributed to the origin of coromuel, the regular clock-like evening breeze from the southwest that sweeps the bay in the afternoon and evenings. A mythical English pirate, Cromwell, is said to have used the winds of the bay well, running and reaching out into the gulf on the evening breeze to surprise and board the

Spanish merchantmen becalmed offshore. Cromwell was so omnipotent in tall tales retold that he became an evil myth, but the wind by which he sailed, the coromuel, is blessed by the inhabitants of La Paz for transforming the otherwise hot and oppressive afternoons into most agreeable and refreshing weather. The legends of pirates and buccaneers at Pichilinque are legion and their buried hordes have been perennially searched for along the shore over the intervening centuries. When the new road bed for the Ferry Terminal was excavated, a large chest of silver and other valuable coins was found by the Mexican workmen and turned over to the Mexican Government. Perhaps there is still an unrecovered cache to be found, a pleasant afternoon's occupation with a modern metal detector.

Immediately adjacent to Pichilinque Harbor off its southern entrance is Bahía Falsa (False Bay), lying in a northeast-southwest orientation and penetrating the shore about ¾ of a mile. False Bay has depths of 5 to 6 fathoms in its outer portion, shoaling to 2 fathoms at its head where a growth of mangrove thicket covers the shore. A white sand beach on the southeastern shore of False Bay affords *good landing* for small boats. Punta Colorado (Colorado Point), the first point southward of Pichilinque Harbor and False Bay, about ¾ mile distant from San Juan Nepomezeino Island, is a bold rocky bluff of reddish color about 50 feet

high with *shoal water* extending about 200 yards off its seaward end. There is a narrow bight on the south side of the point, about ⅓ mile from its outer end, but it is shoal from the mouth to its head.

Punta Prieta (Prieta Point), about 1¾ miles southeastward of Punta Colorado and immediately northward of the entrance to the La Paz access channel, is a sharp vertical gray bluff 32 feet high, with the land rising gradually behind it. A number of oil tanks are located just back of the point and provide an unmistakable landmark. There are outlying rocks close off the point and from it a *rocky shoal* projects about ¼ mile southwestward. Mount Santa María, 1,553 feet high, the highest hill in the vicinity, is situated 3 miles east-northeastward of Punta Prieta. A *navigation light*, 56 feet above the sea, is shown from a white framework tower mounted on the roof of a white wooden house at Punta Prieta and exhibits a **white group flash of three flashes every 10 seconds:** flash 0.5 second, eclipse 1.5 seconds; flash 0.5 second, eclipse 1.5 seconds; flash 0.5 second; eclipse 5.5 seconds. The *light* is visible in the sector 290° through 148° and can be seen for a distance of 13 miles in clear weather. Vessels waiting to enter the channel or intending to remain outside the Port of La Paz may *anchor* anywhere southward of Prieta Point in depths of 7 to 10 fathoms, but the open roadstead northward of El

Punta Base, Isla Lobos in the foreground, Pichilinque Harbor and ferry terminal in middleground

Mogote is exposed and Pichilinque Harbor is preferred for *anchorage* as it offers better shelter.

An oil terminal, the distribution plant for the government-owned Pemex Oil Agency, is established on the southeastern side of Punta Prieta, the entrance to the La Paz access channel. A dozen oil storage tanks of varying sizes, metal sheds and warehouses and a concrete administration building comprise the oiling station complex. A large T-head fueling wharf extends 315 feet into the channel and has a warping face about 65 feet long. Depths of 30 to 33 feet may be carried alongside the head of the wharf. A large white can buoy, used for warping large vessels alongside the face of the pier, is located off the pierhead. Fueling is by gravity only; diesel, fuel oil, gasoline and fresh water are available with permits obtained from the Port Captain at the Port of La Paz. Vessels desiring to take appreciable quantities of fuel or water will find this terminal to be the most efficient loading facility in the La Paz area; small yachts and power-boats with minimal requirements for fuel and water may obtain these supplies from 55 gallon drums off Abaroas' shipyard dock within the port.

Puerto de La Paz (Port of La Paz), which is approached through the Canal de La Paz (La Paz Channel) is situated about 3½ miles southward of Punta Prieta and lies on the eastern side of the fairway at the entrance to a large shallow lagoon, Ensenada de Aripes. The northern side of this lagoon is formed by a low sandy peninsula, El Mogote, which protects the lagoon and La Paz Harbor from the open bay. The harbor, which lies between the eastern end of El Mogote and the mainland opposite, is from ½ to ¼ mile wide and well protected, but it is encumbered with shoals which restrict the anchorage space to a small area.

A narrow channel, with depths of 3 to 4 fathoms, fronts the shore and can be negotiated by small vessels for over 6 miles into the lagoon, where depths of 2 to 3 fathoms may be carried in the deeper parts. The configuration of the entrance channel into La Paz Harbor is such, with maneuvering space so limited, that no vessel over 328 feet may enter the harbor. The least depth in the fairway is about 16 feet and that in the access channel the same; but this depth cannot be depended upon, as seasonal currents alter the configuration of the shoals. Vessels of 31-foot draft or less may negotiate the channel at any stage of the tide; vessels of greater draft should enter at full and flood. A *sand shoal*, with depths of only 1 to 8 feet over it, extends northward from the eastern end of El Mogote spit to within 400 yards of Punta Prieta, protecting La Paz Harbor from the seas built up in the open bay by northwesterly winds.

CHANNEL PILOTS — Pilotage for commercial vessels entering the harbor is compulsory except for Mexican vessels under 500 tons and yachts under cruising permits. Pilots board incoming vessels in the vicinity of Punta Prieta with proper advance notice by radio or signal flag and will

Punta Prieta

take vessels in at night at an overtime charge. *It is not advisable, however, to attempt to enter the harbor access channel after dark without a pilot unless thoroughly familiar with the channel and the marker buoys.* While careful pilotage through the channel is necessary to avoid projecting sand shoals, safe passage may be readily accomplished by small yachts by choosing a time of slack water and conning the channel from aloft.

Canal de La Paz (La Paz Channel), which is entered about 600 yards southeastward of Punta Prieta, runs close inshore for about 3½ miles between the mainland and the eastern edge of the *sand shoal* which extends outward from El Mogote. The channel is narrow with steep banks on either side, the depth in some places shoaling from 16 feet to 3 or 4 feet within a distance of 20 yards. The deep water of the channel and the projecting shoals on either side can be readily distinguished from aloft and a new series of lighted channel buoys (which augment the established range markers) now permit small vessels safe passage with relative ease through the channel. Masters of small vessels familiar with the channel, its range markers and lighted buoys enter and leave the harbor after dark but to caution again, *nighttime passage without thorough familiarity is not recommended.*

The La Paz access channel is marked by light buoys moored along its length from the entrance, about ½ mile southeastward of Punta Prieta, to a position about 1 mile below the main wharf. On entering, odd numbered buoys are painted black and moored to port; even numbered buoys are painted red and moored to starboard. *Navigation note: The channel buoys are somewhat rusty and their respective colors are difficult to ascertain in some cases. Not all the channel buoys are lighted and the fixed range markers only approximate the center line of the channel and must be employed with caution.*

The channel is marked by three pairs of *lighted range beacons* consisting of square concrete towers which in line bear, respectively, 147° and 181° ahead and 27° astern, consecutively; the seaward sides of the beacon structures visible when in line are painted white, the other sides being red. Lights are exhibited at the head of the Municipal Wharf located on the south shore of the inner harbor. The *front beacon* of the outer pair of channel range markers in range 147°, located about 1 mile southeastward of Punta Prieta, exhibits a *light* with a characteristic of a **quick white flash** at an elevation 49 feet above the sea; the *rear beacon,* approximately 180 yards from the front marker, exhibits a **white flash every 5 seconds** at an elevation of 62 feet.

The *front beacon* of the next consecutive pair of range markers in range 181°, located on the shore about 1 mile northeastward of the Municipal Pier at La Paz, exhibits a *light* with a characteristic of a **quick white flash** at an elevation 59 feet above th sea; the *rear beacon of this range,* approximately 1,000 yards from the front marker, exhibits a **flashing white group of two flashes every 5 seconds** at an elevation 105 feet above the sea.

The *front beacon* of the third consecutive pair of range markers in *range 27° astern,* located on the hillside about

½ mile south-southeastward of Caymancito Rock, exhibits a *light* with a characteristic of a **quick white flash** at an elevation 62 feet above the sea; the *rear beacon,* approximately 200 yards from the front marker of this range, exhibits a **flashing white group of three flashes every 6 seconds:** flash 0.5 second, eclipse 1 second; flash 0.5 second, eclipse 1 second; flash 0.5 second, eclipse 2.5 seconds at an elevation of 125 feet above the sea.

A **flashing red light** is shown 28 feet above the sea from a wooden post established on the south angle of the Municipal Mole; a **flashing green light** is shown 26 feet above the sea from a wooden post on the north angle of the mole.

Navigation caution: The positions of the channel range markers as printed on the eleventh edition of H.O. 2103 are only approximately indicated as noted on the chart. The channel buoys may be fairly well relied upon but caution and a lookout aloft is advised as the configuration of the shoals changes somewhat from year to year. The deeper portion of the channel is generally toward the east shore; there are encroaching sand shoals projecting from El Mogote sand spit.

El Caymancito, a large white palatial residence built during the presidency of Miguel Alemán for presidential use during official visits is situated along the eastern shore of the channel; a popular bathing beach of white coral sand and an adjoining pavilion called El Coromuel lie close southward.

Roca Caymancito (Caymancito Rock), above water, lies close inshore on the eastern side of the channel about 1¼ mile south-southeastward of Punta Prieta. Small craft with local knowledge can cross the shoal on the western side of the channel, about ¾ mile southward of Punta Prieta, with Caymancito Rock bearing 129° through a *boat passage* with a least depth of about 9 feet at low water. Another small boat channel, with a least depth of 7 feet at low water, crosses the bank close off the eastern extremity of El Mogote. Local knowledge is necessary to use these passages but they are very convenient as a shortcut to and from the harbor for the shore boats of vessels anchored northward of El Mogote. *However, this boat passage is only approximately charted with patches of uncharted and unmarked shoal water.*

ANCHORAGE — The best anchorage off the town lies about 1,000 yards southwestward of the Municipal Pier in depths of from 3 to 4 fathoms, sand and mud. The holding ground is good and there is very little surge and no swell; however, there being no shelter in the area, vessels are exposed to strong north to northeast winds during the winter months and to strong tidal currents at flood and ebb in the narrow confines of the channel. During inclement weather the *anchorage* is considered uneasy, as vessels are constantly overriding their anchor cables and swinging into one another; mooring fore and aft is helpful but ground tackle should be carefully tended and strain eased when necessary. Vessels drawing less than 13 feet can lie alongside the head of the Municipal Pier long enough to take or discharge supplies with permission of the Port Captain; *anchorage is forbidden off the northern end of the pier.*

The pier, 375 feet long with a 120-foot T-head, extends from the beach in front of the town. A number of vessels may be found warped alongside working cargo a great percentage of the time. Special Quarantine anchorage for vessels entering from foreign ports and calling at La Paz as first port of entry is located abreast the old city limits eastward of the Municipal Wharf; however the Health Officer, when previously notified, usually boards at Punta Prieta and, unless a health problem exists, has cleared the vessel for general anchorage by the time of arrival in the port.

Small yachts usually find *anchorage or mooring* off José and Andrés Abaroas' shipyards in a bight about 1 mile westward of the Municipal Wharf. A number of small vessels lie on *permanent moorings* off the shipyards and on occasion an empty mooring may be had. Small-boat cruising to La Paz has significantly increased in the last few years and the anchorage is generally full of yachts. Lacking an available mooring, *anchorage* may be taken in 2 to 3

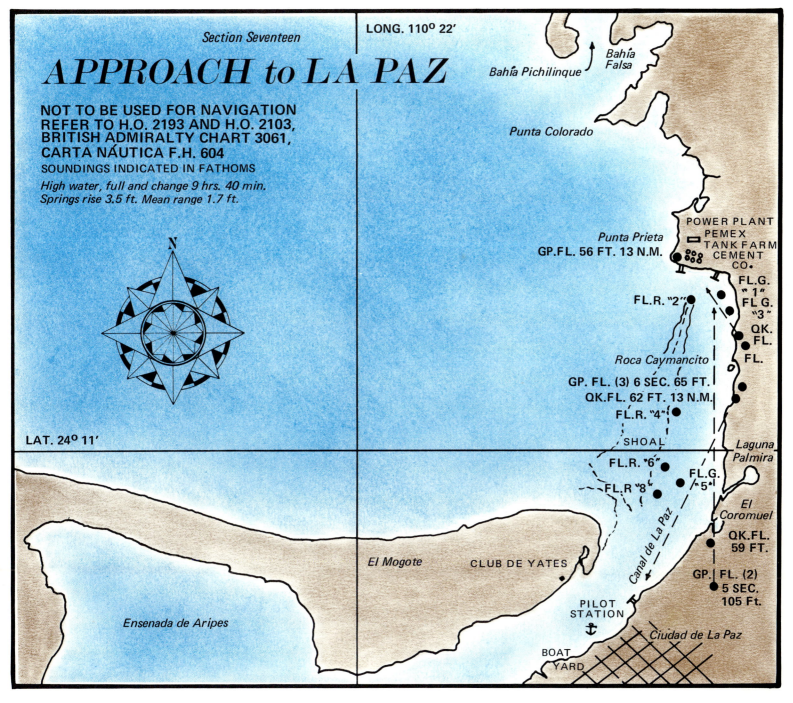

Section Seventeen

APPROACH to LA PAZ

LONG. 110° 22'

NOT TO BE USED FOR NAVIGATION
REFER TO H.O. 2193 AND H.O. 2103,
BRITISH ADMIRALTY CHART 3061,
CARTA NÁUTICA F.H. 604
SOUNDINGS INDICATED IN FATHOMS
*High water, full and change 9 hrs. 40 min.
Springs rise 3.5 ft. Mean range 1.7 ft.*

N

LAT. 24° 11'

Bahía Pichilinque
Bahía Falsa

Punta Colorado

POWER PLANT
PEMEX
TANK FARM
CEMENT CO.

Punta Prieta
GP.FL. 56 FT. 13 N.M.

FL.G. "1"
FL.G. "3"

FL.R. "2"

QK. FL.

FL.

Roca Caymancito
GP. FL. (3) 6 SEC. 65 FT.
QK.FL. 62 FT. 13 N.M.
FL.R. "4"

SHOAL

Laguna Palmira

FL.R. "6"
FL.G. "5"
FL.R "8"

El Coromuel

QK.FL. 59 FT.

El Mogote

CLUB DE YATES

Canal de La Paz

GP. FL. (2) 5 SEC. 105 Ft.

Ensenada de Aripes

PILOT STATION

Ciudad de La Paz

BOAT YARD

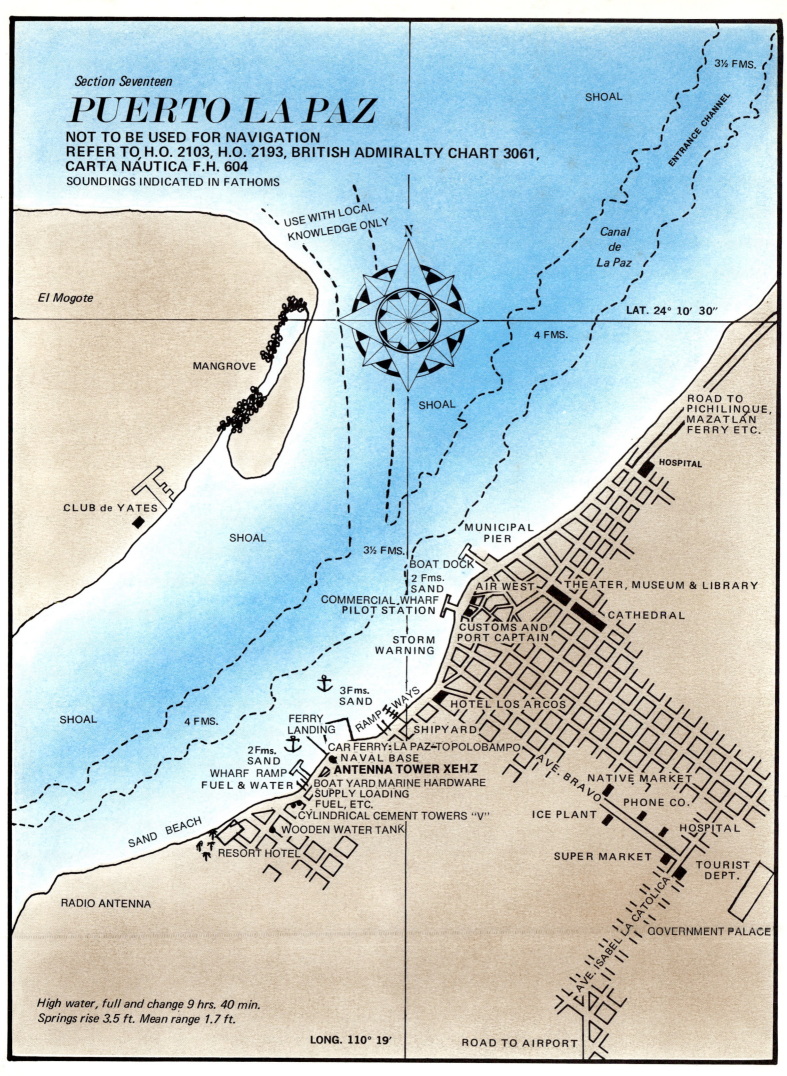

Section Seventeen

PUERTO LA PAZ

NOT TO BE USED FOR NAVIGATION
REFER TO H.O. 2103, H.O. 2193, BRITISH ADMIRALTY CHART 3061,
CARTA NÁUTICA F.H. 604
SOUNDINGS INDICATED IN FATHOMS

3½ FMS.

SHOAL

ENTRANCE CHANNEL

USE WITH LOCAL
KNOWLEDGE ONLY

N

Canal
de
La Paz

El Mogote

LAT. 24° 10' 30"

MANGROVE

4 FMS.

SHOAL

ROAD TO
PICHILINQUE,
MAZATLÁN
FERRY ETC.

SHOAL

HOSPITAL

CLUB de YATES

MUNICIPAL
PIER

SHOAL

BOAT DOCK

3½ FMS.

2 Fms.
SAND

COMMERCIAL WHARF
PILOT STATION

AIR WEST

THEATER, MUSEUM & LIBRARY

CUSTOMS AND
PORT CAPTAIN

CATHEDRAL

STORM
WARNING

3Fms.
SAND

SHOAL

4 FMS.

HOTEL LOS ARCOS

FERRY
LANDING

RAMPWAYS

SHIPYARD

2 Fms.
SAND

CAR FERRY: LA PAZ-TOPOLOBAMPO

AVE. BRAVO

NATIVE MARKET

WHARF RAMP
FUEL & WATER

NAVAL BASE

ANTENNA TOWER XEHZ

PHONE CO.

BOAT YARD MARINE HARDWARE
SUPPLY LOADING
FUEL, ETC.

ICE PLANT

HOSPITAL

CYLINDRICAL CEMENT TOWERS "V"

WOODEN WATER TANK

SUPER MARKET

TOURIST
DEPT.

SAND BEACH

RESORT HOTEL

RADIO ANTENNA

GOVERNMENT PALACE

AVE. ISABEL LA CATOLICA

High water, full and change 9 hrs. 40 min.
Springs rise 3.5 ft. Mean range 1.7 ft.

LONG. 110° 19'

ROAD TO AIRPORT

226

Entrance to La Paz Harbor showing the channel

fathoms over a sand and mud bottom. A short *masonry mole,* angled at its outer end, extends from the beach for a short distance on the eastern side of the shipyards; a *landing* may be made here and fuel, water and provisions loaded. Vessels also lie at anchor well down the channel to the west. Along the shore a number of piers are built out into the channel for private use. The southern side of El Mogote Peninsula across from the town is shoal and grown with mangrove thickets along a sand and mud shore which is flooded at high tide. In these thickets beneath the mud an edible variety of clams can be found in good quantity.

La Paz Yacht Club is situated midway along this shore of El Mogote and is reached by boat or by the ferry that docks adjacent to the two shipyards.

TIDES AND TIDAL STREAMS — Tidal streams in the harbor are considerable and must be taken into account when selecting an anchorage and rigging ground tackle or a permanent mooring. The tidal currents flooding and ebbing Ensenada de Aripes, and constricted by the relatively narrow confines of the access channel which comprises the harbor of La Paz, have a normal rate of about 2 knots,

La Paz Harbor

but driven by wind and accelerated by the higher tides, can reach a maximum rate of about 6 knots past La Paz Municipal Wharf. Ground tackle or mooring lines should be rigged accordingly. The mean high water interval at La Paz is 9 hours 40 minutes; the tide is chiefly diurnal, the spring range is 3.5 feet.

WIND AND WEATHER — The climate of La Paz is warm and dry and healthful during the winter and spring months; from November through May the temperatures range from 50° to 75°. Gentle prevailing winds blow out of the north or northeast but can blow quite violently out of this quarter during winter storms. The summer months are hot and dry; from June through October the temperature range from 75° to 100° or a little more, relieved by a prevailing northwesterly breeze that blows frequently in the moorings until noon. Beginning in the afternoons and persisting until early evening the clock-like *coromuel* breeze blowing off the land from the southwest refreshes the town. In the absence of this breeze, from midday, the city can become hot, breathless and oppressive. The rainy season is from August through October, but 5 inches annual rainfall is considered a big year. The local hurricane winds — *chubascos* or *cordonazos* — may occur any time between June and November but more likely in September or October and can be very devastating; however, it is not unusual for such storms to skip a year or two. Storm signals are flown from the mast above the pilot station alongside the Municipal Wharf.

PORT CAPTAIN — The Port Captain's office is located at the foot of the Municipal Wharf — Capitanía de Puerto, Muelle 13, telephone 2-02-43. Clearance papers from the first point of entry into Mexico or the last foreign port must be presented to the port authorities within 24 hours after arrival and picked up 24 hours before departure. Presented directly to the Captain of the Port, there is no charge for yachts under cruising permits. An agent may be desired for handling the documents and for general translation of the yachtmaster is not conversant with the Spanish language, in which case the Captain of the Port will recommend a proper agent. The charge for this service is about $10.00 U.S. currency. Pilotage is only charged if a pilot's service has been utilized.

FACILITIES — Fronting the southeastern shore of La Paz Harbor there are a number of active marine facilities available to supply and service yachts and small craft; in the town there are competitive and well-equipped machine shops, welding shops, a foundry, electronic sales and service agencies, marine engine parts houses, ship chandlers, refrigeration specialists, laundries and laundromats, as well as a large central market and several small supermarkets where provisions may be obtained.

José and Andrés Abaroas' shipyards, surrounded by a grove of palms, are situated at the foot of the short masonry mole in a small bight about a mile westward of the Municipal Wharf. The location can be easily recognized by the flotilla of yachts and sportfishing cruisers anchored in the roadstead immediately offshore. The mole extends only a short distance offshore having a depth of water at its outer end of about 5 feet. Yachts anchor just off the mole, putting a line ashore and warping the stern as close to the mole as the draft and the tide will allow. Supplies, provisions, water and fuel may be taken to the end of the mole and carried aboard over the stern. The shipyard enterprise has been in existence for two generations; their workmanship is quite good, sometimes lacking only proper materials. Experienced labor is reasonable. Most marine equipment, hardware, paint and supplies required may be obtained either in the shipyards or at one of several supply houses in the town. A portable 10-ton crane is available for rent in the harbor, as well as a small tug. Fairly large vessels up to 80 feet can be hauled out on the marine railway in José Abaroas' yard; smaller vessels up to 35 feet are hauled out in Andrés Abaroas' adjacent yard. However, a docking plan of your vessel's hull should be supplied to expedite cradle adjustment and prevent damage due to blind handling.

Benseman's Machine Shop in the town has a rather large inventory of modern machine tools amidst a generous collection of old iron and discarded equipment. Their work is excellent and they will tackle almost anything in need of repair on a small yacht. Prices are reasonable. There are several other machine shops and boat repair shops with competitive prices in La Paz. A boat builder, Mac Shroyer, operating a marine services company, Yates y Servicios Marinos provides a range of services from repair and parts to yacht charters, provisions and professional skippers familiar with the fishing grounds and skin diving coves.

Butane is available as is diesel, fuel oil and several grades of gasoline. Bulk fuel may be purchased at Pemex (Petróleos Mexicanos) Cinco de Mayo #612, telephone 2-03-21, and taken aboard at the fuel wharf at Punta Prieta, telephone 2-01-49. Butane may be purchased from Distribuidora de Gas, Calle Cinco de Mayo #240, telephone 2-02-05, 2-15-15; Cali Gas, Calle Nicholas Bravo and G. Farias, telephone 2-07-94; Garcia Gas, Cinco de Mayo #1017, telephone 2-05-49. Several large department stores offering a wide variety of hard and soft wares as well as general supplies and provisions are established in the city, the largest among them being Ruffo Brothers, in business for over a century. The Central Commercial Market located at Isabel La Católica 385 Sur, and Supermercado at Zaragoza and Puerto offer domestic and imported supplies and provisions at competitive prices.

La Paz has a new and modern drinking water pumping and treatment plant and city water is potable and safe. There are periods when the water table is low and water scarce, and at such times careful attention to the quality of the water taken into ship's tanks should be observed, tested if possible, and treated if necessary. Fresh water may be obtained at the Municipal Wharf in quantity through a steel pipeline valved at the pierhead; however a 2-inch close nipple and suitable reducers together with an adequate length of filling hose must be provided from ship's stores.

PUBLIC ACCOMMODATIONS — There are six major hotels in La Paz, all on the main street fronting the bay and continuing southwest. La Perla Hotel, with an open-air public dining room at street level, is across from the foot of the main wharf; Los Arcos, with a swimming pool, is located on the same main street a few blocks southwest. Los Cocos, La Posada, Guaycura, and Calafia are grouped together about 2 miles further along the waterfront. These are mostly resort hotels with swimming pools, first-class accommodations and American plan. *Anchorage* may be taken close offshore near this hotel group and *landing* facilities are available. A pier with *landing* dock for dinghies is established in front of the Hotel Los Cocos. There are a number of guest houses and some motels all with clean and comfortable accommodations.

TRANSPORTATION — There are numerous taxis available for hire in the town. Fares are reasonable and transportation from the main part of town to the outlying hotels, the International Airport, the Ferry Terminal at Pichilinque, etc. may be had at any time; longer trips into the country or along the coast may be arranged with short notice. The new International Airport accommodates the largest jet passenger planes in public service. Air West flies from Tucson and Phoenix; Aeronaves de México flies from Los Angeles and Tijuana International Airports to La Paz daily; shuttle flights serve all the resort hotels and sport-fishing resorts along the coast with regular and chartered service from La Paz. The Mazatlán-La Paz Topolobampo Ferry service runs daily between the mainland and the peninsula with special service run at the peak season. The ferries take both passengers and vehicles. The gulf crossing requires 17 hours, leaves La Paz Sundays and Thursdays at 5 p.m. and leaves Mazatlán Saturdays and Tuesdays at 4 p.m. From May to October, ferries leave both ports daily at 5:00 p.m. Arrival 2 hours before sailing time is advised for ticketing and line up. Passenger fares are $5.20 (dollars) to $24.00; auto fares are $3.00 to $44.00.

There is also ferry service between Topolobampo on the Mexican mainland and La Paz carrying both vehicles and

View of the main channel at La Paz

passengers on a regular schedule. The motor vessel *Salvatierra* sails from Topolobampo each Monday, Wednesday and Friday at 9:00 a.m. The return trip leaves La Paz on Tuesday, Thursday and Sunday at 8:00 p.m. and arrives in Topolobampo at 6:30 a.m. the following day. The ferry has space for 370 passengers and 60 autos; fares range from $4.40 to $6.00 for passengers and from $35.00 to $70.00 for cars and trailers. Reservations and further information may be obtained in La Paz by calling at the ferry office, Independencia #107-A, telephone 2-01-09.

Aerolineas del Pacifico provides passenger service between La Paz and Mexicali on Sundays and Fridays.

Baja Flying Service has regular and chartered flights to the peninsula. Call Captain Francisco Muñoz at Tijuana Airport, telephone (903) 385-9110, or (714) 424-8956; address P.O. Box 478, Imperial Beach, California 92032.

Autotransportes Águila offers regularly scheduled bus service from La Paz to San Bartolo, Los Barriles, Buena Vista, San José del Cabo and Cabo San Lucas, and from La Paz to the Santo Domingo Valley.

Autotransportes Estrella de California offers freight-only service from La Paz to San Bartolo, Los Barriles, Buena Vista, San José del Cabo, and from La Paz to Todos Santos and Pescadero.

COMMUNICATIONS — La Paz has landline telephone service to the towns and villages on the peninsula with connections to the national telephone system on the mainland. International telephone service is handled out of La Paz with little or minimum delay, depending on the volume and backlog of message traffic and the availability of clear international trunk lines. Public telephones are located at the major hotels, or calls may be placed at the telephone office, Telephonos de México, Calle Nicolás Bravo #716, telephone 2-00-01.

Public messages are accepted for transmission by the government telegraph agency; those messages with international destinations are routed through Mexico City. The government telegraph administration office is located at Constitución and Revolución Calles, telephone 2-03-22; the government telegraph office is located at Calle Artesanos #8, telephone 2-05-02. Government radio communication to all stations within the Southern Territory of Baja California is under the administration Departmento de Radio offices located in the Government Palace, telephone 2-07-91.

There is daily international airmail service at La Paz. Unicom is operated from the La Paz Airport, and Servicios Aeros communicate on 2620 kHz from the airport.

Broadcast Radio Stations XEHZ, operating on 990 kiloHertz with 1,000 watts power, and XENT, operating on 790 kiloHertz with 1,000 watts power, maintain regular scheduled programming. XHK-TV Channel 10 La Paz Television Station operates regularly scheduled programming. (See Appendix.)

MEDICAL FACILITIES — La Paz has a well-established general hospital, Salvatierra, which will accept seamen, telephone 2-01-38. The Government Health Department is located at Avenue Cinco de Mayo and Altamirano, telephone 2-06-76.

The Social Security Clinic and Hospital is located at Calles Nicolás Bravo and México, telephone 2-12-14; the clinic, telephone 2-07-96.

There are 10 or more practicing medical doctors in La Paz, including general practitioners, a gynocologist and other specialists; there are 5 or more practicing dentists. The Military Infirmary is located on Avenue Madero, telephone 2-04-65.

MARINE EMERGENCIES — Call Mexican Naval Headquarters via 2182 kiloHertz, emergency calling frequency or landline telephone, Sector Naval Militar, 2-02-77 located at Avenue Madero #408.

SOURCES OF ADDITIONAL INFORMATION — Yates y Servicios Marinos, S.A. (Yacht Charters and Marine Services) Apartado Postal #290, La Paz, Baja, California, Mexico; Mazatlán/La Paz/Topolobampo Ferry Service, Caminos y Puentes Federales de Ingresos y Servicios Conexos, Independencía #107-A, La Paz, Baja California, Mexico, telephone 2-01-09 La Paz; José or André Abaroas' Shipyard, La Paz, B. Cfa. Sur, Mexico.

THE PEARLS OF LA PAZ

Pearling has been an attraction in the Gulf of California from the time of the first Cortez expedition to the peninsula in 1533, and La Paz has been its center of activity for over 400 years. It was the pearling concession and exclusive fishery license that was fervently sought from the King of Spain through the Viceroy of Mexico that inspired much of the coastal exploration which was accomplished during the first 200 years of Spanish rule of the Californias. Such was the distraction of the prospect of gaining a fortune in pearls to most of the early explorers sent out by the Spanish Government that orders were specifically written in many cases prohibiting a sojourn for pearl trading until the assigned exploration and mapping tasks were carried out — to act otherwise on pain of death. Considered a mineral deposit, pearls were by regal law property of the Crown and subject to royal control with formal concessions made to individuals or companies for their exploitation.

The Indians valued the shiny nodules incidentally pried from the oysters that they primarily sought for food, and were in possession of a fine collection of large and colorful jewels when the Spanish discovered the beds. Jiménez, Cortez, Ulloa and Alacrón had all brought back marvelous collections of fine pearls that they had traded from the Indians for odds and ends that caught the Indians' fancies. A wealth of pearls was believed to lie hidden in the extensive oyster beds that had been reported to exist in the waters of the gulf, and the subsequent search and exploration for this treasure alone almost wholly occupied the preparations and voyages of most of the explorers well-known to history, as well as the Spanish merchants who financed them. Between 1616 and 1635 Juan de Iturbi, Francisco Ortega and their pilot Esteban Carbonel, while conducting explorations in the Gulf of California, brought back some pearls of rare beauty and size, and of immense value. The Sea of Cortez thereafter became known throughout the world for its extravagant wealth of pearls.

The pearl oyster is known locally in La Paz as "la concha de la perla fina" and the best ones are found in the beds that fringe the lower part of the peninsula from Mulegé around to Magdalena Bay. Other beds, though of less value, are located on the mainland over a stretch of a hundred miles opposite La Paz, and in the Tres Marías Islands. The richest pearl beds are found in the Bay of La Paz; in the vicinity of Loreto; around the southwest point of Carmen Island; in and around Puerto Escondido, Islas Los Coronado Sur, Islas Los Danzantes and the islands of San José and San Marcos. The shells from which these pearls are secured are four to five inches in length, the ones from the mainland being thick and small and gnarled and the meat very good to eat. Those of the peninsula are smooth and flat and thin, as large as a saucer and of delicate construction. In some instances they are found eight or nine inches long, but there is no connection between the size of the oyster and the likelihood of finding a pearl within its shell. The gulf oyster thrives in water temperature around 72° and grows in a range of depths from shallow tidal basins to a 130-foot depth and more. The pearl fishing season opens in May and ends in October and during this time the pearl banks were at one time dotted with small boats carrying a motley crew of divers and their ragged equipment.

The expression "pearl banks" (placers de perlas) is somewhat misleading, as the oyster shells are never exposed on the smooth bottom or on the flat surfaces of underwater reefs but are usually hidden in the crevices of the rocks and reefs. Divers without the aid of suits often descended to depths of 10 to 12 fathoms; great strength was required to extract the oysters from the crevices and the divers frequently emerged with hands and feet bleeding; and in this condition they were quite attractive to the man-eating sharks that hovered in the depths. Yaqui Indians from the mainland were the best divers and as many as 800 were once employed at the height of the pearl fishing industry; but it became increasingly difficult to secure Indians for this task as each season one or two or more of the divers were devoured by sharks.

In order to secure one really valuable pearl, thousands of oysters had to be gathered and opened. The dried meat of the non-pearl bearing oyster was sold to Chinese merchants who shipped the product to their homeland where it brought a fancy price as a delicacy. Because pearls are valuable not only for their beauty but for the fact that they are scarce and fetch a high price, men are not only willing but eager to engage in the laborious and sometimes dangerous pearl trade, more for the promise of a lucky find than the day-to-day profit of their labor or the value of the oyster as food. At long intervals a fortunate individual manages to bring up a highly valuable jewel, whereupon the news gets around and the gambler's spirit, which is at the root of the business, spurs the activity of the entire colony of pearlers to scour the oyster beds anew, venturing further and deeper than before. As a consequence of this often mad rush for elusive riches, over the centuries the oyster beds have been repeatedly scraped clean.

The Indians gathered the pearl oyster for food, using nothing more than a sharp stick about a foot long for the dual purpose of fighting off sharks and prying off shells; the pearls they found were a treasured by-product with which they adorned their bodies or festooned their religious symbols. The early Spanish pearlers soon changed all that, trading for pearls with cheap knives, old clothes and wormy ship's biscuit. When their trading goods ran out, the Spanish extracted the precious jewels from the natives in any way they found necessary, finally pressing them willingly or unwillingly into service to pry the shells from the beds in ever increasing numbers, no longer for food but for the yield of pearls alone. The whereabouts of the legendary "Cave of the Dead Beasts" in which the Cochimi Indians worshipped an age-old trove of the largest, most colorful and exquisite pearls brought up from the depths by their tribe over a period exceeding a thousand years, has to modern knowledge remained undiscovered, a well-kept secret that the last of the tribe took to their graves with their final extinction. Great heaps of shells may be found to this day along the coast from Magdalena Bay around the cape and on the shores of the off-lying islands well up into the gulf, remnant debris of the once-flourishing beds of pearl oysters now virtually disappeared.

In 1826 R.W.H. Hardy, who spent three years reconnoitering the gulf in the 25-ton schooner *Bruija* and the companion vessel *Wolf,* employed an immense diving bell in the vicinity of La Paz in an attempt to improve the laborious method of gathering pearl shells. After repeated experimentation, he found the cumbersome equipment too unwieldy to move around over an irregular bottom and gave up the enterprise, reporting to his employers, The General Pearl and Coral Fishery Association in London, (who had sent him over for the purpose of organizing a pearl fishery in the gulf), that large-scale operations with equipment available would be unprofitable.

In 1874 another English vessel, much larger than the *Bruija* or the *Wolf,* arrived off La Paz and introduced modern diving equipment, which quickly revolutionized the industry and ultimately contributed to the final destruction of the once fabulous oyster beds that had somehow survived all earlier attempts by man to wipe them out. Equipped with machinery for handling six divers and their heavy diving suits at one time and enabling them to work on the bottom for a much longer time and at far greater depths than the bare skin native divers, the English company exploited oyster beds never worked before, completely stripping them of shell. By 1884 the pearl fishery was highly developed as a large-scale commercial enterprise and great quantities of pearl shell were exported to Europe for use in making buttons and ornaments, and the dried meat was exported to the Orient as a highly prized Chinese delicacy.

These wholesale methods drastically changed the character of the pearl fishery at La Paz and, while there were still pearls to be found in commercial quantities, the mechanized divers working in organized groups almost totally displaced the individual native skin diver. Strong cooperative unions gained legal control of the pearl fishery, outlawing all others including the individual native diver. The concessionaire — holder of the government license to exploit a certain coastal area, and usually the financier of the boats and equipment as well — protected the product of his enterprise by demanding that oysters be brought to port whole and unshucked. In a dockside shed in La Paz he had them opened by menial workers under the watchful eye of an overseer. Thus very few of the pearls brought up went astray, but there were those few canny native workers who managed to secrete a few of the precious jewels by swallowing them and smuggling them out of the sheds in their bowels. The divers, however, deprived of the excitement of a "find" and denied the hope of sudden riches which had heretofore driven them in their bare skins to deeper and deeper dives and imbued them with an irresistible urge to stay down ever a little longer until their lungs were ready to burst, were no longer motivated to these greater efforts. The apathy and discouragement engendered by hard and dangerous labor rewarded only by small returns and without the gambler's hope of ever realizing the Great Reward manifested itself in a dwindling collection of shell despite the advantage of the diving suits.

The falling off of the La Paz pearl fishery had to do as well with the overfished and severely depleted oyster beds. A French entrepreneur, Gaston Vives, at the turn of the century attempted to cultivate new oyster beds by planting them in wire cages submerged in great rock-walled lagoons. He did not attempt to culture the pearls but only to cultivate their early growth in protected beds removed from their natural enemies. The young oysters, when sufficiently mature, were to be removed to private coastal beds where the pearls spontaneously produced in the mature oysters could then be harvested. Unfortunately, the sporadic incidence of natural pearls did not lend itself to commercial enterprise and the advent of the Mexican Revolution of 1910 wrecked further hope of experimentation. Vives' site of development, which comprised an extensive investment in large rock-walled seawater basins and ancillary laboratory buildings, was on Expíritu Santo Island and the remains of his enterprise which failed may still be seen at San Gabriel Bay today.

The Mexican Revolution of 1910 upset the entire industry considerably and by 1914 had disrupted its commercial pursuit almost completely. The lone diver began again to pursue the pearling trade, now illegally without a license, but having no investment but that of his skin and occasionally an antiquated diving helmet. Paying no fee and running little risk of being caught in unfrequented parts of the coast, he could dive to the end of his strength and all he brought up was his to keep. Diving went on in this haphazard manner aboard ragged little boats with battered equipment, their crews barely above a survival level, until the ultimate catastrophe overtook the trade: An oyster blight! Some unknown and seemingly mysterious disease, rampaged the beds around 1940 and in a final demise after 400 years of exploitation, the pearl fishery of La Paz came to a commercial end. There are those few who still pursue the diving business in small vessels rigged with old but serviceable equipment, but the contemporary enterprising diver usually invests his time and equipment with a fishing cooperative on the Pacific coast and brings up, instead of oysters, abalone and lobster for which there is a ready cash market at the cannery. Of course, now and then, from an untouched patch hidden in the depths beneath the reefs, baskets of pearl oysters are brought up and opened then and there, with that age-old anticipation of a great find infrequently but exquisitely rewarded.

Pearls of considerable value can still be purchased in La Paz but their price is high and for a truly fine jewel, negotiable by the purchaser only to a small degree. As if lulled into a fantasy of a renaissance of the great pearl market of the past, hawkers on the streets of La Paz offer poor imitations of the iridescent grays and opulent blacks for which the city was once world famous; these "jewels" go for what the market will bear and likely as not they are an oiled bit of shell or a blackened ball bearing. Over the centuries some truly exquisite and valuable pearls were taken from the oyster beds of the gulf, among them being some of the finest crown jewels of Europe. The wife of the President of France cherished a particularly large and lustrous pearl that reputedly had been purchased in La Paz for $30,000 in 1880. Another very fine specimen, but not quite so large, was purchased by the superintendent of the copper mine at Santa Rosalía more recently, about 1940, for $1,500, worth considerably more than that in the European market.

If you have a taste for the meat of the oyster and are lucky enough to discover a patch of unclaimed shells in some out-of-the-way cove tucked under a submerged reef, and the fear of the tintoreo, baracuda or the giant octopus is not discouraging, a dive beneath the surface may be a refreshing experience with the inscrutable reward of a gambler's fortune. And failing that, there is still the undiscovered location of the Indian "Cave of the Dead Beasts," somewhere along the marine cliffs in the vicinity of Loreto.

Porgy

SECTION 18
ISLAS ESPÍRITU SANTO and PARTIDA

Isla Espíritu Santo

Isla del Espíritu Santo is the largest of the islands which shelter Bahía de La Paz from the eastward. The island lies about five miles off the mainland, the southern end forming the northern shore of the San Lorenzo Channel; Espíritu Santo Island is about 18 miles north of La Paz. For navigation see United States Oceanographic Office Chart H.O. 2193, San Lorenzo Channel; H.O. 1664, Magdalena Bay to La Paz; H.O. 621, Cabo San Lázaro to Cabo San Lucas including the Southern Part of the Gulf of California; British Admiralty Charts #3061, Plans in the Golfo de California, Canal San Lorenzo inset; #3053, Bahía La Paz to Bahía Magdalena; Mexican Carta Náutica F.H. 604, Parte Sur del Golfo de California.

Espíritu Santo Island, of volcanic origin and with many steep bluffs and deep arroyos, rises to numerous peaks, the highest of which attains an elevation of 1,951 feet above the sea. Sheer rock walls in many places plunge unbroken into the sea, their faces composed of sharply defined volcanic layers of varicolored strata, red, pink, yellow, pearl-white and jet-black lava bands, an open page of geological history through the ages. In some places the soil of the island is bare but for the most part lightly covered with cactus, thorny brush, and, after the rains of late summer, a sprinkling of brightly colored flowering vines, especially the white flowers of the balloon vine and the bright red queen's wreath. On the western side of the island at the mouths of the deeper arroyos, a number of small mangrove-bordered lagoons penetrate the shoreline and form sheltered coves that afford *good anchorage* for yachts and small coastal vessels, protected from all winds except those from the westerly quadrant.

The island is about 7½ miles long and from 2 to 5 miles wide at its widest point; taken with Isla Partida Sur, a companion island 1,099 feet high separated only by a narrow boat channel off the northwestern end of Espíritu Santo Island, the combined land mass comprises a total length of about 12 miles and appears as a single island in profile, when viewed from a short distance off. In the dim past, geologically speaking, there was an active volcano in this part of the island and, in its eruption, it formed a crater of rather large proportion. In the subsequent subsidence half the volcanic cone sank below the level of the sea. The con-

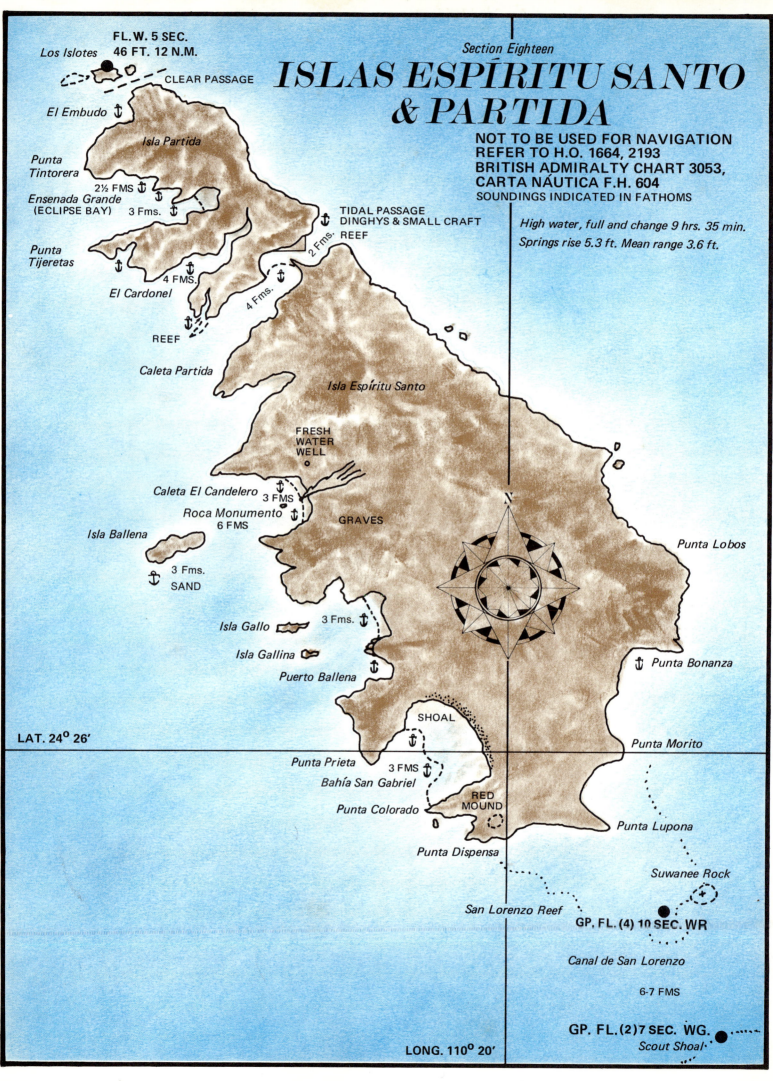

FL.W. 5 SEC.
46 FT. 12 N.M.
Los Islotes

CLEAR PASSAGE

El Embudo ⚓

Isla Partida

Punta
Tintorera

2½ FMS ⚓

Ensenada Grande
(ECLIPSE BAY)
3 Fms. ⚓

⚓
TIDAL PASSAGE
DINGHYS & SMALL CRAFT
REEF

2 Fms. ⚓

Punta
Tijeretas

⚓ REEF

4 FMS. ⚓

4 Fms.

El Cardonel

⚓

REEF

Caleta Partida

Isla Espíritu Santo

FRESH
WATER
WELL
○

Caleta El Candelero
3 FMS ⚓

Isla Ballena

Roca Monumento
6 FMS ⚓

GRAVES

3 Fms. ⚓
SAND

Isla Gallo ▭

3 Fms. ⚓

Isla Gallina ▭

⚓
Puerto Ballena

SHOAL

⚓

Punta Prieta

Bahía San Gabriel

3 FMS ⚓

Punta Colorado

RED
MOUND

Punta Dispensa

Section Eighteen
ISLAS ESPÍRITU SANTO
& PARTIDA

**NOT TO BE USED FOR NAVIGATION
REFER TO H.O. 1664, 2193
BRITISH ADMIRALTY CHART 3053,
CARTA NÁUTICA F.H. 604**
SOUNDINGS INDICATED IN FATHOMS

High water, full and change 9 hrs. 35 min.

Springs rise 5.3 ft. Mean range 3.6 ft.

Punta Lobos

⚓ Punta Bonanza

Punta Morito

Punta Lupona

Suwanee Rock

San Lorenzo Reef

GP. FL. (4) 10 SEC. WR

Canal de San Lorenzo

6-7 FMS

GP. FL. (2) 7 SEC. WG.

Scout Shoal

LAT. 24° 26'

LONG. 110° 20'

stant onslaught of tides and currents breached the east side of the crater to let the sea pour in and form a deep cove, Partida Cove. The sheer lava walls of the old volcano, and the precipitous rock-covered slopes down to the water's edge within the cove, eloquently reveal this geological history. Isla Partida in the Bay of La Paz is given the suffix Isla Partida Sur to distinguish it from its namesake, but much smaller islet located farther northward in the gulf.

Los Islotes, sometimes called Seal Islands, are three flat rocky islets, situated about ½ mile northward of the rocky bluff which forms the northernmost point of Isla Partida; the two larger islets are about 50 feet high with flat tops and perpendicular sides; the third and westernmost is a large rock 5 feet high. The channels between these islets and the passage between the group and Isla Partida are suitable only for small boats. A *navigation light* is shown 46 feet above the sea from a *red tower* on the northwesternmost islet. It exhibits a **white flash every 5 seconds:** flash 0.5 second, eclipse 4.5 seconds, and can be seen in clear weather for a distance of 12 miles. A *25-fathom spot,* reported in 1935, lies approximately 11 miles northeastward of Los Islotes. In fine weather there is suitable *anchorage* for small yachts on Isla Partida, just inside Los Islotes, called El Embudo (The Funnel). *Anchorage* may be taken over a sand bottom in the middle of the funnel, enclosed by vertical walls of rock. At the end of the funnel is a small beach of finely pulverized white coral sand on which a *landing* can be made. Los Islotes hosts an enormous colony of sea lions and the islets are often referred to as Seal Rocks. The splashing and barking of these animals can be heard for miles and, when the wind is wrong, the strong odor of their habitat can be detected for about as far.

The western coast of Isla Espíritu Santo and Isla Partida is comprised of a succession of rocky bluffs penetrated by a series of deep inlets forming bays and coves many of which afford *sheltered anchorage* protected from the prevailing winds. On the western side of Isla Partida, about 2 miles from the rocky bluff that comprises the northern extremity, there is a small inlet called Ensenada Grande where sheltered *anchorage* may be taken. The cove formed within the inlet is protected by Punta Tintorea (Shark Point) on its northwest side and Punta Tijeretas (Frigate Bird Point) on the southwest side. It is a comfortably large triple-headed cove with sandy beaches; standstone formations extend precipitously to the water's edge. Four fathoms are sounded well back into the cove on the southeast side, and *protected anchorage* may be taken in that depth abreast a small beach of dark-colored sand. On the northeastern side of Ensenada Grande, the water shoals to 2½ fathoms off a shallow cove filled to its mouth with a shoal sand bank, but the anchorage here is less well sheltered. At the head of the cove is a clean white beach of soft coral sand. The water at the head of the cove is so shallow that an approach to within 100 yards of the beach cannot be made, with a vessel drawing much more than 2 feet. Here Joseph Wood Krutch, the famed naturalist and chronicler of Baja California, set up camp and observed a full eclipse of the moon March 13, 1959, and bestowed the name Eclipse Bay.

About ½ mile southward of Ensenada Grande, beyond a high spur that runs down from the central ridge of Isla Partida to the sea forming a point, there is a somewhat narrower but deeper cove called El Cardonel. The cove penetrates the shore to almost ⅘ the width of the island at that point and its parallel sides open into a shoal basin at the head. *Anchorage* may be taken well into the mouth of the cove, sheltered on either side by rocky slopes that fall steeply down to the water. *Landing* may be effected in the small inlet at the southeast corner of the basin. Around the southern point of El Cardonel Cove there is a still deeper cove between Isla Partida and Isla Espíritu Santo, comprised of the breached volcanic cone described above. Caleta Partida (Partida Cove) as this indentation is referred to, is actually a narrow strait running east and west between the high hills of the two islands, with passage blocked toward its western end by a low spit of sand and rock that forms the head of the cove. This spit, partially covered by the tide at high water, projecting northward

Partida Cove, west

Partida Cove, east

from the Espíritu Santo shore, overlaps another broader spit projecting in the opposite direction from the Isla Partida shore. A boat passage with 3- to 5-foot depths threads the tidal channel between the two spits, and small fishing skiffs negotiate this passage regularly, passing from one side of the islands to the other without the necessity of rounding the north end of Isla Partida. Prolific colonies of rock oysters, butter clams and long-legged crabs populate this tidal channel. A fish camp is established on the easternmost spit that projects from Isla Partida, and a quantity of market fish is caught, cleaned and transported to La Paz daily. Good sheltered *anchorage* over a sand bottom may be taken in Partida Cove and a *landing* may be made on the sand beach of the spit at the head of the cove. A smaller cove filled with quite shoal water lies indented northward approximately midway through the strait in the Isla Partida shore. A brisk westerly breeze of wind sometimes blows through this strait.

Caution: A dangerous reef about ¼ mile long extends in a southwesterly direction from the northern entrance point of the cove; this reef is covered at high water.

Caleta El Candelero (Candelero Cove), about 1½ miles southward of Partida Cove, lies indented in the shore of Isla Espíritu Santo close northeastward of Islote Ballena. Steep rocky cliffs fall to the water's edge on both sides of the cove. There is a large rock in the middle of the cove with several detached rocks off the inshore side; detached rocks also lie in shoal water just off the point of land dividing the two beaches at the head of the cove. *Anchorage* may be safely taken seaward of the central rock, 6 fathoms being sounded on a line between the two entrance points of the cove, 3 fathoms and less immediately within. There is about 2 fathoms, sand, between the rock and the beach on the port hand closer to the rock; and 2 fathoms, sand, between the rock and the beach on the starboard hand, closer to the beach. The cove affords shelter from north and east winds but is open to the south and west. The southerly

Coromuel winds cause a considerable swell to sweep the anchorage, requiring ground tackle fore and aft to prevent rolling uncomfortably in the trough. *Landing* may be made on either of the beaches but the depth of the water immediately offshore is quite shoal. A small *lagoon* opens in the shore on the south side of the cove with a growth of mangrove thickets around its perimeter. Several varieties of tall cactus and a green growth of bushes fringe the cove. Evidence of Indian graves may be seen back of the small lagoon. The only developed source of water to be found on the island is a *masonry well* constructed by the early inhabitants in the northern canyon leading up from the cove. It is about 20 feet deep and requires a bucket and a length of line to bail the water from it.

Isla Ballena (Whale Island) is a barren rocky island lying about 2 miles southward of the northwestern extremity of Isla Espíritu Santo, close off the western coast and immediately southward of Candelero Cove. This small islet is separated from the larger island by a channel with a width of a little more than ½ mile and depths of 2 to 8 fathoms. Isla Ballena is about ¾ mile long, lying nearly east and west, and ¼ mile wide; its highest peak is 228 feet above the sea.

Two small islets, El Gallo and La Gallina (The Rooster and The Hen) are situated about 1¼ and 1¾ miles, respectively, southeastward of Isla Ballena; abreast these small islets are three deep coves indented in the shore of Isla Espíritu Santo, close southeastward of Isla Ballena. Puerto Ballena is the name given to the anchorage ground to be found in the middle cove which affords partial shelter from the prevailing winds for small yachts and coastal vessels.

Punta Prieta, situated about 1¾ miles south-southeastward of La Gallina islet and 2 miles north-northwestward of Punta Dispensa, is a sharp, dark-colored bluff point which descends in steps from the hills inland. Bahía San

Gabriel (San Gabriel Bay), which is very shallow except at its entrance, lies eastward of Prieta Point, bracketed between that point and Punta Colorado on the southeast side. This bay is of considerable extent but the greater part is filled with a shore bank and the water is shoal. Immediately southeastward of San Gabriel Bay is another smaller bight which is completely filled with a shore bank and has shoal water to its mouth. The best *anchorage* to be had is in the southeastern portion of San Gabriel Bay abreast the old ruins of an experimental pearl fishing station, in about 2 to 3 fathoms over a sand and rock bottom. While this anchorage is well protected from north and east, it is open to the west and to the *Coromuel* winds which rise in the afternoons and persist into the late evenings. *Anchorage* may be taken as well under the lee of Prieta Point on the northwestern side of the bay. A white sand beach is situated at the head of the bay on which a *landing* can be made; clams abound in the shoal water.

TIDES — The mean high water interval at full and change in San Gabriel Bay is 9 hours 35 minutes; the rise and fall of the tide has a spring range of 5.3 feet, and a mean range of 3.6 feet.

Extensive stoneworks of the old tidal basins comprising the oyster ponds of an abandoned pearl fishery are built around a small inlet on the southeastern side of the cove, abreast the preferred anchorage. The ruins of a 6-cornered building and odd pieces of equipment left from this turn-of-the-century enterprise are interesting features to explore at this anchorage. Back of the oyster basins and higher on the island are Indian mounds and caves, blackened by ancient campfires and strewn with shell and bone fragments. Bits of pottery, arrowheads and stone implements may be found as evidence of early native habitation. When it was first discovered by the Spanish in 1533, in spite of the scarcity of fresh water, the island supported several hundred Indians who maintained themselves principally by fishing. Cortez

called the island La Isla de la Perlas, and the extensive oyster beds he found to exist along the western coast are frequently mentioned in early manuscripts. The vicinity of the island was much frequented by Spanish pearling expeditions from the middle of the sixteenth century to the end of the eighteenth century. As previously mentioned, Juan de Iturbi and his pilot Esteban Carbonel, financed and accompanied by Francisco de Ortega, sailed into the gulf in 1631 searching for pearls and spent some time at the island giving it its present name, Isla de Espíritu Santo. They employed a wooden diving bell, weighted with lead and large enough for two people, together with heavy iron drags for scraping oysters from the sea floor. This unwieldy equipment proved impractical as it was soon discovered that oysters for the most part were tightly wedged into the crevices of the rock rather than growing evenly spread on a flat open bottom. In the spring of 1683 Admiral Isidro Otondo y Antillón, accompanied by Fathers Kino, Copart and Goni, while attempting to establish a colony near La Paz, spent a week at Espíritu Santo trading for pearls with the natives before the debacle of the cannonball episode at the mission, which forced them to hastily return to Mexico. In 1720, after finally establishing a mission at La Paz that seemingly would survive, the Fathers induced the Indians of Espíritu Santo to participate in mission work. The Indians traveled across the bay periodically and contributed their labor to the mission enterprise but elected to continue to live on their island. Pearlers still arrived and traded with the Indians for pearls although the missionaries discouraged these visits. After the Pericue Indian rebellion of 1734-36 previously referred to, which saw the destruction and sacking of all the southern missions, the Espíritu Santo Indians disappeared, victims of the Spanish soldiers sent in retribution, and of Spanish diseases contracted from the soldiers in the course of Indian subjugation. Espíritu Santo Island is presently uninhabited except for seasonal fish camps.

The climate of the island is much like that of La Paz:

Ensenada Grande

warm and dry and healthful, receiving only about 5 inches of rain a year. The only permanent fresh water occurs in underground seepages in some of the deeper arroyos on the western side of the island and water can be found sometimes long after a rain in natural rock hollows called tinajas which support the animal life found on the island.

The eastern side of the island is quite spectacular with great sandstone cliffs eroded by eons of wind and wave into strange sculptured rock formations that plunge precipitously into the sea.

Punta Dispensa (Dispensa Point), the southwestern extremity of Espíritu Santo Island, is a rocky bluff of moderate elevation, situated between Punta Colorado, north-northwestward, and Punta Lupona, eastward. The point can be easily recognized by a conspicuous red mound, 213 feet high and composed of lumps of lava, situated about 600 yards northward. Punta Dispensa lies about 4 miles north-northwestward of Punta Arranco Cabello across the San Lorenzo Channel.

Punta Lupona, the southeastern extremity of Espíritu Santo Island, is a low sandy point situated about 1 mile eastward of Punta Dispensa; between these two points the shore recedes to form a bight, from which the coastal bank with depths of less than 3 fathoms over it, extends for as much as ¾ mile offshore; farther southward a *detached 3-fathom patch* lies a little less than a mile southeastward of Punta Dispensa. There are a few scattered bushes between Punta Lupona and the hills to the northward as far as Punta Morito (labeled Bonanza Point on the official navigation charts), situated about 1¾ miles northwestward of Punta Lupona.

Punta Morito (Punta Bonanza) may be recognized as a rocky bluff with a flat-topped hill 100 feet high behind it. The intervening coast is comprised of alternate sand beaches and cliffs. From Punta Morito the coast, consisting of white sand cliffs, trends northward for about 2 miles and then eastward for about ½ mile to the point called by the natives, Punta Bonanza, which may be identified by a *reef of rocks* which extends southeastward for about ¼ mile; at the head of the bay thus formed is a large mound of conspicuous boulders. *Anchorage* may be taken in this bay in the bight southward of the rocky reef with shelter from the

northwesterly winds, in depths of from 5 to 6 fathoms. The unfrequented beaches along this side of the island are formed of great stretches of white sand backed by dunes; swimming is excellent and the water is warm. A *hot salt spring* surrounded by indian rockwork is located on the island a short distance back of the shore.

Punta Lobos, the eastern extremity of Espíritu Santo Island, is a high rocky bluff with the land rising abruptly behind it; the point is steep-to with deep water close around; it is situated about 4¾ miles north-northeastward of Punta Lupona. From Punta Lobos the east coast of the island trends northwestward and westward to the northerly ex-

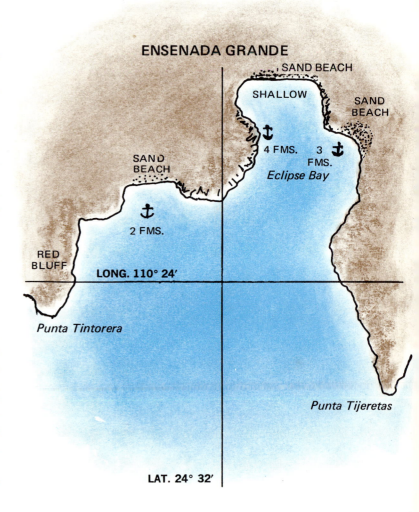

El Embudo, Isla Partida

tremity; the coast is bluff with short stretches of white sand beach at the heads of steep ravines.

A *reef* extends about ¼ mile off a rocky point situated a little less than 4 miles northwestward of Punta Lobos. This rocky reef on the eastern side of the island marks the entrance point of the windward cove formed between Isla Espíritu Santo and Isla Partida; the cove is sharply indented, receding about 1¾ miles to the head where a low sandspit separates the windward cove from the leeward cove on the opposite side of the two islands. The mouth of the windward cove is about 1 mile wide and *anchorage* may be taken under the cliffs on either side, but this ground is subject to gusty, northwesterly winds that sometimes blow through the gap between the two islands. *Landing* may be made on the sandspit at the head of the cove, and at high water the interconnecting channel that winds between the overlapping sandspits may be negotiated to the opposite cove by small boats. A seasonal fish camp is established on the spit within the windward cove.

From the northwestern side of this cove, the west coast of Isla Partida trends northwestward for about 2½ miles under towering cliffs, thence west-northwestward for about 1 mile to its northwestern extremity and off-lying Los Islotes (Seal Islands) whence the island has been circumnavigated.

Los Islotes, Isla Partida

SECTION 19
LA PAZ
to PUNTA SAN MARCIAL

Cabeza de Mechudo—Mechudo Head

The run from La Paz northwestward to Agua Verde Bay, a distance of about 90 miles, is characterized by numerous coves and sheltered bights affording excellent protected anchorage all along the way. Several stretches provide smooth passage in sheltered water in the lee of offshore islands, which in turn offer comfortable anchorage. Emergency gasoline supplies only are available; some water and fresh provisions are to be had at several of the anchorages. For navigation see H.O. 621, Cabo San Lázaro to Cabo San Lucas including the Southern Part of the Gulf of California; H.O. 1664, Magdalena Bay to La Paz; H.O. 850, Western Shore of the Gulf of California from San Marcial Point to San Basilio Bay; British Admiralty Charts #3053, Bahía La Paz to Bahía Magdalena; #2324, Cape San Lucas to San Diego Bay including the Gulf of California; Mexican Carta Náutica, F.H. 604, Cabo San Lázaro a Cabo San Lucas y Parte Sur del Golfo de California.

From the eastern end of the El Mogote peninsula the southern shore of Bahía de La Paz trends westward at first, then in a wide sweep curves gradually northward for a total distance of 27 miles to Punta de Los Reyes (Punta Coyote on the navigation charts; not to be confused with the point of the same name at the western end of the San Lorenzo Channel). The first 6 miles of this stretch of coast are comprised of the low and sandy El Mogote Peninsula covered with bushes and mangrove thickets and backed by the large shallow lagoon, Ensenada de Los Aripes. The next 6 miles

of this curving coast are characterized by sand hills from 15 to 75 feet high. About 12 miles westward of the eastern tip of El Mogote, a cattle ranch, Rancho Rodríguez, is situated on the shore of the bay and nearby, a short distance inland, is the small settlement of El Bosque. A road communicates between these places and several other ranches and settlements around Ensenada de Los Aripes, thence to La Paz.

Navigation caution: Shoals with depths over them from 4 feet to 3 fathoms extend up to 1 mile offshore in several places between 4 and 14 miles westward of the eastern tip of the El Mogote Peninsula; caution should be exercised in accordance with a vessel's draft when navigating throughout this area.

For a distance of about 16 miles southward of Punta de Los Reyes, alternatively called Punta Coyote, the shore is backed by a long tableland from 500 to 1,000 feet high faced with cliffs from 50 to 100 feet high and interspersed with a number of shingle beaches. Rancho San Juan is situated on the shore, about 5½ miles southward of Punta de Los Reyes; it is fronted by a low shingle beach on which a landing can be made; close westward of this place is a remarkable and conspicuous dark-colored peak, 1,431 feet high, that serves well as a coastal landmark. At 2 miles from the shore off this part of the coast depths of 15 to 20 fathoms are sounded. *Navigation note — charting error: A*

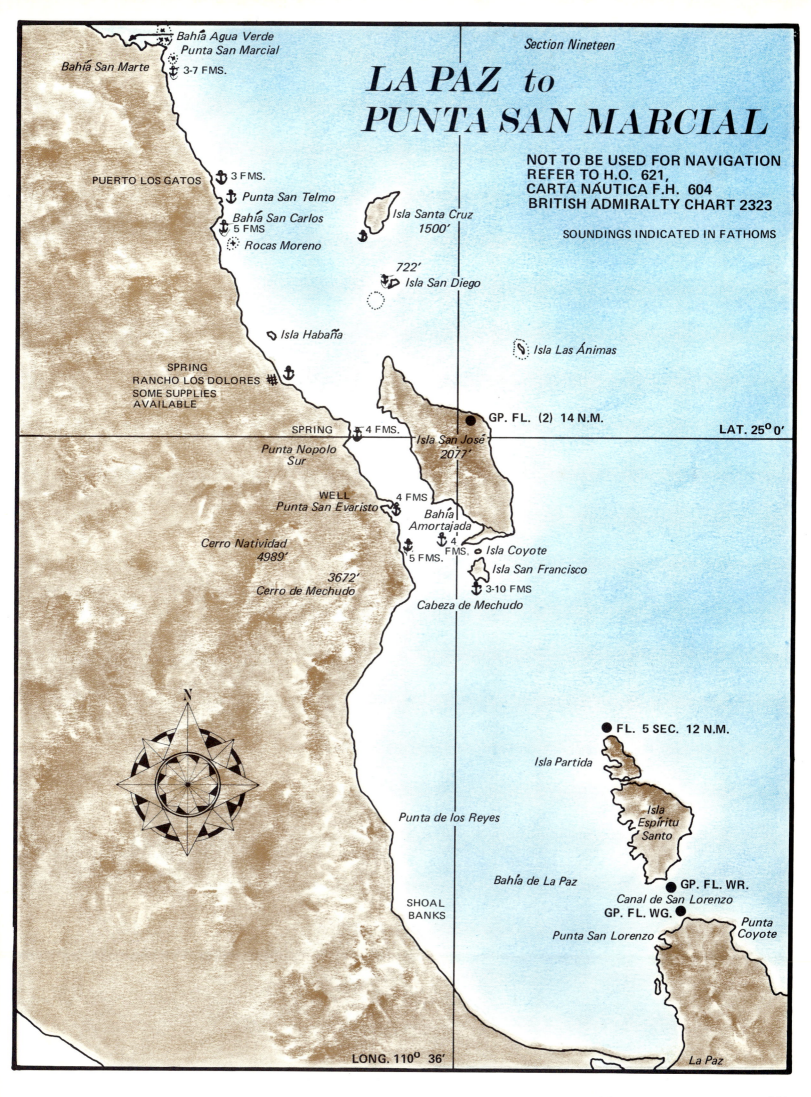

Bahía Agua Verde
Punta San Marcial
Bahía San Marte
3-7 FMS.

LA PAZ to
PUNTA SAN MARCIAL

NOT TO BE USED FOR NAVIGATION
REFER TO H.O. 621,
CARTA NÁUTICA F.H. 604
BRITISH ADMIRALTY CHART 2323

SOUNDINGS INDICATED IN FATHOMS

PUERTO LOS GATOS
3 FMS.
Punta San Telmo
Bahía San Carlos
5 FMS
Rocas Moreno

Isla Santa Cruz
1500'

722'
Isla San Diego

Isla Habaña

Isla Las Ánimas

SPRING
RANCHO LOS DOLORES
SOME SUPPLIES
AVAILABLE

GP. FL. (2) 14 N.M.

LAT. 25° 0'

SPRING
Punta Nopolo
Sur
4 FMS.
Isla San José
2077'

WELL
Punta San Evaristo
4 FMS
Bahía
Amortajada
4
FMS.
Isla Coyote

Cerro Natividad
4989'
5 FMS.
Isla San Francisco
3-10 FMS

3672'
Cerro de Mechudo
Cabeza de Mechudo

N

FL. 5 SEC. 12 N.M.

Isla Partida

Punta de los Reyes

Isla
Espíritu
Santo

Bahía de La Paz
GP. FL. WR.
Canal de San Lorenzo
GP. FL. WG.
Punta
Coyote

SHOAL
BANKS
Punta San Lorenzo

LONG. 110° 36'
La Paz

coastal survey made in 1943 indicates that the coastline in the vicinity of Punta de Los Reyes (Punta Coyote) and southward towards El Mogote is actually about 1 mile farther eastward than charted.

Punta de Los Reyes (Punta Coyote), 27 miles northwestward of La Paz, is a perpendicular, white rocky bluff 150 feet high. Between Punta de Los Reyes and Cabeza del Mechudo, situated about 20 miles northward, the coast recedes forming a bight. Northward of Punta de Los Reyes the bluffs gradually decrease in height and are replaced by sand beaches backed by sand hills. A short distance inland there is a tableland which rises abruptly to heights of 1,500 to 2,000 feet, broken by deep arroyos into a series of short flat mesas. Nearer Cabeza de Mechudo the high land is closer to the coast, and bluffs 150 to 200 feet high replace the sand beaches. Cabeza de Mechudo (Mechudo Head) is a bold perpendicular, stratified cliff 300 feet high surmounted by a dome-shaped hill 750 feet high. Monte del Mechudo rises to an elevation of 3,672 feet about 3½ miles westward of this headland; it is the only prominent peak in the vicinity and is visible for more than 50 miles in clear weather, and together with the headland, provides an excellent landmark at the southern entrance to the San José Channel.

El Mechudo means "the long-haired man" in Spanish and, according to legend, the place was given that name after a diving mishap in the once rich pearl oyster beds along this coast that left an indelible impression on those who survived. It was the time-honored custom among the Indian divers of Loreto, mostly neophytes of the mission, to provide the finest pearl of each day's catch to the safekeeping of the Mission Father in order that the blessing of the Virgin might be invoked to protect the lives of the divers in their dangerous enterprise. However, there were those Indians who clung to their ancient atheistic beliefs, rooted more deeply in a practical appraisal of day-to-day living than the religious concepts inculcated by the Spanish priests. There was one such diver whom Fate blessed with the luck of finding a great lustrous black and very valuable pearl which he immediately declared he would keep for himself. Diving again with the hope of further multiplying his sizable fortune, the Indian diver failed to return to the surface. His companions, searching in the depths to see what had happened, came upon him with his leg trapped in a giant clam, his long black hair undulating in the current and the terror of eternal damnation in his eyes. The prized black pearl was pried from his death-stiffened fingers and duly offered to the Virgin in the sanctuary at Loreto, but the pearl divers thereafter avoided the oyster beds off El Mechudo as an accursed place. John Steinbeck, after a trip on the Western Enterprise with Ed Ricketts to the Gulf of California, hearing of the legend of the cursed great black pearl of Loreto, wrote his classic tale *The Pearl*.

Cabeza Mechudo

The coast for about 1½ miles northward of Cabeza de Mechudo is comprised of high perpendicular cliffs; farther north-northwestward a sand beach, broken only by a short bluff, continues for a distance of about 4½ miles to a sandy point that projects from the general line of the coast about 2 miles southward of Punta San Evaristo. There is *good anchorage* for vessels with local knowledge immediately southward of this sandy point, about ½ mile offshore in depths of from 5 to 6 fathoms.

Punta San Evaristo is a rocky headland, 130 feet high, which projects about ¾ mile from the general line of the coast about 8 miles north-northwestward of Cabeza de Mechudo. Close southward of San Evaristo Point and embraced by the hook of the point is a well protected cove about ¾ mile across and open to the southwest. A crescent sand beach lies at the head of the cove, and several groups of ranch buildings, including a school house, are built back of the beach. *Good all-weather anchorage* may be taken about ½ mile offshore in 5½ fathoms, sand. Smaller vessels may anchor closer to the beach in the northwestern bight in 4 fathoms, sand; or in the southwestern bight in 3 fathoms, sand. *Caution should be observed when making into San Evaristo Cove around the headlands as a reef of rock extends a short distance off the southern point of the cove and a shoal fringes the northern headland.* The holding ground is good and the waters of the bay generally quite smooth, well sheltered from strong northerly winds. Supply vessels load and discharge cargo in the cove by use of lighters. A road crosses the low spur of the headland to a ranch on the northern side of the point. The coast between this cove and the northern end of the sandy beach one mile southward is comprised of rocky bluffs from 20 to 50 feet high. On the northern side of the San Evaristo headland there is an open bight fringed by a stretch of sand beach; back of the beach is a salt evaporating pan in operation by the ranch established at the foot of the hill behind. There is a growth of trees along the far perimeter of the salt pan and around the ranch buildings; a road leads over the low spur behind the headland to the cove southward. Salt is loaded by lighter off the beach to the small coastal vessels that also serve the salt works on San José Island just offshore. *Anchorage* may be taken off the beach in 2½ to 3 fathoms, sand.

From Punta San Evaristo to Punta Nopolo Sur, about 7 miles north-northwestward, the land is high and precipitous, with occasional short stretches of sand beach and deep water close offshore. Punta Nopolo is a great rocky cliff close behind which is a rugged peak, 1,578 feet high. A succession of rocky bluffs, 400 to 500 feet high, extends about 3¼ miles northwestward from the point. Immediately northwestward of Punta Nopolo Sur a deep narrow arroyo, cut into the steep sides of the broken rocky terrain, opens onto the shore in a small cove indented between rocky promontories. Five-foot high letters NOPOLO in white paint on the south side of the cove can be seen for ½ mile when approaching from northward. Two thatched houses are situated above the sandy beach on the same side of the cove; a third house is built back of the shelving gravel beach on the north side. A small *spring* of brackish water

Monte Mechudo

rises among a green growth of foliage and date palms on the flat bottom of the arroyo and is tapped by *two wells* back of the settlement. *Good anchorage* may be taken in 4 fathoms, sand, off the gravel beach on the north side of the cove; or 2½ fathoms, sand, on the south side of the cove about 100 yards offshore close by the white letters NOPOLO. Landing may be easily made anywhere on the beach. *Navigation note: About 78 miles northward along this coast in the vicinity of the town of Loreto, a second point and anchorage bears the same name "Nopolo."* Several other short stretches of sandy beach lie tucked in the hook of the point formed by the ridge of rock that extends into the sea close northward. There is *good shelter* at Nopolo Sur, the people of the fishing village are friendly and hospitable; the cove is a popular anchorage frequented by cruising yachts. Fresh *water* is available here in limited quantities, fuel in emergency and some fresh provisions.

Close westward of Nopolo Point the rocky bluffs give way to an arroyo, the mouth of which opens onto the shore and a fringe of sandy beach. A ranch is established ¼ mile back of the beach and a growth of green foilage may be seen in the flat bottom or the arroyo. *Anchorage* may be taken off this beach and a *landing* effected easily on shore.

Canal de San José (San José Channel) is a navigable channel formed between the coast that runs from Cabeza de Mechudo to Punta Nopolo Sur and the offshore islands, San Francisco and San José, that lie parallel to the mainland at this point. The channel is about 20 miles long with an average width of 4 miles, being that width at the southern entrance between Isla San Francisco and Punta Mechudo; it has a least width of about 2½ miles opposite Punta San Evaristo and also at the northern entrance of the channel. This passage is useful for masters of vessels desiring smooth water protected in the lee when the seas outside are running; masters of sailing vessels beating up the gulf may also choose a course through this channel in order to benefit by the tidal streams which set through at a rate of from 1 to 3 knots, but timing is important. *Sheltered anchorage* can be found in several bights and coves on both sides of the channel in foul weather; however, when navigating

Punta San Evaristo

the channel at night or in thick weather, it is recommended to keep well over toward the western shore which is clear of outlying dangers.

Isla de San Francisco (San Francisco Island) lies on the east side of the southern entrance to the San José Channel, about 4½ miles across from Cabeza de Mechudo and about 1½ miles southward of the southwestern end of Isla de San José. It is a relatively small pile of lava and ash 689 feet high, with an area of about 1½ square miles and of irregular shape. Severe rocky slopes characterize the western side; precipitous cliffs fall steeply to the sea on the eastern side. The shore is comprised principally of rocky bluffs varying in height from 20 to 150 feet, with intervening sand beaches; the southwestern extremity of the island is a windswept rocky head 300 feet high, it is comprised of a barren slope marked by red and yellow bands situated at the seaward end of a curving rocky ridge that connects to the main body of the island by a low sandy isthmus. From the head of the ridge a *rocky reef and sandspit* hooks northwestward; a cove with a white sandy beach fringing its shore is formed within the bight of the hook on the southwestern side of the ridge. *Anchorage* in depths of 5 to 10 fathoms may be taken by large vessels off the sand beach, just westward of the

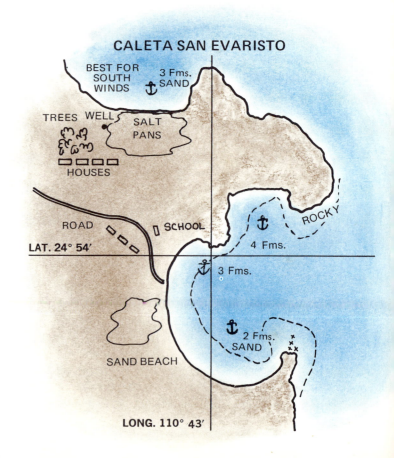

CALETA SAN EVARISTO

BEST FOR SOUTH WINDS

3 Fms. SAND

TREES   WELL

SALT PANS

HOUSES

ROAD   SCHOOL

ROCKY

4 Fms.

LAT. 24° 54′

3 Fms.

2 Fms. SAND

SAND BEACH

LONG. 110° 43′

southeastern point of the island, and by smaller vessels in 3½ fathoms, sand bottom, closer in shore on the northwest side of the cove. Shoal water fills the hook of the bight but good *landing is* afforded by ship's boat on the wide beach.

Sheltered anchorage may also be taken between two bold reefs that extend from the southwest corner of the island immediately northwest of the Isthmus Cove. *Anchorage* may be taken in an open bight on the northwest corner of the island opposite Isla Coyote, sand; an alternative *anchorage* may be had on the eastern side of the isthmus in a depth of 2½ fathoms, sand, with care to avoid the foul ground at the head of the bight. A *rock* that projects 4 feet above high water lies 200 yards from the shore in this bight. Off the northern and southern ends of the island there are *numerous rocks* and care should be taken to avoid them when rounding the island.

Soundings around Isla San Francisco show depths of 3 to 9 fathoms close-to except on the northwest side where

early charts. In 1881, a German, Federico Ernst, discovered a gold and silver vein on the island which he worked successfully for about 5 years, the ore running to about $50 a ton as valued in 1899. The San Francisco Academy of Science expedition to the gulf, in the spring of 1959, found a 10-inch tree on this tiny uninhabited island with the inscription "FR 1886" carved in its trunk.

Rocas del Coyote (Coyote Rocks), sometimes referred to locally as Isla Pardito, are a group of rocks lying about midway between Isla de San Francisco and the sandspit at the southwestern extremity of Isla de San José. The highest rock of the group is 40 feet above the sea and on it are built two houses, though part of one has fallen into the sea. A family with children seasonally occupy the dwellings; they grow no crop of any kind, nor can they do so on this bleak and waterless rock; all the water they drink must be brought from the mainland or from neighboring San José Island. They occupy themselves catching and drying fish which are sold in the market at La Paz,

Coast northward of Punta San Evaristo

there are *shoal depths* of 2½ fathoms ¼ mile offshore; the channel between this shoal area and Coyote Rocks is 3 to 5 fathoms in depth and clear of dangers. Off the northern point of the island there are three dark patches in a group reflecting a grassy bottom covered by 4 fathoms of water. All the anchorages described above are used by local fishermen, by cruising yachtsmen and by sportfishermen from La Paz. Tinajas, pools of brackish water, may be found for some time after the rainy season in the arroyos and their existence is known and utilized by the natives.

Pearling vessels worked this area sporadically from the latter part of the 1500's through the early part of the 1900's, a choice part of the famous pearl banks noted on

and elsewhere on the mainland. *Detached sunken rocks* lie 700 yards northwestward of this highest rock. *Caution: The channels on either side of Coyote Rocks are dangerous and should be used only by masters of vessels thoroughly familiar with the dangers.* The channel between the rocks and the spit off San José Island is less than ½ mile wide with depths of 6 to 7 fathoms; the channel between the rocks and the north end of San Francisco Island is a little over ¾ mile wide with depths of 4 to 5 fathoms but a *shoal* extends into the channel for ⅓ that distance on its southern side. If passage is attempted, it is safest to pass to the north of the patch of rocks and to keep the shore of San José Island aboard. Passage may be made in small vessels through the channel southward of Coyote

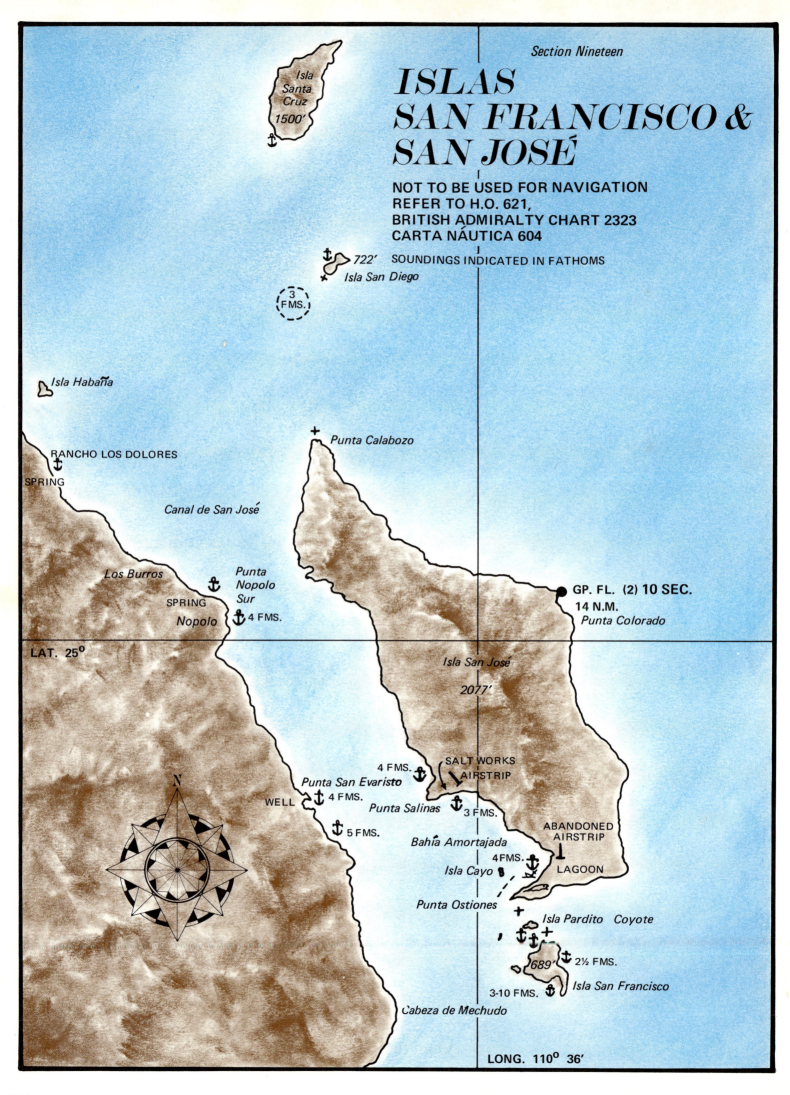

ISLAS SAN FRANCISCO & SAN JOSÉ

**NOT TO BE USED FOR NAVIGATION
REFER TO H.O. 621,
BRITISH ADMIRALTY CHART 2323
CARTA NÁUTICA 604**

Isla
Santa
Cruz
1500'

722' SOUNDINGS INDICATED IN FATHOMS
Isla San Diego

3
FMS.

Isla Habaña

Punta Calabozo

RANCHO LOS DOLORES

SPRING

Canal de San José

Los Burros

Punta Nopolo Sur

SPRING

Nopolo

4 FMS.

GP. FL. (2) **10 SEC.**
14 N.M.
Punta Colorado

LAT. 25°

Isla San José

2077'

4 FMS.

SALT WORKS
AIRSTRIP

Punta San Evaristo

4 FMS.

WELL

Punta Salinas

3 FMS.

ABANDONED
AIRSTRIP

5 FMS.

Bahía Amortajada

4 FMS.

LAGOON

Isla Cayo

Punta Ostiones

Isla Pardito Coyote

689' 2½ FMS.

3-10 FMS. Isla San Francisco

Cabeza de Mechudo

LONG. 110° 36'

Isla San José and Isla San Francisco

Rocks, and *anchorage* is to be had on the western side of the highest islet immediately southward of the first smaller rock.

Rocas de la Foca (Seal Rocks), situated about 1¾ miles westward of Isla de San Francisco, are two flat rocks about 5 feet high with several sunken rocks around them. Depths of 5 to 7 fathoms have been sounded on their south side and the passage between Seal Rocks and the western shore of Isla de San Francisco is clear.

Isla de San José (San José Island; San Josef Island on early American charts) is a rugged island of volcanic uplift lying parellel to the mainland forming the eastern side of the San José Channel. The island is 16½ miles long and 2 to 6 miles wide, being narrowest at its northern end which terminates in a sharp point, Punta Calabozo. The highest elevation near the middle of the island is a conspicuous knob 2,077 feet above the sea; another peak near the northern end rises to an elevation of 1,382 feet. Higher parts of the island are steep brush-covered wastes; the lower coastal slopes are comparatively gentle and more fertile with abundant vegetation, especially in the numerous deep arroyos of the northeastern portion. In spite of the dry and barren appearance of its upper slopes, Isla San José is one of the most fertile islands in the gulf requiring but a small bit of rain to bring out its verdure. Coyotes are numerous and deer at one time were abundant; cattle are run on the island from time-to-time. Small rodents are common and birds nest in great numbers.

The central ridge of the island drops off steeply to the sea on the eastern side, which is comprised of a succession of high rocky bluffs with some intervening sand beaches clear of off-lying dangers except close inshore. Soundings show depths of 50 fathoms and more close offshore. A *navigation light* is exhibited on the northeastern side of the island, about 2 miles northwestward of Punta Colorado (Red Point), the first prominent point about 8 miles from the southeastern end of the island. The *light* is shown 85 feet above the sea from a white tower and exhibits a group characteristic of **two white flashes in a period of 10 seconds:** flash 0.5 second, eclipse 1 second; flash 0.5 second,

eclipse 8 seconds. This light can be seen 14 miles in clear weather. Brackish water standing in pools may be found in the arroyos that open onto the shore in the vicinity of Punta Colorado.

Islotes de las Ánimas are a group of rocky islets off the east coast of Isla San José situated about 6 miles northeastward of Punta Colorado; the islets comprise a patch not more than ¼ mile in extent, including several outlying rocks, the largest and highest of which rises 90 feet above the sea. Between Islotes Las Ánimas and San José Island there is a deep, clear channel. Off-lying the southeast point of Isla San José, about 9 miles southward of Punta Colorado, there are several *detached rocks;* a hill 400 feet high rises abruptly just behind the point. For 5 miles northward of this point the coast consists of a series of inaccessible bluffs 50 to 500 feet high. The southern coast of the island is comprised mostly of a sand beach backed by hills from 100 to 500 feet high.

The coast trends westward from the southeast point for 3½ miles to Punta Los Ostiones (The Oysters) the southwestern point of the island from which a low sand spit projects west-southwestward for 1½ miles. Within the spit there is a lagoon of considerable size extending to within ½ mile of the point, with an opening to the sea on the northern side. Isla de San Francisco and the shoals and rock patches previously described lie southward and southwestward of this point.

The western side of Isla de San José presents a gradual slope from the central ridge to the sea, with a series of sand beaches and coves at the mouths of the arroyos that open onto the shore. Several bays and a number of *good anchorages* are to be found along this western shore; fresh *water* rises at the head of Bahía Amortajada and at the settlement at Punta Salinas.

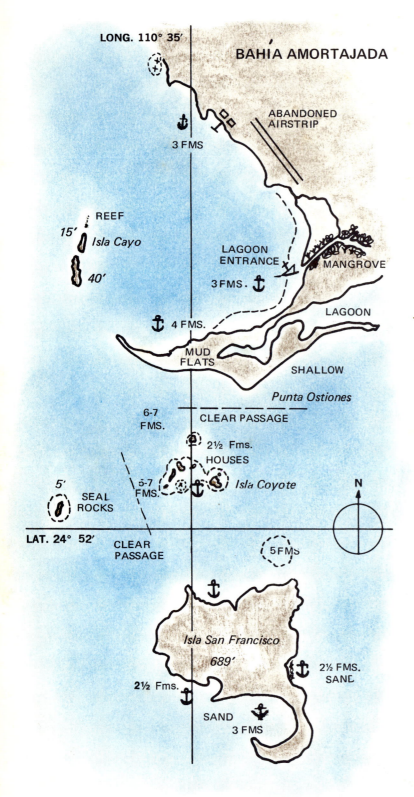

LONG. 110° 35'

BAHÍA AMORTAJADA

ABANDONED AIRSTRIP

3 FMS

REEF
15' Isla Cayo

40'

LAGOON
ENTRANCE
3 FMS.

MANGROVE

4 FMS.

LAGOON

MUD
FLATS

SHALLOW

Punta Ostiones

6-7
FMS.

CLEAR PASSAGE

2½ Fms.

HOUSES

5'

SEAL
ROCKS

5-7
FMS.

Isla Coyote

N

LAT. 24° 52'

CLEAR
PASSAGE

5 FMS

Isla San Francisco
689'

2½ FMS.
SAND

2½ Fms.

SAND
3 FMS

At Los Ostiones Point, a canal 100 yards wide cuts from the main body of the island a triangular portion of land comprised of a great sandspit, a cobbled beach and an extensive lagoon with an intricate maze of tidal canals. This isolated wedge covers 2 or 3 square miles and, in addition, on the easterly side of the channel, there are a thousand acres more of mangrove swamps. The tidal lagoon is located in the center of the spit and is fringed with thickets of mangrove on whose tangle of tide-washed roots grow a thick crop of edible oysters. The lagoon drains thrugh a narrow ½-mile long channel into the main tidal canal and thence into the bay; small boats may enter through this channel and explore the lagoon. The hull of a sizable vessel lies stranded on the sand bar in the mouth of the lagoon. *Landing* may be made near the outer end of the point on an abruptly sloping cobble beach where *anchorage* can be had close inshore. During the spring of the year gnats and mosquitoes thrive in great pestiferous clouds in and around the swamp and lagoon, making a near anchorage or shore reconnaissance a most unpleasant experience. Nevertheless, the lagoon of San José Island is one of the most beautiful spots in the Gulf of California, hosting a myriad of long-legged and exotic birds — herons, ibises and egrets among many other species that nest and feed in the area.

Bahía Amortajada (Shelter Bay) is situated on the western-shore of San José Island, about 3 miles eastward of Punta San Evaristo across the peninsula shore. The bay is formed by a wide indentation embraced between the sandspit and lagoon at the southwestern point of the island, and Punta Salinas, 4 miles northwestward; the bay recedes about 1½ miles from a line joining these two points and includes Islote Cayo (Cayo Islet), lying a little over ¾ mile northwestward of the end of the sandspit.

The islet, about ¼ mile long and 100 yards wide, with a height of 40 feet at its southern end and 10 to 15 feet at its northern end, provides considerable protection against northwesterly winds for the anchorage in Amortajada Bay. Near the middle of the islet there is a break over which the sea washes at high water; a *reef* projects northward for about ¼ mile from the northern end of the islet. The southeastern portion of Bahía Amortajada is a deep bight running northeastward from the sandspit to the mouth of the lagoon entrance channel which drains into the sea at the head of the bay. *Landing* may be easily made on the sand beach anywhere along the shore. An *airstrip* has been constructed on a rise back of the lagoon near the mouth of the entrance channel.

In the vicinity of Amortajada Bay there may be found

the ruins of old barricades, remnant of a time when the island served as a military outpost; the sites of old sentry boxes are still plainly marked. There are a number of old and well-used campsites ranging from the time of the earliest Indian habitation, through the pearling era to present day fishing expeditions of the Vagabundos del Mar. A *well* with brackish water is located back from the shore. From the channel mouth the shore of the bay assumes a northwesterly direction, bringing up at Punta Salinas, a sandy point with a steep hill 50 feet high rising immediately behind it. *Good anchorage* may be had in the southern part of the bay in depths of 7 to 8 fathoms, well protected from prevailing winds and with good shelter from the fierce local storms known as *cordonazos*. *Good anchorage* may also be obtained in the bight southward of Punta Salinas, 200 to 300 yards from shore, in depths of from 6 to 12 fathoms; small vessels may anchor in 4 fathoms or less right off the beach. *Anchorage* may also be had northward of Salinas Point.

Two salt lagoons are situated near Punta Salinas where commercial salt is produced by natural evaporation. A small settlement is established here, and an *airstrip* has been constructed just back of the salt pans. A supply vessel calls monthly from La Paz to deliver supplies and to load salt. Emergency gasoline may be obtained here when sufficient supply is on hand. Behind the lagoons the land rises in broken ridges to a height of 1,830 feet. A low sand beach fringes the shore for about 3¼ miles northward of the point, and at the northern end of the beach there is a small ranch. *Fresh water* is obtained from a well at the ranch.

Eastward of the ranch the island attains its greatest elevation, 2,077 feet. For 2 miles northward of the ranch steep hills rise immediately from the water's edge. Winding between these hills is a deep arroyo, which extends about halfway across the island and opens to the sea at a position about 1 mile north of the ranch. About 2 miles north of the ranch the coast again becomes a low sand beach, which, broken by only a single bluff, extends to a point opposite Nopolo Point, across the San José Channel. Just north of the point on the island is a lagoon with a shallow opening to the sea. Thence to Punta Calabozo, the northern extremity of the island, a distance of about 4 miles, the coast trends northward in an unbroken line of steep, rock, dark-colored bluffs. A *reef of rocks,* partially above water, extends ¼ mile off Punta Calabozo.

Bahia Amortajada, Isla San José

Bahía Los Dolores

Between 1631 and 1633 a Spanish pearling expedition financed by Francisco de Ortega to the Gulf of California worked the rich pearl oyster beds around the island, at which time the island was given the name Isla de San José. The pearl beds were well known to the Spanish and a number of expeditions visited the area during the sixteenth and seventeenth centuries, reaping many beautiful and valuable pearls. The island was originally inhabited by a tribe of Pericue Indians whom the Spanish missionaries were at first unable to successfully proselyte and who persisted in raiding the mission settlements on the mainland. In 1720 Father Bravo succeeded for a time in pacifying them but in the process punitive expeditions of Spanish soldiers, who were sent on several occasions, very nearly wiped out the tribe; the rest mostly succumbed to European diseases introduced by the Spanish colonists and soldiers to the extent that the island was totally depopulated by 1750. Gold, silver and copper mining was pursued without remarkable success on the island during the nineteenth century.

Isla de San Diego (San Diego Island) which lies about 5½ miles northward of Punta Calabozo at the northernmost point of San José Island, has a length of nearly one mile and rises from the sea like the tip of a submerged ridge to a maximum elevation of 722 feet. Isla San Diego is another example of a barren volcanic uplift. A *reef of rocks* on which the sea usually breaks, and which is partly above water, extends southwestward about ¾ mile from the southwestern extremity of San Diego Island and ends in a small *rock awash*. Close to the reef's end there are depths of 4 to 5 fathoms and at nearly ½ mile farther southwestward a depth of 3 fathoms has been sounded, beyond which the depths increase rapidly. Between San Diego and San José Islands there is a passage with a width of 4 miles and

mid-channel depths of 30 to 44 fathoms, apparently clear of dangers. Caution should be exercised when navigating in this vicinity, however, as there may exist submerged dangers as yet uncharted. A *rock* lies several hundred yards offshore on the southeastern side of the island toward its southwestern end. *Anchorage* may be taken in an open bight on the northwestern side of the island just southward of the northwestern tip but the sheer rocky cliffs of the island offer little opportunity to land; access is afforded by a gentler slope on the southwest side. The island has an unusually large population of lizards and deer mice; scorpions are abundant.

Isla de Santa Cruz (Santa Cruz Island) situated about 3½ miles northward of Isla de San Diego and which it exceeds in length by about 4 times and in height by about twice, is a barren granite mass that rises abruptly from deep water. The two islands resemble each other very closely except for size, Santa Cruz being 3¾ miles long and about 1½ miles wide, rising from the sea to a maximum height of 1,500 feet and characterized principally by sheer straight cliffs. The northern end of the island terminates in a sharp point and the western face slopes up from the shore at an angle of 45°. The eastern side is comprised of bold spectacular bluffs 300 to 1,000 feet high, rising almost perpendicularly from the sea, and it is inaccessible; the only landing place on the island is at its southwestern end where there is a short stretch of gravel beach. The channel between Isla San Diego and Isla Santa Cruz is about 4 miles wide and is apparently free of dangers, but passage should be undertaken with due caution as submerged dangers may exist as yet uncharted. No bottom was sounded at 100 fathoms midway between the two islands, and a depth of 195 fathoms, sand, was found 1¼ miles from the shore of Isla de Santa Cruz. A little over 1 mile southwest of the island the water

is over 400 fathoms deep; off Las Ánimas Rocks, a depth of 940 fathoms has been sounded at a distance of 2 miles.

This chain of off-lying islands affords considerable shelter to the stretch of Peninsula coast opposite, and *protected anchorage* may be had in a number of coves both in the lee of the outlying islands and in coves along the peninsula shore. The narrowest part of the San José Channel lies between Lagoon Point on San José Island and Nopolo Point, opposite. Between Nopolo Point and Punta San Telmo, situated about 19 miles north-northwestward, the coast recedes somewhat and is comprised of a succession of rocky bluffs broken by a number of deep arroyos that open onto the shore above stretches of sandy beach. In the mouths of some of these arroyos small ranches are established. A range of mountains rises to an elevation of about 2,500 feet just back of the coast. Close offshore there are several prominent islets and rocks. Rocky bluffs from 300 to 400 feet high extend in succession for about 3¼ miles northwest from Punta Nopolo. Los Burros, a remarkable, broken, rocky cliff that rises from 300 to 500 feet high, projects somewhat from the general line of this coast about 2 miles northward of Punta Nopolo Sur; deep water lies close up to the face of the cliff. The coast northward tends inward forming the long sweeping bight of Bahía Los Burros (Los Burros Bay). A broad arroyo sloping toward the sea opens onto the shore with a long sandy beach at its mouth. Several ranch buildings are situated just back of the beach, with signs of cultivation of the flat arroyo bottom somewhat farther back. *Anchorage* may be taken in the roadstead with indifferent shelter and *landing* effected easily and safely on the shore in good weather.

Punta Dolores is situated about 3 miles farther northward and Bahía Los Dolores lies indented in the coast just northward of this point. The northern entrance of the bay is marked by a prominent red-colored bluff. When approaching from the south, what you first see when you round the headland is a long white sand beach and just back of it a straggling grove of date palms. A white-washed tile-roofed ranch house surrounded by a stand of ragged palms with dusty foliage is situated some distance back from the beach. Radio masts stand athwart the house. The rotting ribs and keel of the *San Diego,* a venerable old gulf fishing vessel, was to be seen for many years wrecked on the beach. This is Rancho Los Dolores, a somewhat larger establishment than the several others along this coast. It occupies a cultivated slope that stretches back to a range of broken mountains and it serves as a supply and trading point for a num-

ber of small ranches in the interior. Fresh provisions as available may be purchased here. *Fresh water* is brought from a *spring* at the old mission site, farther up the arroyo, in a make-shift series of open troughs and pipes to irrigate several hundred acres of citrus trees of various kinds — oranges, lemons and a sweet Mexican lime called limone; mangoes, figs and bananas are also grown here as well as a quantity of grapes. As on every Mexican rancho, there are a few domesticated animals, and chickens are kept for fresh eggs. The life is leisurely, the owner of the ranch quite hospitable, and willing to give permission to camp on his beach to those who respect the natural beauty of the place. The gasoline and diesel supplies stocked at the ranch are brought by boat from La Paz and are intended for the farm machinery used in the cultivation of the orchards and vineyards, and not for sale. There is a radio transmitter in operation at the ranch capable of communicating with coastal vessels and other shore stations and may be used for emergency situations. *Anchorage* may be taken close inshore and *landing* effected anywhere along the sand beach. The bay affords a rather exposed anchorage but is the port of call for several small coastal vessels which use it as a shipping and supply point for ranches in the interior. A number of inland trails converge here at the beach. A dirt track runs

up the canyon and across a pass to La Presa, 20 miles inland, which is connected by road to La Paz. About 3 miles up the arroyo from the ranch there are the ruins of an old dam and irrigation ditch and an ancient orchard of orange and lemon trees; these works and what little can be found of the walls of the old chapel abandoned in 1740, are all that remains of Mission Nuestra Señora de Los Dolores founded in 1721 by Father Guillen. The site of the mission was known to the Indians of the area as Apate and had a spring of sweet water of sufficient flow to irrigate the mission crops. The Los Dolores Mission fields and adjoining land were taken over as a private ranch early in the nineteenth century.

Isla Habaña is a great barren rock 90 feet high and about 1,000 yards long, with its sloping top whitened by birdlime. It lies 1 mile offshore, about 2½ miles northwestward of the red-colored bluff at the northern entrance to Bahía Los Dolores and can be seen from that anchorage; it is about 8¾ miles west-northwestward of Punta Calabozo, the north point of San José Island. Between Habaña Islet and the nearest point of the Baja coast opposite, there is a channel more than a mile wide with depths of 10 to 17 fathoms. On the coast west of Habaña Island there is a small bight with a gravel beach, back of which there is an open valley.

Rocas Moreno (Moreno Rocks) the largest of which is 40 feet high, lie ½ mile offshore, about 5½ miles northwest of Isla Habaña. Between the rocks and the shore of the peninsula there is shoal water; a *reef of rocks,* partly above water, extends about ¼ mile in a southeasterly direction from the largest rock. On the coast about 2 miles southward of these rocks there is a lagoon. The coast in the vicinity of Moreno Rocks is comprised of a pebble beach with occasional bluffs from 10 to 25 feet high of a yellowish and reddish color. A prominent mountain, rising to an elevation of 2,534 feet about 4½ miles inland and 8½ miles south-southwestward of Punta Telmo, provides a good mark.

Roca Negra (Black Rock), sometimes referred to locally as Roca Prieta, is 55 feet high and lies 1 mile offshore, about 2¼ miles northward of Moreno Rocks. The passage between Roca Negra and the coast is safe for small vessels but *caution should be observed when navigating in the vicinity as some shoal spots and hidden dangers may still remain uncharted.*

Bahía San Carlos, (San Carlos Bay), an open roadstead northwestward of Roca Negra affords *good anchorage* in depths of 5 to 7 fathoms. At a point along the shore in the center of the roadstead, a small lagoon formed at the mouth of a seasonal stream lies isolated from the bay by an exposed sandbar connecting long sand beaches on either side. At the north end in a small bight is another somewhat larger lagoon, the narrow entrance to which lies under the hook of the point. Thickets of mangrove and other green and yellow vegetation border the lagoon. The only *airstrip* between Puerto Escondido and Isla San José is a dirt runway back of the center of this bight. A two-story brick house and other buildings of Rancho Tambiche, not visible from the bay, are located on the north side of the runway; a resort is in the planning stage for this area.

Punta San Telmo (San Telmo Point) is a sharp rugged point 30 feet high which extends about ¼ mile from the general line of this coast; close off the point there are *numerous detached rocks.* The bluffs on either side of the point are of a reddish color and a prominent table mountain rises to an elevation of 2,818 feet, 6½ miles westward of the point. Southward of Punta San Telmo, between it and Bahía San Carlos, there are several small coves indented in the shore at the heads of which are white sand beaches off which *anchorage* may be taken and on which *landing* may be effected.

Puerto Los Gatos, immediately northward of Punta San Telmo, is a double-headed open bight with broad white sandy beaches divided by a spur of rocky red cliffs that extend a short distance into the cove, close off which there is a *submerged reef.* Southward of these cliffs another *short reef of rocks* extends into the cove, and between the two reefs the broad sandy beach slopes upward to yellow sand dunes partially covered with desert growth. Southward of this second reef a narrower, steeper beach continues southward to an upthrust of coastal cliffs off which a large, wide, *submerged rocky reef* extends into the cove toward the opposite entrance point, at a position ⅓ of the distance across the mouth. The clarity and color of the

Tambibiche, Bahía San Carlos

252

water usually reveals the presence and extent of this reef. *Caution should be taken to give the shoal water near this danger adequate berth when entering the cove.*

Anchorage may be taken just inside this reef, between it and the next proximate reef, in 3 fathoms, sand, just off the beach. A more spacious *anchorage* with greater swinging area may be taken off the beach in the northwestern part of the cove in 2½ fathoms, sand. A *reef of rocks* extends into the cove for a short distance from the red cliffs that comprise the northern entrance point of the cove.

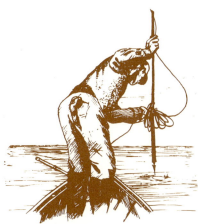

Directions: Due to the projection of these reefs from both entrance points of the bight restricting clear passage into the cove to ½ the distance across the mouth, careful conning to anchorage must be employed. On a course set well off a line connecting the black rocky point on the south side of the cove with the red cliffs on the northern entrance point, run until the middle of the sand beach in the northwestern part of the cove bears 275° magnetic; then bear into the anchorage on this course keeping midway between the submerged reefs on either hand.

Anchorage may be had in 2½ fathoms, sand, close off the beach. Dry washes draining separate arroyos run down to the beaches on either side of the dividing spur. The surrounding land is dry desert terrain with typical scattered desert growth; there is no habitation at Puerto Los Gatos nor any drinking water developed. The anchorage is quite pleasant in fair weather and remote from general coastal traffic.

The coast between Punta San Telmo and Punta San Marcial situated about 13½ miles north-northwestward is generally steep-to and rocky, with bluffs from 75 to 350 feet high interrupted by a few stretches of sand beach. High mountains rise immediately behind this straight stretch of coast. The water is deep close-to; depths of 10 fathoms to more than 30 fathoms are found within ½ mile of shore. There are no charted dangers. Pico Marcial is situated about 5 miles southwestward of Punta San Marcial.

Bahía San Marte (San Marte Bay) is formed by a slight indentation in the coastline between Punta San Marcial and a steep rocky bluff 1¾ miles southward. There is *good anchorage* within 700 yards of a small sand beach at the head of the bay, in depths of from 10 to 12 fathoms; smaller vessels may find good holding ground closer inshore, in 3 to 7 fathoms. When approaching this anchorage from the southward, *caution should be observed to avoid the foul ground in the vicinity of San Marcial Point.* The land behind the anchorage at San Marte Bay is very mountainous.

Punta San Marcial (San Marcial Point) is a moderately high rocky cliff surmounted by a peak 1,131 feet high; a *dangerous reef of rocks* extends about 1,200 yards southeastward from the point, and a *detached rock awash,* on which the sea breaks in any weather, lies about 800 yards farther southeastward. Passing vessels should give Punta San Marcial a berth of at least 2½ miles. Roca San Marcial (San Marcial Rock) 1¼ miles north-northeastward of San Marcial Point, is 25 feet high and of small extent but with numerous smaller rocks surrounding it; *foul ground with rocks awash,* and on which the sea breaks heavily, extends about ¾ mile northwestward. A passage ¾ mile wide and studded with rocks lies between San Marcial Rock and the nearest point on the peninsula shore. *Navigation caution: Owing to off-lying rocks and foul ground, San Marcial Rock should not be approached nearer than 1 mile and the passage between it and the coast should not be attempted except with local knowledge.*

San Marte Bay offers a good anchorage for small vessels with considerable protection from north winds. It may be easily identified from a considerable distance just south of Punta San Marcial. At the head of the cove there is a pleasant sand beach on which a dry landing can be made. This cove offers shelter from the prevailing weather and is an alternate anchorage to Bahia Agua Verde.

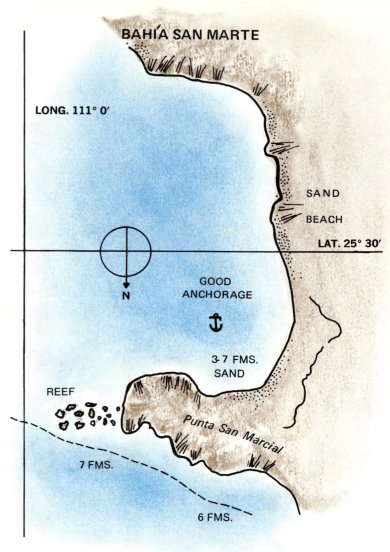

Bahía San Marte, Punta San Marcial

SECTION 20
PUNTA SAN MARCIAL to PUNTA CONCEPCIÓN

La Sentinela

Bahía de Agua Verde

Bahía de Agua Verde (Agua Verde Bay), located a little over 90 miles northwestward of La Paz and somewhat more than 100 miles southeastward of Mulegé, is a very popular and picturesque cove visited by cruising yachts and sportfishermen bound in either direction along this coast. For navigation see H.O. Chart 621, Southern Part of the Gulf of California; H.O. 850, Western Shore of the Gulf of California from Punta San Marcial to Bahía San Basilio with inset plan of Agua Verde Bay; H.O. Chart 849, Western Shore of the Gulf of California from Punta Púlpito to Isla San Marcos including Bahía Concepcíon; British Admiralty Charts #2324, Gulf of California and #2323, Manzanillo Bay to the Gulf of California; Mexican Carta Náutica F.H. 604, Parte Sur del Golfo de California.

Bahía de Agua Verde is a small bay situated about 2½ miles westward of Punta San Marcial. From San Marcial Point the coast trends northward ½ mile then turns abruptly westward for about 2 miles and embraces within this distance several small bights at the heads of which are short strips of white sand beach. Bahía de Agua Verde is the largest of these indentations, being tucked in a bight between two bold points; the northwesternmost, Punta San Pasqual, is a rocky bluff 338 feet high with a large, white needle-shaped pinnacle rock, La Solitaria, 115 feet high, lying about 600 yards off the point and providing an unmistakable landmark from seaward.

Directions: When approaching Agua Verde Bay from the southeast, lay a course to pass well outside San Marcial Rock and reef, no closer than the 10-fathom curve. When the beach through the mouth of the bay bears 240° magnetic, come around to that course and lay directly into the anchorage on a line drawn through the center of the bay between the entrance points, keeping Roca Solitaria on the starboard hand and giving adequate berth to the reef extending into the cove off the spur of rock on the northeast side. Navigators familiar with the dangers of the inside passage may save a good bit of time in calm weather by passing close along the shore and into the bay. When approaching from the northwest, passage may be made into the bay through the clear channel between the northwest entrance point and Roca Solitaria.

Agua Verde Bay affords a secluded and quiet *anchorage* in ordinary weather; its waters are sheltered by Punta Pasqual from the northwest quadrant and by the shores of the bay from the southwest around to the southeast, but the bay is open to the northeast and should be avoided in this weather. Agua Verde Bay can be windy and uncomfortable on occasion. Several adjacent coves offer alternative shelter. The *best anchorage* affording the greatest protection in all weather is a small bight in the northwest corner of the bay off a white sand beach in 3 to 5 fathoms, sand; it is protected on the seaward side by a spur that ends in a high rock, off which a reef extends into

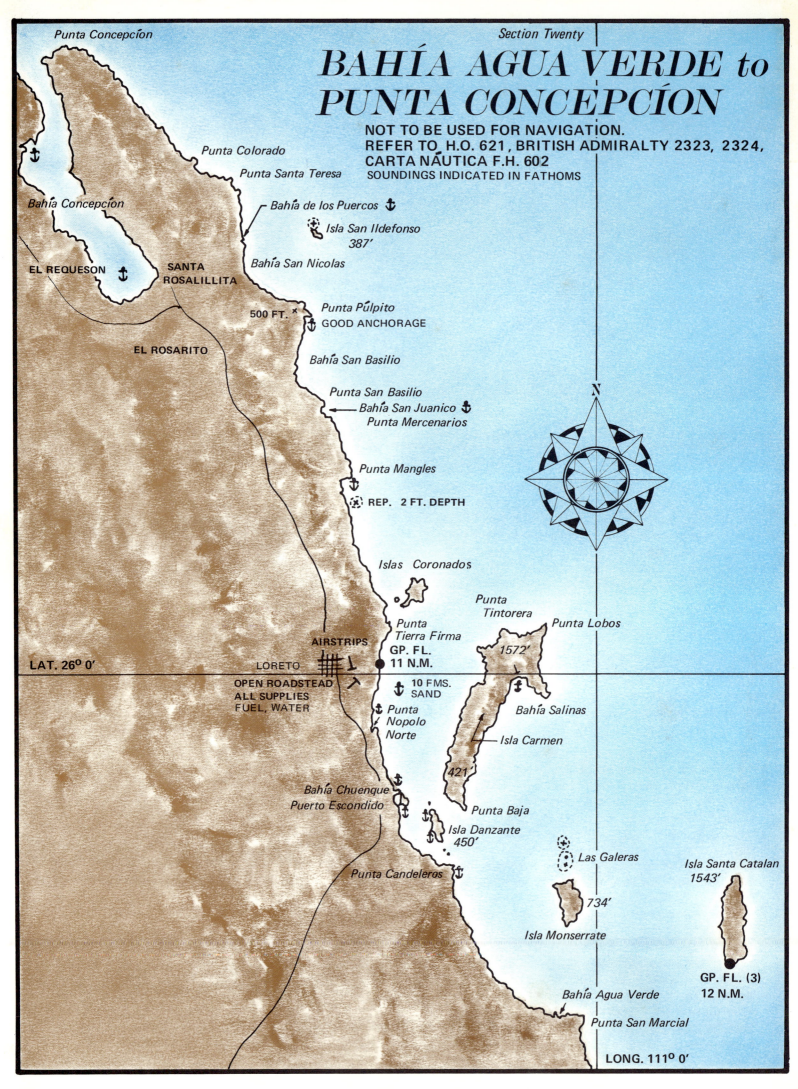

Punta Concepcíon

BAHÍA AGUA VERDE to PUNTA CONCEPCÍON

NOT TO BE USED FOR NAVIGATION.
REFER TO H.O. 621, BRITISH ADMIRALTY 2323, 2324,
CARTA NÁUTICA F.H. 602
SOUNDINGS INDICATED IN FATHOMS

Punta Colorado

Punta Santa Teresa

Bahía Concepcíon

Bahía de los Puercos

Isla San Ildefonso
387'

Bahía San Nicolas

EL REQUESON   SANTA
                ROSALILLITA

500 FT.   Punta Púlpito
           GOOD ANCHORAGE

EL ROSARITO

Bahía San Basilio

Punta San Basilio
Bahía San Juanico
Punta Mercenarios

Punta Mangles

REP. 2 FT. DEPTH

N

Islas Coronados

Punta
Tintorera   Punta Lobos

Punta
Tierra Firma   1572'
GP. FL.
11 N.M.

AIRSTRIPS

LAT. 26° 0'

LORETO   10 FMS.
                SAND
OPEN ROADSTEAD
ALL SUPPLIES   Bahía Salinas
FUEL, WATER
            Punta   Isla Carmen
            Nopolo
            Norte

                        421'

Bahía Chuenque   Punta Baja
Puerto Escondido
            Isla Danzante
            450'

                            Las Galeras
                                            Isla Santa Catalan
                                            1543'
Punta Candeleros

                        734'
                    Isla Monserrate   GP. FL. (3)
                                            12 N.M.

                    Bahía Agua Verde

                    Punta San Marcial

                                    LONG. 111° 0'

Bahía Agua Verde, looking southeast

the cove. *Caution: There is a rocky pinnacle covered 10 feet which lies about 250 yards eastward of the 249-foot hill on the western side of the bight; the pinnacle lies in 3½ fathoms and exhibits a brown patch in otherwise light greenish water. After locating the position of the submerged pinnacle, cast anchor well clear to avoid fouling the ground tackle when swinging.*

From this anchorage Roca San Damien, the pinnacle rock to the northwestward which lies about ½ mile offshore, may be seen across the low sandy isthmus at the head of the bight. *Landing* may easily be made on the beach. *Anchorage* may also be taken on the eastern side of the bay and *landing* effected near a bluff point, close off the northeast side of which there are several *rocks awash* at low water.

Back of the larger of the two white sand beaches in the vicinity of the detached 60-foot high *pinnacle rock* on the southwest shore of the cove there is a small cluster of palms and green foliage; this is the site of a village of thatched houses where several families are engaged in ranching and fishing. There is as well in this small settlement, a school and a church. Brackish but *potable water* is obtained from the shallow well. A trail runs along the coast communicating with a small village 22 miles northward and to which a road connects with Loreto.

Isla Santa Catalan, off-lying Punta San Marcial about 13 miles east-northeastward and situated about 17½ miles north-northwestward of Isla de Santa Cruz, appears from a distance as a cliff-sided island with a high central ridge on which may be seen two pronounced peaks, the highest of which is 1,543 feet above the sea. The island is 7½ miles long lying north and south, and about 2 miles wide. The eastern shore of the island is almost completely formed of lofty rock cliffs that plunge steeply into the sea. The cliffs are steep-to with deep water to their foot, except for a single break about 1 mile east-northeastward of the northern summit where a flat delta formation extends out nearly ½ mile from the shore. This cobbled delta slopes gradually from its seaward end toward a narrow arroyo that opens in the otherwise precipitous wall.

The western coast of the island is also steep-to but less precipitous than the eastern side with several small coves indented between protective points along the shore. A *rock awash* on which the sea breaks lies 300 yards off the more easterly of the two northern points of the island. No soundings are available for the channel between Isla Santa Catalan and Monserrate Island, 12 miles westward. An isolated depth of 18 fathoms, rock, has been sounded and charted about 6 miles southward of Isla Santa Catalan.

A *navigation light* is exhibited 56 feet above the sea from a *white tower* situated on the southern point of the island; the light exhibits a **white group flash of three flashes in a period of 12 seconds:** flash 0.5 second, eclipse 1 second; flash 0.5 second, eclipse 1 second; flash 0.5 second, eclipse 8.5 seconds. The light may be seen for a distance of 12 miles in clear weather. The light structure is set well back of the point. There is a *landing place* on a sandy beach in a small bight just eastward of the light where *anchorage* may be had, protected from northerly weather.

Dusky Shark

257

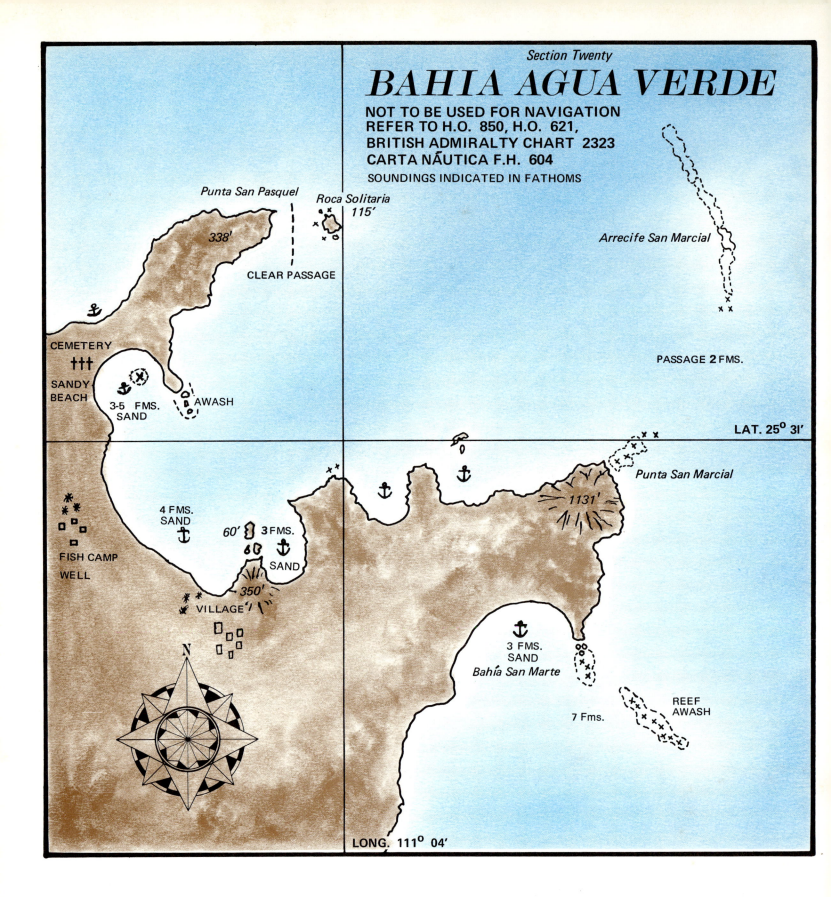

BAHIA AGUA VERDE

NOT TO BE USED FOR NAVIGATION
REFER TO H.O. 850, H.O. 621,
BRITISH ADMIRALTY CHART 2323
CARTA NÁUTICA F.H. 604
SOUNDINGS INDICATED IN FATHOMS

Punta San Pasquel

Roca Solitaria
115'

338'

Arrecife San Marcial

CLEAR PASSAGE

PASSAGE 2 FMS.

CEMETERY

SANDY BEACH

3-5 FMS. SAND

AWASH

LAT. 25° 31'

Punta San Marcial

1131'

4 FMS. SAND

60'   3 FMS.

FISH CAMP WELL

SAND

350'

VILLAGE

N

3 FMS. SAND

Bahía San Marte

REEF AWASH

7 Fms.

LONG. 111° 04'

Vagabundos in pursuit of shark livers and fins occasionally make temporary camp on the island; rotting shark skeletons, an assortment of abandoned and rusting gear as well as graves marked by simple crosses attest to their brief but eventful residence. Sufficient water to support a lengthy stay is always a problem but seasonal tinajas, natural rock basins filled with still water, and two small springs provide a limited source on Isla Catalan; a few stunted palms grow near one of the springs and mark its existence. A rusted beacon tower stands near the shark camp in a cove at the southwest end of the island.

Santa Catalan Island supports various small animals and a variety of vegetation including the largest growth in number and size of the great barrel cactus on any of the Gulf Islands; many specimens reach a height of 10 feet and a diameter exceeding 3 feet. A mature plant may be more than 100 years old, a truly remarkable thing to behold by naturalist and layman alike; rugged and enduring in its natural, unspoiled state it can be mutilated or destroyed with a few hacks of a machete in a moment of thoughtless destruction, lost for the study or enjoyment of the next adventurer to pass this way. There is also on the island a unique rattle-less rattlesnake, discovered by naturalists only a few years ago and somewhat of a curiosity in the animal world. Treks on the island after sundown are avoided due to the danger of stepping on one of these poisonous reptiles in the dark. Such examples of flora and fauna and many others to delight the explorer with an eye to the unique manifestations of countless centuries of isolated evolution are to be seen on many of the uninhabited offshore islands in the Gulf of California and constitute a naturalist's reserve which the Government of Mexico seeks to protect.

Isla Monserrate, its southern end situated about 8½ miles northward of Punta San Marcial and about 7 miles from Punta San Cosme, the nearest point on the mainland, is a barren volcanic and limestone uplift with a relatively level profile, the highest point in its south central part rising 734 feet above the sea. Viewed from a distance, a terraced appearance is readily apparent; the second highest mesa in the southern part of the island is at a 560-foot elevation, and a distinct marine terrace which is now 40 feet above sea level may be seen at various places.

The island is 4 miles long lying in a north-south direction and 2 miles wide at its widest point. Its northern

extremity is formed by a double point. Depths of 50 to 80 fathoms are sounded in the channel between the island and the mainland. The shore of Isla Monserrate is generally steep-to, the southern and eastern sides comprised of a succession of bold rocky bluffs off which, in several places, sunken rocky ledges project ¼ mile seaward. Off the north and northeast points are some *detached rocks*. On the north side of the island there is a small bight with a short stretch of sandy beach near the northwestern point; the western side of the island has a low rocky shore with several points shelving into the sea. Despite dense stands of cacti and thorny scrub, the sterile lava slopes of Isla Monserrate are deeply eroded even though the rainfall is quite minimal and sporadic. The island is uninhabited and rarely visited, a sanctuary for nesting seabirds.

Las Galeras are two rocky islets lying close together about 1¾ miles northward of Isla Monserrate; the easternmost and larger islet is 70 feet high and a *rocky reef* projects southeastward from it for about ½ mile; the western islet is 40 feet high with a passage between the two islets approximately 250 yards wide in which there are many rocky ledges and the soundings irregular. The least depth sounded in the passage between Isla Monserrate and Las Galeras is 7 fathoms. A *dangerous rock*,

Coastline, vicinity of Punta San Cosme

Punta San Cosme, Rocas San Cosme and San Damien

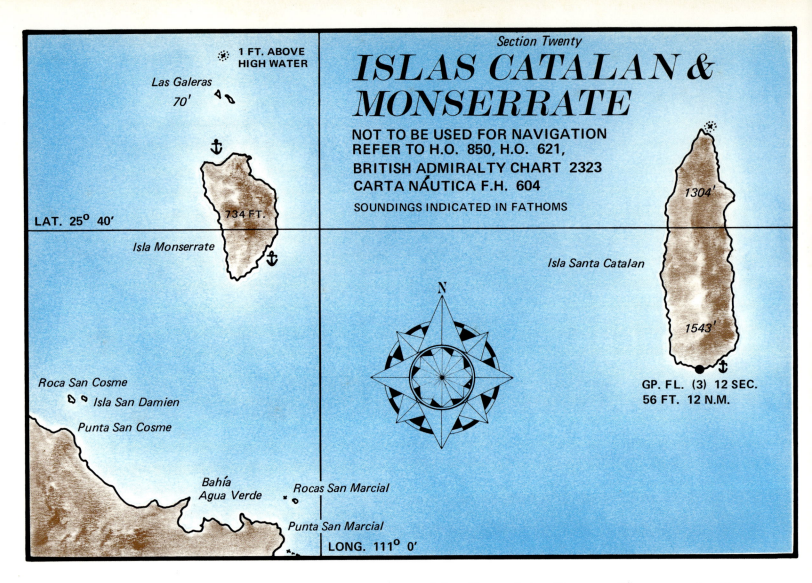

ISLAS CATALAN & MONSERRATE

NOT TO BE USED FOR NAVIGATION
REFER TO H.O. 850, H.O. 621,
BRITISH ADMIRALTY CHART 2323
CARTA NÁUTICA F.H. 604
SOUNDINGS INDICATED IN FATHOMS

1 FT. ABOVE HIGH WATER

Las Galeras 70'

734 FT.

LAT. 25° 40'

Isla Monserrate

Roca San Cosme
Isla San Damien
Punta San Cosme

Bahía Agua Verde
Rocas San Marcial
Punta San Marcial

LONG. 111° 0'

N

1304'

Isla Santa Catalan

1543'

GP. FL. (3) 12 SEC.
56 FT. 12 N.M.

---

1 foot high and surrounded by sunken rocks, lies about 1¼ miles northward of Las Galeras. In the passage between this rock and Las Galeras, depths of 11 to 22 fathoms have been sounded.

Punta San Cosme is situated about 4 miles northwestward of Punta San Pasqual and between them the coast forms a bight. About 1 mile westward of Punta San Pasqual there is another rocky bluff point off which, to the northwest, there are two rocks above water. Westward of the latter point is a stretch of sand beach about 2 miles long, back of which are several ranches and an arroyo that opens onto the shore; beyond the arroyo the coast assumes a northwesterly direction.

Punta San Cosme (San Cosme Point) is a rocky cliff rising abruptly to a hill 225 feet high. Two sharp twin peaks, which rise to an elevation of 3,808 feet about 4 miles southwestward of the point, provide a prominent landmark. A shoal with the least depth over it of 6 feet lies in a position about ¼ mile off the eastern side of Punta San Cosme. A group of rocks lies less than 1 mile northward of Punta San Cosme; Roca San Cosme, the westernmost and largest, rises 75 feet above the sea, and ⅓ mile eastward, San Damien Rock rises 45 feet above the sea. At about 700 yards southwestward of San Damien Rock are several low rocks, 2 to 4 feet high with rocks awash near them. Soundings in the passage between these rocks and the shore show no bottom at 10 fathoms except for the narrow 1-fathom shoal situated ¼ mile eastward

of San Cosme Point. However, this passage should only be attempted with local knowledge.

The coast between Punta San Cosme and Punta Candeleros, situated about 10¾ miles north-northwestward, is comprised of a succession of bluffs alternating with sand beaches, and backed by mountains that rise to an elevation of 2,000 feet. Roca Blanca (White Rock), referred to on some charts as Trinidad Islet, rising 127 feet above the sea and surrounded by a number of smaller rocks, some of which are above water, is situated about 4 miles southeastward of Punta Candeleros and about 2 miles offshore. There is deep water close off these rocks on all sides and a clear passage between them and the mainland westward.

This coast has many unexplored bights with inviting anchorages; however caution should be observed in this area as shoals and submerged dangers may exist as yet uncharted. One small *anchorage* used by sportfishermen and yachtsmen affording shelter from all but northerly weather is tucked snugly into the precipitous coastal cliffs just southward of Punta Candeleros. A prominent high rocky cliff eroded to reveal its elemental strata rises above a sheer broken rocky point protruding somewhat from the general line of the coast. The narrow mouth of a small cove opens on the north side of this point. The steep cliff that drops vertically into the sea for the last 30 feet forms the western wall of the cove; a long narrow spur, connected at its southern end to the point by a low isthmus, forms the

Coastline looking northwest to Punta Candeleros, Roca Blanca

eastern side of the cove and affords protection from the sea, which breaks over the isthmus at high water but disturbs the anchorage very little. A curving sandy beach lies at the head of the cove. *Anchorage* may be taken off the beach in 2½ to 3½ fathoms, sand, employing ground tackle fore and aft. There is only enough room in this cove for one or two vessels at most. A sandy flat, well protected from the weather, extends a short distance beyond the beach. A depth of 15 fathoms has been sounded just outside the entrance to this cove.

Punta Candeleros is a prominent steep-to bluff about 50 feet high behind which the land rises abruptly. The point may be approached closely; depths of 95 fathoms, mud, have been sounded within ½ mile of it.

Los Candeleros (The Candlesticks), are three pinnacle rocks lying northward of Punta Candeleros and between it and the southern extremity of Isla Danzante. The southernmost rock is situated about ¼ mile northward of Punta Candeleros with depths sounded close around it of 18 to 26 fathoms; the middle rock, which is about 100 feet high, lies about ½ mile farther northward with depths sounded immediately around it of 17 to 22 fathoms; there is a small *detached rock* lying close aboard its northwest side and a *rocky reef* about 500 yards off its southwest side. The northernmost rock in the Los Candeleros group, which is about 40 feet high, is situated about ¾ mile northwestward of the middle rock and about the same distance from the southern end of Isla Danzante; depths of 13 to 27 fathoms have been sounded close around this rock, however a group of *submerged rocks* lies off its northern end.

While large deepdraft vessels are advised to avoid passage between the southernmost rock and Punta Candeleros as well as between the northernmost rock and Isla Danzante, small yachts and fishing vessels will find conve-

nient and clear passage through the center of either of these channels employing due care. *Caution: A minimum depth of 10 to 15 fathoms has been sounded in the passage between the southernmost rock and Punta Candeleros with no known dangers; however, when passing between the northernmost rock and Isla Danzante, keep to the center of the channel and give a wide berth both to the rocky reef which extends several hundred yards southeastward from the southern extremity of the island marked halfway along its length by a pinnacle rock that rises 25 feet above water, and, on the southern side of the channel, to the submerged rocks off the northern side of the rock islet. On the northern side of the passage between the middle and southernmost rock there is a rocky reef which lies several hundred yards southwest of the middle rock; by giving this reef adequate berth, a clear channel for safe passage also exists between these two rocks.*

Candeleros Anchorage is a small partially enclosed shallow bay immediately westward of Punta Candeleros. The bay is open to the north-northeast but reasonably sheltered by the off-lying Los Candeleros Rocks, Isla Danzante to the north-northwest and Isla Carmen to the north. This cove affords *good protection* from southerly weather. The best *anchorage* is under the hook of the protecting headland on the southeast side of the cove off a sand beach on which a *landing* can easily be made. The water is quite shoal close to the beach but deepens abreast the sharp rock atop the headland. A sandy flat extends from the beach about ½ mile beyond the berm in this corner of the cove. The beach continues in a sweep around the perimeter of the cove for about ½ mile. A dirt road runs from the cove to the newly paved highway that communicates with Puerto Escondido, about 6 miles northwest.

Bahía Candeleros

The coast between Punta Candeleros and Punta Coyote, situated about 6 miles northwestward, recedes to form a large bay in which there are several isolated rocks and which is sheltered from the northeast around to the southeast by Isla Danzante and Isla Carmen.

Mission San Juan Bautista Malibat, founded in 1705 midway along the shore of Candeleros Bay at a place the Indians called Ligúi, was sustained until 1721 when it was abandoned as too arid to support adequate agriculture and too exposed to the raids of the hostile Pericu Indians from the offshore islands. Traces of the ruins of the main chapel have all but disappeared where they stood on a flat above a fairly good beach. The depths along the shore of this bay are irregular, there being shoal patches of but 2½ fathoms

at ½ mile offshore. A group of rocks, the principal ones of which are 40, 15 and 35 feet high, respectively, from south to north, lie up to one mile offshore in a position about 3½ miles northwestward of Punta Candeleros. Passage between the rocks and the shore should not be attempted as the channels are foul; there are depths of 16 fathoms, however, in the passage between these rocks and Isla Danzante.

Isla Danzante lies close offshore in Candeleros Bay between Punta Candeleros and Punta Coyote; it is about 2½ miles from Puerto Escondido at its closest point and 1½ miles across a navigable channel from the southern end of Isla Carmen. Danzante is a barren, uninhabited island rising to a maximum height of 450 feet toward the southern end, which is situated about 2½ miles from Punta Candeleros

Cove close south of Punta Candeleros

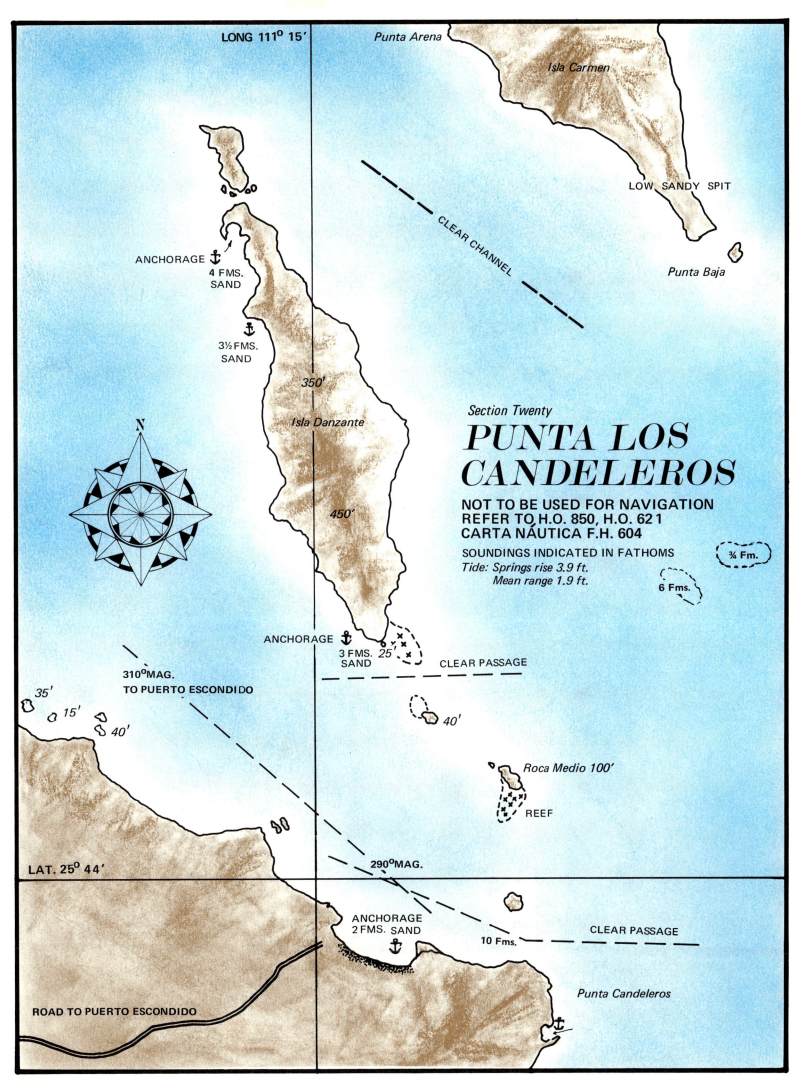

LONG 111° 15'

Punta Arena

Isla Carmen

LOW SANDY SPIT

CLEAR CHANNEL

Punta Baja

ANCHORAGE ⚓
4 FMS.
SAND

⚓
3½ FMS.
SAND

350'

Isla Danzante

450'

Section Twenty

PUNTA LOS CANDELEROS

NOT TO BE USED FOR NAVIGATION
REFER TO H.O. 850, H.O. 621
CARTA NÁUTICA F.H. 604

SOUNDINGS INDICATED IN FATHOMS
Tide: Springs rise 3.9 ft.
Mean range 1.9 ft.

¾ Fm.

6 Fms.

ANCHORAGE ⚓
3 FMS.   25'
SAND   CLEAR PASSAGE

40'

Roca Medio 100'

REEF

310°MAG.
TO PUERTO ESCONDIDO

35'

15'

40'

290°MAG.

LAT. 25° 44'

ANCHORAGE
2 FMS. SAND
⚓

10 Fms.   CLEAR PASSAGE

Punta Candeleros

ROAD TO PUERTO ESCONDIDO

⚓

Isla Danzante, Isla Carmen, Los Candeleros

and 1½ miles from the nearest point on the shore of the bay. There is a detached pinnacle rock, 25 feet high, off the southern end of the island from which a *sunken reef* extends southeastward. Isla Danzante is 3½ miles long, oriented north-northwest by south-southeast; it is almost a mile wide at its widest point in the southern half, tapering in an irregular shape toward the northern end, which is separated in the last half mile from the main body of the island by a shallow channel encumbered with rocks. The coast of the island is mostly comprised of bold rocky bluffs rising precipitously to a layered volcanic uplift from which the island is formed; deep water lies close-to around most of its shoreline.

Anchorage may be had by deepdraft vessels off a strip of sand beach on the southwestern side of the island; a cove located on the northwestern side of the island affords *good anchorage* for small vessels with drafts of 8 feet or less. This latter cove affords excellent protection in all but westerly weather, which rarely blows from that quarter. *Directions: When making for the anchorage, keep to the middle of the entrance midway between the headlands; a sunken reef lies just off the northern entrance point, and a sunken rock off the southern entrance point.*

Best anchorage may be found in the cove on the starboard hand in 2 to 4 fathoms, sand. *Anchorage* may be taken in the cove on the port hand, also sand but shallower. *Landing* may be made on the narrow sand beaches at the heads of the coves with easy access to the interior of the island. Southward of this anchorage area two additional coves afford protection; *anchorage* may be had in the southernmost cove off a narrow sand beach in 3½ fathoms, sand.

The water throughout this area is quite clear; the bottom at the heads of the anchorage coves is shallow and sandy, dropping quickly to greater depths close offshore. Occasionally Vagabundos — shark and turtle fishermen — camp on the island; otherwise it is uninhabited. However, this has not always been so. Evidence of Indian middens may be found in the arroyos back of these coves and beaches.

There is a channel between Isla Danzante and Isla del Carmen, situated northeastward, which is from 1½ to 2¼

miles wide and free of dangers. It is frequently used by vessels coming from the southern part of the gulf and bound for Puerto Escondido or Loreto. Tidal streams in the channel are quite strong and should be taken into account by sailing vessels.

Caution: An isolated rock, with a least depth of 4½ feet and an extent of about 100 yards, lies 3¾ miles eastward of Danzante Island, about 4 miles northeastward of Punta Candeleros and almost 3 miles southeastward of Punta Baja, the southern extremity of Carmen Island. This danger lies in the southeastern approach to the channel between the two islands and is steep-to, affording little or no warning of near approach by depth sounding devices. Depths of 6 fathoms, however, have been sounded as recently as 1965 on a bank about 1½ miles west-southwestward of this isolated rock shoal. The area of the bank is about 1½ miles in length, oriented northwest by southeast, and about ½ mile wide.

Isla Danzante and Isla del Carmen, together with the maze of various offshore islets and rocks, provide considerable shelter for the waters of Candeleros Bay and the excellent enclosed harbor of Escondido at its northern end. The land behind Bahía Candeleros, beyond a relatively level coastal shelf, rises precipitously to rugged and deeply eroded mountains which form the southern portion of Sierra de la Giganta. El Cerro de la Giganta, the highest peak of the range, with an elevation of 5,794 feet and surrounded by several smaller peaks, lies about 24 miles northwestward of Punta Coyote. About 2½ miles southward of Punta Coyote there is a strip of sand beach, behind which there is a fertile green slope with a ranch established at its foot. Punta Coyote, at the northwest end of Candeleros Bay, is a steep bluff rocky headland rising from the sea to a height of 75 feet. It forms the southeastern extremity of an irregularly shaped peninsula, about 1¾ miles long and about a mile wide at its southern end on which there is a hill 350 feet high. The peninsula is joined to the mainland at its northern end by a narrow sandy isthmus on which sand dunes have been

Isla Danzante, Isla Carmen

formed. This peninsula encloses the small land-locked harbor of Puerto Escondido.

Puerto Escondido (Hidden Harbor) is a perfectly land-locked and secure harbor for small vessels in any weather. It is a favorite anchorage for cruising yachtsmen and sportfishermen and an excellent refuge in the severest blow. It is located about 22 miles northwest of Agua Verde Bay and 12½ miles southeast of Loreto. For navigation refer to H.O. Charts 621 and 850; British Admiralty Charts #2323 and #2324; Mexican Carta Náutica F.H. 604.

Channel leading to Puerto Escondido

Puerto Escondido lies immediately westward of Punta Coyote, covered by the hook of the Coyote Peninsula. The semicircular outer bay, about ¾ mile wide, formed between a deeply indented cove behind the hook and the mainland westward, affords *good anchorage* for deep-draft vessels in depths of 6 fathoms, sand. Passage into the outer bay is wide and unencumbered and may be undertaken at any stage of the tide. A concrete jetty with a T-head extends eastward into the bay from the western shore at a position near the entrance to the inner harbor. The outer face of the wharf is 300 feet long, protected along its entire length by rubber tire fenders; there are depths of 4 to 6 fathoms alongside. Back of the concrete wharf several service structures have been built in anticipation of commissioning the harbor facilities.

A *dirt airstrip* has been bulldozed on the south side of the service road that connects to the Loreto/Villa Constitución Highway and has been in use from time to time. (Refer to Appendix.) As late as 1971 there was no activity at the wharf facility and no fuel, provisions, or services to be had, except fresh meat on the hoof from a ranch nearby. The harbor at Puerto Escondido is intended to serve the rich agricultural region newly developed around Villa Constitución, which is also served by the new deepwater port of San Carlos in Magdalena Bay on the Pacific coast. An intercoastal highway has been constructed and has been nearly all paved between these two ports; the same road connects as well to Loreto, 14 miles distant by land. The intended purpose is to save transportation around the cape when shipping products and receiving supplies to and from both mainland Mexico and

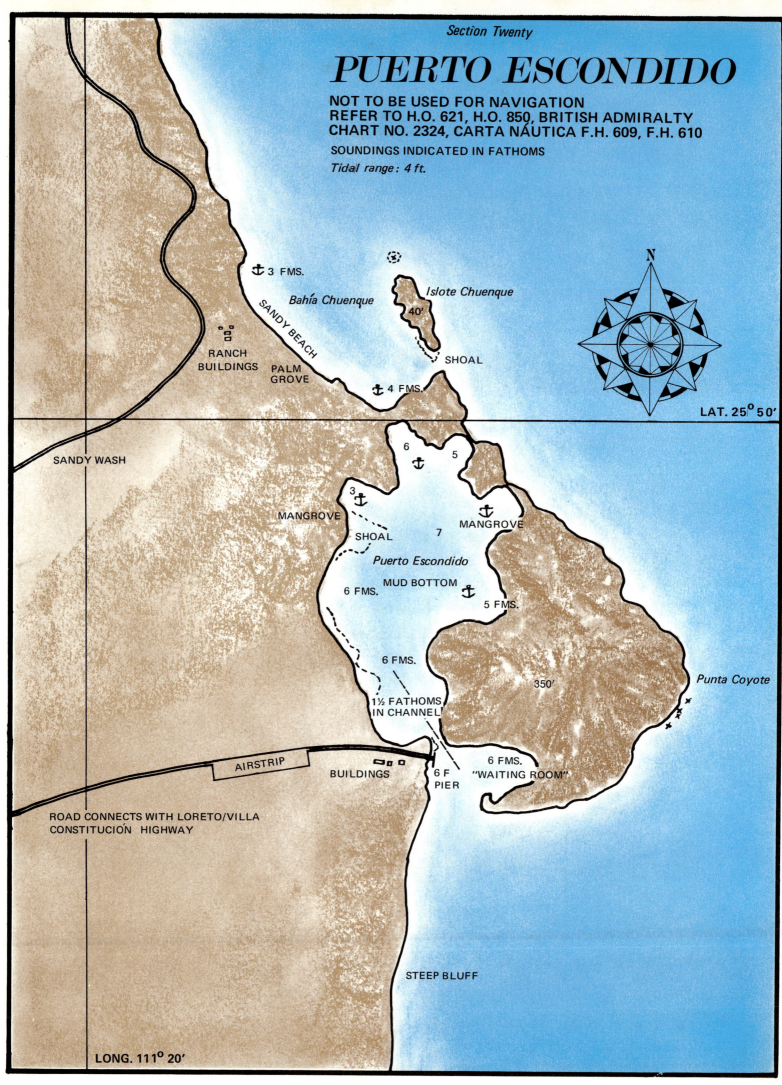

PUERTO ESCONDIDO

NOT TO BE USED FOR NAVIGATION
REFER TO H.O. 621, H.O. 850, BRITISH ADMIRALTY
CHART NO. 2324, CARTA NÁUTICA F.H. 609, F.H. 610
SOUNDINGS INDICATED IN FATHOMS
Tidal range: 4 ft.

⚓ 3 FMS.

Bahía Chuenque   *Islote Chuenque*

40′

SHOAL

SANDY BEACH

RANCH
BUILDINGS   PALM
GROVE

⚓ 4 FMS.

N

LAT. 25° 50′

SANDY WASH

6   5
⚓

3   ⚓
⚓

MANGROVE   MANGROVE

SHOAL   7

Puerto Escondido

MUD BOTTOM   ⚓

6 FMS.   5 FMS.

6 FMS.

350′   Punta Coyote

1½ FATHOMS
IN CHANNEL

AIRSTRIP   6 FMS.
BUILDINGS   6 F   "WAITING ROOM"
PIER

ROAD CONNECTS WITH LORETO/VILLA
CONSTITUCIÓN HIGHWAY

STEEP BLUFF

LONG. 111° 20′

Pacific coastal ports. There is also a plan formulated to build a resort complex on the bay with an improved airstrip and sportfishing facilities.

Inner Harbor — Northward of the concrete T-pier a channel leads to the inner harbor. The entrance is about 75 feet wide from shore to shore with a least depth of 9 feet at low water carried through a navigable channel about 30 feet wide between a sandspit on the south side and a rocky shore on the north side. A light green coloration of the water between the pier and the sandspit reveals a *shoal patch* on the south side of the channel. *Directions: Keep to the northern shore of the outer basin when making for the entrance and pass the shoal on the port hand. The tide ebbs and flows through this narrow pass with a 3- to 4-knot current and it is advisable for deep-keel vessels to await slack water at full and change before attempting the passage.*

TIDES — The tide at Puerto Escondido is chiefly diurnal, the subordinate phase being negligible. Springs rise 3.9 feet; the mean height is 1.9 feet.

The inner basin of the harbor is of irregular shape, about ¼ mile wide and 1 mile long, oriented north and south. The depths range from 4 to 7 fathoms throughout the central area and from 2 to 2½ fathoms along some portions of the shore, mud bottom. While the waters of the bay can be as clear as crystal, they are sometimes turbid and murky due to tidal stirring; the surface of the inner harbor is almost always calm as a lake. During the summer months the weather can be quite hot and airless and a more ventilated anchorage in the outside harbor may be preferred. A *shoal* skirts the shore along the length of a sandy flat on the west side of the basin at the north end of the flat. A *good anchorage* may be had in the northwestern end of the basin in a small cove sheltered by hills on three sides.

There are mangrove thickets along the shore of the bay and at low tide rock oysters may be gathered in clumps from the intertidal branches or from the exposed rocks. The bay is a natural spawning ground for every conceivable form of sea life and a variety of mature species can be seen passing in and out through the narrow

Puerto Escondido

Bahía Chuenque

channel. A windmill sticking up over the tops of a grove of trees marks a small ranch about ½ mile back from the bay. The family operating Rancho Escondido is quite hospitable and they are the only persons living in the vicinity. There is *good water* at this place.

Puerto Escondido was first visited by the Ortega pearling expedition in 1633. At that time entrance to the bay was gained through the north end where the sandspit and cobbles now enclose the harbor. Early reports by the Mission Fathers also describe a navigable mouth in this location. Ortega named the bay Bahía de Los Danzantes (Bay of Dancers) because the Indian inhabitants had greeted his landing with a display of native dances accompanied by the playing of wooden flutes. During Atondo's visit in 1685 the harbor was renamed San Ignacio de Loyola. The Jesuit missionaries utilized Puerto Escondido as a harbor of refuge, built a sizable breakwater, a warehouse, and a large wharf and employed the port as a supply depot for the missions in the interior of the peninsula as far as the west coast. Ruins of the wharf were still visible at the turn of the century. It has been conjectured that it was the Jesuits who engineered the fill across the northern entrance of the bay to create a completely enclosed port, but it is not unreasonable to assume that natural forces, such as the great flood that inundated Loreto in 1827, created the bar from a sudden and voluminous wash.

Bahía de Chuenque (Chinque Bay) is a small crescent bay immediately northward of Bahía Escondido about 1¾ miles northwestward of Punta Coyote. The bay is open to the north and affords shelter from all winds except those blowing into the mouth. On the eastern side of the bay, just off the entrance point, there is a small island, Islote de Chuenque, which is about 650 yards long and 40 feet high. Since the passage between the islet and the mainland point immediately southward is shoal and encumbered with *submerged rocks,* the bay should be entered from the north, rounding well off Islote de Chuenque

to clear a *submerged rock* detached from its northern end.

Anchorage may be taken at the head of the bay anywhere along the white sand beach in depths of 3 fathoms, sand. There is a cluster of palms just back of the beach at its head and a small group of ranch buildings close westward. *Anchorage* may also be had in a snug but narrow cove indented between the rocky hill of the eastern entrance point and a rocky spur close southward in depths of 4 fathoms, sand. *Landing* may be made safely anywhere along the beach. The highway to Loreto passes immediately behind the bay on a roadbed just above the shore; a dirt road runs down to the beach at the west end of the cove. Bahía Chuenque was once a sizable Indian rancheria; there are some old crumbling stone foundations in the vicinity which are the remnants of an early mission visiting station.

Punta Nopolo Norte (Nopolo Point North, distinguished from Punta Nopolo Sur) is a bold rocky knob, 75 feet high, about 7 miles north-northwestward of Punta Coyote and 5½ miles from Loreto. The intervening coast is characterized by bluffs 15 to 75 feet high and pebble beaches with deep water close-to; depths of 10 to 15 fathoms are sounded within 200 yards of the shore, deepening to 120 fathoms at a little more than ½ mile. The rocky knob of Nopolo Point, situated on the north side of the mouth of a river that empties into the sea, is almost an island, connected to a curving beach only by a narrow sandy isthmus. Westward of the point is Ensenada Nopolo, a small shallow cove open to the northward, fringed by a sand beach. *Anchorage* sheltered from southerly winds may be had here over a sand bottom.

The coastal highway runs to Loreto just back of the beach. The cultivated bottom land of a ranch lies a little more than a mile northwest of the cove on the west side of the highway. The coast from Nopolo Point northward, to the anchorage at Loreto, a distance of about 5½ miles, is formed by a low sand beach at the foot of a fertile and well-watered alluvial slope of considerable extent. *Shoal water* extends for nearly ½ mile off this coast for about 2 miles northward of Nopolo Point. Off Punta Primera Agua, a low sandy point which projects but little from the

Punta Nopolo (Norte)

general line of the coast, about 1½ miles southward of Loreto, there is a *shore bank* on which there are depths of 1 to 3 fathoms extending ½ mile seaward between this point and a position close southward of Loreto.

Loreto is a town of some 2,000 population; the number of the citizenry has varied considerably over the 273 years since the time of its founding in the seventeenth century. When Jesuit Father Juan María Salvatierra of Italy first landed on the beach on October 15, 1697, to found a mission, he brought with him a party of 9 men, including a carpenter and a blacksmith and an escort of six soldiers. In 1752, when after great labor the mission buildings had been completed, irrigation systems developed and the lands surrounding tilled, watered and cultivated, as many as 7,000 Indian converts called Loreto their home.

When all the buildings were intact after its completion in 1752, the Loreto Mission comprised the largest settlement on the west coast of North America. The mission complex embraced a comprehensive colonial establishment: It was the center of Government and residence of the Father Superior of all the California missions; it commanded and supported and was in turn protected by a garrison of soldiers, equipped with small arms and brass cannon, who occupied the peninsula's largest presidio; a shipyard for the construction and repair of coastal exploration vessels and supply ships was established on the waterfront and a number of small but quite seaworthy vessels were built and launched here. A navy training school was founded for Indians to prepare them to handle the ships in and across the gulf and around the cape. Salt ponds, located some distance from the village but closeby the shipyards, were employed for seasoning timbers brought from the mainland. The timbers that were placed in these seasoning and preserving ponds were principally "kneed" pieces of oak, huge segments weighing several tons with a natural bend created by the juncture of a limb with the trunk of a tree, especially prized for joining the stem and the sternpost to the keel, or the main deck beams to the frames. Immersed in the salt pond for a year or two, the dense oak turned black and hard, "pickled" and virtually impervious to rot. It is interesting to note that in the official archives in the *Lonja* in Seville, ship-timber seasoning ponds are recorded as having been in use at Loreto, Mexico, and Pensacola, Florida, in 1746. In 1940 the ponds were located by Randolph Leigh when he sailed the gulf in *Lascar II*, at which time he actually examined the timbers remaining in the ponds, forgotten by the Spanish and Mexican Governments for over 200 years and regarded by the villagers as too heavy to be used in any way.

Loreto, as well as being the ecclesiastical, political and military center of operations for all of the peninsula, also controlled all commercial enterprise. Among the latter pursuits which it dominated was the pearl fishery and, before the expulsion of the Jesuits in 1764, Loreto had become the principal pearl market in the region. Profits from pearls alone, based on estimates from payments to the Spanish Crown under the "Kings Fifth" formula, ran to about $25,000 annually, no small sum as calculated in that day. The King's treasure was kept in the Royal Treasure House until ready for shipment to Spain; in Loreto it was comprised of a small one-room structure of stone with iron bars fixed across the windows and located closeby the church. It is still in use today, but in a humbler role, as a residence with a lean-to addition.

Nuestra Señora de Loreto was named for a statue of the Virgin from the Port of Genoa, which was brought intact to the new mission at the time of its founding by Father Salvatierra and probably represents the most interesting artifact to be seen in the church today.

Despite repeated earthquakes, especially the very destructive one of 1877, the church has remained more or less intact, the severest damage suffered being the collapse of about ¼ of the roof, which has since been repaired and replaced. Most of the rest of the mission complex has either crumbled to rubble and disappeared to scavengers or has been rebuilt and utilized for other purposes. Some of this rebuilding has been done with the old ceiling timbers of the chapel and the original oaken beams supporting the church bells.

Carved in the stone of the arch above the entrance to the church are the words: "Cabeza y Madre de la Missiones de Las Californias." ("Head and Mother of the Missions of the Californias.") Father Salvatierra established Loreto as the principal mission center for the colonization of California, and from this base of operations over a period of 70 years, the Jesuits founded 21 other missions throughout Baja California.

Loreto was now to serve as a frontier base of operations for the exploration and settlement of Alta California. This was the starting point for the historic overland trek of the Gaspar Portola and Junípero Serra party in 1769, which ultimately led to the establishment of the Nuevo California Missions and to the discovery of San Francisco Bay. It was the object of this party to establish settlements at both ends of the Northern Territory, at Monterey and at San Diego, and at San Buenaventura midway between, so as to render the Northern Territory securely under the dominion of Spain. Two brigantines, the *San Carlos* and the *San Antonio,* left Loreto a month apart to support the overland party with supplies by sea, and a third vessel, the ill-fated *San José,* after several false starts, got underway a year later, only to be wrecked in a storm without reaching her destination. The efforts, hardships

Ciudad de Loreto

and successes along the way are told elsewhere but the results of this expedition are eloquently manifest in the chain of missions that held sway for a half century and shaped the stable society which the United States inherited with the purchase of California from Mexico under the treaty of Guadalupe Hidalgo in 1848.

Through a turbulent and trying 132 years as Capitol of California, Loreto was the pivotal point of exploration and development activity throughout the Californias. During the Spanish regime, a messenger left Guaymas once a month, crossed the gulf in a small boat, and landed at Loreto, carrying the mail for all of California. From Loreto the letters and packets were carried overland to the various missions as far away as Monterey. After the demise of the mission system, this mail service was discontinued and for many years an entire year would pass without news from California or communication with mainland Mexico, except for that carried sporadically by the masters of trading vessels calling for water, firewood or fresh provisions.

Little remains in Loreto's present somnolent and dusty state to remind one of its distinguished role in the development of California or the longevity of its importance as the seat of central government. But a sharp eye for historical artifacts can turn up a wealth of memorabilia here and there in the village and on the surrounding ranches.

Loreto, the oldest continually occupied town in Baja California, is situated approximately midway between Punta Nopolo Norte and Punta Tierra Firma at the foot of a fertile alluvial plain which slopes inland to the sharply pinnacled mountain range of Sierra de la Giganta. The highest peak of this range, La Giganta, rises to an elevation of 5,794 feet, and stands as the most prominent landmark back of this stretch of coast. The village is fronted by what is essentially an open roadstead, called, however, Bahía Paniacis. It is partially protected from winds by Punta Tierra Firma, while 20-mile long Carmen Island, which lies roughly parallel to the coastal plain in a position about 8 miles offshore, breaks the force of the winds from the south and east. Punta Coyote at Bahía Escondido lies 12 miles southward; the southeast point of the larger of the two Coronados Islands lies 7 miles northeastward. For navigation see H.O. 850, Western Shore of the Gulf of California; British Admiralty Chart #2324, Cape San Lucas to San Diego Bay, with the Gulf of California; Mexican Carta Náutica F.H. 604, Parte Sur del Golfo de California.

A great grove of palms clustered all along the shore of the village site shades whitewashed and red-tiled roofs of the numerous houses. Through the southern portion of the village runs a watercourse, Arroyo de las Parras, a brackish estuary closed off from the sea at its mouth most of the year by a sandbar. A *submerged sandspit,* with 2 fathoms of water over it, extends out nearly ½ mile from the shore, close southward of the mouth of the estuary. A *navigation light,* shown 39 feet above the sea, is exhibited from a red metal framework tower close eastward of Loreto Village. The light exhibits a **white group flash of two flashes in a period of 10 seconds:** flash 0.3 second, eclipse 1 second; flash 0.3 second, eclipse 8.4 seconds; and is visible for 11 miles in clear weather in the sector 181° to 273°.

Anchorage is in the open roadstead, ½ mile off the village, in depths of 8 to 9 fathoms, with good holding ground in sand. *Directions: Bring the church to bear in range 256° with Pilón de Parras (Sugarloaf Peak) 3,674 feet high, situated about 8½ miles inland. This anchorage is exposed to winds from the north, northeast and southeast and when blowing from these quarters send heavy seas sweeping across the anchorage, rendering it quite uncomfortable; at such times it is advisable to seek shelter in the lee of Isla Carmen at Puerto Ballandra about 7 miles offshore.* The anchorage is good in ordinary weather and the usual practice is to arrive at Loreto in the early morning, obtain supplies and fuel and conduct ship's business before noon, leaving before the prevailing northeast wind springs up in the afternoon. *Anchorage may also be had about ¾ mile southward of the church dome about ½ mile off the end of the pier at the Flying Sportsman's Lodge.* Loreto is a port of entry, and yacht cruising permits must be cleared with the Captain of the Port upon arrival. His office is located on the quay, a one-room adobe building marked by a flagpole in front.

TIDES — The tide at Loreto is chiefly diurnal, as it is along most of the peninsular coastline north of La Paz, the range being around 4 feet.

FACILITIES — General provisions, fresh fruits and vegetables, meat and eggs are available in quantities dictated by seasonal supply. Throughout the fertile countryside quantities of produce are cultivated sufficient to export to other parts of the peninsula, and to the mainland as well. There are several stores which carry a variety of soft goods, hardware and miscellaneous supplies and which dispense gasoline from a pump. Diesel fuel is available and aircraft gasoline is stocked in several octanes, but in limited supply. Aircraft gasoline is dispensed from two large tanks above ground at the Flying Sportsman's Lodge on the south side of town; regular gasoline may be had at the pump in town or in 55-gallon drums, stored several places in the town for vehicular and marine use. Since it is trucked from La Paz, it is sometimes in short supply but every ranch keeps what it needs for its own use and when unobtainable in sufficient quantities in the town, gasoline can very often be procured from the ranchers. However, one must bring his own container or rent an empty drum, wherever available, for use in transporting fuel to the dock. A full gasoline drum will float in seawater and can be rolled to the end of the dock, cast into the water and towed to the vessel at anchor, probably as simply as any other method of handling. A double bight of ¾-inch manila or nylon line, fastened securely to the deck and passed underneath and around the drum, will handily suffice as an efficient purchase to roll the drum up out of the water and onto the vessel; a heavy canvas folded beneath the drum may be employed as a fender. (The circumference of the drum provides adequate leverage and acts as a rolling sheave.)

Engine room supplies, lubricating oil and a limited number of parts are available in this port. Special parts can be ordered from Mazatlán, La Paz, Guaymas, or San Diego and flown in by scheduled or chartered aircraft.

A T-head masonry jetty extends a considerable distance into the bay before the town and serves as the main wharf. A smaller stone jetty is built out from the Flying Sportsman's Lodge to the southward and serves as a sport-fishing wharf. *Good water* is available but should be tested for purity and if necessary boiled or chemically treated before drinking or used in cooking. Water obtained in the town must be carried in a vessel's own portable containers. Treated and bottled water is available at the Flying Sportsman's Lodge. There are *two airfields* at Loreto: a municipal hard-packed dirt field on the north side of town and a private dirt field at Flying Sportsman's Lodge on the south side of town; the latter has not been in use recently. (See Appendix.) A municipal diesel-electric plant furnishes power to the city and operates for a limited time each day.

While Loreto has never been known as a commercial fishing port and supports only a small canoe fleet for its local fishery, construction of an elaborate filleting, freezing and fish-meal plant was commenced in 1965, with the intention of developing the port as a fish food producing center. The offices, ice-making plant, freezer, cold storage, and power plant are virtually complete, housed in well-constructed buildings. Most of the machinery is on the site but the untimely death of the developer brought the project to a halt, where it stands waiting to be completed.

PUBLIC ACCOMMODATIONS — There are several sportfishing resorts offering overnight accommodations and meals. The Flying Sportsman's Lodge, a motel-like cluster of concrete block cottages with hot and cold showers, maid service, and al fresco dining patio, swimming pool and sportfishing dock, is located about 1 mile south of the center of the town. Sportfishing launches are operated for charter by the lodge. Hotel Oasis is located in the town and offers similar accommodations and facilities. Pensión Doña Blanca, across from the church, offers lodging and meals in town. The above accommodations are listed in a descending order of cost but all are comfortable and hospitable.

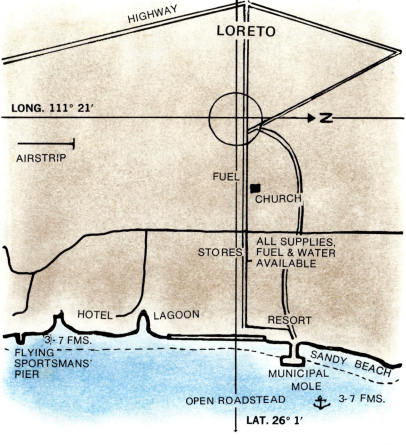

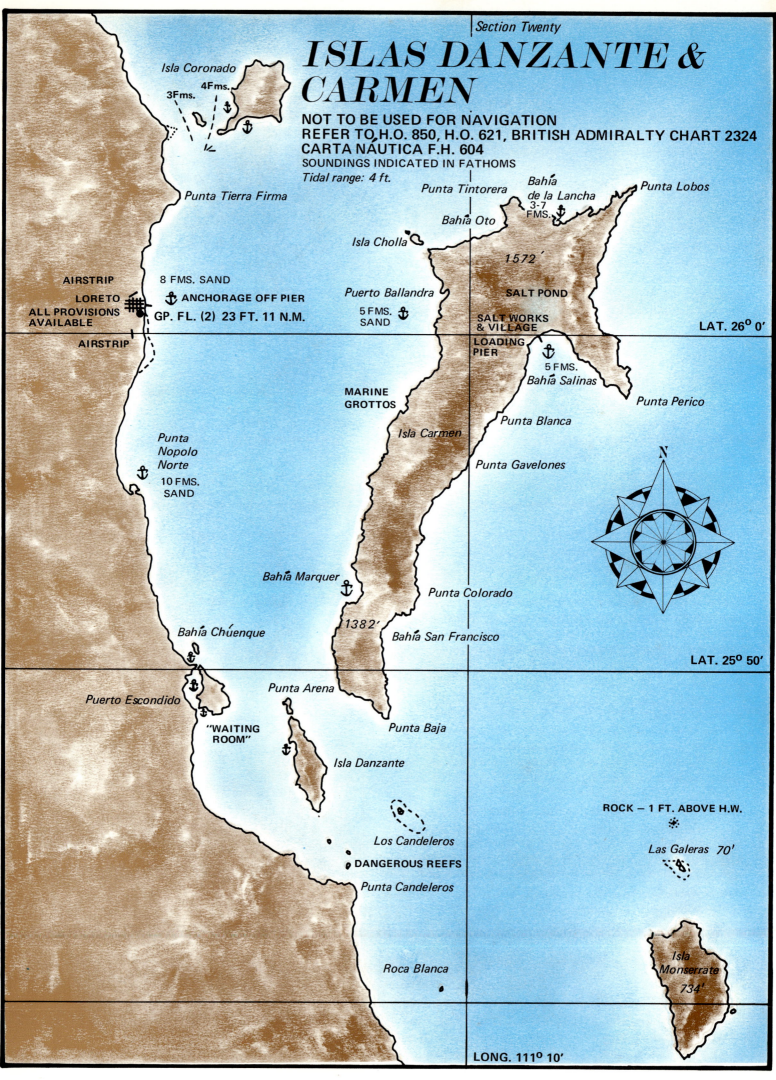

Section Twenty

ISLAS DANZANTE & CARMEN

NOT TO BE USED FOR NAVIGATION
REFER TO H.O. 850, H.O. 621, BRITISH ADMIRALTY CHART 2324
CARTA NÁUTICA F.H. 604
SOUNDINGS INDICATED IN FATHOMS
Tidal range: 4 ft.

Isla Coronado

3 Fms.   4 Fms.

Punta Tierra Firma

Punta Tintorera   Bahía de la Lancha   Punta Lobos
3-7 FMS.

Bahía Oto

Isla Cholla   1572'

AIRSTRIP
LORETO
ALL PROVISIONS
AVAILABLE

8 FMS. SAND
ANCHORAGE OFF PIER
GP. FL. (2) 23 FT. 11 N.M.

Puerto Ballandra
5 FMS.
SAND

SALT POND

SALT WORKS
& VILLAGE

LAT. 26° 0'

AIRSTRIP

LOADING
PIER

5 FMS.
Bahía Salinas

Punta Perico

MARINE
GROTTOS

Punta Blanca

Isla Carmen

Punta
Nopolo
Norte
10 FMS.
SAND

Punta Gavelones

N

Bahía Marquer

1382'

Punta Colorado

Bahía San Francisco

LAT. 25° 50'

Bahía Chúenque

Puerto Escondido

Punta Arena

"WAITING
ROOM"

Punta Baja

ROCK – 1 FT. ABOVE H.W.

Isla Danzante

Las Galeras 70'

Los Candeleros

DANGEROUS REEFS

Punta Candeleros

Isla
Monserrate
734'

Roca Blanca

LONG. 111° 10'

COMMUNICATIONS — There is a new post office with frequent, regularly scheduled mail pickup and delivery by air. There is a government radio and landline telegraph office, located across from the plaza, which accepts public messages to all points both domestic and foreign. A good road runs inland 32 miles to Commondú in the Santo Domingo Valley, a rich agricultural center; a new coastal highway communicates with Mulegé and Santa Rosalía to the north, Puerto Escondido, La Paz, Villa Constitución to the south and Magdalena Bay on the Pacific coast. Taxis are for hire in the town, buses run between the various towns of the peninsula on a loose schedule, the ubiquitous Mexican cargo truck carries a variety of produce and supplies to and from Loreto weekly and a regularly scheduled airline serves the town. Charter flights and private planes make frequent visits to Loreto. A ferry communicates regularly to Guaymas across the gulf. Cargo and fishing vessels call at the port and salt is regularly loaded and transported from Salinas Bay, Carmen Island, a few miles offshore.

MARINE EMERGENCIES — Aid in marine emergencies may best be obtained from local commercial fishing vessels, cruising yachts in the vicinity, sportfishing launches docked or cruising off the resorts, and from Mexican Naval vessels stationed at Guaymas or La Paz or on patrol in the vicinity. Ship-to-shore frequencies 2182, 2638 and 2620 kiloHertz are actively monitored by all the foregoing vessels and by shore stations along the coast. Flying Sportsman's Lodge monitors UNICOM aircraft frequency 122.8 megaHertz, as do a majority of the other gulf resorts. A good practice is to always maintain a daily or twice daily schedule with several coastal or mobile stations within communicating distance for safety.

MEDICAL FACILITIES — There is a doctor in Loreto and a new government hospital. There are first aid treatment facilities at Salinas Bay, Carmen Island, offshore. Regularly scheduled aircraft passenger service leaves Loreto for La Paz, Guaymas, Mazatlán and San Diego, where more extensive medical facilities are available.

SOURCES OF ADDITIONAL INFORMATION — Flying Sportsman's Lodge, 510 West Sixth Street, Suite 418, Los Angeles, California, phone (213) 625-1551.

Isla del Carmen (Carmen Island) is one of the largest islands in the Gulf of California; it lies elongated northnortheast and south-southwest in contrast to the north-south trend of the neighboring Baja California coastline, forming a 20-mile long wedge-shaped coastal channel that shelters the mainland from Puerto Escondido to Punta Tierra Firma. The island lies offshore a little more than 3 miles, measured between Punta Coyote and Punta Arena, at the southern end of the intervening channel. The northern end of the channel has a width of a little more than 5 miles between the eastern tip of Isla Coronados and Cholla Islet off the westernmost point of Carmen Island; the island's closest approach to Loreto is about 8 miles.

Carmen Island is of volcanic origin and of irregular outline; a range of peaks runs its entire length of 17½ miles, and the island rises to a maximum elevation of 1,572 feet about 7 miles from the northern end. It is approximately 2 miles wide for the most part of its length, widening to 5 miles toward Salinas Bay, with a maximum width of 7 miles measured across its northern and broadest portion. The island affords *numerous sheltered anchorages* and has a number of protected bays and coves, the most important of which are Puerto Ballandra, Bahía Salinas and Puerto de la Lancha. At first glance the island gives the appearance of a barrenness verging on sterility but in the arroyos there is some considerable growth of cactus and brush, revealing the presence of ground water; here and there a mangrovebordered tidal lagoon, rich with birdlife, cuts back at the head of a cove. Several *springs of fresh water* that run year around are to be found on the island.

Punta Baja, the southernmost point of Carmen Island, lies about 5 miles north-northeastward of Punta Candeleros on the mainland and is comprised of a low gravel spit; *shoal water* over a stony bottom extends over ¼ mile off this point. The land behind the point slopes gradually upward toward the hills and is covered with grass and low bushes. The western coast from Punta Baja to Punta Arena, a distance of about 2¼ miles, consists of a sand and gravel beach with a few *detached rocks* close-to near Punta Arena, but with deep water a short distance offshore. Several sharp peaks, 600 to 900 feet high, rise close behind the shore. Punta Arena is low and sandy; on the beach near the point are some huts.

Bahía Marquer (alternately called Bahía Marqués), located about 3 miles northward of Punta Arena, is a small inlet at the head of which there is a short sand beach; back of the beach there are some huts and close off the northern point of the bay there are some *detached rocks*. The intervening coast is comprised of steep rocky bluffs and deep arroyos. The remainder of the western and northern coasts of the island is comprised mostly of rocky bluffs with a few intervening sand beaches; *detached rocks* lie close inshore in places, but moderately deep water is sounded close-to.

Puerto Ballandro (alternately called Puerto Ballandra) is a small, well-sheltered cove situated about 12½ miles northward of Punta Baja, in a position about 1¾ miles southward of the bluff northwestern point of Isla del Carmen. This snug *anchorage* is reached through a relatively narrow entrance about 600 yards wide, situated between two moderately high promontories which open into a roughly circular basin a little over ½ mile across. The two headlands are connected within by a sweeping arc of sand; along the shore of the bay, at the mouth of an arroyo which opens onto a sandy beach, there are two small mangrove-bordered tidal lagoons. The bay has a depth of 5 to 5½ fathoms in most parts, with a moderately deep submarine canyon running from the entrance across the basin in a northeasterly direction almost to the beach. *Anchorage* may be taken on the north side in 3 to 4 fathoms, white sand, very close to the beach and well sheltered from northerly weather; for shelter from southerly weather *anchorage* may be taken in a small bight on the southwest side of the basin, or, alternatively, near the rusty wreck of a half sunken vessel that lies just off the beach in the shallows near the southern shore. Puerto Ballandro is both a popular anchorage in fair weather for cruising yachtsmen and sportfishermen, and a sheltered haven in which to wait out foul weather from every point of the compass except the west. A sizable arroyo runs back from the bay and, after passing through a narrow gorge where two great walls of red lava blown with potholes almost close the gap, it opens into quite an extensive valley. A wide bed of gravel winds down from the hills in a dry riverbed. At the mouth of the valley is a small ranch with a corral. Puerto Ballandro is connected with the village at Bahía Salinas, located on the eastern side of the island, by a trail that leads through a system of valleys to the opposite side of the island.

Isla Cholla (Cholla Islet) is a small, low sand islet about ⅓ mile long, rising 20 feet above the water and situated about 1¾ miles northward of Puerto Ballandro, at a position ¼ mile off a bluff point at the northwestern extremity of Carmen Island. Off the northwestern end of Cholla Islet are some *detached rocks*. Between this islet and Punta Tintorera, situated about 2¾ miles northeastward, the coast turns sharply eastward for about 1¼ miles and then curves again to the north, forming Bahía de Oto, an open inlet in which vessels may *anchor* sheltered from southerly winds. Near the mouth of an arroyo which opens on the shore at the head of this bay are some seasonally occupied huts.

Marine grottos, carved in the lava cliffs by the constant onslaught of the sea, may be found along the north shore of Carmen Island. Large enough to be explored by dinghy for a considerable distance within the sea wall, these grottos offer a unique combination of submarine gardens, and fascinating sea life beautifully modulated by a filtering of sunlight for undersea photography.

Punta Tintorera is a steep bluff about 80 feet high with detached rocks lying close offshore. Between this point and Punta Lobos, situated about 3¾ miles eastward, there is a small open semicircular bay called Puerto de la Lancha, the shores of which are mostly gravel beaches and where *sheltered anchorage* can be obtained from southerly winds in depths of 2½ to 7 fathoms.

Timber Hitch

Close eastward of Puerto de la Lancha is another small *landlocked cove,* the entrance to which is about 200 yards wide. The cove is about ¼ mile long with depths throughout of 3 to 5 fathoms. The mouth of an arroyo opens into the cove and a small stream runs seasonally across the gravel beach. Seasonally occupied huts are built just back of the beach at the head of the cove. *Anchorage,* sheltered from southerly winds, may be taken here by small vessels. A trail runs from this cove to Bahía Salinas on the opposite side of the island.

Punta Lobos, the northwestern extremity of Isla del Carmen, is comprised of a rocky headland about 125 feet high, surrounded by *detached rocks* and connected with the main body of the island by a low narrow strip of land. From Lobos Point the coast turns abruptly southward, and from there to Punta Perico, a distance of about 6 miles, there is a succession of rocky bluffs with occasional *detached rocks* close offshore.

Punta Perico (Perico Point) is a sharp, rocky cliff surmounted by a reddish-colored peak 460 feet high. *Navigation danger: A detached rock 30 feet high lies very near the point; 150 yards southward of this rock is another submerged rock; a shoal bank with a depth of 6 fathoms over its outer end extends from the western side of the point.*

Bahía de Salinas (Salinas Bay) is entered between Punta Blanca, situated about 10 miles north-northeastward of Punta Baja, and Punta Perico, lying about 3½ miles further eastward. From Perico Point the coast tends sharply northwestward for about 2½ miles, then westward, then gradually curves southward to Punta Blanca, forming the deep indentation of Salinas Bay. Punta Blanca at the southwestern entrance to the bay is a steep bluff surmounted by a hill; *detached rocks* extend about 200 yards out from the point. The bay affords *good anchorage* in depths of 5 to 6 fathoms with excellent holding ground in sand over heavy mud, sheltered from all winds except those from the southeast around to the south-southwest. While the bay offers shelter from the severe northerlies that sometimes blow in this region, its shallow waters can become quite rough due to winds funneling down the arroyo at the head of the bay. Small vessels are advised to seek anchorage close to the shore under these conditions; however, the anchorage is only clear of dangers outside the 3-fathom curve. Occasional squalls blowing into the bay may be expected in August and September.

BAHIA SALINAS

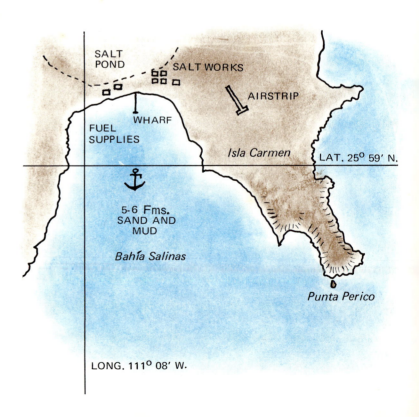

SALT POND

SALT WORKS

AIRSTRIP

WHARF

FUEL SUPPLIES

Isla Carmen

LAT. 25° 59′ N.

5-6 Fms. SAND AND MUD

Bahía Salinas

Punta Perico

LONG. 111° 08′ W.

At the head of the bay, separated from the sea by a shingle beach and cradled in the sunken crater of an extinct volcano, is a large and ancient salt pond, the level of which rises and falls with the tide. The pond, occupying a large portion of the valley that runs back from the bay, is about 1½ miles long and 1 mile wide. The salt pond has been the source of commercial salt for several centuries and constitutes one of the finest and purest salt deposits in the world. A salt works is established here and a small village is located back of the beach at the head of the bay. A wharf utilized for loading salt into lighters for transfer to vessels at anchor offshore extends into a depth of 3 fathoms before the village. A narrow gauge railway runs from the salt works to the end of the wharf. Some provisions may be purchased at the general store in the village but fresh water brought in from Loreto is in short supply. There is a radio station in the village which communicates with incoming vessels, aircraft and shore stations.

The solar salt plant operated here by a Mexican company, Salinas del Pacifico, produces a very pure grade salt for domestic and foreign markets and employs several hundred workers who reside on the island. The hot, dry climate is ideal for salt production with evaporation said to be as much as 8 feet per year. Although the ponds are capable of producing as much as 200,000 tons annually, output is less than ¼ that capacity. The oldest ship in the Mexican merchant marine, the picturesque steamer *San Luciano*, loads salt from Carmen Island for mainland ports.

Since these deposits have been worked from the time the Spanish first settled Baja California in the sixteenth century, the salt would have been exhausted long ago save for the tidal replenishment through an old wooden pipe which communicates with the sea. Widely distributed evidence of coral reefs and associated sea shells around the margins of the salt deposits indicate an ancient origin to these salt beds. Recently a geological team drilled a test hole to a depth of 40 feet at the bottom of the shallow pond which revealed many horizontal layers of marine sands impregnated with salt alternating with mud and sand washed down from the surrounding hills.

Bahía Salinas

Punta Gavelones (Gavelones Point) is situated about 2 miles southward of Punta Blanca, the intervening coast between these points being steep and rocky. A sharp peak 1,491 feet high is situated 1¾ miles north-northwestward of this point. Southward of Punta Gavelones the coast recedes somewhat and is comprised mostly of steep bluffs. A small stream, that flows during the rainy season, discharges into the sea through a short strip of sand beach at a position about 2 miles southward of Punta Gavelones. About 1½ miles farther southward the mouth of Arroyo Blanco opens onto the shore.

Punta Colorado (Red Point), a little more than 1¼ miles southward of Arroyo Blanco, is a bluff point of moderate elevation and of a reddish color; close to the point there are some *detached rocks*.

Bahía San Francisco (San Francisco Bay) is a large open bight formed by the coast receding considerably between Punta Colorado and Punta Baja. Southward of Punta Colorado the bluffs become lower, finally terminating in a sand beach which extends to Punta Baja, and a complete circumnavigation of the island. The coast for a distance of at least 1½ miles northward of that point is skirted by a *shore bank* that extends outward for as much as ½ mile and should be given adequate berth. *Navigation note: A current set of about 1¼ knots southwestward has been experienced by navigators 10 miles eastward of Carmen Island.*

The run from Loreto to Punta Concepción, at the mouth of Bahía Concepción, covers a distance of about 60 miles and includes several excellent coves and bays and offshore islands where sheltered anchorage may be obtained.

The coast between the Loreto Anchorage and Punta Tierra Firma, situated about 4 miles to the northward, is low and sandy. There is good *anchorage* anywhere along this coast within ½ mile of the beach in depths of from 3 to 7 fathoms. A round building stands on the point. Low bluffs begin a little northward of Punta Tierra Firma and at about 2 miles northward there is a low bluff point with an arroyo opening onto the shore on its southern side. A *shore bank*, with depths of 3 fathoms at its outer edge, extends from ¼ mile to ½ mile offshore for about 1½ miles southward and 2 miles northward of Punta Tierra Firma; outside this bank the soundings increase rapidly, 120 fathoms being sounded at 1½ miles off the point.

Islas Coronados (Coronados Islands) are comprised of a small volcanic island and an adjacent low rocky islet situated close offshore about 3 miles northeastward of Punta Tierra Firma; the southwestern extremity of the island lies but 1½ miles eastward of the low bluff point near the arroyo mentioned above, a narrow and shoal passage intervenes between the island and the mainland, suitable only for small vessels. The larger island is of irregular contour, about 1¾ miles long, oriented north and south, and 1½ miles wide at its widest part, rising from the sea to a height of 928 feet near its northern end; an extinct volcano forming the main part of the island is capped by a cinder cone at this summit. A low, flat segment of the island, ending in a sandspit mixed with stones, extends about ¾ mile from its southwestern side; off the point of the spit are some

Islas Los Coronados, Sea of Cortez

detached rocks and a reef. The remainder of the coastline of the island is characterized by steep rocky bluffs. Two marine terraces are readily discernible at 100 feet and 140 feet above the present sea level.

A low sandy islet, surrounded by shoal water that plainly reveals its shallow depth by a light green coloration, lies about midway between Islas Coronados and the mainland, dividing the passage into two channels. The passage westward of this islet, between it and the mainland, is about 800 yards wide with a least depth of 3 to 3½ fathoms; the passage eastward of the islet is about ¼ mile wide with depths in it of 4 to 5 fathoms. These passages, as previously noted, are suitable only for small vessels, and when using them one should keep to mid-channel. There is an *excellent anchorage* for riding out severe southeasterly weather in the open bight close northward of the low sandspit that makes off from the southwest side of Isla Coronado, in 2 to 3 fathoms, sand. There are sandy beaches along the shore of the bight formed by the hook of the spit and a seasonal fish camp is located on the northeastern side. *Shoal water* skirts the shore of the bight but can be plainly made out by its light green hue. There is a clear channel leading to this *anchorage* between the south side of the small islet and the reef extending off the spit, and by keeping midway between the two, shoal water may be avoided. *Anchorage* may be taken, as well, on the south side of the spit, or off the sand beach on the south side of the small islet, in a depth of 3 fathoms.

Francisco Ortega visited this island group during his pearling expedition in 1633 and bestowed the name Islas de los Coronados. Limestone deposits found on the islands were utilized by the Jesuit missionaries in the preparation of mortar for the masonry of their church buildings in Loreto.

The coast between the low bluff westward of Islas Coronados and Punta Mangleres (Mangles Point) situated about 12 miles northward is, with the exception of the fertile valley and plain of San Bruno, generally bold and rocky with high land rising to heights of 2,000 feet immediately behind. The mouth of Arroyo de San Bruno is situated about 7 miles northwestward of Islas Coronados but it is difficult to make out at a distance as the course of the San Bruno Creek, which flows through the arroyo for about 1½ miles above its mouth, lies very nearly parallel to the coastline and is screened from seaward by high hills situated on the intervening land.

The entrance to San Bruno Creek is quite narrow and shoal water extends about ¼ mile offshore. A grove of palms stands close along the shore; a branch road communicating with the coastal highway runs down to the shore to a place called Buena Vista and thence to a white sand beach south of the mouth of the San Bruno Creek. About 2 miles farther southward, situated on a low point overlooking the sea, is a grove of date palms among which may be found the ruins of the San Bruno Mission. In an attempt to colonize Baja California in 1683, prior to the establishment of the Loreto Mission, Father Eusebio Francisco Kino and Admiral Atondo landed 200 colonists and supplies at San Bruno and proceeded to build a chapel, a triangular fort, corrals, houses and various other buildings. Supply of the colonists in their first attempt to become self-sufficient

Mangles Anchorage

restocking of ships' water supplies. The name "Mangles" derived from the thickets of mangroves growing in the estuary at the mouth of San Bruno Creek. An H.O. publication, 2181, Anchorages in the Gulf of California, showing Mangles Anchorage in detail, was published for many years by the Hydrographic Office but has been discontinued.

The coast between Punta Mangleres and Punta Púlpito situated about 14½ miles northward is, in general, steep-to, with rocky bluffs, close off which are some detached rocks and islets.

Punta Los Mercenarios (Mercenaries Point) about 4½ miles northward of Punta Mangles is a rocky cliff of dark sandstone surmounted by a reddish conical hill 519 feet high; about ¾ mile northwestward of Mercenarios Point is a short sandy point with a jagged rocky bluff about 50 feet high at its outer end. Close off this point are *two small islets* 10 and 30 feet high, respectively; ¼ mile eastward of the point is a *rock* 6 feet high; between this rock and the shore there are depths of 7½ fathoms. The shoreline between the two points recedes a little and is comprised of a sand beach with an arroyo opening onto the shore a little more than halfway from Mercenarios Point.

Punta San Basilio (San Basilio Point) situated about 2½ miles north-northwestward of Punta Mercenarios, is a steep-to rocky cliff of red sandstone about 50 feet high, surmounted by a hill 450 feet high; *detached rocks* lie off this point with deep water close-to.

Caleta de San Juanico (San Juanico Cove), southward of Punta San Basilio, is a large open cove about 1½ miles in extent, the shores of which are comprised of yellow bluffs and sand beaches; back of one of these beaches is an attractive valley. There are a number of *detached rocks,* some submerged and some projecting above water, in the western

failed for lack of adequate transport across the gulf, and after a precarious 19 months of existence, the colony was abandoned in 1685. The ruins of this first settlement may be plainly seen today almost 300 years later.

Punta Mangleres (Mangles Point) is a moderately high bluff surmounted by a hill rising steeply to a height of about 100 feet; it comprises the southern end of a succession of cliffs of variegated colors, from 200 to 300 feet high. A double peak, 2,368 feet high, about 3 miles westward of the point, provides a good landmark. Some *detached rocks* lie close off the point, and there is an *isolated shoal* about ¼ mile southeastward of it, over which there is a depth of 7 fathoms. A *group of rocks lies awash* about ¾ mile offshore about 2¼ miles south-southeastward of Punta Mangleres.

Good anchorage, with shelter from northwesterly winds can be obtained about ½ mile offshore southward of Punta Mangles, in depths of from 5 to 9 fathoms, rock; smaller vessels may *anchor* closer to shore in the bight just westward of the cliffs in 3 to 4 fathoms, gravel with some rock, being careful to avoid *foul ground* that skirts the shore on both sides of the head of the bight. At times the anchorage is subject to surge that requires anchoring bow and stern to prevent uncomfortable rolling in the trough. *Navigation caution: In making for Mangles Anchorage from the southward, care must be taken to avoid the rocks awash that lie about 2¼ miles south-southwestward of the point and about ¾ mile offshore. These rocks cover an area that extends westward several hundred yards.* As there are no dangers outside 200 yards of Mangles Point, vessels arriving from the northward may haul close around it.

Mangles Anchorage was much used in early days by pearl fishing vessels and in later times by whaling vessels as a regular stopover point. Firewood was abundant ashore, and fresh water, available from San Bruno Creek nearby, enabled

Caleta San Juanico

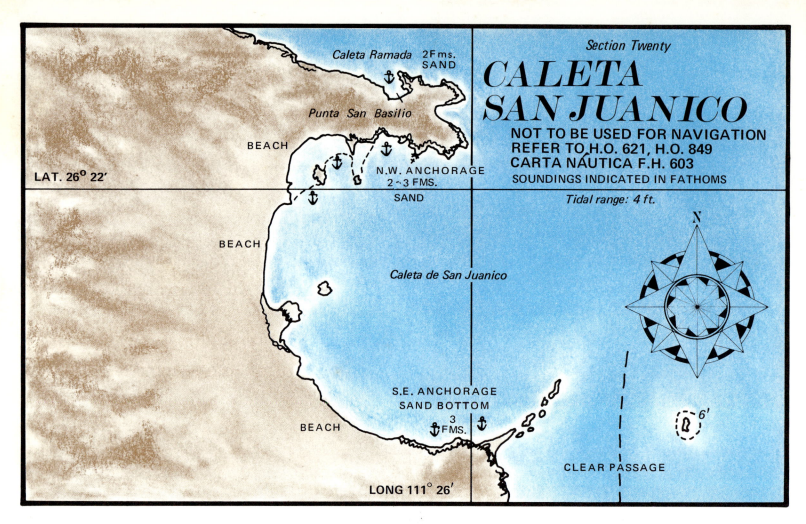

Caleta Ramada 2 Fms.
SAND

Punta San Basilio

BEACH

LAT. 26° 22'

N.W. ANCHORAGE
2 - 3 FMS.

SAND

BEACH

BEACH

Caleta de San Juanico

S.E. ANCHORAGE
SAND BOTTOM

BEACH
3 FMS.

LONG 111° 26'

CLEAR PASSAGE

6'

N

Section Twenty

CALETA SAN JUANICO

NOT TO BE USED FOR NAVIGATION
REFER TO H.O. 621, H.O. 849
CARTA NÁUTICA F.H. 603
SOUNDINGS INDICATED IN FATHOMS

Tidal range: 4 ft.

and northern parts of the cove. The entrance to San Juanico Cove and the land within is characterized by unusually striking pinnacle formations; while the anchorage is otherwise somewhat difficult to find when making from either northward or southward because of the indistinctness of San Basilio Point, the cove may easily be recognized close-to by these pinnacle formations. The cove is about 1½ miles across from the southeast to the northeast anchorage.

Anchorage may be taken in 3 to 4 fathoms, sand, on the southeast side of the cove, or in shallower depths, on the northwest side, well protected from southeasterly winds; however there is a great deal of kelp. *Landing* may be easily made on the sandy beaches with access to the interior valley. *Fresh water* may be found in a shallow depression during the rainy season just back of the beach.

Ramada Cove, just northwest of Punta San Basilio, affords a *protected anchorage* from southerly winds in 2 fathoms, sand; there is a fine white sand beach here on which a *landing* can be made.

Northward of Punta San Basilio the coast recedes considerably, forming the open bay of Bahía de San Basilio (San Basilio Bay) which lies between the point and Rocas de La Gaviota, situated close inshore about 5 miles north-northwestward. The shores of this bay are comprised of low bluffs alternating with sand and pebble beaches. Approximately 3 miles northwestward of Punta San Basilio there is a small cove indented in the coast that may be recognized by a grove of trees standing on the rim at the southern side. There are *detached submerged rocks* on both sides of the cove and at its head. *Anchorage* may be taken here,

but neither the character of the bottom nor the depths have been reported by mariners. *Landing* may be made on a narrow sand beach at the foot of the steep sides of the cove or in a smaller sandy cove immediately around the south entrance point. *Caution: Submerged dangers, as yet uncharted, may exist along this shore.*

Punta Púlpito (Púlpito Point) is a bold and remarkable headland about 470 feet high situated about 7¾ miles northward of Punta San Basilio and 2¾ miles north-northeastward of Rocas de La Gaviota. The point terminates in a great, round rocky knob with sheer sides at the outer end of a peninsula which projects about ½ mile from the general line of the coast and is connected to the mainland westward by a low neck. Punta Púlpito appears as an island when first sighted approaching from the south. This point can clearly

Caleta de San Juanico, northwest Anchorage

Punta Púlpito, looking south

Punta Púlpito, looking north toward Punta San Antonio

be made out at a considerable distance from any direction; the origin of its name is evident in its unique shape. *Detached rocks,* both above and below water, extend about 200 yards off the point; outside these rocks the water deepens abruptly to 15 and 20 fathoms. A remarkable triple-peak rises to an elevation of 1,640 feet about 3¾ miles southwestward of the point and provides a good landmark for navigating in the locality.

Fondeadero del Púlpito (Púlpito Anchorage) has been used by vessels large and small over several centuries for shelter from northwesterly winds, and was at one time included on H.O. Chart 2181, now discontinued as obsolete. *Good anchorage* may be obtained for large vessels in a position about ¼ mile offshore and about 1,200 yards southward of the point in depths of from 5 to 10 fathoms. Along the western shore of the anchorage are numerous *detached rocks,* some of them more than 300 yards offshore. In the northern part of the bight in the lee of the point there is a sand beach which provides a *good landing place.* Small vessels may obtain *anchorage* close off this beach in 3 fathoms, sand, fair holding ground. There is considerable surge in the anchorage from swells diffracted around the point and ground tackle should be set accordingly, to minimize uncomfortable rolling. *Navigation note: Tidal streams run with considerable strength in this vicinity.*

Punta Santa Antonita (Santa Antonita Point) is a low rocky bluff about 15 feet high, situated about 1¼ miles northwestward of Punta Púlpito; a *shoal* on which the sea breaks extends northward from the point for about ¼ mile. *Anchorage,* protected from southerly winds, may be obtained by small vessels on the northwest side of this point close off a sand beach in 4 fathoms, sand. The surge in this locality is considerable and anchoring fore and aft is required to stay any length of time in comfort. Punta Santa Antonita forms the southeastern limit of San Nicolás Bay which lies between this point and Punta Santa Teresa, situated about 10 miles further north-northwestward.

Black Sea Bass

Cove in Bahía San Nicolas

Northward of Punta Santa Antonita the coast falls away to the westward forming the large open bay of Bahía San Nicolás (San Nicolás Bay). The southern shore is comprised of low land extending well into the interior which is cut by several small arroyos that, during the rainy season, carry small streams which empty into the bay; the western shore consists of bluffs backed by high land cut by several deep arroyos. Off the western shore of the bay are a number of *detached rocks*.

Isla Ildefonso (Ildefonso Island) lies offshore about 6 miles at the midway point of the bay (see below). The small ranching settlement of San Nicolás is located in the bottom land of an arroyo that breaks onto the shore of San Nicolás Bay west-northwestward of Punta Santa Antonita. A small lagoon lies immediately back of the sand berm at the mouth of the arroyo and the ranch occupies the flat land a little farther up the arroyo. Cultivation is evident and a grove of trees stands near the dwellings. *Water* is obtained from several wells in the arroyo. An *airstrip* is bulldozed on the flat on the northwest side of the arroyo and is suitable for small planes. (See Appendix.) San Nicolás Bay is shown on early charts as Bahía de Comondú.

A small semicircular cove opens in the shore northwestward of the San Nicolás Ranch; the shore of the cove is comprised of a sand beach, and a small arroyo breaks through from the surrounding hills at the head of the cove. Some green foliage may be seen back of the beach at the mouth of the arroyo. *Detached rocks,* on which the sea breaks, lie close off the southern entrance point to the cove. *Anchorage* for small vessels may be had here with some protection from the coastal winds; however, neither bottom characteristics nor depths have been reported by mariners.

About 4 miles southward of Punta Santa Teresa is Bahía de los Puercos, a small cove affording *sheltered anchorage* to small vessels, protected from both northerly and southerly winds. Off the southern entrance point to the cove there is a heavy growth of kelp concealing some *detached rocks* on which the sea sometimes breaks; kelp fringes the northern shore of the cove, as well and conceals *detached rocks*. The head of the cove is clear, and while room to swing is tight, a snug *anchorage* may be had in 4 fathoms, sand. Several houses are built back of the beach in the bottom of the arroyo that opens into the cove. A green growth of foliage may be seen in the arroyo and some *fresh water* is available.

Caleta de los Puercos

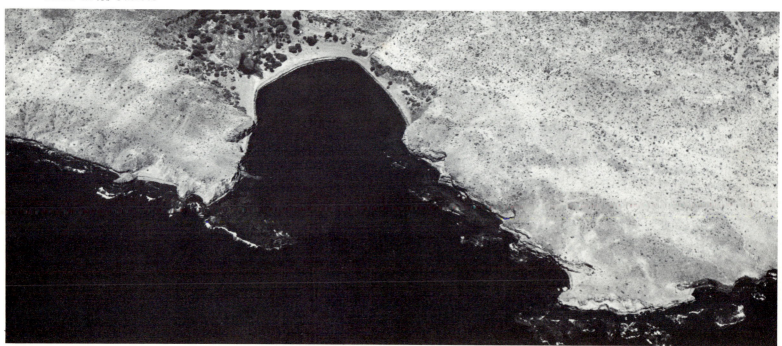

Isla Ildefonso

A road connects from this place westward to the head of Bahía Concepción, a distance as the crow flies of 7½ miles, thence northwestward to Mulegé and Santa Rosalía.

Punta Santa Teresa (Santa Teresa Point), 10¾ miles north-northwestward of Santa Antonita Point is a rocky point surmounted by a small, sharp hill; a conspicuous peak 955 feet high is situated about 1 mile southwestward of the point. *Detached rocks* lie off the point.

Isla San Ildefonso (Ildefonso Island), lying offshore in a position about 5½ miles north-northeastward of Punta Santa Antonita, is a steep-to, barren and rocky islet with a flat profile that rises 387 feet above the sea. The island is about 1½ miles long and ½ mile wide; a *reef of rocks*

Bahía San Lino and Punta Colorado

Punta Santa Teresa

Bahía San Nicolas

projects out about ¼ mile from its northern end. There are no beaches; the entire coastline of the island is comprised of ragged lava and steep cliffs and *landing* is difficult but possible in several places. Soundings along the eastern shore show deep water close-to; between the island and the mainland there is a deep passage that is free of dangers.

Isla San Ildefonso is characterized more by the myriad of birdlife it supports than for any other part it has ever played in the ongoing life of the gulf. Clouds of birds wheel and turn over its terrain of steep cliffs; thousands more nest in its gas-blown potholes and shallow caves, still others are to be found among the splay of lava boulders piled on the island or in whatever thin crust of soft earth can be found along its flat, rolling top. Brewster and blue-footed booby, craveri murrelets, heermann gulls, sparrow-hawks and burrowing owls, western gulls and ravens, osprey, rock wrens and great blue herons all struggle for existence; duck hawks hover over the eastern slopes and brown pelicans occupy the southeastern corner of the island. Sea lions add their throaty voices to the chorus of bird cries but are relegated to a definite minority under the fleeting shadows of the aerial population.

Seabirds prefer small barren islands because they are free of predators and San Ildefonso Island is one of a dozen such perfect nesting platforms scattered among the various islands of the gulf. The tide pools are rich with sea life as well; seaweeds hide a collector's trove. Bottom fish abound. There is a strong movement among naturalists to have San Ildefonso Island included as a sanctuary along with Islas Raza and Guadalupe to preserve this untrammeled treasure of wildlife. In the meantime the responsibility for careful conservation depends on the increasing numbers of cruising yachtsmen and sportfishermen who have the extremely good fortune to explore these waters.

Francisco Ortega, in search of pearls in 1636, visited the island and gave it its name after a rather obscure Spanish bishop of the seventh century. Ortega describes the island as being considerably larger than it is now and inhabited by Indians who had wells of brackish water on the beach. Either there is some discrepancy through mistaken description in Ortega's original log, in its subsequent transcription and translation, or Isla San Ildefonso in sinking into the sea.

The coast between Punta Santa Teresa and Punta Concepción, situated about 19 miles northwestward, is high and rocky. *Note: Great patches of red water, a curious phenomenon noted by the earliest Spanish navigators and which gave rise to the name Vermillion Sea, is prevalent along this part of the coast. Scientific investigations of these broad red patches attribute them to the presence of countless numbers of miniscule organisms that flourish during certain seasons of the year, suspended some distance below the surface; in the case of the brick-colored and corrosive waters of some portions of the upper gulf, it is due to the presence of similar concentrations of organisms floating on the surface giving it a milky-red color.*

Between Punta Teresa and Punta Colorado, situated about 4½ miles northwestward, there are several minor points of land, off which *rocks,* some above water and some submerged, extend for as much as ¼ mile. Punta Colorado (Colorado Point) is a high, reddish-colored bluff fringed with *detached rocks.*

Bahía de San Lino (San Lino Bay) is situated in the curve of the coastline lying southward of Punta Colorado and affords shelter from southeasterly and westerly winds but is open to the northwest. A small lagoon of brackish

water is formed back of a sand beach at the head of the cove. *Anchorage* in the bay may be obtained in a range of depths between 4 and 7 fathoms. Pico Colorado, 1,605 feet high, is situated about 4 miles westward of Punta Colorado. A remarkable mountain of whitish appearance rises to an elevation of 2,434 feet about 5¼ miles northwestward of Pico Colorado and provides a good navigational landmark along this part of the coast. About 3½ miles northwestward of Punta Colorado is a low point with a gravel beach to either side; a *reef* projects about ¼ mile seaward from this point and shallow water extends some distance beyond the reef. *Shoal water and reefs* extend up to nearly ½ mile offshore between positions about 4 and 6 miles further northwestward, and should be given adequate berth when coasting this shore. Soundings taken at a distance of 1 mile offshore show depths of 20 to 40 fathoms.

Punta Concepción (Point Concepción), the northernmost point of the peninsula which forms the eastern side of Bahía Concepción, is an ill-defined bluff point about 30 feet high with numerous *detached rocks* lying northward and westward of it.

Navigation note: Punta Concepción has been reported to give good radar returns up to 17 miles; it is not lighted and navigators should lay their courses well off the point, and be wary of the possible set of tidal currents.

From Punta Concepción the coast trends southwestward for about 2 miles, receding slightly to Punta Aguja, which,

with Punta Santo Domingo ½ mile beyond, forms the northeastern entrance point of Bahía Concepción.

Punta Aguja (Aguja Point) is a sharp rocky bluff off which *detached rocks and shallow water* extend a short distance. *Navigation caution: Prior to 1880, a rock with depths of 3 fathoms over it was reported to lie about 1 mile northeastward of Punta Gallito, situated on the mainland opposite Punta Santo Domingo; however, a careful search for it by navigators over subsequent years has not confirmed its existence.*

Mission at Loreto

Punta Concepción

Bahía Concepción, looking to the south

SECTION 21
PUNTA CONCEPCIÓN to PUNTA CHIVATO
(Including Mulegé)

Bahía Concepción (Concepción Bay) is one of the most popular areas in the Gulf of California regularly visited by cruising yachts and sportfishing vessels and embraces within its 100 square miles of generally calm and sheltered waters some of the most beautiful coves and bays in Baja California. It is a short run from the town of Mulegé in Bahía Santa Inés, a little over two miles northwestward around the bay's northern entrance point, and about 60 miles from Loreto, southeastward. For navigation refer to U.S. Naval Oceanographic Charts H.O. 621; H.O. 849; Mexican Carta Náutica F.H. 602.

Bahía Concepción is entered between Punta Aguja, situated about 2 miles southwestward of Punta Concepción, and Punta Gallito, situated about 3¼ miles westward across the mouth of the bay. Punta Aguja is a sharp rocky bluff off which detached rocks and shoal water extend for a short distance; Punta Santo Domingo, comprising the southwestern projection of this entrance point, is situated about ½ mile beyond. Punta Gallito may be recognized by a dark-colored conical rock connected to the mainland by a low sandspit; a sand-covered islet, terminating at its outer end in a rocky bluff, lies separated from the point by a shoal channel several yards wide. The point and islet are almost com-

pletely surrounded by shoal water. *Navigation note: Prior to 1880, a submerged rock with depths of 3 fathoms over it was reported to lie about 1 mile northeastward of Punta Gallito just outside the entrance to Bahía Concepción; navigators have subsequently been unable to relocate or verify the existence of this rock.*

Anchorage may be obtained eastward of Punta Aguja or southward of Punta Santo Domingo, the choice between the two depending principally upon the wind and weather. While the seas at the entrance to Bahía Concepción are often quite flat and the wind moderate, a stiff blow can whip up a short chop from which one may wish to seek quick shelter. *Anchorage* southward of Punta Santo Domingo may be obtained off a low red bluff in 2 fathoms, sand, just outside the shore bank; *Anchorage* may also be taken close off the white sand beach just southward in 2 fathoms, sand. The southern limit of the cove is marked by a grey bluff at the southern end of the sand beach. *Navigation caution: When making into the anchorage, give Punta Santo Domingo and its outlying reef adequate berth, as well as the shore bank extending southward from the point to the northern end of the sand beach. This anchorage is fairly well protected; however, the eastward fetch from*

Western shore, Punta Concepción

across the bay is almost 3 miles and wind from this quarter can whip up rough seas, and a sharp, steep swell. *Landing may be made anywhere along the sandy beach.*

Bahía Concepción, 3¼ miles wide at its mouth, lies oriented in a south-southeast — north-northwest direction, penetrating the surrounding land for a distance of 22 miles. It is a long narrow bay characterized by almost straight, parallel sides. For the first 5 miles from the entrance the bay gradually narrows to a minimum width of 2 miles, then opens out to a width of from 3 to 4 miles. There is a least width of 1¼ miles and a least depth of 5 fathoms in the navigable channel at the narrowest part of the bay. Concepción Bay is relatively shallow; the depth does not exceed 20 fathoms and varies but little over its entire length. Bahía Concepción affords *sheltered anchorage* in several coves well protected from all weather except gales blowing directly out of the north; a northerly, blowing from just the right direction, will sweep unchecked down the bay, building sharp, steep waves in the shallow waters to a considerable height and fury. Fortunately, such gales are rare and for the most part the waters of the bay are still and placid, affording one of the best shelters along the coast between Bahía Escondido and Santa Rosalía. *Navigation caution: An obstruction with less than 1 fathom covering it was reported in 1961 to be situated in the center of the bay southwestward of Punta Santa Rosalía with 14 or 15 fathoms all around.*

The eastern shore of the bay trends south-southeastward for about 2¾ miles from Punta Santo Domingo to Punta Guadalupe; thence 3½ miles to Punta Las Ornillas. Deep water is found close-to for a short distance on either side of Punta Las Ornillas; except for this short stretch of coast, however, the entire eastern shore of the bay is skirted by a *shoal bank* ¼ to ¾ mile wide. A peak, 2,434 feet high and of a whitish appearance, rises on the peninsula a little over two miles eastward of Punta Las Ornillas. The eastern shore is comprised of sand and pebble beaches from which the land slopes gradually to the mountains situated along the spine of the peninsula, separating the bay from the gulf eastward.

Punta San Ignacio is situated 3¾ miles south-southeastward of Punta Las Ornillas, and ½ mile farther are a ranch and a small stream of fresh water which runs during the rainy season; a fish camp and dirt *airstrip* are located here. Punta Santa Rosalía is located about 2 miles farther southeastward and a group of ranch buildings are established immediately southeastward. *Navigation note: The shore bank with 1 to 1½ fathoms of water covering it, extends almost ¾ mile between Punta San Ignacio and Punta Santa Rosalía and should be given adequate berth.*

The head of the bay, 10 miles farther southeastward of Punta Santa Rosalía, is called La Passajera and, like the eastern shore, is low and sandy; it is a flattened semicircular continuation of the shore beaches. The shoaling of the southern end of the bay is very gradual to the outer edge of a shore bank fronting the beach. There is a lagoon at the western end of which the bank extends to a distance of about ½ mile. The Loreto-Mulegé road skirts the head of the bay with a branch road connecting to the ranching settlement of Santa Rosalillita at the eastern corner; an aban-

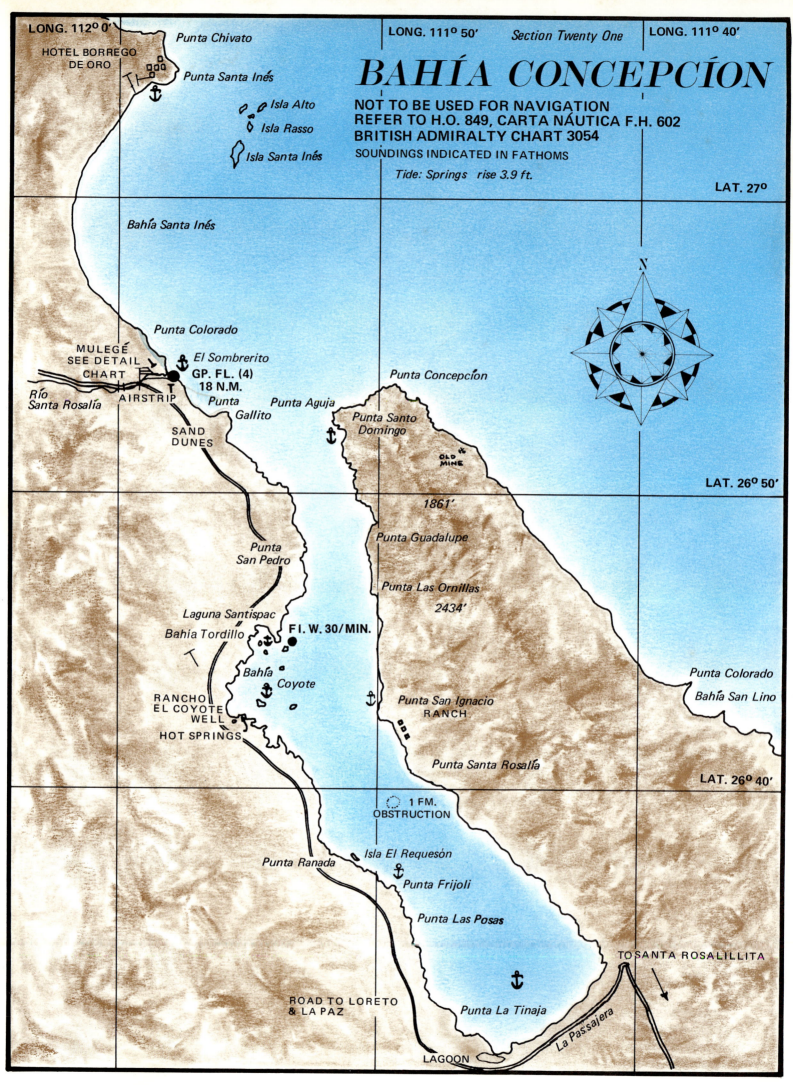

Punta Chivato

HOTEL BORREGO DE ORO

Punta Santa Inés

BAHÍA CONCEPCÍON

NOT TO BE USED FOR NAVIGATION
REFER TO H.O. 849, CARTA NÁUTICA F.H. 602
BRITISH ADMIRALTY CHART 3054
SOUNDINGS INDICATED IN FATHOMS

Tide: Springs rise 3.9 ft.

Isla Alto

Isla Rasso

Isla Santa Inés

LAT. 27°

Bahía Santa Inés

N

Punta Colorado

MULEGÉ
SEE DETAIL
CHART

El Sombrerito
GP. FL. (4)
18 N.M.

Punta Concepcíon

Río
Santa Rosalía

AIRSTRIP

Punta
Gallito

Punta Aguja

Punta Santo
Domingo

OLD
MINE

SAND
DUNES

1861'

LAT. 26° 50'

Punta Guadalupe

Punta
San Pedro

Punta Las Ornillas

2434'

Laguna Santispac

Bahía Tordillo

Fl. W. 30/MIN.

Bahía
Coyote

Punta Colorado

Bahía San Lino

RANCHO
EL COYOTE
WELL

Punta San Ignacio
RANCH

HOT SPRINGS

Punta Santa Rosalía

LAT. 26° 40'

1 FM.
OBSTRUCTION

Punta Ranada

Isla El Requesón

Punta Frijoli

TO SANTA ROSALILLITA

Punta Las Posas

ROAD TO LORETO
& LA PAZ

Punta La Tinaja

La Passajera

LAGOON

doned road runs northwestward along the peninsula to Punta Concepción where there was at one time a manganese mine, the ore reputedly 52 percent pure; the main road follows the western shore within a mile or less of the coast, sometimes dipping close to the beach. A forest of cactus of considerable size grows abundantly back of the head of the bay, and in this area deer are numerous.

The western shore of the bay is in marked contrast to its eastern shore having an irregular configuration characterized by a series of promontories and high bluffs with intervening bights and inlets dotted with small islets in places. At the north end of the bay the irregular character of the shore disappears, the coast once again becoming low, shelving to sand and pebble beaches with shoal water extending well offshore.

From a position about 1 mile southward of Punta Gallito, a sand beach extends for 1 mile southeastward followed by bluffs of moderate height for the next 1½ miles; thence a low pebble beach continues for 1¾ miles interrupted by a solitary knob, then continues for 1¾ miles to Punta San Pedro. There is a *hot spring* in this vicinity.

Punta San Pedro (San Pedro Point) is a bold headland about 100 feet high, situated about 5½ miles southeastward of Punta Gallito; a shore bank, which is covered by shoal water sounded to depths of 1 to 1½ fathoms, extends about ¾ mile off this part of the coast, from about 2 miles northward to 1½ miles southward of Punta San Pedro. Vessels entering the bay should keep to the center of the channel. About 3 miles southward of Punta San Pedro is a bold rocky headland elongated north-northwestward, about 200 feet high and connected to the mainland by a low sandspit. Shoal water surrounds this point and extends off it for some distance; the point forms the northern limit of Coyote Bay.

Immediately west of the northern entrance point to Coyote Bay lies Santispac Cove. At the cove's mouth are an islet and a shoal, and in the center of the cove lies a small islet. At the cove's head lies a shallow circular lagoon, Laguna Santispac, rimmed by a mangrove thicket. Oysters cling to the mangrove roots and may be gathered at low tide. Small butter clams also may be found in great abundance in the sand. Santispac Cove offers good protection from northerly weather and an anchorage at its head in 4 fathoms, sand. Southwest of Laguna Santispac is a small cove with a mud beach above which a trailer park is being built. This spot is called Tordillo Bay and will provide trailer camping and fishing facilities.

Bahía Coyote (Coyote Bay) is a popular rendezvous for cruising yachts and sportfishing launches and offers a sheltered and convenient *anchorage* with ready access to the gulf for the coastal fleet of commercial shrimpers. The bay is entered between the two aforementioned points through the clear channels that lead among the several islands in the compass of the bay. Coyote Bay is encumbered with a number of these small islets and rocks from 30 to 100 feet high and navigation among them must be undertaken with caution, especially in the northern part of the bay, as existing official navigation charts fix their locations with only rough approximation and, in some instances, considerable discrepancy. When making into Coyote Bay any of the channels between the islands or between the entrance points and the islands may be used by keeping to the middle of these channels; shoal water and submerged rocks can clearly be identified during daylight hours by the light blue-green hue fringing these dangers; movement within the bay at night is not advised except by those intimately familiar through long experience with the channels and submerged dangers. There are several small islets in the northern part of the bay 30 to 40 feet high, surrounded by *reefs and sunken rocks* and separated by narrow but navigable channels 5 to 10 fathoms deep. The outermost of these islets, rising 35 feet above the sea, lies ½ mile southeast of the northern entrance point of the bay and marked by a navigation light flashing white 30 times per minute.

Isla Blanca and an off-lying rock are situated in a position about ⅔ mile farther southward; in all there are ½ dozen of these islands, several shoals and a number of rocks, both submerged and above water, scattered in Coyote Bay and off Laguna Santispac. Traces of man's food and pearl gathering activities, both recent and ancient, are plainly evident. There are to be found in the vicinity great mounds of a large species of clam shells as well as the shells of pearl-bearing oysters piled in heaps on the islands and in the mouths of caves ashore; the caves bear the indelible traces of habitation by man over many centuries. Petroglyphs can be clearly seen on large boulders located at the mouth of a short arroyo near Coyote Bay. The history of the region records Bahía Concepción as one of the earliest areas to be explored and exploited for pearl oysters.

Isla Coyote, rising 35 feet above the sea, is situated on the southern side of the mouth of Santispac Bay at the northern end of Bahía Coyote. A *shoal with rocks submerged* lies in a position just eastward of Isla Coyote in the mouth of Santispac Cove.

Isla Barga (Bargo), rising 100 feet above the surface of the sea in a position about 800 yards from the southern shore, is the largest of the islets in Coyote Bay; it is a boomerang-shaped, barren rocky islet, enclosing in its arms on the northern side, a pocket beach of fine white sand shoaling gradually toward deep water. The turquoise-blue of the water off this beach is characteristic of the shallow water around the other islets, shoals and rocks in Bahía Concepción. *Landing* may be easily made on this beach; *anchorage* may be obtained just offshore. Two *detached rocks* stand above water off the western side of the islet and are connected to its shore by a white sand shoal that reflects the same turquoise-blue. In the passage between Barga Island and the mainland there are depths of 7 to 10 fathoms.

North end, Bahía Coyote

Isla Guapa, rising 80 feet above the sea, stands in a position about ¾ mile eastward of Barga Island and about 1 mile southward of Blanca Island. Official nagivation chart H.O. 849, published by the Naval Oceanographic Office in Washington, D.C. and based on U.S. Naval Surveys between 1873 and 1875, incorrectly charts the position of Isla Guapa displaced approximately ¾ mile southward. Both radar and photographic observations indicate that Guapa Island lies only about 1 mile southward of Blanca Island. *Submerged rocks* lie close off both the northern and southern shore of the island; a *solitary rock,* 50 feet high, lies in a position about 1,200 yards south-southeastward of the eastern end of Barga Island and about 600 yards from the point at the southern limit of Coyote Bay; the *rock,* surrounded by shoal water, lies directly in the mouth of a small cove. A shore bank extends several hundred yards off the beach at the head of this cove and a small tidal lagoon is situated in the southern corner of the cove.

Directions: When entering this cove keep to the deep channel midway between either entrance point and the islet, with care to avoid the shore bank on the northern side of the cove extending outward around the point; the channel southward is the wider of the two channels and clear of the shore bank and therefore recommended.

Anchorage, sheltered from southerly weather, may be obtained off a sand beach in a small cove in the southern part of Coyote Bay; a red rocky headland affords shelter from the southeast. *Landing* may be made anywhere along the sandy shore. At the north end of the beach are a grove of palms and other green foliage shading a whitewashed ranch building with a red-tiled roof. Other buildings of the El Coyote Ranch and fish camp are located back of the beach in the mouth of an arroyo which opens onto the cove. *Fresh water* and some supplies are available at the ranch, and rowboats and tackle are offered for rent; there is a good beach with some shade trees. There is a blacksmith with a forge at Coyote Bay and his ability as an iron worker is uncommonly good. A *hot spring* is located in the southeast side of the bay and inquiry at the landing will enable one to enjoy its therapeutic warmth. The Loreto-Mulegé road runs close along the shore in this vicinity and a government mail truck calls weekly. A refrigerated cargo truck serves the fishing cooperative in operation at Coyote Bay. A *landing strip* in the bed of a dry lagoon nearby is used by freight planes to pick up part of the catch of this sea-food operation. (See Appendix.)

Legend supports the existence of the wreck of a pirate vessel that went aground close southward of Coyote Bay, having entered Bahía Concepción to escape pursuit. Treasure hunting for the wreck and its imagined cargo occupies the local population when picnicking in the vicinity.

The shore for about 7 miles southeastward of Bahía Coyote is comprised of a series of rocky bluffs with intervening sand beaches, and is fronted by a shore bank to a distance of about ½ mile offshore in places. The remainder of the western shore is steep-to. *Repeat, navigation caution:*

Section Twenty-One

BAHIA COYOTE

NOT TO BE USED FOR NAVIGATION
REFER TO H.O. 849,
SOUNDINGS INDICATED IN FATHOMS

ROAD TO MULEGE

Laguna Santispac

Caleta Santispac

Caleta Tordillo

SAND 4 Fms.

REEF

Isla Coyote 35'

35' Fl. W. 30/MIN.
LIGHT
CLEAR PASSAGE

Isla sin nombre

9-10 Fms.

Isla Blanca

LAT. 26° 44'

Bahía Coyote

N

FISH CAMP

Isla Guapa 80'

3 Fms. SAND

Isla Bargo 100'

7-10 Fms.

RANCHO EL COYOTE

SAND BEACH

WELL
BLACKSMITH

HOT SPRING

50'
+++

Tide-Springs rise 3.9 ft.

ROAD TO LORETO AND LA PAZ

LONG. 111° 53'

In 1961 an obstruction with a depth over it of less than 1 fathom with 14 to 15 fathoms all around was reported to exist in the center of the bay about 7 miles southward of Punta San Pedro.

Punta Ranada, comprised of a low bluff at the foot of some hills and situated about 4½ miles southeastward of the southern point of Bahía Coyote, encloses a bight northward filled almost entirely by a shore bank, the depths of which have been sounded at 2½ fathoms along its outer edge. The shore of the cove formed in the bight is sandy; a tidal estuary penetrates the shore at the northern end of the beach and a small ranch is established at its mouth; *fresh water* is available at this place.

Isla El Requeson (Ricason), rising 50 feet in elevation, is situated about 800 yards eastward of Punta Ranada and is connected to the shore by a narrow spit of white sand over which the tide flows. The island is ½ mile long, about 200 yards wide and 50 feet high. Shallow lagoons are formed on either side of the spit in the arms of the elongated island, between it and the mainland shore along which it lies parallel. *Anchorage* may be taken off the mouth of the southern lagoon in the lee of the island and *landing* effected on the sandy beach which rims the lagoon and comprises the spit. The road runs close along the shore at this place through a small settlement called El Requeson.

Punta Frigoli (Frijoli), a sharp bluff about 40 feet high, situated a little over 1¼ miles southeastward of Isla Requeson, brackets a small white sand beach pocketed on the northwest side of the point. *Landing* may be easily made here and *anchorage* obtained off the beach. Tidal channels and a small lagoon lie northwestward along the shore, which is low and sandy and which is fronted by a shore bank that extends off ½ mile. Las Posas Point is situated about 1½

South end, Bahía Coyote

miles southward, closely backed by a hill 750 feet high.

Punta La Tinaja is situated about 3¼ miles farther southward; *fresh water* is located in the vicinity. A hill 500 feet high lies immediately south-southwestward of the point. The shore between Punta Frigoli and Punta La Tinaja is low and sandy and nearly straight with deep water close-to. Southward of Punta La Tinaja is the aforementioned lagoon in the southwestern corner at the head of Bahía Concepción. Some small islands stand off the entrance to the lagoon and shoal water extends ½ mile offshore. A ranch is located back of the sizable basins of the lagoon on the western shore; *fresh water* may be obtained at the ranch.

In fine weather a vessel may find *anchorage* almost anywhere in the bay but with northerly gales and a heavy sea setting into the bay *sheltered anchorage* may be found under the lee of one of the islands in Coyote Bay. The bottom throughout Bahía Concepción is nearly everywhere of sand, white and fine, affording good holding ground and reflecting enough light to be visible at a depth exceeding several fathoms.

TIDES — There is very little tidal movement within the bay and the currents are for the most part inappreciable. The tide is chiefly diurnal, the spring range being 3.9 feet; the mean tide level is 1.9 feet.

Bahía Concepción was first discovered for the Spanish by Francisco Ulloa during his first expedition to explore the gulf in 1539. Sebastián Vizcaíno took shelter in Bahía Coyote from the severe weather of a fierce *cordonazo* that overtook his vessels in 1596. Don Francisco Luzenilla, captain of a pearling expedition, visited the bay in 1668 and reported that white-skinned Indians lived along the shores of the bay and subsided on wild fruit and shellfish; the bay was called Mulegé by the Indians. The same Indians were subsequently Christianized by Father Basualda of the Mulegé Mission who opened the first trail along the western shore of Bahía Concepción in 1705. These apparently

Isla Requeson

Isla Bargo

La Passajera, south end of Bahía Concepción

unique Indians soon succumbed to disease, dying out completely without a trace of folklore or history to record their former idyllic life.

In September, 1914, shortly after the declaration of World War I by the British and French against Germany and Austria, the German light cruiser *Leipzig* was playing cat-and-mouse with Australian and Canadian men-of-war. The *Leipzig,* badly in need of bunker fuel to make good her escape from the gulf and continue her forays against Allied shipping on the Pacific coast, stood into Bahía Concepción and, under guidance from a Mexican pilot from Mulegé, anchored in Coyote Bay, well hidden from seaward.

Mulegé is one of the oldest and continuously occupied colonial towns of Baja California. It is situated at the mouth of Arroyo de Santa Rosalía which breaks through the coastal hills and forms a narrow lagoon over a mile long, opening into the gulf approximately 70 miles northwestward of Loreto, and 34 miles southeastward of Puerto Santa Rosalía.

The site of an ancient Indian settlement for countless centuries, the port was first established in its modern context as a mission ranch in 1705 and has endured since as a semi-somnolent agricultural village emerging in the last decade as a major gulf resort, sportfishing center and popular way port for cruising yachts. For navigation see U.S. Naval Oceanographic Office Charts H.O. 620, Golfo de California, Northern Part; H.O. 849, Western Shore of the Gulf of California from Punta Púlpito to San Marcos Island; British Admiralty Chart #2324, Cape San Lucas to San Diego Bay with Gulf of California; Mexican Carta Náutica F.H. 603, Golfo de California, Parte Norte.

When approaching from the south, the coast, for 2¼ miles between Punta Gallito and Roca Equipalito northwestward, at the entrance to the Mulegé estuary, is low and sandy. Equipalito Rock, which lies on the south side of the Río Santa Rosalía, closely resembles Punta Gallito at the entrance to Bahía Concepción; the land westward of the

rock being low and swampy with several small lagoons. A shallow bank extends fully ¾ mile offshore for a distance of about 1¼ miles southeastward of Roca Equipalito; when standing in for an anchorage, Pico Colorado, which rises to an elevation of 836 feet about 1¼ miles westward of the river mouth, should be held to a bearing nothing northward of 276° in order to avoid the shoal water near the coast southward of that bearing line. Pico Colorado is of a distinctly reddish color and is an excellent landmark when navigating in this vicinity.

Punta El Sombrerito (Sombrerito Point) is a great felt-colored rock pyramid, standing 119 feet high above a round base on the north side of the mouth of the river; it very much suggests the shape of a huge sombrero with a broad brim. El Sombrerito Point is almost an island, connected to the mainland northwestward by a low sandy spit, over which the river occasionally breaks. Punta Prieta is a low dark-colored bluff about ¾ mile northward; shoal water extends for a short distance off its northern side.

There is a *navigation light* on Punta El Sombrerito shown at a height of 138 feet above the sea from atop a small white concrete building; the *light* exhibits a **group flash of four white flashes** visible for 18 miles seaward in clear weather in the sector 181° through 273°. When approaching Mulegé from well offshore during daylight hours, the *lighthouse* may be seen as a small white spot apparently on the side of a mountain. Closer in, it may easily be distinguished in its position atop the articulated point. There is a semaphore painted gray on the western side of the *lighthouse*.

Once inside the lagoon, sportfishing launches may be seen tied up stern-to off the rocky shore and alongside the small dock of the Loma Linda Landing. Haul-out facilities over the beach are constructed here and several launches may usually be seen out of water for repair and painting. At high water vessels of 25- to 30-foot length can be safely taken over the bar that extends from Punta El Sombrerito to the far shore southward; within the estuary small boats may negotiate the river for a considerable distance where depths of from 2 to 5 feet prevail between shoal places. Service docks extend into the deeper portions of these channels in front of the several resorts on both sides of the river.

TIDES — The high water interval at full and change is approximately 7 hours; springs rise about 4 feet.

Fondeadero Mulegé (Mulegé Anchorage), suitable for large vessels, is situated in the open roadstead between Punta El Sombrerito and Punta Prieta where *anchorage* may be taken in depths of from 5 to 8 fathoms about ½ mile from shore; small vessels may anchor closer in about 100 yards off the beach in 3 to 3½ fathoms, sand. This anchorage is poor, being exposed to the prevailing winds and subject to strong currents; northerly winds create a lee shore and an on-board anchor watch at all times is advised. *Caution: This anchorage is entirely unsafe in northerly gales and should be left immediately for better protection when severe weather from this quarter threatens.*

Alternative anchorage, sheltered from northerly winds, may be had in Bahía Concepción southward, in the northern corner of Santa Inés Bay northward, or in the lee of San Marcos Island, offshore. Small vessels of light draft may enter the mouth of the Mulegé estuary for a more *sheltered anchorage* under the lee of Punta El Sombrerito but the Santa Rosalía River mouth is shallow and encumbered with rocks, requiring caution with safe passage only at high water. Boats and shallow draft vessels desiring to enter the inner lagoon should approach the entrance channel northward of El Sombrerito Point rounding close southward the *reef* on which the sea breaks and which can clearly be seen extending off the southeast extremity of the lighthouse headland, giving it a berth of no more than 25 feet. A rocky islet around which the sea breaks, and connected to the south shore by a submerged sandbar, stands off the southern side of the mouth of the estuary; shoal water skirts the shore in this vicinity. The navigable channel, clearly showing deep blue between lighter colored shoal water to either side, may be followed close around El Sombrerito for a distance of about 50 yards to the end of the sheer headland cliffs, which must be kept close aboard on the starboard hand; an *uncharted rock* and *shoal submerged* on the south side of the channel should be watched for and given an adequate berth.

A long, low, narrow islet divides the estuary into two reaches; the northern reach leads up the river to the town of Mulegé about 2 miles distant. The Club Aero de Mulegé (Rancho Loma Linda), a modern first-class resort hotel now operated as a private club is built on a bluff overlooking the estuary on the north shore about ½ mile from the mouth. A dirt path leads from the boat dock on the estuary bank to the hotel above. A green metal water tank stands on the east side of the red-tile roofed hotel buildings. A swimming pool, focused in the gentle curve of the architectural line of the buildings, occupies the center of a palm-treed patio in front. The runway of a dirt *airstrip* for small planes is bulldozed in a terrace immediately above the hotel to the east; the larger *Mulegé airstrip* is cut into a second terrace above and back of the club complex just below Pico Colorado. Scheduled air transport service from Tijuana calls three times weekly. (See Appendix.) The club offers sportfishing launches for hire. A resort called Serenidad Mulegé occupies lower land on the south side of the estuary above a boat dock that extends from the bank. An *airstrip* neatly marked off with whitewashed rocks is situated alongside the resort buildings to accommodate small planes. The letter "S" in a size easily discernible by overflying aircraft is laid out in white rocks on a small hillock alongside the runway. The resort offers a sandy beach and sportfishing launches for hire.

Playa de Mulegé, a third resort complex of thatched ramadas, occupies the shelf above the beach outside the lagoon entrance, just southward of the reef in the lee of the rocky islet. Sportfishing launches are moored just off shore in front of the resort.

Beyond the resort establishments, away from the mouth of the estuary, the river bends between a lush growth of date palms thickly grown on both banks. The sterile quality of the bare rocky red earth along the coast is suddenly

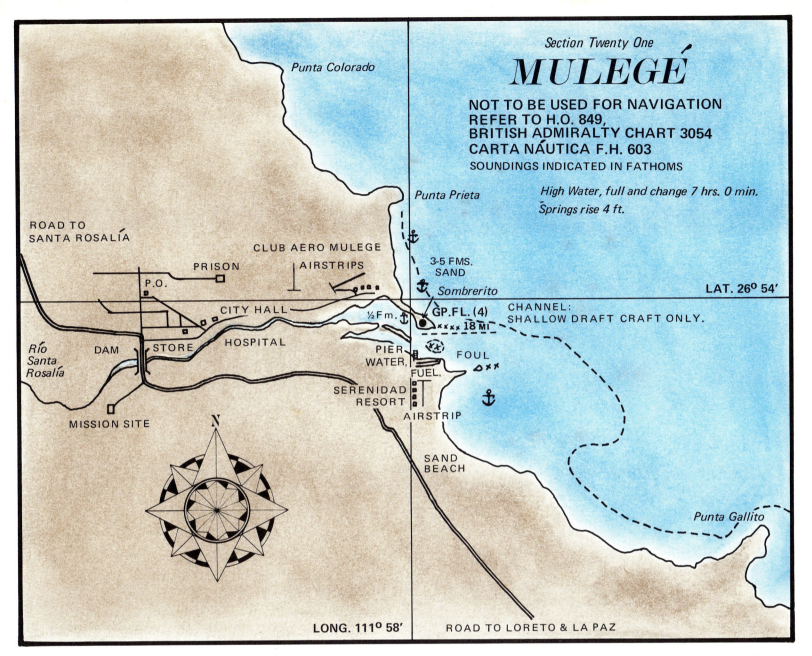

MULEGÉ

NOT TO BE USED FOR NAVIGATION
REFER TO H.O. 849,
BRITISH ADMIRALTY CHART 3054
CARTA NÁUTICA F.H. 603
SOUNDINGS INDICATED IN FATHOMS

High Water, full and change 7 hrs. 0 min.
Springs rise 4 ft.

Punta Colorado

Punta Prieta

LAT. 26° 54'

ROAD TO
SANTA ROSALÍA

PRISON

CLUB AERO MULEGE

AIRSTRIPS

P.O.

3-5 FMS.
SAND

Sombrerito

CITY HALL

½ Fm.

GP.FL. (4)

CHANNEL:
SHALLOW DRAFT CRAFT ONLY.

18 MI

Río
Santa
Rosalía

DAM

STORE

HOSPITAL

PIER
WATER,

FOUL

FUEL,

MISSION SITE

SERENIDAD
RESORT

AIRSTRIP

N

SAND
BEACH

Punta Gallito

LONG. 111° 58'

ROAD TO LORETO & LA PAZ

transformed up this river into a surprisingly tropical setting. The luxuriant foliage of the date palms, pressing in on the waters of the lagoon-like river, gives one the pleasurable sensation of a South Seas locale. The river, which is actually a tidal estuary for at least half the distance to the village, is shallow but broad; it is fresh water fed by one of the several great artesian springs that rise along the coast at the foot of the lofty range of mountains that form the spine of the Baja Peninsula. A variety of giant black snook, called locally róbalo prieta, populate the waters of this estuary and are a sportsman's challenge and delight. Along this same waterway, beneath a great rock outcropping, a *hot spring* rises to fill a sylvan pool with clear warm water, ideal for bathing. Along each side of the estuary runs a dirt road that communicates between the village and the airstrips as well as the resorts at the mouth. The valley of the arroyo widens from a few hundred feet near the gulf to ½ mile or more at the village near the head of the lagoon, about 2 miles from the mouth. Just above the village is a concrete dam which impounds the water from the stream bed and provides ample irrigation for the orchards and farms of the valley.

Before one arrives at the village an immense whitewashed quadrangle mud-brick building with rampart corner towers may be seen standing on a high hill to the north. It is the Carcel de Cananea, the territorial penitentiary occupied today by surprisingly few inmates under an equally surprising humane and progressive penal system. Those prisoners qualifying by good behavior are allowed their freedom each day to labor on the surrounding farms and at various trades in the village, returning to their cells each afternoon at a blown signal. The wives and families of the inmates occupy residences in the village or thatched adobes closeby the prison. A small Mexican Army garrison supervises the prison and guards the town.

On the opposite side of the waterway, perched high above the village on a hill near a masonry dam and its small lake, the Mission Santa Rosalía de Moliege, founded originally in 1705 by a Sicilian Jesuit, Father Juan Manuel Basualda, surveys the wide vista of the fertile valley once completely under its sovereign aegis. The first location of the mission was nearby on the site of an Indian ranchería called Caamanc-ca-Caleja, washed out by a great flood in 1770. The present mission church, since repaired and remodeled several times, was built by Jesuit Father Escalante in 1766 and was continuously in use until 1845; after a period of disrepair it was refurbished and now serves as one of the village churches. The building is a neat masonry patchwork laid up with white lime mortar. An ancient lime kiln still stands behind the mission where ingredients for an excellent mortar and a very durable concrete were manufactured to a special formula under direction of the mission fathers. It is a spot well worth visiting. Closeby, during the great *chubasco* of 1959, a fierce onslaught of high winds and heavy rains uncovered a great field of interesting and valuable artifacts in an ancient Indian midden. Some 2,000 or more Indians occupied the valley at the time of the founding of the mission in 1705; by 1782 they had dwindled from disease and other casualties to less than 100.

Below the mission church and dam, situated on a slight elevation on the left bank of the arroyo, the village of Mulegé, with a population of around 750 persons, centers around a small plaza. The main street edges along a few blocks of solidly built adobe walls, one house running into another with a mix of various commercial establishments and homes. The public school is one of the most imposing buildings. There are two general stores with a surprisingly large stock of food staples, hardware and drygoods. Gasoline, lubricating oil, engine and mechanical parts are available in the town but marine fuel is more readily obtainable at the resort hotels at the mouth of the lagoon. There are two tourist hotels in the town where comfortable rooms and meals may be had. The surrounding well-irrigated farms produce a large variety of tropical and subtropical fresh fruits and vegetables including mangoes, bananas, oranges, olives, limónes, figs, dates, pomegranates, grapes, sugarcane, beans, sweet potatoes, and alfalfa forage. The date crop is by far the largest commercial crop grown and exported, the original palms having been brought to Mulegé and planted by the missionary founders. The date crop is at the height of its harvest toward the end of each year and the drying and packing sheds are a beehive of activity. Cattle are run and milk cows, rarely seen in this region, are kept.

Esteban Carbonelli first discovered the Mulegé Lagoon in 1536 and found that the natives had been gathering pearl oysters for food for centuries and had amassed a fabulous collection of priceless pearls as a casual by-product; immediately, a Spanish pearl rush to the gulf ensued and the region around Mulegé, especially in nearby Concepción Bay, proved a bonanza to the firstcomers. For 170 years thereafter the coast in the vicinity of Bahía Concepción and Bahía Santa Inés was frequented by pearlers, both legitimate ones and poachers.

It was here in Mulegé, shortly after the founding of the mission, that an event occurred that indelibly marks a place in maritime history. The port will be most eminently remembered as the site of the first shipyard in California, and for *El Triunfo de la Cruz,* the staunch vessel built there that served so ably and so long the needs of the Baja California missions.

In order to maintain communication and transport across the gulf, Father Juan Ugarte, then in charge of the California missions and in residence at Loreto, undertook to build a seaworthy ship, an art with which he had no familiarity whatsoever. Ugarte was a resourceful man, however, having already proven his remarkable ability for organization. Procuring the services of a shipwright from across the gulf, a laborious trek into the high mountains was made in search

of suitable trees from which to cut timbers for a ship. After several trips to the tree-bearing craggy slopes some 200 miles from Loreto, sufficient pine trees were felled and an adequate number of rough timbers hewn for the job. The incredible labor of carrying and dragging this material out of the mountains began, and Mulegé, being only 90 miles distant from the forest where the trees were felled, was chosen for the shipyard site. In a short time, with the aid of two carpenters and the labor of the mission Indians, Ugarte's vessel grew ready to launch. In September, 1719, Ugarte nailed a cross upon the bowsprit and christened his ship *El Triunfo de la Cruz (The Triumph of the Cross).* The ship, compared to other vessels then in use, was of considerable size and judged to be well built by those contemporaries knowledgeable about marine architecture. It was pronounced, in fact, superior to any other vessel of its kind that had ever before been seen in those waters. For a number of years *El Triunfo de la Cruz* continued to be the only ship in the services of the missionaries and was almost constantly voyaging to one place or another. Father Ugarte died in 1731 but his vessel, first ship to be constructed in California — built and launched in Mulegé — saw many more years of useful service before it succumbed to the elements and was lost in a severe storm.

Mulegé

FACILITIES — At the mouth of the lagoon under the lee of El Sombrerito Point there is a dock extending a short distance out into shoal water before the Loma Linda Landing; fuel in drums is sometimes available here. A second dock in the left reach of the estuary before the Serenidad Mulegé Resort extends into shoal water and can accommodate small boats and launches; fuel is available for purchase at the *airstrip* near the hotel and may be transported over the dock. *Fresh water* is available at the hotel as well. A third dock extends into somewhat deeper water below the Club Aero in the main reach of the estuary on the starboard hand when entering. Fuel is available at the hotel's *airstrip* and may be transported down the trail and over the dock; *fresh water* is also available. Gasoline is stocked in 100, 90 and 80 octanes, principally for airplanes but regular motor fuel and diesel may be obtained in the village behind the large general store, about 2 miles up the estuary. Transportation by truck to the hotels can be arranged.

Shipmaster's note: The Captain of the Port issues permits to masters of vessels desiring to take stores, water or fuel, and ship's papers must be presented to him upon arrival in any event. Mulegé is noted for its warm hospitality and consideration is rendered in return for respect.

Mulegé Entrance Channel

TRANSPORTATION — Taxis are available at the hotels and in the town. Bus service connects Mulegé with Loreto and La Paz to the south, and to Santa Rosalía, northward. Air transportation by scheduled flights may be had three times weekly to Tijuana and flights are available also to Loreto, La Paz, Santa Rosalía and Los Angeles Bay. Cargo trucks carry supplies and produce to and from Mulegé weekly. Small coasters call in the roadstead at frequent intervals. Private planes and boats may be expected throughout the year with heavier traffic during the winter.

COMMUNICATIONS — Telegraph and telephone lines link Mulegé with Santa Rosalía, Loreto and La Paz, and from these places to international points. The telegraph office is open for acceptance of public messages. The resort hotels, Club Aero and Serenidad Mulegé, maintain UHF UNICOM watch on 122.8 kiloHertz for incoming planes. Ship-to-shore watch is maintained on 2128, 2638, 2738 and 2620 kiloHertz.

PUBLIC ACCOMMODATIONS — There are five hotels in the Mulegé area: Club Aero de Mulegé (Rancho Loma Linda) on the north side of the estuary, situated on a bluff overlooking the mouth of the lagoon, offers first-class accommodations, American plan, by reservation. Casual diners from pleasure yachts are welcome in the dining room and bar; the other facilities of the hotel are available to them depending on space. Serenidad Mulegé, situated on the south side of the estuary near the mouth of the lagoon, offers first-class accommodations, American plan, by reservation. Casual diners from pleasure yachts are welcome in the dining room and bar and the other facilities of the hotel are available depending upon space.

Playa de Mulegé, a budget-priced resort of grass ramadas located on the beach just outside the mouth of the lagoon on the south side of the estuary entrance, offers meals, a bar, and comfortable cots under the protection of thatched huts. Casual visitors from pleasure yachts are welcome as space and meals may be available.

Old Hacienda Mulegé, offering comfortable accommodations at a budget price, is located in the town, two miles up the river. Meals are served and there is a bar.

Las Casitas, also located in the town, offers comfortable accommodations and meals at a budget price.

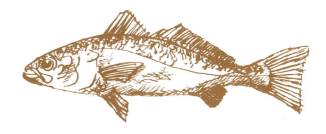

MARINE EMERGENCIES — Government Navy and Coast Guard vessels are stationed in the Port of Santa Rosalía, 34 miles northwestward. They may be contacted on the emergency ship-to-shore frequency of 2182 kiloHertz, or a message may be relayed by other vessels in the vicinity.

MEDICAL FACILITIES — There is a small clinic and hospital in Mulegé Village, attended by a nurse. Larger hospital facilities with the service of a doctor are available in Puerto Santa Rosalía, 34 miles to the northwest. A second emergency hospital facility is located on the south end of San Marcos Island at the Kaiser Gypsum Works, about 22 miles northwestward and offshore. There is a resident dentist at Santa Rosalía.

SOURCES OF ADDITIONAL INFORMATION — Club Aero de Mulegé, 4325 Sepulveda Boulevard, Culver City, California 90230, telephone (213) 473-3343; Serenidad Mulegé, 4305 Donald Douglas Drive, Long Beach, California 90808, telephone (213) 774-2257; Old Hacienda Mulegé, 1025 Cypress Avenue, Imperial Beach, California 92032, telephone (714) 424-8956 or 385-9110.

Río Santa Rosalía, Mulegé

Bahía de Santa Inés (Santa Inéz Bay) is a great open bay formed by the semicircular sweep of the coast between Punta Prieta and Punta Santa Inés, situated about 9 miles northward. The shore of this bay is generally low and sandy, backed by low hills. Punta Colorado is a moderately high reddish-colored bluff at the foot of a lateral spur of the hills, about 1 mile northwestward of Punta Prieta. A monument erected at Latitude 27° 00′ north, Longitude 112° 01′ west, marking the southern boundary of the Santa Magdalena Plain, stands on the beach about 6½ miles northwestward of Punta Prieta and 5½ miles north-northwestward of Punta Colorado. The plain, dry, barren, and covered with rock, is several miles in width and extends along the coast northward of the monument. In the latter part of the 1800's a rash of land promotions was capitalized in San Francisco, trading on the combination of the vast and empty acres of the Baja California Peninsula and the adventurous spirit of Americans eager for the riskiest of speculations that promised cheap land or quick riches.

Near Punta Santa Inés are some conspicuous table-topped hills known as Las Barracas, the highest being 300 feet in elevation; these hills are separated from the coastal range by a valley.

Punta Santa Inés (Santa Inéz Point) is a blunt cape comprised of four rocky headlands embracing three sandy beaches. The point, forming the northern boundary of Santa Inés Bay, is low and rocky and surmounted by a small hill. A sandspit with a narrow waist extends in an easterly direc-

Islas Santa Ines

Punta Chivato, Bahía Santa Inés

tion off the point terminating in a T-shaped configuration at its extremity; ¼ mile northward, a volcanic ridge extends several hundred yards seaward and a smaller finger of rock extends into the sea northward of the ridge. The sand beaches inbetween these rocky projections are a creamy white in sharp contrast to the surrounding dark volcanic flows. About ½ mile westward of the T-shaped projection of the point, detached rocks lie close inshore. A resort hotel complex, Borrego de Oro, is built on a low promontory about 1 mile westward of the point, its buildings plainly visible from offshore during the day and its lights clearly marking its position at night. *Anchorage* may be taken under the lee of Punta Santa Inés, sheltered against northwesterly winds about ½ mile offshore in depths of 4½ to 5 fathoms; sportfishing launches belonging to the resort are moored in the open bight immediately westward of the hotel in 2 fathoms, sand. A short breakwater has been constructed, extending off the hotel point to provide some protection from southeasterly weather as the anchorage is exposed to winds from that quarter.

The soundings in the southern part of Bahía de Santa Inés range from 5 fathoms close inshore to 18 to 20 fathoms at about ½ mile off; the northern portion of the bay is shallower, there being depths of 3 fathoms or less at ¾ mile offshore, deepening to 5 to 8 fathoms between the mainland and Santa Inés Islands.

Islas de Santa Inés (Santa Inéz Islands) situated on the rim of the bay from 2 to 3 miles southeastward of Punta Santa Inés are comprised of three low flat islets surrounded by shoals and sunken rocks; between the islands and the point, however, there is a clear passage with depths of 4½ to 5 fathoms. The southernmost and largest island, Isla Santa Inés, is about 1 mile long and ⅓ that wide, a mere speck of barren land raised above the water about 30 feet and perched on the brink of a shelf that slopes into the depths of the outer gulf. The southern point of the islet is low and rocky with a scattering of *exposed rocks* in shoal water extending off for about ½ mile. *Shoal water* skirts the

western side with a growth of seaweed over a sandy bottom; on this side there is a small cove with a sandy beach frequented by local native fishermen. At one time two wooden cross-marked graves could be seen on the skyline of the island; above the landing beach a 40-foot stone wall, carefully built in the shape of a right angle, subtended a wide lane marked by large isolated stones leading to the two graves. The graves were 3- by 10-foot rectangles of stones ornamented with pearl shells but with no indication as to the names of the occupants of these plots nor the circumstances of their deaths, a casual mystery of the eternal flow of life and death in the grand compass of the gulf. The central and smallest islet of this group, Isla Rasso, is but 6 feet above sea level and separated from its larger neighbor by *submerged rocks* on a shoal ridge; the northernmost islet, Isla Alto, is raised only 15 feet above the sea and is of small

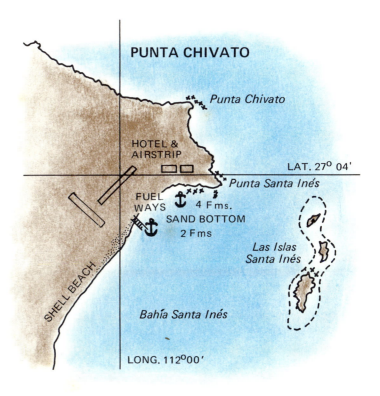

297

Borrego de Oro Hotel and anchorage

extent; its center lies 2 miles east-southeastward of Santa Inés Point. Depths increase rapidly eastward of the group.

Navigation caution: A 3 fathom shoal 1¼ miles long, oriented north-northwest and south-southeast, and ½ mile wide lies within 1½ miles of the southernmost island. Eastward of the islets the depths increase rapidly. The natives conduct an extensive turtle fishery in the bay and nearby waters of the gulf supplying the tasty "caguama" meat to the local market and resort hotels. Turtle meat is considered a delicacy preferred by many to Mexican beef.

One of the most remarkable occurrences in the Bay of Santa Inés is the great abundance of a variety of exquisite sea shells to be found on the beaches. Here indeed, is a shell collector's paradise; a scattering of sea shells of every conceivable size, shape and color, and combination of colors to challenge the catalogues of the most assiduous conchologist and weary his back with the irresistible enticement of a host of species. Fossil shells are to be had as well, imbedded in the shale of the water-cut ledges of the low cliffs that rim the shore; layer upon layer of shell-turned-to-stone through untold thousands of years are revealed as each new storm exposes a deeper deposit.

Borrego De Oro (Golden Bighorn) or Hotel Punta Chivato as it is more commonly referred to, is a first-class luxury resort situated on a rise overlooking the bay about a mile westward of Punta Santa Inés. The buildings are of modern colonial masonry construction, embracing a fresh water swimming pool and attractive landscaped grounds. Sportfishing launches are rented and a small fleet of them lies moored in the bay before the hotel. A marine railway has been constructed to haul out the launches for repair and painting, and it is designed to service vessels up to 32 feet in length. Two lighted, hardpacked *airstrips* serve the resort; 80- and 100-octane aviation fuel is available; marine gasoline and diesel fuel are also carried. UNICOM radio 122.8 kHz. communication is maintained for aircraft, and high frequency side-band equipment is in operation for

radiotelephone communication internationally; the radio equipment is capable of ship-to-shore communication on 2182, 2620 and 2738 kHz. Scuba diving in the bay is a popular sport and a variety of equipment as well as compressed air is available at the hotel.

There are a few *detached rocks* close offshore between Punta Santa Inés and Punta Chivato, situated about 1¾ miles northward; one of these off-lying rocks, 25 feet high, is due eastward of a conspicuous white bluff.

Punta Chivato (Chivato Point) is a low bluff with a tableland 40 to 60 feet high behind it; many *detached rocks* lie off the point. At Chivato Point the coast turns sharply westward and assumes a general northwesterly trend as far as the entrance to Caleta San Lucas (San Lucas Cove), a distance of about 15 miles. This coastline is generally low and sandy with occasional bluffs and is fronted by a shore bank which extends from 600 to 800 yards offshore in places.

SECTION 22
PUNTA CHIVATO to
PUNTA SAN FRANCISQUITO

Isla San Marcos showing Roca Lobos

Isla San Marcos (San Marcos Island) is a large, dry and barren island that lies off the coast midway between Punta Chivato and Caleta de San Lucas. The island is about 5½ miles long, oriented approximately north and south, and from 1¼ to 2½ miles wide. It is quite hilly rather than mountainous, rising to a height very nearly in the center of 891 feet. Its color and vegetation are those of the neighboring mainland. Except for the salt works on Carmen Island, it is the only island in the gulf on which there is an industry of any considerable proportion, having an extensive gypsum mine, a processing plant and loading facilities on the western side near its southern end. For navigation see H.O. 620, H.O. 849; British Admiralty Charts #2324, #3061; Mexican Carta Náutica F.H. 603.

The island is separated from the coast of the peninsula by Canal de San Marcos (Craig Channel) which has a least navigable width of 1 mile and clear channel depths of 3½ to 4½ fathoms. *Vessels using this channel must employ due caution to avoid the long tail of the shoal that makes off from the south point of the island, and the coastal shore bank opposite, as well.* The southern point of Isla San Marcos is a low, sandy tongue nearly ½ mile long from which a *rocky reef,* with depths of less than 3 fathoms over its outer edge, extends about 1¼ miles southward to within just a little over a mile of the Peninsula coast, defining the San Marcos Channel. Eastward of the low sandspit, the south coast of the island is comprised of a series of sheer bluffs about 30 feet high, with shoal water extending off for nearly ½ mile.

Roca de Los Lobos (Lobos Rock), a small rock about ¼ mile long and 20 feet high, lies on the eastern side of this bank, about ¾ mile northward of its southern extremity, and ½ mile from the southern tip of San Marcos Island; numerous *sunken rocks* surround it and not more than 1½ fathoms can be carried through the passage between it and the island. *A detached and isolated 3-fathom shoal* lies about 1 mile east-northeastward of Lobos Rock. The southern end of San Marcos Island, between positions on the eastern and western sides, respectively, about 2¼ and 1¼ miles from its southern extremity, is fringed by a *shore bank* with depths over it of less than 3 fathoms and which extends offshore for as much as 600 yards in places. There is a *good anchorage* eastward of Lobos Rock, between it and the isolated 3-fathom shoal situated about 1 mile east-northeastward, in depths of from 5 to 7 fathoms. Small vessels may seek more sheltered *anchorage* from northerly weather closer to the island, within the cove embraced by the reef which extends off the southern tip of the island and a point surrounded by kelp beds close eastward. There is good holding ground, sand bottom, in from 2½ to 4 fathoms about ¼ mile, or less, from the prominent bluffs that back the cove. A *landing* may be made on the rocky beach at the foot of the bluffs in calm weather, although a swell sometimes renders this operation a bit wet. A trail leads from the anchorage to the village located at the gypsum mine, entailing about a 15 minute hike.

There is a large gypsum deposit (yeso in Spanish) on San Marcos Island that has been mined since 1925. The

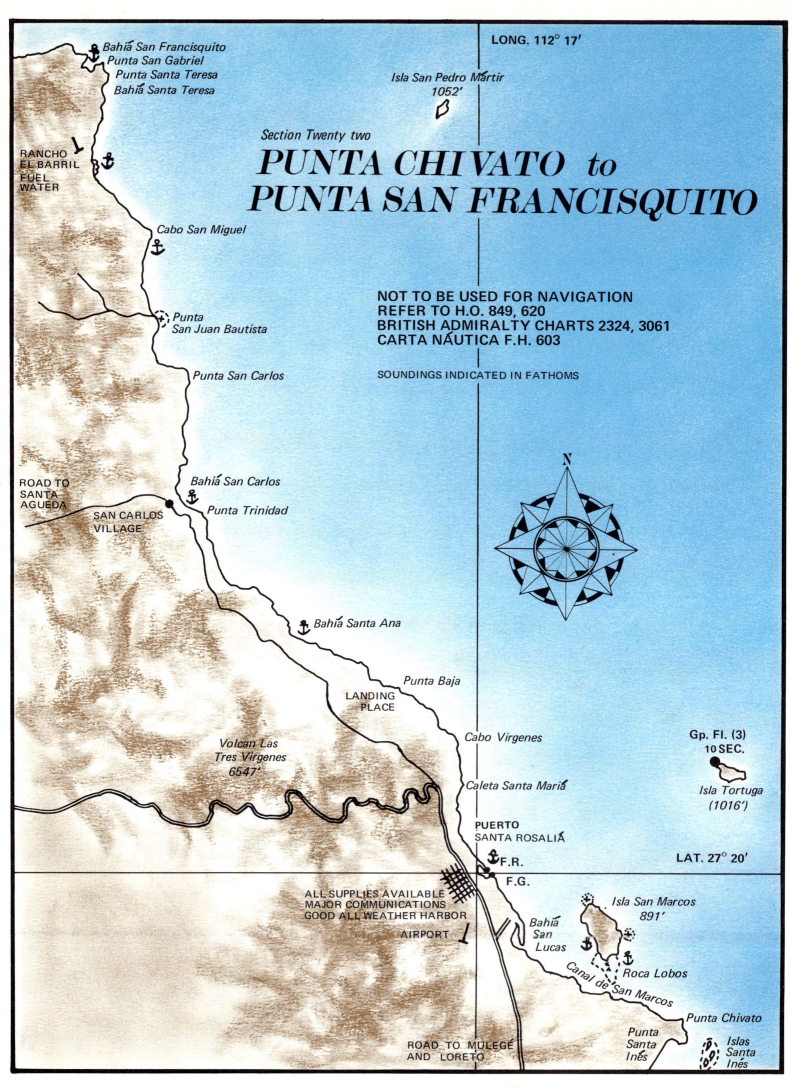

Bahía San Francisquito
Punta San Gabriel
Punta Santa Teresa
Bahía Santa Teresa

Isla San Pedro Mártir
1052'

LONG. 112° 17'

RANCHO
EL BARRIL
FUEL
WATER

Cabo San Miguel

Section Twenty two

PUNTA CHIVATO to PUNTA SAN FRANCISQUITO

Punta
San Juan Bautista

Punta San Carlos

**NOT TO BE USED FOR NAVIGATION
REFER TO H.O. 849, 620
BRITISH ADMIRALTY CHARTS 2324, 3061
CARTA NÁUTICA F.H. 603**

SOUNDINGS INDICATED IN FATHOMS

N

ROAD TO
SANTA
AGUEDA

Bahía San Carlos

SAN CARLOS
VILLAGE

Punta Trinidad

Bahía Santa Ana

Punta Baja

LANDING
PLACE

Cabo Virgenes

Gp. Fl. (3)
10 SEC.

Volcan Las
Tres Virgenes
6547'

Caleta Santa María

Isla Tortuga
(1016')

PUERTO
SANTA ROSALIA

F.R.

LAT. 27° 20'

F.G.

ALL SUPPLIES AVAILABLE
MAJOR COMMUNICATIONS
GOOD ALL WEATHER HARBOR

AIRPORT

Bahía
San
Lucas

Isla San Marcos
891'

Roca Lobos

Canal de San Marcos

Punta Chivato

ROAD TO MULEGÉ
AND LORETO

Punta
Santa
Inés

Islas
Santa
Inés

Isla San Marcos   Gypsum loading pier

gypsum beds are exposed in the central part of the south-ern end of the island and the material is mined north of the village near the southwestern corner. The area being worked has a decidedly whitish appearance in contrast to the darker surrounding hills, and serves as a distinctive landmark when approaching from southward or westward.

An ancient saline lake or lagoon in which the gypsum or calcium sulfate accumulated, possibly supplied by hy-drothermal springs connected with volcanic activity, is found as much as 400 feet thick in the quarry. Modern pit-mining machinery and earth-moving equipment is em-ployed together with conventional blasting techniques. Freighters call at the island about every two to three weeks to load a cargo of bulk gypsum, working several hatches simultaneously by utilizing modern bulk loading equipment installed on the wharf. Loading proceeds at a rate of 1,200 to 1,300 tons per hour and a vessel which arrives by eight in the morning may be ready to leave by the next afternoon.

Several brackish wells are located on the island; how-ever all drinking water, supplies, and fuel needed at the mines and in the village are brought by the gypsum freight-ers in ballast from North American ports. About 800,000 tons of the mined product per year are shipped to all parts of the Pacific basin.

WHARF AND VILLAGE — A T-head pier, measur-ing 320 feet along its outer face, extends about 300 yards from the shore of the mine cove; there are depths of 42 feet along the northern arm of the pier and 32 feet along the southern arm. Dolphins stand about 250 feet off each end of the berth for mooring and shifting. *Pilotage* is compul-sory for vessels proceeding to this berth although smaller vessels may approach the cove and *anchor* ½ mile north-westward of the pier in 8 to 10 fathoms, sand, without a pilot. There is frequently a surge in this anchorage and

ground tackle is advised fore and aft to avoid uncomfort-able rolling. Smaller vessels may obtain *anchorage* south-eastward of the pier in shoaler water with ready access to a *landing place* on shore.

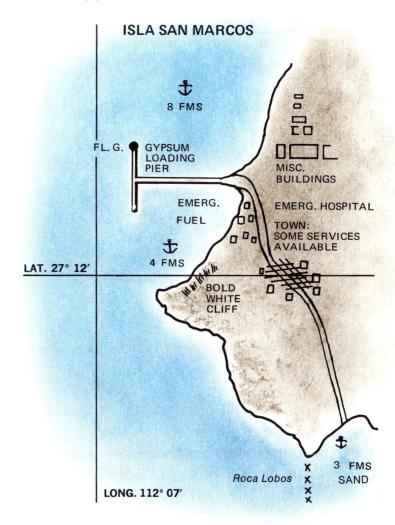

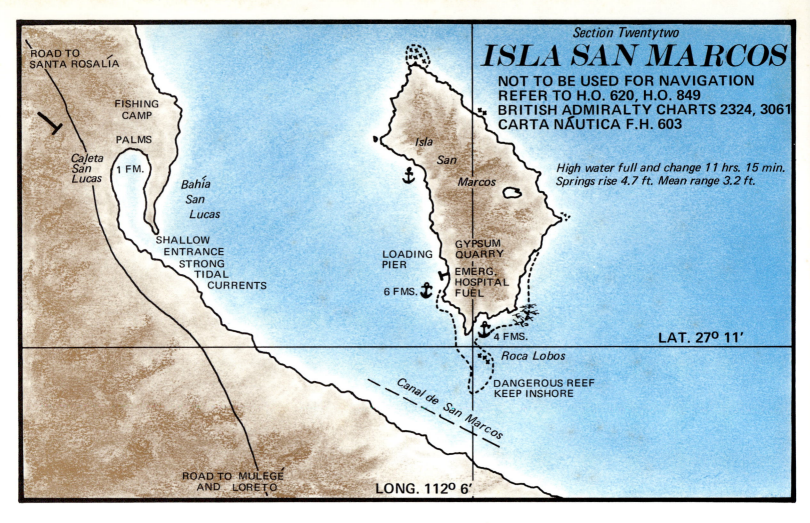

Section Twentytwo

ISLA SAN MARCOS

**NOT TO BE USED FOR NAVIGATION
REFER TO H.O. 620, H.O. 849
BRITISH ADMIRALTY CHARTS 2324, 3061
CARTA NÁUTICA F.H. 603**

*High water full and change 11 hrs. 15 min.
Springs rise 4.7 ft. Mean range 3.2 ft.*

ROAD TO
SANTA ROSALÍA

FISHING
CAMP

PALMS

Caleta
San
Lucas

1 FM.

Bahía
San
Lucas

SHALLOW
ENTRANCE
STRONG
TIDAL
CURRENTS

Isla

San

Marcos

GYPSUM
QUARRY

LOADING
PIER

EMERG.
HOSPITAL
FUEL

6 FMS.

4 FMS.

LAT. 27° 11'

Roca Lobos

DANGEROUS REEF
KEEP INSHORE

Canal de San Marcos

ROAD TO MULEGÉ
AND LORETO

LONG. 112° 6'

Navigation lights are exhibited 36 feet above the water **flashing red** from a dolphin standing on the southern end of the T-pier, and **flashing green** from a dolphin on the northern end of the pier; the *lights* can be seen in clear weather for 9 miles but may be obscured when a large freighter is moored alongside the pierhead.

San Marcos Island is a port of entry for foreign vessels and entering or clearing procedures may be officially transacted if the port is first or last port of call in Mexico. Various supplies and provisions may be purchased in the village and a limited amount of diesel fuel may be obtained from the company stocks in emergency. There is a blacksmith shop and a machine shop where minor repairs can be made and some engine parts are stocked. Company mechanics may be called upon in emergency for engine or machinery repair or adjustment. Metal warehouse sheds and company buildings are located on the shelf just back of the shore northward of the pier; a complete company village, including shops and barracks for the workers, is situated in a protected draw southward of the pier.

There is a *hospital* in the village with 4 beds and an attendant doctor; a *dentist* whose office is in Santa Rosalía, makes regular visits across the channel to the island; a larger *hospital* facility is located at Santa Rosalía where scheduled air transportation is available to other parts of the peninsula, Mexico and the United States. A pilot launch makes a weekly trip 15 miles across the channel to Santa Rosalía for supplies and mail. Some 250 employees of the Companía Mexicana Occidental, S.A., which is organized under the laws of Mexico but affiliated with Kaiser Gypsum Company of the United States, live and work on the island.

Northward beyond the company gypsum mine a third *anchorage,* with some shelter from the prevailing winds, may be had in a small cove a little over 2 miles north of the pier on the west side of the island. From the southern point of the island to its western extremity, the shore is comprised of sand beaches and bluffs 15 to 20 feet high, behind which the hills rise to the top of the island. The northwest side of San Marcos Island is comprised of steep bluffs off which there are a number of detached rocks and islets that lie up to ¼ mile offshore at some points; the most conspicuous of these outlying rocky islets are 40 feet high at the northwestern point of the island and 25 feet high midway between this point and the northern point of the island.

Off the north point of San Marcos Island, which is surmounted by a sharp hill, three whitish islets 10 to 40 feet high and a number of *detached rocks* extend about ½ mile northward. The east side of San Marcos is comprised chiefly of rocky bluffs 20 to 300 feet high. Near the southeastern point of the island there is a strip of sand and gravel beach about 1 mile long; on the northeastern side there is a similar beach ¾ mile long, off which are a number of *detached rocks,* the highest of which is 8 feet above water. A *rocky reef* projects a short distance from the easternmost point of the island.

San Marcos Island appeared on early charts of the gulf as Isla de Galápagos and was, and sometimes still is, referred to as Galápagos Island because of the large number of marine turtles frequently to be found in the waters around the island. In the latter part of the 1800's, during the height of a land promotion scheme on the nearby Magdalena Plain, the off-lying island was referred to as San Marcos Island after the name of the model community proposed for the prospective coastal colonists. An outlying but smaller island is named Isla Tortuga, which is yet another Spanish name for turtle.

When first discovered by the Spanish, a small tribe of Indians lived on San Marcos Island, subsisting quite adequately as fishermen on the product of their daily catch. They fared rather badly at the hands of the early Spanish pearlers, however, and when the mission at Mulegé was established, the San Marcos tribe was removed to that coastal village. Father Basaulda, finding calcium sulfate deposits on the island in the form of natural translucent sheets, transported some of the material to the mission and used it for windows in his church at Mulegé, in lieu of glass.

Isla de Tortuga (Tortuga Island), situated about 22 miles off the coast of the peninsula and lying in a position approximately 15 miles northeastward of the northern end of San Marcos Island, is an oval-shaped, steep-to volcanic pinnacle that rises abruptly from the deep waters of the surrounding gulf, showing only the very top of the volcano from which the land was formed. It is hilly and barren, about 2 miles in length and a little over 1 mile in width. The highest peak near the southern shore rises to an elevation of 1,016 feet above the sea, which has a depth in this part of the gulf of over 5,000 feet. The center

of the island is comprised of a broad volcanic crater and the entire island is covered with a mantle of sharp, dark, lava rock making landing and penetration to its interior a difficult task. There is no known fresh water source and, because of its parched condition, very little vegetation. The volcano appears to have erupted in fairly recent geological times and is considered by geologists to be the youngest island in the gulf.

A *navigation light* is shown from the northern coast near the western end of the island, exhibiting a **white group flash of three flashes in a period of 10 seconds:** flash 0.3 second, eclipse 1.7 seconds; flash 0.3 second, eclipse 1.7 seconds; flash 0.3 second, eclipse 5.7 seconds. The *light* is shown 105 feet above the sea from a metal tower and can be seen for a distance of 6 miles.

Caleta San Lucas (San Lucas Cove), situated about 15 miles northwestward of Punta Chivato and about 10 miles southward of Santa Rosalía, is a roomy but shallow cove bordered by date palms; it offers safe all-weather protection for small vessels of 5-foot draft or less. A long spit, extending south-southwestward, nearly encloses a rather large shoal lagoon about 2 miles long, oriented north and south, and ½ to ¾ mile wide. The entrance channel, in which the ebb and flow of the tide can be of considerable strength, is close northward of a sand islet situated in the middle of a narrow entrance; this channel, which has depths in it at low water of 1 to 1½ fathoms, parallels the shore behind a mud bank, then doglegs close along the inside of the arm of the spit, finally opening into an oval basin surrounded by shoal banks; inside the lagoon the depths range from ½ to 1 fathom. A small estuary opens off the basin at the mouth of a stream which empties into the lagoon.

Caleta San Lucas

The configuration of the mud bar fronting the access channel outside the harbor varies from season to season, and at times it will allow a draft of as much as 6 feet to be carried over close aboard the south end of the spit at high water; at other times the depth over the bar at this position is severely limited and access must be found around the southern end of the bar.

TIDES — The mean high water interval at full and change at San Lucas Cove is 11 hours 15 minutes; the spring range is 4.7 feet, the mean range 3.2 feet. At low tide some of the tastiest rock oysters and clams in the gulf can be gathered from the mud flats surrounding the San Lucas lagoon.

FACILITIES — There is a fishing camp located on the shore, where gasoline may sometimes be obtained. A community of small ranches grows truck garden produce and cultivates date palms. A sizable *airstrip* is in use just back of the shore of the lagoon along its western side; medium-size multi-engine passenger planes land here from Loreto,

Santa Agueda. Depths of 20 to 40 fathoms are sounded at a mile offshore.

Punta Santa Agueda is low and sandy with a shoal extending about 200 yards north-northwestward, beyond which the depths increase rapidly. The point lies on the eastern side of the mouth of the Santa Agueda Lagoon, the mouth of which is awash at low water; most of the shallow lagoon within dries at that stage. An islet, Islote Santa Agueda, lies close inshore about 400 yards westward of Punta Santa Agueda.

Between Punta Santa Agueda and Punta Blanca, situated about 2½ miles northwestward, the coast recedes to form a bight at the center of which lies Puerto de Santa Rosalía. The coast is steep-to and deep between Punta Santa Agueda and Puerto de Santa Rosalía, but shoals rapidly to a shore bank extending offshore about 400 yards between Santa Rosalía and Punta Blanca northward; for this reason vessels approaching the coast are advised to take frequent or continual soundings.

Guaymas, La Paz and Tijuana, serving the scheduled transportation needs of the town of Santa Rosalía about 7 miles north. Refreshment stands are located near the airstrip. The newly graded and paved coastal road runs close by Caleta San Lucas.

From the entrance to San Lucas Cove northward about 3 miles, the coast is low and sandy with a bank skirting the shore as far as a prominent point surmounted by a red mound about 60 feet high; thence the coast trends northwestward for about 5 miles to Punta Santa Agueda. This stretch of coast is comprised of bluffs of moderate height with intervening sand beaches backed by land rising gradually to a high range of mountains in the interior. For the first mile northward of the Red Mound Point, a bank extends about 500 yards offshore; the remainder of this distance is steep-to except for some *detached rocks* lying close inshore, from 1 mile to ½ mile southward of Punta

Santa Rosalía was founded in the 1870's as a result of a chance discovery of some of the richest copper bearing ore in Mexico. In 1866, José Rosa Villavincencio, a rancher in nearby Santa Agueda, discovered on the desolate coast near the mouth of the Arroyo del Purgatorio a rather large field of curious, rough, ball-shaped fragments called boleos in Spanish. The boleos lay in a jumble of purplish lava slag, which, when assayed in Guaymas, proved to be carbonates and oxides of copper combined in an ore of incredible purity. Immediately a rush of prospectors came to the area and a number of claimants started a crude frontier mining operation in the hills, just back of the coast near the Santa Agueda Ranch. The mining area was simply referred to as the Santa Agueda District and, as it proved itself to be more than a minor scratching on the surface, the claims were soon bought up by German interests in Guaymas.

The first commercial quantity of the richest ore from

Puerto Santa Rosalía

the surface was loaded in a chartered square-rigger and shipped around the Horn to Europe. It was of such purity that the initial 6,000 tons delivered to the European smelter was said to be valued at 480,000 pesos, no mean sum in the 1870's. In 1884 the German holdings were bought by a French syndicate, Le Compagnie du Boleo, and serious operations began. By 1886, with sizable profits from the ore alone and generous concessions from the the Mexican Government under President Porfirio Días, Compañía de Boleo installed their first smelter at the mine. Thus began a stream of sailing ships around the Horn bearing thousands of tons of coal and coke for the insatiable maw of a somewhat inefficient smelting furnace, but one that was unceasingly stoked to pour out an unending stream of pure copper ingots for the owners.

From its crude frontier beginnings an orderly company town rose up. Track was laid from the mine heads to the smelter, thence to the waterfront, and a steam locomotive and ore cars were employed to transport the ever increasing stream of ore. The copper output in all forms steadily rose over the years to an astounding peak of 3,000 tons a month, the second largest copper mine in Mexico, out-produced only by the fabulously rich Cananea district in Sonora.

For this considerable production, enormous quantities of coal and coke were consumed, as much as 6,000 tons per month. A square-rigged collier left a north European port for Santa Rosalía on the average of one every eleven days, and with luck rounded Cape Horn, sailed up the long coast of Chile, Peru, Ecuador, Central America, and beat up the Gulf of California in from 120 to 150 days; some ships, taking the longer way around the Cape of Good Hope and across the Indian Ocean, took 200 to 250 days from point of departure to their destination on the Gulf of California. Once arrived they would cast anchor in the open roadstead at the rapidly growing port now called Santa Rosalía, a name borrowed from the Mission Santa Rosalía de Mulegé nearby. The Indian workers and local ranchers reverent to the mission referred to the new mining town as "Cachanilla," or simply "El Boleo"; but, by whatever name, the place became a well-known deepwater port throughout the maritime world.

The last of their breed, the great iron squareriggers — profitable for nothing save nitrates from the west coast of Chile or grain from the Pacific Northwest or Australia — came endlessly to the Santa Rosalía roadstead. In fact, Santa Rosalía's demands for smelter fuel was a principal sustaining source of revenue for the obsolescent sailing ship fleets that plodded across the world's seas in search of cargoes. But smelter fuel was only a one-way cargo, for the copper ingot output of the Santa Rosalía mines — too valuable to trust to slow and chancy windships — was shipped by steam vessel to Guaymas, thence overland by rail to New Orleans, where it was transhipped by steam vessels in regular Atlantic trade. From Pacific ports came other ships, both sail and steam, bringing cement, brick, lumber, machinery, and steel rails.

As ship traffic piled up on this open and unprotected coast, shipwrecks mounted with first this one, then that one going aground and stranding ashore in the occasional but fearful southeasters called aptly then and now, cordonazos (The Lash). After a rash of costly wrecks, the Compañía de Boleo began construction of a breakwater from the slag cast out by the smelters. The base of the mole that was to be a breakwater began at the smelter site, jutting out from a point close to the smelter itself and running eastward for a few hundred yards, then swinging in a wide arc southward for a distance of about ¼ mile. The breakwater building material consisted mostly of slag from the smelter, poured hot and steaming into the sea from railroad cars that traversed track laid atop the ever-lengthening mole. By 1910 the harbor was completed, the south mole built right over one of the unfortunate vessels left derelict aground. Thereafter the practice of discharging cargo from the roadstead was mostly discontinued.

From 1906 to 1916 Santa Rosalía was in her heyday; the copper ore was topping a half dozen mine heads at an unprecedented rate. Compañía de Boleo, at the outset of its most profitable production years, had purchased a steam vessel of 201 gross tons, the *Korrigan,* and employed it to transport its valuable ingots across the gulf to Guaymas. In 1907 this vessel was wrecked ashore on the beach north of the village, where her rusted remains may still be seen today, embedded in the sand. In 1898 the company purchased a second and larger vessel, the *Korrigan II,* and in 1912, still another, the *Korrigan III,* a ship of 916 tons, the latter two used to carry partially refined ore out of the gulf and up the Pacific coast to Tacoma for final smelting.

By 1954 the richest ore body of the mining property was gone and the "poorer" stock piles had been processed. The Government of Mexico had been pressing the Compañía de Boleo to relinquish its mining rights and at this low point in their long producing history they elected to discontinue their operation in the Gulf of California. A Mexican company was formed, Boleo Estudios e Inversiones Mineras, S.A., called locally still by the old familiar name used for almost a hundred years, El Boleo.

The whitish plume from the hillside stack still blows in the direction of the prevailing breeze or floats in the still air above the town, a telltale signal to seamen that here indeed still lives the gulfside town of Santa Rosalía, happily unchanged in most ways from its picturesque frontier beginnings. There's more history and romance of the sea in a single grain of Santa Rosalía's mine-stack soot than in all the rest of the gulf ports combined. It is a port well worth a visit and boasts the only enclosed deepwater harbor in the gulf; a good place for shelter when the sea is up.

Rolling Hitch

Puerto de Santa Rosalía (Port Santa Rosalía), about 1½ miles northwestward of Punta Santa Agueda, can be recognized from a good distance off by the telltale smelting stack plume of smoke that rises skyward. The stack discharge is piped to the top of a hill northwestward of the mine works in order to disperse it away from the village. Close in, this stack can be readily made out, with a large above-ground duct snaking over the hills leading to a tall adobe brick smokestack ½ mile from the town.

It provides an excellent landmark. The glow of the fires at the smelter and the twinkle of electric lights at the mine works are readily seen at night. Between Santa Agueda and Caleta Santa María (Santa María Cove), about 5½ miles northward, there are six arroyos spaced about 1 mile apart, opening onto the shore, in each of which mining activity is carried on. Across the mouths of the arroyos, trestles of the mine railroad show to seaward. Vessels bound for Santa Rosalía generally raise Tortuga Island, then when abreast take their departure steering for the landmarks of the port. When calling at this port, reference should be made to H.O. 620, H.O. 849; British Admiralty #2323, and #3061; and Mexican Carta Náutica F.H. 603.

Puerto de Santa Rosalía is a small but well-protected artificial harbor, enclosed by two masonry faced mine-slag moles that are so configured as to surround an inner basin and serve as effective breakwaters against the sea. The easternmost and principal mole extends out nearly at right angles from the shore on the northwestern side of the harbor, then bends sharply to the southeastward, paralleling the shore and forming an effective breakwater against the sea. Two piers project inward from this mole, affording berths for vessels, but except alongside these two piers, the mole is foul with debris and encumbered with mostly inoperative heavy equipment. The southern mole projects out in a northeasterly direction from the shore, abreast the seaward end of the outer breakwater, leaving a narrow entrance, about 140 yards wide, between the two. The entrance channel is dredged from time-to-time to eliminate a shoal that tends to accumulate westward and southward from the head of the outer mole; the entrance channel is sometimes considerably narrowed to as little as 200 feet, by the incursion of this shoal between dredging periods. The harbor thus enclosed is roughly rectangular in shape with a length of about 500 yards and a width of about 350 yards.

Navigation lights are exhibited at the heads of the two moles. A **flashing red light** is shown 43 feet above the sea from a *white concrete tower* on the south end of the outer breakwater and has a range of 9 miles. A **flashing green light** is shown 43 feet above the sea from a *white iron mast* at the head of the south mole and has a range of 10 miles. A **flashing white light** is set atop the Port Captain's office, on the south mole, *on a white metal column.*

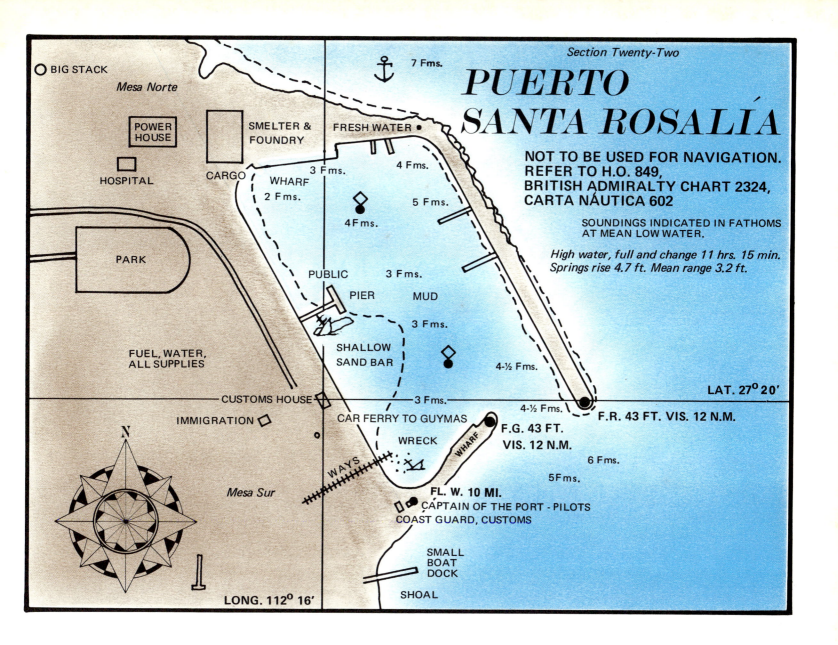

Section Twenty-Two

PUERTO SANTA ROSALÍA

NOT TO BE USED FOR NAVIGATION. REFER TO H.O. 849, BRITISH ADMIRALTY CHART 2324, CARTA NÁUTICA 602

SOUNDINGS INDICATED IN FATHOMS AT MEAN LOW WATER.

High water, full and change 11 hrs. 15 min. Springs rise 4.7 ft. Mean range 3.2 ft.

BIG STACK
Mesa Norte
POWER HOUSE
SMELTER & FOUNDRY
FRESH WATER
7 Fms.
HOSPITAL
CARGO
WHARF
3 Fms.
4 Fms.
2 Fms.
5 Fms.
4 Fms.
PARK
PUBLIC PIER
3 Fms.
MUD
3 Fms.
FUEL, WATER, ALL SUPPLIES
SHALLOW SAND BAR
3 Fms.
4-½ Fms.
CUSTOMS HOUSE
3 Fms.
4-½ Fms.
F.R. 43 FT. VIS. 12 N.M.
LAT. 27° 20'
IMMIGRATION
CAR FERRY TO GUYMAS
WRECK
WAYS
WHARF
F.G. 43 FT. VIS. 12 N.M.
6 Fms.
5 Fms.
Mesa Sur
FL. W. 10 MI.
CAPTAIN OF THE PORT - PILOTS COAST GUARD, CUSTOMS
N
SMALL BOAT DOCK
SHOAL
LONG. 112° 16'

Pilotage for large vessels is compulsory; the pilot comes out to the roadstead in a small, white open motorboat and boards well off the entrance. Small cruising yachts and sportfishing launches are exempted and may enter or leave the harbor freely when larger vessels are not maneuvering.

PORT OF ENTRY — Santa Rosalía is an official port of entry for Mexico and all foreign vessels must present their papers for both Customs and Quarantine clearance through the Captain of the Port.

HARBOR ENTRANCE — There are depths of 26 feet (when recently dredged) in the entrance channel at mean low water; inside the basin the deepest part is on the eastern side off the outer mole where there are general depths ranging from 26 to 15 feet; vessels of 27½-foot draft have been accommodated. Two can buoys are moored inside the harbor at either end of the basin. The western side of the harbor, westward of a line between the two cans, is quite shoal with *submerged dangers*. A *wreck* lies stranded at the inner end of the south mole; another *wreck* is stranded on the eastern end of the shoal that extends outward midway along the western wall of the basin.

TEMPORARY BERTH — Cruising yachts and sportfishing launches may find temporary berth on the port hand just inside the harbor entrance at the wooden wharf along the inner face of the south mole, convenient to the office of the Captain of the Port at the foot of the mole. An entering vessel may also come alongside the dilapidated pier near the hulk of a stranded steel freighter midway along the waterfront. Proper anchorage in the harbor will be designated by the Port Captain, usually in the basin in the southwest corner of the harbor close northwestward of the south mole.

Navigation warning: While the entrance channel always has depths of 20 feet or more, the western half of the harbor basin is foul with shoals, submerged pilings, submerged wrecks and inoperative heavy equipment. Proceed with caution. A small native boat dock is situated outside the harbor in the corner between the southern face of the south mole and the beach, but the water is shoal.

SEA AND WEATHER CONDITIONS — The prevailing winds throughout the year are from the general direction of north, swinging alternately from northwest to northeast. Summer winds blowing from the southeast and east occasionally bring tropical rainstorms from across the gulf but rainfall is infrequent at Santa Rosalía and the region suffers from an almost continuous dry spell; only 4.2 inches of rain can be expected on the average annually. Flooding down the arroyo through the center of town, while rare, is not altogether unknown. In 1911 a flash flood cascaded a sea of mud and boulders down the middle of the town, wreaking great damage to houses and shops in its path. Such conditions, however, vary from the norm; generally the surrounding hills remain almost dry and bare of green growth and only in the town are trees and shrubs to be seen, as the result of careful irrigation with precious fresh water.

The summers are exceedingly hot with little relief from the warm, dry northeast desert winds that blow across the hills. A particularly severe condition sometimes occurs during the months of May and June, when a nighttime offshore breeze occasionally blows from the west with great intensity, 40 to 50 knots, or greater, being not uncommon. At such time vessels underway should proceed along a course laid as close to the shore as depths and dangers will allow, in order to avoid the offshore fetch and to take advantage of the calmer waters close inshore. When at anchor under these severely windy conditions, ground tackle should be doubled up and the rode veered to a safe scope. Readiness to ride out such a sharp offshore blow can only be hampered by surprise.

Fall and winter months, as well, bring stiff winds that generally blow along the shore out of the northerly quadrant, raising a seaway that is uncomfortable to small boats but not dangerous to shipping. Easterly and northeasterly gales make the roadstead an insecure anchorage in winter.

ANCHORAGE — Outside the harbor, anchorage may be had by large vessels close inshore in depths of 7 to 13 fathoms, good holding ground; inside the 20-fathom curve the bottom shoals rapidly. The best anchorage during heavy weather is close northward of the port in 8 fathoms, with the two chimneys of the smelting works in range 249°.

FACILITIES — Considerable improvements have been made to both the port and the town over the intervening years. The town is divided into three sections: Mesa Norte or Mesa Francesa, a shelf of land above the harbor on the north, where the offices and houses of the mining officials are located; Mesa Sur (South Mesa), a similar elevation on the south side of the central arroyo, occupied by government offices, the military garrison and some houses of the workers; La Playa, the main part of the town on the bottom land of the arroyo, where most of the mine workers live in company-built houses arranged in mathematically uniform rows.

There are several small parks, a school, a kindergarten, several general stores, two public markets, several cafes and cantinas, a barber shop, a drug store, a French bakery, a Pemex gas station, a *hospital,* a *dentist's office,* an agency of Banco National de México, a relatively new Government Building, a theater, two hotels and a pre-

fabricated church manufactured in Belgium and brought around the Horn in a square-rigger in the late 1800's. The church still serves its function well and remains in reasonably good condition, the conversation piece of the town.

There is a complete system of electrical lighting in the town and the stores and shops are a beehive of activity until perhaps 10 p.m. every night. General supplies and a variety of dried and canned provisions are available at reasonable prices in the several general stores; fresh meats, fruits and vegetables are brought to the municipal markets daily from Santa Agueda and the surrounding farms. There are several small garages and shops where machine and engine parts can be procured; special parts may be flown in from Guaymas, La Paz or San Diego. The mining company maintains a large machine shop and foundry that may be utilized for emergency repair. The Pemex gasoline station, located on the main street three blocks up from the plaza, dispenses 70-octane gasoline which can be purchased for marine use by bringing a suitable container; 100- and 80-octane aircraft gasoline may be obtained at the *airstrip* on the South Mesa about 1½ miles from the town. Diesel fuel may be obtained in the harbor alongside the dock and permits for its purchase are issued by the Captain of the Port. *Water* is available from a pipeline at the dock but it is of poor quality for drinking and should be boiled or treated before using. Fishing supplies, butane gas and ice are available. There are several floating cranes in the harbor and dock-mounted hoists for heavy equipment and engine work. A marine ways capable of dry-docking vessels of up to 300 tons is operative with hull repair facilities.

PUBLIC ACCOMMODATIONS — There are two hotels in Santa Rosalía: the company Hotel Français, on Mesa Norte near the mine works, offers good accommodations on the American plan at quite reasonable prices; there is a good restaurant in the hotel. The Hotel Central, on the Plaza, offers accommodations on the European plan at equally reasonable rates.

TRANSPORTATION — There are a surprising number of good automobiles in this small remote town and several taxis available for transport of provisions and gasoline to the waterfront. A good road connects inland to the newly constructed, well-graded and partially paved coastal highway. Scheduled air transportation may be booked at the airline office for Guaymas, Loreto, La Paz and Tijuana, leaving from the *airport* at Caleta San Lucas, about 15 miles south of town; taxis are available to the airport. There is an *airstrip* on the South Mesa about 1½ miles south of town, where mining company and private planes land. A venerable old ferry, *Viosca,* makes a round trip weekly across the gulf to Guaymas,

Punta Santa Ana

Salt pan north of Punta Santa Ana

carrying passengers, supplies and mail; a single auto-mobile may be carried on the after hatch as deck cargo; the crossing takes about 12 hours. The company steamer makes irregular trips to Guaymas and up the Pacific coast to United States ports.

COMMUNICATIONS — There. is a Government Post Office near the Plaza with airmail service several times weekly; there is telegraph service to Mulegé, La Paz, and Loreto, with international connections. High frequency single side-band radio equipment communicates with international radiotelephone circuits. There is UNICOM communication on 122.8 megaHertz with incoming aircraft. The marine band, 2182, 2638, 2738, and 2620 kiloHertz, is monitored.

MARINE EMERGENCIES — Mexican Government vessels are frequently on station in the harbor and can be contacted on the emergency ship-to-shore radio frequency of 2182 kiloHertz. Fishing vessels and freighters in the vicinity may be contacted for help or message relay. The Mexican Navy maintains a base at Guaymas.

MEDICAL FACILITIES — There is a 15-bed hospital in Santa Rosalía, with attendant medical staff and modern equipment. Emergencies beyond the scope of the local hospital are flown to Guaymas, La Paz or San Diego. The hospital is located on Mesa Norte near the mine works and the Hotel Français.

SOURCES OF ADDITIONAL INFORMATION — Captain of the Port, Operación Porturía, Santa Rosalía,

B. Cfa., Mexico; Boleo Estudios e Invérsiones Mineras, S.A., Santa Rosalía, B. Cfa., Mexico.

The coast between Puerto Santa Rosalía and Caleta Santa María, about 5½ miles north-northwestward, is comprised of a succession of bluffs separating a series of arroyos, the sandy mouths of which open onto the shore. This particular part of the coast is fronted by a *shore bank* extending offshore for a distance of about ¼ mile in places. A group of mine buildings stands on a flat bench overlooking the sea, a little over a mile northward of the Santa Rosalía Harbor; a road runs along the foot of the cliffs close to the shore.

Caleta de Santa María (Santa María Cove), about ¾ mile wide, is indented about ¼ mile inside a line joining its entrance points. The southern entrance point is low and rocky, blending into rocky bluffs with low hills behind on the southern side of the cove; the northern side of the cove is hilly, terminating in a sharp bluff point 70 feet high, off which lie numerous *detached rocks*. At the head of the cove is a sand and shingle beach called "Biarritz."

Anchorage sheltered from northwesterly winds, but exposed to southeasters, may be taken about ¼ mile offshore in the middle of the cove, in depths of from 5 to 6 fathoms, with the highest peak of Las Tres Vírgenes bearing 277°, distant about 15 miles, and the highest peak of Isla Tortuga bearing 97°. Smaller vessels may *anchor* closer to the head of the beach in 2½ to 3½ fathoms, sand. On an earlier H.O. Chart 0639, Anchorages in the Gulf of California (now discontinued), Santa María Cove is shown in plan with numerous soundings within the points of the cove.

The coast northward of Santa María Cove, comprised of bluffs from 30 to 200 feet high, broken occasionally by deep arroyos with gravel beaches at their mouths, trends northward for about 5½ miles, then gradually falls away northwestward for another 2½ miles to Cabo Vírgenes. The land slopes steeply to Monte Santa María, which rises to an elevation of 4,302 feet about 3½ miles inland, its ridge running parallel with the coast for several miles. A *monument* is charted on the shore about 5 miles northward of Santa María Cove. The depths off this part of the coast are considerable; soundings within 1¼ miles of the shore are greater than 300 fathoms.

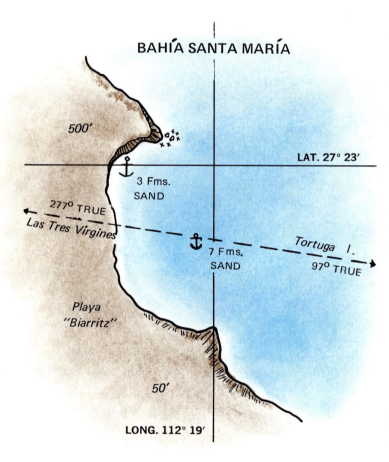

Las Tres Vírgenes are three remarkable mountains about 14 miles inland from the *monument,* the southernmost and highest of which attains an elevation of 6,547 feet. Volcanic activity within recent times was reported by the Spanish missionaries in 1746 to have occurred amongst these lofty peaks and there is abundant evidence of recent lava flow on the slopes of the volcano.

Cabo Vírgenes (Cape Vírgenes), a rocky cliff 200 feet high surmounted by a hill with an elevation of 600 feet, is backed by a high coastal range a short distance inland. Soundings off the cape show depths of 5 fathoms close-to,

deepening to 130 fathoms at about 1 mile offshore. Northwestward of Cabo Vírgenes the coast is generally low and the mountain range lies several miles inland. As is characteristic around almost all capes where the general trend of the coast bulges outward to form a land prominence, one may expect a high percentage of brisk winds. The meeting of several prevailing gulf currents often produces an abnormally confused sea in a stretch about 5 miles on either side of the cape, causing severe tidal rips and rough, steep waves. When wind driven, these seas can be especially uncomfortable for small vessels; this turbulence may be avoided by passing well off the land.

Punta Baja, 4½ miles northwestward of Cabo Vírgenes, is a shingle point off which a *shoal* extends a short distance. Just southward of the point is the mouth of an arroyo which leads up to an old silver mine. About ¾ mile southeastward of the point is a *landing place* marked by a flagstaff. Punta Santa Ana, situated about 7 miles west-northwestward of Punta Baja, is steep and closely backed by hills about 400 feet high; the point forms the eastern entrance of Bahía de Santa Ana.

Bahía de Santa Ana (Santa Ana Bay) is a slight indentation in the coast, about 3½ miles wide, westward of Punta de Santa Ana. The southern and western shores of the bay are comprised of sand and shingle beaches; a fresh water creek, which may be identified by the grass and trees on its banks, empties into a small lagoon that opens at the western point of the bay. *Anchorage* may be taken in the bay protected from southeasterly winds; soundings show very deep water within a short distance off the shore. The western entrance point of the bay, situated about 3½ miles westward of Punta Santa Ana, is a low shingle point from which shoal water extends more than ¼ mile. About 2¾ miles northwestward of the western entrance point of Bahía de Santa Ana is the mouth of a lagoon at another low point fringed by shoal water.

Punta Trinidad (Trinidad Point) is a prominent headland, 250 feet high, surmounted by moderately high bluffs, situated about 13½ miles northwestward of Punta Santa Ana; several *detached rocks* lie off the headland. The coast between these two points is for the most part bluff with a range of hills rising immediately behind. *Detached rocks* lie off this stretch of coast. A salt flat is situated immediately back of the point; the small settlement of San Carlos, marked by a grove of palm trees, is located close southeastward at the head of a narrow cove in the mouth of which there is a small islet. A road connecting to Santa Rosalía runs along the shore to San Carlos, then turns inland. An *indifferent anchorage,* sheltered from the north wind, may be taken southeastward of the point; equal shelter from the south wind may be had northwestward of the point in the lee of the off-lying Seal Rocks.

Bahía de San Carlos (San Carlos Bay) is an open bay situated northwestward of Punta Trinidad. A *rocky islet* about 6 feet high and of whitish color, around which shoal water extends for a short distance on all sides, lies close inshore about 1¾ miles north-northwestward of Punta Trinidad; between the islet and the point is a sandy

Cabo San Miguel

bight in which shoal water extends about ½ mile offshore. About 3¾ miles northward of the whitish islet is a *rocky point* surrounded by *detached rocks;* a *large rock,* about 6 feet high, lies ½ mile offshore northward of this point.

Punta San Carlos is a low sand and shingle point, about 12 miles northward of Punta Trinidad, which may be identified by a sharp peak rising to an elevation of 5,000 feet about 10 miles westward. *Natural phenomena: Numerous and extensive patches of reddish-colored water have been observed off this part of the coast: soundings made while traversing these patches give no bottom at 55 fathoms. This curious phenomenon, analyzed by oceanographers as a concentration of great numbers of minute organisms coalescing in a seasonal burst of life just beneath the surface of the sea, was noted by early Spanish navigators at numerous places in the Gulf of California and gave rise to its earliest name — Mar Vermilio (The Vermillion Sea).*

The coast for about 9½ miles northward of Punta San Carlos is for the most part low, with sand and gravel beaches and an occasional low bluff, but from that position to Cabo San Miguel, a further distance of about 2½ miles, the coast is formed of an almost continuous bluff, about 50 feet high. The country inland is covered with bushes and cactus and slopes gradually upwards to the hills.

Punta San Juan Bautista (San Juan Bautista Point), situated 4¾ miles northward of Punta San Carlos, is a low sand and gravel point off which shoal water extends for about ¼ mile.

Bahía de San Juan Bautista (San Juan Bautista Bay) is an open indentation receding about 1 mile between Punta San Carlos and Punta San Juan Bautista. At a short distance northward of Punta San Juan Bautista the hills approach the coast, ending in bluffs. A dirt road runs out to the point, communicating with the settlement of Santa Gertrudis and Las Legunitas, about 15 and 18 miles inland, respectively.

Cabo San Miguel (San Miguel Cape), situated about 7 miles northward of Punta San Juan Bautista, is a bold rocky bluff, 150 feet high, close eastward of which are several *detached rocks.* A remarkable group of mountains rises to an elevation of 3,504 feet about 5 miles westward of the cape, and serves as an excellent landmark for taking bearings along this part of the coast. *Navigation note: From a position about 1 mile southward of Cabo San Miguel, thence to a position 2 miles southward, a shore bank extends seaward from ¼ to ½ mile; there are depths of only 2¼ fathoms along its seaward edge.*

Rancho El Barril

Several *fair anchorages* are available for shelter from northwesterly winds southward of the cape. Large vessels may obtain *anchorage* immediately southward of the cape in depths of 7 to 8 fathoms at about ½ mile offshore. Smaller vessels may obtain *anchorage* in the second cove southward of Cabo San Miguel, beyond a *rocky reef* lying off a red rock promontory; the best position is several hundred yards off the sandstone cliffs in 2 fathoms, sand and rock bottom. *Landing* may be made on the sand beach at the foot of the cliffs. Shelter from winds out of the southerly quadrant may be obtained in an *anchorage* in the large bight northward of the cape off a sandy beach tucked into the cliffs behind the cape.

Between Cabo San Miguel and Punta Santa Teresa, situated about 13½ miles northward, the coast recedes and is comprised of low bluffs alternating with sand beaches. A *white rock,* 5 feet high, lies close inshore about 1½ miles northwestward of Cabo San Miguel. The coastal range rises a short distance back of the shore and a remarkable sharp peak, 6,258 feet high, about 33 miles westward of Punta Santa Teresa, is plainly visible from

the offing. Immediately northward of Cabo San Miguel the coast trends westward forming a large open bay.

Rancho El Barril (El Barril Ranch), situated approximately midway along the shore of this bay about 7 miles northward of Punta San Miguel and 6½ miles southward of Punta Santa Teresa, is an old *watering place* for ships plying the gulf. It may be recognized by its windmill, some old abandoned houses and green foilage that surrounds the mouth of a small stream that opens onto the shore. Several Mexican families live here and recently the place has developed into an oasis of hospitality. There is an *airstrip* capable of accommodating small planes (see Appendix), meals are served at the ranch, horses and small boats are available to rent, gasoline is kept on hand to supply small boats calling from Kino Bay across the gulf, and *good water* is to be had.

Anchorage is in the open roadstead, northward of a shoal that extends from a round bluff point southward of the ranch to the mouth of the stream; when swells are running onto the beach the *shoal* off the mouth of the stream breaks. *Landing* may be made on a sandy beach just north of the ranch at the mouth of a small arroyo. Rancho Barril is the first and closest fuel stop and supply point to the cross-gulf destination port of Bahía San Francisquito, 9 miles northward, where there are no improvements at the present time.

Punta de Santa Teresa is a rocky bluff about 40 feet high, rising abruptly to a hill 567 feet high. Bahía de Santa Teresa (Santa Teresa Bay), located southward of Santa Teresa Point, is a small open bay at the head of which is a sand beach backed by low land that extends across to the head of Bahía de San Francisquito; on the low neck of land between Bahía de Santa Teresa and Bahía de San Francisquito is a low flat bed of a fresh water pond which is dry for the most part of the year. A brackish water seepage emanates from the hillside on the south side of this dry depression near the beach; the *spring* is surrounded by a green growth of foilage. At one time there was a small ranch on the shores of the bay occupied by a Mexican family who ran a few cattle, cared for shipments to and from a small mine in the interior and supplied water to vessels that occasionally called along the coast. A *landing strip* of questionable maintenance has been utilized in this dry bed over the years. (See Appendix.)

The shore along the southern part of the bay is comprised of bluffs, backed by hills about 150 feet high and fronted by *detached rocks*. *Anchorage* sheltered from northwesterly winds may be taken about ¼ mile offshore in depths of from 7 to 8 fathoms, with Punta Santa Teresa, bearing about 28°, distant 600 to 800 yards. Smaller vessels may obtain *anchorage* closer inshore off the beach in the center of the bay, or at the head of the bight immediately southward of the point, in 2 to 3 fathoms, sand.

Northward of Punta Santa Teresa, between it and Bahía de San Francisquito, is a prominent headland with barren hills 300 to 500 feet high and a rugged bluff coast. Punta San Gabriel, situated nearly 1¼ miles northward of Punta Santa Teresa, is the northeastern point of this headland; it is a rocky bluff 45 feet high with high volcanic hills just behind, and with numerous *detached rocks* surrounding it. Just westward of the point is a strip of sand beach ¼ mile long, at the western end of which is a rocky point similar to Punta San Gabriel that forms the eastern entrance point of Bahía de San Francisquito.

As a destination port for cross-gulf cruising boats, Bahía de San Francisquito is approximately 55 miles from Kino Bay on the Sonora side of the gulf, with the several "midriff" islands providing relatively short open gulf hops of 10, 12 and 14 miles between sheltered lees. While the crossing is relatively safe in favorable weather, the wind can kick up suddenly and severely in the open channels; that eventuality should always be of prime consideration when making the crossing. Severe winds encountered beyond the lee of the shelter islands on any leg of the crossing should be interpreted as a strong indication to return to the nearest shelter to await more favorable weather. Small outboard or inboard launches should never venture on the open gulf unless in pairs and then only with adequate radio communication between one another and with shore stations. Float plans should always be filed before leaving the last improved port. (See Appendix.)

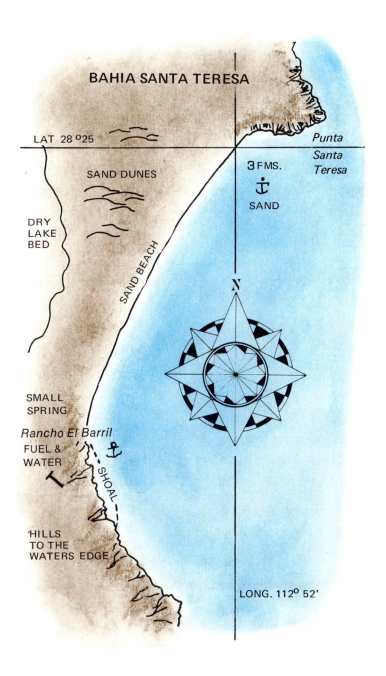

BAHIA SANTA TERESA

LAT 28°25

SAND DUNES

DRY LAKE BED

SMALL SPRING

Rancho El Barril
FUEL & WATER

SHOAL

HILLS TO THE WATERS EDGE

3 FMS.

SAND

Punta Santa Teresa

N

LONG. 112° 52'

SECTION 23
PUNTA SAN FRANCISQUITO to
BAHÍA SAN LUIS GONZAGA

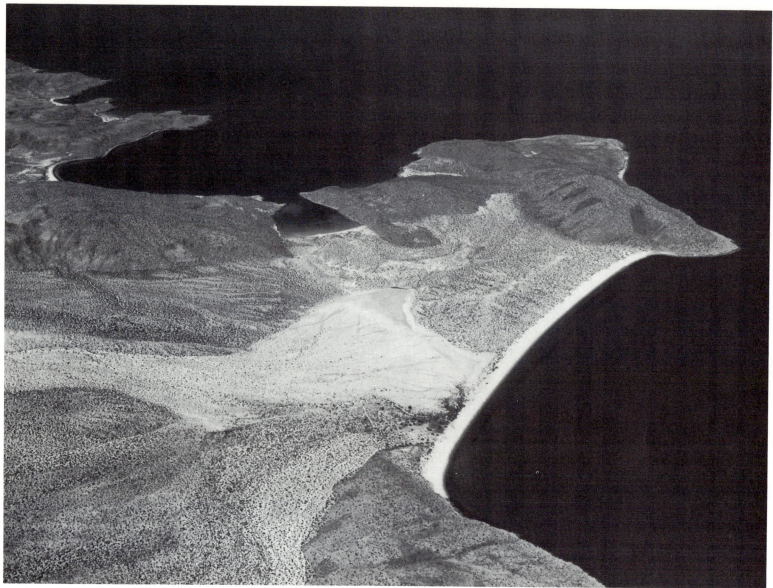

Bahía Santa Teresa, Bahía de San Francisquito

From the northwest point of the entrance to Bahía de San Francisquito to Punta de San Francisquito, a distance of nearly two miles, the coast is comprised chiefly of steep bluffs that are closely backed by a tableland 300 to 400 feet high. Punta de San Francisquito is a low, rocky bluff with a number of detached rocks lying close off it. There are three small coves with white sand beaches on the northern approaches to Bahía de San Francisquito; *detached rocks* must be given a safe berth when approaching the heads of these coves.

Bahía de San Francisquito (San Francisquito Bay) is a well-protected and deeply indented bay providing excellent shelter along an otherwise open stretch of coast at the narrowest waist, La Cintura (midriff), of the Gulf of California. It is a popular destination port for both

coastal and cross-gulf cruising boats. It is situated at Latitude 28° 26′ north, Longitude 112° 53′ west, with the wide mouth of the bay open to the northeast between Punta San Gabriel on the south and Punta San Francisquito on the north. The settlement of Rancho Barril is located approximately 8 miles south; the Port of Santa Rosalía approximately 76 miles southeastward. Bahía de Los Angeles is the nearest settlement northwestward, a distance of approximately 45 miles. For navigation see H.O. 638, Anchorages in the Gulf of California or Birtish Admiralty Chart #3061, Plans in the Gulf of California.

San Francisquito Bay is a squarish basin about 1 mile in extent, open northward and northeastward but affording good protection from both the prevailing northwesterly and southwesterly winds of the outside gulf. Within the

314

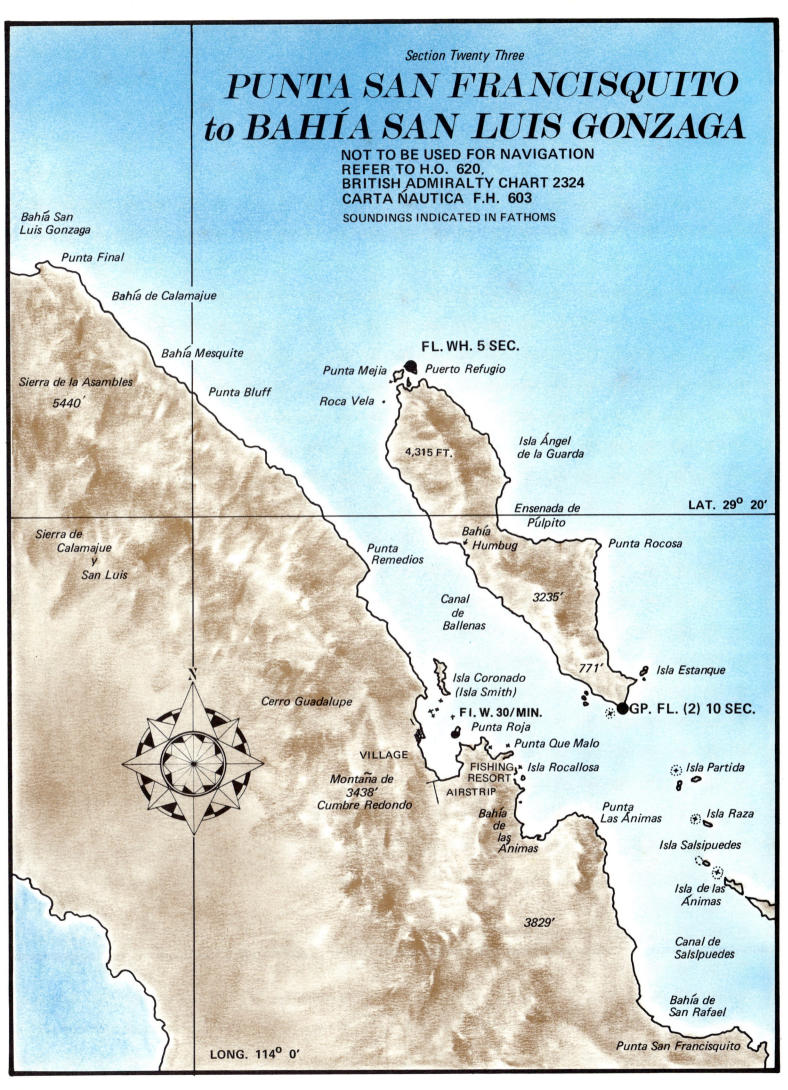

PUNTA SAN FRANCISQUITO
to BAHÍA SAN LUIS GONZAGA

NOT TO BE USED FOR NAVIGATION
REFER TO H.O. 620,
BRITISH ADMIRALTY CHART 2324
CARTA ÑAUTICA F.H. 603
SOUNDINGS INDICATED IN FATHOMS

Bahía San
Luis Gonzaga

Punta Final

Bahía de Calamajue

Bahía Mesquite

Sierra de la Asambles
5440´

Punta Bluff

Punta Mejia   Puerto Refugio

FL. WH. 5 SEC.

Roca Vela

4,315 FT.

Isla Ángel
de la Guarda

Ensenada de
Púlpito

LAT. 29° 20'

Sierra de
Calamajue
y
San Luis

Punta
Remedios

Bahía
Humbug

Punta Rocosa

Canal
de
Ballenas

3235´

Cerro Guadalupe

Isla Coronado
(Isla Smith)

Fl. W. 30/MIN.

Punta Roja

771´

Isla Estanque

GP. FL. (2) 10 SEC.

N

Punta Que Malo

VILLAGE

FISHING
RESORT

Isla Rocallosa

Isla Partida

Montaña de
3438´
Cumbre Redondo

AIRSTRIP

Bahía
de
las
Ánimas

Punta
Las Ánimas

Isla Raza

Isla Salsipuedes

3829´

Isla de las
Ánimas

Canal de
Salsipuedes

Bahía de
San Rafael

LONG. 114° 0'

Punta San Francisquito

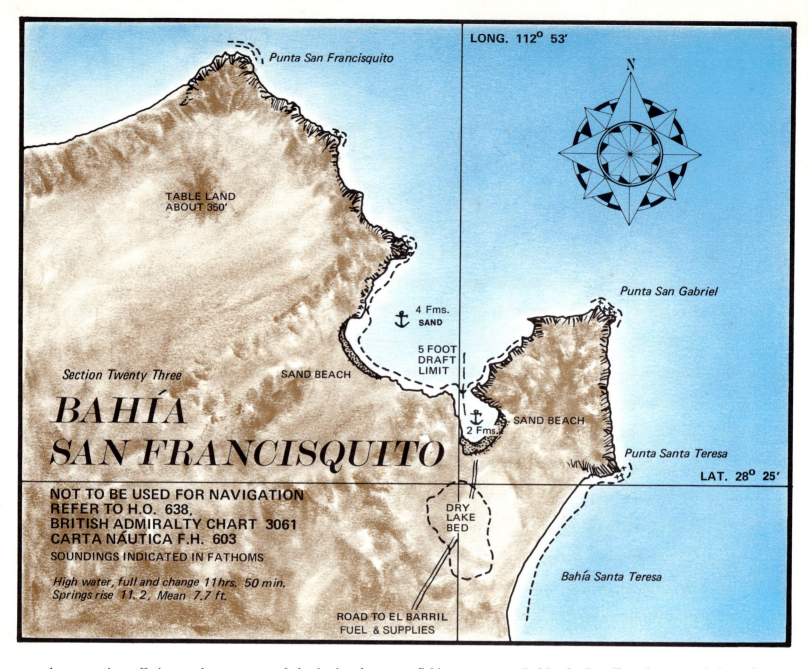

LONG. 112° 53'

Punta San Franciquito

TABLE LAND
ABOUT 350'

4 Fms.
SAND

Punta San Gabriel

5 FOOT
DRAFT
LIMIT

Section Twenty Three

SAND BEACH

2 Fms.

SAND BEACH

BAHÍA
SAN FRANCISQUITO

Punta Santa Teresa

LAT. 28° 25'

NOT TO BE USED FOR NAVIGATION
REFER TO H.O. 638,
BRITISH ADMIRALTY CHART 3061
CARTA NÁUTICA F.H. 603
SOUNDINGS INDICATED IN FATHOMS

*High water, full and change 11 hrs. 50 min.
Springs rise 11.2, Mean 7.7 ft.*

DRY
LAKE
BED

Bahía Santa Teresa

ROAD TO EL BARRIL
FUEL & SUPPLIES

bay, opening off the southern corner of the basin, there is a shallow landlocked secondary basin eminently suitable as an *anchorage* for small vessels. Its entrance, between two rocky points about 300 yards apart, is *shoal and rocky;* the passage narrows to about 100 yards with a depth of a fathom or less at low water. This basin is protected from all winds; the sand bottom has a few patches of weed-covered rock and offers good holding ground throughout.

Good anchorage may be taken in the southwestern part of the outer bay, in depths of 5 to 6 fathoms, about ¼ mile off the ½-mile long sand beach flanked by rocky bluffs; the entire bay is clear of dangers. *Excellent anchorage* within the inner basin may be had in from 1 to 2 fathoms, sand, but the state of the tide must de observed when carrying greater than 5-foot draft through the entrance.

TIDES — The mean high water interval at full and change at San Francisquito Bay is 11 hours 50 minutes; the spring range is 11.2 feet; the mean range is 7.7 feet.

There are no improvements at Bahía de San Francisquito the present time. There are plans afoot for a major

fishing resort at Bahía de San Francisco, consisting of a marina, a regular fuel and provision stop for cruising vessels, an improved airstrip and a resort motel. Fishing and skin diving is excellent in the area and there are great rock oysters to be gathered along the tidal shallows.

Bahía de San Rafael (San Rafael Bay) is a large open bay situated between Punta de San Francisquito and a point about 16 miles northwestward; the shores of the bay are comprised chiefly of sand beaches, and the land, intersected by numerous arroyos and covered with desert vegetation, rises gradually toward the interior. The bay affords good protection against southerly winds. In the southern part there are depths of 40 fathoms at a mile from the shore, while in the northern and western portions, at the same distance offshore, the depths range from 10 to 20 fathoms. The coast is comprised of bluffs closely backed by mountains from San Rafael Bay to Punta de las Animas, 14 miles northwestward.

Rocas Bernarbé (Barnaby Rocks) are two rocks only 2 feet above water, lying between 600 and 800 yards off a low point situated about 3½ miles southeastward of Punta de las Ánimas; between these rocks and the shore there

Bahía de San Francisquito

is a shallow rocky channel, a passage suitable only for small boats. There is a *fair anchorage* southward of Barnaby Rocks, about ¼ mile from the beach, in depths of 7 to 8 fathoms, coarse sand.

Canal de Sal Si Puedes, which lies between the mainland on the west and the chain of islands composed of San Lorenzo, Sal Si Puedes, Raza, and Partida on the east, is a wide, deep channel through which tidal currents set strongly, especially with an ebb tide and a northwesterly wind, against which combination sailing vessels and underpowered launches find it almost impossible to make any headway. Soundings in the northern part of the channel, 2½ miles from the shore, near Punta Las Ánimas, show a depth of 716 fathoms; in several places between the island of San Lorenzo and the mainland, no bottom was found at 320 fathoms.

Ballenas Channel, running between the mainland and Isla Ángel de la Guarda, is a continuation of this channel. *Anchorage* may be taken near the western shore to await favorable tidal periods for easy passage, and *anchorage* may also be found in the vicinity of Isla Raza and Isla Partida, but owing to the great depths there are few such places in the channel proper.

TIDAL STREAMS — The tidal currents in the vicinity of these islands, and in the channel between them and the peninsula, are extremely strong, sometimes producing heavy tide rips, whirlpools, upwellings and overflowing patches of confused water that led early Spanish navigators to report their small vessels in danger of being "gulped down into great and fearful maws" of the Vermilion Sea. Velocities of surface currents during the extreme periods of the lunar tide at full or new moon may reach the incredible strength of greater than 6 knots in certain constricted channels.

Canal de Ballenas (Ballenas Channel), running between the mainland of the peninsula and Isla Ángel de la Guarda,

is about 45 miles long and 8 to 13 miles wide. Charts developed by the early whalers designated the channel "Whale Channel," both a translation of the Spanish name and a reflection of a fishing ground where great pods of catchable whales were regularly encountered. Soundings throughout the channel show great depths; those obtained within less than a mile from the shore of the island indicate over 200 fathoms, and at the southern entrance depths exceeding 650 fathoms have been recorded. The natural stricture of the channel, and a considerable depth gradient between the north and south ends, combine with a substantial tidal differential approximating 12 feet during extreme lunar periods, to produce strong tidal currents of 3 knots, or greater. Northwesterly winds sometimes blow through the Ballenas Channel with considerable force, raising steep, heavy seas. If a wind condition occurs at such a period, so as to reinforce the maximum tidal streams, vessels can make but little headway against the wind and current. At such times it is advisable to anchor in any one of several *sheltered coves* along the shore and lay over until the advent of more favorable conditions.

Punta de Las Ánimas (Las Ánimas Point) marks northern entrance on the western shore to Ballenas Channel. It is a bold rocky bluff, 75 to 125 feet high, with a rocky shelf lying close-to. Back of the point steep hills of a reddish color rise abruptly to heights ranging from 300 to 500 feet, with mountains rising to more than 2,000 feet a short distance inland. The point is steep-to with depths of 60 fathoms sounded at a distance off of less than ½ mile.

Bahía de las Ánimas (Las Ánimas Bay) is a large, well-sheltered bay lying indented southwestward of Las Ánimas Point. From the point the coast trends southwestward for 5½ miles to the mouth of a small lagoon, whence it sweeps around to the western entrance point, Punta El Alacrán, 6½ miles westward of Las Ánimas Point, forming the bay. Between Las Ánimas Point and the small lagoon within the bay, the shore is comprised of sandy beaches interrupted by several bluffs. The entrance to the lagoon, which dries at half tide, is marked by a thicket of mangrove. About 2 miles northwestward of the lagoon entrance there is a steep bluff point that is surmounted by a brownish-colored mound, 80 feet high, off which there are situated several islets from 30 to 75 feet in height. The bay affords *good anchorage* well sheltered against the prevailing winds; the best *anchorage* is in the southern part in depths of 6 to 12 fathoms, nearly on a line between the off-lying islets and the lagoon entrance. Small vessels may find *anchorage* in shoaler water closer to shore.

Navigation caution: The lagoon mouth must not be approached closer than ¾ mile due to shoal water and foul ground; there are several rocky islets situated close off the lagoon entrance.

Punta El Alacrán (Point Alacrán), the northwest entrance point of Las Ánimas Bay, is a sharp rocky bluff 25 to 40 feet high, surmounted by a dark hill 100 feet high. About ½ mile northward of the point, and connected with it by a *rocky shoal,* is a low islet only 2 feet high, situated in the mouth of a small bight. The bight is formed by the coastal indentation between Punta Alacrán and Punta Isla Viejo, a prominent, sharp, bluff point formed by a spur of reddish hills 200 to 300 feet high, about 1½ miles northwestward. There is a sand beach at the head of the bight.

Bahía Pescado (Pescado Bay) is situated at the northern end of the bight formed between Punta Isla Viejo and Punta Soledad, about 2 miles northwestward.

Isla Rocallosa (Rocallosa Islet), a barren rocky islet 75 feet high, 1½ miles northwestward of Punta Isla Viejo, lies offshore in the mouth of Bahía Pescado, providing a protected anchorage over a sand bottom in its lee. The head of the cove is comprised of a sand beach backed by low sand dunes. *Landing* can be easily effected anywhere in the cove. On the flat above the cliff located on the southeastern side of the cove a pattern in 8 inch rocks is carefully laid out as illustrated:

Puerto Don Juan, situated in a deeply indented narrow cove immediately westward of Punta Que Malo, affords *good anchorage* protected from all winds, in 2½ to 7 fathoms, sand bottom at its southwestern end. The head of the cove is shoal but *anchorage* may be taken anywhere within its long narrow entrance. *Navigation caution: Detached rocks lie close off all the prominent points between Isla Rocallosa and Punta Roja, the southern entrance to Bahía de Los Angeles.*

Bahía de Los Angeles (Los Angeles Bay) is located about 50 miles northwestward of Bahía de San Francisquito and about 65 miles southeastward of Bahía San Luis Gonzaga, in a position on the western shore of Canal de Ballenas approximately opposite the southeastern end of Isla Ángel de la Guarda. For navigation see United States Oceanographic Charts H.O. 620, Golfo de California, Northern Part; British Admiralty Chart #2324, Cape San Lucas to San Diego Bay with the Gulf of California; Mexican Carta Náutica F.H. 603, Golfo de California, Parte Norte.

The bay, covering an area of approximately 25 square miles, is almost completely landlocked between Punta Roja on the southeastern side and Punta Gringa on the northwestern side; it is protected from northward and northeastward by 15 islands and islets of varying sizes spread across the mouth. There are three deep, safe passages into the harbor but they should only be attempted with adequate knowledge. The shores of the bay are for the most part sandy, with beaches interrupted by several rocky bluffs. Shallow water extends some distance offshore in the southern part of the bay. Montaña de Cumbre Redondo (Round Top Mountain), 3,423 feet high, situated about 2 miles inland on the southwestern side of the bay in a position about 8 miles westward of Punta Roja, provides an excellent landmark from seaward.

Three deep, safe passages lead into the bay: When approaching from southeastward, Isla de Cabeza de Caballo, (Cabeza de Caballo Island) of dark-reddish color and 225 feet high, and its two small satellites lying close southward, Islas de los Gemelos (or Los Hermanitos), 50 to 70 feet high, define the southernmost passage into Bahía de Los Angeles. The channel, which is clear of dangers and which has depths in it of 20 to 30 fathoms, lies between Punta Roja, a reddish rocky bluff, and the two small islets, Los Gemelos, about 600 yards northward. A navigation light flashing white 30 times per minute is exhibited from an orange and white banded concrete column established on the easternmost islet. The light can be seen for 10 miles in clear weather. A second safe passage, about ½ mile wide with mid-channel depths of 20 to 30 fathoms, lies northward of the two small islets, between them and Isla de Cabeza de Caballo, on the southern side of which a stone monument stands atop a 225-foot hill. The 2-mile wide passage immediately northwestward of Isla de Cabeza de Caballo, between it and Isla La Ventana, is *unsafe* due to the many dangerous *sunken rocks and rocks awash* with deep water all around. *Directions: Southernmost Passage — Steer for Montaña de Cumbre Redondo (Round Top Mountain) on course 251° until nearly abreast Punta Roja (Red Point) then keeping to mid-channel, make good a course of 270° for the anchorage.*

Northward of Isla de Cabeza de Caballo, on the north side of the dangerous passage previously mentioned, there is a group of 8 islands 90 to 125 feet high, the largest and most southerly of which is Isla La Ventana, so named for a remarkable rocky formation through which a sizable

Isla Coronadito

1554'

CLEAR PASSAGE

Isla
Mitlan

Isla Coronado (Smith Island)

Punta Toro

Punta
La Gringa

Isla Jorobado

Isla Flecha   Isla Pata

Isla San
Aremar   Isla Calaveras

Isla Llave   Isla
Isla Cerraja   Bota

Isla
La Ventana

AIRSTRIPS

CLAMS

PUEBLO DE
BAHÍA
DE   4 Fms.   SURF FISHING
LOS ANGELES   MOLE   Punta Arena

Isla Piojo
125'

MOST SUPPLIES
AVAILABLE
FUEL, WATER

FOUL PASSAGE

Isla Cabeza
de Caballo
225'

20-30 Fms.

FI. W. 30/MIN.   Islas de los
Gemelos

LONG. 113° 30'   Punta Rojo   20-30 Fms.   CLEAR PASSAGE

LAT. 29° 0'

ANCHORAGE
2 - 3 Fms. SAND

El Límona   Punta que Malo

Puerto
Don Juan

Laguna de Marea

FISHING RESORT

Punta Soledad

Section Twenty Three
BAHÍA de
LOS ANGELES
NOT TO BE USED FOR NAVIGATION
REFER TO H.O. 620,
BRITISH ADMIRALTY CHART 2324,
CARTA NÁUTICA F.H. 603
SOUNDINGS INDICATED IN FATHOMS

High water full and change 0 hrs., 25 min.
Spring rise 11.8 ft., Mean range 8.1 ft.

Isla Rocallosa

Bahía Pescado

Punta Isla Viejo

Caleta Alacran

Southeastern Entrance Channel to Bahía de Los Angeles

fissure or "window" has been worked at sea level by the continual action of wind and wave. Eastward of this group is an outlying flat-topped island, Isla Piojo, 125 feet high, and situated in the most northerly position of the group of islands fronting Bahía de Los Angeles is the largest island, Isla Coronado (Isla Smith).

Isla Coronado is a 4-mile long, flat-topped island 1,554 feet high, with a width ¼ to ¾ mile. Off its northwestern and highest end, and separated from it by a narrow boat channel, stands Isla Coronadito, 60 feet high; another islet, Isla Mitlan, 75 feet high, lies in a position about midway along the western shore of Isla Coronado, being connected to the island by a rocky shoal. Some *dangerous rocks* lie about ½ mile northwestward of this islet. A *white rock,* Isla Calaveras, 40 feet high, lies a little more than ½ mile southward of Isla Coronado (Isla Smith); the small flat-topped island, Isla Piojo previously mentioned, is situated about 1¼ miles southeastward of the southern extremity of the larger island.

The northern passage, which is deep and safe and more than a mile wide, although somewhat intricate, leads between Isla Coronado (Isla Smith) and a low, narrow neck of land that extends southeastward from the shore, terminating in a rocky bluff; thence a clear channel leads between the bluff and the group of eight islands close southeastward. This passage is free of submerged dangers except where some *dangerous rocks,* lying in a position 1,500 yards off the middle of the west side of Isla Coronado, narrow the channel to 1,800 yards. A least depth of 10 fathoms has been sounded in this passage; there are no dangers between the group of eight islands and the long neck of land previously described.

Directions: Northerly Passage — When approaching the bay from the north keep well over toward the mainland *side of the passage, to give the dangerous rocks westward of Isla Coronado (Smith Island) adequate berth. After passing between the extremity of the long narrow neck on the shore side and the group of islets southward, keep a distance of at least 1 mile from the western shore, to avoid a shoal that projects out from it. When the seaward extremity of the low sand point called Punta Gringa bears 282°, steer for the anchorage.*

Navigation caution: These passages may be used in safety when weather conditions render the landmarks plainly distinguishable, but only locally acquainted masters and pilots should attempt entrance into the bay under adverse conditions of visibility.

The best *anchorage* is to be had in the western part of the bay in depths of 8 fathoms off the mouth of a small cove formed by Punta Arena, a low sandspit which extends southward from the shore; small vessels may find secure *anchorage* in shallower water in the lee of the sandspit closer inshore. This cove lies about 3½ miles northeastward of Montaña de Cumbre Redondo and fronts a settlement, Pueblo de Bahía de Los Angeles, comprised of a fishing village, a sportfishing resort, a general supply point and a fuel stop for small vessels plying the gulf. A stone mole is built into the basin of the cove from the shore at the foot of the village. El Limóna, a cove at the mouth of a small lagoon, Laguna de Marea, about 2¼ miles southeastward of the first anchorage, affords an alternative *anchorage* in the bay.

Pueblo de Bahía de Los Angeles is a small settlement occupying the coastal flat at the head of the bight formed behind the long arm of the sandspit, Punta Arena. The village is nestled at the foot of a high hill and its several dozen houses and buildings are surrounded by a scattering of green foliage. A rock mole extends into the bay,

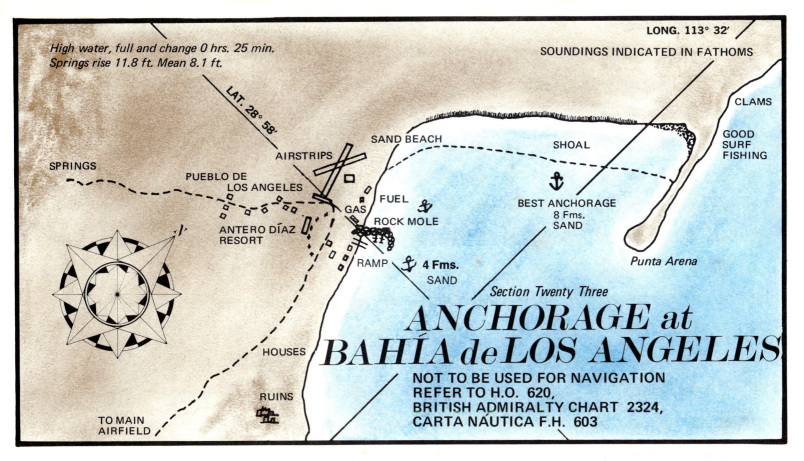

High water, full and change 0 hrs. 25 min.
Springs rise 11.8 ft. Mean 8.1 ft.

LONG. 113° 32'

SOUNDINGS INDICATED IN FATHOMS

LAT. 28° 58'

SPRINGS

AIRSTRIPS

SAND BEACH

CLAMS

GOOD
SURF
FISHING

SHOAL

PUEBLO DE
LOS ANGELES

FUEL

GAS

ROCK MOLE

BEST ANCHORAGE
8 Fms.
SAND

ANTERO DÍAZ
RESORT

RAMP

4 Fms.
SAND

Punta Arena

Section Twenty Three

ANCHORAGE at BAHÍA de LOS ANGELES

HOUSES

RUINS

NOT TO BE USED FOR NAVIGATION
REFER TO H.O. 620,
BRITISH ADMIRALTY CHART 2324,
CARTA NÁUTICA F.H. 603

TO MAIN
AIRFIELD

curving in a sharp hook at its outer end to form a short breakwater. Small motor vessels dock within the protection of the breakwater to take passengers, provisions and fuel. Several small buildings and a large metal warehouse stand alongside the foot of the mole. Just back of the landing and extending northward along the shore from the north side of the village is an *aircraft landing strip* used by small planes. Four miles southward of the village a longer *airstrip* used by larger multi-engine aircraft is bull-dozed into the plain.

The village itself consists of a comfortable resort motel, a grocery store, where general supplies and provisions may be obtained, several private residences and about 20 other houses and shacks occupied by the local turtle fishermen and resort workers and their families. The present population of the village is about 100. Turtle fishing is the principal occupation aside from tourist accommodation and sportfishing services. The turtles are of the green variety, shipped live by truck to Ensenada for lack of mobile refrigeration facilities, and highly prized for the quality of their meat, which excels that of the larger scaled brown turtles of the more southerly ports. For the sport-fishermen, outboard boats are for rent and an 85-foot diesel vessel with overnight accommodations is for charter. The Baja Flying Service lands at Bahía de Los Angeles on its regular run from Tijuana to Mulegé and return; there is a taxi to and from the airstrip where the passenger planes land. The San Diego Natural History Museum maintains a scientific station at Bahía de Los Angeles, referred to as the Vermilion Sea Field Station and uses the building and facilities as a base of operations for its active ongoing studies of both the peninsula and the gulf. *Good water* is piped from a *spring* back of the village, which has supplied fresh water to the local inhabitants and to travelers on land and sea for centuries; the spring was called Aguaje San Juan by the early Spanish settlers and the

general area was often referred to by the same name. Water is also obtained from several wells in the vicinity.

The bay was first visited in 1539 by the Spanish explorer Francisco de Ulloa, who called it Puerto de Lobos after the many California sea lions he found sporting in the water and on the beaches. Jesuit Padre Fernando Consag visited and gave the bay its present name in 1746, on one of his exploration voyages to the upper gulf; he reported that there was a large Indian ranchería established on the shores of the bay and that the Indians lived principally on shellfish. Upon the establishment of the Mission of San Borja in 1762, about 22 miles inland, Bahía de Los Angeles became a visiting station of the mission and its principal supply and shipping point. Shortly thereafter the native population of the bay was moved inland to labor at the mission which, at its peak, supported 3,000 Indians. In the 1890's and later, supplies for a number of mines operating in the vicinity of the bay were regularly landed at Bahía de Los Angeles and over $2,000,000 worth of silver bars were shipped out from one mine alone. Rusted machinery, an abandoned steam locomotive, partially collapsed mine workings and a white masonry calabozo (jail), still standing in good repair, may be seen in the near locality. The settlement as it exists today dates from the early 1930's with many of the improvements developed since 1951.

SEA AND WEATHER CONDITIONS — During the late spring and early summer months, an afternoon breeze, often to 20 knots, springs up from the northeast, cooling the otherwise hot, still climate of the bay and providing excellent day sailing; this breeze generally gives way to an offshore westerly which occasionally becomes very intense, but lasts generally for a period of only 2 or 3 hours. These winds at the peak of their intensity can render the anchorage somewhat uncomfortable.

Looking northward from Bahía de Los Angeles

Punta la Gringa

FACILITIES — Fuel, water and provisions may be taken aboard alongside the masonry mole that extends into the bay in front of the village. Diesel and several grades of gasoline are loaded from 55-gallon drums stored in the metal warehouse at the foot of the mole. Aircraft gasoline in 80- and 100-octane grades is available. Provisions may be purchased at the store connected with the motel; canned foods, fresh vegetables, fresh meat and fish are available at reasonable prices depending on current supply. Turtle meat is generally available throughout most of the year. Outboard boats with motors are for rent; fishing tackle and ammunition are available. Guides may be hired. An 85-foot diesel vessel with overnight accommodations is for charter. Some automobile and marine engine parts are stocked and a motor mechanic is available. Parts unavailable in the village may be ordered and received in a few hours or days by truck or plane from La Paz, Santa Rosalía, Ensenada or San Diego.

PUBLIC ACCOMMODATIONS — The Casa Díaz run by Sr. Antero Díaz and his wife offers comfortable accommodations with private rooms and fresh water showers in a resort-style motel. The dining room is open to guests and to all travelers, and serves good meals at reasonable prices. Reservations for motel space should be made in advance, especially during the fishing and hunting seasons.

TRANSPORTATION — The Baja Flying Service lands at Bahía de Los Angeles on its regular run from Tijuana to Mulegé and return; there is scheduled semiweekly ser-

vice. Taxis are available in the village with service to the airport or to outlying points of interest. A 4-wheel drive vehicle is for hire to hunting parties. Private planes may land at the dirt *airstrip* closeby the village.

COMMUNICATIONS — There is no landline telegraph or telephone service to Bahía de Los Angeles but surface and airmail service are rapid and regular. Both low frequency and high frequency radiotelephone equipment is operated from aboard the 85-foot diesel vessel, *San Augustin II,* anchored in the bay off the village. Ship-to-shore and inter-ship communication is maintained but not on a regular communication schedule; Oakland Radio KMI can be contacted on high frequency any time of the day or night and radiotelephone messages handled to international circuits.

MARINE EMERGENCIES — The 85-foot diesel vessel, *San Augustin II,* regularly operating from Bahía de Los Angeles, may be depended upon for aid in emergency. Closest harbors from which tugs, Mexican Naval vessels, or other sea-bound aid may be summoned are Santa Rosalía, 120 miles to the southward, Guaymas, 160 miles across the gulf, or San Felipe, 145 miles northwestward. There is considerable coastal traffic comprised of pleasure and fishing vessels plying the gulf, and aid may be re-

Punta Arena, Bahía de Los Angeles

quested by marine radio directly, or by relay, generally on 2182, 2638, 2738 kiloHertz, but increasingly on citizen's band radio, although exclusive reliance on this band is not prudent.

MEDICAL FACILITIES — First aid can be rendered at Bahía de Los Angeles; more serious medical emergencies can be handled at Santa Rosalía, 120 miles southward, Guaymas, 160 miles across the gulf, or San Felipe, 145 miles northward. Aircraft can be summoned by radio for medical flights to centers more elaborately equipped for medical emergency. This bay is a regular stop on the medical circuit of the Flying Samaritans.

SOURCES OF ADDITIONAL INFORMATION — Casa Díaz, Antero Díaz, P.O. Box 579, Ensenada, B. CFA., Mexico; Baja Flying Service; Francisco Muñoz, P.O. Box 478, Imperial Beach, California 93032, telephone (714) 424-8956 or (903) 385-9110.

From the rocky bluff opposite the northwestern end of Isla Coronado (Isla Smith) the coast northward of Bahía de Los Angeles trends north-northwestward for about 12½ miles to within 3 miles of Punta Remedios and is comprised of rocky bluffs, alternating with short stretches of pebble beaches; thence a sand and pebble beach extends to Punta Remedios. A small lagoon, Laguna Salina, ½ mile in length, penetrates the shore about 1½ miles northwestward of a position opposite the northwestern end of Isla Coronado (Smith). The land back of the coast is broken and backed by mountains 1,500 to 2,000 feet high. Near the northern end of this rocky stretch of coastline, and lying close inshire, are three small islets

about 1¼ miles apart and 15 to 30 feet high; the two southernmost are covered with birdlime and have a whitish color.

Punta Remedios (Remedios Point) is a low sandy point closely backed by hills northward and westward, which quickly rise to the lofty coastal range situated only a short distance inland. Bahía de los Remedios (Remedios Bay), south of Punta Remedios, is an open bay just southward of the point that affords shelter from northwesterly winds. A sand and pebble beach extends about 3 miles from the point and near its southern limit is a small lagoon. The best position in which to seek *anchorage* is about 700 yards off the beach in 10 fathoms, abreast a reddish-colored hill 200 feet high, with Punta Remedios bearing 30°, distant about 1¾ miles. *Navigation caution: There is a small cove in the bight about 200 yards southwestward of Punta Remedios but in it, about 100 yards offshore, there is a submerged rock that dries 3 feet, as well as other submerged rocks in the vicinity.*

Between Punta Remedios and Punta Acantilado, situated about 26 miles northwestward, there is no anchorage nor shelter to be had, except *indifferent protection* for small vessels in a cove called La Botica (The Drug Store) approximately opposite the northwestern end of Isla Ángel de La Guarda, where a small lagoon sheltered behind a sand dune opens to the sea but is accessible only at high water. Otherwise this stretch of coast is an almost unbroken succession of high rocky bluffs 50 to 150 feet high, rising to the coastal range immediately behind.

Punta Acantilado (Bluff Point) situated on the western side of the northern entrance to Canal de las Ballenas (Ballenas Channel) is a bold rocky bluff about 100 feet high and may be identified from a distance by Sharp Peak, 3,189 feet high, which lies about 6½ miles west-south-westward; Double Peak, 5,440 feet high in a position about 9 miles southward of Sharp Peak, is situated about 13½ miles south-southwestward of Punta Acantilado. The coast between Punta Acantilado and Punta Final, situated about 21 miles to the northwest, is generally high, rocky and precipitous, except for a short stretch of low beach situated about 5 miles northward of Punta Acantilado.

Bahía Mesquite (Mesquite Bay), westward of Punta Acantilado, affords *fair anchorage* in depths of 7 fathoms about ¼ mile off a pink-colored cliff in the northern part of the bay. As the *anchorage* is approached, the soundings decrease suddenly from 16 to 10 fathoms, then gradually to 5 fathoms close off a gravel beach.

Isla Piojo, looking northward

Bahía de Calamajue (Calamajue Bay), situated about 14 miles northwestward of Punta Acantilado and 6 miles southeastward of Punta Final, offers *good anchorage* in depths of 9 fathoms, about ¾ mile off the sandy beach at the head of the bay; *landing* can be easily effected on this beach. Back of the beach in the middle of the plain at the mouth of the Calamajue Arroyo is a red-colored hill, a conspicuous identifying landmark. The bay is open to the north but affords some protection from southeasters. There is a small inlet on the western end of the beach where the sand meets the rocky bluff of the western headland. A few small shacks of a seasonal fish camp and a *well* of strongly alkaline water may be found in this portion of the landing about ¾ mile back of the shore. Just behind the beach there is an *aircraft landing strip* in the bed of a dry lagoon. (See Appendix.)

Old Puerto Calamajue, as the bay was called in early Spanish colonial days, was first discovered by Padre Fernando Consag in his explorations of the upper gulf region in 1753. The cove was developed as a visiting station of the San Borja Mission and used as such until 1766 when Spanish Padres Arnes and Diez founded the Calamajue Mission here. Their crops were unsuccessful because of the lack of good water; that which was to be had was so strongly alkaline that it killed the half-grown crops. After 18 months of fruitless effort, the mission site was abandoned and the mission enterprise moved north to Santa María. At the present time the adobe ruins of the old mission are barely discernible on the terraced banks on the east side of the Calamajue Arroyo. Across the arroyo and overlooking it, near the edge of a low bluff, is an abandoned gold ore mill, Molino de Calamajue. A dirt road leads up the arroyo from the cove to the main Peninsular Highway.

Pueblo de Bahía de Los Angeles

Punta Bluff

Puerto Calamajue

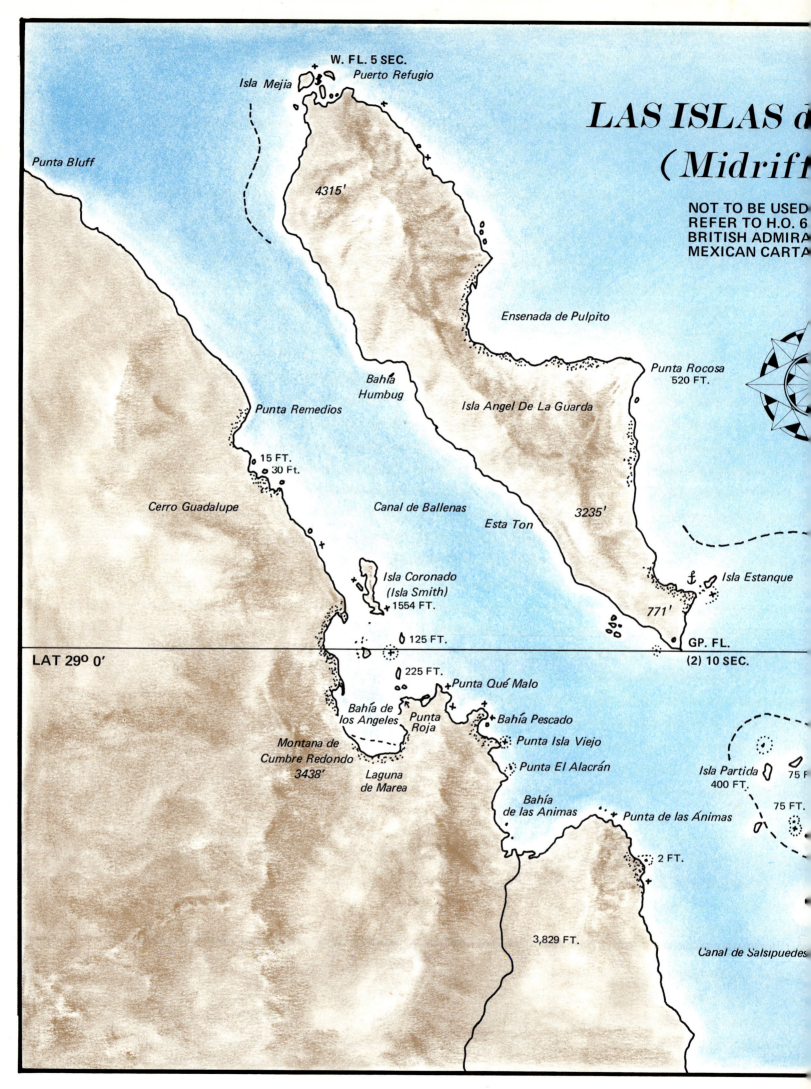

LAS ISLAS d
(Midrift

NOT TO BE USED
REFER TO H.O. 6
BRITISH ADMIRA
MEXICAN CARTA

W. FL. 5 SEC.

Isla Mejia   Puerto Refugio

Punta Bluff

4315'

Ensenada de Pulpito

Punta Rocosa
520 FT.

Bahía
Humbug

Punta Remedios

Isla Angel De La Guarda

15 FT.
30 Ft.

Cerro Guadalupe

Canal de Ballenas

Esta Ton

3235'

Isla Estanque

Isla Coronado
(Isla Smith)
1554 FT.

771'

125 FT.

GP. FL.

LAT 29° 0'

(2) 10 SEC.

225 FT.

Punta Qué Malo

Bahía de
los Angeles

Punta
Roja

Bahía Pescado

Punta Isla Viejo

Montana de
Cumbre Redondo
3438'

Laguna
de Marea

Punta El Alacrán

Isla Partida
400 FT.

75 F

75 FT.

Bahía
de las Animas

Punta de las Ánimas

2 FT.

3,829 FT.

Canal de Salsipuedes

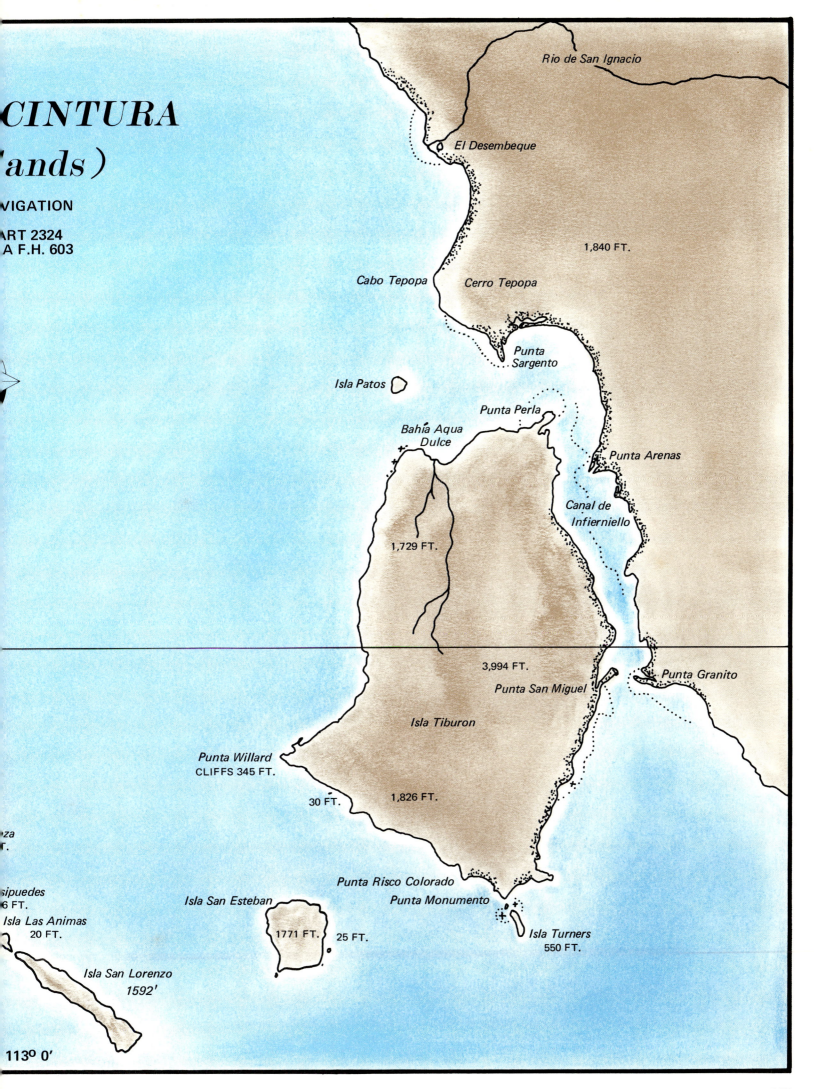

CINTURA

(ands)

VIGATION

ART 2324
A F.H. 603

Rio de San Ignacio

El Desembeque

1,840 FT.

Cabo Tepopa   Cerro Tepopa

Punta
Sargento

Isla Patos

Punta Perla

Bahía Aqua
Dulce

Punta Arenas

Canal de
Infierniello

1,729 FT.

3,994 FT.

Punta San Miguel   Punta Granito

Isla Tiburon

Punta Willard
CLIFFS 345 FT.

30 FT.   1,826 FT.

za
T.

Punta Risco Colorado

sipuedes
6 FT.

Punta Monumento

Isla Las Animas
20 FT.

Isla San Esteban

1771 FT.   25 FT.

Isla Turners
550 FT.

Isla San Lorenzo
1592'

113° 0'

SECTION 24
LAS ISLAS de la CINTURA (midriff)

Isla San Estéban

Isla San Pedro Mártir (San Pedro Mártir Island), isolated in mid-gulf at Latitude 28° 23' north, Longitude 112° 20' west, lies about 28 miles due east of Punta de Santa Teresa on the peninsula shore, 22 miles southward of Monument Point, the southern extremity of Tiburon Island, and 28 miles southwestward of Kino Point on the Sonora shore. For navigation see H.O. 620, Gulf of California, Northern Part; Mexican Carta Náutica, F.H. 603, Golfo de California, Parte Norte; British Admiralty #2324, Cabo San Lucas to San Diego Bay. The island is triangular-shaped measuring less than a mile in extent either way, with a maximum elevation above the sea of 1,052 feet. There are several *detached rocks* within a distance of about ½ mile of the southern side of the island. A *lee,* protected from the prevailing wind, may be found in small indentations on each of the three sides of the island, affording shelter from the weather blowing from any direction.

The rocky character of the island supports a desert vegetation, including a forest of dwarfed *cardon,* a type of fruit-bearing cactus. The early Spanish missionaries, apt students of native Indian lore, boiled down the juice squeezed from the stem of the *cardon* to obtain a balsam highly effective in the healing of cuts and bruises. The fruit of this cactus is also boiled down and, without the addition of sugar, makes a quite palatable jelly used in native family medicine as a remedy for dysentery. There is no evidence of Indian occupation of San Pedro Mártir Island but the *cardonal* is extensive, growing over a great portion of the rocky slopes.

A *bank,* with an area of about 3 square miles, having depths over it of 15 to 23 fathoms, soft mud, lies about 8 miles north-northwestward of Isla de San Pedro Mártir; 2 miles westward of this bank the depths increase abruptly to

no bottom sounded at 100 fathoms. The full extent of this bank has yet to be completely determined and accurately charted. The waters around the island and in the vicinity of the adjacent bank are particularly rich in sea life. It and San Lorenzo Island to the north are breeding grounds for the brown pelican, one of the species of sea birds seriously theatened by the widespread use of pesticides on California coastal farms. The U.S. fish and wildlife service in cooperation with the government of Mexico has recently conducted a pelican tagging program in the upper gulf in a scientific program designed to study the habits of these birds.

Isla de San Esteban is a barren, rocky island of volcanic origin rising from the sea to a height of 1,772 feet in a position about 9½ miles eastward of Isla San Lorenzo, 21 miles northwestward of Isla San Pedro Mártir and 12 miles westward of Isla Turners and the southern extremity of Isla Tiburon. The island is about 4 miles long oriented north and south, and is about 3 miles wide. A rock, 25 feet high and connected to the shore westward by a rocky reef, lies about ¼ mile offshore in a position about 1 mile northward of the southeasternmost point of the island; immediately northward of this reef is a gravel beach from which a valley slopes up into the interior. The remaining portion of the coast around the island is comprised of almost perpendicular bluffs from 100 to 500 feet high, separated by short stretches of gravel and shingle beaches.

On the southwest corner of Isla San Esteban, a low shingle spit extends ¾ mile seaward to form a bight in which *anchorage* with some shelter close under a bluff may be obtained; however, this anchorage is untenable in unfavorable winds. A bank, steep-to and with depths of 6 fathoms over it, extends more than ½ mile offshore at the northeastern extremity of the island. The intervening channels between Isla San Esteban and Isla Tiburon, and that between Isla San Esteban and Isla San Lorenzo are deep and clear dangers. Small power boats trailered to Kino Bay on the Sonora shore of the Mexican mainland frequently undertake a gulf crossing to Bahía San Francisquito by island hopping to Isla Turners, Isla Tiburon, Isla San Esteban, Isla San Lorenzo and their Baja peninsula destination.

Islas de San Lorenzo (San Lorenzo Islands) are comprised of a long, narrow island chain lying parallel to the trend of the coast; the southeastern extremity of the southernmost island is situated about 9 miles northeastward of Punta de San Francisquito. The islands, consisting of a high, barren volcanic uplift, are separated into three unequal parts, the southern island being by far the largest, nearly 10 miles long with a maximum width of 2 miles and an elevation of 1,592 feet at the highest peak near its southern end. This island, called Isla de San Lorenzo on modern navigation charts, is a veritable knifeblade segment of land whose sheer sides drop almost unbroken into the sea and even then continuing precipitously downwards with soundings of

2,000 feet to be found within less than a mile of the shore.

A boat passage separates the southern island from the next island segment northward, Las Ánimas Island. Taken together the two segments have a combined length of 12¼ miles. The islands are quite barren, supporting almost no vegetation; however, along the narrow bottoms of the arroyos that corrugate the islands' sides are low stands of brush with various kinds of cacti clinging to the precipitous declivities. Spits of cobble, half a dozen or more, run out at right angles to the western side, and there are in places, narrow gravel beaches between the island's seawall and the water.

About 3 miles southeastward of the boat passage, on the western side of San Lorenzo Island, there is a slightly projecting sand beach where a *landing* may be effected in fair

Isla San Lorenzo looking due east

Isla de las Ánimas, looking eastward

weather; at the southeast extremity of this island there is another small strip of sand beach which, during northwesterly winds, affords a *good landing place*. With the exception of these several narrow shelves along the shore, the sides of the island are bold rocky bluffs inaccessible from the sea. *Anchorage* with shelter from northerly winds may be obtained in two small coves on the southwestern side of Isla San Lorenzo toward the southern tip. *Anchorage* sheltered from southerly weather may be obtained on the northern side of the boat passage between Isla San Lorenzo and Isla de las Ánimas. The northern end of San Lorenzo Island is an excellent spot to dive for lobster.

There are several indentations along the northeastern shore of Isla de las Ánimas, where sheltered anchorage may be obtained. Anchorage protected from all but northerly weather may be taken in a small cove on the northeastern side of the island, toward its northwestern extremity. *Shelter* is also afforded in a small cove on the southern shore of the island just southward of its northwestern end. A white rock, 20 feet high, is situated about 300 yards offshore approximately 1¾ miles southeastward of the northwestern extremity of Isla de las Ánimas. *Detached rocks* lie close off the northwestern end of the island.

Isla Sal Si Puedes (Sal Si Puedes Island) lying about 1 mile northwestward of Isla de las Ánimas and comprising

the third island of the chain is about 1½ miles long with a maximum width of ½ mile; the island's highest peak near the southern end rises 376 feet above the sea. Close off the island are two sizable *detached rocks* and several smaller ones; the largest of these, about ½ mile from the northwest extremity and lying off the southwestern side, is 50 feet high. Between Sal Si Puedes Island and Las Ánimas Island there is a passage but it is foul with dangers projecting from a *submerged reef;* a *rock awash* lies in the middle of the passage, somewhat closer to Sal Si Puedes Island. *A clear channel* with depths of 10 fathoms, which follows close along the shore of Isla Sal Si Puedes, affords safe passage from one side of the islands to the other.

The southeastern ⅓ of the island is connected to the remaining ⅔ portion by a low narrow ridge that divides the two deeply indented coves thus formed. *Anchorage* may be taken on either the north or south sides of the island within these long narrow coves with ground tackle rigged fore and aft and spring lines run ashore and made fast to the rock outcroppings on either hand. The bottom at both anchorages is of sand with a depth of about 3 fathoms at the mouth of the southern cove and 4 fathoms at the mouth of the cove on the northern side of the island.

Isla Raza

Isla Raza (Raza Island), a small island barely 100 feet high, ¾ mile long, oriented east and west and no more than ½ mile wide, is situated between Isla Sal Si Puedes and Isla Partida, being about 4¾ miles northward of the former. The island, less than ⅓ of a mile square, is whitened by birdlime — the deposit of countless thousands of seabirds that frequent its rocky terrain — but the island is nevertheless difficult to make out until closely approached. Among neighboring islands principally of volcanic origin, Isla Raza appears to be of non-volcanic character. The shores consist chiefly of moderately high bluffs with detached rocks close-to; a *reef,* which extends for a short distance from its southeastern end, should be given a wide berth. *Fair anchorage* can be obtained about 600 yards offshore on the south side of the island, in depths of 5 to 8 fathoms over a gravel and rocky bottom, with a cautious eye to the *reef of rocks* previously mentioned, which projects a short distance off the island's southeastern end. Abreast this anchorage ground there was a landing pier at one time, near which could be seen a house with a flagstaff.

Isla Raza is a Wildlife Preserve — a migratory waterfowl sanctuary — dedicated on May 30, 1964, by President López Mateos, in a decree promulgated in response to a proposition by Lewis Wayne Walker, then assistant director of the Arizona-Sonora Desert Museum in Tucson; he and other naturalists were concerned with the preservation of a unique breeding ground for large numbers of a variety of seabirds whose continued existence was seriously threatened by the indiscriminate incursions of man. The island is a nesting ground admirably suited to the breeding habits of terns, gulls, petrel, pelicans, grebes, and other species that return to the island year after year in response to an unvarying primordial instinct; it is the setting for tens of thousands of breeding pairs of seabirds between April and June of each season. During this period the birds literally cover every square inch of available space on the flat surfaces of the land with their nests, and eggs.

At one time every canoe and boat, within miles of Raza Island, capable of navigating across the intervening waters from the Peninsular coast was paddled out to this bird island; egg collectors, bent on scooping up every last bird egg laid, put ashore to gather up a valuable boat load for sale in the coastal markets at San Felipe, Santa Rosalía, Mulegé, La Paz, Guaymas and Hermosillo. Each egger in the course of a season was responsible for taking as many as from 30,000 to 50,000 eggs, a quantity, when multiplied by the number of eggers, that the bird population could not accommodate and survive.

During the nesting season great clouds of seabirds wheel and turn over the small island, then alight almost simultaneously, each on his pre-claimed several-inch-square nesting territory, carefully folding his outstretched wings while miraculously avoiding entanglement with his neighbors performing the same choreographic trick quite close all around. For visitors to the island (and under the Wildlife Sanctuary rules, visitors are allowed with camera and guide) the sight of Raza's 7-acre flat interior valley, covered every inch with nesting birds, is never to be forgotten. Naturalists' sightseeing trips can be arranged at Bahía de Los Angeles and leave from that port.

Isla Raza

Isla Partida

Besides the natural grandeur of the myriads of breeding seabirds on Raza Island, there is also the mystery of the orderly piles of stones and extensive hand-laid breast-high dry-rock walls that occupy acres of the island. An ancient legend attributes the origin of the hundreds of conical piles of stones to a Seri Indian use of the island as a sacred burial ground, a sort of cemetery annex of Tiburon Island on the Sonora coast which they occupied for centuries. The stones on Raza Island are not haphazardly heaped in a few random piles but laid up with the great care of practiced stone masons in even, conical piles, each rock carefully fitted beside its neighbor and each course resting in geometric precision on the one beneath. Some of the piles, once precisely stacked have, in the course of time, fallen or been knocked over and lie scattered about the still obvious pattern of their base. The rock walls are laid up of larger boulders in the same careful manner, meeting other courses of rock at true 90° corners.

The Seri Indian myth being what it is — an unsubstantiated folk legend — scientists have ventured other theories attributing the piles of stones to early guano gatherers cultivating the largest bare expanse of land for scraping and raking their valued product together by removing the randomly scattered stones of the island to concentrated piles; a similar theory applies to the egg gatherers desirous of making as much clear area available to the egg laying birds as possible. Neither theory adequately explains the stonemason-like rock work or the extensive courses of stone walls erected on certain parts of the island.

The dead are buried on Raza Island, whether beneath the conical piles of stones or not. In a hollow depression near the south side of the island stand three weathered wooden crosses nailed through with square-cut boat nails. Perhaps the crosses mark the graves of unlucky members of a whaling ship, or perhaps the graves of some of the crew of an early Spanish pearler, having succumbed to the deadly ravages of scurvy. Such markers as these wooden crosses, standing their lonely vigil, have the universal respect of man, and their preservation against all but the ravages of time is an unwritten rule carefully adhered to by all those still fortunate enough to be observers.

Roca Raza (Raza Rock) is the isolated rocky projection above water of a submerged peak rising out of the sea a little over a mile northwestward of the northwestern point of Isla Raza. It is a bare, wind-swept irregular pyramid of a weather-worn stone, standing 75 feet high and providing in its various crevices and small benches safe nesting places for numerous seabirds. Its sides, though quite steep, are climbable and scientists investigating its geological incongruity and its precariously situated flora and fauna have clambered over most of its surface. The rock is steep-to with deep water all around, except on its southwestern side where, at a distance of about 400 yards, there is a *rock awash* with depths of 20 fathoms sounded close-to. Raza Rock, a marine

Isla Salsipuedes, Isla de las Ánimas and Isla San Lorenzo

monument of solid stone, stands as a lonely sentinel among its neighboring islands and islets whose volcanic uplifts of conglomerate and sandstone strata are in sharp geological contrast.

Isla Partida (Partida Island), sometimes referred to as Isla Cordonazo, situated about 4½ miles northwestward of Isla Raza, appears as two islands when observed at a distance, an optical effect due to its peculiar configuration of two 400-foot high peaks separated by a low narrow strip of land. The island is about 1¼ miles long and ½ mile wide, enclosing in a crescent-shaped cove on its northwestern side a rocky islet 85 feet high, which is situated off the steep bluff point of the cove's western headland. *Anchorage* may be taken in the fine little harbor formed within the crescent, in depths of from 3 to 8 fathoms, sand bottom, open to the northward but well sheltered from the other weather quadrants by the long arms of the cove's headlands. For the most part, this cove provides a serene and *comfortable anchorage* but the sea-battered cliffs and well-weathered headlands are mute evidence of the cordonazos, the fierce northers that seasonally lash the cove with high winds and great waves.

On the southeastern side of Partida Island, an islet 75 feet high, is situated about 700 yards offshore and *anchorage,* sheltered from northwesterly winds, may be taken in depths of from 4 to 20 fathoms in the channel between the two; the bottom is mixed rock and sand, with the western side of the anchorage providing the clearest anchoring ground. Small vessels may anchor close off the sand beach on the large island in depths of 2½ fathoms. The sandy character of the bottom reflects a light green hue in the

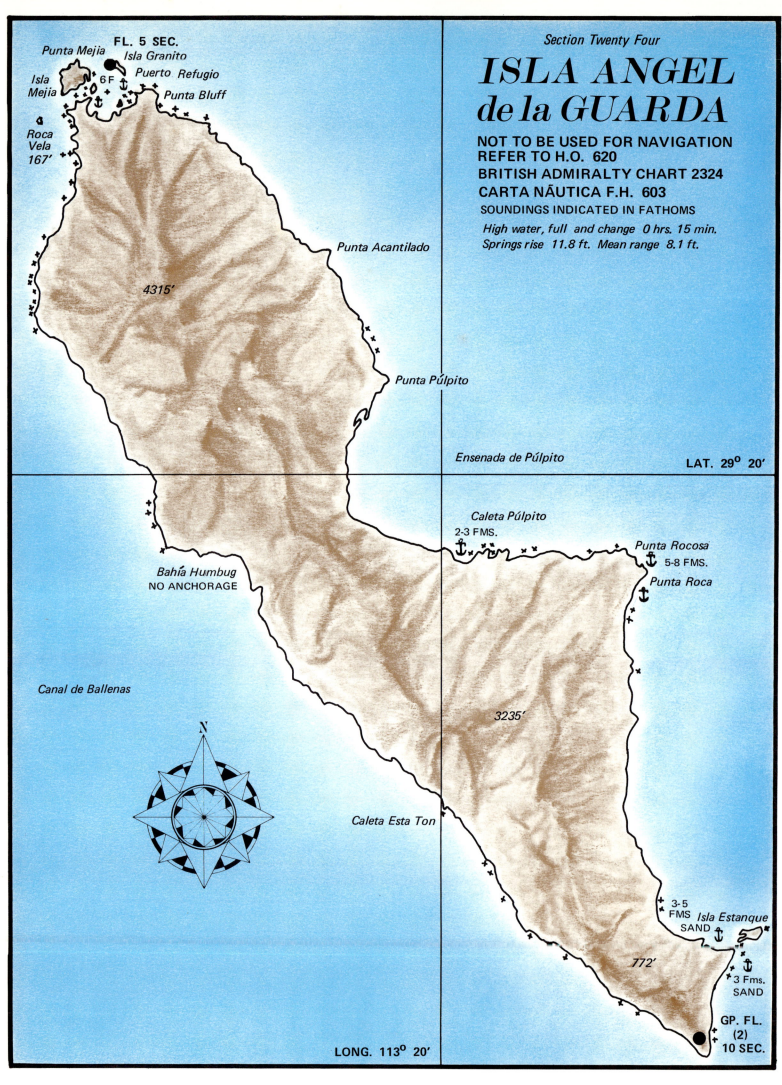

FL. 5 SEC.

Punta Mejia

Isla Granito

Puerto Refugio

Isla
Mejia

6 F

Punta Bluff

Roca
Vela
167'

Punta Acantilado

4315'

Punta Púlpito

Ensenada de Púlpito

Section Twenty Four

ISLA ANGEL
de la GUARDA

NOT TO BE USED FOR NAVIGATION
REFER TO H.O. 620
BRITISH ADMIRALTY CHART 2324
CARTA NÁUTICA F.H. 603
SOUNDINGS INDICATED IN FATHOMS

High water, full and change 0 hrs. 15 min.
Springs rise 11.8 ft. Mean range 8.1 ft.

LAT. 29° 20'

Caleta Púlpito
2-3 FMS.

Punta Rocosa
5-8 FMS.

Punta Roca

Bahía Humbug
NO ANCHORAGE

Canal de Ballenas

3235'

N

Caleta Esta Ton

3-5
FMS

Isla Estanque
SAND

772'

3 Fms.
SAND

GP. FL.
(2)
10 SEC.

LONG. 113° 20'

anchoring ground but no shoal dangers have been reported to exist. Over quite an extent of the southeastern side of the large island, and along the northwestern beach of the small islet, the sandstone seawall has been considerably undermined by the onslaught of the sea, resulting in random landslides of stratified debris sloping up from the water's edge to the seawalls.

Isla Partida is principally comprised of volcanic ash mixed with strata of sandstone; its typical desert vegetation is a somewhat heavier growth than found on neighboring islands but not of any height, nor is it difficult to penetrate upon landing to reconnoiter the island. The beaches are mostly rocky.

Roca Blanca (White Rock), situated about 800 yards northward of Isla Partida, is a steep-sided rocky monument, well covered with birdlime, giving it the whitish appearance for which it is named. A *reef with a rock,* projecting 2 feet above water at its outer end, extends about 700 yards northward from White Rock; the soundings are irregular and the bottom rocky for about 1¼ miles further northward, beyond which the depths increase rapidly.

WINDS AND CURRENTS — Tidal streams in the vicinity of the southeastern and central groups of these offshore islands run with sometimes considerable velocity, frequently producing strong tidal rips, whirlpools with swift vortexes and upwellings of considerable turbulence that are wise to avoid in small craft. Winds from the northwesterly quadrant generally prevail from November to June and frequently blow in this area with considerable force for 2 or 3 days at a time.

Isla San Lorenzo, bearing 147° T.

Isla Ángel de la Guarda (Ángel de la Guarda Island), a long, high, volcanic island lying parallel to the peninsular coast which at its closest proximity is 7½ miles across the Ballenas Channel, is the second largest land mass in the Gulf of California. Its high central range of mountains rises from 3,000 to 4,315 feet above the sea and runs in a continuous ridge from one end of the island to the other, dipping to a comparatively low point about the middle of the island's 42-mile length. There are neither foothills, benches nor extensive valleys; the sides of the long, high central ridges drop, for the most part, directly into the sea. The island is rocky, relatively barren except for typical desert growth and low bushes in the vicinity of the few arroyos; it is entirely uninhabited because of the lack of any viable water source. In the northeastern corner there is a small valley through which a seasonal stream flows immediately after the rains, then as quickly dries up to the parched condition that prevails throughout most of each year. Small hollows and tinajas collect and hold rain water to the extent sufficient to support a small population of coyotes, as well as the smaller animals and birds on which they live; iguanas, smaller lizards and rattlesnakes abound.

The eastern coast of the Ángel de la Guarda Island has a very irregular configuration with several open bays, and one enclosed, where vessels may *anchor* sheltered from the prevailing winds. The eastern shore is generally bold with rocky bluffs predominating. The southern point of the island is a sharp bluff, one mile northward of which is a hill 772 feet high that falls away abruptly to the shore on the east and west sides of the island. A *navigation light* is shown 131 feet above the sea from a metal tower on this point; it exhibits a **white group flash of two flashes every 10 seconds:** flash 0.5 second, eclipse 1.5 seconds; flash 0.5 second, eclipse 8 seconds. About 3 miles northward of the southern point, on the eastern side of the island, there is a small sandy beach off which *anchorage* may be obtained ¼ mile offshore in depths of 7 to 9 fathoms, with protection from northwesterly winds. Here the coast becomes low and curves northeastward to a sharp point; from this point a *rocky reef,* which dries in places, extends about a mile offshore to Pond Island.

Isla Estanque (Pond Island), sometimes referred to as Isla La Bibera, is a small island about 1 mile long and ¼ mile wide that rises to an elevation of no more than 400 feet above the sea. Its seawall rises in nearly perpendicular cliffs almost all around the circumference of the island, but on its southwestern side there is a small enclosed basin where small craft may anchor and find shelter. Along the south side of the island a 20-foot high rock pile gradually diminishes in height and tapers to a partially *submerged reef* that reaches southwestward almost a mile to the shore of Isla Ángel de la Guarda. A large *white rock* 80 feet high lies detached about 300 yards southeastward of this reef, and between it and the reef there is a *rock awash.* Three *submerged rocks* are situated about 250 yards off the southeastern side of Estanque Island and some *detached rocks* lie close off its northeastern side. A small *white rock* lies along the line of the reef.

Anchorage may be taken on the southern side of Estanque Island, close off its rocky shore, several hundred yards eastward of the foot of the reef in 3 to 4 fathoms, sand, sheltered from the west around to the northeast. The southwestern end of Estanque Island encloses a landlocked basin providing *excellent anchorage* for small craft, protected all around from the sea and sheltered especially from northerly winds by the hill on the northwestern side that rises to a high bluff facing the sea.

The southeast point of Ángel de la Guarda

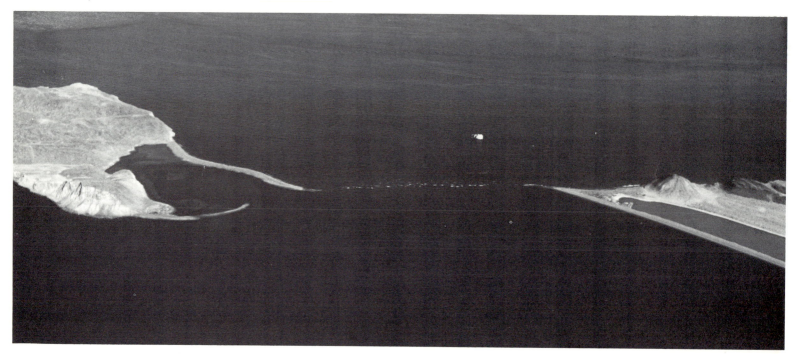

Isla Estanque; southeast point, Ángel de la Guarda

Directions: Access to this basin may be had only from the northern side of the island, and when approaching from the south a course must be laid around the northeastern extremity of the island as there is no passage through the reef. To enter the basin from the north, proceed southward toward the rocky reef extending between the two islands; it can be easily made out by the projecting rocks, and the sea and tidal currents washing upon it. A white rock projects a few feet above water about midway along the reef; the 80-foot high white rock, previously described and constituting a good landmark, lies about 300 yards southeastward beyond the reef. Approach the reef in deep water to within 100 to 200 feet; then sail parallel to it rounding up northward with a course laid through the narrow entrance channel between the northeastern foot of the reef and the

rocky spit on the port hand, curving toward it from the northwestern side of the basin. Enter and leave the basin at high or medium tide as the passage is shoal at low tide.

Anchorage may be taken within the basin in 2½ to 4 fathoms, sand bottom. At certain times of the lunar month tidal currents run with considerable velocity in the vicinity of the reef and must be taken into account when navigating in the area.

TIDES — The tidal interval at high water at full and change is 0 hours, 25 minutes; the spring range is 11.8 feet, the mean range, 8.1 feet.

In the northwest bight formed by the hook of the point at

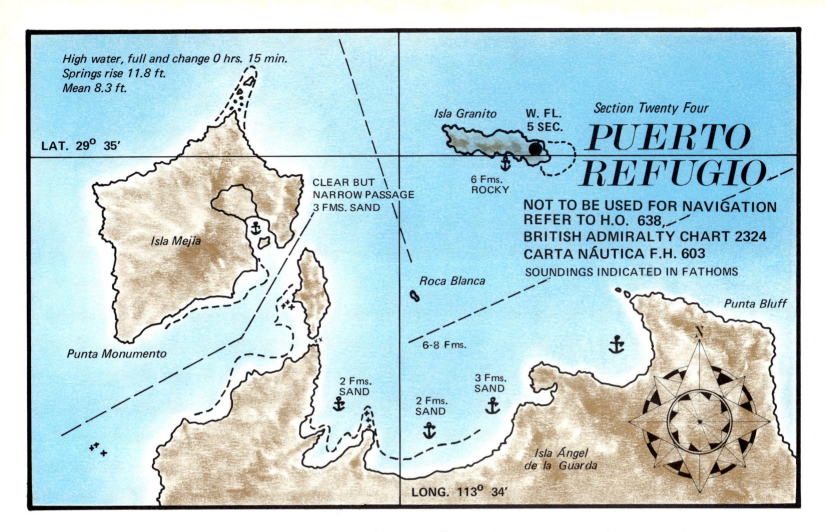

High water, full and change 0 hrs. 15 min.
Springs rise 11.8 ft.
Mean 8.3 ft.

LAT. 29° 35'

Isla Mejia

Punta Monumento

CLEAR BUT
NARROW PASSAGE
3 FMS. SAND

Isla Granito   W. FL. 5 SEC.

6 Fms.
ROCKY

Roca Blanca

NOT TO BE USED FOR NAVIGATION
REFER TO H.O. 638,
BRITISH ADMIRALTY CHART 2324
CARTA NÁUTICA F.H. 603
SOUNDINGS INDICATED IN FATHOMS

Punta Bluff

6-8 Fms.

2 Fms.
SAND

2 Fms.
SAND

3 Fms.
SAND

Isla Ángel
de la Guarda

LONG. 113° 34'

the western extremity of the Pond Island Reef, as it abuts the eastern shore of Isla Ángel de la Guarda, *anchorage* may be taken off a long sand beach in 3 to 5 fathoms, sand. Back of the beach, separated from the sea by a narrow sandy berm, is a long, narrow salt water lagoon, completely enclosed in the land. At the northwestern end of the lagoon a short dark lava bluff rises just back of the beach; immediately northward of this bluff a small circular sandy cove, protected on either side by headlands, opens to the sea. *Anchorage* may be taken in the mouth of this cove and *landing* easily effected on the shelving sandy shore.

The eastern shore of Isla Ángel de la Guarda between Pond Island and Punta Roca, situated about 13½ miles north-northwestward, recedes to the westward, forming a large open bay in the southern part of which there is *good anchorage* sheltered from southeasterly winds. The shore in the vicinity of this anchorage is comprised of a sand and gravel beach from which the depths increase gradually seaward. *Anchorage,* with some protection from northerly winds, may be obtained abreast a white sand beach immediately southwestward of Punta Roca.

Punta Roca (Rocky Point), sometimes referred to as Punta del Diablo, is a bold headland surmounted by a hill 1,948 feet high at the northeastern end of a spur running down from the central mountain ridge and ending in a cliff 520 feet high. Northwestward of Punta Roca about 1 mile, a secondary point, Punta Rocosa, comprises the northwestern headland of this promontory. *Anchorage,* sheltered from the northwesterly winds, may be obtained northward of Punta Roca in a position immediately southward of Punta Rocosa, close inshore in depths of 5 to 8 fathoms.

Between Punta Rocosa and the next prominent point to the northwest, Punta Púlpito, a distance of about 10½ miles, the coast recedes westward about 4 miles, forming the large open bay of Ensenada del Púlpito, the shores of which are comprised chiefly of pebble beaches with a few small bluff points in the southern portion. The land, sloping upward to a moderately high tableland, is covered with typical desert growth, including large cactus. *Good anchorage* may be obtained on the southern shore of this bay in Caleta Púlpito (Púlpito Cove), a small deep cove situated about 6 miles westward of Punta Rocosa; the cove is open to the north but affords excellent protection from southerly and westerly winds. *Anchorage* may be taken in the center of the cove in depths of 2 to 2½ fathoms, sand, abreast a white sand beach at its head. An arroyo leading down from the central ridge of the island opens onto the shore of the cove and affords access to the interior. Caleta Púlpito may be recognized by the contrasting red and white cliffs comprising the western headland. About 2 miles southward of Punta Púlpito a small lagoon, which dries at low water, has a narrow entrance that opens to the sea. Good, edible clams are to be found here. Between Punta Púlpito at the northern end of Ensenada del Púlpito and Punta Acantilado, situated about 13½ miles northwestward, the coast is a succession of rocky bluffs. About 5 miles southward of Punta Acantilado there is a low, slightly projecting point at which location an arroyo opens onto the shore.

Punta Acantilado (Bluff Point) is the northeastern extremity of a bold rocky headland 720 feet high, which forms the northern end of Ángel de la Guarda Island; rocky bluffs, 100 to 300 feet high, extend a mile to either side of the point. Westward of Punta Acantilado approximately 1 mile, Puerto

Roca Vela, Isla Mejia, Punta Monumento, northwest end of Isla Angel de la Guarda

Refugio opens at the northern end of the island.

Puerto Refugio (Refuge Bay) is formed between the northern end of Isla Ángel de la Guarda and the adjacent islands of Isla Granito and Isla Mejia; the harbor is formed by two basins connected by a narrow channel, both of which afford *good anchorage* sheltered from all winds, and are easily accessible from either side of the island. The eastern side of the harbor, which has the larger basin of the two and measures about 1¾ miles across, is entirely clear of submerged dangers. A spur of hills running down from a peak 720 feet high, situated about ½ mile westward of Acantilado Point, terminates in a rocky bluff point that forms the eastern arm of the basin; the point projects northwestward from the southern shore of the bay about ¼ mile and a *rocky reef, with detached rocks* lying on it, extends outward for another 300 yards. A *navigation light,* shown 46 feet above the sea from a metal tower standing on the southeast point of Isla Granito, exhibits a **white flash for one-half second every 5 seconds.** The *light* can be seen in clear weather for a distance off of 6 miles. Piedra Blanca (White Rock) is a jagged rock of whitish color, 41 feet high and steep-to, situated nearly in the center of the eastern basin; depths of 7 to 13 fathoms surround this rock.

The eastern basin of Puerto Refugio is entered from the east, between Isla Granito and the eastern arm of the harbor; from the north the basin is entered between Isla Granito and Isla Mejia. Both of these passages are deep and more than ¾ mile wide. *Directions: When entering the eastern basin through either of the passages, bring Piedra Blanca (White Rock) to bear about midway of the entrance and steer for it until within a reasonable distance, then steer for the anchorage.*

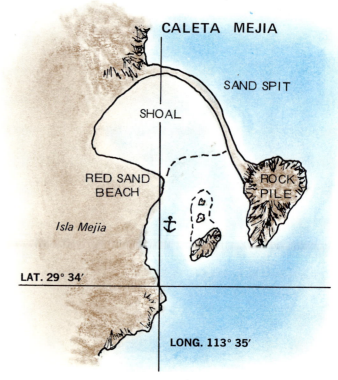

CALETA MEJIA

SAND SPIT

SHOAL

ROCK PILE

RED SAND BEACH

Isla Mejia

LAT. 29° 34'

LONG. 113° 35'

When entering by the eastern passage, adequate berth must be given the *reef,* which extends 300 yards northwestward from the eastern entrance point, and the *rocky shoal,* which extends about 300 yards northward from a point on the southern shore, near the southwestern corner of the basin. When entering by the northern passage, adequate berth must be given to the *reef* which extends northward from the northern extremity of Mejia Island. *Anchorage* may be taken southward of Isla Granito in depths of from 8 to 12 fathoms but the bottom is mostly rocky. The *best anchorage* will be found in the southern part of the basin in depths of 6 to 8 fathoms, sand, with White Rock bearing

000° distant ¾ mile; small vessels may work closer to the head of the cove and anchor in 2 to 3 fathoms, sand. A smaller cove immediately westward may be entered by shoal draft vessels and *safe anchorage* taken in 2 to 3 fathoms, sand; however, a *reef* extends off the intervening point and must be avoided as well as a *rock awash* at high water, situated just to one side of the center of the smaller cove's entrance.

TIDES — The high water interval at full and change at Puerto Refugio is 0 hours, 25 minutes; the spring range is 11.8 feet, the mean range 8.1 feet. Since the range of the

Southwestern Entrance to Puerto Refugio

Isla Mejia

337

tides in this vicinity is considerably more pronounced than the range of those encountered southward toward the mouth of the gulf, care should be exercised when selecting a suitable anchorage for the draft of the vessel.

Isla Granito (Granite Island), which fronts the eastern side of Puerto Refugio in a position about 2 miles northwestward of Punta Acantilado, is a narrow, rocky island with three prominent peaks: 172 feet high on the western end, 227 feet high in the middle and 281 feet high near the eastern end. The island is about ¾ mile long and 300 yards in width and is covered with a sparse growth of cactus and desert vegetation. The eastern point of the island terminates in a low, lava-strewn tongue at the root of which is a fine white sand beach, stretching from one side to the other. A *detached white rock* 15 feet high stands on a *rock reef,* partly awash, which extends eastward off the northeastward side of the tongue. A *landing* may be made in the small cove westward of the hook of the tongue although the beach is quite rocky; the sandy beach on the opposite side of the tongue, behind the white rock and reef, offers a clearer *landing.* Immediately westward of the high central peak of the island, a small cove with a white sand beach opens onto the southern shore; a *landing* can be made in this cove and access to the opposite side of the island effected by hiking over the low land back of the cove; a large bight with a sand beach at its head, on which a *landing* can be made, lies across the island at this point. Off the southwestern end of the island there are several *detached rocks awash and submerged;* a *reef,* on which stands a rock 13 feet high, extends about 200 yards from the northwestern point. The passages on either side of Granite Island are more than ¾ mile wide, clear of dangers, and have depths of 15 to 30 fathoms. The 39-foot high pyramidal metal tower of the *navigation light* may be seen standing on the southeast point of the island. Isla Granito is the year around home for a sizable colony of California sea lions.

Roca Vela (Sail Rock), on the western side of Isla Ángel de la Guarda, is a sharp conical rock of whitish appearance, covered by birdlime. Steep-to, it stands 167 feet above the sea in a position about 1¾ miles southwestward of Punta Monumento, the southwest point of Mejia Island. Roca Vela provides an excellent landmark when approaching Puerto Refugio from the west. Depths of 16 fathoms have been sounded close around this rock.

Isla Mejia (Mejia Island), which forms the northern side of the western basin of Puerto Refugio, is situated about ½ mile northward of the northwestern end of Isla Ángel de la Guarda. The island, a little over 1½ miles long and 1 mile wide, rises to a peak of 857 feet near its northwestern extremity. It is hilly and barren, except for some cactus and other desert vegetation, and its weather-sculptured sides fall precipitously into the sea. With the exception of some sandy beaches on its southeastern side, the coast of the island is a continuous rocky cliff which attains a height of 500 feet on its northwestern side. *Detached rocks* lie close off all the prominent points and a *dangerous reef* of rocks,

partly above water, extends about 800 yards northward from the northern point of the island. A shallow cove with some small islets in it penetrates more than halfway across the island from a position southward of its eastern extremity. Between the eastern end of Isla Mejia and the northern end of Ángel de la Guarda, and connected to the latter by a *rocky reef,* is a small islet 250 feet high, with a length of ½ mile and a width of about 400 yards. This islet separates the two basins of Puerto Refugio but there is a narrow channel 150 yards wide, with clear mid-channel depths of

Puerto Refugio, Isla Granito in foreground

Cove, northeastern shore, Angel de la Guarda

7 to 10 fathoms between it and Isla Mejia, which enables passage between the eastern and western basins; a gravel shoal prevents passage between the southern end of this islet and the large island.

Directions: — To pass through into the eastern basin from the anchorage in the western basin, steer for the northern extremity of the small islet that separates the two basins until the middle of the channel between that islet and Isla Mejia bears 27°; this course leads through the channel in a depth of not less than 4 fathoms. A small cove on the southern side of Isla Mejia, which opens onto the passage between the two basins, offers *good anchorage* to small craft. A small islet and several *detached rocks,* above water, lie in the middle of the entrance to this cove, but a clear basin is formed behind the islet, where *anchorage* may be taken off a sand beach. The shore material is composed of a fine red mud-like sand and its deep-toned hue is in colorful contrast to the blue-green water in the cove. The western basin of Puerto Refugio lies between the southern side of Isla Mejia and the northwestern point of Ángel de la Guarda. *Caution: A dangerous group of rocks some of which are awash lies between ¼ mile and ½ mile west-northwestward of the southern point of the entrance. The entrance channel to the southwest end of the basin lies between these rocks and Punta Monumento, the southwestern point of Isla Mejia; although a mid-channel depth of 10 fathoms has been sounded, the passage between the rocks and the main island is not recommended, lacking local knowledge.* Entrance to the northeast end of the basin may be made through the passage that connects the two basins as previously described.

Directions: A vessel entering the western basin of Puerto Refugio should pass northward of Roca Vela (Sail Rock) then *steer for the middle of the entrance, keeping Piedra Blanca (White Rock), situated in the eastern basin, in line with the southern extremity of the islet that separates the two basins in a range bearing about 72°, which leads clear of all dangers to the anchorage.* The best *anchorage* in the western basin is in a depth of 6 to 7 fathoms, sand and shell, in the outer part of the basin, with the southwest tangent of Isla Mejia bearing 37° and Piedra Blanca (White Rock) in line with the southern extremity of the islet that separates the eastern and western basins.

Puerto Refugio affords good protection from all prevailing winds and offers quiet anchorage in smooth water. *Landing* may be made on any of several sandy beaches on the main island or the smaller off-lying islets. The character of the land is quite stark but geologically colorful; there are good beaches on which to camp but no sweet water except that which is preserved in tinajas or natural basins formed in the rock and filled during infrequent rains. The surrounding waters abound in sealife of every description. Numerous varieties of bottom fish may be found in every season and sportfish feeding on the seasonal schools of small bait are abundant. Shark are numerous, and whales frequent the vicinity of the island much of the year. Of all the marine animals, however, none is more evident than the California sea lion, who as a permanent resident of the gulf, seems to gather in the largest numbers at Puerto Refugio. So far as is known, there has never been permanent Indian habitation on Isla Ángel de la Guarda due to the lack of water.

The island was discovered by Francisco de Ulloa during his exploration of the upper Gulf in 1539. No attempt was made to colonize the island or exploit its territory and in fact it was rarely visited. In 1765, on the strength of a rumor that fires had been seen burning on Ángel de la Guarda, the Jesuit priest, Padre Link, embarked from Bahía de Los Angeles and explored most of the island but found it barren of human habitation, animals or fresh water. The western side of Isla Ángel de la Guarda, fronting the Ballenas Channel, is most inaccessible and lacking in good anchorage. However, about 14 miles northwestward of the southeast extremity of the island, there is a small cove known as Esta Ton, which offers shelter from all but southerly weather in a small enclosed basin; however, the narrow entrance to the cove is somewhat difficult to find. *Anchorage* may be taken over a sand bottom and *landing* effected on a coarse white sand beach at the head of the cove.

Bahía Humbug (Humbug Bay), approximately midway the length of the western side of Ángel de la Guarda at the waist or narrowest part of the island is well named. The bay presents a picture of a fine looking anchorage with a steep sandy shore but the depths are too great for anchoring, even close to the beach. The lead finds no bottom at 40 fathoms and thus did the bay gain its name — Humbug. There is *no anchorage* here, although one may *land* and gain access to the interior of the island up a steep, broad arroyo that leads over the central ridge of the island to Bahía Púlpito on the eastern shore. Immediately northward of Humbug Bay is a bold, bluff point; between this point and Punta Remedios on the peninsula opposite is the narrowest part of the Ballenas Channel, about 8 miles wide.

SECTION 25
BAHÍA SAN LUIS GONZAGA to BOCA de COLORADO

Bahía San Luis Gonzaga and Bahía Willard

Close northward of Punta Willard the mouth of the Arroyo San Luis opens in a broad and flat sandy plain onto the shore. A brackish well midst an oasis of green foliage is located on the south side of the arroyo about ½ mile inland. Punta Bufeo is the northwestern headland of Arroyo San Luis; Isla San Luis lies about 2½ miles offshore opposite this point.

The coast between Punta Willard and Punta San Fermín situated about 38 miles north-northwestward is, except for a few bluffs, low and sandy; the land back of the shore slopes upward to broken hills and tablelands 1,000 to 1,500 feet high. Several islets lie off this part of the coast in a chain between Punta Bufeo and Punta Fermín. The depths offshore are comparatively shoal with but 12 fathoms sounded at 2½ miles, and 15 fathoms at 5 miles.

Punta Final (Point Final) is a rocky bluff of moderate height with low land to the southwest. Bahía San Luis Gonzaga (San Luis Gonzaga Bay) is an open bay which lies between Punta Final and Willard Point, situated about 4½ miles west-northwestward. From Punta Final the coast turns sharply southwestward and, sweeping around in a semicircle, forms the bay which is open to the north but affords *good anchorage* about ½ mile offshore, in depths of 8 fathoms during southeasterly winds. The shore of the bay is comprised of a long sweep of low sand and gravel beach. A rocky head, connected to the beach by a short sandspit, extends from the shore near the southeastern end of the bay, forming a small baylet between it and Punta Final, called Ensenada de San Francisquito; there are several small coves with sandy beaches at their heads in this part of the bay, one of which, not more than 50 yards wide, is called Caleta de San Francisquito (San Francisquito Cove).

Villa Mar y Sol, a sportfishing resort catering to trailers and trailered boats, is established closeby the sandspit on its northwestern side. Close southeastward an *aircraft landing strip* suitable for light planes serves the resort. (See Appendix.) Lodging, meals, fishing supplies and some provisions are available here. Outboard motorboats are for rent.

On the northwestern end of the bay a larger fishing resort, Hotel Casa Alfonsina, is established along the sandy shore, closeby the spit connecting to the island. An *aircraft landing strip* suitable for small planes is located parallel to the beach, immediately behind the resort. (See Appendix.) Outboard motorboats are for rent, tackle is available, accommodations offered and the dining room is open to guests and travelers alike. Aircraft and marine

ROAD TO MEXICALI

Punta Sargento

Salinas de Omatepec

Estero la
Ramada

Bahía de Adair

**OMNI 112.1 mHz
PPE**

Roca del Toro

R. bn. 318 kHz
Punta Penasco
GP.Fl. W. (2) 5 SEC.
20 MI

Playa Las Almejas
La Escondida

Rocas Consag

LA PONDEROSA FISH CAMP ⊙ 286'

Punta El Machorro

El Paraiso

SAN FELIPE

Bahía de San Felipe

AIRSTRIP

FL. W. 12 MI.

Punta San Felipe
Punta Estrella
Punta Diggs

N

LAT. 31° 0'

Laguna Percebu
Bahía Santa María
Nuevo Mazatlan
Agua Chale

Section Twenty Five

BAHÍA
SAN LUIS GONZAGA to
BOCA de COLORADO

NOT TO BE USED FOR NAVIGATION
REFER TO H.O. 620,
BRITISH ADMIRALTY CHART 2324
CARTA NÁUTICA F.H. 603
Tide-Springs rise 18 ft., (approx.)

**COLORADITO
FISH CAMP**

Punta
San Fermin

WELL

Puertecitos

HOT SPRINGS

Acantilado Rojo

Punta Isabel

**CAMPO
HUERFANITO**

El Huerfanito

Isla Miramar

ROCK RUINS

AIRSTRIPS

Isla Lobos

OKIE'S LANDING

Isla Encantada

LAT. 30° 0'

Isla Pomo
Isla San Luis

CAMPO SALVATIERRA

Punta Bufeo
GP. FL. (4) 12 SEC.

**PAPA
FERNANDEZ
RESORT**

Punta Willard

Bahía San Luis Gonzaga

AIRSTRIP

Punta Final

LONG. 114° 0'

341

Bahía Willard

gasoline is available.

Punta Willard (Willard Point), situated 8 miles northwestward of Punta Final and close northwestward of an island nearly joined to the shore southwestward, is 185 feet high and forms the northern headland of Bahía Willard, a small landlocked bay immediately northwestward of Bahía San Luis Gonzaga. A *navigation light* is shown 59 feet above the sea from a metal tower on the point and exhibits a **white group flash of four flashes every 12 seconds:** flash 0.5 second, eclipse 1.5 seconds; flash 0.5 second, eclipse 1.5 seconds; flash 0.5 second, eclipse 1.5 seconds; flash 0.5 second, eclipse 5.5 seconds. The light can be seen for a distance of 6 miles in clear weather. *Navigation note: On some charts Punta Willard is considered to be the eastern extremity of the island lying within Willard Bay, that point of land showing seaward being the most distinctive landmark along this shoreline.*

Bahía Willard (Willard Bay), an almost completely landlocked bay westward of the island, affords excellent protection under all conditions of sea and wind, is free of hidden dangers, and constitutes the northernmost *all-weather anchorage* on the western shore of the gulf. At the head of the bay in the shelter of the island, a shallow lagoon lies back of a spit of sand; a *sand shoal* extends from the island to the mouth of the lagoon, and the spit connecting the island to the shore dries at low water. Small

Caleta de San Francisquito

shoal draft vessels and boats may enter Willard Bay from San Luis Gonzaga Bay between the island and the spit, at high water; larger vessels enter through a deep clear channel immediately south of Punta Willard and north of the island. Depths in the harbor range from 5 to 10 fathoms with a depth of 5 fathoms sounded at about ¼ mile off the lagoon entrance. The tidal interval at full and change is about 1 hour, 20 minutes; springs rise about 14 feet.

Anchorage may be taken off the mouth of the lagoon in a cove under the lee of the island's southwest shore; *anchorage* may also be obtained on the northwestern side of the bay in a bight under the lee of Willard Point; *landing* may be effected on the sand beach at the head of the bight. A *shoal* extends outward from the shore immediately southwestward of this anchorage and care should be exercised to give it adequate berth when maneuvering in the harbor. Anchorage position should be carefully selected and depth accurately sounded as the ebb tide, dropping as much as 15 feet, may leave a vessel stranded on the mud bottom during slack water.

At the head of the bight close under the lee of Willard Point, there is a sportfishing resort called Papa Fernandez's, and sometimes referred to as Papa Gorgonio's, owned by one and the same man, Sr. Gorgonio Fernandez. An *aircraft landing strip* suitable for light planes is located on the flat plain back of the resort immediately southwestward of a small hill. There is a masonry-walled well, Pozo de los Frailes, constructed during the Spanish colonial period and still in use, 1 mile north of the resort; a stone building, dating from the early eighteenth century, stand nearby along the shore. Quite a good automobile road connects southward to Las Arrastras, thence to Santa Rosalía, Mulegé and La Paz; a lesser road connects northward to Puertecitos and San Felipe.

The land surrounding Bahía San Luis Gonzaga and Bahía Willard is of an undistinguished desert character, a vista of low mesas and small hills with dry, scattered desert vegetation. The arroyos that run back from the sea are soon lost in the angular hills, and the watersheds they drain, under the prevailing conditions of sparse rainfall are of too small an extent to support living streams. What moisture there is stored beneath their coarse gravels is too heavily laden with alkali to be of much use. Sand generally replaces alluvial silt, and what soil there is has little fertility. The sea alone and its fringing shore offer an abundance of life and a delightful climate; sportfishing and cruising is popular along this coast and commercial fishing boats range throughout the headwaters of the gulf.

Okie's Landing is situated in a small cove with a shingle beach, under the lee of a rocky point about 14 miles northwestward of Punta Bufeo and 5 miles northwestward of Campo Salvatierra. The landing is sheltered by the high land of the coastal range and Las Encantadas Islands offshore. It has been used off and on for many years as a sportfishing resort where motorboats may be rented, fishing tackle, bait and outboard fuel purchased and where some few refreshments and provisions are available. Trailer space and sleeping shelters are available when the camp is in operation.

ISLA SAN LUIS
REEF
LAVA FLOW
730'
SHOAL
3 Fms.
SAND
LAGOON
BLUFF
SAND
LAT. 29° 58'
LONG. 114° 21'
REEF AND SANDSPIT

Isla San Luis

About ½ mile north of Okie's Landing, on the east side of the road near the mouth of Arroyo Miramar and roughly opposite Isla El Muerto, there is a group of ancient Indian rock rings, the ruins of housing sites of a small village. In the mouth of an arroyo that opens onto the shore about 2 miles southward of this place and ¼ mile inland is an *aircraft landing strip* (See Appendix) suitable for small planes. Situated closeby is a mining operation called La Mina de Judas Tadeo. A mine building stands near the runway, and a *spring* of fresh water is located about ½ mile south of the mine and ¼ mile west of the connecting road.

Campo Huerfanito, a sportfishing resort consisting of several concrete block buildings and space for a number of trailers, as well as various other wooden shacks, is situated on the shore opposite Isla Huerfanito. There is a launching ramp for outboard motorboats here; outboard motor fuel is available as well as fishing tackle, bait, refreshments and some few provisions. The coastal road to Puertecitos and San Felipe runs along the shore back of the resort. An *aircraft landing strip* suitable for light planes is situated on the west side of the road near the resort. (See Appendix.)

Punta Isabel (Isabel Point) lies in a position about 2½ miles northward of Isla Huerfanito; Acantilado Rojo (Red Bluff), a remarkable reddish-colored bluff 100 feet high, protrudes from the coastal range below Cerro Prieto (Prieto Mountain), about 3½ miles further northward, and provides an excellent navigational landmark along this part of the coast. The shore falls to a low shelf on either side of the bluff; immediately southward is a natural evaporating

tidal basin glistening white with desiccated salt. On the northern side a large arroyo opens onto the shore and from its mouth a low, flat delta extends several hundred yards seaward from the general line of the coast and has a fringing shore bank. The coast between Acantilado Rojo and Puertecitos, about 7 miles northward, is comprised of a series of low bluffs with intervening arroyos that penetrate only a short distance into hills that rise steeply from the shore. The mouths of the arroyos form small coves in some of which are seasonal fish camps and sportfishing resorts. The coastal road threads its course along the seaward face of the hills, dipping down occasionally to provide access to the major coves and landings. *Detached rocks* lie close offshore in several places.

The six islands lying offshore along a 15-mile stretch of coast, between points just northwestward of Bahía Willard and just southeastward of Punta Isabel, comprise the northernmost group of Gulf islands and are characterized by their volcanic features and great flocks of seabirds. These islands collectively are called by the natives, Islas Las Encantadas (The Enchanted Islands).

Isla San Luis is an island of volcanic origin rising from the sea to a height of 729 feet and lying nearly 3 miles off Punta Bufeo, in a position about 13 miles northwestward of Punta Final at Latitude 29° 58′ north, Longitude 114° 25′ west. The island is separated from the mainland by a clear channel 1¼ miles wide. A low sandspit extends more than a mile from the southwestern side of the island, and on either side of the spit *shoal depths* extend for a distance of

½ mile. *Good anchorage* can be obtained on either side of the spit, protected from northwesterly winds on one side and from southeasterly winds on the other, but in either case care must be taken not to approach closer than ½ mile.

The eastern side of the island is a great concave cratered bluff of black lava, its half shell open to the sea; a broad black lava flow issues from a vent in the north side of the crater and fringes the sea off the north point of the island. The beaches are of black lava sand and that same rock generally characterizes most of the island's surface forcing its way through the layers of ash to emerge as low outcroppings and pinnacles. A thin fringe of sturdy brush borders the western side of the island but overall there is a scarcity of vegetation. The island is easily accessible in most of its parts from several good landing points. There is a small lagoon that changes with the ebb and flow of the 15-foot tide from a mud basin to a considerable lake. All of the other islands in the Encantadas group may be viewed northwestward from a lofty vantage point on Isla San Luis.

On the seaward side of San Luis Island, about ½ mile from its northern end and connected to it by a *reef* that dries at low water, is a small islet 478 feet high, remarkable in that it is composed almost entirely of one monolithic chunk of pumice and therefrom derives its Spanish name Isla La Pomo (Pomo Island). It is alternatively called Isla Encantada (or Cantada Island) but this name is currently given on modern charts to the next island northwestward, 2½ miles distant. The pumice material comprising the lofty and sheer cliffs of Pomo Island that plunge straight-sided into the sea has the curious character of being lighter by volume than water; chunks of the island that drop off float around and are carried by the tidal currents among the other islands of the group, curiosities of the gulf, and doubtless attributed by early and unscientific observers to some kind of exotic enchantment. *Navigation warning: A dangerous rock, awash at low water, lies 1 mile northward of the northwestern end of Isla San Luis; another dangerous rock that dries 3 feet and is steep-to, with 19 fathoms sounded close around, lies 1¼ miles northward of Isla La Pomo.*

Isla El Cholludo (Referred to on the navigation charts as Isla La Encantada), a small rocky island rising 354 feet above the sea in a position about 2½ miles northwestward of Isla San Luis, lies a little over 3 miles offshore at Latitude 30° 01' north, Longitude 114° 29' west. The island is oriented northwest and southeast with a central ridge running from one end to the other; its deeply eroded sides fall steeply to the sea. A large *detached rock*, whitened by birdlime and separated into two parts by a narrow channel, lies about 700 yards eastward. *Navigation warning: About 1¼ miles eastward of Isla El Cholludo and 2½ miles northwestward of Isla Pomo there is a large reef of rocks, some sunken, some awash, occupying a roughly circular area that has a diameter of about ½ mile; soundings do not give a warning of near approach to this isolated reef as it is steep-to with deep water all around.*

Okie's Landing, the fishing resort previously referred to, is situated in the small cove lying opposite Cholludo Island on the mainland shore.

Isla Los Lobos (Isla Coloradito or Isla Salvatierra), ris-

ing 559 feet above the sea, lies about 1½ miles northwestward of Isla El Cholludo in a position about 4 miles offshore at Latitude 30° 03' north, Longitude 114° 29' west. A low *sandspit and shoal* extend more than ½ mile southwestward from the island. The island has an uppermost band of reddish lava, separated in a distinctive layer from whitish material beneath, which provides a good landmark for identification.

Isla El Muerto (Isla Miramar), about 3½ miles westnorthwestward of Isla Los Lobos, lies approximately 2½ miles offshore and rises out of the sea to a height of 626 feet. On its southwestern side, two deep indentations form coves which offer *shelter* from northeasterly and southeasterly weather.

Isla El Huerfanito (Little Orphan Island), a mere hump of a rock 75 feet high, lies a little less than 1 mile offshore in a position about 5 miles northwestward of Isla El Muerto, and constitutes the northernmost island of Islas Las Encantadas. The northern end of the island is a bluff point with a whitish cliff on the inshore side; the southern end falls more gently from the single central ridge of the island's hump. Low spits of land extend a short distance outward from either end of the island. Campo Huerfanito, the sportfishing resort previously referred to, is situated on the mainland shore opposite the island.

Puertecitos (Little Ports) lies in a position about 13 miles northward of Isla Huerfanito, about 45 miles northward of Bahía San Luis Gonzaga, and 45 miles southward of San Felipe; it is a deep, rectangular indentation in the rocky, terraced coastal bluffs, open to the southeastward with a sand beach at its head. The cove affords protection from northerly weather but only shallow draft vessels may enter the mouth; deepdraft vessels must anchor outside and the extreme rise and fall of the tide must be taken carefully into account.

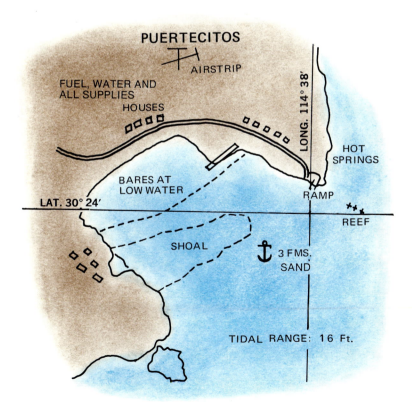

Puertecitos

Acantilado Rojo

Puertecitos is a popular sportfishing center with a considerable number of resort buildings, houses and other improvements built along the shore at the head of the cove, as well as on the seaward headland. There is a launching ramp for trailered boats; provisions and supplies, gasoline, ice, butane, several cafes and restaurants, refreshment stands, skiffs and outboard motorboats, and resort cabins are·all provided for sportfishermen visiting the area. An *aircraft landing strip* suitable for small planes is built on the flat back of the beach. (See Appendix.) The concrete *launching ramp* is located at the seaward end of the outer arm of the headland. On the seaward side of this headland, a *hot sulfur spring* rises among the rocks in three separate pools of varying temperature at the high tide line. From the seaward side of the cove a short masonry breakwater, submerged at high water, extends into the inner basin, which dries at low water. The coastal road dips down to the cove and passes through to one side of the settlement.

Immediately northward of Puertecitos, and open to the west, is a similar cove, though not as deeply indented, with a sand beach at its head called locally Bomber Beach because of the wreck of a military aircraft, during World War II, on the slope of the beach. A *reef of rock* extends seaward from the outer headland and the cove is unprotected from the prevailing wind, which drives the surf onto the beach. Several houses are built just back of the shore at the head of this cove, as well as in the adjacent cove close westward. About three miles northward of Puertecitos is an open bight with a sand beach at its head, called Caleta Corvina (Corvina Cove), which is the site of a sportfishing camp; several shacks are built on the shore near the water's edge, refresh-

ments are for sale, and trailer camp sites are for rent. A *well* is located on the west side of the coastal road close northward of Corvina Beach.

Punta San Fermín, about 7 miles northward of Puertecitos, is a low sand point poorly defined and not readily made out from seaward; Cerro Fermín (Canelo or Rugged Peak), rising to an elevation of 3,413 feet about 11 miles west-southwestward of the point, serves as a good landmark. *Anchorage* with some protection from northwesterly winds may be had in a narrow inlet immediately southward of the point. *Navigation caution: spring tides rise about 18 feet in the vicinity of Punta San Fermín.* The old settlement and water hole of Tinaja Somez is located along the coastal road closeby the point.

The coast from Punta San Fermín trends northward as far as Punta Diggs, a distance of about 27 miles; the shore throughout this entire distance is low and sandy, with the coastal range of mountains rising to an elevation of about 1,000 feet a few miles inland. *Soundings* taken at 2½ to 4 miles offshore give depths of 8 to 15 fathoms. The Arroyo Matomi opens on the coast in a large wash, close northward of Punta San Fermín; the Coloradito Fish Camp is located on the north side of the wash. A *well* of sweet water may be found on the north side of the wash, east of the coastal road.

Agua de Chale, situated about 14 miles northward of Punta San Fermín, is a small cove with a sand beach at its head; the name derives from a *well* of sweet water located close by. Nuevo Mazatlán, in the same vicinity, is the site of a fish camp in a cove with a sandy beach; fresh water is

Isla Lobos

Isla Encantada, Isla Lobos

available here. Back of Campo Nuevo Mazatlán is an abandoned sulfur mine with discarded and rusting machinery. Close northward along the coast is an open bight, Bahía Santa María, where trailer camp sites are for rent and refreshments are sold. Approximately 8½ miles north of Nuevo Mazatlán is Laguna Percebú, situated at the northern end of a semicircular cove which penetrates the low, flat land of the shore, creating a small tidal lagoon. At the southern end of the cove a spit of sand and rock extends northward partially sheltering the mouth of the cove; rocks *covered and awash* at high tide are exposed at low tide off the northern end of the spit. A second small inlet penetrates the shore back of a rift of sand dunes in the lee of the spit at the southern end of the cove; small shoal draft boats can negotiate the entrance and anchor within the shelter of the inlet at high water. There is a palm ramada built on the beach at the head of the cove.

For almost a mile northward of Percebú Lagoon another narrow, long lagoon, separated from the sea by a barrier spit of sand parallels the shore and opens at its northern end; the entrance is shoal with a breaking bar when the sea is running. Punta Diggs, situated about 4 miles north-ward, is low and sandy, projecting only slightly from the general line of the coast. Playa Estrella is a sandy beach in an open bight immediately southward of Punta Diggs, and is a popular camping and fishing location. Punta Estrella is situated about 2½ miles north of Punta Diggs, and Punta San Felipe is located about 2 miles farther north where the coast breaks toward the west. A navigation light flashing white from a white and orange banded column stands on the point just south of San Felipe at Lat. 30° 55′ north, Long. 114° 43′ west. The light has a 12 mile range. A small hill, rising to a height of 1,033 feet about 1¼ miles inland, is situated just back of the coastline behind Punta Estrella. *Navigation note: Punta San Felipe, as labeled on official navigation charts, is immediately northward of the town; it is the point which Mexican Government charts designate Punta El Machorro; Punta San Felipe, according to the same Mexican charts, is situated southward of Punta El Machorro about 8½ miles, as previously described.*

Isla Miramar

Punta El Machorro (San Felipe on the official navigation charts) Latitude 31° 03′ north, Longitude 114° 50′ west, situated about 8½ miles northwestward of Punta San Felipe across Bahía San Felipe, is a rocky headland with a dark hill, Cerro El Machorro, 940 feet high, rising abruptly from it. Punta El Machorro is the most significant and conspicuous headland along this part of the coast and provides an unmistakeable landmark when approaching San Felipe Bay. La Encantada Peak (also marked on the charts as Montaña Calamajue), the highest mountain in Baja California, rises to an elevation of 10,126 feet about 28 miles westward of Punta El Machorro; it has a whitish appearance and a jagged summit and on clear days it can be seen for a distance of over 100 miles.

Bahía San Felipe (San Felipe Bay), which lies southward of Punta Machorro, affords some shelter from northwesterly winds; the bay is quite shallow with depths of 3 fathoms sounded at 1 mile offshore. The shore, for the most part, is low and sandy but rocky bluffs lie along the northwestern part. *The best anchorage is in the northern part of the bay in depths of 4 to 5 fathoms, mud, with the 940-foot summit of the dark hill over Punta El Machorro bearing 325°, and a sharp white peak 4,288 feet high bearing 244°.* An unofficial *navigation light* at San Felipe, built by the villagers and maintained by the church, has only a small lens mounted on a latticework iron tower standing alongside a dome-shaped religious shrine. At one time an open fire was burned at night on the rock where the light now stands to guide fishermen home.

TIDES — The tidal interval at high water full and change is 9 hours, 55 minutes. The tide is chiefly diurnal; springs rise approximately 17½ feet, and extreme tides reach as much as 22½ feet, or a little more above mean low water. The mean range is 11.8 feet. High water occurs about 5.5 hours later than at the mouth of the Gulf; low water approximately 6 hours later. The timing is such that when there is high water at one end of the Gulf, there is low water at the other. Mean low water springs occur a day or two after the moon is new or full. The greatest tides will coincide with the new or full moons. Currents northward of Las Islas de la Cintura (Midriff Islands) are mostly tidal in nature, up to 6 knots at full and change of the moon, a sufficiently strong velocity to be reckoned with.

Tidal measurements in the upper Gulf for the last few years have been made under the direction of Dr. Donald A. Thompson, Department of Biological Sciences, University of Arizona and the results published in a yearly tidal calendar obtainable for $1.50 from Bureau of Mimeography and Multilithing, The University of Arizona, Tucson, Arizona 85721. A tidal station has been established at Puerto Penasco on the Sonora shore and the tidal curves have been found to be in phase from the mouth of the Colorado River to Kino Bay; however, at Guaymas, less than 100 miles from Kino Bay, the times of low and high water are about 6 hours earlier. Ideally additional stations need to be established for observation in the upper Gulf to produce more comprehensive forecasts useful for all of the principal points of marine activity on both shores;

WEATHER — The climate of the region is pleasant in the winter and spring but becomes rather hot and still during the summer months. During summer, gusty and hot desert winds are frequently encountered in the upper third of the Gulf. In the more offshore regions, northwesterly winds prevail from November to May, and southeasterly ones during the rest of the year. Moderate northwest gales that last two or three days at a time are frequently experienced. Infrequently a fierce storm sweeps through the upper Gulf with high winds driving the shallow water into short, steep punishing waves. The most recent *cordonazo* struck San Felipe in July, 1967, driving anchored fishing vessels in the bay well up into the town; roads were washed out, buildings destroyed, automobiles buried in the silt and debris, and damage to a considerable degree was inflicted on the settlement. Fortunately, these fierce storms of hurricane force are of a sporadic nature with many years between their occurrence.

Isla El Huerfanito

San Felipe

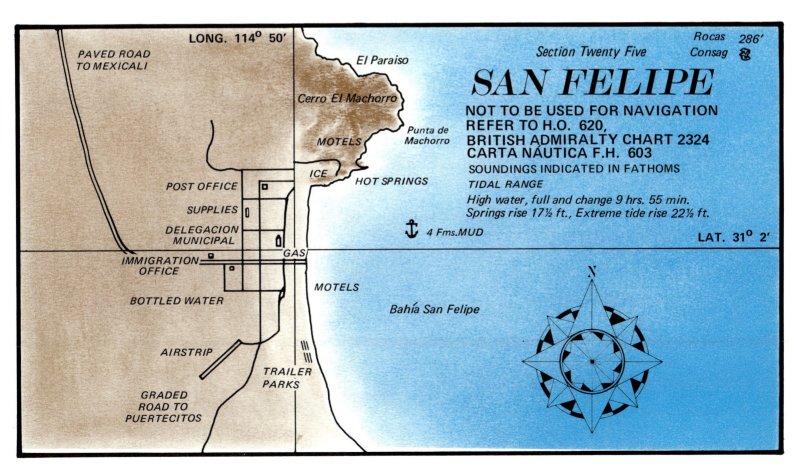

PAVED ROAD
TO MEXICALI

LONG. 114° 50'

El Paraiso

Cerro El Machorro

Punta de
Machorro

MOTELS

ICE

HOT SPRINGS

POST OFFICE

SUPPLIES

DELEGACION
MUNICIPAL

GAS

IMMIGRATION
OFFICE

BOTTLED WATER

MOTELS

AIRSTRIP

TRAILER
PARKS

GRADED
ROAD TO
PUERTECITOS

Bahía San Felipe

Rocas   286'
Consag

Section Twenty Five

SAN FELIPE

**NOT TO BE USED FOR NAVIGATION
REFER TO H.O. 620,
BRITISH ADMIRALTY CHART 2324
CARTA NÁUTICA F.H. 603**
SOUNDINGS INDICATED IN FATHOMS
TIDAL RANGE
*High water, full and change 9 hrs. 55 min.
Springs rise 17½ ft., Extreme tide rise 22½ ft.*

⚓ 4 Fms. MUD

LAT. 31° 2'

N

Punta de Machorro

The bay and waterhole of San Felipe was named by Jesuit Padre Fernando Consag in 1746 at which time he inscribed a chart of his making "San Phelipe de IHS." The bay was used toward the end of the eighteenth century as a supply point for the northern Dominican Missions. Development as a port began around 1858 at which time some temporary shacks were built along the waterfront. Permanent inhabitants settled around 1920 and large-scale commercial fishing operations began about 1942 at the beginning of World War II. San Felipe has recently became a popular sportfishing center since the completion of the paved highway from Mexicali.

FACILITIES — There is an extensive settlement on the shores of San Felipe Bay, chiefly comprised of commercial fishing enterprises; a large number of fishing vessels operate out of the bay. Sportfishing facilities, offering charter boats of all types, and resort accommodations for travelers with trailered launches are numerous. Several grades of gasoline are available, as well as diesel fuel, lubricating oil and butane. Engine and marine parts may be purchased from stock and marine mechanics may be hired. Ways facilities consist of flat tidal work areas where vessels are floated at high tide, and shored up as the tide ebbs regularly 18 feet. Many vessels are allowed to merely lay over on the turn of their bilges, one side to be worked on at one tide and the other side to be exposed for repair on another tide. There are no docks along the waterfront; flat-bottomed freighters anchor in the shallow roadstead and wait for the tide to recede, which leaves them high and dry on the tidal flats; cargo and cattle are then worked from the beach.

Fresh water, supplies and provisions are available in the village. Trucks make daily runs with frozen fish products to Mexicali and the United States, about 125 miles distant; special orders may be obtained on their return trip. A commercial icehouse on the northeast side of the harbor supplies crushed ice from a chute to commercial fishing boats moored below the cliff. Block ice may also be obtained here. Liquor stores, grocery stores, meat markets, sportfishing and tackle shops, and the inevitable tourist curio shops are located in the town. There are three Pemex gasoline service stations, selling several grades of gasoline to 100 octane. There are no street lights in the town by government decree; this condition has been created to prevent optical interference with astronomical observations being carried on at the National Observatory recently constructed on Encantada Peak, high in the mountain range back of the town.

PUBLIC ACCOMMODATIONS — There are 6 hotels with 95 rooms and baths at reasonable rates; there are 6 trailer and camper courts offering cabañas, water, electricity and sewer connections, toilets and showers; three of the trailer courts have concrete launching ramps across the beach. There are several restaurants, cafes and bars. There is a plaza, a public library, a movie theater, and the usual government buildings. A sulfur hot springs is located near the ice house below the cliffs on the northeast side of the bay.

Reservations and information regarding hotels, trailer courts and boat charter may be obtained from the following establishments: Augie's Riviera Hotel (rooms, restaurant, bar, and boats for charter), P.O. Box 642, Calexico, California; El Cortez Motel and Trailer Park (rooms, restaurant, boats for charter, bait and tackle available), P.O. Box 1227, Calexico, California; Arnold's Del Mar Motel and Cafe (rooms, showers, cafe adjoining); Motel El Cortez (rooms, baths, kitchens, patio, restaurant, bar and concrete launching ramp for trailered boats), P.O. Box 1227, Calexico, California; Villa Del Mar Motel (rooms, hot water showers, restaurant, adjoining bar); Costa Azul Trailer Park; Miramar Trailer Park; Club de Pesca Trailer Park; Las Arenas Trailer Park.

COMMUNICATIONS — Landline telephone service connects San Felipe with the mexican mainland, the United States and international circuits; telegraph service also extends to the town. The telephone office is located at Oaxaca

El Paraiso

and Hidalgo Streets. There is a government Post Office in the town and mail delivery is rapid and regular by land and air. A good paved road, Mexico #5, communicates with Mexicali, Calexico and El Centro; the border is about 127 miles distant.

TRANSPORTATION — Commercial truck traffic between San Felipe and Mexicali is relatively heavy and frequent; public bus service runs between the two towns, connecting to cities across the border in the United States. Taxi service is readily available in San Felipe and to outlying resorts and beaches. Two *airstrips* serve the town.

MEDICAL FACILITIES — There are several private doctors and dentists in San Felipe. The government Social Security Hospital is located on the south side of the plaza.

The Coast northward of San Felipe is largely comprised of low tidal land to the mouth of the Colorado River. Immediately westward of Punta El Machorro there is an open bight beneath the dark hill of Cerro El Machorro with a broad sandy beach along its shore. This cove is called El Paraíso and there is a trailer park established here of the same name. There is a small museum connected with the trailer park, featuring curious seashells and oddities of the Sea of Cortez. The water off the beach is shoal but shallow draft boats may approach the shore closely at high water. The rise and fall of the tides should be carefully watched everywhere along this part of the gulf to avoid stranding. A fishing camp called La Ponderosa is located several miles northward of El Paraíso. Trailer space is for rent, there is a launching ramp for trailered boats and refreshments are available. Several miles northward of La Ponderosa, Estero La Ramada opens through a sand bar to the sea; tidal flats cover many square miles of the coastal shelf along this stretch of the shore to Bahía Ometepec and Isla Gore at

the mouth of the Colorado River. Mud flats and shoals that dry at low water extend offshore 1½ to 6 miles; the flats are backed by plains that rise gradually toward the mountain range in the interior.

Roca Consag (Consag Rock), situated offshore about 18½ miles east-northeastward of Punta El Machorro and Bahía San Felipe, rises 286 feet above the sea and is whitened by birdlime to such an extent that from a distance it resembles a ship under sail, and is sometimes referred to as Ship Rock. A tongue of boulders runs westward from its base; a number of *detached rocks,* some of them more than 25 feet high, lie ¼ to ½ mile westward of the main rock. Soundings close around the rock show depths of 5 to 7 fathoms, deepening to 19 and 20 fathoms ½ mile off; soundings between Roca Consag and Punta El Machorro, at the northeastern end of Bahía San Felipe, show depths of 10 to 15 fathoms, generally mud.

Fish camp at los Almejas

El Moreno

Sportfishing boats use Roca Consag as a convenient mark in navigating offshore in search of game schools. It provides an excellent point of departure for shaping a course for the mouth of the Río Colorado; the rock lies in a position about 35 miles southeastward of the river entrance. *Caution: The ebb and flow of the great tides at this extreme point in the gulf produce heavy rips in the vicinity of Consag Rock.*

Consag Rock is strangely of sedimentary material in a vast surrounding land comprised mostly of volcanic rock. Its sides are scaled with fragments on the verge of breaking loose and plunging into the sea; its top is a jumble of broken and loose material. It can be climbed, however, and has been a number of times for the sake of scientific investigation. Recent scientific observations of the earthquake-triggering San Andreas fault that runs the entire length of California, locate its southern extremity in the gulf about 60 miles off the mouth of the Colorado River.

For navigation beyond this point and along the eastern side of the Gulf of California reference is made to United States Oceanographic Office Publication H.O. 26, Sailing Directions for the West Coasts of Mexico and Central America.

From the time of the Cortez expedition across the Vermillion Sea in the early part of the sixteenth century to a more thorough exploration by Fathers Kino and Consag in the seventeenth and early part of the eighteenth centuries, one of the two principal focal points for expeditionary parties was the head of the Gulf of California: First, to determine the insularity of California, firmly believed to be an island; then to search out the possibility of a continuous waterway through the fabled Straits of Anian, across or around the North American continent to the Atlantic — a shortcut to Europe. What a bonanza that would have been! It was doggedly believed by the leading geographers of the day that no one continent could begin at Latitude 55° south, as the tip of South America does, and run in an uninterrupted coastline without a single pass for well over 10,000 miles to the high northern latitudes. The answer to this riddle was sought at the headwaters of the Vermillion Sea. Thus was early and thorough exploration of the region accomplished. The story of the many expeditions to the head of the Gulf of California and up the Río Colorado is a book unto itself and there is one that eminently deals with the subject: *The Grand Colorado* by Tom H. Watkins; I commend it to you.

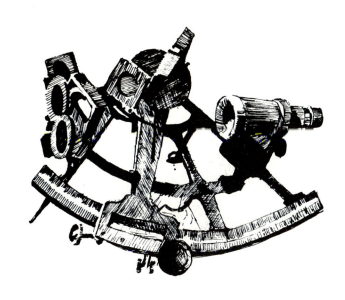

APPENDICES

Before the advent of radio, ships left port and were seldom heard from again until they were sighted entering port. Occasionally they were never seen again, the fate of crew and ship being shrouded in mystery forever. All the perils of the sea had to be faced alone, unless by the rarest luck another vessel chanced within hailing distance. At such times the masters and crew were so hungry for news that they nearly always hove-to and "spoke" one another; the outward bound giving latest news from her home port and the world at large; the homeward bound giving news of other ships and taking mail ashore.

Today shipboard radio equipment operated in connection with established communications networks provides a means for calling assistance to any ship in distress, and for notifying all other ships in the immediate area of an emergency lifesaving or salvage service they may be in a position to render. Investigation of various maritime disasters and of spectacular and successful rescue of lives and property has made it clear that in most cases it has been a radio link — or lack of it — responsible for the outcome. Modern medium

and high frequency radiotelephone communications networks operated in conjunction with the established landline telephone circuits enable people aboard ships at sea to communicate readily with those ashore to tell the progress of the voyage, and that all is well.

By the time a boat owner and his crew are ready to undertake an extended voyage down the Baja California coast they should be completely familiar with basic marine radio operating procedures and practiced in readily establishing contact with shore stations, as well as with other vessels. Equipment reliability and effectiveness for long range communications should be the primary consideration. It is well to bear in mind that shipboard radio sometimes affords the only link upon which you may need to depend while cruising in Baja waters, remote from the normal emergency aid generally available to mariners along more highly populated coastlines.

The following marine radio information is offered to enable you to exploit the full possibilities inherent in the communication equipment installed aboard your vessel and to objectively appraise its adequacy for both short and long range communication.

GENERAL RULES FOR RELIABLE COMMUNICATION IN BAJA CALIFORNIA

Several simple self-disciplined rules for reliable communications have been found advantageous to ship's safety by experienced Baja hands.

1. Know your radio equipment and its capability fully; understand its use and operation thoroughly. 2. Maintain radio power supply from storage batteries separate from starting or lighting source. 3. Acquaint yourself with other radio-equipped vessels traveling in the same area; establish regular radio schedules and check in several times a day. 4. Test your transmitting range for each current cruising locality; utilize relay procedure through other stations to extend your communicating range. 5. Explore all available radio channels utilized on a regular basis in your cruising area; *provide your equipment with crystals for all frequencies necessary to communicate on these channels. Utilize relay procedure to communicate if*

necessary. 6. Read the roll call from shore stations KMI-Pt. Reyes and KOU-San Pedro regularly. 7. Maintain a regular radio weather watch. 8. Understand the use and application of the radio direction-finder installed aboard; familiarize yourself with its particular bearing deviation characteristics through practice. 9. Keep a radio log in a permanent bound book with pages numbered consecutively to comply with the law and for reference.

CAUTION: The radio data contained in this Appendix has been drawn from original sources and reprinted with careful attention to currency and accuracy, but errors may exist; the data, therefore, should be used accordingly. Masters of vessels using this book as reference are advised to check all information against official government publications or original commercial sources.

SHIP-TO-SHIP/SHIP-TO-SHORE MEDIUM FREQUENCY SINGLE SIDEBAND (SSB):

2065.0 kHz	Ship-to-ship/ship-to-shore (only in geographic areas where operation will not interfere with Canadian stations).
2079.0 kHz	
2082.5 kHz	Ship-to-ship working frequency/coast-to-ship commercial traffic and safety communications.
2093.0 kHz	Ship-to-ship, commercial fishing only.
2096.5 kHz	Ship-to-ship working frequency: coast-to-ship commercial traffic limited to 150 watts and A3A (pilot carrier) or A3J (no carrier) emission.
2687.4 kHz	Coast Guard communication only; working frequencies.
2660.4 kHz	

NOTE: SSB equipment may be used on all presently authorized intermediate frequencies (2142, 2638, 2670, 2694, 2704, 2738 kHz) except 2182 kHz where A3H (AM equivalent) emission is mandatory. A series of higher frequencies is also allocated to SSB operation enabling "high seas" long distance intership and ship-to-shore communication.

SHIP-TO-SHIP/SHIP-TO-SHORE MEDIUM FREQUENCY DOUBLE SIDEBAND (DSB) (To be eliminated January 1, 1977)

United States Frequencies:

2142 kHtz	Ship-to-Ship working frequency (daytime only).
2182 kHtz	Distress, Coast Guard, Calling frequency.
2638 kHz	Ship-to-Ship working frequency.
2670 kHtz	Coast Guard: Broadcast Notice to Mariners, working frequency.
2694 kHtz	Coast Guard intercommunication only.
2704 kHtz	Special ocean racing and Coast Guard.
2716 kHz	Coast Guard liaison.
2738 kHtz	Ship-to-shore working frequency.

Mexican Frequencies:

2182 kHz	Ensenada Radio XFE.
2715 kHtz	Mazatlán Radio: Weather 9:10 and 11:10 a.m.
2660 kHtz	Mazatlán Radio: Weather 12:00 Noon
2523 kHz	Manzanillo Radio
2620 kHz	Baja California Hotels
2875 kHz	La Paz International Airport-Air Services
2830 kHz	"C" Band
2238 kHtz	"Banana Band"

DISTRESS FREQUENCIES AND MEDICAL ADVICE
2182 kHz/156.8 mHz

The Federal Communications Commission and the United States Coast Guard both approve the use of a two-tone self-generated audio signal transmitted to alert attention preceding a distress message, and to actuate automatic alarm detection devices. The two-tone signal can be immediately identified, recognized as a distress signal and sorted from the other traffic. The Radiotelephone Alarm Signal should be transmitted prior to a DISTRESS CALL for approximately one minute and used only to announce that a DISTRESS CALL or MESSAGE is about to follow.

NOTE: Maintaining a close watch on the DISTRESS and EMERGENCY frequencies, 2182 kHz and 156.8 mHz, while the radio equipment is not otherwise employed, assures your participation as a possible lifesaving unit or relay link in the event of a marine emergency.

MEDICAL ADVICE

Emergency medical advice by radio may be obtained from the United States Public Health Service through Coast Guard Radio NMQ Long Beach, NMC San Francisco or through commercial coastal stations KOU San Pedro or KMI San Francisco. Specify complete description of sick person and his symptoms in first message.

SHIP-TO-SHIP / SHIP-TO-SHORE VHF-FM LINE-OF-SIGHT MARINE RADIO COMMUNICATIONS CHANNELS

CHANNEL	FREQUENCY mHz	MODE/USE	APPLICATION
6	156.3	Ship-To-Ship, simplex	Intership Safety, Pilots; All Vessels; Mandatory
7A	156.35	Ship-To-Ship/Ship-To-Shore	Commercial ship's business
8	156.4	Ship-To-Ship, simplex	Commercial ship's business
9	156.45	Ship-To-Shore	Yacht clubs/pleasure craft
10	156.5	Ship-To-Ship/Ship-To-Shore	Commercial ship's business
11	156.55	Ship-To-Ship/Ship-To-Shore	Commercial ship's business
12	156.6	Ship-To-Ship/Ship-To-Shore	Port operations, Harbor Masters, Coast Guard Liaison
13	156.65	Ship-To-Ship/Ship-To-Shore	Navigational, Ship's position or movements
14	156.7	Ship-To-Ship/Ship-To-Shore	Port Operations, ship's movements
15	156.75	Shore Station	Weather, navigational hazards, Notice to Mariners
16	156.8	Ship-To-Ship/Ship-To-Shore	Distress, Safety, Calling All Vessels, Mandatory
17	156.85	Ship-To-Shore	State agencies/recreational boating
18A	156.9	Ship-To-Ship/Ship-To-Shore	Commercial ship's business
19A	156.95	Ship-To-Ship/Ship-To-Shore	Commercial ship's business
20	157.0/161.6	Ship-To-Ship/Ship-To-Shore, duplex	Port Operations
21	157.05		Coast Guard
22	157.1/161.7	Ship-To-Shore, duplex	Coast Guard
22A	157.1		Coast Guard
23	157.15/161.75	Ship-To-Shore, duplex	Public telephone channels
23A	157.175	Ship-To-Ship/Ship-To-Shore	Coast Guard Auxiliary
24	157.2/161.8	Ship-To-Shore, duplex	Public telephone channels
25	157.25/161.85	Ship-To-Shore, duplex	Public telephone channels
26	157.3/161.9	Ship-To-Shore, duplex	Public telephone channels
27	157.35/161.95	Ship-To-Shore, duplex	Public telephone channels
28	157.4/162.0	Ship-To-Shore, duplex	Public telephone channels
65A	156.275	Ship-To-Ship/Ship-To-Shore	Port Operations, Ship Movements
66A	156.325	Ship-To-Ship/Ship-To-Shore	Port Operations, Ship Movements
67	156.375	Ship-To-Ship	Commercial, Ship's business
68	156.425	Ship-To-Shore	Yacht clubs/pleasure craft
69	156.475	Ship-To-Shore	Yacht clubs/pleasure craft
70	156.525	Ship-To-Ship	Pleasure craft, working frequency
71	156.575	Ship-To-Shore	Yacht clubs/pleasure craft
72	156.625	Ship-To-Ship	Pleasure craft, working frequency
74	156.725	Ship-To-Ship/Ship-To-Shore	Port Operations, ship's movements
77	156.875	Ship-To-Ship	Commercial, ship's business
78	156.925	Ship-To-Shore	Yacht clubs/pleasure craft
79A	156.975	Ship-To-Ship/Ship-To-Shore	Commercial, ship's business
80A	157.025	Ship-To-Ship/Ship-To-Shore	Commercial, ship's business
83B	157.175		Coast Guard Auxiliary
84	157.225/161.825	Ship-To-Shore, duplex	Public telephone channels
85	157.275/161.875	Ship-To-Shore, duplex	Public telephone channels
86	157.325/161.925	Ship-To-Shore, duplex	Public telephone channels
87	157.375/161.975	Ship-To-Shore, duplex	Public telephone channels
88A	157.425	Ship-To-Ship/Ship-To-Plane	Commercial, fish spotting
WX-1	162.55	Coast Station KWO-37 (L.A.)	24-hour National Weather Service
WX-2	162.4	Coast Station KEC-62 (S.D.)	24-hour National Weather Service

CITIZENS' BAND NON-LICENSED VHF COMMUNICATIONS

Citizens' Band radiotelephone equipment operating on 27 mHz may be used on shipboard without station or operator licensing. The equipment is relatively inexpensive but effective at sea only over short distances. Many small craft owners utilize Citizens' Band equipment for auxiliary communications capability to provide a radio link between boats in close proximity, in order to relieve the burden on the already overcrowded 2 to 3 kHz marine band. However, such limited auxiliary equipment should not be employed as the sole radio capability aboard a vessel whose range requires proper radio communication for marine emergencies. Channel 9 has been designated an emergency frequency but should not be considered a substitute for the authorized marine VHF-FM distress frequency, as it is not monitored by the Coast Guard. Citizens' Band offers 23 channels of communication over a range of frequencies from 26.965 mHz to 27.255 mHz.

AMATEUR RADIO NETWORKS

Radio "Hams" in the United States maintain several active nets with "Radio Aficionados" in Baja California and provide still another reliable link of communication to many places otherwise too remote for regular commercial landline connections. The amateur radio operators and their sometimes formidable communications capabilities have many times aided in communications emergencies. In California there is an all-day net established on 7.255 mHz., SSB which can handle messages to most cities in the west. On weekday evenings another net operates on 3.960 mHz., SSB, clearing traffic at 7 p.m. Pacific standard time during winter months and at 9 p.m. daylight savings time during summer months. There is an amateur Mexican radio station at the Melling Ranch near Cabo Colnett in the upper Baja Peninsula and one located at Bahia Los Dolores on the Gulf coast near Isla San Jose. Further information is easy to achieve by either tuning in on the nets or working the frequencies.

HIGH SEAS MARITIME MOBILE RADIOTELEPHONE SERVICE

Reliable two-way radiotelephone communication service is offered by the Bell System between vessels or aircraft and the established landline telephone system through its coastal radio station KMI and High Seas Marine Operator Pt. Reyes, California. The service is designed to provide reliable duplex voice communication for ships and aircraft in transoceanic travel or in remote areas beyond the range of the regular intermediate frequency marine band; it is also applicable to short and medium range communications as well. Compatible shipboard radio equipment capable of A3A type emission (SSB) on the high frequency 4, 8, 12, 16 and 22 mHtz. bands is required to be installed and maintained by the owner of the vessel or aircraft.

The coastal station KMI – Pt. Reyes is manned at all times and continuously monitors ship frequencies, alert for incoming calls. At scheduled intervals (usually the first five minutes of each hour) the station broadcasts a test transmission and announces a roll call of vessels for which shore traffic is being held. Automatic signalling equipment is available which will provide an audible alarm when a particular coded number is dialed by the KMI technical operator. U.S. weather broadcasts are also transmitted at regular intervals.

Additionally, the station is always available for radio transmission checks, message traffic checks, Coast Guard emergencies, and distress traffic. The coast station has a multiple array of directional rhombic antennas which are selected to provide the best signal.

Calls are placed by choosing the optimum paired frequencies assigned to the station as determined by propagation conditions, the vessel's geographic position, time of the day or night and by experience. Service charges are based upon ship's position relative to established geographic zones and minutes of conversation. Shipboard calls may be charged to landline numbers. Operating procedures and a rate schedule may be obtained in a booklet available free of charge from Pacific Tel. & Tel. Co., Maritime Mobile Radiotelephone Service, 153 Kearney Street, Rm. 209, San Francisco, California 94105, telephone (415) 399-3081, 986-5216 or 361-0900; Pacific Telephone & Telegraph Company, P.O. Box 5868, Los Angeles, California 90055, telephone (213) 621-5624; for technical assistance American Telephone and Telegraph Company, 1587 Franklin Street, Room 2514, Oakland, California 94612, telephone (415) 836-2711. (Call collect.)

KMI CALLING AND WORKING FREQUENCIES — Coastal Station, San Francisco, California

Best Baja Frequencies

As far south as:	Ship (kHtz)	KMI (kHtz)	Operating Code	Ship (kHtz)	KMI (kHtz)	Operating Code
	Primary calling and working frequencies:			*Secondary calling and working frequencies:*		
Asuncion Bay — night.	4072.4	4371.0	4-1 (S + D)	4101.2	4399.8	4-2 (S)
Cedros Island — day.	8204.4	8738.4	8-1 (S + D)	8201.2	8735.2	8-2 (S)
Magdalena Bay — day, evening, night.	12382.5	13161.5	13-1 (S + D)	12372.0	13151.0	13-2 (S)
Cabo San Lucas — evening, night.	16512.5	17307.5	17-1 (S + D)	16509.0	17304.0	17-2 (S)
Cabo San Lucas — any time.	22045.5	22671.0	22-1 (S + D)	22042.0	22667.5	22-2 (S)

S—Single Sideband   D—Double Sideband

NOTE: Radiotelephone calls for vessels at sea are broadcast by KMI at regular intervals (usually first 5 minutes of each hour). Both ship and shore stations must transmit on paired frequencies as shown in the list; cross-band operation is not permitted by F.C.C. regulations.

HOTELS AND STATIONS UTILIZING 2620 kHtz

All Baja Hotels and Resorts welcome cruising yachts in their anchorages; yacht crews are equally welcome ashore to avail themselves of refreshment, dining room service and overnight accommodations depending upon available space. Hotel and Resort management request adequate prior arrangements, however, as to number of dinner guests and approximate arrival time so that adequate preparations may be made for extra service. Nearly all resort establishments maintain an extended radio watch on aircraft UNICOM 122.8 mHtz and on the Marine Band, 2182, 2638 or 2620 kHtz.

CODE		STATION: Frequency 2620 kHtz
0	(cero)	Servicios Aereos, S.A., La Paz Airport
1	(uno)	Hotel Rancho Las Cruces
2	(dos)	Hotel Palmilla
3	(tres)	Hotel Camino Real Cabo San Lucas
4	(cuatro)	Compania de Productos Marinos (Cannery at Cabo San Lucas)
5	(cinco)	Hotel Bahia de Palmas
5.5	(cinco y medio)	Hotel Punta Pescadero
6	(seis)	Hotel Cabo San Lucas
6.5	(seis y medio)	Hotel Bajo Colorado
7	(siete)	Hotel Buena Vista
8	(ocho)	Hotel Punta Colorada
10	(diez)	Hotel Finisterra
11	(once)	Office in La Paz of Hotel Cabo San Lucas
13	(trece)	Office in La Paz of Hotel Buena Vista

KOU MARINE RADIOTELEPHONE OPERATOR
Coastal Station, San Pedro, California.

INTERMEDIATE FREQUENCY (DUPLEX)

CHANNEL	SHIP	KOU	PERIOD
1	2009 kHz	2566 kHz	24 hours
2	2126 kHz	2522 kHz	Daytime only 7 am to 7 pm PST
3	2206 kHz	2598 kHz	Daytime only 7 am to 7 pm PST
4	2382 kHz	2466 kHz	24-hour service

NOTE: Radiotelephone calls for vessels at sea are broadcast by KOU at regular intervals (usually first 5 minutes of each hour).

VHF/FM (DUPLEX)

CHANNEL	SHIP	SHORE STATION	AREA
26	157.3 mHz	161.9 mHz	San Pedro
27	157.35 mHz	161.95 mHz	Santa Barbara, Marina Del Rey, Dana Point
28	157.4 mHz	162.0 mHz	Santa Barbara, San Diego

NOTE: VHF Channels 26 and 28 rotate over the United States in communications satellites providing marine radiotelephone links from any coastal point.

SAN DIEGO TO ENSENADA

POINT LOMA LIGHT STATION "C" (— · — ·) 302 kHtz. Range: 150 miles Group Sequence I & IV. Longitude 117° 14.5′ north, Latitude 32° 39.9′ west.
Characteristic "C" (— · — ·) 50 seconds. Long dash (———) 10 seconds. Silent 300 seconds. Each sequence, 6 minutes (360 seconds). Repeat twice each six minute period. Hours of transmission: continuous.

SAN CLEMENTE ISLAND "NUC" (— · · · — — · — ·) 350 kHz. N33° 01.6′ W118° 34.2′.

SAN DIEGO "SA" (· · · · —) 269 kHz; AN (· — — ·) 245 kHz.

TIJUANA "TIJ" (— · · — — —) 393 kHz N32° 32′ W116° 59′
    "UN" (· · — — —) 381 kHz N32° 32′ W117° 02′

ENSENADA RADIO "XFE" (— · · — · · — · ·) 308 kHz. If this radiobeacon is not operating, a call to the harbor master on 156.8 mHtz or 2182 kHtz requesting its operation will cause the facility to be turned on. 308 kHz. Range: 180 miles, Longitude 116° 35′ west, Latitude 31° 52′ north. "XFE" plus two 8-second tones.

TODOS SANTOS "TS" (— · · ·) 292 kHtz.
Distance Finding Station, (DFS.) Range: 200 miles, Longitude 116° 48.8′ west, Latitude 31° 48.8′ north. "TS" (— · · ·) 2 times, duration 6 seconds; 18 dashes (— — — —), duration 16 seconds; Long dash (———), duration 24 seconds. "TS" (— · · ·) 2 times, duration 6 seconds; silent 8 seconds: Period 1 minute (60 seconds). Hours of transmission: continuous. The radiobeacon signal and the fog signal are synchronized for distance-finding. The first blast of the fog signal begins simultaneously with the group of 18 dashes. Distance from the beacon may be determined from the number of dashes received before the fog signal is heard; each dash corresponds to 1/6 mile.

ESTERO DE PUNTA BANDA "EN - ES" (· — · · · · ·) 305 kHtz. Range: 12 miles Longitude 116° 37.3′ west, Latitude 31° 46.9′ north. Directional. To the southward of the bearing line, 124° towards the radiobeacon, "ES" (· · · ·) will be heard with a stronger signal than "EN" (· — ·); to the north-ward of the bearing line "EN" will be heard stronger. On the bearing line both signals will be heard equal strength. DASHES: North of bearing line (— — — — — — — —) etc. On bearing line (5° width) (— — — — — — — —) etc. South of bearing line (— — — — — — — —) etc.
Hours of transmission: During periods of low visibility: continuous; during clear weather, none by day, continuous at night.

BAJA RADIO BEACONS

Tijuana	TIJ	(— · · — — —)	393 kHz	Omni 113.8 mHz	N32° 31′ W 116° 59′
Todos Santos	TS	(— · · ·)	292 kHz	Dist. Fnding. Stn.	N31° 48.8′ W116° 48.8′
Ensenada	XFE	(— · · — · · — ·)	308 kHz		N31° 52′ W 116° 35′
La Paz	XFK	(— · · — · · — · — ·)	295 kHz		N24° 08′ W 110° 17′
La Paz	LAP	(· — · · — · — ·)	373 kHz	Omni 112.3 mHz	N24° 04′ W 110° 21′
Punta Penasco	PPE	(· — — · — — ·)	318 kHz	Omni 112.1 mHz	N31° 23′ W 113° 30′
Hermosillo	HMO	(· · · · — — — —)	415 kHz	Omni 112.8 mHz	
Guaymas	XFY	(— · · — · · — · — —)	321 kHz		N27° 57′ W 109° 48′
Guaymas	GYM	(— — · — · · — — —)	368 kHz		
Ciudad Obregon	CEN	(— · — · · — ·)	354 kHz	Omni 115.1 mHz	N27° 24′ W 129° 50′
Los Mochis	LMM	(· — · · — — — —)	227 kHz	Omni 115.5 mHz	N25° 51′ W 108° 58′
Culiacan	CUL	(— · — · · — · — —)	225 kHz	Omni 112.1 mHz	N24° 46′ W 107° 29′
Mazatlan	XFL	(— · · — · · — · — · ·)	309 kHz		N23° 14′ W 106° 27′
Mazatlan	MZT	(— — — — · · —)	285 kHz	Omni 114.9 mHz	N23° 10′ W 106° 16′

MEXICAN BROADCAST STATIONS

XETRA		
Tijuana	690 kHz	N 32° 25.2′ W 117° 05.5′
XEMMM		
Tijuana	800 kHz	N 32° 30.8′ W 117° 01.1′
XEMO		
Tijuana	860 kHz	N 32° 30′ W 116° 57.2′
XEGM		
Tijuana	950 kHz	N 32° 25.5′ W 117° 05.3′
XEAZ		
Tijuana	1270 kHz	N 32° 32.3′ W 117° 02.7′
XEC		
Tijuana	1310 kHz	N 32° 30′ W 117° 01′
XEXX		
Tijuana	1420 kHz	N 32° 30.8′ W 116° 57.2′
XENT		
La Paz	790 kHz	N 24° 09.8′ W 110° 18.9′
XEHZ		
La Paz	990 kHz	N 24° 05.4′ W 110° 20.0′

XHK-TV		
La Paz	Channel 10	
XEVSD		
Villa Constitucion	1440 kHz	N 25° 35.0′ W 111° 45.0′
XEBBC		
Tijuana	1470 kHz	N 32° 30′ W 116° 57.7′
XEBG		
Tijuana	1550 kHz	N 32° 30.8′ W 117° 01.1′
XERB		
Rosarito Beach	1090 kHz	N 32° 21.2′ W 117° 03.7′
XEPF		
Ensenada	1400 kHz	N 31° 52.7′ W 117° 03.7′
XESS		
Ensenada	1450 kHz	N 31° 51.5′ W 116° 38.4′
XEDX		
El Sauzal	1010 kHz	N 31° 55.8′ W 116° 42.2′
XEHC		
Ensenada	1590 kHz	N 31° 51.2′ W 116° 38.0′
XESR		
Santa Rosalia	1320 kHz	

WEATHER FORECASTS, STORM AND HURRICANE WARNINGS ON VOICE FREQUENCIES

KEC-62 San Diego 162.40 mHz; KWO-37 Los Angeles 162.55 mHz: U.S. Weather Bureau continuous broadcast 24 hours, Point Conception to Mexican Border (Voice).

NMQ Long Beach Coast Guard Radio 2670 kHz: Daily 6:30 a.m., 11:00 a.m., 3:00 p.m., 9:00 p.m.

NMC San Francisco Coast Guard Radio: 8765.4 kHz, 13148.9 kHz, 17294.9 kHz at 0500 GMT; 4385.2 kHz, 8765.4 kHz, 13148.9 kHz at 0135, 0410, 0515, 0805, 0935, 1205, 1335 GMT; 13148.9 kHz, 17294.9 kHz, 22644.9 kHz at 1605, 1710, 2005, 2135 GMT. (Equator to 30°N and east of 140°W.) (Voice, single side band.)

KMI Point Reyes: commercial coast station 8738.1 kHz, 8735.2 kHz, 13161.5 kHz, 13151.0 kHz at 0500 GMT and each odd hour to 1500 GMT; 13161.5 kHz, 13151.0 kHz, 17307.5 kHz, 17304.0 kHz at 1700 GMT and each odd hour to 0300 GMT.

KOU San Pedro: commercial coast station 2466 kHz and 2566 kHz daily 8:00 a.m. and 8:00 p.m.; antenna located at longitude 118° 20' west, latitude 33° 43.6' north (Voice).

WWV and WWVH Fort Collins, Colorado and Maui, Hawaii: National Bureau of Standards 2.5 mHz, 5.0 mHz, 10.0 mHz, 15.0 mHz, 20.0 mHz, 25 mHz. Time-Ticks, storm and hurricane warnings, oceanographic phenomena on the hour.

WEATHER FORECASTS, STORM AND HURRICANE WARNINGS ON BROADCAST FREQUENCIES

SAN DIEGO:

Station	Frequency		Coordinates
KOGO	600	kHtz	N 32° 43.3′ W 117° 04.2′
KFMB	760	kHtz	N 32° 50.5′ W 117° 01.5′
KSDO	1130	kHtz	N 32° 47.9′ W 117° 06.7′
KCBQ	1170	kHtz	N 32° 50.4′ W 116° 59.5′
KSON	1240	kHtz	N 32° 41.7′ W 117° 07.3′
KGB	1360	kHtz	N 32° 43.8′ W 117° 05.0′
KFMB-FM	100.7 mHtz		
KGB-FM	101.5 mHtz		

TIME SIGNALS

The National Bureau of Standards broadcasts accurate time signals continuously from its radio stations WWV, Fort Collins, Colorado and WWVH, Maui, Hawaii on the following frequencies:

2.5 mHz	15 mHz
5 mHz	20 mHz
10 mHz	25 mHz

For explanation, analysis and use of time-tick signals see H.O. publication 117-B, "Radio Navigational Aids" or the National Bureau of Standards publication No. 236, U.S. Department of Commerce, Washington D.C. 20234.

NEW FEDERAL COMMUNICATIONS RULES AND REGULATIONS GOVERNING MARINE BAND SHIP-TO-SHIP/SHIP-TO-SHORE OPERATING FREQUENCIES

New International Radio Regulations were adopted during The World Administrative Radio Conference held in Geneva in 1967. In an effort to resolve some of the many problems caused by overcrowding of present internationally assigned radio communications bands, regulations were promulgated to phase out the amplitude modulation (AM) 2 to 3 kHtz. marine band; it will be replaced with a more efficient system of single-sideband (SSB) transmission and more frequencies on which to communicate. AM radio equipment operating on the current 2 to 3 kHtz. marine band will not be licensed after January 1, 1972 and not permitted after January 1, 1977. Existing and currently licensed marine AM stations may continue to operate until this latter date, but not thereafter. Currently licensed AM stations may be moved from boat to boat by the original licensee, but not transferred to a new licensee. During this five year interim period new owners of transferred boats cannot transfer or renew the radio station license of installed AM equipment, but must conform to the new VHF-FM and SSB equipment Federal Communications Commission rules.

After January 1, 1972 all new radio equipment installed aboard vessels for short range communications (50 miles) will be in the new VHF-FM (Frequency Modulation) band; SSB equipment for long range communications may be licensed only to vessels with VHF-FM short range equipment. The intent of the new regulations is to channel all short range communications to VHF-FM line-of-sight frequencies and thereby prevent overcrowding on SSB long range frequencies, the problem which is now extant on the old 2-3 kHtz. band. The new VHF-FM band of 39 separate operating channels occupies a range of frequencies from 156 to 162 mHtz. utilizing a frequency modulation system of transmission which affords sharp, clear communications free of electrical interference and bothersome static.

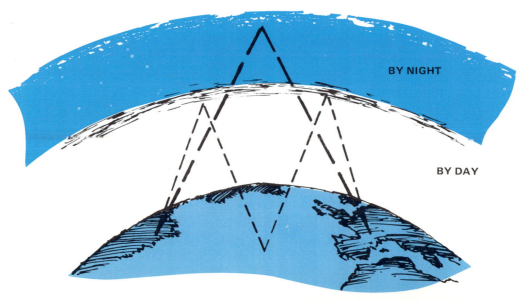

BY NIGHT

BY DAY

CLEARING — All vessels leaving an American port destined for a foreign port as their first port of call must obtain proper clearance papers. The exception is for countries which participate with the United States in reciprocal cruising privileges for yachts such as Canada, or the Bahamas. In the case of Mexico or for any of the the other countries of Central or South America, or of the Pacific islands (other than those administered by the United States) a Consulate clearance of the country of first destination is required. If a vessel's cruising itinerary anticipates a series of stop-overs in one country on the way to a final port in that same country, clearance to the final port may be obtained via the way ports.

Mexico and the United States honor reciprocal cruising permits issued at the first port of call and good for the entire course of the voyage within a period of six months. Under such a permit U.S. yachts enjoy all privileges accorded those of Mexican nationality while cruising in Mexican waters; the reciprocal privilege is extended to yachts of Mexican nationality while cruising in United States waters.

Pleasure craft leaving the United States are not required to clear Customs but must do so at the first American port of reentry; however, if valuable foreign-made equipment such as cameras, tape recorders, field glasses, etc, or firearms are to be carried into Mexico aboard the vessel it is wise to declare and register such items at the U.S. Customs House before leaving the last American port so that upon returning there will be evidence of prior American ownership obviating any levy of duty for importation.

In obtaining clearance papers for Mexico, a certified crew list is the single most important document required. The crew list must include the name of the vessel, name and address of the owner, the vessel's registration or documentation number and port of registry, the name of each member of the crew, or guest, his age, sex, nationality and position aboard the vessel (Captain, cook, engineer, radio operator, seaman, etc) and the vessel's destination via wayports, if any. If passports are carried by any of the crew members, the passport number should be entered after his name. The crew list must be visaed by the Consulate of the country for which the vessel is bound; for Mexico, the clearance papers must be rendered in Spanish.

**CREW LIST IN SPANISH TO BE
PRESENTED AT FIRST MEXICAN PORT**

ESTADOS UNIDOS MEXICANOS

SECRETARIA DE LA MARINA NACIONAL
DIRECCION DE MARINA MERCANTE

MARINA MERCANTE   ROL DE TRIPULANTES   NUMERAL _____

PUERTO DE ENSENADA, B. Cfa.

ROL de las personas con que navega ___ Yate Americano" IDALIA "

matricula de ___ San Francisco Calif. ___ del porte de ___ -34- ___ toneladas

brutas de arqueo, al mando de su Capitán, ___ LEE LEWIS.

que zarpa para el puerto de ___ SAN DIEGO CALIF., E.U.A.

NOMBRE	Nacionalidad por nacimiento	Titulo Profesional	Cargo que desempeña	Edad	SUELDOS Pesos | Cts.
1.- LEE LEWIS	AMERICANA.		CAPITAN	24	
2.- JAMES VOORHEES	"		MARINERO	24	
3.- HELEN LEVENSON	"		"	32	
4.- MEL LEVENSON	"		"	42	
5.- TOM WILLIAMS.	"		"	45	
6.- DOROTHY WILLIAMS.	"		"	38	
7.- MURREY MELNER	"		"	43	
8.- SHIRLEY MELNER	"		"	39	
9.- HAROLD MORSE	"		"	35	
10.- LILLIAN MORSE	"		"	29	
11.- RAY KLETTER	"		"	35	
12.- EDWARD KLETTER	"		"	39	
13.- EDWARD JUSTICIE	"		"	23	
14.- GEORGE BOOTH	"		"	19	

Visado de conformidad en la fecha por esta Oficina de Población, con __14__ tripulantes, inclusive el Capitán.

Ensenada, B. Cfa., ___ agto 12. 66

El ~~Inspector~~ del Servicio.
Jefe.

Registrado a fojas _____ del libro respectivo, haciendo constar que me han sido presentados y están en vigor su Patente de Navegación, certificados de navegabilidad y de máquinas y que reune los requisitos necesarios para garantizar la vida del hombre en el mar.

Comprende este ROL los asientos de _____ individuos, y siendo de mi satisfacción, como Capitán que soy, me obligo al exacto cumplimiento de cuanto disponen las leyes y reglamentos del legítimo comercio nacional y demás disposiciones vigentes que me sean prevenidas por las Autoridades Marítimas de los puertos nacionales.

ENSENADA, B. Cfa., __Agosto 12__ de 19 66

por ___ EL CAPITAN. ___ Agente.

EL CAPITAN DEL PUERTO.

These clearing procedures and the proper paperwork in quadruplicate may be accomplished through the Mexican Consular Service, or a reputable Customs House broker; or by the master of the vessel himself if he is sufficiently conversant with the law, the language, the form, and the proper procedure. Consular fees for this service are 500 Mexican pesos, or $40.00 (dollars). Brokerage fees are added to this sum if a Custom House Broker is employed to do the leg work, the total amounting to around $25.00. The Mexican Consular Service or Broker will also provide necessary forms for fishing or hunting licenses.

While traveling aboard a vessel of United States registry in Mexico a tourist card or passport is not required so long as the crew members confine their activities to the immediate vicinity of the ports of call; if, however, they intend to make trips inland or between ports by land, a tourist card is required and therefore advisable at the outset of the voyage. Proof of citizenship such as a birth certificate or a notarized attestation of nationality by a responsible authority plus two passport photos are required to obtain the tourist card. Tourist cards permitting travel in Mexico are limited, as well, to a six month period; this time limit has always been strictly adhered to, however a new tourist card can be obtained for another six month period, but only at the Mexican border. The time limit for the cruising permit aboard yachts has only been recently enforced, eliminating protracted voyages into Mexico. Since flying or driving to the border for renewal of a tourist card is quite a different sort of undertaking than returning by water with one's vessel for renewal of a cruising permit, it is hoped that some remedy for practically extending the cruising permit will be arranged by Mexican authorities.

SEA STORES — Vessels bound on extended voyages to foreign waters are entitled to take sea stores, tax free. Tobacco, cigarettes, liquor and other alcoholic beverages are usually those items desired, as shorn of federal tax, they are surprisingly cheap commodities. Sea stores may be obtained through the Customs House and arrangements made by the ship's broker; however it is incumbent upon the ship's master to provide a sea stores locker capable of being sealed while in domestic ports. It has been difficult for yachts to qualify for sea stores as their voyages are usually of such short duration that sea stores taken are rarely consumed before returning to an American port, the remaining stores then posing a problem of remaining sealed and untouched until the next foreign voyage. However, a yacht destined for an extended foreign voyage is as entitled to take sea stores as any other vessel providing it meets specifications as required by the Customs Service.

ENTERING — All vessels entering a foreign port (with the exception of those countries which extend reciprocal cruising privileges) must present their clearance papers for examination, must clear pratique through the health department and secure validation for the next port of call. When entering Mexico, the first port of call must be one officially authorized for port clearance and only thereafter may wayports, islands, anchorages and remote places be visited. Immediately upon arrival at the first port of call in Mexico, ship's papers should be presented to the Departmento de Migración (Department of Immigration), Departmento de Salubridad Publica (Department of Public Health) and the Capitania de Puerto (Captain of the Port) for examination and issuance of a cruising permit.

It is advisable at the outset of a voyage to secure a dozen or more sets of copies of all required ship's papers as each port authority in every port visited will require one or two copies for validation and record; generally, two copies are delivered to the Captain of the Port and one to the Department of Immigration. The documents will be processed and, if everything is in order, will be returned with permission to continue the voyage to the next port. With local knowledge and an adequate command of the language the business of port clearance may be transacted directly with the port authorities involved, but maritime brokers specializing in ship and yacht clearing procedures are available in most ports of entry. Their services generally include help in obtaining fuel, water, provisions and repair and are usually reasonable.

Mexican law relating to yachts of U.S. nationality has been considerably liberalized in many respects in the last few years. The health requirements now pertain only to the first port of call and are dispensed with thereafter. Tourist cards are not required for the crew to disembark and to visit the environs of the port but, as previously advised, should be obtained to render cruising plans and crew itinerary more flexible. According to Mexican law, U.S. yachts after securing validation of the cruising permit at the first port of entry are to be accorded the same freedom of travel between ports as a yacht of Mexican nationality, but in practice and through courtesy, validation of the vessel's papers is rendered at each port of call. In the matter of port clearance, it is the responsibility of the vessel's master to present his ship's papers to the proper authorities, rather than the duty of the port officials to obtain them. It is also wise to consider the normal working hours of the port officials and to plan the ship's arrival in the port well within that period to avoid payment of additional fees for overtime.

At the end of the voyage, before leaving the last Mexican port of call, clearance out of the country is required entailing similar procedures as upon entering, and presents no more problem than wayport validation. The cost of the revenue stamps on the various final documents amounts to about $3.00 (dollars); brokerage fees amount to about $10.00 or $12.00 (dollars).

RE-ENTERING FIRST AMERICAN PORT — All vessels including yachts and other pleasure craft from foreign ports arriving at their first American port of call are required to obtain inspection and clearance within 24 hours after arrival from Quarantine, Customs, Immigration and Department of Agriculture. In San Diego this may be accomplished either at the Customs Dock at the western entrance to the Shelter Island Marina on the north side of the main ship channel, or at the Embarcadero fronting the City Hall. The department of Agriculture publishes a list of plants, fruits and vegetables admissible at Mexican border ports of entry; only those items on the list (which changes from time to time) may be brought back aboard a returning vessel, and then only upon specific inspection. The State of California has its own additional restrictions. Any item prohibited must not be brought into the United States, even if it was previously purchased in the United States and carried into Mexico on the same vessel just returning. No alcoholic beverages or liquors, in any quantity, opened or unopened, may be imported into California ports, and all such remaining aboard at time of entry must be surrendered to the Customs agent. Foreign made goods up to a value of $100.00 each 31-day voyage period may be brought back exempt of duties except for those restricted trademarked items including certain perfumes and cameras. All items must be declared whether exempt or not; a fine or seizure of the offending vessel may be levied for failure to comply with these requirements.

Aliens may not be brought back as crew members unless with proper entry papers. Resident aliens sailing from an American port to a foreign port must have proper identification and copies of valid resident permits to gain re-entry. The master of the vessel is ultimately responsible for the actions of his crew, and the ship itself is subject to seizure for serious violations.

CLEARANCE FROM LAST MEXICAN PORT

OFFICIAL PORTS OF ENTRY IN BAJA CALIFORNIA — Ensenada/Isla Cedros/Puerto San Carlos, Puerto Cortez-Bahia Magdalena/Cabo San Lucas/La Paz/Loreto/Santa Rosalia/San Felipe.

SPORTFISHING IN MEXICAN WATERS — Owners of yachts interested in sportfishing in Mexican waters are required to obtain a fishing license for their vessel and each individual aboard. These may be obtained at the Mexican Fish Commission, 233 "A" Street, San Diego, or at the Broadway Pier Building, Room 313. In San Pedro, Mexican Fish Commission Offices are located at 305 West 6th Street, Room 3.

CUSTOM HOUSE BROKERS — A mimeographed page of information on the subject of yacht clearance into Mexico is available from the Consulate General of Mexico at 601 West 5th Street, Los Angeles, California 90012, telephone (213) 624-3261.

Wilmington	Howard Hartry, Inc., 301 West B Street (213) 830-1010
	Williams, Clarke Co., Inc., 603 North Fries Avenue. (213) TE-46458
San Pedro	Guy B. Barham Co., 22 West 8th Street. (213) TE-24273
	W. J. Byrnes & Co., 136 West 8th Street. (213) TE-24219
	Arthur J. Fritz & Co., Inc., 1300 South Beacon Street. (213) 831-0274
	Gene Miller, 224 West 8th Street. (213) 833-5213
	Stephen M. Stambuk, 123 West 8th Street. (213) 832-2008
	Wayne N. Withrow & Co., 1300 South Beacon Street. (213) 775-6663
Long Beach	James Loudon & Co., Inc., 110 West Ocean Blvd. (213) 437-0736
San Diego	George Salazar, 1030 West Broadway. (714) 232-2023
	Shreve & Hays, B Street Pier, (714) 232-6547
Ensenada	Gil Ojeda, Comisionista y Agente de Buques (Ship Agent) Apartada Posta 22, Avenido Frente 485, telephone 8-3615 or (residence) 8-2738.
	Agencias Maritimas del Pacifico (Ship Agent) Ruiz 52-E, telephone 8-2648 or 8-1753

TRAILER BOATS — Under a recently liberalized Mexican customs law, trailered boats under 22 feet in length may enter any part of Mexico without bond; however, trailered boats of any size may enter without bond into the free zones which include Baja California, and a small portion of the Sonora coast bordering the Gulf of California. Trailered boats over 22 feet entering Mexico beyond the free zones must be bonded for the purpose of preventing illegal chartering or sale of the vessel in Mexico. The cost of the bond, when required, relates to the value of the boat and may be obtained through a regular Customs House Broker at the border crossing.

Note: Under a program called Operation Cooperation called for by the U.S. Government to prevent illegal importation of narcotics, the military and naval forces of Mexico patrol their coast, and will hail, board and inspect yachts of every nationality as they deem necessary, in much the same manner as our Coast Guard conducts inspections for safety pleasure craft along our own coast. Courtesy and respect are mutual lubricants for such an encounter; having proper ship's papers easily accessible will expedite the inspection. The presence of Mexican military coastal patrols for the stated purpose will at the same time afford a search and rescue capability to provide against marine losses.

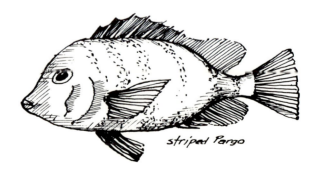

striped Pargo

WHALE WATCH

The Department of the Navy, Naval Undersea Research and Development Center, San Diego, California is conducting a basic research program on the prevalence of whales and other marine mammals which are common to the coasts and offshore waters of Baja California and the Sea of Cortez. There are approximately 20 species of these marine animals currently under study. Four are Pinnipeds, members of the animal order that includes seals, sea lions and walruses; the remainder are Cetaceans, the order that includes porpoises, dolphins and whales. Relatively little is known about the habits of most of these animals in much of this coastal area. For this reason, reliable reports of their sighting, singly or in groups, by commercial fishermen or mariners plying Baja California waters can contribute significantly to the scientific body of knowledge. The form below is provided for all those wishing to participate in the sighting program; reports will be acknowledged with identification or corroboration of what you have seen insofar as the reported detail allows. Photographs, where possible, will permit more certain identification.

Copies of this form together with a pamphlet describing and illustrating the marine mammals under study to facilitate their identification may be obtained by writing to Whale Watch, Naval Undersea Research & Development Center, San Diego, California 92132.

There is presently in preparation and soon to be published an illustrated book, Whales and Porpoises of the Eastern North Pacific — A Guide to Their Identification in the Water, by Steve Leatherwood, William E. Evans, Marine Life Sciences Laboratory, Ocean Sciences Department, Naval Undersea Research & Development Center, San Diego, California 92132 and Dale W. Rice, National Oceanic and Atmospheric Administration, National Marine Fisheries Service, Fishery Oceanography Center, La Jolla, California 92037.

WHALE IDENTIFICATION CHART

RIGHT

GRAY

BLUE

FINBACK

SEI

BRYDE'S

HUMPBACK

MINKE

SPERM

SURFACING & BLOWING   BEGINNING THE DIVE   DIVING

WHALE WATCH SIGHTING REPORT

Date & Local Time:_____

Location: _____ Lat. _____ Long.

Identification: _____

_____

_____

_____

_____

_____

_____

_____

_____

Identify each species sighted by common and scientific name, if known. Describe its profile or striking features. Sketch or photograph if possible.

Number of Whales sighted:_____

Heading of Whale(s): _____ Magnetic.

Estimated speed of Whale(s): _____ knots.

Associated birds, fishes or other mammals: _____

_____

Remarks:_____

_____

_____

_____

_____

_____

_____

_____

Observer:_____

_____

Mailing Address:_____

_____

_____

NOTE: Xerox this form and mail with observed data to WHALE WATCH, Department of the Navy, Naval Undersea Research and Development Center, San Diego, California 92132.

SEA GUIDE

BAJA CALIFORNIA

SECTION REFERENCE CHART

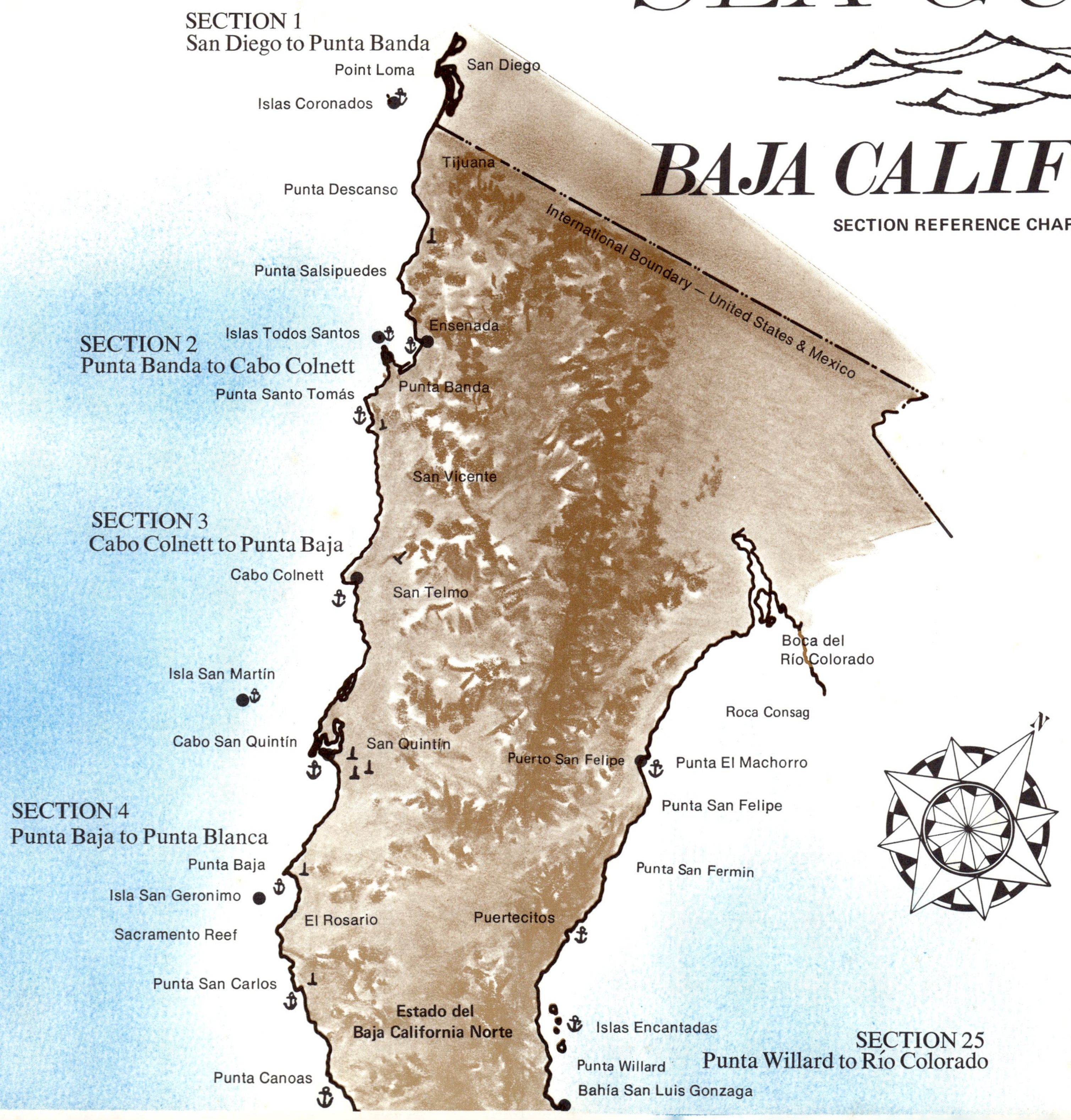

N

International Boundary – United States & Mexico

SECTION 1
San Diego to Punta Banda

San Diego
Point Loma
Islas Coronados
Tijuana
Punta Descanso
Punta Salsipuedes
Ensenada

SECTION 2
Punta Banda to Cabo Colnett

Islas Todos Santos
Punta Banda
Punta Santo Tomás

SECTION 3
Cabo Colnett to Punta Baja

San Vicente
San Telmo
Cabo Colnett
Isla San Martín
San Quintín
Cabo San Quintín

SECTION 4
Punta Baja to Punta Blanca

Punta Baja
Isla San Geronimo
El Rosario
Sacramento Reef
Punta San Carlos
Punta Canoas

Estado del Baja California Norte

Boca del Río Colorado
Roca Consag
Punta El Machorro
Punta San Felipe
Punta San Fermín
Puerto San Felipe
Puertecitos

SECTION 25
Punta Willard to Río Colorado

Islas Encantadas
Punta Willard
Bahía San Luis Gonzaga

SAILING SHIP ROUTES

Pacific Ocean, vicinity of Baja California Peninsula.
From British Admiralty Chart #5308.

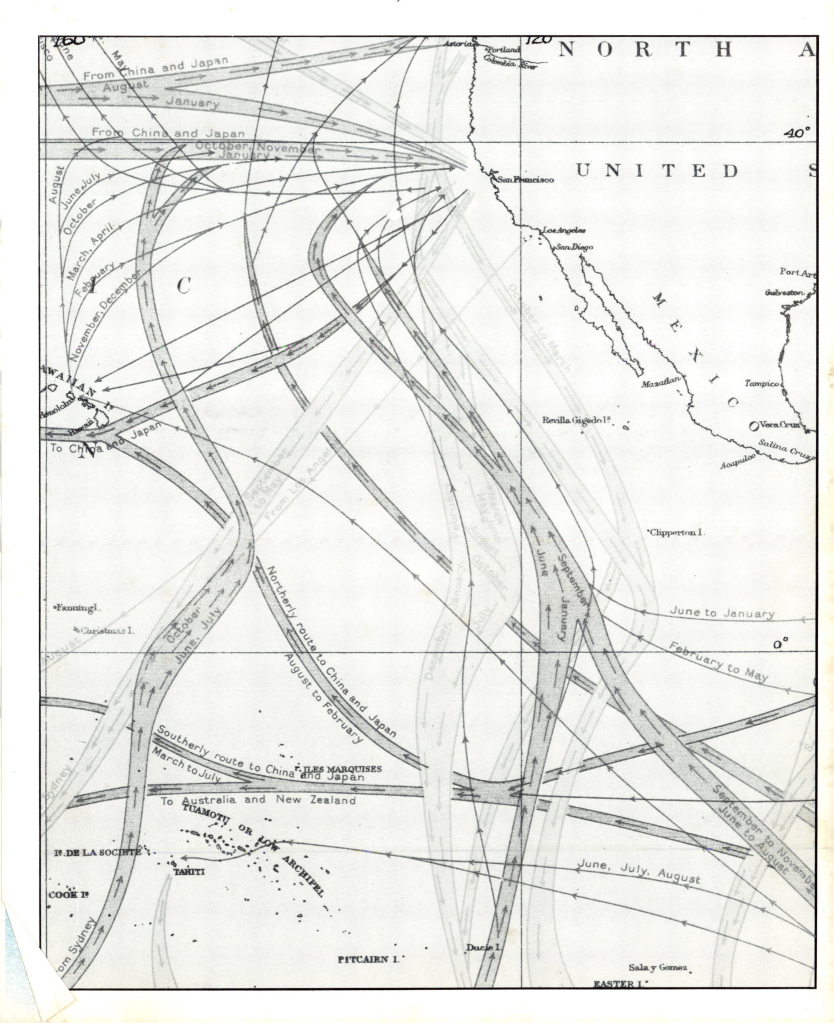

STEAMSHIP ROUTES

Pacific Ocean vicinity of Baja California Peninsula.
From British Admiralty Chart #5307.

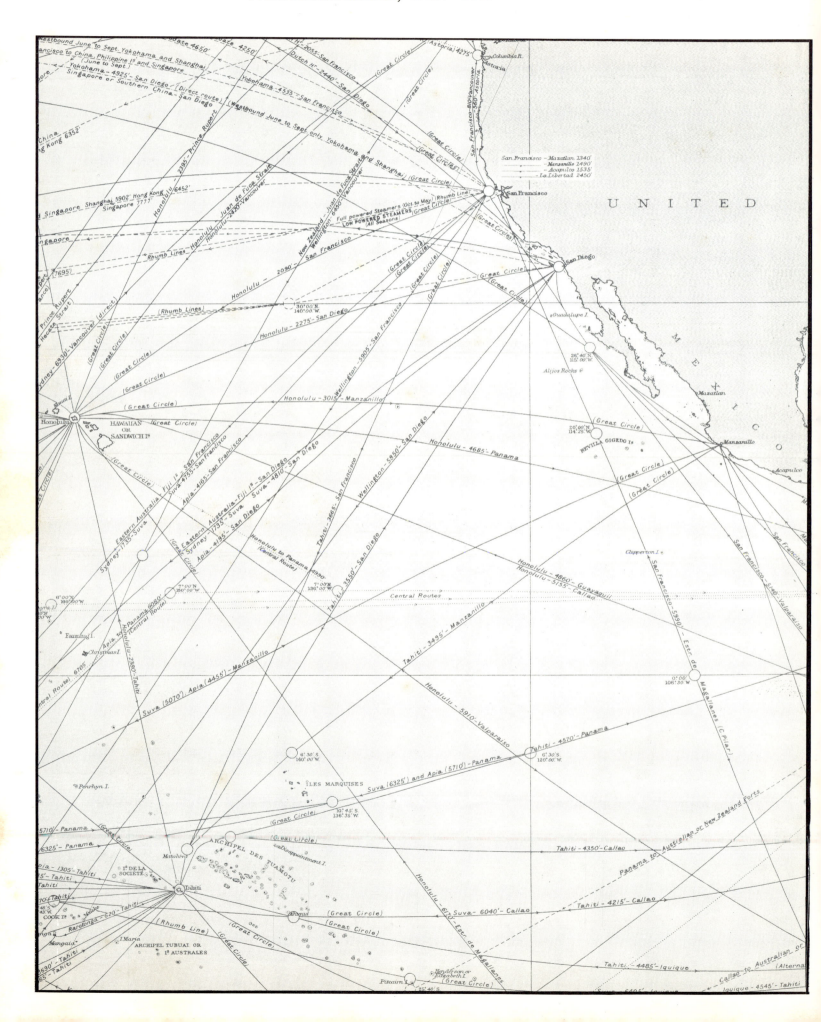

SECTION 5
Punta Blanca to Morro Santo Domingo

Punta Blanca

Punta Acantilado

Islas San Benito

Puerto Refugio

Bahía Playa María

Isla Ángel de la Guarda

SECTION 7
Islas San Benito,
Cedros, Natividad

Isla Cedros

SECTION 6
Morro Santo Domingo
to Punta Eugenio

Morro
Santo
Domingo

Bahía de
Los Ángeles

Isla Natividad

SECTION 24
Las Islas de la Cintura — Midriff Islands

SECTION 8
Punta Eugenio
to Punta Abreojos

Punta San Eugenio

Bahía de
las Ánimas

Bahía
San Bartolomé

Isla
San
Lorenzo

Isla Tiburon

Bahía de
San Rafael

Laguna Guerrero Negro

Isla
San
Esteban

Punta San Pablo

Laguna Ojo de Liebre
Scammon's Lagoon

Punta
San Francisquito

Isla San Pedro Mártir

SECTION 23

Punta San Roque

Punta San Francisquito to Bahía San Luis Gonzaga

Isla Asunción

Punta San Carlos

Territorio del
Baja California Sur

Punta San Hipolito

Punta Trinidad

Latitude 28° North

SECTION 9
Punta Abreojos
to Punta San Juanico

Punta Baja

Punta Abreojos

Laguna San Ignacio

Santa Rosalía

Isla Tortuga

Bahía Ballenas

Isla San Marcos

SECTION 22
Punta Chivato to Bahía San Franciquito

Punta Chivato

Mulege

Punta Santo Domingo

Punta Concepción

Punta Pequeña

SECTION 21
Bahía Concepción to Punta Chivato

SECTION 10
Punta San Juanico to Cabo San Lázaro

Bahía
Concepción

Punta Santa Teresa

Punta San Juanico

Punta Púlpito

Boca de Santo Domingo

Isla Coronado

Loreto

SECTION 11
Cabo San Lázaro
to Cabo Tosco

Boca de Soledad

Isla Carmen

Bahía Escondido

Matancitas

Punta Candeleros

Bahía
Agua Verde

Isla Monserrate

SECTION 20
Bahía de Agua Verde a Punta Concepción

Cabo San Lázaro
Bahía Santa María

Puerto San Carlos

Punta
San Marcial

Isla Catalan

Bahía
los Dolores

Isla Santa Cruz

Bahía Magdalena

Isla San Diego

Isla Santa Margarita

SECTION 12
Cabo Tosco to Cabo San Lucas

Puerto Cortez

Punta
Nopolo Sur
Punta
San Evaristo

Isla de los Ánimas

Cabo Tosco

Isla San José

Boca Flor de Malba

Isla San Francisco

Punta Marquis

Cabeza de Mechudo

SECTION 19
La Paz to Punta San Marcial

Isla Partida

Isla Espíritu Santo

SECTION 18
Islas Espíritu Santo and Partida

Punta Coyote
Rancho de las Cruces

SECTION 17
La Paz
and Environs

Isla Cerralvo

La Paz

Punta Arena de la Ventana
Punta Pericc
Bahía Los Muertos

SECTION 13
Oceanic Islands

Punta Lobos

Todos Santos

Punta Pescadero

Bahía de las Palmas

SECTION 16

Isla Guadalupe   Roca Partida
Rocas Alijos   Isla de Socorro
Isla Clarion   Isla de San Benedicto

Bahia Los Muertos to Canal de San Lorenzo

Punta Arena

SECTION 15
Los Frailes to Bahía Los Muertos

San José
del Cabo

Bahía Los Frailes

SECTION 14
Cabo San Lucas to Los Frailes

Cabo Falso
Cabo San Lucas

Puerto Chileno
Punta Palmilla

Boca de Tule

TROPIC OF CANCER LAT. 23° 27' N.

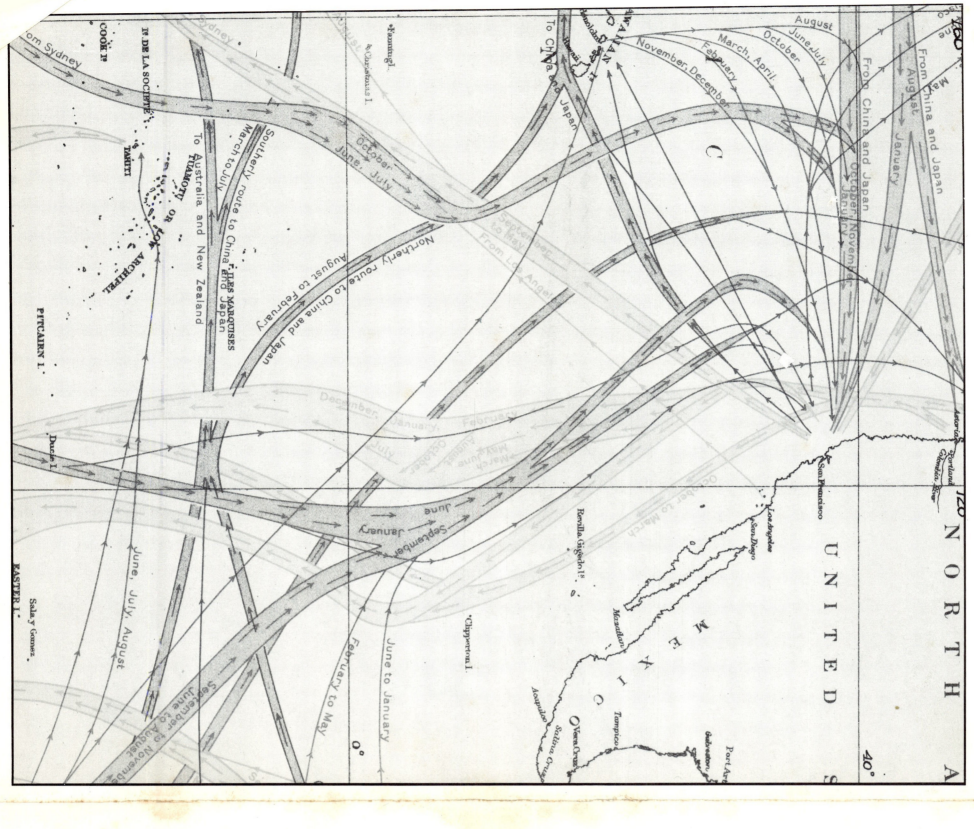

Pacific Ocean, vicinity of Baja California Peninsula.
From British Admiralty Chart #5308.

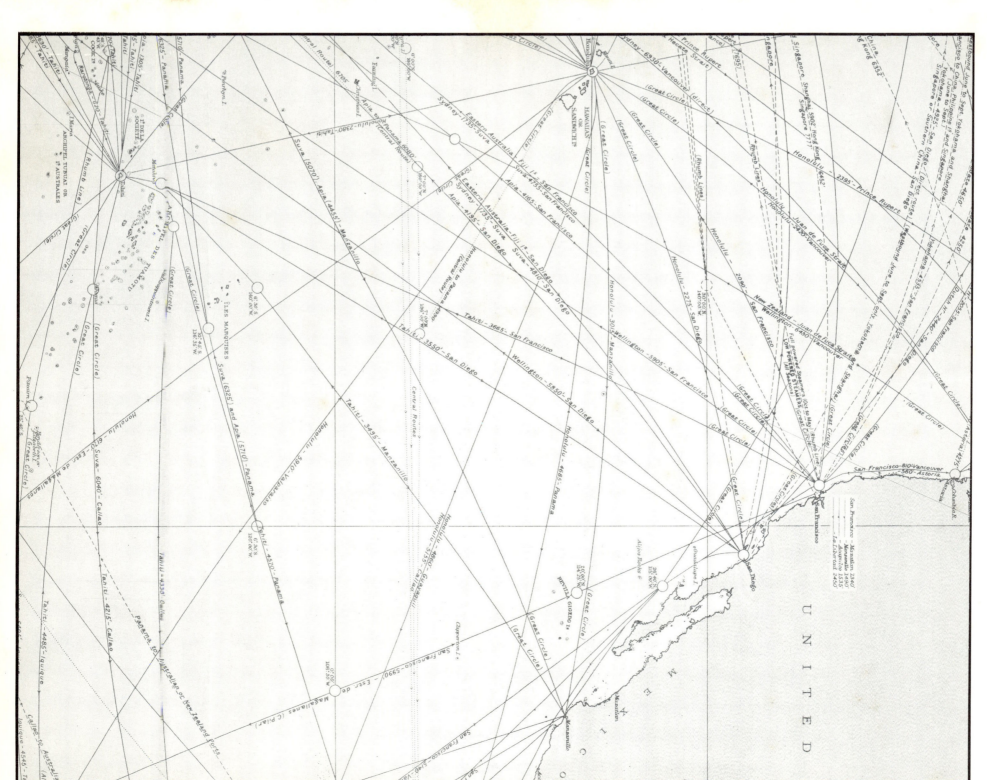

Pacific Ocean, vicinity of Baja California Peninsula.
From British Admiralty Chart #5307.

INDEX

366

SOURCES OF ADDITIONAL INFORMATION

Sea Boating Almanac for the current year published by Sea Publications, Inc., 1499 Monrovia Avenue, Newport Beach, California 92663; "Sea of Cortez" by Ray Canon, published by Lane Book Company, Middlefield and Willow Roads, Menlo Park, California; "Cruising the Pacific Coast" by Jack and Carolyn West, published by Sea Publications, Inc., 1499 Monrovia Avenue, Newport Beach California 92663; "Cruising the Sea of Cortez" by Spencer Murray and Ralph Poole, published by Best-West Publications, Palm Desert, California; "Baja California" by Ralph Hancock, published by the Academy Press, 5299 Fountain Avenue, Los Angeles, California; "Lower California Guide Book" by Peter Gerhard and Howard Gulick, publishes by The Arthur H. Clark Company, Glendale, California; Kym's Guide No. 6, No. 7, No. 55, No. 56, No. 57; published by the Triumph Press, Inc., P.O. Box 75445, Sanford Station, Los Angeles, California 90005; "Guide to Baja California del Norte," "Guide to Baja California del Sur" published by the Automobile Club of Southern California, 2601 South Figueroa Street, Los Angeles, California 90054; "Cruising the East Coast of Baja" by Vern Jones, published by Yates y Servicios Marinos, S.A. Apartado Postal 290, La Paz, Baja California Sur, Mexico; "Baja Cruising Notes" by Vern Jones, published by SeaBreez Publications, Box 1741, Thousand Oaks, California 91360; "Sea of Cortez Cruising Guide" by Captain Allan Douglas, published by the author, 15717 Indiana Avenue, Paramount, California 90723;

"Baja California, Mexico by Road, Airplane and Boat" by Cliff Cross, Cliff Cross Guide Books, Box 301, North Palm Springs, California 92258; "Airports of Baja California" and (separately) "The Complete Map for Air Navigation in Baja" by Arnold Senterfitt, published by the author, Star Route, Lakeside California 92040; "Baja by Air" by Allen R. and Phyllis T. Ellis, published by Pan American Navigation Service, 12021 Ventura Blvd., North Hollywood, California 91604; U.S. Naval Oceanographic Office, H.O. Publication No. 26, "Sailing Directions for the West Coasts of Mexico and Central America" available at all official U.S. Government Hydrographic Chart Distribution Agencies or by mail from Naval Oceanographic Distribution Office, Clearfield, Utah 84016; British Admiralty "West Coast of Central America Pilot," available from Official U.S. Chart Agencies or by mail from Hydrographer of the Navy, Hydrographic Department, Ministry of Defense, Taunton, Somerset, England; Director General de Turismo, Palacio de Gobierno, La Paz, B. Cfa., Mexico; Mexican National Tourist Council, 9445 Wilshire Blvd., Beverly Hills, California; The Consulate General of Mexico, 125 East Sunset Blvd., Los Angeles, California 90012; Sea Guide, Volume I, covering the waters of Southern California from Point Arguello to Punta Banda, distributed by Sea Publications, Inc., 1499 Monrovia Avenue, Newport Beach, California 92663; "Marine Mammals of the Pacific Coast" by Charles Scammon, published by Manessier Publishing Company, Box 5517 Riverside, California 92507.

REQUEST FOR CORRECTIVE INFORMATION

Mariners are invited to cooperate in corrective revisions of this Pilot by reporting all discrepancies between published information and conditions actually observed or encountered by forwarding appropriate additions, deletions, improvements and descriptions of any new facilities.

Observer: _____

Ship's Name: _____ Master: _____

Mailing Address: _____

_____

_____

Date of Observation: _____

Position: Long. _____ Lat. _____ GMT: _____

If Correction, SEA GUIDE Page No. _____ Chart: _____

Details of Information Reported: (Use additional space if necessary) _____

_____

_____

_____

_____

_____

_____

_____

MAILING INSTRUCTIONS

Please mail a xerox copy of this form, together with other available material (Photos, sketches, publications, etc.,) to:
SEA GUIDE, Route 1, Box 46, Carmel, California 93921

ACKNOWLEDGEMENTS

In the preparation of this Pilot the generous cooperation of many professional and scientific men and women has been heavily depended upon. There have been many small gestures of assistance and some major efforts expended in searching out accurate information on behalf of the contents. To all these people — far too many to acknowledge by name in the space allotted I offer my utmost gratitude for their generosity and help. A special expression of gratitude, however, is due certain men whose sustained support in this long project, and the importance of their contributions made the work possible. Dr. Carl Hubbs, Professor Emeritus, Scripps Institution of Oceanography is one of those remarkably responsive natural scientists to whom I am deeply indebted, and no less his wife, both prodigiously generous contributors of their time and knowledge.

Inspiration is an ingredient as important as the content — the leavening in the loaf that gives rise to form and finished product: To Dr. Joseph Wood Krutch, Rockwell Kent, and Dr. Dallas Hanna, all since commended to the deep, I owe a debt for their priceless kind of contribution. To name but a few more people who contributed their time and knowledge of Baja generously, I must include Dr. George Lindsay, Kenneth K. and Nancy Bechtel, Dr. Eric Barham, Dr. Louis Wayne Walker, Dr. Adrian Richards, Dr. Gordon Gastil, John Minch, Dr. Reid Moran, Dr. W. B. Bryan, Dr. Wheeler J. North, James L. Squire, Doyle E. Gates, Harry M. Johnson, John Carmack, Steve Leatherwood, Joan Perkal, Dr. Robert L. Eberhart, Peggy Slater, Alberto Alvarez Morphy and Ambassador Fulton Freeman.

Research depends on libraries and ready access to pertinent materials depended in my case on the generous and interested help of several outstanding librarians: Alan Baldridge of Hopkins Marine Station, Paul Spinks of the Naval Post Graduate School at Monterey, Ray Brian of the California Academy of Science, John Barr Tomkins, Bancroft Library and Ronald L. Silveira de Bragnanza of the University of California at San Diego all gave unstintingly of their time and knowledge on behalf of my project.

Aerial photography played an important part in the production of this book, and I owe a special debt of gratitude to Morrie Camhi for his advice, direction and excellent handling of the negatives as well as for his general inspiration; also to Cole Weston, Craig Sharp, Nils Ibsen, Al Weber and Harold Price for their generous contributions of time, material and general helpfulness. A special thanks to Arnold Senterfitt for his valuable knowledge of flying in Baja and his extensive experience in aerial photography which he generously shared with the author. Appreciation is given as well to Richard Webb for providing the opportunity for the photographic flight, to Carl Mall for technical help in flight, and to Peter Poland, Baja pilot par excellence.

Thanks in a large measure is due last but not least to my wife, Judy, for her sustained support through a prodigiously long project and for her own, not inconsequential efforts in preparing the index, no mean job in itself; to Judy Phillips, a tireless colleague for an accurate and excellent typescript and to Ray Poulter, publisher's representative, for his patient understanding and forebearance through a period of creative gestation far more protracted than originally forecast. Thanks to all who have participated in this work and made its final publication possible.

Introduction, in part, from "Rutters of the Sea": Thanks to Commander David W. Waters, National Maritime Museum, Greenwich, England.

PHOTO CREDITS

National Aeronautics and Space Administration	Frontispiece
Eric Barham	127
Nancy Bechtel	190 (2), 295
W. B. Bryan	183
Homer Dana	175 (2)
Les Herling	57
Carl Hubbs	160
Red Humphreys	160
George Lindsay	158, 164, 165, 166 (2)
Los Angeles Times	163
Carl Mall	305
H. Petrie	171
Adrian Richards	167 (2), 168, (2), 172 (2), 175, 180, 182 (3)
Arnold Senterfitt	© 79, © 92, © 124, © 198, © 248, © 252, © 275, © 303, © 314 © 323, © 324, © 340
U. S. Navy	158, 160, 167 (2), 168 (2), 169, 172 (4), 173, 175, 176, 177, 179 (2), 180

All other photos taken by author.

CHART CREDITS

Page 363, Courtesy of the British Admiralty
End Papers, Courtesy, Director, Huntington Library
Pages 72, 75, Courtesy, Director, Bancroft Library

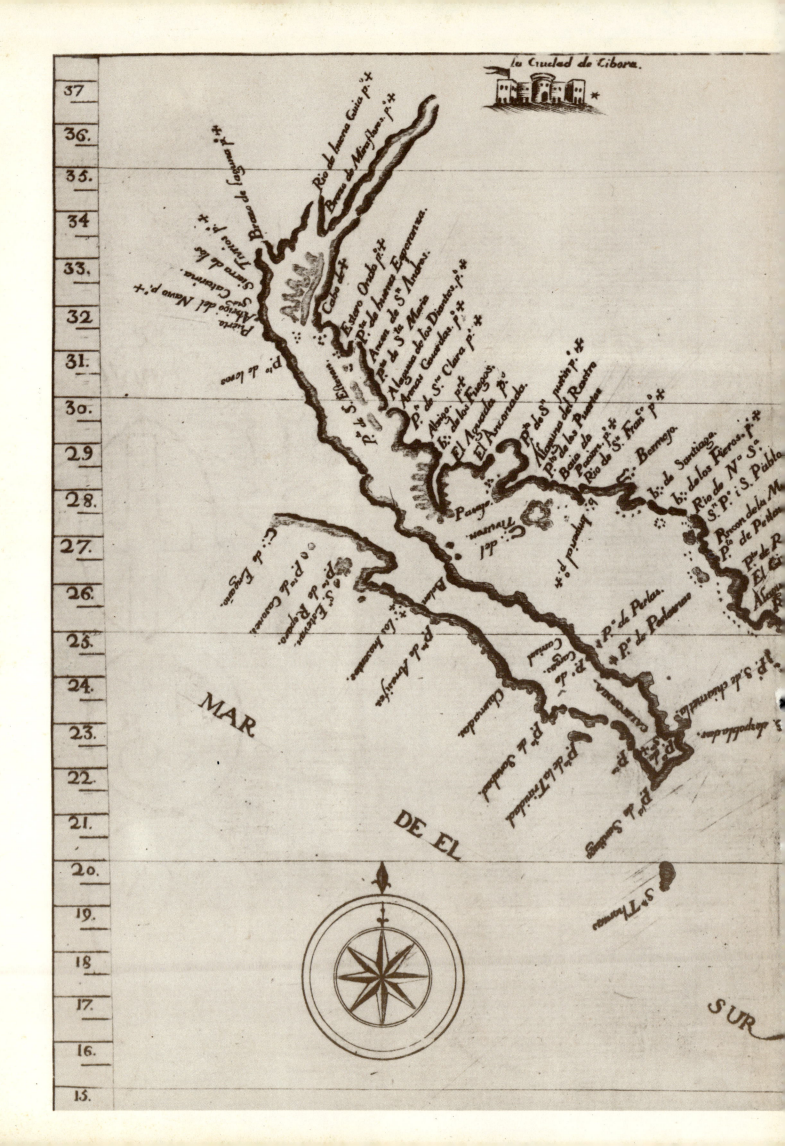